The **Roug**

Slovenia

written and researched by

Norm Longley

www.roughguides.com

Contents

The Great Outdoors
colour section
following p.144

Subterranean Slovenia
colour section
following p.272

Introduction to
Slovenia

Sporting a geographical diversity unmatched in many countries twice its size, Slovenia is a country of endless variety, a magical landscape embracing imperious white limestone mountains, spectacular underground curiosities, sweeping vineyards, and a craggy coastline punctuated by historic coastal resorts. Since breaking free from the yoke of the old Yugoslav alliance, Slovenia has settled down to life in the new European order with ease; politically and economically stable, this tiny country of less than two million people constantly delights with its understated charm.

Dominated by Germanic and, to a lesser extent, Hungarian and Italian influences from the Middle Ages until the end of World War I, Slovenia spent the best part of the next seventy years locked into a less than harmonious **Yugoslav federation**. When the federation began to fracture in the late 1980s, Slovenia was the first to secede; save for the so-called **Ten-Day War** of independence in the summer of 1991, the country emerged more or less unscathed from the bloodbath that tragically engulfed Croatia and Bosnia. Slovenia was by far and away the most **liberal** and **progressive** of Yugoslavia's erstwhile republics, which partly accounted for its relatively painless transition from one-party rule to multiparty democracy, and from communist to market economy, following independence. Having escaped the shackles, the country's long-held desire to cement its place within the wider international community was finally achieved in 2004 with **European Union membership**, followed in 2007 with the introduction of the euro, while there was further prestige in 2008 when it became the first of the former communist states to hold the EU presidency.

While all this appears to have made little tangible difference to the lives of most Slovenes, it has helped raise the country's profile in a big way. Prior to the dismemberment of Yugoslavia, Slovenia, along with Croatia,

Fact file

• With an **area** of less than 21,000 square kilometres (roughly the size of Wales), and a **population** of just two million, Slovenia is one of Europe's smallest nations. Forty percent of the country is **mountainous**, around a quarter of which is alpine, with three major mountain groups: the Julian Alps, the Kamniške-Savinja Alps and the Karavanke mountains. The highest peak is Triglav (2864m) in the Julian Alps. The remainder of the country comprises subalpine hills, karst plateaus, forests and flat plains, whilst the coastline, facing the Adriatic, is just 47km long.

• The country is divided into eight geographical **regions** – Bela Krajina, Dolenjska, Gorenjska, Koroška, Notranjska, Prekmurje, Primorska and Štajerska – the boundaries of which are very fluid.

• On June 25, 1991, Slovenia became an **independent republic** for the very first time. The 1991 constitution set in place a **parliamentary system of government**, elected every four years, with the prime minister at its head. The head of state, the president, is elected every five years. Slovenia became a full member of the EU in May, 2004.

• **Tourism** is one of the fastest growing sectors of the Slovenian economy, with alpine, coastal and spa resorts absorbing the bulk of the country's tourist traffic. Slovenia's most important **exports** are vehicles, electrical appliances and pharmaceutical goods, and its main trading partners are Germany and Italy.

could always boast the lion's share of the federation's tourist traffic, though this was almost completely decimated during the regional conflicts of the 1990s. In recent years, however, the country has managed to re-establish itself in style, and visitors will be struck by the quality of the **tourist facilities** on offer, be it a tourist farm, ski centre or spa resort. Indeed, Slovenia's pristine environment reflects the quality of life here, and there's an atmosphere of order that wouldn't seem out of place in Scandinavia, while a good proportion of the population speak perfect English.

As appealing as many of Slovenia's towns and cities are, especially the enchanting capital Ljubljana, the country's greatest asset is its magnificent, and astonishingly varied, natural heritage; as one of Europe's greenest nations – over half the country is forested – there are limitless opportunities for **outdoor**

◄ Mountain hut, Julian Alps

pursuits: skiing, climbing and trekking in the mountains, whitewater rafting, kayaking and canyoning on the country's many rivers, cycling through rolling hills and forests, or riding cross-country on a Lipizzaner, to name but a few. And with distances so small, in a single day you could be hiking in the Alps in the morning, downing a few glasses of wine in a local cellar over lunch, and relaxing by the beach at the end of the day.

Where to go

Most visitors to Slovenia begin with a trip to the country's sophisticated capital, **Ljubljana**, whose engaging blend of Baroque and Habsburg architecture, and river cafés and restaurants, could quite happily detain you for a few days. From here it is customary to make a beeline for the stunning alpine lakes and mountains northwest of the capital, namely **Lake Bled**, with its fairy-tale island church and cliff-top castle, and the even more beautiful **Lake Bohinj**, less than 40km to the west. Both lakes lie on the fringe of the **Julian Alps**, whose magisterial peaks are as popular with climbers and hikers in the summer as they are with skiers in the winter. Most of the Alps are contained within **Triglav National Park**, which extends south to the imperious **Soča Valley**, whose eponymous river draws adventure sports enthusiasts to its foaming waters each summer.

Slovenian wine

Slovenian wine (*vino*) is little known beyond the country's borders, yet vineyards here cover roughly the same area as the Bordeaux region in France and produce about half the quantity of wine of that region, much of which is of extremely high quality. Slovenia has three distinct wine-producing regions, each of which is subdivided into separate districts (there are fourteen in total): the largest of these regions is **Podravje** in the northeast, where white wines such as Laški Rizling, Sauvignon and Šipon predominate; whereas the **Posavje** region in the southeastern corner of the country is known for its reds, in particular the rich and velvety Metliška črnina from Bela Krajina, and the blended, juice-like **Cvicek** from Dolenjska. The Primorje, or coastal, region yields a prolific number of both red and white wines, foremost of which are the excellent Merlot, the straw-yellow Zlata ("Golden") Rebula, and the dry Tokaj, all of which emanate from the gorgeous Goriška Brda hills bordering Italy. Meanwhile, no visit to the Karst region is complete without a drop of the full-blooded, ruby-red **Teran** wine.

By far the most enjoyable place to sample wine is in one of the many **wine cellars** (*vinska klet*) that abound along the country's twenty or so **wine roads** (*vinske ceste*). Alternatively, most towns and cities have a *vinoteka* (wine shop), where you may be offered tastings, and most decent restaurants will have a healthy complement of Slovenian wines.

South of the Soča Valley, beyond the captivating **Goriška Brda** and **Vipava Valley** wine-growing regions, you'll find the **Karst**. This rugged limestone plateau is scattered with ancient stone villages, such as **Štanjel**, but is famed above all for its dramatic underground rivers, streams and depressions, manifested most spectacularly in the **Škocjan Caves**. The Karst is also home to the world-famous **Lipica stud farm**, the original home of the Lipizzaner.

Although just 47km long, the Slovenian **coast** packs in a multiplicity of little resorts, the most enjoyable being **Piran**, a town brimming with Venetian architecture, and **Portorož**, the country's major beach resort. A short way north of these is the workaday port town of **Koper**, which conceals an appealing medieval centre.

Returning inland, there are more subterranean wonders to explore, few of which can hold a candle to the breathtaking **Postojna Caves**, which lie within striking distance of another of Slovenia's remarkable natural phenomena, the "disappearing" **Lake Cerknica**. South of here, the dark forests and deep river valleys ranged along the Croatian border offer further possibilities for outdoor pursuits, whilst those seeking cultural diversions can take their pick from a rich tapestry of historical sites – churches, castles and ancient monasteries.

By comparison, the eastern part of the country is much less visited, and though it might not possess the clear-cut attractions of other regions, there are some hugely rewarding places to visit. Chief among these is the country's most historic, and prettiest town, **Ptuj**, which is also the setting for the marvellous Pust carnival, Slovenia's most exuberant annual event. Just a short ride away is the country's second city, **Maribor**, and the sprawling **Pohorje Massif**, a major summer and winter recreational resort. Eastern Slovenia abounds in **spas**, the most popular of which are **Rogaška Slatina** and **Čatež**, two of the largest in the country. Moving further east, across the Mura River and towards the Hungarian border, the undulating hills of the **Podravje** wine-growing districts give way to the flat plains of **Prekmurje**, a lovely, rural region of smooth fields interspersed with attractive villages distinguished by Hungarian-style farmhouses and little white churches.

When to go

Most visitors come to Slovenia in summer, when the weather is at its most reliable, the full range of sights are open, and the country's numerous festivals are in full swing. However, many of Slovenia's attractions, including the capital, are just as enjoyable outside the peak summer months, and in particular during spring and autumn, when the countryside colours are at their most resplendent, hotel prices (at least in the resort areas) are slightly lower and the crowds are a little thinner. Slovenia's climate follows three distinctive patterns: in the northwest, an **alpine** climate predominates, characterized by very cold winters, often with heavy rainfall and snow, and moderately warm

Ptuj

www.roughguides.com

9

▲ Mountain biking, Triglav National Park

summers, occasionally interspersed with short, violent storms. However, with the wide range of pursuits on offer here – skiing between December and March, and climbing, hiking and adventure sports between April and September – a visit to the mountain regions can be enjoyed at pretty much any time of the year. Aside from Kranjska Gora in the winter, and Lake Bled and Lake Bohinj in the height of summer, few resorts get so full that finding accommodation becomes a problem.

The Primorska region (from the Soča Valley down to the coast) has a typically **Mediterranean** climate – very warm summers with consistent sunshine, and pleasantly cool winters; this is the one part of the country that can feel a little pressured by crowds, particularly in August when hordes of vacationing Italians arrive from just across the border. Booking accommodation around this time is therefore recommended. Whatever the season, there's a good chance you'll experience the infamous *burja*, a vicious wind that whips down through the Karst on its way to the Bay of Trieste.

The remainder of the country subscribes to a **continental** climate of hot, dry summers – particularly in the south and east of the country – and bitterly cold winters.

Average monthly temperatures

	Jan	Feb	Mar	Apr	May	Jun	Jul	Aug	Sep	Oct	Nov	Dec
Črnomelj												
Temp °C	1	4	7	11	16	19	21	20	16	11	6	2
Temp °F	34	40	46	52	61	66	70	68	61	52	43	36
Koper												
Temp °C	5	6	9	12	17	20	23	23	20	16	10	7
Temp °F	41	43	48	54	62	68	74	74	68	61	50	46
Ljubljana												
Temp °C	-1	0	5	9	14	17	19	19	15	10	4	0
Temp °F	30	33	41	48	57	62	66	66	60	50	40	33
Maribor												
Temp °C	-3	-1	4	9	14	17	19	18	14	9	3	-1
Temp °F	26	30	40	48	57	62	66	64	57	48	37	30

things not to miss

It's not possible to see everything that Slovenia has to offer in one trip – and we don't suggest you try. What follows is a selective taste of the country's highlights: outstanding architecture, natural wonders and historic sites. They're arranged in five colour-coded categories, which you can browse through to find the very best things to see and experience. All highlights have a page reference to take you straight into the Guide, where you can find out more.

01 **Adventure sports on the Soča** Page **151** • This fabulous, foaming river is a first-rate venue for any number of adventure sports, from whitewater rafting, kayaking and canoeing to hydrospeeding.

02 **Lake Bohinj** Page **123** • Encircled by majestic mountains, Bohinj is the pearl of the alpine lakes, less visited and more serene than Lake Bled.

03 **Planica ski-jumping** Page **139** • Enjoy daring feats, beer and music at one of the world's great ski-jumping venues.

04 **The Karst** Page **183** • Explore dry-stone villages and head underground to a mysterious subterranean world of rivers, streams and caverns.

05 **Škocjan Caves** Page **188** • Carved out by the thrashing Reka River, the world's largest underground canyon is Slovenia's most amazing natural wonder.

07 **Kurent** Page **304** • Slovenia's most vibrant and entertaining winter spectacle, featuring spooky masked figures dressed in chunky costumes parading through town.

06 **Ljubljana's Old Town**
Page **60** • Enjoy fabulous Baroque and Habsburg architecture, a hilltop castle and leafy riverside cafés in the enchanting Slovene capital.

08 **Lake Bled** Page **112** • Fairytale lake complete with island church and atmospheric castle – take a dip, a stroll or just kick back on a gondola.

09 **Wine** Page **8** • From the sunny Goriška Brda hills in the west to the beautiful Ljutomer–Ormož vineyards in the east, Slovenia possesses some terrific wine-growing regions.

10 **Piran** Page **199** • An atmospheric coastal resort strewn with gorgeous Gothic–Venetian architecture, pretty little churches and quaint squares.

11 **Soča Valley** Page **149** • Snow-dusted peaks, a magical river and a raft of historical sites combine to make this a truly memorable place.

12 **Hiking in the Julian Alps** Page **130** • One of Europe's most stunning and least spoilt mountain ranges, these mountain wilds are Slovenia's prime hiking region, with trails to suit walkers of all abilities.

14 **Predjama Castle** Page **221** • Dramatically sited castle with a labyrinth of rooms, secret passages and underground caves.

15 **Prekmurje** Page **308** • Lush green fields, picturesque villages and storks characterize Slovenia's easternmost region.

13 **Ptuj** Page **298** • Slovenia's oldest and most appealing town is run through with over two thousand years of history.

16 **Logar Valley** Page **279** • Impossibly picturesque glacial valley, carpeted with meadows and forests and hemmed in by the raw peaks of the Kamniške-Savinja Alps.

17 **Skiing** Page **136** • Take your pick from over twenty ski resorts, with slopes and facilities to suit all abilities.

Basics

Basics

Getting there

Flying is the easiest way to reach Slovenia, with a couple of airlines now flying direct from airports in the UK and Ireland. Flying from North America, Australasia or South Africa will entail one or more changes. With a rail pass you can take in Slovenia as part of a wider European trip, but travelling to Slovenia by train from the UK is a rather long haul. Another option is to drive, a journey of some 1500km from the UK, best covered slowly over a couple of days.

Air fares are highest from June to August, and drop during the "shoulder" seasons – March to May and September to October. The best prices are found during the low season, from November to February, excluding Christmas and New Year when prices are hiked up and seats are at a premium.

You can often cut costs by going through **a specialist flight agent**, who in addition to dealing with discounted flights may also offer student and youth fares and travel insurance, rail passes, car rentals, tours and the like. Some agents specialize in charter flights, which may be cheaper than scheduled flights, but departure dates are fixed and cancellation penalties are high.

Flights from the UK and Ireland

Flying to Slovenia from the UK takes approximately two hours. Adria Airways, the Slovenian national carrier, operates one daily flight from London Gatwick to the capital, Ljubljana, and, between May and September, twice-weekly flights from Manchester to Ljubljana. Expect to pay around £120–140 return in low season and £180–200 in high season. In addition, easyJet operates one daily flight from Stansted to Ljubljana, fares for which can be obtained for as little as £70–80 return, including tax.

If you're struggling to get a direct flight, there is the option of flying into one of the neighbouring countries – in fact this can actually work out better, depending on which part of Slovenia you are intending to visit (see "overland from neighbouring countries" p.21).

From Ireland, Adria Airways operates one flight a week from Dublin to Ljubljana between May and September, with fares from around €180–260.

Flights from the US and Canada

There are no direct flights from the US or Canada to Slovenia, so you'll have to fly into a major European hub and continue the journey from there. Lufthansa, for example, offers low-season midweek return fares to Budapest (via Frankfurt) from around US$650 from New York and US$850 from West Coast cities, rising to around US$850 and US$1250 respectively during high season. From Canada, Lufthansa (via Frankfurt) offers return fares to Budapest from around Can$1250 low season, and Can$1600 high season.

Flights from Australia, New Zealand and South Africa

There are **no direct flights** to Slovenia from Australia or New Zealand, so you'll have to change airlines, either in Asia or Europe, although the best option is to fly to a Western European gateway and get a connecting flight from there. A standard return fare from eastern Australia to Ljubljana, via London, with Qantas, is around Aus$2200 low season and Aus$2700 high season. The same routes apply for flights from New Zealand, with a standard return fare from Auckland, with Air New Zealand, from around NZ$2800 low season, and NZ$3500 high season.

Similarly, there are no direct flights to Slovenia from South Africa, so you'll have to change airlines at one of the main European gateways. A standard return fare from Johannesburg to Ljubljana, via Frankfurt or Vienna (with South African Airways or a leading European airline), is around ZAR9000 low season and ZAR11000 high season.

By train

Travelling by train to Slovenia is likely to be considerably more expensive than flying, though it can be a leisurely way of getting to the country if you plan to stop off in other parts of Europe along the way. The shortest journey from London's St Pancras International to Ljubljana takes around eighteen hours; a standard second-class return ticket on this route, incorporating Eurostar via Paris or Brussels, will cost around £350.

Deutsche Bahn is the best option for making seat reservations on continental trains and its website (see p.22) is an excellent resource for checking railway timetables, while the website of The Man in Seat Sixty-One (see p.23) is an excellent source of information on most aspects of rail travel in Europe. Thomas Cook's red-covered European Rail Timetable, which details schedules of the main Slovenian train service, is the most useful printed source for timetables; the same publisher also produces the Rail Map of Europe.

Rail passes

If you're taking in Slovenia as part of a wider trip, there are a number of rail passes available. The InterRail Pass (@www .interrail.net) is available to European residents only (or those who have been resident in a European country for at least six months), and you will be asked to provide proof of residency before being allowed to buy one. They come in over-26 and (cheaper) under-26 versions, and cover thirty countries, of which Slovenia is one.

Six steps to a better kind of travel

At Rough Guides we are passionately committed to travel. We feel strongly that only through travelling do we truly come to understand the world we live in and the people we share it with – plus tourism has brought a great deal of **benefit** to developing economies around the world over the last few decades. But the extraordinary growth in tourism has also damaged some places irreparably, and of course **climate change** is exacerbated by most forms of transport, especially flying. This means that now more than ever it's important to **travel thoughtfully** and **responsibly**, with respect for the cultures you're visiting – not only to derive the most benefit from your trip but also to preserve the best bits of the planet for everyone to enjoy. At Rough Guides we feel there are six main areas in which you can make a difference:

- Consider what you're contributing to the **local economy**, and how much the services you use do the same, whether it's through employing local workers and guides or sourcing locally grown produce and local services.
- Consider the **environment** on holiday as well as at home. Water is scarce in many developing destinations, and the biodiversity of local flora and fauna can be adversely affected by tourism. Try to patronize businesses that take account of this.
- Travel with a purpose, not just to tick off experiences. Consider **spending longer** in a place, and getting to know it and its people.
- Give thought to how often you **fly**. Try to avoid short hops by air and more harmful night flights.
- Consider **alternatives to flying**, travelling instead by bus, train, boat and even by bike or on foot where possible.
- Make your trips "**climate neutral**" via a reputable carbon offset scheme. All Rough Guide flights are offset, and every year we donate money to a variety of charities devoted to combating the effects of climate change.

There are two types of pass. The Global Pass covers all thirty countries (one month of continuous use costs €599 for over 26s/€399 for under 26s; 22 days' continuous use €469/309; ten days' use in a period of 22 days €359/239; five days in ten days €249/159). InterRail Passes do not include travel between Britain and the Continent although holders are eligible for discounts on rail travel in Britain and Northern Ireland and cross-Channel ferries, as well as reduced rates on the London–Paris Eurostar service.

The other InterRail scheme is the One-Country Pass which allows you to travel for a certain number of days during a one-month period in one country depending on which pass you buy. For Slovenia, eight days in one month costs €119 for over 26s/€77 for under 26s; six days in one month €99/64; four days in one month €69/45; three days in one month €49/32.

Non-European residents qualify for the Eurail Pass (⊛www.eurail.com), which must be bought before arrival in Europe (or from RailEurope in the UK). The Global Pass allows for unlimited rail travel in Slovenia and twenty other countries, and is available in increments of fifteen days (€511 for over 26s/€332 for under 26s), 21 days (€662/429), one month (€822/535), two months (€1161/755) and three months (€1432/€933).

The One-Country Pass allows unlimited second-class train travel on a select number of days within one month, starting at three days within one month (€49/33), up to eight days within one month (€118/77), within Slovenia. Furthermore, there's the Select Pass, which allows travel in three (from €211), four (from €235) or five (from €260) bordering countries over a selected period of time (five, six, eight or ten days within a two-month period); and a Regional Austria–Croatia–Slovenia Pass (from €191), which allows unlimited free first-class train travel between four and ten days within two months in these three countries.

By car

If you have the time and inclination, driving to Slovenia, a distance of 1500km from London, can be a pleasant proposition. However, it's really only worth considering if you are planning to travel around Slovenia extensively, or want to take advantage of various stopovers en route.

Once across the channel, the most direct route to Ljubljana (around 30hr at a leisurely pace with plenty of stops) is via Brussels, Stuttgart, Munich and Salzburg before crossing into Slovenia at the Karavanke Tunnel border. Detailed printouts of the route can be obtained from the websites of Michelin (⊛www.viamichelin.com), the AA (⊛www.theaa.com) or the RAC (⊛www.rac.co.uk). See p.25 for details of driving within Slovenia.

Overland from neighbouring countries

Slovenia is conveniently placed for easy access from a number of neighbouring countries. Travellers from the UK (or Ireland) on a low-cost flight (to Budapest, Graz, Trieste, Venice or Zagreb) can continue the onward journey by bus or train. Travellers from North America or Australia/New Zealand are likely to fly into one of the European gateway cities (for example Paris or Frankfurt), also necessitating an onward journey to Slovenia by train or bus.

From Graz six trains a day make the short one-hour journey to Maribor, two of which continue on to Ljubljana. From Venice there are three daily trains to Ljubljana, all of which stop in the border town, Villa Opicina. Alternatively there are regular buses from Trieste to Koper, which is well connected to the capital by bus and train. From Budapest (Keleti and Deli stations) there are half a dozen trains a day to Ljubljana, with a journey time of around nine hours. From Zagreb, there are currently eight trains a day to Ljubljana (2hr 30min).

Airlines, agents and operators

Airlines

Adria Airways ⊛www.adria-airways.com.
Air France ⊛www.airfrance.com.
Air New Zealand ⊛www.airnz.co.nz.
British Airways ⊛www.ba.com.
easyJet ⊛www.easyjet.com.
KLM (Royal Dutch Airlines) ⊛www.klm.com.
Lufthansa ⊛www.lufthansa.com.

Malev Hungarian Airlines ⓦ www.malev.hu.
Qantas Airways ⓦ www.qantas.com.
Ryanair ⓦ www.ryanair.com.
South African Airways ⓦ www.flysaa.com.
Wizz Air ⓦ www.wizzair.com.

Agents and operators

North South Travel UK ☎ 01245/608291,
ⓦ www.northsouthtravel.co.uk. Friendly, competitive
travel agency, offering discounted fares worldwide.
Profits are used to support projects in the developing
world, especially the promotion of sustainable tourism.
STA Travel US ☎ 1-800/781-4040, UK
☎ 0871/230 0040, Australia ☎ 134 782,
New Zealand ☎ 0800/474400, South Africa
☎ 0861/781781; ⓦ www.statravel.com.
Worldwide specialists in independent travel;
also student IDs, travel insurance, car rental, rail
passes, and more. Good discounts for students and
under-26s.
Trailfinders UK ☎ 0845/058 5858, Ireland
☎ 01/677 7888, Australia ☎ 1300/780212;
ⓦ www.trailfinders.com. One of the best-informed
and most efficient agents for independent travellers.

Specialist operators

Activities Abroad ☎ 01670/789991, ⓦ www
.activitiesabroad.com. Four- to ten-day multi-activity
holidays in the Julian Alps and Soča Valley, including
canyoning, caving, cycling, kayaking and rafting;
from £425.
Adventure Center ☎ 1-800/228-8747 or
510/654-1879, ⓦ www.adventurecenter.com.
Variety of eight- to ten-day tours of the mountains and
lakes, including water activities and skiing, as well as
cultural and wine tours.
Balkan Holidays ☎ 0845/130 1114, ⓦ www
.balkanholidays.co.uk. Southeastern Europe
specialists, offering package deals to Bled, Bohinj,
Kranjska Gora and Portorož. Ski package and flight-
only deals available too.
Beyond Slovenia Australia ☎ 02/9651 3177,
ⓦ www.beyondslovenia.com. Slovene specialists
who can assist with any aspect of travel to
the country, including tailor-made packages,
accommodation and tours.
Crystal Holidays ☎ 0870/166 4951, ⓦ www
.crystalholidays.co.uk. Summer and winter (ski)
package deals to Bled, Bohinj, Bovec, Kranjska Gora
and the Adriatic Coast. Flight-only deals too.
Eastern Eurotours Australia ☎ 1800/242353 or
07/5526 2855, ⓦ www.easterneurotours.com.au.
Several excellent week-long escorted tours throughout
the country, including the Alps and Slovenian castles,
as well as ski holidays in Kranjska Gora.

Exodus ☎ 0845/863 9600, ⓦ www.exodus.co.uk.
Wide range of eight-day tours, including multi-activity
(whitewater adventure sports on the Soča River in
summer, cross-country skiing and snowshoeing in
the Julian Alps in winter), trekking/climbing (including
an ascent of Mount Triglav), and family adventure
holidays, all from around £850.
Explore Worldwide ☎ 0870/3334001, ⓦ www
.explore.co.uk. Eight-day Alpine Lakes tour taking in
Ljubljana, the Julian Alps and the Adriatic coast; and a
same-length, family-oriented Caves and Castles tour
which includes various activities; both from £850.
Headwater ☎ 01606/720199, ⓦ www.headwater
.com. Eight- and nine-day guided and self-guided
walking holidays (easy to moderate) in the Julian Alps,
with stays in high-end hotels; from £880.
Hooked on Cycling ☎ 01501/740985, ⓦ www
.hookedoncycling.co.uk. Various week-long self-
guided cycling trips, including tours of the Julian Alps,
Karst and coast, and eastern Slovenia; from around
£500. They also offer a range of seven-day, self-
guided hiking trips from around £475.
Inghams ☎ 020/8780 4400, ⓦ www.inghams.co.uk.
Seven- to fourteen-day summer (lakes, mountains and
coast) and winter (skiing) package tours.
Inntravel ☎ 01653/617946, ⓦ www.inntravel
.co.uk. Seven-day walking and cycling tours including
the Karst and Coast (from £530), Lakes and Alps
(from £800), and northwestern Slovenia (£750).
Just Slovenia ☎ 01373/814230, ⓦ www
.justslovenia.co.uk. UK's premier Slovenia specialist,
offering tailor-made holidays, including fights,
accommodation (including tourist farms), sports and
activities/recreational pursuits, and car rental.
Saddle Skedaddle ☎ 0191/265 1110, ⓦ www
.skedaddle.co.uk. Eight-day, self-guided cycling tour of
the Julian Alps, Soča Valley, Karst and coast; from £995.
Thermalia Travel ☎ 0870/165 9420, ⓦ www
.kingdomholidayhealth.com. Spa holiday specialists
offering a range of five-, seven- and ten-day
treatment programmes at the Rogaška Slatina,
Šmarješke Toplice and Strunjan spas.
Vamos Travel ☎ 0870/762 4017, ⓦ www
.vamostravel.com. Excellent Central and Eastern
Europe specialist offering tailor-made tours to
Ljubljana and Bled, multi-activity adventure holidays,
ski breaks, and much more.
Wilderness Travel US ☎ 1-800/368-2794,
ⓦ www.wildernesstravel.com. Eleven-day hiking trip
(moderate to difficult) through western Slovenia, taking
in the Julian Alps, Logar Valley, Soča Valley and Piran.

Rail contacts

Deutsche Bahn ⓦ www.bahn.de. The German
national rail website is the best source of international
timetabling information.

European Rail UK ☎020/7619 1083, ⓦwww
.europeanrail.com. Independent specialist offering a
range of European rail tickets, including InterRail.
Europrail International Canada ☎1-888/667-
9734, ⓦwww.europrail.net. Eurail and country passes.
Eurostar UK ☎0870/518 6186, outside UK
☎+44/1233 617575; ⓦwww.eurostar.com. High-
speed train links from London St Pancras International
to Paris, Lille and Brussels.
Rail Europe UK ☎0844/848 4064, US ☎1-888/
382-7245, Canada ☎1-800/361-7245, Australia
☎03/9642 8644, New Zealand ☎09/377 5415,
South Africa ☎011/628 2319; ⓦwww
.raileurope.com. Wide range of European passes,
including InterRail, and Eurostar tickets.

The Man in Seat Sixty-One ⓦwww.seat61.com.
Excellent website detailing routes, timings and fares
across Europe.

Ferry contacts

Eurotunnel UK ☎0870/535 3535, ⓦwww
.eurotunnel.com. Drive-on, drive-off shuttle trains for
vehicles from Folkestone to Coquelles, near Calais.
P&O Ferries UK ☎0871/664 5645, ⓦwww
.poferries.com. Dover to Calais.
Sea France UK ☎0871/663 2546, ⓦwww
.seafrance.com. Dover to Calais.
Stena Line UK ☎0870/570 7070, ⓦwww
.stenaline.co.uk. Harwich to Hook of Holland.

Getting around

Whether you travel by train, bus or car, almost any journey you take around
Slovenia will be wonderfully scenic; moreover, the country's tiny scale means that
you'll never have to travel long distances. On the whole, both trains and buses are
clean, reliable and inexpensive; although trains are cheaper, buses do cover a far
greater number of destinations. Driving brings the obvious advantages of allowing
you to visit pretty much anywhere you please, and in your own good time.
Approximate times and frequencies are given in the "Travel Details" section at the
end of each guide chapter.

By rail

Slovene railways (*Slovenske železnice*) runs
a smooth, efficient and inexpensive service
covering a modest 1200 kilometres, almost
half of which is electrified. All the key lines,
as well as international trains, run through
Ljubljana. Even if you're not intending to
travel to the capital, you'll often save
yourself a lot of hassle by heading to
Ljubljana first and changing there, instead of
messing about changing at a host of small
regional stops.

Trains (*vlaki*) are divided into **slow trains**
(*potniški*), which stop at every halt, **Intercity
trains** ("IC") which are faster, more comfortable, and stop at fewer stations, and the
very fast, **Inter City Slovenia** ("ICS"), three-
carriage tilting trains which run between
Maribor and Ljubljana (1hr 45min) stopping

at Pragersko, Celje and Zidani Most – at
weekends between mid-June and August
this train runs once daily between Maribor
and Koper. These trains are air-conditioned,
have catering and are wheelchair accessible.
For information on the car (Bohinjska Bistrica
to Most na Soči) and museum (Jesenice to
Most na Soči) trains see p.125 and p.163.
There are no domestic overnight trains.

Although there are no special carriages,
bicycles (*kolo*) can be carried on all trains
(except the ICS), for which you have to pay
an extra €3.

Most **timetables** (*vozni red*) have explanations in English; the yellow boards with
Odhodi are departures, the white boards
with *Prihodi* arrivals. Timetable leaflets,
which only indicate routes that trains from
that particular station take, are sometimes

Driving distances (km)

Bled	Bovec	Celje	Čronmelj	Koper	Kranj	Kranjska Gora	Ljubljana	Maribor
...	99	114	164	162	23	35	53	162
	...	187	216	166	122	44	125	243
		...	130	194	82	161	77	68
			...	185	117	202	91	188
				...	...	198	117	250
					...	58	26	138
						...	88	221
							...	133
								...

available from counters, but if you're planning to travel extensively on the railways you might want to invest in a national timetable (*Vozni Red Slovenske Železniške*; €4), available from the bigger stations. You can also check train information on the website Ⓦ www.slo-zeleznice.si, which has good English explanations. There are left-luggage lockers (*garderoba*; €2 for 24hr) at the following stations: Celje, Divača, Koper, Ljubljana, Maribor, Nova Gorica, Postojna and Sežana.

Tickets

Tickets for domestic train services can be bought at the station (*železniška postaja*) on the day of departure and up to two months in advance. If you enter a train without a ticket (for a good reason) you will have to pay a supplement of €2.50. Otherwise, fare dodging (not advised) will cost you €40. Most town and city stations now accept payment by credit card for both domestic and international tickets.

Fares are calculated by distance travelled, with a return ticket (*povratna vozovnica*) exactly double that of a single (*enosmerna vozovnica*). To give you some idea, a journey of 50km costs around €4 (€6 first class), a journey of 100km, €6 (€9 first class), and a journey of 200km, €10 (€15 first class). ICS trains, however, are more expensive; the second class fare for the journey between Ljubljana and Maribor (156km) is around €14 (€20 first class, which includes a snack and drink). **Concessionary fares** on domestic services are available for children under the age of 6 (free), and for children aged between 6 and 12 (half-price).

Seat reservations (*rezervacije*; €3.50) are obligatory for services marked on a timetable with a boxed R (in effect all ICS trains and some international services), and optional for those designated by an R. Slovenian railways do not issue any passes for travel within the country. However the country is part of the InterRail and Eurail systems, both of which also incorporate more Slovenia-specific passes (see p.20).

By bus

Slovenia's **bus network** consists of a slightly confusing, but generally well-coordinated, array of small local companies. On the whole, buses are clean, reasonably comfortable, and, except for some departing on a Friday evening, rarely crowded. They also have the advantage of being able to reach significantly more destinations than trains; moreover, services tend to be more frequent. That said, services, particularly those on rural routes, are dramatically reduced (or even nonexistent) at weekends, and especially on Sundays.

Towns such as Ljubljana, Maribor and Koper have large bus stations (*avtobusna postaja*) with computerized booking facilities where you can buy your tickets hours (if not

Murska Sobota	Nova Gorica	Novo Mesto	Postojna	Ptuj	Slovenj Gradec	
291	159	127	102	165	143	Bled
299	76	198	121	246	215	Bovec
103	165	100	130	59	49	Celje
232	173	37	121	179	179	Črnomelj
306	90	181	64	253	223	Koper
194	102	99	79	141	108	Kranj
281	120	157	140	216	187	Kranjska Gora
191	113	73	53	136	114	Ljubljana
56	224	139	186	26	71	Maribor
...	268	195	242	54	126	Murska Sobota
	...	161	62	224	194	Nova Gorica
		...	111	148	130	Novo Mesto
			...	189	161	Postojna
				...	74	Ptuj
					...	Slovenj Gradec

days) in advance – recommended if you're travelling between Ljubljana and the coast in high season. Otherwise, simply pile onto the bus and pay the driver or conductor. If you need to store items of baggage in the hold you'll be charged a little extra. Like trains, **fares** are calculated according to distance travelled; typical fares are around €6 for 50km and €12 for 100km.

By car

All things considered, driving in Slovenia is a joy. Despite the country's high level of car ownership, Slovenia's well-surfaced roads often seem blissfully traffic-free, and you'll be endlessly distracted by the scenery. Neither is driving likely to tire you out, such are the short distances between destinations. If driving in the mountainous regions, bear in mind that some of the higher passes, such as the Vršič Pass in the Julian Alps, are often closed for days or weeks at a time during periods of heavy snowfall.

The country is crossed by two **motorway** corridors (*avtocesta*): the A1 which runs in an east–west direction from Šentilj, just north of Maribor, down to Koper on the coast (there's also a short stretch from Postojna up to Nova Gorica, the H4), and the A2 which runs north–south from the Karavanke Tunnel on the Austrian border to Obrežje on the Croatian border (and continuing down to Zagreb). There are, though, still incomplete sections on the latter route; both these motorways pass through Ljubljana. In order to travel on the motorways you must purchase a **vignette** (sticker) in advance; these cost €15 for a week and €30 for a month, and can be purchased at petrol stations and post offices. Lesser **highways**, linking the major centres, are numbered with a single digit, while secondary or tertiary roads are identified by two or three digit numbers.

Petrol stations (*bencinska črpalka*) can be found everywhere, even in the most rural backwaters. Although most open from around 6 or 7am to 9 or 10pm, there are now quite a few 24-hour service stations, usually located on the outskirts of larger towns and cities, and around resort areas. Lead-free fuel (*neosvinčen bencin*), which costs around €1 per litre, is the most commonly used. Credit cards are accepted at most stations.

In cities, **parking** in white zones (marked with white lines) is permitted for up to two

Bus timetables

Bus timetables can be difficult to comprehend, as there's often little by way of English explanation. However, the following letters indicate those days that buses operate: V (every day); D (Mon–Fri); D+ (Mon–Sat); SO (Sat); N (Sun); NP (Sun & holidays); ŠP (school days).

hours (typically €0.60, though it will cost more down on the coast), while you can stay in a "blue zone" for up thirty minutes (free). *Brezplačno* means free parking. Parking in car parks (*parkirišče*) normally costs around €1 per hour.

For information on any aspect of driving within Slovenia, you can contact the Automobile Association of Slovenia (Avto-moto zveza Slovenije or AMZS), based in Ljubljana at Dunajska 128 (☎01/530-5100). Their information centre (daily 5.30am–11pm; ☎01/530-5300) provides information and assistance, while their website (🌐www.amzs.si) tells you all you need to know about driving in Slovenia and provides up-to-the-minute information on road traffic conditions. They also publish a 1:270,000 tourist road map of Slovenia.

In the event of a **breakdown**, call AMZS's Assistance-Information Service (SPI) on the 24-hour emergency number ☎1987. There are 24-hour technical centres in Celje, Koper, Kranj, Ljubljana, Maribor, Otočec and Postojna, with technical units (open 7am–8pm) in the other major towns; the addresses and telephone numbers of all centres can be found on the AMZS website (see above). All accidents should be reported to the police on ☎113.

Hitchhiking is widely practised by Slovenes, and you'll often see queues of students lining roadsides on the outskirts of Ljubljana and other towns on a Friday evening in a quest to get home. Avoid these places at these times and you shouldn't have too much of a problem getting a ride with someone. As anywhere, however, it's not a foolproof pursuit, so caution should be exercised.

Rules and regulations

Traffic drives on the right and **speed limits** for vehicles are 130kph on motorways, 90kph on secondary and tertiary roads, and 50kph in built-up areas. Otherwise, the most important rules are the prohibitions against sounding the horn in a built-up area (unless to avert accidents) and using a hand-held mobile while driving. It is compulsory for driver and passengers to wear seatbelts, to use dipped headlights when travelling on all roads at all times of the day, and to keep a triangular breakdown sign in the car.

Between mid-November and mid-March you're required to carry snow chains.

Random stops by the police are quite common and if you are stopped – you'll often see police vehicles on approaches to villages and built-up areas – you'll be required to show all your **documents**, so make sure you have them in the car at all times. The police are extremely hot on road traffic violations and any offence committed (speeding, not wearing a seatbelt, illegal parking and the like) is subject to an on-the-spot **fine**, which can be anything between €40 and €250, depending on the offence. It goes without saying that **drinking and driving** do not go hand-in-hand; the permitted blood-alcohol level for drivers is 0.05mg per 100ml of blood, although you may still be liable to a €130 fine if caught with this amount. Any amount over this means a fine of anything up to €500.

Car rental

Renting a car is simple enough, provided you are 21 or older, and hold a valid national driving licence. You can order a car through rental agencies in your own country, which sometimes works out cheaper, particularly if you book online. Most of the major companies have an outlet in Ljubljana (see p.81), including the airport, as well as in some of the major towns and cities.

Car rental **costs** are not especially cheap; expect to pay around €45–50 for a day (unlimited mileage) and around €35–40 per day for seven days or more. You may find that local companies, such as ABC Cars in Ljubljana, offer better deals, so it's worth looking around before deciding which company to use. Before signing, check on any mileage limits or other restrictions, extras, and what you're covered for in the event of an accident. You may be able to take the car into neighbouring countries, although most companies charge extra for this.

Car rental agencies

ABC Cars 🌐 www.europcar.si.
Alamo 🌐 www.alamo.com.
Auto Europe 🌐 www.autoeurope.com.
Avis 🌐 www.avis.com.
Budget 🌐 www.budget.com.
Dollar 🌐 www.dollar.com.

Addresses

Following the Slovenian address system is not difficult. The most **common terms** are: *ulica* (street), *cesta* (road), *pot* (trail), *steza* (path) and *trg* (square). The street name always comes before the number. In some smaller towns and most villages throughout Slovenia there is no street name at all, just a house number; where no street name is given in the guide, assume it's because there isn't one.

Enterprise Rent-a-Car ⓦ www.enterprise.com.
Europcar ⓦ www.europcar.com.
Hertz ⓦ www.hertz.com.
Holiday Autos ⓦ www.holidayautos.co.uk.
Irish Car Rentals ⓦ www.irishcarrentals.ie.
National ⓦ www.nationalcar.com.
SIXT ⓦ www.sixt.com.
Thrifty ⓦ www.thrifty.com.

Cycling

Slovenia's wonderfully varied topography presents endless opportunities for cyclists. From the tough mountain climbs in Triglav National Park to the iron-flat landscapes of Prekmurje, there are a number of well-organized recreational routes and trails all over the country. Otherwise, cycling is permitted on all roads except motorways. Most urban centres have, to a greater or lesser degree, well-integrated cycle lanes or paths, though the traffic in towns and cities is rarely threatening. On a practical note, bikes can be taken onto trains, except ICS, for a small fee, while some buses might allow you to store your bike in the luggage compartment.

Accommodation

Slovenia has a healthy range of accommodation to suit all tastes and budgets; hotels abound and there are an increasing number of good-value pensions to choose from. For those with less cash to spend, there are plenty of private rooms to go around, particularly in the more popular areas such as Bled, Bohinj and the coast, while a stay on a tourist farm provides an attractive, affordable and peaceful alternative. There's a good spread of decent campsites across the country, as there are hostels and student dorms.

Reservations for all types of accommodation are advisable during high season in the capital and more popular places (June–Aug & Dec–Feb in the ski resorts), or if you're bound for somewhere with limited possibilities. Details of all Slovenia's hotels, private rooms, tourist farms and campsites are listed in booklets available from the Slovenia Tourist Board; you can view the same contents online at ⓦ www.slovenia .info.

Hotels and pensions

Slovenian hotels use the traditional **five-star grading system** for classification, although in many cases this only gives a vague idea of prices, which can vary dramatically according to the locality and season. Generally speaking, prices in the capital, along the coast and in the major resorts, such as Bled, Bohinj and Kranjska Gora, are higher than elsewhere. Do bear in mind that ratings are not always indicative of the quality of a place – for example, three-star places can, and do, vary appreciably from one place to another.

Unfortunately, Slovenia's city **hotels** tend to be heavily geared towards the business traveller – in Ljubljana, for example, budget or medium-priced hotels are few and far between, a situation common to other places like Maribor, Celje and Nova Gorica. Many of the hotels in key resorts such as Bled, Bohinj or Portorož are aimed squarely at the package-tourist – the same goes for the growing number of spa hotels in Slovenia. That said there are an increasing number of **family-run hotels** and **pensions** (*penzion*) which, in most cases, offer much better value than a hotel of a similar price and invariably come with a more personal touch. Some pensions are more commonly known as **gostišče**, not to be confused with a *gostilna* (which is an eating establishment), but these are usually found in smaller towns and more rural areas.

Slovenia can count less than a handful of five-star establishments, some of which have been incorporated into historic buildings, for example at Mokrice and Otočec castles. Most four-star hotels have all the luxuries you'd expect, with modern, and in many cases, renovated, rooms, with satellite TV and wi-fi – moreover, many now possess some sort of spa/health facility, such as a pool, sauna or gym. The vast majority of the country's hotels are in the three-star category, and this is where standards can vary. However, in most cases the rooms are reliably comfortable and come with TV, minibar and internet access. More predictably, one- and two-star hotels – of which there are actually very few – can be tatty, soulless places (and sometimes come without private bathroom) but are usually clean and bearable. Most hotels include **breakfast** in the price, but this is not always clear and it's worth checking.

Private rooms and apartments

Hostels aside, taking a **private room** (*zasebne sobe*) is the cheapest option available, particularly if there are two of you sharing. Few towns and cities are well stocked with private rooms, but you'll find that there are plenty to go around in the busier lake and coastal resorts. Rooms are **categorized** from one to three stars; a one-star place is very basic and comes with shared shower and toilets, a two-star usually has private shower and toilet, and a three-star comes with plusher furnishings and sometimes a television.

As a rough guideline, **prices** start at around €20 for a double room in a category-one place, €25 for a category-two place, and €35 for a category-three place. Not included in the price is tourist tax, which is usually around €2 per person; nor is breakfast included. Moreover, in most places, prices are subject to a thirty percent surcharge if you stay fewer than three nights. Rented out in the same way as private rooms, **apartments** (*apartmaji*) are a reasonably cheap alternative, particularly if there are a few of you. A standard four-bed apartment in Bohinj or on the coast will cost in the region of €65–70, a six-bed place around €80–90 per night.

With the odd exception (for example in Bohinj) very few tourist offices administer bookings for private rooms; these are usually handled by local agencies. Larger agencies such as Kompas have branches in several towns and resorts.

Accommodation price codes

Accommodation in this guide is graded according to the price bands below. Note that prices refer to the **cheapest available double room in high season (June–Aug)**. For hostels and dorms, the price per bed has been given.

❶ €25 and under	❹ €46–55	❼ €86–100
❷ €26–35	❺ €56–70	❽ €101–120
❸ €36–45	❻ €71–85	❾ €121 and over

Tourist farms

Farm tourism (*turističnih kmetji*) is a thriving sector in Slovenia, and if you're looking for a restful night, then these rural retreats are perfect. Note though that their very isolation means that, unless you have your own means of transport, they can often be quite difficult to reach.

Despite a **classification system** (denoted by apples), there is often little distinction between the highest grade (four apples) and a lower grade, though most farms offer reasonably sized, modestly furnished rooms with bathroom. Farms with four apples invariably have larger, slightly better furnished rooms, sometimes with television. Although there are no hard and fast rules regarding **pricing**, as a guide a double room on a farm with three or four apples will cost around €45–55, two apples around €35–45, and one, or unclassified, farms around €30. All prices include breakfast, which is a wholesome affair, typically consisting of tea, coffee, juice, cereal, home-made bread, jam, cheese and ham; in some places you may also get a cooked breakfast. Most farms offer a half-board option for about €8 extra, which is exceptional value given that the cooking is invariably superb – many also produce their own wine.

You can do activities, such as horse riding, cycling and tennis at some farms, while others allow you to help out on the farm – from preparing foodstuffs (baking bread or making jam), to milking the cows or feeding the calves. The Association of Tourist Farms of Slovenia has an excellent website (Ⓦ www.farmtourism.si) which lists and describes every one of the country's tourist farms.

Mountain huts

There are some 170 **mountain huts** (*Planinarski Domovi*; see box, p.142) scattered across Slovenia's hills and mountains, ranging from the most basic refuges with huge dorms and cold running water, to more comfortable alpine villas offering a wider range of cosier rooms, hot water and other amenities. In any case, most huts are convivial places, where hikers share a beer or two and exchange information about trails or the weather before pushing on.

The majority of huts, especially those at higher altitudes, are open between June and September, while some are open a month or two longer than this, and a few year-round; if you're planning to spend any length of time in the more popular hiking areas, for example around Triglav, you'd be wise to book ahead. Depending on the type of hut and its location, you'll pay anything between €10 and €20 for a bed; UIAA-affiliated members are entitled to a discount. The useful, if very dated, *Mountain Huts* book, published by the Slovene Alpine Association, lists every hut, together with routes and approaches to the next lodge.

Hostels and dorms

Slovenia now has a reasonably good spread of **youth hostels** (*mladinski hotel*), with several excellent ones in Ljubljana There are also well-equipped hostels in Bled, the Karst (Pliskovica), Piran and Ptuj – uniformly excellent, and with comprehensive amenities, each of these hostels has rooms sleeping between two and six people (some also have fourteen bed dorms), and charges around €20 per person, including breakfast. Most offer discounts to HI card holders.

Another possibility are **student dorms** (*dijaški dom*), which are generally of a decent standard, but usually only open in July and August once the students have packed up (although quite a few keep some beds aside during the rest of the year, but these are usually available at weekends only); expect to pay around €10–15 for a bed. The website Ⓦ www.youth-hostel.si has details on all Slovenia's hostels, as does Ⓦ www .hostelworld.com.

Youth hostel associations

US and Canada

Hostelling International–American Youth Hostels US ☏ 1-301/495-1240, Ⓦ www.hiusa.org. **Hostelling International Canada** ☏ 1-800/663-5777, Ⓦ www.hihostels.ca.

UK and Ireland

Youth Hostel Association (YHA) UK ☏ 01629/592700, Ⓦ www.yha.org.uk. **Scottish Youth Hostel Association** ☏ 0845/293 7373, Ⓦ www.syha.org.uk.

Irish Youth Hostel Association Ireland ☎01/830 4555, ⓦwww.anoige.ie.
Hostelling International Northern Ireland Northern Ireland ☎028/9032 4733, ⓦwww.hini .org.uk.

Australia, New Zealand and South Africa

Australia Youth Hostels Association Australia ☎02/ 9565 1699, ⓦwww.yha.com.au.
Youth Hostelling Association New Zealand New Zealand ☎0800/278299 or 03/379 9970, ⓦwww.yha.co.nz.

Camping

Slovenia has a good, if rather uneven, spread of **camping grounds** (*kampi*) across the country. Most campsites, whatever their size, are clean and well-appointed places, while the better ones (sites are categorized from between one and three stars), such as those in Bled and Bohinj, have excellent amenities – more often than not with restaurants, shops, sports facilities and children's play areas. Nearly all sites have hot water.

Expect to pay around €2–3 for ground rent plus €8–10 per person per night and slightly more at the better sites. Prices are reduced slightly outside July and August. The majority of sites are open from April or May to September or October, with a handful open year-round. Note that **camping rough** is illegal.

If you're planning to do a lot of camping, an **international camping carnet** is a good investment. The carnet gives discounts at member sites and serves as useful identification. Many campsites will take it instead of making you surrender your passport during your stay, and it covers you for third-party insurance when camping. In the UK and Ireland, the carnet is available to members of the AA or the RAC, or for members of the Camping and Caravanning Club (☎024/7669 4995, ⓦwww.campingandcaravanningclub .co.uk), the CTC (☎0870/873 0061, ⓦwww .ctc.org.uk) or the foreign touring arm of the same company, the **Carefree Travel Service** (☎024/7642 2024), which provides the carnet free if you take out insurance with them. In the US and Canada, the carnet is available from home motoring organizations, or from Family Campers and RVers (FCRV; ☎1-800/245-9755 or 716/668-6242, ⓦwww.fcrv.org).

Food and drink

Slovenia straddles several culinary cultures, absorbing Austrian, Balkan, Mediterranean and Pannonian influences. That said, and despite the increasing internationalization of restaurants and cafés, there remains a strong native Slovene tradition based on age-old peasant recipes. For a full glossary of food and drink terms, see pp.347–349.

Breakfasts, snacks and sandwiches

Breakfast (*zajtrk*) in your average hotel typically consists of bread or rolls with jam or marmalade, and sometimes cereal and yoghurt – only in the better hotels will you be offered a full buffet complement, with cooked food, pastries or croissants and fresh fruit. Breakfast on a tourist farm is invariably an enjoyable, wholesome affair, with everything from bread and milk to jams and cheeses prepared on the farm.

The best places for **snacks** are *okrepčevalnice* (snack bars) and street kiosks, which dole out *burek*, a flaky and often very greasy pastry filled with cheese (*burek z sirom*) or meat (*burek z mesom*). Sausages come in various forms, most commonly hot dogs, *hrenovke* (Slovene frankfurters), or the much tastier *kranjska* *klobasa* (big spicy sausages). A popular light lunchtime meal is *malica*, a filling two or three-course meal with drink usually served from 11am or midday until 3pm, and costing around €3–4.

Slovenia's **supermarkets** (*trgovina*) and delicatessens (*delikatesa*) are good places to stock up on sandwich and picnic ingredients, like local cheese (*sir*) and salami. You can buy fresh fruit and vegetables here too but, if possible, try and get your produce from outdoor markets (*tržnica*) or roadside stalls. Bread is best bought from bakeries (*pekarna*), most of which usually sell a decent range of croissants and sandwiches – which makes them the best place to head for if you've not been offered breakfast at your hotel or lodging. In a similar vein is the almost impossible to pronounce *slaščičarna* (patisserie), where you can indulge in all sorts of sweet-toothed delights.

Restaurants and meals

The most common type of eating establishment in Slovenia is a **restavracija** (restaurant). These can be found everywhere, though the quality is often variable, from the down-at-heel to the very classy. Although there are plenty of restaurants in the larger towns and cities (Ljubljana and Maribor specifically), you'll often find that choices are extremely limited in smaller towns. Invariably more atmospheric is a **gostilna**, an inn-type place which is usually, but not always, located on the outskirts of town and in more rural areas; along the same lines, a **gostišče** serves food and also has some accommodation available. If possible, don't pass up the opportunity to eat on a tourist farm, where you'll find Slovenian home cooking at its finest, with ingredients usually harvested on the farm itself.

Generally speaking, **menus** vary little wherever you eat, and are invariably dominated by meat dishes (*mesne jedi*), mostly schnitzels (*zrezek*), beef (*govedina*), pork (*svinjina*) and veal (*teletina*). However, the tasty southern Balkan meats *čevapčiči* (grilled rolls of minced meat) and *sarma* (cabbage stuffed with meat and rice) frequently make their way onto menus. One particularly curious Slovene speciality is horse steak (*žrebičkov zrezek*), and neither

are Slovenes squeamish about offal – liver (*jetra*) and grilled or fried brains (*možgani*) are popular standbys in cheaper restaurants. The majority of menus in classier restaurants will often feature game, with Slovenes particularly partial to bear (*medved*), deer (srna), pheasant (*fazan*) and rabbit (*zajec*). Soup (*juha*) is a standard **starter** – in Primorska try *jota* (beans and sauerkraut), and in Štajerska, *kisla juha* (pigs' knuckles and head with sour cream); delicious dry-cured ham (*pršut*) from the Karst is another good appetizer. Two of the most **traditional Slovene dishes** are *žlikrofi*, ravioli filled with potato, onion and bacon; and *žganci*, once the staple diet of rural Slovenes, a buckwheat or maize porridge often served with sauerkraut.

On the coast you'll find plenty of fish dishes (*ribje jedi*), with mussels (*školjke*), shrimps (*škampi*) and squid (*lignji*) particularly prominent. If you're anywhere near the Soča Valley (and in particular Kobarid, which has three of the country's best restaurants), do try the fabulous freshwater trout (*postrvi*) from the local Soča River, the king of which is the superb, and much sought-after, marble trout. Otherwise, Italian pasta dishes appear on many restaurant menus, while goulash (*golaž*) is found almost everywhere; *segedin* is goulash with lashings of sauerkraut.

Typical **desserts** include solid Central European favourites such as strudel and *štruklji* (dumplings with fruit filling); the two most traditional Slovene sweets are *potica*, a doughy roll filled with nuts, tarragon and honey; and, from the Prekmurje region, *gibanica*, a delicious layered pastry consisting of poppy seeds, walnuts, apple and cream. For something more straightforward you can't go wrong with *palačinke*, pancakes with a choice of fillings, or ice cream (*sladoled*).

Inevitably, standards of **service** vary depending on the type of establishment you are dining in, but by and large you'll find waiting staff courteous and friendly; and you'll rarely have trouble making yourself understood as most waiting staff speak a good standard of English. If you think it's merited, a ten percent tip would be standard.

Vegetarians and vegans

Although the situation for vegetarians and vegans is no longer the disaster zone it once was, the options, except in better restaurants, are usually both meagre and fairly predictable. Aside from the usual salads, vegetable and omelette dishes, Slovenian specialities to look out for are *štruklji* (dumplings with cheese or fruit filling), *ocvrti sir* (cheese fried in breadcrumbs) and *gobova rižota* (mushroom risotto) – the latter is usually excellent; in the better restaurants, you'll find upmarket variations on the above plus, possibly, one or two other dishes.

Drinking

Daytime drinking takes place in small **café-bars**, or in a *kavarna*, where you might also find a range of cakes, pastries and ice cream on offer. Coffee (*kava*) is usually served black unless specified otherwise – ask for *mleko* (milk) or *smetana* (cream) – and often drunk alongside a glass of mineral water (*mineralna voda*), the most popular of which is Radenska, from the spa town Radenci. Cappucinos are a hit-or-miss affair, ranging from good quality to little more than a regular coffee with a dollop of whipped cream on top. Tea (*čaj*) drinkers are in a minority here, although its popularity is growing and there are a couple of fantastic little teahouses (*čajna hiša*) in Ljubljana and Maribor.

Evening drinking usually goes on in small European-style bars or the more traditional *pivnica* (beer hall) or *vinarna* (wine cellar). **Slovene beer** (*pivo*) is of the Pilsner type and is not bad at all – in fact it was always considered among the best of the many beers brewed in any of the ex-Yugoslav republics. The two dominant breweries are Laško, based in the town of the same name and producer of Zlatorog (the mythical chamois), and the Ljubljana-based Union; opinion varies as to which is the best though, on balance, the more flavoursome Laško probably has the edge; both breweries also produce *temno pivo* (literally "dark beer"), a Guinness-like stout.

Although excellent, **Slovenian wine** (*vino*) is little known – it rarely makes it onto the shelves of Western supermarkets – but its reputation is growing. White wine (*belo*) predominates; particularly worth trying are Beli Pinot and Šipon, and there are some fine reds (*črno*) too, notably Cabernet Sauvignon and Merlot from the Vipava Valley, and the dark, acidic Kraški teran from the Karst. For more on Slovenian wine, see the boxes on p.171, p.258 and p.298. You shouldn't leave the country without trying one of the fiery brandies: *slivovka* (plum brandy), *viljamovka* (pear brandy), *sadjevec*, a brandy made from various fruits, and the gin-like juniper-based *brinovec*.

The media

Despite 45 years of communism, the Slovene media always had the most balanced and pluralistic coverage of the ex-Yugoslav republics. Given its size, though, it's not surprising that the country has fewer daily newspapers in circulation than just about any other European nation; its television coverage, meanwhile, differs little from that in any other central-east European country, with foreign cable and satellite television having made huge inroads in recent years.

Television

As in most countries, national TV is a rather bland, often unedifying diet of dull movies, game shows and soaps, although many households now subscribe to satellite channels. The public service broadcaster, RTV Slovenija (Radio-Television Slovenia), transmits on two channels, while the chief commercial channels are Kanal A and Pop TV, both of which broadcast the standard diet of foreign movies, soaps, sit-coms and music. RTV Slovenija also broadcasts the country's three major radio channels.

Most hotels have satellite TV, though most channels are German or Italian, while the better-quality hotels will usually have English language channels such as CNN, Sky News and BBC World.

The press

Among the five major dailies, the most widely read by the urban population is the mildly pro-government *Delo*, which is also considered the most sophisticated read; this is followed by *Dnevnik* (daily), and the Maribor-based *Večer* (evening). Closest to western tabloids in style is *Slovenske Novice*, full of the usual sensationalist trash stories.

With the exception of some of the major bookshops and more upmarket hotels in Ljubljana, English dailies are difficult (if not impossible) to come by. There are, however, a couple of decent English-language publications worth seeking out: the informative *Slovenia Times* (Wwww.sloveniatimes.com), and the more politically oriented *Slovenia News* (Wwww.ukom.si/en/news).

The **BBC** (Wwww.bbc.co.uk/worldservice), **Radio Canada** (Wwww.rcinet.ca) and **Voice of America** (Wwww.voa.gov) list all the world service radio frequencies around the globe.

Festivals

The Slovenian calendar is littered with some marvellous festivals and events. While a good number of these take place in the larger cities such as Ljubljana and Maribor, there's an excellent spread of local events throughout the rest of the country. Neither are these entirely confined to the summer: Slovenia has several strongly rooted seasonal traditions, none more so than the "Pust" in February, which is perhaps the most uniquely Slovenian celebration.

Most cities, and many of the larger towns, stage some form of **Summer Festival**, which invariably incorporates a colourful mix of classical and contemporary music, art and theatrical performances. Moreover, there is a terrific range of music festivals, from jazz and rock to classical, the latter being particularly prominent, both in the capital and elsewhere. A number of the country's castles stage classical music concerts on summer evenings. A great deal of fun are the **Medieval Days Festivals**, which seek to recreate life in the Middle Ages in the form of medieval crafts markets, song and dance, and knights' games; the two highest-profile ones are held in the historic towns of Kamnik and Škofja Loka in June.

The country's strong wine-growing tradition is manifest in its many **wine-related events**, which occur throughout the major wine-producing centres, such as Brda and Jeruzalem, between May and September; the main collective wine celebration is St Martin's Day, on November 11. Aside from the festivals listed below – each of which is covered in greater detail in their respective chapters – there are dozens of other, more local, events taking place across the country, some of which are also described in this guide.

January

King Matjaž Snow Castle Festival Črna na Koroškem, last weekend in January. Hugely popular snow castle building competition in the Koroška mountains.

February

Kurentovanje Ptuj Sunday before Shrove Tuesday and Shrove Tuesday. The most famous of Slovenia's

pre-Lent carnivals, featuring riotous displays of masked revelry; the other major Pust carnivals take place in Cerkno and Cerknica.

March

Ski-jumping World Championships Planica (Kranjska Gora), mid-March. The climax to the World Ski-Jumping Championship at Planica is a high-octane weekend of top-class sport, music and lots of beer.

April

Festival of Salt-making Piran and Sečovlje, end of April. Taking place in town and at the salt pans themselves, the festival incorporates a series of events to celebrate the start of the salt-making season.

May

Druga Godba Ljubljana, end of May for one week. Superb, alternative/world music festival with a strong line-up of both Slovene and international artists.
International Flower Festival Bohinj, end of May for two weeks. Celebrating the wild flowers of the Julian Alps, this colourful event features exhibitions, workshops, a flower market, and tours of flowers in their natural habitat.

June

Festival Brežice in Brežice and other venues across Slovenia, end of June to the end of August. Prestigious classical music festival of ancient Baroque music, starring some of Europe's finest singers, orchestras and musicians.
Lent Festival Maribor, end of June for two weeks. Massive gathering of popular and serious music, dance and ballet, street and puppet theatre, and folkloric events down by the Drava River.
Ljubljana Jazz Festival Ljubljana, end of June. Slovenia's premier jazz festival features five days of

world-class concerts, most of which take place in the atmospheric surrounds of the Križanke.

Rock Otočec Otočec (Novo Mesto), last weekend of June. The country's largest rock festival, with a cool line-up of both Slovenian and international artists.

July

Ana Desetnica Street Theatre Ljubljana, beginning of July. Colourful and enjoyable street theatre performances in the Old Town and surrounds.

Bled Days Bled, mid-July. Weekend fair and crafts stalls down by the lake, culminating in a spectacular fireworks display and thousands of candles on the lake.

Knights' Tournament Predjama Castle, mid-July. One-day jousting tournament plus large doses of medieval merriment.

Ljubljana Festival Ljubljana, July to mid-September. More than two months of top-notch opera, classical music, ballet and theatre in the capital's key cultural happening.

Mediterranean Festival Izola, July. World, ethno and folk music festival on an open-air stage in Izola's Old Town.

Primorska Summer Festival Izola, Koper and Portorož, July to August. Open-air stage and street theatre performances, some of which take place in unusual locations such as a disused railway tunnel and the Sečovlje saltpans.

August

Etno Festival Bled, first week in August. International and domestic folk music gathering.

Festival Radovljica mid-August. High-class international festival of ancient classical music.

TrnFest Ljubljana, August. Cracking, small-scale festival with gigs, exhibitions and workshops (some for kids) organized by the KUD cultural centre.

Tartini Festival Piran, end of August for two weeks. Top class classical fare in honour of the town's most famous former resident.

September

Kravji Bal (Cow's Ball) Lake Bohinj, second or third weekend in September. Mass booze-up to celebrate the return of the cows from the mountains.

National Costumes Festival Kamnik, second weekend in September. Song, dance and colourful finery from Slovenia's multifarious regions.

Festival of the Old Vine Maribor, mid-September for nine days. Superb gastronomic offerings in this lively affair celebrating the ceremonial harvesting of the world's oldest vine.

November

St Martin's Day Countrywide, November 11. Nationwide wine celebrations.

LIFFe Ljubljana, mid-November. The Ljubljana International Film Festival is Slovenia's premier film gathering, showcasing both domestic and international movies.

December

Christmas Celebrations Countrywide. A month of yuletide celebrations kick off on December 6 (St Nicholas's Day) with the giving of gifts to children.

Sports and the outdoors

Given its size and resources, Slovenia's sporting pedigree is impressive, many of its sportsmen and women having achieved notable successes in a number of sports since the split with Yugoslavia in 1991. The most high-profile sporting event in the Slovenian calendar is the World Ski-Jumping Championships at Planica in March.

The country's finest moment came at the 2000 Sydney Olympics, when it captured its first-ever gold medal courtesy of the rowers Iztok Čop and Luka Špik; indeed, **rowing** has been Slovenia's most prominent summer sport since the times of the former Yugoslavia, and now, as then, several major regattas are held each summer on Lake

Bled. Given the country's excellent facilities, it's little surprise that Slovenia has produced a legion of fine **skiers** and **ski-jumpers** – the Yugoslav national ski team was almost always made up exclusively of Slovenes – and there's been a healthy measure of Olympic and World Championship success over the past decade. Indeed, the current star of Slovenian sport is hammer thrower, Primoz Kozmuž, who became the country's first ever track and field gold medallist at the 2008 Beijing Olympics.

In popular **team sports** such as basketball, handball and water polo – traditionally very strong sports in the former Yugoslavia – Slovenia has been left somewhat in the slipstream of Serbia and Croatia, but its teams still manage to perform creditably at European level. In spite of a desperately weak domestic league Slovenia's footballers have massively overachieved in recent years, qualifying for both the European Championship Finals in Holland and Belgium in 2000, and then the 2002 World Cup in Japan – the first time it had qualified for either finals.

There are few more active nations in Europe than Slovenia, most of whose inhabitants begin trekking, climbing and skiing at a very early age. The country's mountains, forests, hills, rivers and lakes offer unlimited potential to indulge in a wide range of **outdoor pursuits** – hiking and skiing in the Julian Alps, whitewater rafting or kayaking in the Soča Valley, cycling through the rolling hills of Dolenjska, or riding through the Logarska Dolina Valley, to name just a few. Moreover, just about any of these activities can be done as part of an organized group, usually with gear supplied. Before taking part in any adventure activities, check your insurance cover. For more on all these activities see the *The Great Outdoors* colour section.

Although a mere 46km long, the Slovene coast offers possibilities to indulge in a number of **watersports**: scuba diving (*potapljanje*) in the waters around Piran, as well as sailing (*jadranje*) and windsurfing (*surfanje*). The coastal waters are perfectly safe for swimming (*plavanje*), but if you fancy something a little bit warmer you should be able to track down a local indoor pool in most towns of a reasonable size. Some of the better hotels, particularly those on the coast, have their own pools that can be used for a small fee by non-guests.

There are currently around a dozen **golf** courses in Slovenia, some of which, like those at Bled and Voljči Potok, can be played out against stunning alpine backdrops. You can find **tennis courts** in most places.

Travel essentials

Costs

Although Slovenia can by no means be classified as a bargain destination, it's still very good value on the whole, though prices in the capital, as well as in some of the more popular destinations like Bled, Bohinj and some of the coastal resorts are invariably higher than the rest of the country.

If you're on a tight budget, you could get by on around £25/€30/$40 a day, staying in a hostel or private accommodation, eating in cheap diners and using public transport. Those on a moderate to mid-range budget (cheap to mid-range hotel, better restaurants plus car rental) can expect to spend around £70/€85/$110. If you want to splash out on the best hotels and restaurants and rent a car count on spending upwards of £100/€120/$150 per day. You'll find food in supermarkets and convenience stores on a par with prices in many Western European countries.

Museum admission charges are reasonable, the typical entrance fee being around €2–4, although you'll pay considerably more for some of the star attractions such as the Postojna or Škocjan Caves, which charge in excess of €15

Crime

Slovenia has a very **low crime rate** and it's extremely unlikely that you'll have any problems; violent crime against tourists is almost nonexistent and petty crime rare. Of course, the usual common-sense precautions apply: watching where you walk late at night, keeping an eye on valuables, particularly in crowded buses, and locking your car at all times when unattended.

In the unlikely event of any dealings with the police (*policija*), you'll generally find them easy-going, approachable and likely to speak some basic English. The only time you may be asked to provide some form of identification is if stopped while driving, which is quite likely. If you do have anything stolen while in Slovenia, you'll need to go to the police and file a report, which your insurance company will require before paying out for any claims made on your policy. Should you be arrested or need legal advice, ask to contact your embassy or consulate in Ljubljana (see p.81). To call the police dial ☎113.

Electricity

Wall sockets in Slovenia operate at **220 volts** and take round, two-pin plugs. A standard continental adaptor allows the use of 13-amp, square-pin plugs.

Entry requirements

Citizens of the EU, Australia, Canada, New Zealand and the US can enter Slovenia with just a passport and may stay in the country for up to ninety days, while citizens of some neighbouring countries, such as Italy and Austria, require only an identity card. Citizens of South Africa require a **visa**. All the latest information can be obtained from the Slovene Foreign Ministry website at ⊛www.mzz.gov.si.

If you do require a visa, applications can be made to any Slovenian consulate abroad in person, or by post. Ninety-day stay tourist visas, with the option of single, double or multiple entry, currently cost €35; transit visas, valid for five days, cost €15.

Slovenian embassies and consulates abroad

Australia Embassy: Level 6, St George's Building, 60 Marcus Clarke St, Canberra ACT 2601 ☎02/6243 4830, ⓔvca@gov.si; Consulate: 86 Parramatta Rd, Sydney NSW 2050 ☎02/9517 1591.
Britain Embassy: 10 Little College St, London SW1P 3SH ☎020/7222 5400, ⓔvlo@gov.si.
Canada Embassy: 150 Metcalfe St, Suite 2200, Ottawa, Ontario K2P 1P1 ☎613/565-5781, ⓔvot@gov.si; Consulate: 747 Browns Line, 2nd Floor, Etobicoke, Toronto, Ontario M8W 3V7 ☎416/201-8307.
Ireland Embassy: Morrison Chambers, 2nd Floor, 32 Nassau St, Dublin 2 ☎01/670 5240, ⓔvdb@gov.si.
New Zealand Embassy: Level 6, St George's Building, 60 Marcus Clarke St, Canberra ACT 2601 Australia ☎02/6243 4830, ⓔvca@gov.si.
US Embassy: 2410 California St NW, Washington, DC 20008 ☎202/667-5363, ⓔvwa@gov.si; Consulate: 600 Third Avenue, 21st Floor, New York, NY 10016 ☎212/370-3006, ⓔkny@gov.si.

Gay and lesbian travellers

Slovenia was always the most tolerant of the ex-Yugoslav republics, with an active gay and lesbian movement in existence since the mid-1980s, though that's not to say gays and lesbians have had an easy time of it. Although attitudes have softened slightly in recent years, the majority of the population remains largely unsympathetic towards the gay and lesbian community.

Not surprisingly, Ljubljana is the centre of the gay and lesbian scene in Slovenia, and manifestations of gay life beyond the capital are almost nonexistent. A number of events now take place in Ljubljana, the most prominent of which are the annual **Gay Pride Parade** (late June or early July) – first organized in 2001 and now an established fixture in the capital's festival calendar – and the **Gay and Lesbian Film Festival** at the beginning of December, which has been running for more than 25 years.

Both of these events are organized by the proactive gay association **Roza Klub**, itself just one wing of the autonomous, alternative cultural society Škuc, based at Kersnikova 4

(☎01/430-4740, ☻www.ljudmila.org/siqrd). Roza Klub also runs Galfon, a gay and lesbian advice line (☎01/432-4089; daily 7–10pm), organizes club nights, and publishes several magazines and fanzines. The group **Out in Slovenija**, at Kašeljska 121 (☎041/562-375, ☻www.outinslovenija .com), organizes numerous sport and recreational activities – hiking, cycling, skiing and the like – for gays and lesbians.

Health

Travelling in Slovenia should present few problems: the country has high standards of hygiene and health care, inoculations are not necessary and tap water is safe everywhere. Most problems tend to be weather-related; summers can be blisteringly hot, particularly in central, southern and eastern regions, so a high-factor sun cream is essential. Conversely, inclement weather in the mountainous regions, particularly at higher altitudes, can present potentially serious dangers – so the usual provisos apply, namely, suitable clothing, sufficient provisions and equipment, and a watchful eye on the forecast. If you're planning to spend time in the mountains or forested areas, you may wish to consider being inoculated against tick-borne encephalitis.

All towns and most villages have a **pharmacy** (*lekarna*), with highly trained staff, most of whom invariably speak a good standard of English. Opening hours are normally from 7am to 7 or 8pm; signs in the window give the location or telephone number of the nearest all-night pharmacy (*dežurna lekarna*). In emergencies dial ☎112 for the ambulance service, who will whisk you off to the hospital (*bolnica*) where you should be attended to fairly rapidly.

Insurance

Even though EU health-care privileges apply in Slovenia, you'd do well to take out an insurance policy before travelling to cover against theft, loss, and illness or injury. A typical travel **insurance policy** usually provides cover for the loss of baggage, tickets and – up to a certain limit – cash or cheques, as well as cancellation or curtailment of your journey. Most of them exclude so-called dangerous sports unless an extra premium is paid: in Slovenia this could mean, for example, skiing, scuba diving, whitewater rafting and trekking.

Internet

In most towns and cities, internet cafés are the exception rather than the rule; where you do manage to find a place to log on, expect to pay anywhere between €1 and €3 for one hour. That said, the majority of tourist offices now offer free use of a terminal, while another option is the local library, although these are usually closed at weekends. Wi-fi is now widespread throughout the country. The Slovenian public wireless network Neowlan (☻www.neowlan.net) offers internet connection use for around €3 for thirty minutes and €9 for two hours; these pre-paid cards can be purchased at post offices and kiosks. Many hotels offer free wi-fi for their guests (either in the lobby or, in the better hotels at least, in the rooms themselves), while there are an increasing number of free wi-fi public locations in Ljubljana and some of the larger towns.

Laundry

Self-service laundries (*pralnica*) are nigh-on impossible to find in Slovenia, even in the larger towns and cities. Your options are, therefore, usually limited to hotels, some hostels and campsites.

Living and working in Slovenia

Opportunities for working in Slovenia are few and far between, especially in the most traditional form of work abroad, **teaching English**. International House (ⓣ01/300-4300, ⓦwww .mint.si), in Ljubljana, is the only international private language school in the country, though there are a few small private language schools in the capital and Maribor.

For those keen to pick up a new language – or brush up on existing skills – there's a well-established language centre at the Centre for Slovene as a Second Foreign Language, based within Ljubljana University's Faculty of Arts Department. Their annual summer school, with courses available at all levels from beginners to advanced, and covering a range of topics from Slovene literature and culture, to business Slovene and theatre workshops, run for either two (€530) or four (€900) weeks throughout July. The course also incorporates a varied social programme, which may include, for example, a two-day mountain trip, local workshops, and evening entertainment. Registration is required by the end of May for participation that summer; accommodation can also be arranged. They also offer a two-week winter course at the end of January (€530), while there are a number of more straightforward language courses at the university available throughout the year, lasting from two weeks up to a year. For more information contact the centre at Kongresni trg 12 (ⓣ01/241-8677, ⓦwww .centerslo.net).

An organization called Voluntariat, working in conjunction with local organizations, coordinates around a dozen **work camps** throughout Slovenia, with projects as varied as working with Roma, in Prekmurje, to working on the saltpans near Portorož. In theory these programmes, which can last from two weeks to several months, are available year-round, but most volunteers work in the period between May and September. The only cost involved is a participation fee (around €80), payable on registration; thereafter all board and lodgings are paid for. If you are involved in a longer-term project (several months), you may also receive pocket money. To find out more contact Voluntariat at Resljeva 20, Ljubljana (ⓣ01/239-1623, ⓔinfo@zavod-voluntariat.si).

Mail

The Slovene postal service (*Pošta Slovenije*) is a well-run, efficient organization. **Post offices** (*pošta*), rarely crowded, are orderly places and are usually open Monday to Friday 8am to 6 or 7pm and until noon or 1pm on Saturday, although in Ljubljana and some of the coastal resorts you'll find that the main post offices keep longer hours. **Stamps** (*znamke*) can be bought at the post office and at newsstands.

Maps

The best country maps are the 1:300,000 Freytag & Berndt map of Slovenia, while the 1:300,000 GeoCenter Euro Map of the Dalmatian Coast and Croatia (which also covers Slovenia) is particularly useful if you're thinking of combining the two countries. There are now some good hiking maps published by The Alpine Association of Slovenia (Paninska zveze Slovenije: PZS), such as the 1:50,000 ones of Triglav National Park, the Julian Alps and the Karavanke mountains. The best current road map available is the 1:270,000 Tourist Road Map (*turistična avtokarta*) published by the national motoring organization AMZS. Most tourist offices can give you a basic town or city map, but for more detailed ones, and regional maps, expect to pay around €5–6. If you haven't bought maps in advance of your trip, you're best off trying the bookshops in Ljubljana (see p.80).

Money

Slovenia's unit of currency is the **euro**, which officially changed over from the tolar in 2007. The euro is split into 100 cents. There are seven euro **notes** – in denominations of 500, 200, 100, 50, 20, 10 and 5 euros, each a different colour and size – and eight different **coin** denominations, including 2 and 1 euros, then 50, 20, 10, 5, 2 and 1 cents. Euro coins feature a common EU design on one face, but different country-specific designs on the other. For currency rates check out ⓦwww .xe.com or ⓦwww.oanda.com.

As a rule you're best off **changing money** in banks (*banka*), which you can find just about everywhere and which are generally open 8.30am to 12.30pm and 2 to 5pm weekdays, and 8.30 to 11am or noon on Saturdays. Otherwise, you can change money at numerous small exchange offices (*menjalnice*), tourist offices, tourist agencies, post offices and hotels, though you may end up paying considerably more in commission.

Credit cards are now accepted in most hotels, restaurants and shops, and you'll have little trouble finding **ATMs** (*bančni avtomat*), even in the smallest towns. Note that if your debit or credit card won't work in a particular ATM, it is worth trying another – not all of the smaller banks are connected to the right global clearing system.

By far the most recognized **travellers' cheques** are American Express, whether sterling or dollars. Although it may not be required in all instances, make sure you have your passport when changing travellers' cheques (or cash). Also note that, in some banks, you may have to show the receipt from the issuing bank, or another cheque to prove continuity of serial numbers. In the event of lost or stolen cheques, report the loss forthwith to the American Express office in Ljubljana, which is opposite the train station at Kolodvorska 16 (Mon–Fri 8am–5pm; ☎01/430-7720); lost or stolen cheques can usually be replaced within 24 hours.

Opening hours and public holidays

Most **shops** open Monday to Friday from 8am to 7pm and on Saturdays from 8am to 1pm, with some (usually the mall-type places in bigger towns and cities) open on Sundays between 11am and 5pm. There are also an increasing number of 24-hour food shops open throughout the country.

Museums are generally open Tuesday to Sunday 9 or 10am to 5 or 6pm, with shorter hours in winter, while some close down altogether during this period; there are, of course, exceptions to the above but in any case all times are detailed throughout the guide. For the opening hours of post offices, banks, pharmacies and tourist offices, see the relevant sections.

Slovenia counts no fewer than **fourteen public holidays,** a number of which celebrate important milestones in the country's history. Should any of these fall on a Sunday, then the Monday becomes the holiday. Don't expect much to be open on the following days; January 1 & 2 New Year; February 8 Day of Slovene Culture (Prešeren Day); Easter Monday; April 27 Resistance Day; May 1 & 2 Labour Day Holidays; June 25 Slovenia Day; August 15 Assumption Day; October 31 Reformation Day; November 1 All Saints' Day; December 25 Christmas Day; December 26 Independence Day.

Phones

Public phone boxes, found just about everywhere, use **phonecards** (*telekartice*), which currently come in denominations of €3, €4, €7 and €14; you can buy these from post offices, newspaper kiosks and tobacco shops. If making long-distance and international calls it's usually easier to go to the post office, where you're assigned to a cabin and given the bill afterwards. All Slovenian land line numbers are seven-digit, and are preceded by two-digit **regional codes** – of which there are six (☎01 for Ljubljana, up to ☎07, but no

Calling home from Slovenia

Note that the initial zero is omitted from the area code when dialling the UK, Ireland, Australia and New Zealand from abroad.

Australia international access code + 61
New Zealand international access code + 64
UK international access code + 44
US and Canada international access code + 1
Ireland international access code + 353
South Africa international access code + 27

☏06). To make a direct call to somewhere outside the area you are in, you must use the regional code.

The main **mobile phone** providers in Slovenia are Debitel, Mobitel and Vodafone Simobil; numbers have nine digits, including one of these prefixes: ☏031, ☏041, ☏051 or ☏040. Calling a mobile from a public or private phone you must dial all the numbers; when calling from abroad drop the 0.

Shopping

Just about all of Slovenia's cities and bigger towns now have at least one **shopping mall** – invariably incorporated within a multi-purpose entertainment complex – the result being that traditional town centre shopping areas are shrinking. Slovenia's rich **folk art** tradition – manifest most obviously in the painted beehive panels, woodenware from Ribnica, lace from Idrija and black pottery from Prekmurje – is a good source of ideas for souvenir gifts; more often than not, such items can be found in the museums where they are actually exhibited, though there are occasional shops where you can pick up these things. Whether buying for yourself or as a gift, Slovenia's excellent wine makes a terrific purchase; this is best bought from a *vinoteka* (wine shop) or *vinska klet* (wine cellar). **Flea markets** are few and far between, though the Sunday morning one on the banks of the Ljubljanica, in Ljubljana, is definitely worth a browse, particularly for its communist-era knick-knacks (see p.80).

Smoking

In common with all those countries from the former Yugoslavia, smoking is commonplace, although it is now prohibited in restaurants and other public places.

Time

Slovenia is one hour ahead of GMT, six hours ahead of Eastern Standard Time and nine ahead of Western Standard Time. It is ten hours behind Australian Eastern Standard Time and twelve hours behind New Zealand.

Tipping

Although tipping is not obligatory, it is polite to round the bill up to a convenient figure in restaurants and when taking a taxi.

Toilets

Public toilets (*javno stranišče*), which can be found in most train and bus stations, are, on the whole, clean, though you'd do well to carry your own paper; most charge around €0.50. *Moški* means men and *Zenske* means women.

Tourist information

A large number of free brochures and special-interest pamphlets are produced by the Slovenian Tourist Board (ⓦwww .slovenia.info), and distributed by their offices abroad as well as their excellent, and extensive, network of local-authority-run tourist offices within Slovenia. Almost without exception the staff, most of whom speak excellent English, are extremely knowledgeable and helpful. Inevitably, tourist office opening times vary greatly, depending on both their location and the season; some keep impossibly convoluted hours, but as a rule you'll find most open between 9am and 6 or 7pm (til 8 or 9pm in more popular areas) over summer. Similarly, tourist agencies' opening hours vary enormously, depending on the time of year; during high season, some stay open as late as 10pm, though may close an hour or so earlier, or later, than the scheduled time, depending on custom.

The tourist board's main publication is the *Next Exit* tourist map, which plots six different routes throughout the country, each of which lists tourist offices, places to eat and sleep and key sites of natural and cultural interest – many off the beaten track. Although there are exceptions, and these are listed throughout the guide, tourist offices do not deal in private accommodation (see p.28); for this you're best off heading to local tourist agencies, which can be found in most towns and cities – again, these are listed where relevant.

In Britain you can contact the Slovenian Embassy, 10 Little College Street, London SW1P 3SH (℡020/7222 5400, ✉vol@gov .si) for tourist information.

Travellers with disabilities

Although progress is being made, Slovenia remains dreadfully slow in acknowledging the needs of the disabled traveller, and you shouldn't expect much in the way of special facilities. Few places are well equipped, or have facilities, for disabled travellers and, aside from the better ones, access to hotels and public buildings is generally poor, even in Ljubljana. Public transport is little better, although the Inter City Slovenije trains between Maribor and Ljubljana do have wheelchair facilities and specially adapted toilets, while an increasing number of train stations provide ramps for access to platforms. Similarly, most museums are ill equipped to deal with wheelchair users. The Slovene Disabled Association (Zveza Paraplegikov Slovenije) at Štihova ulica 14

(℡01/432-7138, ✇www.zveza-paraplegikov .si) can assist with any specific queries you may have about travelling in Slovenia.

Travelling with children

From a practical point of view travelling with children in Slovenia will present no obvious problems. Most of the better-quality hotels are well disposed to catering for children, while most restaurants (at least those of a decent standard) should be able to provide highchairs for younger children and babies. Most car-rental firms provide child or baby seats for a small extra charge. All supermarkets, and many smaller shops, are well stocked with the requisite nappies, baby food and so on.

Your biggest challenge will be keeping the kids entertained; bar the odd zoo there are few attractions specifically targeted at children, though there are enough things to see and do in Ljubljana to keep the young ones happy. Otherwise, the most obvious destinations are the **beaches** along the coast which, on the whole, are clean and safe (most bathing areas are roped off), while many have grassy areas with sporting and play facilities.

Another thing that might appeal to adults as well as kids is **puppetry**, a popular and well-regarded form of entertainment in Slovenia; there are particularly good theatres in Ljubljana and Maribor, details of which are given in the relevant sections.

Beyond this, you'll find that some of the country's **festivals** (see p.34) also incorporate elements specifically designed with children in mind; foremost among these is the excellent TrnFest, which takes place in Ljubljana in August, and the Pippi Longstocking Festival in Velenje in late September, featuring music, cinema, theatre and dozens of workshops for kids.

Guide

Guide

Ljubljana

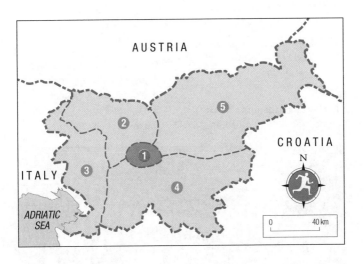

CHAPTER 1 # Highlights

* **Jože Plečnik** Stunning architecture at almost every turn from the nation's greatest architect. See p.60

* **The Old Town** With Baroque churches, elegant town houses and cool cafés, the Old Town has charm in spades. See p.60

* **Ljubljana Castle** Looming high above the Old Town; climb the clocktower and take in the magnificent views of the Alps. See p.63

* **Križanke** Take in a jazz or rock concert at the atmospheric, Plečnik-designed open-air theatre. See p.66

* **The City Museum** The city's most absorbing museum brings together a terrific array of cultural heritage from both Slovenia and non-European lands. See p.66

* **Trnovo** Roman ruins, Plečnik oddities and riverside cafés in this green and peaceful suburb. See p.68

* **Tivoli Park** The city's green heart, affording easy promenade strolls or more exerting hillside walks. See p.71

* **Drinking by the Ljubljanica** Enjoy a beer at sundown in one of the many bars along the willow-fringed banks of the river. See p.76

▲ Ljubljanica

Ljubljana

L JUBLJANA is one of Europe's brightest and most engaging small cities, a destination that has managed to retain its low-key charm despite a significant increase in its profile in recent years. Situated in the southern part of the Ljubljana river basin, at the juncture of the Alps and Dinaric mountain ranges, pretty much everything converges here: all major transport links, industry and commerce, culture, politics and power. However, with a population of less than 300,000 – which easily makes it one of Europe's smallest capital cities – Ljubljana retains a distinctly languorous and provincial air.

As the former Yugoslavia imploded in the early 1990s, Ljubljana suffered few of the traumas that befell neighbouring Zagreb, its path smoothed by a relatively sound economic and political infrastructure. Now some twenty years later – as a European Union capital – Ljubljana is a prosperous, self-assured place, its slick veneer of sophistication masking a disparate number of outside influences – Austrian, Balkan and Mediterranean – subtly absorbed and tinkered with over the years.

The city's tremendously compact centre lends itself perfectly to discovery by foot and it's unlikely you'll need, or want, to use the refreshingly clean and efficient public transport system. While the city boasts a number of eminently enjoyable museums and galleries – the City Museum, Ethnographic Museum and National Gallery chief among them – its real charms lie outdoors. Ljubljana's central core is a showcase of princely Baroque and Secessionist edifices, while the legacy of magnificent buildings, bridges and pathways bequeathed by Jože Plečnik, Slovenia's greatest architect, is difficult to overestimate, transforming as it did the entire fabric of the city between the two world wars. Its churches too reveal dazzling artistry, from Francesco Robba's extraordinary altar sculptures to Quaglio's resplendent frescoes.

Fundamental to the city's layout and history is the slender **Ljubljanica**, a once navigable waterway, but now sprinkled with several fine-looking bridges. On both the left and right banks vestiges of the city's Roman and medieval past can be detected, but it's the splendid Baroque town houses and maze-like streets of the majestic **Old Town**, lorded over by the landmark castle, which exerts the greatest pull. Furthermore, the splashes of greenery – such as **Tivoli Park** – give just a hint of what lies beyond the city's boundaries. Above all though, Ljubljana is a sociable city, a place to come and meet people, dip in and out of its enchanting riverside cafés, and engage in the nightlife.

Owing to both the country's size and the city's central location, it's perfectly feasible to do a day-trip from here to just about any of the country's principal attractions, be it the mountain lakes of Bled and Bohinj to the northwest, the karst and coast to the south and west, or the castles and spas to the east.

Some history

Though sources first mention Ljubljana in 1144, the history of settlement here goes as far back as 2000 BC, when lake-dwellers inhabited the marshy area to the south of the city. They were closely followed by the **Illyrians** and **Celts**, though it was the **Romans** who engineered the first major commune, constructing a fortified military encampment on the left bank of the Ljubljanica around 50 BC. It was given the name **Emona** and inhabited by some five thousand civilians until Emona was sacked in around 450 AD; remnants of this period can still be seen in the form of several sections of the city walls, as well as archeological sites in the city.

Next up were the **Slavs**, who settled here at the tail end of the sixth century in what is now Stari trg and Mestni trg. During the twelfth century this evolved into Ljubljana's **medieval** core, and was given the German name Laibach in 1144, before assuming its Slovenian name, Luwigana, in 1146. Following their arrival in the thirteenth century, the **Spanheim** family of **Carinthian dukes** granted the municipality city rights, and in 1243 the name **Ljubljana** first appeared; at around the same time, the city became the capital of the Carniola province, before falling under the jurisdiction of the **Habsburgs** in 1335.

A catastrophic **earthquake** in 1511, which left little of the city standing, coincided with Ljubljana becoming the leading centre of the **Reformation** in

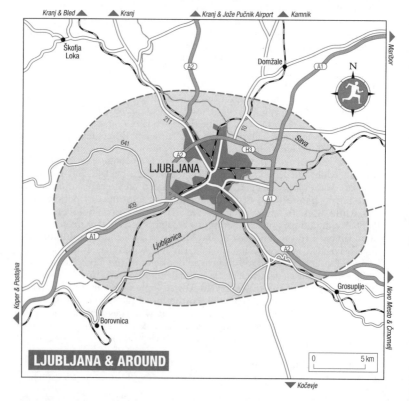

LJUBLJANA & AROUND

0   5 km

Slovenia. This period was marked by significant spiritual and cultural progression, thanks largely to leading reformers such as Primož Trubar, who sought to promote literacy among the populace and who published the first Slovene book – the primer, *Abecedarium* – in 1550; at this time the city also gained its first college and public library. The Reformation was successfully snuffed out at the end of the sixteenth century, a period that saw the arrival of the **Jesuits** (1597), who reorganized the city's educational system, and established many religious buildings. The city's cultural pulse quickened further with the establishment of the Academia Operosorum – the first society of scholars and intellectuals – in 1693, and the Academia Philharmonicorum in 1701, one of the first musical institutions in Europe. Alongside this new Catholic order, a distinct architectural style, **Ljubljana Baroque**, emerged, expressed most sublimely in the city's four principal churches: St James's (1615); the Annunciation (1660); St Nicholas's (1706); and Ursuline (1726), as well as Robba's outstanding Fountain of the Three Rivers.

Between 1809 and 1814, Ljubljana was designated the capital of Napoleon's **Illyrian Provinces**, the city deemed a geographically convenient location for Napoleon in his attempt to prevent the Habsburgs accessing the Adriatic. A few years after his downfall Ljubljana was chosen to host the prestigious **Congress of the Holy Alliance** (1821), a gathering of the triumphant monarchy states that had defeated the French. During the mid-nineteenth century, and despite continued political repression, the city experienced something of an **industrial revolution** – the catalyst for which was the completion of the Vienna–Ljubljana–Trieste rail line in 1857. The city began to emerge from its provincialized cultural and political strait-jacket in the 1880s, while a raft of cultural institutions, including the Opera House (1892) and National House (1896), were established. In 1895, a second, and equally destructive earthquake necessitated yet more wholesale reconstruction, though this time it was Vienna and the Secessionist school which provided the inspiration – the results of which are particularly outstanding along Miklošičeva ulica.

With the creation of the **Kingdom of Serbs, Croats and Slovenes** in 1918 – recast as the Kingdom of **Yugoslavia** in 1929 – power transferred from Vienna to Belgrade, though this left Ljubljana no better off than when under Habsburg rule. Nevertheless, the founding of the National Gallery (1918), University (1919) and Academy of Sciences and Arts (1938) was confirmation of the city's continuing cultural efflorescence. During this interwar period, the city also experienced an architectural revolution, thanks to **Jože Plečnik**, whose work completely transformed the city landscape. With every justification, the city was dubbed "Plečnik's Ljubljana". Following **World War II**, a period during which the city was occupied by both Italians and Germans before being liberated by the Partisans, it became the capital of the Republic of Slovenia, one of the six federal republics of the Federal People's Republic of Yugoslavia, and then, in 1963, the Socialist Federal Republic of Yugoslavia.

After Tito's death in 1980, relations between Ljubljana and Belgrade gradually worsened, coming to a head in 1988 with the staging of the "**Ljubljana Four Trial**" (see p.328), a case many at the time regarded as the final denouement in Slovene–Serb relations (and by implication the end of Yugoslavia). At around the same time, Ljubljana was at the forefront of Yugoslavia's intoxicating **alternative cultural scene**, thanks in no small part to the controversial and provocative arts collective Neue Slowenische Kunst (NSK), or New Slovene Art, the core of which was the anarchic rock group Laibach. They, and other alternative movements were fundamental in stimulating debate on social and political issues, prescient given the deepening tensions between Ljubljana and Belgrade.

On June 26, 1991, the day after Slovenia had officially declared its **independence**, thousands gathered on Republic Square to celebrate – somewhat prematurely as it turned out – unaware that Yugoslav Army (JNA) tank units were closing in on Brnik airport, just 23km away. However, the subsequent **ten-day war** had little direct effect on the city and on July 7 it was able, finally, to rejoice in its status as the capital of a new **republic**.

Arrival, information and city transport

Ljubljana's Jože Pučnik **airport** is in Brnik, 23km north of the city, and connected to the main bus station by a number of buses operated by various companies. The best option is the private shuttle bus, which has frequent daily departures both to (5.20am–10.30pm) and from (5.50am–10.55pm) the airport (30min; €5). Otherwise, there are public buses (Mon–Fri hourly 5am–8pm, Sat & Sun 7am, then every 2hr 10am–8pm; 45min; €4.20), which arrive at bay 28 of the bus station from where they also leave (Mon–Fri 5.20am, then hourly 6.10am–8.10pm, Sat & Sun 6.10am, then every 2hr 9.10am–7.10pm). Adria Airways operates ten buses a day from Brnik (7.40am–midnight; 30min; €5) to their terminal at the bus station, and the same number in the opposite direction (5.20am–10.30pm). Adria also offers a minibus shuttle service (€10), which operates around the clock and can drop you off anywhere in the city; reservations are required if travelling from the city to the airport (☎041/362-079). A taxi to or from the airport will cost around €35.

The **train** (*Železniška postaja*) and **bus stations** (*Avtobusna postaja*) are next to each other on Trg Osvobodilne fronte, from where it's a ten-minute walk south into the centre. The excellent facilities at the train station include a train information office (daily 5.30am–9.30pm), tourist information office (June–Sept daily 8am–10pm; Oct–May Mon–Fri 10am–7pm, Sat 8am–3pm), exchange desk (daily 5.30am–10pm) and 24-hour left-luggage lockers. The bus station ticket office is open daily from 5am to 10.30pm.

Information, maps and tours

The excellent **Slovenian Tourist Information Centre (STIC)** at Krekov trg 10 (June–Sept daily 8am–9pm; Oct–May Mon–Fri 8am–7pm, Sat 8am–3pm; ☎01/306-4576, ⊕www.visitljubljana.si/) can assist with information on any aspect of travel within the country, including the capital. The main city **Tourist Information Centre (TIC)** is in the Old Town on Stritarjeva next to the Triple Bridge (daily: June–Sept 8am–9pm; Oct–May 8am–7pm; ☎01/306-1215, same website). Both of these provide comprehensive information on the city (in several languages, including English), have free, detailed **maps** to give away, and can book private accommodation (see p.28). The office on Stritarjeva also has a ticketing centre, where you can buy tickets for cultural and sporting events, both in the city and throughout the country. There is also an information office at the train station and an information desk at the airport (daily 11am–5.30pm). Worth picking up at any of these is the monthly *Where To?* pamphlet, which has museum and gallery listings as well as events and performances for that month. If you're planning on staying in the city for a few days, consider investing in the **Ljubljana Tourist Card** (€13), which entitles you to unlimited travel on all the city's buses, and offers discounted entrance fees to selected museums, galleries, restaurants and bars; it's valid for three days and can be obtained from all of the city's tourist information centres or online at ⊕www.visitljubljana.si.

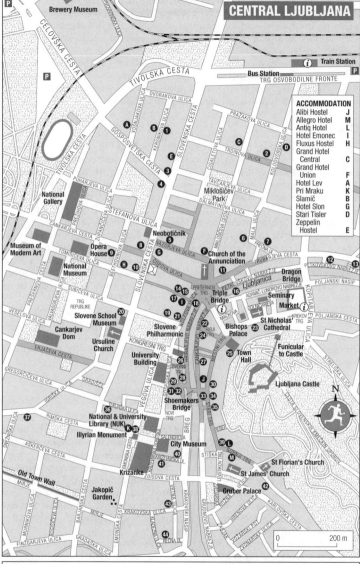

CENTRAL LJUBLJANA

ACCOMMODATION

Alibi Hostel	J
Allegro Hotel	M
Antiq Hotel	L
Hotel Emonec	I
Fluxus Hostel	H
Grand Hotel Central	C
Grand Hotel Union	F
Hotel Lev	A
Pri Mraku	K
Slamič	B
Hotel Slon	G
Stari Tisler	D
Zeppelin Hostel	E

RESTAURANTS

Abecedarium	22	Harambaša		Pri Škofu	44
Ajdovo Zrno	11	Okrepčevapnica	43	Pri Vitezu	40
Ambient	2	Joe Pena's	8	Ribca	16
Gostilna As	14	Julija	34	Romeo	33
Cantina Mexicana	15	Kavalino	13	Shambala	41
Falafel	12	Ljubljanski Dvor	26	Gostilna Sokol	23
Figovec	4	Paninoteka	29	Špajza	42
Foculus	36	Pasta Nona	3	Tomato	20
		Pr' Potic	39	Zlata Ribica	24

CAFÉS, BARS & CLUBS

Café Antico	35	Maček	27
Bachus	19	Movia	25
Bi-Ko-Fe	31	Patrick's	7
Café Gaudi	5	Roxly	6
Čajna Hiša	30	Slamič	B
Cutty Sark	17	Top	10
Dvorni Bar	28	Tromostovje	18
Jazz Club Gajo	9	Zlata Ladjica	32
Le Petit Café	38	Zmauc	37
K4	1	Zvezda	21

The tourist office offers two-hour **sightseeing tours** (daily: April–Sept 10am; Oct–March 11am; €10) of the city, starting at the Town Hall and finishing with a ride on the funicular up to the castle. It also organizes a number of special interest tours, including Baroque Ljubljana, Secessionist Ljubljana and Plečnik's Ljubljana (€50 for groups up to five, €60 for groups up to ten). Tickets can be purchased on the spot (in front of the Town Hall on Mestni trg) or from the tourist offices on Krekov trg and Stritarjeva. A fabulous source of information is the entertaining and on-the-ball *Ljubljana In Your Pocket* (€2.90), which is available from the information centres and most hotels.

City transport

The city **buses**, run by Ljubljanski Potniški Promet (LPP), are clean, cheap and frequent; there are 22 bus lines, the majority of which operate between 5am and 10.30pm, with the most important lines (#1, #2, #3, #6 & #11) starting at 3.15am and running until midnight – each stop clearly indicates which buses stop there. Entering via the front door only, you pay in cash by depositing the exact amount in the box next to the driver (a one-way journey costs a flat **fare** of €1 or by using the slightly cheaper plastic tokens (*žetoni*; €0.80), which are bought in advance from newspaper kiosks and post offices). Each payment or token is valid for one unbroken journey only. Daily (*dnevna vozovnica*; €4) and weekly (*tedenska vozovnica*; €15) tickets can be bought from the LPP kiosks at Trdinova ulica 3 and Bavarski Dvor, Slovenska cesta 55, and the main bus station. The useful fold-up LPP **map**, which clearly denotes the various bus lines and all the stops, can be obtained from the kiosks mentioned above and the tourist offices.

It's unlikely that you'll have much call for a **taxi**, but if you do, expect to pay around €1–1.50 per kilometre – ordering by phone will work out slightly cheaper, but taxis can also be flagged in the street or found at ranks by the train station, outside the *Hotel Slon* and near Prešernov trg – the most reliable company is Rumeni Taxis (☏041/731-831).

Accommodation

Ljubljana's **hotel** possibilities are, for the most part, concentrated at the upper end of the price range, but there is an excellent spread of **youth hostels** and **student dorms** around town, while **private accommodation** is another option – if the latter is your preferred choice, head to the tourist office on Stritarjeva, who should be able to arrange something close to the centre. More often than not, rooms (❷) come with shared bathroom facilities and without breakfast. You could also try Tour AS at Mala ulica 8 (☏01/434-2660, ⓦwww .apartmaji.si); though they deal predominantly with apartments (❺–❽), they have a handful of private rooms too (❸).

The city's one **campsite** is 4km north of the centre in Ježica (buses #6 or #8), at the Ljubljana Resort (☏01/568-3913, ⓦwww.ljubljanaresort.si). This large and clean year-round site by the Sava River also has a decent hotel (❻), and fully-furnished, self-catering chalets sleeping up to four people (❾) – the resort's superb facilities include the Laguna water park, beach volleyball courts, children's play area and restaurant.

Hostels

Ljubljana now has an excellent clutch of **youth hostels**, most of which have internet and kitchen facilities – where breakfast is not included in the price, expect to pay around €5. If you can't bag a bed at any of these, there are four clean and well-run **student hostels** (*Dijaški dom*), with beds available between mid-June and August: *Dijaški dom Bežigrad*, Kardeljeva ploščad 28 (℡01/534-2867, ⓔdd .lj-bezigrad@guest.arnes.si; bus #6 or #8 to stop Mercator); *Dijaški dom Ivana Cankarja*, Poljanska 26 (℡01/474-8600, ⓔdd.lj-ic@guest.arnes.si; bus #5 to Ambrožev trg); *Dijaški dom Poljane*, Potočnikova 3 (℡01/300-3137, ⓔdd .poljane@guest.arnes.si; bus #5 to Gornje Poljane); and *Dijaški dom Tabor*, Vidovdanska 7 (℡01/234-8840, ⓔssljddta1s@guest.arnes.si) – expect to pay around €10 per person for a dorm bed and €15 for a bed in a single or double room; breakfast is not included. Note that the prices given below are all per person.

Alibi Hostel Cankarjevo nabrežje 27 ℡01/251-1244, ⓦwww.alibi.si. This colourful and friendly hostel, in a super Old Town location overlooking the Ljubljanica, has four- to eight-bed dorms (€18), as well as double rooms (€25), spread over several floors. Breakfast is not available.

Celica Metelkova 8 ℡01/230-9700, ⓦwww.hostelcelica.com. Brilliantly original hostel constructed from the remnants of a military prison (see p.57). The twenty "cells", individually designed and each with a different theme, sleep two to three people (€22–27) – shower facilities are shared; there are also four- and five-bed rooms (€25) and a twelve-bed dorm (€20). As well as a small art gallery, facilities include a café and bicycle rental. Breakfast included.

Fluxus Hostel Tomšičeva 4 ℡01/251-5760, ⓦwww.fluxus-hostel.com. The smallest of Ljubljana's hostels is a warm, welcoming place

with six- and eight-bed dorms (€22), and one double room (€30). Breakfast is extra.

Stari Tisler Kolodvorska 8 ℡01/430-3370, ⓦwww.stari-tisler.com. Handy for the stations, this quiet and agreeable inn-type place has a handful of clean and simply furnished double and triple rooms (€22), all with shared shower facilities. Breakfast is extra.

Vila Veselova Veselova 14 ℡059/926-721, ⓦwww.v-v.si. Pleasant and unassuming hostel in an old villa in the embassy district with four- to eight-bed, colour-themed dorms (€18–22), and one double (€28). Breakfast is extra.

Zeppelin Hostel Slovenska 47 ℡051/637-436, ⓦwww.zeppelinhostel.com. Bright, breezy and very sociable hostel just a five-minute walk from the bus and train stations on the city's main thoroughfare; four-, six- and eight-bed dorms (€20–22) and one double (€28). Breakfast included.

Hotels

The majority of Ljubljana's **hotels** are patronized in the main by business people, and with prices that reflect this. Most establishments are pretty central and can be easily reached on foot from the train and bus stations. All include **breakfast** in the price and have internet access of some sort (either cable or wi-fi).

Allegro Hotel Gornji trg 6 ℡01/59 119-620, ⓦwww.allegrohotel.si. Plum in the heart of the Old Town, this superbly restored town house boasts twelve gorgeous, variously sized and individually furnished rooms, each in a different colour scheme. To cap it off, there's a superb buffet breakfast in the brightly decorated cellar. ⓨ

Antiq Hotel Gornji trg 3 ℡01/421-3560, ⓦwww .antiqhotel.si. Directly opposite the *Allegro*, the sixteen highly idiosyncratic rooms in this wonderful, rambling boutique hotel all feature gorgeous wooden beds, patterned carpets and sophisticated furnishings; rooms either have views up to the castle or looking over the pretty rose garden. ⓨ

Austria Trend Dunajska 154 ℡01/588-2500, ⓦwww.austria-trend.at/lju. The city's most technologically advanced hotel possesses immaculate,

designer-furnished rooms, each with a huge plasma screen which allows you to access the internet and receive online video games and digital movies; the remote also allows you to control all facilities within the room (locks, lights, a/c etc). ⓨ

BIT Center Hotel Litijska 57 ℡01/548-0055, ⓦwww.bit-center.net. Busy and lively sports hotel 2km east of the centre, which has no-frills en-suite doubles, in addition to hostel dorms with shared shower facilities (€18); fifty-percent discount on use of sporting facilities (squash, badminton and fitness centre). Buses #5, #9, #13 and #22. ❹

Grand Hotel Central Miklošičeva 9 ℡01/308-4300, ⓦwww.centralhotel.si. Just 300m south of the bus and train stations, this hotel is aimed squarely at the business traveller. The rooms, decorated in a sunny yellow and green colour scheme, are well furnished, with stylish and comfortable beds, a little sofa, minibar and safe. ❾

Grand Hotel Union Miklošičeva 1 ☏01/308-1270, ⓦ www.gh-union.si. This Art Nouveau building actually houses two splendid hotels; the Executive has generously sized and splendidly furnished rooms, some with a balcony looking up to the castle. Rooms in the adjoining Business hotel are similar, though the colour scheme is somewhat dowdy. In addition to the fitness centre and sauna, it's the only hotel in town with a swimming pool (on the rooftop). Both ❾

Hotel Emonec Wolfova 12 ☏01/200-1520, ⓦ www.hotel-emonec.com. Cracking-value place in a quiet off-street location in the heart of town (no parking); the blue and white decorated rooms (including triples and quads) are simple, but fresh and modern looking, while the bathrooms are beautifully designed. ❺–❼

Hotel Lev Vošnjakova 1 ☏01/433-2155, ⓦ www .hotel-lev.si. This gleaming glass high-rise, a five-minute walk west of the bus and train stations opposite Tivoli Park, is the most expensive hotel in town; the lavish, but surprisingly modestly sized rooms, boast smart oak chairs and desks and soundproof windows. ❾

Hotel Park Tabor 9 ☏01/300-2500, ⓦ www .hotelpark.si. Located amid a jumble of apartment buildings a few blocks east of the station, this high rise place has a variety of (overpriced) two- and three-star rooms, some with a/c and internet; as well as two- and four-bed hostel rooms, some with TV and shower (€20–30 plus €7 for breakfast). ❼–❽

Hotel Slon Slovenska 34 ☏01/470-1100, ⓦ www.hotelslon.com. The "Hotel Elephant" is so named after Archduke Maximilian who, with elephant in tow, allegedly stayed at an inn on this site en route to Vienna in 1552. Glass doors lead into sumptuous, parquet-floored bedrooms, with flat screen TV, DVD player, coffee- and tea-making facilities – and even a "pillow menu" to choose from. The hotel houses a magnificent breakfast room, a chic lounge café/ bar and confectioners. ❾

M Hotel Derčeva 4 ☏01/513-7000, ⓦ www .m-hotel.si. Though somewhat lacking in character, this large hotel 2km northwest of the centre has modern, spruce and spacious rooms painted in gentle blue tones as well as a pleasant breakfast terrace. Buses #1, #3, #15 and #16 to stop Kino Šiška. ❼

Pension Tavčar Cesta v Šmartno 7 ☏01/546-6970, ⓦ www.penzion-tavcar.com. Neat, bright and reasonably priced little pension 2km northeast of the city centre. Take bus #12 to stop Hrastje, walk back 200m and take a right. ❻

Pri Mraku Rimska 4 ☏01/421-9600, ⓦ www .daj-dam.si. In a prime downtown location near Križanke, this enjoyable – though extremely expensive – pension has warm, exuberantly coloured rooms (including triples), some with a/c. ❽

Slamič Kersnikova 1 ☏01/433-8233, ⓦ www .slamic.si. A delightful B&B just a stone's throw from the bus and train stations with eleven smartly designed rooms decked out in smooth cream colours and cool wrought-iron furnishings; the in-house café is a little gem too (see p.76). ❼

The City

Geographically and socially, the heart of the city is **Prešernov trg**, a small, animated square on the left bank of the **Ljubljanica**. Several important streets converge here while just about all the major sights and points of interest are within comfortable walking distance. With the exception of **Miklošičeva ulica** – a street rampant with extraordinary Secessionist architecture – and one or two other sights around, such as Metelkova, the commercial district north of Prešernov trg is largely devoid of worthwhile sights.

In any case, most people head straight for the magical **Old Town** on the right bank of the Ljubljanica: strewn with gorgeous Baroque town houses and stately churches, all wrapped around a regal **castle-topped hill**, it is easily the most appealing part of the city. The left bank too has more than its fair share of fine architecture, notably south of the main square **Kongresni trg**, beyond which are the delightful village-like suburbs of **Krakovo** and **Trnovo**.

Most of the city's key museums and galleries are concentrated within a compact area between **Slovenska cesta**, the busy main thoroughfare west of

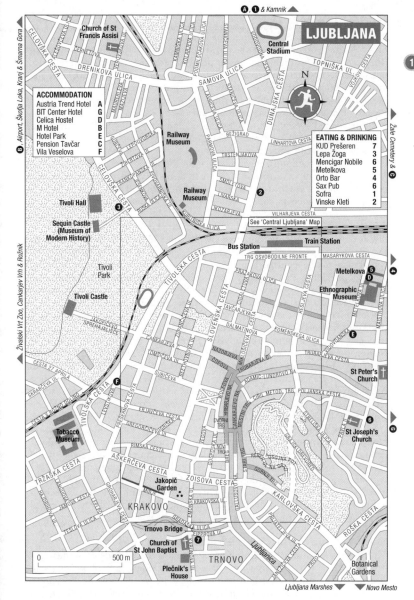

Kongresni trg, and **Tivoli Park**, the city's engaging green pocket and something of a ramblers' paradise. Beyond the central zone, and especially to the north and south, there are a handful of further sights worthy of investigation, including some fabulous churches, a castle and some splendid natural heritage, notably the Ljubljana Marshes.

Prešernov trg

Flanked on three sides by distinguished buildings and busy streets, and on the other by the gently curving sweep of the Ljubljanica, cobbled **Prešernov trg** (Prešeren Square) is Ljubljana's major point of reference, an atmospheric space where open-air cafés do a cracking trade and street theatre performers and musicians keep the punters entertained during the summer months. Presiding over all this activity, on the east side of the square, is the **monument to France Prešeren**, Slovenia's national poet (see box, p.121), after whom the square is named. Designed by Maks Fabiani and Ivan Zajec in 1905, the large, rather scruffy-looking bronze monument has a straight-backed Prešeren standing underneath a naked muse holding a laurel wreath – the circular plinth underneath is a traditional meeting place for locals and tourists alike.

On the north side, a three-part staircase leads up to the Baroque seventeenth-century Franciscan **Church of the Annunciation** (Frančiškanska Cerkev Marijnega oznanjenja; daily 10am–6pm), its striking sandy-red exterior providing a marvellous backdrop to the square. The first church on this site – this is the third – was erected in 1329 by the Augustins, but following the dissolution of the order by Emperor Joseph II in 1784, it was taken over by the Franciscans, who made several significant alterations to the structure and appearance of the church. The centrepiece of a rather gloomy and weary-looking interior is Francesco Robba's eighteenth-century marble high altar, richly adorned with spiral columns and plastic figurines. The illusionist frescoes on the nave and presbytery vaults are by Matevž Langus and Matej Sternen.

A few paces east of the church is the **Urbanc House**, also known as **Centro-merkur**, Ljubljana's oldest department store, built in 1903 by Friedrich Sigmund of Graz. The focal points of this fine Secessionist building are the narrow clamshell-shaped glass canopy shading the entrance and the statue of Mercury, the Roman god of commerce, standing atop the narrow frontage. While the goods now on offer are unremarkable, it's worth having a look inside to view the superb Art Nouveau interior – the elegant staircase and gallery, the allegorical statue representing craft (fabric has long been sold here) and the beautifully polished wood furnishings, most of which are original. On the opposite side of the square, a few steps down Wolfova ulica to the left of the four-storey Secessionist **Hauptman House**, you'll notice a terracotta window framing a relief of Julija Primic, gazing across to Prešeren, her life-long admirer. To the right of the Hauptman House is Čopova ulica, a lively pedestrianized shopping street, but with few shops actually worth venturing into. However, do take a look at the street's one outstanding building, the **City Savings Bank** at no. 3, featuring a prominent glass and wrought-iron canopy, either side of which are allegorical statues symbolizing trade and commerce.

Miklošičeva cesta and Slovenska cesta

The main street spearing north from Prešernov trg, **Miklošičeva cesta**, is strewn with a raft of marvellous Secessionist buildings, all of which were designed following the earthquake in 1895. Directly behind the Franciscan church stands the handsome **Grand Hotel Union** completed in 1905 by the same architect who designed the City Savings Bank, the Croatian Josip Vancaš – hence the striking similarities. Opposite the *Grand Hotel Union*, at no. 8, is the wildly colourful **Cooperative Bank** (Zadružna gospodarska banka). Designed in 1922 by the Slovene Ivan Vurnik, and painted by his wife Helena, the geometric folk-patterned decoration marks this building out as one of the most outstanding in the city; the interior, with a display of national motifs, is no less spectacular. Two hundred metres further on is **Miklošič Park**, laid out in 1899 by Maks Fabiani, a student of Otto Wagner and the Secessionist school of architecture in Vienna. Immediately after the earthquake, Fabiani was assigned the task of reshaping the entire area, a task he accomplished with astonishing speed. Formerly called Slovenski trg, the square was renamed Miklošič Park in 1991 on the hundredth anniversary of the death of the philologist Fran Miklošič.

Built for the well-known Ljubljana printer Otomar Bamberg in 1907, the **Bamberg House** (Bambergova hiša) at no. 16 is one of Fabiani's more restrained pieces of work, consisting of a simple, rather plain design, but worth a glance for the ceramic reliefs of several eminent printers along the top. On the opposite side of the road, at no. 20, is another, earlier Fabiani building, the **Krisper House** (Krisperjeva hiša). Built in 1901, it was the first building to be designed within his overall concept of the square, and features garland-like, botanical decoration running along the entire length of the facade and a turret under a bell-shaped roof – note how, with the exception of the Bamberg House, all the buildings standing at the corners of the square have corner turrets, another Fabiani concept. The northern side of the square is consumed by the monumental Neoclassical **Court Building**, from where it's a short walk west to the **Čuden House** (Čudnova hiša) at Cigaletova ulica 3, perhaps the most flamboyant example of Secessionist architecture in the area.

Running parallel to Miklošičeva ulica is the broad slash of **Slovenska** cesta, the city's busy main north–south thoroughfare. There's little to see here, though, save for the chunky seventy-metre-high tower block, **Neobotičnik** (also known as "Skyscraper"), standing at the corner of Slovenska cesta and Štefanova ulica. Commissioned by the Slovenian Pension Fund for the purpose of housing offices and apartments – and built in response to the American Art Deco skyscrapers of that period – it was, at the time of its completion in 1933, one of the highest residential buildings in Europe, and the first multistorey building in the Balkans; take a peek inside at the impressive marble lobby and monumental spiral staircase.

Prešernov trg to Metelkova

The area east of Prešernov trg is fairly low-key, but contains one or two sights which make its investigation worthwhile. Due east of the square is **Trubarjeva cesta**, a long, narrow, winding street packed with an eclectic mix of cafés, bars and shops. Midway down Trubarjeva, shortly after crossing Resljeva cesta, take a left up Vidovdanska cesta towards the *Hotel Park*, and carry on until you hit **Metelkova ulica**. Up on the right-hand side is the barracks complex of the former Yugoslav People's Army (JNA).

Metelkova's history is a fascinating one: up until the moment the JNA withdrew in the autumn of 1991, Metelkova had served as a barracks for over one hundred years, having been initially commissioned by Vienna for the Austro-Hungarian army. In December 1990, on the same day that the plebiscite for independence was held, the Network for Metelkova – an organization born out of several student and cultural movements – was established, its express aim being to convert the barracks into Ljubljana's alternative cultural hub. However, after three years of frustrating negotiations with the authorities, the Network finally carried out their threats to squat. In the event, and after further crises, various groups and societies gradually established their own territories within the complex, and there now exists, among the still half-wrecked and rubble-strewn buildings, a cosmopolitan gang of bars, clubs, galleries and independent societies, collectively known as Metelkova (see p.78). Located at the entrance to the site is the **Hostel Celica**, (see p.53), something of an attraction itself having been converted from the gutted remains of the former military prison. Even if you're not staying here, it's worth a look around (tour daily, 2pm, free) just to see the wonderful, artistically designed "cells", which now function as rooms.

At no. 2, the **Ethnographic Museum** (Etnografski muzej; Tues–Sun 10am–6pm; €4.50; ⓦ www.etno-muzej.si) holds a captivating collection of both Slovene and non-Slovene exhibits. The first part of the museum is dedicated to the peoples of Asia, Africa and the Americas, with particularly enlightening expositions on the lives of the Mestizo peoples and the Meso-American Indians – don't miss the extraordinary, and really quite spooky, shrunken head from Ecuador – complete with some intriguing archive video footage. The Slovene collection comprises a beautiful assortment of artefacts and treasures, from regional costumes and items representing prominent eighteenth- and nineteenth-century industries – such as pottery, blacksmithing, clockmaking and shoemaking – to the ever amusing, beehive panels, as well as masks from the Kurent festival in Ptuj and Laufarija festival in Cerkno. During the summer, different craftsmen (typically potters and weavers) give demonstrations in the on-site workshops, while the lovely museum café is an enjoyable spot to rest up afterwards.

Two hundred metres beyond the end of Trubarjeva is **St Peter's Church** (Cerkev Sv Petra), built between 1729 and 1733 according to the designs of the Trieste architect Giovanni Fusconi. Its flat, rectangular facade, with two identical bell towers, is enlivened by several dazzling mosaics created by Ivan and Helena Vurnik, including one of St Peter above the main portal. Inside, the central cupola and vaults were beautifully frescoed by the local artisan Franc Jelovšek with scenes depicting the life of St Peter.

Triple Bridge, Marketplace and around

Linking Prešernov trg and the right bank of the **Ljubljanica** is the enchanting **Triple Bridge** (Tromostovje), a brilliant piece of architecture and Ljubljana's most photographed landmark. In 1929, Plečnik decided to broaden the existing central bridge, which dates from 1842, with two lateral footbridges, in order to make access to the Old Town safer and more convenient for pedestrians; to top it off he added the Renaissance balustrades, based on the rising bridges of Venice's waterways, and rows of lamps, all of which gives the bridge a magical appearance at night. Once across the bridge, turn left onto Adamič-Lundrovo nabrežje and you're immediately confronted with another Plečnik masterpiece – the splendid **Market Colonnade**, an elongated, gently curving pavilion harbouring a galaxy of excellent food shops (see p.75) and a downstairs fish market. The colonnade runs along the length of the riverbank from the Triple Bridge to the **Dragon Bridge** (Zmajski most), a quite beautiful piece of Secessionist architecture completed in 1901 by the Croatian Jurij Zaninovich, another student of the school of architecture in Vienna. Sitting atop the chunky pylons at each corner of the bridge are four carved, spitting, swirly-tailed dragons – the city symbol.

The two squares adjacent to the Colonnade, **Pogačarjev trg** and the much larger **Vodnikov trg**, have been the site of the brash and colourful city **market** (Mon–Sat 8am–3pm) for over a century; it's a terrific place to stock up on fresh produce, particularly on a Saturday morning when it seems that half the city congregates here. On the southern side of Pogačarjev trg stands the Renaissance-style **Bishop's Palace** (Škofijski dvorec), one of the oldest buildings in the city, dating back to 1512. Once a residence for distinguished guests – Napoleon stayed here in 1797, as did Tsar Alexander I in 1821 – its outstanding feature is the Baroque seventeenth-century arcaded courtyard. On the eastern side of the same square is the **Seminary** (Semenišče), built

▲ Crossing the Triple Bridge

between 1708 and 1714 and still used by theology students from the dioceses of Koper and Ljubljana; the seminary houses the oldest library in the city, a quite stunning union of Baroque oak-wood furnishings and sky-blue ceiling frescoes representing Theology, Faith and Love by Giulio Quaglio. The stone portal on the southern side – by the flower market – is flanked by two lumbering giants carved by Angelo Pozzo. Visits to the library can be made by contacting the tourist information centre (☎01/306-1215).

St Nicholas's Cathedral

Lording it over Pogačarjev trg, the Baroque **St Nicholas's Cathedral** (Stolnica Sv Nikolaja; daily 6am–noon & 3–6pm), easily spotted from all over town due to its enormous twin bell towers and 24-metre-high dome, is Ljubljana's most important and best-preserved ecclesiastical building. Dedicated to St Nicholas, the patron saint of fishermen and sailors – many of whom lived in the suburb of Krakovo – the present building, designed by Andrea Pozzo from Rome and completed in 1706, stands on the site of a thirteenth-century basilica. Entering through the weighty **bronze door**, designed in 1996 to commemorate the pope's visit and bearing an impressive relief portraying over a thousand years of Slovene Christianity, you're presented with a riot of fine architecture, immaculate carvings and vibrant frescoes. The cathedral really owes its reputation to the **frescoes** painted by Quaglio between 1703 and 1706, but restored in 2006; these vivid paintings illustrate the many sea-bound miracles of St Nicholas, such as the one depicting him steering a ship full of sailors to safety during a particularly nasty storm. Remarkably, Quaglio painted the presbytery vault, showing the scene of the Establishment of the Ljubljana bishopric, in just twelve days. The most impressive **altar** is in the northern wing of the transept, decorated by an oil painting of the Three Magi by Matevž Langus and further embellished with Robba's delightfully sculpted angels and cherubs. In the opposite, southern wing, is a copy of the *Virgin Mary of Brezje* (see p.111), held within a magnificent frame. Note, too, the fine Baroque choir seats with gilded reliefs of Christ and the Apostles, and the splendid pulpit,

Jože Plečnik

Jože Plečnik (1872–1957) was a world-class architect, who transformed Ljubljana into an architectural and urban planning phenomenon. His immense body of work encompasses churches and their interior furnishings, town squares and parks, public buildings, and a scattering of columns, pillars and obelisks.

Plečnik studied at the School of Architecture at the Vienna Academy of Fine Arts under the tutelage of **Otto Wagner**, whom he would later work with for a brief period. For the most part, though, Plečnik worked independently, renovating numerous buildings and concerning himself with interior design projects. Disillusioned with the growing tide of German nationalism, and the increasingly oppressive atmosphere in the Austrian capital, Plečnik moved to **Prague** in 1911, where his burgeoning reputation was further enhanced following the execution of several key projects, including the restoration of Hradčany Castle, the latter at the request of President Masaryk.

In 1921 the lure of a professorship in his home town compelled him to return to **Ljubljana University** to become head of the school of architecture; moreover, his return presented him with the opportunity to map out and implement his grand vision for the city. Over the next twenty years, despite extremely limited financial resources, Plečnik married classical architectural forms with his own richly imaginative ideas to create a series of monumental new buildings (including Market Colonnade, National and University Library, Žale Cemetery), bridges (Triple Bridge, Shoemakers' Bridge) and churches (St Francis in Šiška, St Michael on the Marsh). A key component of his blueprint for this new cityscape was the redesign of large segments of the city, including numerous park areas, squares and streets.

Despite his extraordinary range and output, Plečnik's work was not appreciated by everybody, not least his contemporaries, most of whom were wed to the more traditional, functionalist principles of architecture. Indeed it wasn't until some thirty years after his death that he received the recognition his work deserved.

whose author is unknown. Inevitably, Plečnik also had a hand in the proceedings, designing the baptismal font and bishop's throne.

East of Vodnikov trg

The area east of Vodnikov trg is fairly nondescript, though there are a couple of buildings that might be of interest, particularly to fans of Plečnik. At the beginning of Poljanska cesta, you'll pass Plečnik's **Flat Iron Building** (Peglezen), so named after its extraordinary tapered shape; originally constructed as a municipal building in 1934, it now accommodates a shop on the ground floor, and apartments and a winter garden on the floors above. A few minutes further on, take a right turn down Ulica Janeza Pavla II towards the huge neo-Romanesque **St Joseph's Church** (Cerkev Sv Jožefa), completed in 1922 by the Jesuits. The vast interior is remarkably bare and, aside from Plečnik's monumental semicircular altar, there is literally nothing to see – which probably explains why it was used as a film studio from the end of World War II until its return to a monastery in 1996.

The Old Town

Defined by a tangle of narrow streets, handsome orange-and-red-roofed town houses, and neat rows of compact pavement cafés, Ljubljana's fabulous **Old Town** is for many the most enjoyable part of the city. Heavily fortified in the twelfth century by the Carinthian dukes, the Old Town – cobbled and mercifully free of traffic – extends from **Mestni trg**, across from the Triple Bridge, south down **Stari trg** to **Levstikov trg** and **Gornji trg**; the entire district is wedged between the Ljubljanica to the west and the castle-topped hill to the east.

Mestni trg

After crossing the Triple Bridge and walking to the end of Stritarjeva, you enter elegant **Mestni trg** (Town Square), the first of three medieval squares that form the backbone of the Old Town. Located on the square's northern fringe is a copy of Robba's majestic Baroque **Fountain of the Three Carniolan Rivers**, the original having recently been moved to the entrance hall of the National Gallery following years of debate (see p.68).

The square's most prominent and important building is the white- and grey-brick **Town Hall** (Magistrat) at no. 1, dating from 1719 and one of the most identifiably Baroque buildings in the city. Sporting a gently protruding balcony and impressive clocktower, the building's most interesting features lie within, namely the arcaded inner courtyards adorned with sgraffiti (a decorative technique whereby one colour is laid over another and the top coat is then partly etched away to create a design) and featuring two sculptures: the fountain of Narcissus by Robba, and a statue of Hercules, which previously stood in a fountain outside the Stična Mansion on Stari trg. Hour long tours of the town hall, which include viewings of the banquet and wedding halls, and grand council chamber, take place at 1pm every Saturday between April and September (€2). Of the many other fine buildings on the square, take a look at no. 24, the **Souvan House** (Souvanova hiša), whose frontage is the most outstanding example of Biedermeier to be found anywhere in the city – note the stucco reliefs under the third-floor windows representing agriculture, art and trade. Opposite the town hall a narrow passageway leads to **Ribji trg** (Fisherman's Square), a small, cobbled square where, during the sixteenth century, the fishermen of Krakovo would bring their freshly caught haul from the Ljubljanica to sell to the local inns and houses. Points of interest here include the house (now a restaurant – see p.76) at no. 2, which dates from 1528 (as indicated by its coat of arms), making it one of the oldest residences in the city, and the Neoclassical fountain in the centre featuring a gilded statue of a girl pouring water from a pitcher. The square opens up onto **Cankarjevo nabrežje**, an engaging riverside parade home to some of the city's busiest and most vibrant bars and cafés, and site of the terrific Sunday flea market (see p.80).

Stari trg to Levstikov trg

Mestni trg gradually tapers southwards towards **Stari trg** (Old Square), Ljubljana's oldest medieval square, a slight misnomer for this narrow, gently curving street. With a sprightly assortment of cafés, restaurants and ice-cream parlours, it's the ideal place to re-energize yourself before pressing on with sightseeing.

Shortly after entering Stari trg, take a right down Pod Trančo – formerly the site of a jail – which opens up onto the expansive **Shoemakers' Bridge** (Čevljarski most), so named after a group of local cobblers set up their trading booths here. Prior to their arrival, the bridge was settled by a group of butchers, but so troubled were the locals by the stench that the then emperor, Maximilian I, paid them all off to relocate elsewhere. Remarkably, there has been a bridge of sorts here since the thirteenth century, though this, the second of Plečnik's bridges, was built in 1932.

Back on Stari trg, at no. 11a, is the **Schweiger House**, showcasing a splendid Rococo facade. The stone telamon supporting the wrought-iron balcony above the main portal has a finger raised to his lips in an apparent request for silence – Schweiger, the name of the German owner, meaning "the silent one". The house was later owned by the poet Lily Nova, a bust of whom sits to the left of the main entrance. A few doors down at no. 21 is the **Škuc Gallery** (Tues–Sun noon–8pm; free), a wing of the Škuc Cultural Society, formed in 1978 as a counterpoint to the exhibition policies of the then-dominant state cultural institutions; the gallery hosts imaginative temporary exhibitions by both local and foreign artists.

Beyond the gallery, Stari trg opens up into **Levstikov trg** (Levstik Square), considered to be the true centre of the Old Town and bounded by some notable buildings and monuments. In the centre of the square is the **Hercules Fountain**, a 1991 copy of the original, now in the town hall. A few paces west of the fountain, the **Stična Mansion** (Stiški dvorec), built as a town residence for the abbots of the Stična Monastery in 1630 (which was abolished in 1784) now houses the Academy of Music. During the Counter-Reformation period, the Jesuits settled in and around the square. Their main legacy was **St James's Church** (Cerkev Sv Jakoba), the first Jesuit church in Slovenia, a bright lemon-yellow structure completed in 1615 and festooned with some outstanding sculptures. Retaining only the presbytery from the preceding Gothic church, the present layout is unusual, comprising a Baroque nave with rows of lateral chapels either side, each adorned with colourful Venetian-style stone altars designed by the local stonemason Luka Mislej, the author of most of the altar sculptures. The high altar, another by Robba, is a far more modest take on his other works, but no less impressive – he also made the marvellous sculptures in the Altar of St Anne, the third chapel on the left. The church's most significant addition, the octagonal chapel of St Francis Xavier, was completed in 1670, and features another marble altar with unusual statues of a "White Queen" and "Black King". The church is more often than not closed, so try and visit during daily evening mass (6.30pm) or one of the several Sunday morning services. Next to the church stands the slender column of the Virgin Mary, erected in 1682 in honour of victory over the Turks at Monošter (now Szentgotthard) in Hungary; the pedestal with four saints, underneath the bronze figure of Mary, was added by Plečnik when he redesigned the square between the two world wars.

Across the two busy main road is the custard-coloured pile of the **Gruber Palace** (Gruberjeva palača), built by the Jesuit Gabriel Gruber between 1773 and 1781 for the purposes of research into mechanics and hydraulics; it now houses the National Archives of Slovenia. However, its real architectural delights are concealed within, in particular a decorative Baroque oval staircase with stucco flower plaits, the dome with an allegorical fresco representing trade, craft and technology, and the chapel on the second floor with oil paintings by the Austrian Kremser-Schmidt. Visits, which are free, can be arranged by appointment (☎01/241-4200).

Gornji trg

Arching eastwards from Levstikov trg is **Gornji trg** (Upper Square), a lovely, gently inclining street whose dwellings, notwithstanding the Baroque elements, have retained a number of medieval characteristics – three windows, wide with triangular gables, slightly set back from each other and separated by narrow passageways. As you walk along the street, keep your eye out for a number of interesting details, notably the rustic stone relief of St Christopher, thought to date from around 1530, on the front of the house at no. 1; the bronze plaque with a portrait of the historian Baltazar Haquet at no. 4; and, at no. 16, the sign on the portal denoting that the painter Valentin Metzinger once lived here.

Crowning the upper end of the street is **St Florian's Church** (Cerkev sv Florijana), built in 1672 following a fire twelve years earlier that wiped out the majority of houses along here – St Florian is the patron saint of firefighters and protection from fires. Above all else, the church has some intriguing external elements: in the 1930s Plečnik moved the entrance so that the statue of the Bohemian prelate St John of Nepomuk was placed in front of the original, now walled up, portal. Robba's dramatic relief, in the niche under the pedestal, is of St John being thrown from the Charles Bridge into the Vltava River in Prague. Look out too for the built-in head of an Emona citizen, thought to date from 2 AD; the two niches with badly damaged statues of Charles the Great and St Charles of Borromeo; and the fountain with a portrait of a mask from whence water spouts. Beyond the church, the building at no. 27 features a late-Baroque statue of the Virgin and Child; at one stage it was an orphanage, which earned it the rather disdainful slur, "the shitty school".

Ljubljana Castle

Peeking out above lush woodland high above the Old Town on Castle Hill, **Ljubljana Castle** (Ljubljanski Grad; daily: May–Sept 9am–11pm; Oct–April 10am–9pm; free), with its immaculate whitewashed walls and silky, manicured lawns, does little to give the impression of a residence dating back to the twelfth century, although much of what remains today is actually sixteenth-century, following the earthquake in 1511. Its first inhabitants were the Spanheim family of Carinthian dukes who settled here during the twelfth century, before the provincial lords of the Carniolan province, along with the Habsburgs, took over residence in the fourteenth century. Thereafter, the castle was used as a military fortress, a provincial jail and as a refuge for the poor. Crossing the bridge into the castle, you can see, on the right, the remains of the cells where prisoners were held. In 1905 the castle was taken over by the municipal authorities, with the intention of using it as a cultural centre, although in the event it continued to house convicts, including the writer Ivan Cankar who was imprisoned here for six weeks in 1914. Furthermore, the chronic housing shortage in the city meant that additional tenements had to be constructed, most of which remained occupied until the 1960s.

The castle's chief attraction is the **Virtual Museum** (Virtualni muzej; daily: May–Sept 9am–9pm; Oct–April 10am–6pm; €4, which includes entrance to the clocktower), which is not a museum in the conventional sense, but rather an enlightening twenty-minute 3D visual presentation chronicling the city's urban and architectural development and its cultural and economic growth. Aside from the museum there's not an awful lot to see, though the fifteenth-century Gothic **Chapel of St George** on the western side of the courtyard – one of the oldest remaining parts of the castle – is worth a look for its colourful and remarkably intact coats of arms, representing the Carniolan provincial governors. Most visitors, though, come here to climb the landmark **Clocktower**, built in 1848 but subsequently raised, and now affording wide and superlative views of the city and the Kamniške Alps to the north. The vast courtyard, meanwhile, stages many of the city's principal cultural happenings, including a good number of events connected to the International Summer Festival (see box, p.79).

A **funicular** (*vzpenjai*; every 10min; €3 return) on Krekov trg, transports visitors into the heart of the castle, but if you fancy walking, three paths wind up to the top, each a stiff fifteen-minute climb: south of Vodnikov trg follow the path up Študentovska ulica; on Stari trg follow Reber Way and then Osojna steza; and from St Florian's Church on Gornji trg take Ulica na Grad.

Left bank of the Ljubljanica

The left bank of the Ljubljanica, defined here as the area between **Kongresni trg** and **Zoisova cesta** to the south, holds more magnificent architectural set-pieces, as well as vestiges from Roman Emona and some of Plečnik's greatest work. Its medieval heritage is most pronounced in **Novi trg**, the second oldest square in the city – it too was once surrounded by ramparts which extended as far south as Zoisova cesta.

Kongresni trg and around

From Prešernov trg, Wolfova ulica leads south to **Kongresni trg** (Congress Square), a popular, grassy park shaded by leafy plane trees and fringed by a number of venerable architectural gems. Also called Zvezda ("Star"), on account of its vaguely star-shaped path design, the square was laid out in 1821 to stage the Congress of the Holy Alliance, before which time it was the site of a Capuchin Monastery. Occupying the northwestern corner of the square is the **Kazina** (Casino), a lovely Classicist mansion built in 1837 by the Kazina Society for the purposes of entertaining the Ljubljana elite, largely in the form of dances, evenings of song and other prestigious social events. Among the society's more distinguished patrons was France Prešeren, who spent many an evening here with his contemporaries; the Kazina is even recalled in several of his poems. The building's present-day functions as bookshop and dance school are somewhat more prosaic. Between the two world wars, the Kazina also accommodated the posh *Café Zvezda* – its rather less refined modern-day equivalent, located a little further down on the northeastern corner, serves up some of the best cakes and desserts in town (see p.76).

Recessed within a row of buildings on the western side of the square (across the road) is the **Ursuline Church of the Holy Trinity** (Uršulinska Cerkev Sv Trojice), completed in 1726 and perhaps the most original Baroque statement in Ljubljana. Its fading coffee-coloured frontage, incorporating six thick columns and a graceful triangular ridged gable containing Gothic arches, is designed in Palladian style – its curved side wings serve as the entrances. The bright, airy interior, unpainted and completely white, is rather less elaborate, the exception being Robba's dazzling high altar; made from multicoloured African marble and adorned with the allegorical figures of Faith, Hope and Charity, it ranks alongside his most distinguished work. Other notable artwork includes the side altar paintings by Metzinger, and the wooden altar of Ecce Homo with a relief of the Virgin and Child, dating from 1638.

Next to the church on the corner of Slovenska cesta and Plečnikov trg, the little known **Slovene School Museum** (Slovenski Šolski Muzej; Mon–Fri 9am–1pm; free) charts the history of Slovene schooling from the Middle Ages to the end of the twentieth century. Its displays, divided by periods, include a diverse selection of educational memorabilia, ranging from books and reports to teaching aids and uniforms, as well as a couple of mock-up classrooms complete with chalkboards and desks. Alas, the absence of English captions makes what would otherwise be an engaging visit somewhat frustrating.

The square's most prepossessing building is the buttermilk-coloured **Slovene Philharmonic Hall** (Slovenska filharmonija), whose orchestra, in its various guises, has been performing on this site for over three hundred years; although this building only dates from 1892, it's one of the oldest musical institutions in Europe. Given its modest size, Slovenia's musical heritage is remarkably strong. The Academia Philharmonicorum, established in 1701, was the forerunner to today's Philharmonic, which subsequently became one of the foremost musical institutions in the Habsburg Empire. Its reputation was further enhanced by a roll call of distinguished honorary members – Haydn, Beethoven and Mozart to name just three – and it employed Gustav Mahler to conduct here for the 1881–1882 season. For more information on attending a performance, see p.80. Diagonally across from the Philharmonic, the immense neo-Renaissance **University building**, built between 1899 and 1902, has functioned as the main seat of the university since 1919, and today also houses the Faculty of Law. Busts of academic luminaries, including one of Pleinik, form a semicircular sweep around the entrance.

South of Kongresni trg

Vegova ulica, the main street darting southwards from Kongresni trg, was once the westernmost boundary of the medieval city walls. It received its present appearance during the interwar period courtesy of Plečnik, who rearranged the entire street, punctuating it with several of his greatest monuments. The first building of note, on the right-hand side at no. 4, is the **Faculty of Engineering**, its stately neo-Romanesque facade and thrusting corner towers more than a match for the university building opposite. Across the road is the **Music School** (Glasbena Matica), distinguished by portrait reliefs on the facade, and busts of Slovene musicians – as well as a Croat and a Serb – lining the wall in front of the building; although Plečnik's idea, they were sculpted by his colleague Lojze Dolinar.

Taking five years to complete (1936–41), the **National and University Library** (Narodna in univerzitetna knjižnica; Mon–Tues & Thurs–Sat 2–6pm, Wed 4–6pm, Sun 9am–5pm; free; Ⓦwww.nuk.uni-lj.si), occupying the entire block between Turjaška ulica and the Križanke, is Plečnik's most lauded piece of work. Built on the site of a former palace, its extraordinary, variegated facade, consisting of rough grey stone quarried from Vrhnika and smooth orange brick from Podpeč is one of the city's most outstanding, and conspicuous, landmarks. Upon entering the building from Turjaška ulica – note the smart bronze horse-head handles on the copper-covered wooden door – you're confronted with a dark staircase ascending to a vestibule lined with black marble columns, the walk up symbolically meant to represent the journey from darkness to light, or, from ignorance to knowledge. Beyond here, and filling the entire width of one wing of the building, is the grand reading room, worth visiting for its furnishings, and in particular its "catherine wheel" chandeliers and industrial-style reading lamps.

Treasures of the Ljubljanica

The languid, muddy-green waters of the Ljubljanica have for centuries concealed one of Slovenia's most unlikely, and extraordinary, archeological sites. Over the past thirty years or so a remarkable number of ancient artefacts have been retrieved from the riverbed, including Bronze Age sickles and helmets, Iron Age spearheads, 2000-year-old Hallstatt bracelets, Roman pots, and medieval swords and brooches, proof, if any were needed, that the river was a key centre of activity and movement long before its heyday in the seventeenth and eighteenth centuries.

Some of these items, many of which have been superbly preserved owing to centuries of submersion, are held at the National Museum (see p.70), though many more have been gathered up by amateur archeologists, and hence reside in private collections. If you fancy taking a trip along a stretch of the river, there are one-hour guided excursions during the summer, embarking from Ribji trg (daily: April–Sept noon & 4pm; €10). Tickets are available from the departure point or the tourist information centres.

Vegova ulica winds up at **Trg Francoske revolucije** (French Revolution Square), whose main point of reference is the stern, square-shaped **Illyrian Monument**, designed by Plečnik in 1929 in belated recognition of Ljubljana's short-lived stint as the capital of Napoleon's Illyrian Provinces (1809–13). The obelisk, made from white marble from the island of Hvar in Croatia, is embellished with the Illyrian coat of arms – a crescent moon with three stars – and gilded bronze masks of Napoleon and Illyria. Retained within the core of the monument are the ashes of an unknown French soldier, killed in battle in 1813. The **Friedl-Rechar House**, the curved, crumbling building on the western corner of the square, was once a palace accommodating shops and apartments; its ground floor now houses *Le Petit Café*, one of Ljubljana's most frequented and atmospheric haunts (see p.76).

A few paces south of here is the majestic **Križanke**, formerly the monastic complex of the Teutonic knights but now the setting for the city's prestigious summer festival and other major concerts (see box, p.79). Its present appearance dates from the mid-1950s, when Plečnik, in his final contribution to the city – he was 80 upon its completion – set about transforming the abandoned monastery into an open-air theatre and festival space. The complex's original Gothic details were gradually usurped by Renaissance and Baroque elements, which can be most clearly seen in the main courtyard, which also features shallow archways and exuberantly coloured sgraffiti. Next door, the amphitheatre-like southern courtyard, with its vast retractable canopy, is a superb venue for classical, jazz and rock concerts. Plečnik also designed the **Devil's Courtyard** (Peklensko dvorišče), accessible through the non-descript restaurant and spotted with neat rows of weird-looking wall lamps.

The City Museum

Between Križanke and the Ljubljanica the chief attraction is the **Auersperg Mansion** (Auerspergova palača), adjacent to Križanke at Gosposka ulica 15. After residing here for over three hundred years, the Turjak counts, a noble Slovene family with roots going back to the eleventh century, sold the palace to the city authorities who subsequently used the premises for the **City Museum** (Mestni Muzej; Tues–Sun 10am–6pm; €4). During a painstaking, decade-long renovation programme, an impressive stock of archeological remains were uncovered, including part of the original Roman road that once linked Emona to the port on the Ljubljanica, which can now be viewed down in the basement.

The greater part of this excellent museum is given over to the lives and the people (*ljubljaniani*) who have inhabited the city over the course of time. Entitled "Faces of Ljubljana", the highlight of this entertaining trawl is the wartime coverage, which features a section of barbed wire used to surround the city by occupying Italian forces between 1942 and 1945, an event commemorated each year with an annual walk. Elsewhere, due deference is paid to Tito, in the form of portraits, busts and street signs, plus some rare archive footage of the former president giving a speech from the balcony of the nearby University building.

Up on the second floor, in the protocol (or Mayoral) room, take a look at the statues of Adam and Eve, sculpted by Janez Lipec in 1484, and a portrait of Ljubljana's most revered mayor, Ivan Hribar (1851–1941), painted by Slovenia's greatest female artist Ivana Kobilca, more of whose work can be seen at the National Gallery (see p.68). There's a very pleasant café on site too.

Novi trg and around

Continuing along Gosposka ulica, which runs parallel to Vegova ulica, you'll pass the eastern side of the National and University Library – and, above its second entrance, a dramatic sculpture of Moses, by Dolinar – before reaching **Novi trg** (New Square), a rectangular, sloping space extending down to the Ljubljanica. The square is framed by some wonderful seventeenth- and eighteenth-century mansions, the best example of which is the **Lontovž** on the corner at no. 3; built in 1790, the Slovenian Academy of Arts and Sciences has been based here since 1938. In its courtyard stands a resplendent fountain of Neptune, the precursor to Robba's fountain on Mestni trg (see p.61).

By taking a left turn at the bottom of Novi trg, and walking on a few paces, you'll find yourself back at the Shoemakers' Bridge, which lies next to another, smaller square, Jurčičev trg. **Židovska steža** (Jewish Lane) and **Židovska ulica** (Jewish Street), immediately west of the bridge, together once comprised Ljubljana's small Jewish ghetto. Neither the synagogue, which once stood at Židovska steža 4, nor any other original tenements remain, although a new synagogue – Slovenia's third – was opened in 2003; it's a ten-minute walk southwest of the centre at Tržaška cesta 2. Jews have played little more than a walk-on role in Slovenian history and it remains unclear as to when they first settled in the country, though it is believed that there was a Jewish presence here in the twelfth century. What is known is that following an edict by Emperor Maximilian in 1515, all Jews were banished from Ljubljana, with the majority fleeing to neighbouring Italy and Hungary, and some being dispersed to Slovene villages. Today, it is estimated that around three hundred Jews live in Slovenia, most of whom have settled in Ljubljana.

Turning right at the bottom of Novi trg brings you to **Breg** (Embankment), a river wharf in the fourteenth century when the Ljubljanica was a navigable waterway. Indeed, the river remained the city's principal transport artery, with Breg as its chief port, until the end of the eighteenth century, when the widespread construction of the railways – and in particular the building of the Vienna–Trieste line – spelt its death knell. The boats and ships that used to dock here would sail up from Vrhnika, near its source 20km south of Ljubljana, laden with wood, salt and other goods from the Mediterranean.

Krakovo

A short walk south of Breg is the genteel suburb of Krakovo, reachable from either Emonska ulica – an extension of Vegova ulica – or from Breg, both routes crossing busy Zoisova cesta. During the Middle Ages Krakovo was largely settled by fishermen, many of whom supplemented their income by working as pelajhtarji (torch bearers), which entailed escorting the local citizens home late at night from the theatre or the inn. Horticulture is now the prime activity here and one of the first things you'll notice are the strips of carefully tended vegetable plots, the results of which sustain the daily market on Vodnikov trg.

In parts, the area still retains a medieval-village-like character and this is especially true of Krakovska ulica, with its handsome, one- and two-storey squat houses; the street was once the haunt of prominent town artists, including the celebrated Slovenian Impressionist painter Rihard Jakopič (1869–1943) who was born at no. 11. Jakopič actually worked a short walk west of Krakovska at Mirje 4, in what is now called the **Jakopič Garden** (Jakopičev vrt), site of some Roman ruins including black and white mosaics and the remains of a complex heating system. If you wish to visit, then contact the City Museum (☎01/241-2506). West of the garden, across Barjanska cesta and spanning almost the entire length of Mirje, is a reconstructed section of the **Roman city wall** (Rimski Zid), topped with an incongruous looking pyramid – one of Plečnik's less-inspired concepts.

Trnovo

"Trnovo, a place of miserable name", the great Slovenian poet Prešeren once wrote of Krakovo's attractive neighbouring suburb. It can be reasonably assumed that the motive for this mildly apoplectic outburst was an unrequited love affair, for it was here in 1833 that Prešeren met his great love Julija Primic, who, tragically, never reciprocated his feelings. Prešeren first set eyes on Primic in the towering neo-Romanesque **Church of St John the Baptist**, built in 1855 but radically altered following the 1895 earthquake. The stark, bare interior has few highlights, though the presbytery ceiling frescoes by Matej Sternen are worth a look. The bronze relief plate to the right of the main door features portraits of Plečnik and the parish priest and writer Franc Finžgar. With the exception of Mass, the church is usually closed, so try calling at the priest's door to the right of the church if you wish to have a look. Facing the church is the Plečnik-designed **Trnovo Bridge**, completed in 1932 and incorporating several ungainly stone pyramids, a statue of St John the Baptist and rows of birch trees on either side. Leafy Eipprova ulica, the street running eastwards from the bridge along the Gradaščica canal's southern embankment, is well worth checking out for its delightfully quirky cafés and bars (see p.76).

Directly behind the church at Karunova ulica 4 is **Plečnik's House** (Plečnikova hiša; Tues–Thurs 10am–6pm, Sat 9am–3pm; the house can only be visited on guided tours which take place on the hour; €4), where the great man lived from 1921 until his death in 1957. Most of this fascinating and neatly preserved collection of equipment, books, plans and furniture is located in the cylindrical annexe which Plečnik purposely built to house his studio. The house exemplifies Plečnik's extraordinary commitment to modesty, each room practically yet creatively schemed. Among the more interesting rooms are his studio, with desks bearing numerous instruments, plans and models; the spartan-looking bathroom complete with ingenious wood-heated shower; the small reception room, where he would receive friends and colleagues – note the stove with its built-in copper kettle; and the kitchen, containing his special chair that enabled him to eat and work at the same time. Having browsed around the house, it's hard to reconcile such a modest man with the grand structures that have left such an indelible mark on this city.

West of Slovenska cesta

The neatly ordered district west of Slovenska cesta contains some of the city's most significant museums. Heading west along Cankarjeva cesta, you'll pass the horseshoe-shaped, neo-Renaissance **Opera House**, constructed in 1892 and home to the Slovenian National Opera and Ballet companies (see p.80). Within the impressive tympanum above the main entrance are the figures of Poetry and Glory, above which is a statue of Genius; in the niches in the facade either side of the main entrance stand the allegorical figures of Comedy and Tragedy.

The National Gallery

At the end of Cankarjeva ulica is the **National Gallery** (Narodna galerija; Tues–Sun 10am–6pm, Thurs till 8pm; €5; ⓦ www.ng-slo.si), whose modest but rewarding two-part collection makes this one of the city's more deserving visits. The collection is actually spread over two buildings: you'll find the exhibition of Slovenian painting in Slovenski Dom (National House), a grandiloquent, Habsburg-era pile facing Cankarjeva ulica, while the exhibition of European painting is in the northern extension, a stark postmodernist building around the corner on Prešernova ulica.

Entering via the latter, you're confronted by Robba's **Fountain of the Three Carniolan Rivers**. Its removal from Mestni trg in 2006 (and placement here in 2009) has undoubtedly diluted its impact, though it remains a spectacular piece of work. Allegedly modelled on Bernini's Fountain of the Four Rivers in Rome's Piazza Navona (it is strikingly similar), the fountain, completed in 1751, symbolizes the meeting of the rivers Sava, Krka and Ljubljanica, as represented by three muscular tritons grasping oval jugs, with dolphins splashing at their feet.

The Slovene collection kicks off with **medieval art** and a superb display of Gothic statuary and frescoes, the most interesting of which are located immediately to the left and right as you enter; the most renowned piece is the exquisite, almost porcelain-like *Standing Madonna* (minus Jesus, who was cut off) from the Ptujska gora workshop, thought to date from around 1410. Other notable pieces here include the tympanum with the relief *Madonna on Solomon's Throne*, which once stood in Križanke, and the fragment of the fresco *Madonna and Child*, from the late fourteenth century. From here, you enter the grand main hall containing paintings from the **Baroque** and **Neoclassical** periods. Its highlight is the *Cardplayers* by Almanach, considered to be the most important seventeenth-century group portrait in the country (this Dutch piece is included here, rather than in the European section, as Almanach worked extensively in the former Slovene province of Carniola). There is also an impressive clutch of paintings by Valentin Metzinger and Franc Jelovšek, two of the country's foremost exponents of eighteenth-century church painting – the former was principally concerned with oils, whereas Jelovšek was almost entirely devoted to painting wall and ceiling frescoes. Next up after a rather ordinary collection of **Biedermeiers** are the **Realists**, with a superb offering by its leading representatives, Janez and Jurij Šubic, including the fine *Before the Hunt* and the melancholic *Alone*, both by Jurij. One of the more curious pieces here is by Jožef Petkovšek, whose bleak *At Home* is notable for the missing arm and lower body of his mother – it's believed he'd gone mad by the time he painted this. There is also a wonderful collection by Ivana Kobilca (1861–1926), Slovenia's most celebrated female painter; among her finest works are the cheeky-looking *Woman Drinking Coffee* and the joyous *Summer*.

After passing through a room of bronze busts and statues, the exhibition finishes on a high, with an outstanding collection of work from Slovenia's highly revered **Impressionist** painters. This distinguished group of four artists was led by Ivan Grohar (1867–1911), renowned for investing such emotion in his dreamlike landscapes, such as the masterful *Sower* and *Škofja Loka in Snowstorm*. Rihard Jakopič, a close colleague of Grohar, was a painter of bolder, more expressionist works, as shown in his paintings *Memories* and *The Green Veil/Girl with Crown*. The third and fourth members of this quartet, Matej Sternen and Matija Jama, produced works of a brighter, more orthodox bent, for example in Sternen's *The Red Parasol* and Jama's *Village in Winter*.

The **European collection** is a less thrilling affair, although there are one or two notable pieces, such as another *Cardplayers* by Almanach – the players in this one considerably more worse for wear. One of the collection's most prestigious paintings is *Empress Maria Theresa* by Martin van Meytens, in the Central European section.

The Museum of Modern Art

Diagonally across from the National Gallery, the **Museum of Modern Art** (Moderna galerija; Tues–Sat 10am–6pm; €3; ⓦ www.mg-lj.si) takes over from where the National Gallery left off, namely Slovene art from the 1950s onwards. However, it's a bit of a mixed bag and comes as something of a disappointment after its counterpart. It does, however, stage excellent temporary exhibitions. The highlights from the first hall are the smooth sculptures by Zdenko Kalin and Jakob Savinšek, while the second hall is the most heterogeneous – by virtue of the fact that the work on display spans the 1960s to the 1980s. The most intriguing pieces are Lojze Spacal's wooden sculpture of Downing Street and Rudolf Kotnik's series of oddly shaped canvases interwoven with metal plates and wires. Also worth taking a look at are the exhibits by the retro-avant-garde collective Irwin, who cofounded the controversial and influential Neue Slowenische Kunst or NSK (New Slovene Art) movement in the mid-1980s. The exhibition winds up with a bunch of odd, media-inspired pieces from the 1990s and a more sobering piece of work – a vase created from a mortar shell that fell on Sarajevo.

The National Museum and the Natural History Museum

A short walk southeast of the Museum of Modern Art, at Prešernova 20, lies the **National Museum** (Narodni muzej; Tues–Sun 10am–6pm, Thurs till 8pm; €3; ⓦ www.nms.si), housed in this handsome Rudolfinum building since 1888 and graced at the entrance by four allegorical figures representing Art, History, Natural History and Labour. Inside there's a magnificent double staircase with smooth sculptures of reclining muses, and ceiling frescoes executed by the Šubic brothers. The collection itself is somewhat narrow, focusing almost exclusively on an extensive stockpile of archeological treasures, the most noteworthy item being the Neanderthal flute discovered at the Divje Babe Cave near Cerkno in 1995 (see p.182); there is also a hoard of finds excavated from the unlikely source of the Ljubljanica (see box, p.65), as well as a tremendous stash of Stone Age pottery and tools, Copper Age vessels and implements from the Ljubljana Marshes, and Celtic weaponry and jewellery.

On the second floor of the building is the **Natural History Museum** (Prirodoslovni muzej; same hours and ticket; ⓦ www.pms-lj.si), featuring an almost complete twenty-thousand-year-old skeleton of a mammoth found near Kamnik in 1938, and a two-hundred-million-year-old fossilized fish skeleton found near Triglav. The museum's most impressive assemblage, and one of the most important collections of its kind in Slovenia, is the Zois Collection of Minerals, named after the eminent mineralogist Žiga Zois. To round things off, there is a small multimedia presentation of the extraordinary Proteus Anguinus (aka "The Human Fish"), the largest cave-dwelling vertebrate in the world (see the *Subterranean Slovenia* colour section).

Trg Republike and around

South of the National Museum is the vast concrete car park of **Trg Republike** (Republic Square), the largest and, by some distance the ugliest square in the city, embraced by unsightly postmodern buildings. Shadowing the south side are two towering office blocks, behind which is **Cankarjev Dom**, the country's most capacious cultural and congress centre, named in honour of the celebrated Slovene novelist Ivan Cankar; the centre's two galleries regularly host top-class exhibitions (Tues–Sat 10am–7pm, Sun 10am–2pm; free; ⓦ www.cd-cc.si). Residing on the north side is the unexceptional **Parliament** building, worth a glance for its portal, framed by blackened statues depicting the working-class family and various industries. It was in front of here, on the night of June 26, 1991, that President Milan Kučan unfurled the new Slovene flag and pronounced, "This evening dreams are allowed, tomorrow is a new day" – the thousands celebrating on the square oblivious to the fact that, in a matter of hours, they would be at war (see box, p.329).

Between the two office blocks, across Erjavčeva ulica and behind the primary school, are further **ruins** of Emona. Discovered during excavations in 1969, the finds included part of a baptistry and portico, as well as some lovely mosaics. The gate is likely to be closed but it is possible to see a reasonable amount from a distance. However, if you wish to see it close up contact the City Museum (☏01/241-2506). East along Erjavčeva cesta, on the corner of Slovenska cesta, is the muddy-green **Slovene National Theatre** (Narodno Gledališče), also known as the German Theatre – on account of the fact that it was initially intended for German-speaking audiences only, with Slovenian performances taking place in the Opera House.

A five-minute walk southwest of Erjavčeva at Tobačna ulica 5 is the enlightening **Tobacco Museum** (Tobačni muzej; first Wed and third Thurs of each month 10am–6pm; free; ⊛www.tobacna.si), housed in the Ljubljana Tobacco company building. The collection, neatly presented in gleaming glass cabinets, documents the processing and use of tobacco from the factory's establishment from 1871 to the present day, as well as the lives of those who worked in the factory. Prior to the introduction of machines at the beginning of the twentieth century, the factory employed mainly women (known as *cigarice* or "cigar ladies") as they were deemed to be more dextrous, a prerequisite for the delicate task of hand-rolling hundreds of cigars each day. Aside from photographs and documents there are some fascinating tobacco products, including a superb display of beautifully crafted pipes, cigar holders and snuff boxes.

Tivoli Park

If you're looking for a bit of peace and relaxation you won't have to go far. To the west of Trg Republike, beyond Tivolski cesta, is Tivoli Park, a lush expanse of greenery carved up by broad promenades and backed by dense woodland and hills; it's also a major recreation and sporting centre. The park is accessible from a number of routes, though the most direct is via the subway by the Museum of Modern Art. Exiting the subway, head up Jakopič Promenade, laid out by Plečnik and split down the middle by a row of shabby lampposts, towards **Tivoli Castle** (Tivolski Grad). Since being transformed into a mansion by the Jesuits in 1713, it has been used as a military hospital and barracks, and as a residence for city officials. Local rumour has it that the creator of the cast-iron dogs by the staircase, Anton Fernkorn, was so disturbed by omitting their tongues that – in what might be construed as an over-reaction – he shot himself. The mansion is now the permanent home of the **International Centre of Graphic Arts** (Mednarodni Grafični Likovni Center; Wed–Sun 11am–6pm; €3.50; ⊛www.mglc-lj.si), an enterprising institution devoted to the promotion and printing of graphic art. Its chief activity, however, is the organization of the International Graphic Arts Biennial, the world's longest-running graphic-arts exhibition – a prestigious, three-month-long event taking place in September and October every odd-numbered year.

Up on the northern edge of the park is the brilliant-white Baroque mansion of the **Sequin Castle** (Cekinov grad), which, since 1951, has been home to the enlightening **Museum of Modern History** (Muzej novejše zgodovine; Tues–Sun 10am–6pm; €4; ⊛www.muzej-nz.si). The collection, much of it presented in multimedia form, is arranged chronologically, each room representing a period of twentieth-century Slovenia. The starting point is World War I, featuring several mock-up shelters and a remarkable display of photos and mementoes from the battlefields. The collection moves swiftly on to the interwar period, and illustrates the struggle to establish the country within the new Kingdom of Serbs, Croats and Slovenes. This first part concludes with World War II and a rapid-fire projection of 1500 photos onto the surrounding walls, accompanied by thunderous sound effects. Among the more interesting exhibits in this room, which includes uniforms from the warring sides, is a chess set made from bread and saliva by a prisoner of war. More revealing, however, are a clutch of items (pocket watches, jewellery, gold false teeth) belonging to civilian and political prisoners who had been dumped into mass graves (such as Kočevski Rog, see p.232) following the war's end.

The following rooms are devoted to war damage reconstruction and daily life in socialist Yugoslavia, with particular emphasis on the Slovenian economy. The exhibition winds up by documenting the events leading up to Slovenian independence in 1991, including the accompanying Ten Days' War (see box, p.329); exhibits include a JNA sentry box and items dumped by the army as they retreated – the tank outside the entrance, meanwhile, was one of those used during the war.

Rožnik Hill and the Zoo

Bunched up behind Tivoli Park are a number of modest peaks, sewn together by a network of tidy, well-signposted tracks. The most popular short hike (approx 45min) is up to **Rožnik Hill**, accessible via a number of paths, the best of which begins from behind Tivoli Castle. Having made it to the top, you can take a break and buy some refreshments at the **Cankar Inn**, once periodically the home of novelist Ivan Cankar; opposite is a memorial room (Tues–Fri 9am–1pm Sat & Sun 2–4pm; free) containing a few of his personal effects and some original furniture. The **Church of St Mary's Visitation**, just down from the inn, was built in 1740 – the high altar has a particularly fine painting by Jurij Šubic (visits during Mass only; May–Sept 10.30am).

Nestling in thick woodland on the southern slope of the hill is the city **Zoo** (Živalski vrt; daily: May–Aug 9am–7pm; April & Sept till 6pm; Oct–March till 4pm; €6), an impressively landscaped park, with more than a few steep paths and an exhaustive range of animals, which will at least keep the kids happy. No buses head this way, though the #14 passes through the suburb of Vič, a fifteen-minute walk south (alight at Cesta XV); otherwise, from Tivoli Castle it's a thirty-minute walk around the southern rim of Tivoli Park (along Cesta 27 aprila then Večna pot).

North of the centre

Otherwise unexceptional, the area north of the centre has a few sights worthy of exploration, most of which, inevitably, bear Plečnik's unmistakable stamp. West of the train station, at the intersection of Celovška cesta and Ruska ulica (opposite Tivoli Park), is the **Brewery Museum** (Pivovarski muzej; first Tues of the month by appointment; €3; ☎01/471-7330, ⓦwww.pivo-union.si), located in the old malt-house of the sprawling Union Brewery – founded in 1864 by the cartographer Peter Kosler and one of the two largest breweries in the country. The two-part visit first takes in a tour of the filtration and bottling plants where some sixty thousand bottles are filled each hour, followed by the museum proper, whose exhibits include century-old wooden barrels, carts for carrying crates and a fine collection of beer mugs and tankards.

Close by is the **Railway Museum** (Železniški muzej; Tues–Sun 10am–6pm; €3), which is actually split between two locations. In the roundhouse at Parmova ulica 35 is a marvellous collection of old steam locomotives and rolling stock – sure to get rail buffs misty-eyed – while 300m further south, at Kurilniška ulica 3, there is a more straightforward exhibition presenting the history and development of the Slovenian rail network.

A fifteen-minute walk north of these museums in the suburb of Šiška is the first of the city's two Plečnik-designed churches, the **Church of St Francis of Assisi** (Cerkev Sv Frančiška Asiškega), Verovškova ulica (bus #22 to Drenikova ulica), distinguished by its double-storey, cylindrical belfry topped with a cone. Completed in 1931, this is the least conventional of Ljubljana's churches, its square main hall with a high, flat wooden ceiling and rows of square windows more redolent of a school gymnasium than your average place of worship. A colonnade of chunky, circular brick pillars forms a kind of inner square, in the centre of which is a pyramid-shaped altar; both this and the chandeliers are classic Plečnik.

From the church, head eastwards along Drenikova ulica, and then Samova ulica, for twenty minutes (or take bus #22 from Drenikova) until you reach Dunajska cesta in the suburb of Bežigrad. On your left is the modestly sized **Central Stadium** (Centralni Stadion), formerly home to the city's main football team, Olimpija Ljubljana (who now play elsewhere), but which now sits idle. It's rare for sports stadiums to be given such a classy touch, but here Plečnik embellished the arena using his favoured motif of columns in both the interior (the elegant pavilion) and the exterior (the colonnade) – unfortunately, you can only catch a glimpse of the pavilion through the gates.

One and a half kilometres east of the stadium is **Žale Cemetery** (Pokopališče Žale), announced by a magnificent entrance in the form of a bright, two-storeyed arcade split by a graceful ceremonial arch – meant to symbolize the border between the city of the living and that of the dead. In the park through the entrance there are a number of funeral chapels dedicated to patron saints, part of Plečnik's overall concept for the entire complex. The cemetery itself is immaculate – Plečnik's grave, is to the left of the entrance in Plot 6. From the centre of town, bus #2 stops outside the entrance.

Around the city centre

While it's unlikely you'll be in any hurry to escape the city centre, there are some very enjoyable visits to be had not too far away. Just under 1km south of the centre, and easily reached on foot (along busy Karlovška cesta or, more peacefully, along the banks of the Ljubljanica), are the university's **Botanical Gardens**, at Ižanska cesta 15 (Botanični vrt; daily: April–Oct 7am–7pm; Nov–March 7am–5pm; free; bus #3 to Strelišče). Established in 1810 by the Slovene botanist Franc Hladnik, there are now more than fifty thousand species of plants, shrubs and trees, representing every continent, in these colourful gardens.

Covering an area of over 160 square kilometres, the **Ljubljana Marshes** (Ljubljansko barje), 2km south of the Botanical Gardens, originated some two million years ago and are believed to have been the site of the first settlement in the city. The marshes are now a protected area, noted for their tremendously varied flora and fauna, with excellent opportunities for birdwatching, particularly around Kozlerjeva gošča, near the village of **Črna Vas** (Black Village) on the eastern extremes. The marshes are also something of a fertile hunting ground for archeologists, having yielded innumerable objects since extensive research began here soon after World War II; the latest significant find, in 2002, was a wooden wheel believed to be over fifty thousand years old, making it the oldest such wheel ever discovered. In the centre of Črna Vas is Plečnik's **Church of St Michael on the Marsh** (Cerkev Sv Mihaela na Barju), built in 1938 – some ten years later than the Church of St Francis of Assisi (see p.73) but perhaps even more bewitching. The stone-built exterior, bridge-style staircase and detached hollow belfry are all instantly recognizable as Plečnik's work, as is the extraordinary, largely wooden interior, with its cupboard-shaped altar and Turkish-style lamps. The marshy ground necessitated construction on solid eight-metre-long oak piles, while the hall was elevated to the second floor because of the dangers of flooding. To be sure of getting a look-in, try and visit during Mass (Sat & Sun 10am). To get to the church from the centre take bus #19 to the last stop, Barje, walk back across the junction, and it's 500m ahead; to return, take the same bus from the same stop.

Two kilometres east of the centre, in the suburb of Studenec, is **Fužine Castle** (Grad Fužine), a handsome, Renaissance structure dating from the mid-sixteenth century. The castle was named after the old iron foundry near Polje pri Ljubljani – Fužine means "smelter" – and was originally intended to house a glassworks and paper mill, its location on the Ljubljanica ideal for such industries. Over the centuries, and under various owners, it was rearranged, modified and tinkered with, and there is now very little of interest to see, save for the chapel interior which has some fresco remains. In one wing of the castle is the **Architectural Museum** (Arhitekturni muzej; Mon–Fri 9am–3pm, Sat 10am–6pm, Sun 10am–3pm; €3) – a slight misnomer for what is no more than an exhibition of Plečnik's oeuvre, consisting of photos, illustrations and models of some of his projects. The display is actually a condensed edition of a larger exhibition held in 1986 at the Pompidou Centre in Paris. To get here take bus #20 to the last stop and it's a five-minute walk.

Šmarna gora, some 10km northwest of the centre, is extremely popular with Ljubljančani, many of whom come here after work to pound up and down this isolated 669-metre-high hill. At the summit, a partly preserved fifteenth-century wall is evidence that the hill was once a fortified camp providing protection from the rampaging Turks, though in the event it was never conquered. The **Pilgrimage Church of the Holy Mother**, first mentioned in 1314, was built on the old ruins in 1729 and has some lovely frescoes by Matevž Langus, though the only chance you'll get to see these is by visiting during Mass, each Sunday at 11am. Once you've reached the top, which takes around 45 minutes up one of the steep and bumpy tracks, give the bell-rope a sharp tug, partake in a sweet cup of tea, available from the hilltop hut, and take in the terrific views of the city and Sava Plain spread out below. To get to the hill take bus #8 to Brod and it's a five-minute walk to the start of the main trail.

Eating and drinking

As befits its sophisticated image, Ljubljana is able to boast a tight concentration of first-rate **restaurants**, most of which offer excellent value for money. Although the majority of Ljubljana's restaurants deal predominantly in Slovene, Balkan and international fare, there are a growing number of Asian restaurants to be found. During the summer al fresco dining is extremely popular among Ljubljančani, and many of the restaurants listed offer outdoor seating in the warmer summer months. Although prices here are higher than in most other places, you can still eat well without having to break the bank:

▲ Fruit and vegetable stall in the central market

expect to pay around €14–18 for a two-course meal with a glass of wine in an average establishment, and around €20–25 in the most expensive places. Phone numbers are included where booking is advisable.

The best choice for quick-fix **snacks** are those kiosks and stands opposite the stations, such as *Ajda* and *Konkurenca* (both 24hr), and at the northern end of Miklošičeva, all selling delicious savoury snacks including *burek*, *pljeskavica*, *čevapi* and hot dogs.

Plečnik's splendid **Market Colonnade**, curving along the east bank of the Ljubljanica between the Triple Bridge and the Dragon Bridge, houses dozens of excellent little food shops (Mon–Fri 7am–4pm, Sat 7am–2pm), selling a wide range of breads, cheeses, sandwiches, cakes and confectionery. The large and colourful outdoor **market** (Mon–Sat 6am–2pm), opposite the Colonnade on Vodnikov trg, is the best place to stock up on fresh produce, and there are fish, meat and dairy products down in the basement of the Seminary building on adjacent Pogačarjev trg. There are also plenty of well-stocked **supermarkets** around town, the most central and largest of which is the one in the basement of the Maximarket shopping centre on Trg Republike (Mon–Fri 9am–7pm, Sat 8am–7pm). Down in the basement is the *Restaurant 2000*, a popular **self-service** canteen offering simple three course meals for around €6 (Mon–Fri 9am–7pm, Sat 9am–4pm).

Snacks, sandwiches and fast food

Ajdovo Zrno Trubarjeva 7. A convenient spot for lunch, this bright and cheerful vegetarian place, in an off-street courtyard, has a fresh salad bar, tasty soups, tortillas and tofu. Sit down or takeaway.

Falafel Trubarjeva 40. Popular little sit down or takeaway joint offering all manner of delicious falafel-based snacks, as well as sandwiches, kebabs, salads and baklava.

Paninoteka Jurčičev trg 3. In a super location down by the Shoemakers' Bridge, this cool little sandwich bar serves up a wide range of piping hot paninis and ciabattas, wraps, toasts and salads. Sit down or takeaway.

Pasta Nona Gosposvetska 2. Attractive, informal bistro offering a choice of two or three different pasta, soup and salad dishes each day, one of which is usually vegetarian. Sit down only. Daily noon–5pm.

Ribca Market Colonnade. Terrific fish snack bar on the lower floor of the colonnade, serving generous plates of grilled and fried squid, sardines and seafood salads. Sit down or takeaway.

Tomato Šubičeva 2. Lively diner-style joint which knocks out cheap and filling sandwiches, rolls and grilled snacks, as well as simple cooked breakfasts alongside fresh juices and pastries. Sit down or takeaway. Mon–Fri 7am–9pm.

Cafés and bars

Café Antico Stari trg 27. Bare wooden floors, high tables and stools, and pastel-vaulted ceiling give this popular Old Town hangout a pleasantly dated ambience; there are a couple of little coves for more cosy drinking.

Bi-Ko-Fe Židovska steza 1. Artsy, colourful and chilled-out café with an imaginative range of coffees (iced, chocolate and so on), as well as teas and alcoholic drinks.

Čajna Hiša Stari trg 3. Bijou tea house offering a superb range of teas from around the world, excellent sandwiches and cakes and decent breakfasts. Deservedly one of the most popular places with the locals. Closed Sun.

Cutty Sark Knafljev prehod 1. Opposite *Cantina Mexicana*, this lively, Brit-fashioned pub has a more raucous atmosphere than most places in town, with good beers on tap and regular live music.

Dvorni Bar Dvorni trg 2. Classy wine bar in a lovely location by the Ljubljanica, with tables spilling across the square and down to the river; excellent selection of wines available, as well as a good choice of snacks to munch on.

Café Gaudi Nazorjeva 10. A delightful, quirky interior and seductive range of coffees – alcoholic, iced, chocolate – makes this a terrific place for a quick coffee stop.

Lepa Žoga Celovška 43. Small sports café-bar near Tivoli Park, with shirts and other parapher-nalia of the good and great (mostly foreign sports stars) draped along the walls, and a constant diet of live TV sports, including English football on Sunday afternoons.

Le Petit Café Trg francoske revolucije 4. A small slice of Paris at this eternally busy and wonderfully atmospheric street corner café opposite Križanke; perfect for a coffee and croissant for breakfast or a glass of wine in the evening.

Maček Krojaška 5. The most popular of the string of hip cafés on the right bank of the Ljubljanica, the exuberant terrace of *Maček* is the place to see and be seen, and consequently always crammed.

Movia Mestni trg 2. This snug little wine bar next to the Town Hall is the best place in town to sample Slovenian wine. The friendly, knowledgeable staff can assist with vintages from every Slovene wine-producing region, including those from their own winery in Goriška Brda (see p.171). Closed Sun.

Patrick's Prečna 6. Up a little side street off Trubarjeva, the city's token Irish pub is not a bad place at all, though the draught beers (Guinness, Murphy's, Kilkenny) are as expensive as you'd expect.

Roxly Mala ulica 5. Laid-back café-bar with smooth red and black leather seating and rock star pictures splayed across the walls. There's live rock music at weekends. Closed Sun.

Sax Pub Eipprova 7. The colourful, spray-painted *Sax* is just one of several cool cafés and bars in this idyllic canal-side street five minutes walk south of Breg. Occasional live jazz too.

Slamič Kersnikova 1. Although not as engaging as *Čajna Hiša*, this pleasant, restful little teahouse has a similarly varied range of brews, in addition to coffee and ice cream.

Tromostovje Prešernov trg. Permanently crowded summer-only outdoor café on the busy main square, which also has a terrific ice-cream parlour; on the opposite side of the square is *Cacao*, another popular spot which also has excellent ice cream.

Zlata Ladjica Jurčičev trg 1. Fun, energetic pub, with an enormous terrace, next to the Shoemakers' Bridge on the left bank of the Ljubljanica; if you're here during winter, try the delicious mulled wine.

Zmauc Rimska 21. The graffiti-painted exterior of this happy, hippy dive gives some indication of what to expect – the small, buzzy terrace is packed with locals at pretty much any time of the day.

Zvezda Wolfova 14. Named after the eponymous pre-World War II café in the Kazina building further up on Kongresni trg, this hugely popular hangout is the place to come for ices and pastries.

Restaurants

Abecedarium Ribji trg 2. Named after the first Slovene book, and located in the former residence of its author, Primož Trubar, this informal café/restaurant combines an interesting selection of regional specialities, such as the *bograč* (meaty casserole) from Prekmurje, *žlikrofi* (potato balls in pastry) from Idrija, and *polenta* from the Karst, with lots of quality meat dishes (beef, lamb and wild boar); there's also an appealing breakfast menu.

Ambient Čufarjeva 2. Funky, bright orange bistro whose comfortable, loungey interior and smart outdoor terrace draws a hip lunchtime and evening crowd. The menu, which is regularly changed (curry risotto, beef gnocchi and grilled pork ribs are typical dishes), is top-notch, and the service warm; for breakfast try the omelettes with truffles alongside a big mug of coffee. Closed Sun.

Cantina Mexicana Wolfova 4 (via Knafljev prehod). Flashy and fun Mexican restaurant just across from *As* in this bustling courtyard area – the menu differs little from your average Mexican, but the food is well cooked and presented with style; there's a fancy cocktail bar too.

Figovec Gosposvetska 1. Charmingly old-fashioned downtown restaurant specializing in pony steaks, horsemeat goulash and traditional Slovene standards. The terrace is fine, so long as you don't mind the incessant traffic streaming by.

Foculus Gregorčičeva 3. Long-standing and flamboyantly decorated pizzeria offering an exhaustive range of pizzas in lively surroundings, including a better-than-average vegetarian and seafood selection, and a generous salad buffet.

Gostilna As Čopova 5 (via Knafljev prehod) ☎01/425-8822. A perennial favourite among local politicians and bigwigs, *As* is as posh and as expensive as it gets in Ljubljana. The food's not bad either, with seafood and risotto dishes the main staples, complemented by some fine Slovene vintages. The bistro dining area offers simpler, more affordable eating (salads, pizza and pastas).

Gostilna Sokol Ciril Metodov trg 18. As close to a traditional countryside *gostilna* as you'll get in Ljubljana; the thick wooden benches of this labyrinthine establishment provide a congenial setting for hearty portions of regional Slovene food – for example, ham and olives from the Karst, trout from Primorska, and *gibanica* from Prekmurje. Try, too, a bottle of the domestic Sokol *pivo* in the downstairs bar.

Harambaša Okrepčevalnica Vrtna 8. Replicating a traditional Bosnian tavern, with low wooden tables and stools and kitsch knick-knacks, this place is great fun; the menu features a handful of classic Bosnian dishes such as *pljeskavica* (oversized hamburger) and *čevapčiči* (rissoles of spiced minced meat) served with *kajmak* (creamy cheese) and *lepinja* (doughy bread), while you can round things off with a cup of Turkish coffee and a piece of Turkish delight.

Joe Pena's Cankarjeva 6. Although not as flash as *Cantina Mexicana*, the food – tacos, fajitas, burritos and, more unusually, hot spiced red snapper fillet – at this breezy, and justifiably popular, Mexican restaurant is no less enjoyable.

Julija Stari trg 9. A bright, simple eatery in a central Old Town location, with decent salads, pasta, risotto and Mediterranean dishes. During the summer, the tables strung along the cobbled street outside are an enormously popular place to eat.

Kavalino Trubarjeva 52. Hidden away down a cobblestone alley just off the main street, the cool and airy, split-level *Kavalino* serves up pizzas and much more besides, such as pastas, risottos and noodles; there's also a great value lunchtime menu (€6). Closed Sun.

Ljubljanski Dvor Dvorni trg 1. Alongside *Foculus*, this is the pick of the city's pizzerias; *Dvor* counts some one hundred pizzas, including the best vegetarian choice in town, while the expansive patio area overlooking the Ljubljanica, and with views up to the castle, is terrific.

Mencigar Nobile Zarnikova 3. Incongruously situated in a residential street behind St Joseph's church, this warm, restful establishment offers high class traditional cuisine from the Prekmurje region, such as *bograč*, buckwheat porridge, poppy seed noodles, plum dumplings and *gibanica*; the delightful interior, meanwhile, comprises three countrified rooms painted in gentle pastel colours and decorated with utensils and pottery. Closed Sun.

Pr' Potic Stari trg 21. Furnished with elegant simplicity – red painted walls, cream drapes and smart, neatly covered wooden tables and chairs – this cosy and very welcoming Old Town restaurant boasts a colourful menu featuring some terrific regional specialities, with ingredients freshly sourced from the market on Vodnikov trg.

Pri Škofu Rečna cesta 6 ☎01/426-4508. Secreted away in a quiet street in Krakovo, this is one of the city's most enjoyable restaurants; if you don't fancy anything from the daily menu, ask for one of the house specialities – black risotto (*črna rižota*), pepper-encrusted tenderloin medallions (*biftek škof*) or grilled aubergine with rice and buckwheat (*malancani damjana*). The small, warm terrace and simple, sunny interior round things off beautifully.

Pri Vitezu Breg 20 ☎01/426-6058. *Pri Vitezu* ("At the Knight") is another of Ljubljana's top-end restaurants, a warm, classy place with a creditably distinguished Italian/Slovene-fashioned menu including, for appetizers, swordfish, scallops and snails, and for mains, seafood black risotto, duck breast and horse fillets. Closed Sun.

Romeo Stari trg 6. Located opposite *Julija*, naturally, *Romeo*'s wideranging, if slightly less sophisticated, menu slants obviously towards Mexican – tacos, burritos and the like. Good for late-night munchies.

Shambala Križevniška 12. A cut above any of the city's other Asian restaurants, the beautifully conceived restaurant offers food from several countries, with Vietnamese salad rolls, Thai red and green curry, Japanese Miso soup and vegetable tempura forming the mainstays of an otherwise seasonal menu. Closed Sun.

Sofra Dunajska 145. Despite its unattractive and awkward location some 1.5km north of the centre, it's well worth making the trek to this cheery Bosnian restaurant for its fantastically juicy Balkan staples likes čevapčiči (rissoles of spiced minced meat), karadjordje (breaded veal cutlet rolled and stuffed with cheese), pasulj (oven-cooked beans), not to mention the best roasted lamb in Ljubljana. Closed Sun.

Špajza Gornji trg 28 ☎01/425-3094. Sited at the top of Gornji trg, the elegant rustic trappings of this homely restaurant complement the expertly cooked Slovene food superbly; fish

(sea bass, sole, monkfish), veal medallions with wild berries, and beef fillet with truffles are just some of the treats on offer. First-class selection of wines too.

Vinske Kleti Dunajska 18. Given that the adjoining wine shop is the oldest and largest in the country, it's little surprise that the wine is as important as the food here; high-class culinary delights, meanwhile, include polenta with asparagus rolls, wild boar in pear sauce, and strawberry truffle. Located in the basement of the large circular building by the entrance to the Ljubljana showground. Closed Sat & Sun.

Zlata Ribica Cankarjevo nabrežje 5. Occupying one of the best outdoor dining areas in the city, this modest and inexpensive fish restaurant facing the Ljubljanica, on the corner of Ribji trg, is delightful.

Nightlife

While Ljubljana's **nightlife** cannot match the vibrancy or diversity of larger cities, a drink on a warm summer's evening in one of the many convivial **cafés and bars** strung along the banks of the Ljubljanica is one of the joys of being in this city. Alternatively, a wander up and down Mestni trg and Stari trg will yield an interesting locale every fifty yards or so, while the clutch of energetic bars in Knafljev prehod (the courtyard area between Wolfova ulica and Slovenska cesta) are usually packed to the rafters. Ljubljana's limited, but eclectic, bunch of **clubs** – some of which double up as multicultural, arts–type centres – are more widely dispersed throughout town, although all are within walking distance of the centre.

Festival seasons aside, the city offers a reasonable, if rather Balkan-centric, diet of **live music**, though it does suffer from having few decent **gig venues** to call on; bigger names play at the Hippodrome north of the centre or Tivoli Hall, in Tivoli Park, while the two other principal venues are Cankarjev Dom on Trg republike and the marvellous open-air Križanke complex on Trg francoske revolucije.

Clubs

Bachus Kongresni trg 3. Swanky three-in-one club, lounge bar and restaurant; the banging club features different music on different nights of the week (Thurs disco, Fri hip-hop, Sat R&B), while the lounge bar is great for a daytime coffee or shake, or an evening beer.

Jazz Club Gajo Beethovnova 8. Refined late-night jazz club with regular quality appearances by both domestic and foreign acts. Jam sessions on Mondays from 9pm. Between mid-May and September the club has performances at a fabulous outdoor garden on Cankarjeva cesta, across from the National Gallery. ⓦwww.jazzclubgajo.com.

K4 Kersnikova 4 Stalwart of Ljubljana's alternative scene, offering some of the best music in the city – mainly electronic, but also rock, jazz, hip-hop and

folk, plus gay night on Sundays. Student parties and performance art too. ⓦwww.klubk4.org.

KUD Prešeren Karunova 14. Superb, long-standing gig venue in the Trnovo district that also organizes regular literary events, workshops (including some for kids) and art exhibitions. There's a fine little café here too. Also stages the excellent *Trnfest* festival in August (see box opposite).

Metelkova mesto Metelkova cesta. Ljubljana's legendary alternative cultural centre consisting of a cosmopolitan gang of clubs, bars and NGOs (collectively entitled Metelkova) is located in the former army barracks near the Hostel Celica; venues include Channel Zero (dance), Gala Hala (punk/metal), Mizzart (low-fi), Klub Monokel (lesbian only), Tiffany (gay) and Gromki (performance).

Orto Bar Grablovičeva 1. This good-time haunt a couple of blocks east of the train station has regular late-night club evenings; it's also the city's main small live-rock venue, and you can bank on finding at least a couple of gigs a week here.

Top Slovenska (top of the Nama department store). Lots of spangly silver and gold decor in the city's most straightforward club venue, with different themed nights (Wed R&B, Fri house/dance, Sat retro night). Access is via the glass lift on the street. ⓦ www.klubtop.si.

Entertainment

For a relatively small city, Ljubljana offers a surprisingly rich diet of **classical culture**, with well-established orchestral, operatic and theatrical companies, and there's a good chance you'll catch something whatever time of the year you're here; although most of these institutions close down in July and August, by way of compensation there's plenty going on as part of the annual Ljubljana Festival (see box below).

Classical music, ballet, opera and theatre

Cankarjev Dom, the enormous arts and convention centre on Trg Republike, is the scene of major orchestral and theatrical events, folk and jazz concerts and all manner of art exhibitions (the box office is in the nearby Maximarket shopping centre Mon–Fri 11am–1pm & 3–8pm, Sat 11am–1pm; also 1hr before each performance; ⓣ01/241-7299, ⓦ www.cd-cc.si). Ljubljana's energetic and highly

---

Festivals and events: the Ljubljana year

The festival year in Ljubljana kicks off in spring with **Slovenian Musical Days**, four or five days (usually at the end of March) of concerts performed principally by the Slovene philharmonic and RTV symphonic orchestras. One of the year's most enjoyable music events is the ethno-alternative music festival **Druga Godba** ("The Other Music"), held at the end of May in the wonderful surrounds of Križanke, and featuring a terrific line-up of both domestic and foreign musicians and bands. There's more world class music at the end of June courtesy of the **Ljubljana Jazz Festival**, with five days of concerts staged at Križanke and Cankarjev Dom.

Taking place throughout July and August, the **Ljubljana Festival** has been the city's major annual event for over fifty years, comprising all genres of music, art, theatre and dance. Also in July is the **Ana Desetnica Festival of Street Theatre**, in which the streets of the Old Town are the setting for a varied programme of wonderful and often wacky street performances; and the **Viticulture and Winegrowers Fair**, staged at the Ljubljana Exhibition Grounds, which might appeal, particularly if you're unable to get to any of Slovenia's wine regions – there's plenty of tasting to be had.

Trnfest, a smaller-scale summer festival, runs throughout August, with gigs, exhibitions, workshops and video screenings – there's a good programme for kids here too. The city's foremost artistic event (albeit occurring every odd-numbered year) is the **International Biennial of Graphic Arts**, held throughout September and October at Tivoli Castle, a prestigious affair rated as one of the premier exhibitions of its kind in Europe.

Rounding off the year is the **City of Women International Festival of Contemporary Art**, ten days of female artists' exhibitions, as well as theatre and performance, taking place in the middle of October. The **Ljubljana International Film Festival (LIFFe)** presents a wide selection of primarily European films for two weeks during November at Cankarjev Dom.

regarded **symphony orchestra**, the Slovenska Filharmonija, performs at the Philharmonic Hall on Kongresni trg (℡01/241-0800, ⓦwww.filharmonija.si), while the republic's **opera and ballet** companies are housed in the National Opera and Ballet Theatre, Župančičeva 1 (ticket office Mon–Fri 1–5pm, Sat 11am–1pm; also 1hr before each performance; ℡01/241-1766, ⓦwww.opera .si). **Theatrical** productions take place at the National Drama Theatre (Narodno Gledališče), Erjavčeva 1 (ticket office Mon–Fri 2–5pm & 6–8pm, Sat 6–8pm; also 1hr before each performance; ℡01/252-1511, ⓦwww.drama.si), while the extremely popular **puppet theatre** (Lutkovno Gledališče), Krekov trg 2 (ticket office Mon–Fri 4–6pm, Sat 10am–noon; also 1hr before each performance; ℡01/300-0970, ⓦwww.lgl.si), puts on a regular programme of shows throughout the year.

There's an outstanding programme of pop, classical and orchestral concerts as part of the **Ljubljana Festival** (see box, p.79) taking place in July and August; the festival box office is at Križanke (Mon–Fri 10am–1.30pm & 4–8pm, Sat 10am–1pm; also 1hr before each performance; ℡01/241-6026, ⓦwww .ljublanafestival.si).

Cinema

The majority of **cinema**-(kino) goers now make the trek out to the **Kolosej multiplex** at the BTC shopping complex 1.5km east of the centre on Šmartinska cesta (bus #2 or #7). The best of the few remaining downtown cinemas are the excellent art cinema, Kinodvor, across from the train station at Kolodvorska 13; Kinoteka, at Miklošičeva 28, which screens premieres, cult classics and retrospectives, and Komuna, at Cankarjeva cesta 1; tickets for all cinemas cost around €4–5. There are occasional screenings at Cankarjev Dom (see p.79), which is also the principal venue for the two-week **Ljubljana International Film Festival** (LIFFe) in November (see box, p.79).

Shopping

There are few **shopping areas** of note within the city centre itself, although a wander up and down Čopova ulica, Trubarjeva cesta or Mestni trg might yield the odd find. Otherwise, most of the city folk do their shopping out at the enormous and ever-expanding BTC shopping complex (Mon–Sat 9am–8pm), 1.5km east of town on Šmartinska cesta. A great place to browse on a Sunday morning is the **flea market** along the right bank of the Ljubljanica, between the Triple Bridge and the Shoemakers' Bridge; here you can find just about anything and everything, from old records, books and stamps to furniture, musical instruments and Tito-era memorabilia.

There are several excellent **bookshops** in town, all of which stock a wide-ranging selection of English-language books: the two best ones are Mladinska at Slovenska 29 (Mon–Fri 9am–7.30pm, Sat 9am–2pm), and the smaller Novak at Wolfova 8 (Mon–Fri 10am–10pm, Sat 10am–2pm). Both Kod & Kam, just down from Križanke at Trg francoske revolucije 7 (Mon–Fri 8am–8pm, Sat 8am–1pm), and Geonavtik, at Kongresni trg 1 (Mon–Fri 8.30am–8.30pm, Sat 8.30am–4pm), have a comprehensive stock of **maps**. If you're on the lookout for **music** try Spin Vinyl, at Gallusovo nabrežje 13 (Mon–Fri 10.30am–7pm, Sat & Sun 10.30am–2pm); Vom, at Čopova 14 (Mon–Fri 10am–7pm, Sat 10am–1pm), or Music Box, at Levstikov trg 4a (Mon–Sat 10am–9pm, Sun 4–8pm), all of which have a decent selection of music from both Slovenia and the other ex-Yugoslav republics.

Ljubljana listings

Airlines Adria, Gosposvetska 6 ☎01/239-1910; Austrian Airlines, Čopova 11 ☎01/244-3060; Lufthansa, Gosposvetska 8 ☎01/434-7246.

Banks and exchange Money can be exchanged at all banks, and the post offices, while the exchange office in the train station is useful if arriving early or late (daily 5.30am–10pm). There are several exchange bureaus (*menjalnica*) throughout the city, most of which offer good rates – one of the best is on Pogačarjev trg (Mon–Fri 7am–7pm, Sat 7am–2pm).

Bicycles From mid-April to October the excellent "Ljubljana Cycle" programme offers cheap bike rental (€1 for 1hr, €5 for the day); bikes, which must be returned by 7pm, can be rented from a number of locations, including the Slovenian Tourist Information Centre, the *Antiq*, *Central* and *Grand Union* hotels, *Hostel Celica* and Ljubljana Resort.

Car rental ABC/Europcar, Dalmatinova 15 (*City Hotel*) ☎031/382-052 and airport ☎04/236-7990; Avis, Čufarjeva 2 ☎01/583-8772 and airport ☎04/236-5000; Budget, Miklošičeva 3 (*Grand Hotel Union*) ☎01/421-7340 and airport ☎04/201-4300; Golftourist, Trdinova 4 ☎01/430-6780; Hertz, Trdinova 9 ☎01/434-0147 and airport ☎01/201-6999; Sixt, Trg Osvobodilne fronte ☎01/234-4650 and airport ☎04/238-2414.

Embassies and consulates Australia, Dunajska 50 ☎01/425-4252; Canada, Trg republike 3 ☎01/252-4444; Ireland, Poljanski nasip 6 ☎01/300-8970; UK, Trg republike 3/IV ☎01/200-3910; US, Prešernova 31 ☎01/200-5500.

Emergencies Ambulance ☎112; police ☎113; fire service ☎112.

Hospitals The main hospital is at Bohoričeva 4 ☎01/232-3060, while emergency treatment is also available from the Klinični center at Zaloška cesta 2 ☎01/522-5050. There is also a dental clinic (Stomatološka klinika) here ☎01/431-3113.

Internet access Slovenian Tourist Information Centre, Krekov trg 10 (daily June–Sept 8am–9pm, Oct–May till 7pm; eight terminals); *Cyber Café Xplorer*, Petkovškovo nabrežje 23 (Mon–Fri 10am–10pm, Sat & Sun 2–10pm); *Kiber Pipa*, in the student centre at Kersnikova 6 (Mon–Fri 10am–10pm; free); three terminals inside the bus station ticket office; and the small library in the train station underpass (Mon–Fri 8am–8pm) which allows just fifteen minutes surf time, but at no cost.

Laundry Chemo Express, Wolfova 12 (service washes only; Mon–Fri 7am–6pm; ☎01/251-4404).

Left luggage Lockers at the train station (open 24hr; €2).

Petrol Several petrol stations open 24hrs; Celovška 226; Dunajska 130; Tivolska 43; Tržaška 130; Šmartinska 130.

Pharmacies Central Pharmacy, Prešernov trg 5 (Mon–Fri 7.30am–8pm, Sat 8am–1pm; ☎01/244 2360); Lekarna Ljubljana, Prisoga 7 (☎01/230-6230), has a 24hr duty service.

Police For accidents and emergencies go to Trdinova 10 ☎01/432-0341.

Post office The main office/poste restante is at Slovenska 32 (Mon–Fri 8am–7pm, Sat 8am–1pm), though the office at Trg Osvobodilne fronte, next to the train station, keeps longer hours (Mon–Fri 7am–8pm, Sat 7am–6pm).

Telephones International calls can be made from any phone box on the street, or from booths inside the two post offices (see above).

Travel agencies Specializing in travel for those under 27, the friendly Erazem agency, Miklošičeva 26 (☎01/430-5537, ⓦ www.erazem.net), makes hotel and hostel reservations, issues ISIC and hostel cards, and sells domestic and international tickets (for all forms of transport); outdoor pursuits specialist TrekTrek, Bičevje 5 (☎01/425-1392, ⓦ www.trektrek.si), offers a wide range of adventure-sports activities in the Julian Alps.

Travel details

Trains

Ljubljana to: Bled-Lesce (hourly; 45min–1hr); Brežice (7–13 daily; 1hr 45min–2hr); Celje (every 30min–2hr; 1hr–1hr 40min); Črnomelj (5–9 daily; 2hr 10min–2hr 45min); Divača (every 40min–1hr; 1hr 30min); Kamnik (hourly; 50min); Koper (3–5 daily; 2hr–2hr 30min); Kranj (hourly; 25–35min); Litija (every 30min–2hr; 30min); Maribor (every 30min–2hr; 1hr 45min–2hr 45min); Metlika (5–9 daily; 2hr 30min–3hr); Novo Mesto (7–13 daily; 1hr 20min–2hr); Postojna (every 40min–1hr; 1hr); Sežana (hourly; 1hr 40min–2hr); Ptuj (5–9 daily; 2hr 30min–3hr); Zidani Most (every 30min–1hr; 45min–1hr).

Buses

Ljubljana to: Bled (hourly; 1hr 20min); Celje (Mon–Fri 8 daily, Sat & Sun 3 daily; 1hr 35min); Idrija (Mon–Fri every 1–2hr, Sat & Sun 6 daily; 1hr 15min); Ivančna Gorica (hourly; 50min); Kamnik (every 15–30min; 35min); Kočevje (hourly; 1hr 30min); Koper (Mon–Fri 9 daily, Sat & Sun 5 daily; 2hr 20min); Kranj (every 30min–1hr; 40min); Kranjska Gora (hourly; 2hr); Maribor (4 daily; 2hr 20min–3hr 10min); Murska Sobota (2 daily; 3hr 30min); Nova Gorica (Mon–Fri hourly, Sat & Sun 6 daily; 2hr 30min); Novo Mesto (Mon–Fri 8 daily, Sat & Sun 4 daily; 1hr 10min); Piran (Mon–Fri 6 daily, Sat & Sun 4 daily; 2hr 40min); Postojna (Mon–Fri every 30min–1hr, Sat & Sun 8 daily; 1hr); Radovljica (every 30min–1hr; 1hr); Ribčev Laz (Lake Bohinj) (hourly; 2hr); Škofja Loka (every 30min–1hr; 40min).

International trains

Ljubljana to: Belgrade (3 daily; 8hr 30min); Budapest (3 daily; 8hr 45min); Munich (2 daily; 6hr 30min); Rijeka (2 daily; 2hr 35min); Trieste (2 daily; 3hr); Venice (2 daily; 6hr); Vienna (1 daily; 6hr 15min); Zagreb (6 daily; 2hr 15min).

International buses

Ljubljana to: Rijeka (1 daily; 2hr 30min); Trieste (1 daily; 2hr 30min); Zagreb (3 daily; 2hr 50min).

2

Northwest Slovenia

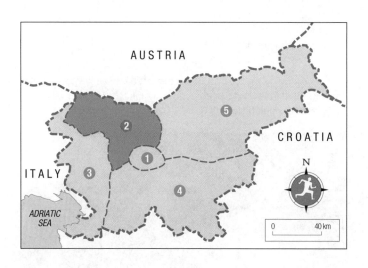

CHAPTER 2 # Highlights

✳ **Velika Planina** This alluring highland plain is spotted with shepherd's huts, and offers great walking opportunities. See p.91

✳ **Škofja Loka** Compact and elegant Škofja Loka is one of Slovenia's most beautifully preserved medieval towns. See p.93

✳ **Kropa** Comely one-street village whose iron-forging traditions are manifest in a superb museum and several other technical monuments See p.110

✳ **Lake Bled** This fairytale lake comes complete with a romantic island church and cliff-top castle. See p.112

✳ **Lake Bohinj** Fish, swim, take a boat ride, or just stroll around Slovenia's most stunning lake. See p.123

✳ **Hiking in the Julian Alps** Superb hiking and climbing including, for the more adventurous, Mount Triglav, the country's highest peak. See p.130

✳ **Vršič Pass** Slovenia's most spectacular mountain pass incorporates nearly fifty hairpin bends, with dozens of attractions along the way. See p.141

▲ Capuchin Bridge, Škofja Loka

Northwest Slovenia

W ith by far the highest profile of any of the country's regions, Gorenjska, Slovenia's northwestern province, offers an outstanding synthesis of natural and cultural heritage, from dramatic alpine mountains, valleys and lakes to startlingly pretty medieval towns and villages. The defining feature of the region is the Julian Alps, a majestic limestone range packed with sawtoothed peaks, fantastically shaped gorges and ravines, deep mountain lakes, and dozens of waterfalls. Most of the Slovene part of the Julians – a small portion spills over into neighbouring Italy – fall within Triglav National Park, Slovenia's only designated national park, at the heart of which is Mount Triglav, the country's highest and most exalted peak. Bordering Austria to the north are two further mountain ranges: the slender Karavanke chain, and, east of here, the Kamniške Alps, whose gloriously tapered peaks strongly resemble the Julians in parts. The tangle of well-worn paths furrowed across these three ranges heaves with hikers during the summer, though the crowds, rarely oppressive, are easily avoided. Hiking aside, the region present stacks of opportunities for adrenaline-fuelled activities – typically, whitewater rafting, canyoning, hydrospeed and paragliding – as well as more traditional pursuits such as cycling, horseriding, fishing and swimming. Moreover, Gorenjska possesses the country's densest concentration of ski resorts, the largest and most popular of which is in Kranjska Gora, squeezed up against the Italian and Austrian borders in the extreme northwestern corner of the country. Located at the tail end of the Alps are Slovenia's celebrated alpine resorts, the most known and visited of which is Bled, a once fashionable health resort whose enchanting lake now ranks as one of the country's premier attractions. For many though, Lake Bled is surpassed by Lake Bohinj, a fjord-like body of water settled amidst gorgeous mountain scenery and bound by a huddle of sleepy villages.

Gorenjska is also sprinkled with a few small towns: the most engaging of these are the medieval settlements of **Kamnik**, sheltered under the Kamniške Alps a short way north of Ljubljana, and **Škofja Loka**, to the west of Ljubljana on the fringe of some delightful, rolling countryside; meanwhile, **Kranj**, Gorenjska's largest city and its key commercial and industrial centre, though initially uninviting, masks a surprisingly endearing old core. Pushing on towards the mountains – as most travellers are apt to do as quickly as possible – the town of **Radovljica** is worthy of a stop-off thanks to its fascinating Beekeeping Museum. Close by are the exquisite villages of **Kropa** and **Begunje**, both of which offer a couple of excellent museums, and **Brezje**, the site of Slovenia's most important pilgrimage church.

Just about all of these places can be reached from Ljubljana with minimum fuss and, with the exception of the park interior, **getting around** the region is easy. Although trains serve most places – and there is the useful **car train** (see box, p.125), which runs between Bohinj Bistrica and Most na Soči – you're best off sticking to buses, which offer faster and more frequent connections. Save for a couple of key roads, most notably the serpentine **Vršič Pass**, which forges a spectacularly scenic route across the mountains between Kranjska Gora and Bovec (in the Soča Valley), access within Triglav

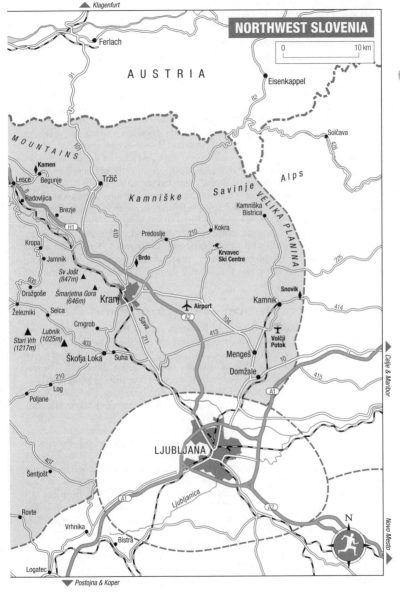

Klagenfurt

NORTHWEST SLOVENIA

Ferlach

0   10 km

AUSTRIA

Eisenkappel

Solčava

MOUNTAINS

Kamen

Lesce   Begunje   Tržič

Radovljica

Brezje

Kamniške

Savinje   ALPS

VELIKA PLANINA

Kamniška
Bistrica

H1

Predoslje   Kokra

Kropa

Jamnik   Brdo

Krvavec
Ski Centre

Sv Jošt
(847m)

Dražgoše   Šmarjetna Gora
(646m)   Kranj

Snovik

Železniki   Selca

Airport   Kamnik

Crngrob

Sava

Lubnik
(1025m)

Stari Vrh
(1217m)

Volčji
Potok

Škofja Loka   Suha

Mengeš

Log   Domžale

Poljane

A1

LJUBLJANA

Šentjošt

Celje & Maribor

Rovte

Vrhnika

Ljubljanica

Bistra

A1   A2

N

Logatec

Novo Mesto

Postojna & Koper

Park is fairly limited – having your own wheels, however, will make life
much easier. There are also quick and easy crossings into Italy and Austria,
the former reached via the main road that bypasses Kranjska Gora, and the
latter via the Karavanke tunnel, under the mountains near Jesenice, and the
Ljubelj tunnel north of Tržič.

Kamnik and around

Hemmed in by thick forests at the foot of the Kamniške Alps, **KAMNIK** – 23km north of Ljubljana – is one of Slovenia's prettiest medieval towns and a major staging post for hikers and skiiers heading onwards to the nearby alpine resorts. A market borough in the thirteenth century, the town established itself as a key trade and crafts centre during the Middle Ages, though the later creation of alternative routes left the town somewhat out on a limb. Industrialization and the construction of the Ljubljana–Kamnik railway in the nineteenth century played a part in its revival, as did the popularity of its thermal spas, frequented by both Ljubljančani and Austrians. Nowadays, Kamnik is a sleepy, old-fashioned place which really only ever comes alive during the staging of the town's three major festivals. Nevertheless, its spruce, neatly preserved medieval old town, castles and museums warrant a trip any time.

Each year the town plays host to three very lively festivals. **Medieval Days**, taking place on the second weekend of June, involves a mock medieval market, trades and crafts shows and medieval sports such as sword fighting and archery. **Kamfest**, in August, constitutes three weeks of music and dance centred on Mali Grad, while the **National Costumes Festival**, on the second weekend of September, sees groups from Slovenia's multifarious regions dress up in their most colourful finery. Naturally, there is much merriment at all three.

Arrival, information and accommodation

The town's main **train station** is on Kranjska cesta, a five-minute walk south of the main street, Šutna, but you're better off alighting at the next stop, Kamnik-Mesto, a short stroll west of Glavni trg (main square) on Kolodvorska ulica; Kamnik-Graben, a couple of minutes further down the line, is the last stop. From the **bus station** on Maistrova ulica, it's a five-minute walk to Glavni trg and the **tourist office** at no. 2 (June–Sept daily 9am–8pm; Oct–May Mon–Sat 10am–6pm, Sun 10am–2pm; ☎01/831-8250, ⓦwww.kamnik-tourism.si), which has **internet** as well as bikes for rent (€5 for 4hr, €8 for the day). The **post office** is at Glavni trg 27 (Mon–Fri 8am–6pm, Sat 8am–noon).

Kamnik has more than enough **accommodation** to go around if you wish to stay, including the decent *Pod Skalo* **hostel** (☎01/839-1233, ⓦwww.hi-kamnik.si; ❶–❷), which has en-suite doubles and triples and is a five-minute walk northeast of the bus station on the busy main road, Maistrova ulica.

The town's one **hotel** is the superb *Malograjski Dvor*, a few paces from the bus station at Maistrova ulica 13 (☎01/830-3100, ⓦwww.hotelkamnik.si; ❼), whose sumptuous, lime-green/lemon-coloured rooms come with antique style furnishings. Otherwise, there are a couple of rather dull, and identically priced, pensions; the *Kamrica*, beneath Mali Grad at Trg svobode 2 (☎01/831-7707; ❺), and the similarly furnished *Pri Cesarju*, a five-minute walk north of Glavni trg at Tunjiška cesta 1 (☎01/839-2917; ❺), which also has triples and quads; the crowns on the doors are in tribute to the time when Emperor Franz Jozef allegedly stayed here. Directly opposite the hostel is the town's small and basic *Resnik* **campsite** (May–Sept; ☎01/831-7314).

The Town

Most of Kamnik's attractions lie east and south of **Glavni trg** (Main Square), part square, part street, and the town's focal point. On the east side of the square, at no. 2, is the **Miha Maleš Gallery** (Tues–Sat 9am–1pm & 4–7pm; €2.50),

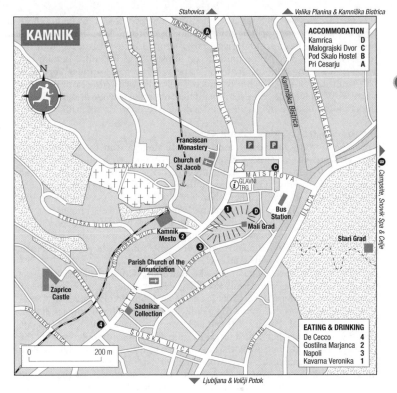

named after the twentieth-century painter but actually hosting temporary exhibitions by other local artists. A short walk west of Glavni trg is the **Franciscan Monastery** (Frančiškanski samostan), dating from 1495, whose library holds a fine collection of handwritten and printed manuscripts from the Middle Ages (contact the tourist office if you wish to visit). Adjoining the monastery, the **Church of St Jacob** (Cerkev Sv Jakoba) was also built in the fifteenth century but redesigned in Baroque style; otherwise unexceptional, the church is a must-see for Plečnik's extraordinary **Chapel of the Holy Grave**, positioned to the right of the high altar – charged with images of war, the great architect (see box, p.60) cast the altar in the shape of a bullet, lined the walls with rows of studded lights (meant to represent helmets), and shaped the door-knob into a dove's head, to symbolize peace.

Mali Grad

Occupying a hillock south of Glavni trg is **Mali Grad** (Little Castle), the town's most evocative and identifiable building. At the summit, on the eastern tip of the ruins, sits the whitewashed, two-storey **Romanesque chapel and crypt** (daily June–Aug 9am–7pm; €3), parts of which date from the eleventh century, making it one of Slovenia's oldest surviving ecclesiastical monuments. The exquisite chapel, much strengthened and remodelled, contains remnants of some superb fifteenth-century late-Gothic frescoes illustrating several venerated saints, as well as paintings by Janez Potočnik. Step outside onto the balcony and there are some fantastic views of the Alps.

Three decades of ongoing research have revealed some intriguing finds around the castle site, including the remains of a **Stone Age settlement** and some 27 graves from an Old Slavic burial ground believed to date from the tenth century – some of the finds are on display at the Kamnik Museum (see below). According to local myth the castle is home to **Countess Veronika**, half-woman, half-snake, who is said to jealously guard the castle's hidden treasures. Whatever the truth, her legend lives on in the town seal, and each year she's brought back to life during the Medieval Days festival (see p.88).

From Šutna to the Stari Grad

From the bottom of the castle continue south along **Šutna**, the town's attractive, crescent-shaped main street, which is lined with neat two-storey Baroque buildings. Midway along the street, the **Parish Church of the Annunciation**, along with its enormous detached Gothic belfry, looms into sight. Preceded by two earlier churches, this eighteenth-century building features a Renaissance-style altar by Ivan Vurnik – well known for his decorative work in Ljubljana – while the frescoes on the presbytery walls, illustrating various feast days, are by Matija Kozelj who also painted the nave and chapels. Note too the intricately cut relief above the portal entrance, which depicts a lamb with vine leaves.

A little further down at no. 33 is the **Sadnikar Collection** (Sadnikarjeva muzejska zbirka), a wonderful assemblage of antique furniture, porcelain, weapons and sacral art, amassed by local vet Dr Josip Nikolaj Sadnikar (1863–1952), the man who discovered the woolly mammoth skeleton now residing in Ljubljana's Natural History Museum. Among its many priceless items are paintings by Metzinger and Tintoretto (the latter one of only two in the country), and a bust by Ivan Mestrovič, Croatia's greatest sculptor. Take a close look at the magnificent carved wooden door leading into the main room, inscribed with the date August 12, 1936, to commemorate the day the King of Yugoslavia came to the house. Visits must be arranged through the tourist office (€2 per person).

Two hundred metres south of here, on a gently sloping hillside across the rail tracks, is the sixteenth-century **Zaprice Castle** (Grad Zaprice), later renovated into a Baroque mansion and now housing the **Kamnik Museum** (Tues–Fri 8am–1pm & 4–7pm, Sat 10am–1pm & 4–6pm, Sun 10am–1pm; €3). It's particularly worth visiting for its exhibition on the excavations at Mali Grad (see p.89), which includes an old Slavic skeleton discovered in 1990 and various other prehistoric relics. Elsewhere, there's an exhibition of Bentwood furniture, whose pioneer, Michael Thonet, was the first to use wood-bending techniques for the purpose of crafting chairs and tables, and an exhibition on Kamnik bourgeois life in the nineteenth century. On the overgrown lawn in front of the museum are four one- and two-cell *kašče* or **granaries** – squat, thatched-roof structures which served as storehouses for alpine herdsmen as they went about their work in the mountain valleys. Prevalent in the nearby Tuhinj Valley (from where these are taken), this particular form of peasant architecture is common throughout the country.

Atop the 585-metre-high Bergantov Hill, east of the Kamniška Bistrica river, is **Stari Grad** (Old Castle), dating from the twelfth century but abandoned in the sixteenth century. Although there's now little to see except a desolate heap of ruins, the reward for the tough little walk to reach them – which begins 100m south along the main road opposite the bus station – is some fine **views** of the town and Alps. You can also reach the castle by car, taking the road beginning in the suburb of Novi Trg.

Eating and drinking

The choice of places to **eat** in Kamnik is very limited. Your best bet is *Gostilna Marjanca* at Kolodvorska 5, which offers an exhaustive Slovene menu. Otherwise there's *Napoli*, a decent pizzeria located on the south side of Mali Grad at Sadnikarjeva 5, and *De Cecco* at Šutna 68, a colourful little spaghetteria which also offers a number of fondues (closed Sun). *Kavarna Veronika*, tucked away in a fabulous spot underneath Mali Grad, on the corner of Glavni trg and Japljeva ulica, is, day or night, the town's premier meeting place, serving up some lovely **coffees** as well as a tempting selection of cakes.

Volčji Potok and the Snovik Thermal Spa

Four kilometres south of Kamnik, near the village of Radomlje, is the **Volčji Potok Arboretum** (daily: April–Aug 8am–8pm; Sept–Nov & March 8am–6pm; €6; ⓦ www.arboretum-vp.si), Slovenia's largest and most important horticultural park. Volčji Potok, meaning "Wolf's Brook", had a number of proprietors over the centuries, before the park was created under the auspices of Ljubljana University in 1952.

The Slovene polymath Janez Vajkard Valvasor (see box, p.237) once described the park as "a great and fertile place, boasting superb meadows and most fruitful fields". It is no less appealing today, home to over three thousand species of plants, shrubs and trees, all sensitively assimilated into the surrounding woodland. However, it's the neatly manicured **French Garden** that most people make a beeline for, though just as lovely is the landscaped **English Park**, with its silky, perfectly trimmed lawns, and the **beech forests** which are ideal for a gentle ramble. Although a beautiful place to visit at any time of year, the best time to come is in spring, when the daffodils and tulips are in full bloom. The bizarre and, quite frankly, useless bus schedule has five buses a day making the trip from Kamnik on weekdays (5.55am, 8am, 1.15pm, 2.45pm & 7.10pm), but only one on Saturdays (4.50pm) and Sundays (4pm). Coming back, there are just two a day on weekdays (7.35am & 5.58pm), with one on Saturdays (9.48am), and on Sundays (9.38am). The fantastically scenic **Golf Course Arboretum**, right next to the park, is a very tight eighteen-hole course, guaranteed to satisfy even the most demanding of golfers (€40 per round; ☏01/831-8080, ✉igrisce@golfarboretum.si).

If you fancy something slightly more relaxing, head to the **Snovik Thermal Spa** (☏01/834-4100, ⓦ www.terme-snovik.si), located in a peaceful spot 9km east of Kamnik out on the road towards Celje. One of Slovenia's newest spas, it incorporates indoor and outdoor pools (Mon–Thurs & Sun 9am–8pm, Fri–Sat till 10pm; €9 for 2hr, €12 day ticket), saunas and steam baths; there are also apartments sleeping two to five people (❻–❽) – the price includes entry to the spa. From Kamnik there are just three buses a day on weekdays (9am, 10.30am & 12.30pm) and one on Saturdays and Sundays (10am), with two return buses Monday to Saturday (1.15pm & 4.48pm) and one on Sundays (3.38pm).

Velika Planina

Velika Planina, a broad alpine plateau comprising grassy slopes, sinkholes and clusters of dwarf pines, is one of Slovenia's prime dairy farming regions as well as a hugely popular destination for skiers and walkers. Touching a height of 1666m, the plain, also known as the Great Highlands, was once a heavily forested area – as evidenced by the remaining clumps of trees scattered across the terrain – but is now given over to a group of small settlements (Velika

Planina, Mala Planina, Tiha Dolina and others), distinguished by dozens of silvery-grey wooden huts, unique for their conical, shingled roofs which extend like witches' hats almost all the way down to ground level. The plateau is at its busiest during the summer months, when walkers, loaded with picnic supplies, trek the well-worn, marked paths between settlements, occasionally stopping off to buy cheese or milk from the shepherds. There are three **mountain huts** (see box, p.142) on Mala Planina; *Jarški Dom* (☏041/676-254; open all year), *Domžalski Dom* (☏051/340-730; open all year) and *Črnuški Dom* (☏041/621-735; June–Sept daily; Oct–May Sat & Sun), all of which have **accommodation** in multi-bedded rooms, and offer hot food.

The most satisfying way to visit Velika Planina is to hike up and take the **cable car** down. The cable car (*žičnica*; June to mid-Sept hourly Mon–Thurs 8am–6pm, Fri–Sun 8am–8pm; mid-Sept to May hourly Mon–Thurs 8am–4pm, Fri–Sun 8am–6pm; €12 return) starts 11km north of Kamnik and ascends to 1407m, from where there are chairlifts up to the top of the plateau – the area known as **Gradišče**; alternatively, or if the chairlift is not operating, you can walk, though it is a steep and gruelling climb. You will be rewarded, however, by the presence of the *Zeleni Rob* snack bar at the top (June–Aug daily; Sept–May Fri–Sun). The main trail begins at the village of **Stahovica**, 5km north of Kamnik and 6km south of the cable car station, a most enjoyable hike which takes around three hours at a steady pace; after about an hour, a sign diverts you to the fifteenth-century **Church of St Primoz** (Cerkev Sv Primoz), a convenient spot to pause and take in the glorious views, before pushing on towards Mala Planina.

Bikes can be taken on the cable car, which is useful as there is a good, and fairly demanding, cycle track on Velika Planina itself – a cycle map detailing a number of routes in the region can be obtained from the tourist office in Kamnik (see p.88). There's a small **campsite** (☏051/307-299; June–Sept) next to the cable car station.

Kamniška Bistrica

Three kilometres north of the cable car station is the tiny settlement of **KAMNIŠKA BISTRICA**, an idyllic recreation spot lying at the head of the Kamniške Alps and a key starting point for **hikes** up into the central tract of the mountains. Note that the following routes are all one way. The two most popular hikes from here, which should suit walkers of all abilities, are **Kamniško Sedlo** to the north (1884m; 3hr 30min) and **Kokrško Sedlo** to the northwest (1793m; 3hr 30min) – both have mountain huts open between June and mid-October. There are several longer and more demanding hikes just over a kilometre back down towards the cable car station, beginning at a track just before the stone bridge; the track, which heads eastwards up the **Kamniška Bela Valley** (you must also cross the brook, which may be tricky if there has been rain), leads to **Presedelj** (1613m; 3hr), **Korošica** (1910m; 4hr 45min) – there's a hut here open between June and September – and **Ojstrica** (2350m; 6hr). If you don't fancy one of these hikes, take the same path for about 25 minutes until you come to a fork – the rocky path to the left will shortly bring you to the **Orglice Waterfall** (Slap Orglice), partly concealed but still an impressive sight. Back in Kamniška Bistrica, **refreshments** can be taken at the *Dom v Kamniški Bistrici*, which also offers dorm **accommodation** (☏01/832-5544; open all year). From Kamnik to Kamniška Bistrica, there are three **buses** a day on weekdays (7am, 11.30am & 4.52pm) and two on Saturdays (7.20am & 4.45pm) and Sundays (7.50am & 4.55pm). The return buses are: weekdays (7.35am, 12.05pm & 5.15pm), Saturdays (8.25am & 5.20pm) and Sundays (8.40am & 5.30pm).

Škofja Loka and around

Not to be outdone by Kamnik, **ŠKOFJA LOKA** (Bishop's Meadow), 19km northwest of Ljubljana, lays fair claim to being one of the oldest and loveliest settlements in Slovenia. Lying at the confluence of the two branches of the Sora River, Škofja Loka was first documented in 973 AD, when the settlement of Stara Loka, along with the Selška Dolina and Poljanska Dolina valleys, was conferred on the bishops of Freising, who would oversee town rule for the next eight centuries. During the early fourteenth century the town was fortified with a five-gate wall – parts of which can still be seen – while the ancient core was "parcelled" into segments. However, despite being pillaged by both the counts of Celje and the Turks, the town layout has changed remarkably little.

For such a modestly sized town, its sights are reasonably well dispersed, from Mestni trg and the handsome town castle in the centre to Stara Loka in the north, and the suburb of Puštal to the southeast. Beyond here, in **Crngrob** and **Suha**, are two of the finest frescoed churches in Slovenia. The town's major annual happening, at the end of June, is the **Medieval Days Festival**, a week of medieval-themed events similar to those which take place in Kamnik. Škofja

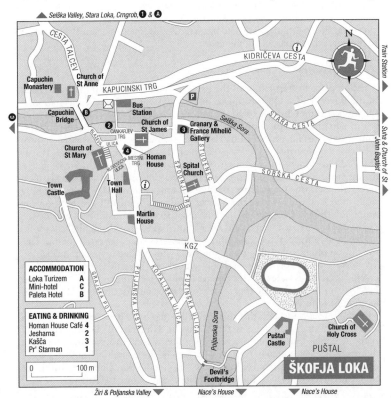

Loka can easily be done as a half- or full-day trip from Ljubljana or alternatively en route to Bled or Bohinj via Kranj.

Arrival, information and accommodation

The **train station** is 3km northeast of town and connected to the centre by hourly buses (none Sun). Far more conveniently, the **bus station** is on Kapucinski trg, just a few paces from the old town across the river; it has a left-luggage office (daily 6am–6pm; €2). The main **tourist office** is a five-minute walk east of the bus station at Kidričeva cesta 1a (May–Sept Mon–Fri 8am–7pm, Sat & Sun 9am–2pm; Oct–April Mon–Fri 8am–4pm, Sat 9am–2pm; ℡04/517-0600, Ⓦwww.skofjaloka.info); they also have **bikes** for rent (€5 for half a day, €8 for a full day). There's another, less useful branch of the tourist office at Mestni trg 7 (May–Sept Mon–Fri 8am–8pm, Sat & Sun 8.30am–12.30pm & 4–8pm; Oct–May Mon–Fri 8.30am–7pm, Sat 8.30am–12.30pm; ℡04/512-0268). The **post office** is next to the bus station (Mon–Fri 8am–7pm, Sat 8am–noon).

The only **hotel** in the centre of town is the quaint, family-run *Paleta*, down by the Capuchin bridge at Kapucinski trg 17 (℡04/512-6400, Ⓦwww.paleta -skofjaloka.si; ❺), which has six colourful rooms (doubles and quads) overlooking the river. Otherwise there's the modern and very homely *Loka Turizem* tourist farm situated a ten-minute walk north of the bus station at Stara Loka 8 (℡04/515-0986, Ⓦwww.loka.si; ❺), and the *Mini-hotel*, 1.5km west of the centre at Vincarje 47 (℡04/515-0540, Ⓔmetka@minihotel.si; ❺), whose comfortably furnished rooms have fabulous views of the Alps; the hotel also has tennis and squash courts, sauna and fitness facilities; from the bus station, cross the Capuchin Bridge, take a right turn and continue along the road.

The Town

The best place to start a tour of the town is Kapucinski trg on the north bank of the River Selška. On this square, and a few steps west of the bus station, is the modest little **Church of St Anne**, consecrated in 1713. More interesting is the adjoining **Capuchin Monastery**, and its library (Mon, Wed & Fri 9am–2pm, at other times call ℡04/596-3005), whose priceless collection of medieval manuscripts includes a copy of the celebrated *Škofjeloški Pasijon* (*Škofja Loka Passion*), the oldest written dramatic text in the Slovene language, dating from 1721 (see box opposite). From the monastery proceed south across the narrow **Capuchin Bridge** (Kapucinski most), whose stunning stone arch is reminiscent of the Mostar Bridge in Bosnia. It was built on the orders of Bishop Leopold in the fourteenth century, making it one of the oldest of its type in Europe, and later named after the Capuchin friars who settled here in the eighteenth century. Some years later, in a cruel twist of fate, the bishop plunged headlong into the river while riding across the bridge on his horse – an incident that probably would not have occurred had he also erected iron balustrades of the type that now line either side of the bridge. Perched on a pedestal in the centre of the bridge is a statue of a wistful looking St John Nepomuk.

Passing through the arch that once served as the town gate, you enter the old town. The first site of note is the **Convent Church of St Mary**, whose Baroque design came about as a result of a fire in 1669 that destroyed much of the original 1358 building. A short walk east of the church is Cankarjev trg, a nondescript square partly redeemed by the late-Gothic **Parish Church of St James** (Cerkev Sv Jakob), most of which dates from 1471. Its untidy grey

Škofja Loka Passion Play

Performed for the first time in over 270 years in 1999, and then again in 2009, the **Skofjeloški pasijon** (*Škofja Loka Passion Play*) is one of Slovenia's most remarkable, albeit rarely seen, spectacles. Written by Friar Romauld Marušič in 1721, it was the first dramatic text in the Slovenian language, a form of medieval and Baroque theatre comprising biblical stories or allegories pertaining to the suffering of Christ – hence its staging around the Good Friday period.

The tone of the play (it's actually more of a procession) is set by the Starbearer – dressed in a red habit to symbolize the impending, bloody agony – followed by Death, Hell and a total of seventeen other scenes, or tableaux, such as the Last Supper, Judgement Day and the Crucifixion. Aside from its slight contemporary twist, and the introduction of a musical element, the play has otherwise remained faithful to its original eighteenth-century production, based on a similar order of events, an almost identical text, and use of the original language.

Such is the organization and finance involved – some six hundred amateur actors, eighty horses, and carefully constructed stage sets at various locations around town are required – that the event is staged only every few years, with the next one scheduled for 2015.

exterior contrasts sharply with the interior, which, though eerily dark, features a magnificent stellar rib-vaulted ceiling embellished with stone bosses showing portraits of church patrons and the town guilds. Other notable works include the black marble Renaissance altars dating from 1694, and the chandeliers and baptismal font by Plečnik. Note too the splendid late-Gothic tympanum above the main entrance.

Mestni trg and Spodnji trg

From Cankarjev trg the street narrows before opening up into **Mestni trg** (Town Square), the town's old medieval market place, an atmospheric, rectangular space framed by many-coloured three-storey burgher houses, almost every other one marked with a plaque denoting its historical significance. Occupying a prime spot at the square's north end is the **Homan House** (Homanova hiša), an exceptional amalgam of Gothic and Renaissance styles, featuring a turret-like corner projection and sixteenth-century frescoes of St Christopher and the bottom half of a warrior, only discovered in 1970. Its outdoor **café**, shaded by a magnificent linden tree, is the most popular meeting place in town; Ivan Grohar, the outstanding Impressionist painter, was a regular at the inn and completed his celebrated *Loka in Snow*, now hanging in the National Gallery in Ljubljana, from here. Further Baroque frescoes were revealed in 1972 on the facade of no. 35 – the former **town hall** (Rotovž) – which also possesses a fine Gothic portal and Renaissance-style arcaded courtyard. Opposite the town hall is the **Plague Pillar**, erected in 1751 by the townspeople in gratitude for their deliverance from fire and plague. Heading down through the square, other buildings worth a glance include the **Žigon House** (Žigonova hiša) at no. 15, formerly a sixteenth-century trade house, and the **Martin House** (Martinova hiša), the last house on the right at no. 26, which was built on top of a section of the old town walls.

Running parallel to Mestni trg to the east is **Spodnji trg** (Lower Square), formerly a residential area for the poorer townsfolk, but now a downtrodden, traffic-filled thoroughfare. At its extreme northern end is the **town granary** (Kašča), a sturdy old building used during the Middle Ages for collecting taxes, which usually took the form of grain or cheese; the granary now houses a good restaurant (see opposite) and the **France Mihelič Gallery** (Galerija Franceta Miheliča; Tues–Sun 10am–noon; free), featuring a superb exhibition of the artist's work from the 1970s. His apocalyptic themes of disintegration, decay and disappearance are embodied in a series of disturbing, surrealist paintings of dismembered bodies and rotting organisms; of particular interest are his paintings of scenes from the Ptuj Kurent (see box, p.304).

Škofja Loka Castle

Mounted on a low grassy hill to the west of Mestni trg is Škofja Loka's majestic medieval **town castle** (Loški Grad), first mentioned in 1215 as "castrum firmissimum Lonca" (strongly fortified castle), though most of what you see today dates from the beginning of the sixteenth century, following the earthquake of 1511. The main reason for visiting the castle is its **Town Museum** (Loški Muzej; Tues–Sun: May–Sept 10am–6pm; Oct–April 10am–4pm; €3), which holds a comprehensive, and occasionally enlightening, collection of local and regional exhibits. Before entering the museum proper, pop into the **castle chapel**, which holds four spectacular Baroque gilded altars rescued from the church in the village of Dražgoše, near Železniki, which was destroyed by the Germans during World War II.

The first three rooms, given over to the dominion of Škofja Loka, are unspectacular, save for a superb votive oil painting depicting the great town fire of August 19, 1698. The next room charts the rise of the town craftsmen and their **guilds**, set up in and around Škofja Loka in the fifteenth century in order to protect the interests of blacksmiths, tanners, tailors and other trades from both local and foreign competition; the assemblage of deeds, chests and banners is very impressive. Guilds were eventually abolished in 1859, owing to a combination of increased free-marketing practices and the French Revolution, although many of their customs were preserved until World War II in the form of guild fraternities. Elsewhere on the ground floor, look out for some possessions of the acclaimed Slovene writer Ivan Tavčar, and painted peasant furniture belonging to the Kalan family, whom Tavčar wrote about in his acclaimed novel *Visoška kronika* (*Visoko Chronicle*; see p.101).

Heading upstairs, make for the excellent **ethnographical collection**, which illustrates the ways and means of peasant living before industrialization, with a fine display of agricultural tools and objects, models of buildings indigenous to the Loka region, and a mock-up of a typical "black" kitchen (a superb real-life example of which can be seen in Nace's House; see opposite). The remaining rooms catalogue the importance to the region of crafts such as lace-making, millinery and dyeing, many of which have long since disappeared. The last room is dedicated to the art of making honey bread using ornate wooden moulds, a practice known as "Mali Kruhek" ("Small Loaves"); on display is a collection of the types of moulds – typically made from pear- or plum-tree wood and featuring motifs of a secular or figural design – used to shape the bread, traditionally baked for holidays and religious feasts. The castle is reachable via two footpaths: from Klobovsova ulica just to the west of the Homan House, or from the path at the southern end of Mestni trg.

Stara Loka and Pustal

The suburb of **Stara Loka** (Old Loka), a short walk north of Kapucinski trg, stakes its claim to be one of the oldest localities in Slovenia, with origins dating from 973 AD. In the centre of the district is the lesser-known **Old Loka Castle**, thought to have evolved from the Bishop's Palace around the beginning of the fifteenth century, but which, save for the round towers, has retained few of its

Hiking and cycling around Škofja Loka

The **Škofja Loka Hills** to the west of town present some terrific opportunities for hiking and cycling. The most popular local excursion is the two-hour **hike** to Lubnik (1025m), reachable via footpaths from Vincarje or from Škofja Loka Castle, passing by the castle ruins and the hamlet of Grabovo. The *Dom na Lubnik* mountain hut at the summit has beds and serves hot food (☎04/512-0501; March–Dec Tues–Sun; Jan & Feb Sat & Sun only). The further west you go, the higher the peaks, culminating in **Stari Vrh**, a small ski resort where you'll find the *Koča Stari Vrh* hut (☎041/682-082; open all year) and **Blegoš**, the region's highest peak at 1562m – where there's the *Koča na Blegošu* hut (☎051/614-587; May–Oct Tues–Sun; Nov–April Sat & Sun only). The 1:50,000 map *Škofjeloško in Cerkljansko Hribovje* (€7), available from the tourist offices, details all routes.

A superb network of **cycling tracks** has now been established in the hills, with routes designed to suit riders of all abilities. The entire track covers an area of some 300km, divided into twelve stages, with each trail clearly marked by green boards attached to posts. The excellent *Loka's Cycling Track* (€2) map, available from the tourist offices, details all stages, indicating elevation, degree of difficulty and sights along the way. **Bikes** can be rented from the tourist office on Kidričeva cesta (see p.94).

---

original features. The greater part of the castle is now occupied by the Centre for the Blind and Partially Sighted – look out for the unique sundial for the blind at the entrance. Opposite the castle stands the neo-Romanesque **Church of St George** (Cerkev Sv Jurij), built in 1865 and unremarkable save for some impressive sixteenth- and seventeenth-century tombstones along the side chapels.

The peaceful suburb of **Puštal**, on the right bank of the Poljanska Sora River, is a lovely place for a stroll and also contains one of the town's best sights. Crossing the wooden **Hudičeva brv** (Devil's Footbridge), a ten-minute walk south of Spodnji trg, follow the road south until you arrive at Puštal 74, otherwise known as **Nace's House** (Nacetova hiša; to visit call ☎04/236-6640 or contact the tourist office; €3.50). Named after its first owner, Ignacij "Nace" Homan, this almost perfectly preserved eighteenth-century Slovene homestead is predominantly of Baroque appearance, though its stone-vaulted cellar and two "black kitchens" (see p.129) are evidence of fifteenth- and sixteenth-century elements. Its furnishings, including a fine maple-wood table, carved chairs and a ceramic heating stove featuring a motifed tile from 1417, are all original; take a look, too, at the skilfully crafted iron grilles (gatri) adorning the windows.

From the house, head north towards the main road; on the left-hand side is **Puštal Castle** (Puštal Grad), dating from around 1220 and now housing a music school. Two hundred metres east of the castle, a gravelly path breaks off from the main road and spirals steeply up to the simple Baroque **Church of the Holy Cross** (Cerkev Sv Križ), from where there are wonderful views of the town and castle (you can get the key to the church from the house just below).

Eating and drinking

The best **restaurant**, in a town where there are few, is *Kašča*, housed in the basement of the old granary at Spodnji trg 2 (closed Sun), which serves tasty stews, such as *Kašča pot*, to augment its impressive stock of fish and grilled-meat dishes – this is also the place to head to for wine. Two other reasonable places are *Pr' Starman*, just down from the old castle at Stara Loka 22 (closed Sun), where you can tuck into wholesome Slovene grub; and *Jesharna*, a simple but welcoming pizzeria across the bridge from the bus station. Comfortably the best

drinking spot in town is *Homan House Café* whose outdoor terrace – enveloped by a huge linden tree – is a lovely place to relax, day or night.

Suha and the Church of St John the Baptist

Standing anonymously in a field 2.5km east of town on the outskirts of the village of **SUHA** is the diminutive **Church of St John the Baptist** (Cerkev Sv Janez Krstnik), acclaimed for its outstanding medieval paintings. On entering this small fifteenth-century church, you are immediately drawn to the stellar rib-vaulted presbytery, coated with stunning frescoes depicting scenes from the life of Christ and the Virgin Mary (surrounded by evangelists, angels and various Apostles peering through columns). The lower panels depict the sixteenth-century painter Jernej of Loka's images of the wise and foolish maidens and the holy martyrs. On the inner wall of the triumphal arch is a representation of the Last Judgement. There is no public transport to the village (and buses do not stop on the nearby main road), so if you don't have your own transport rent a bike from the tourist office in Škofja Loka to avoid a long and draining walk. The key to the church can be obtained from no. 32, approximately 150m down from the church.

Crngrob and the Church of the Annunciation

Four kilometres north of Škofja Loka, in the tiny settlement of **CRNGOB** (Black Grave), is the fourteenth-century pilgrimage **Church of the Annunciation** (Marijino oznanenje), regarded as one of Slovenia's most significant monuments and distinguished by some matchless **frescoes**. Completed in the seventeenth century, but originating in the thirteenth century, the church manifests a variety of styles – Romanesque, Gothic and Baroque – though its outward form is predominantly Gothic. The nineteenth-century neo-Gothic columned portico at the western end of the church reveals one of the finest frescoes in Slovenia, the partly effaced *Holy Sunday* (*Sveta Nedelja*), completed in around 1470 by the workshop of Janez Ljubljanski. More than forty scenes portray a series of tasks which good Christians are obliged to do on the Sabbath – pray, assist the sick, and so on, as well as what they should not be doing – gambling, drinking and the like. To the left is *The Passion of Christ*, an earlier work completed by the Friulian masters.

Though on a much larger scale, the church interior is strikingly similar to that of the parish church in Škofja Loka, its shadowy tripartite nave giving way to a sumptuously light chancel supported by six octagonal columns and featuring a delightful pale red-, yellow- and blue-painted rib-vaulted ceiling. Completed by Ljubljana craftsman Jurij Skarnos in 1652, the profoundly ornate **high altar** – the largest Baroque gilded altar in the country – is festooned with almost one hundred statuettes and pillars and rounded off with an oil painting by Leopold Layer. The fabulous organ dates from 1753, and the immense bell tower, featuring a large fresco of St Christopher on its south wall, was raised to its present height of 62m in 1666. If the church is locked you can obtain the key from the house below (no. 10). The church can be reached via a monotonous, straggling road which extends northwards from Groharjevo naselje in Stara Loka (a 1hr walk). Alternatively, take the Kranj bus and alight at the village of **Dorfarje**, from where it's a twenty-minute walk to the church. If you fancy a rural stopover, there is the wonderfully comfortable *Pri Marku* **tourist farm** just down from the church at no. 5 (T04/513-1626, Wwww.pri-marku-porenta.si; ❸) – you can even sleep in the hay barn. Refreshments can be had at the *gostilna* just a few paces from the church (closed Wed).

The Selška valley

The **Selška Valley**, which fans out northwest from Škofja Loka, is often ignored in favour of the region's more obvious attractions a short way north. This is unfortunate, as there are several lovely villages here and some of the scenery is immensely rewarding. Although there are a few buses serving most of these places, having your own transport will enable you to see a lot more.

Selca and Železniki

Twisting its way north out of Škofja Loka, the narrow, flat-bottomed **Selška Valley** stretches for some 34km between the northern flank of the Škofja Loka Hills and the southern ridge of the forested Jelovica plateau. Twelve kilometres up the valley is the quaint village of **SELCA** (from where the valley took its name), distinguished by the Baroque **Church of St Peter** (Cerkev Sv Petra), rebuilt in 1767 after having been burnt down on two previous occasions; the centrepiece of the church is the high altar, featuring a fine painting by Langus, depicting Christ bestowing power upon Peter. Five kilometres further west is **ŽELEZNIKI**, the valley's key economic centre. This spindly three-kilometre-long town, made up of several interconnected settlements, has been shaped by its centuries-old iron-smelting industry, which reached its peak here in the seventeenth century when two blast furnaces and more than sixty workshops were operational. Technological advances throughout Europe at the end of the nineteenth century, coupled with the depletion of iron-ore stocks, brought about the demise of the industry and the last furnace was decommissioned in 1902.

The one remaining **blast furnace** (*plavž*), dating from 1826 and the only preserved technical monument of its kind in the country, is situated at the western end of town and stands as a fitting memorial to a bygone era. The town's industrial heritage is thoroughly documented in the **Železniki Museum** (April–Oct Tues–Thurs 9am–3pm, Fri 9am–5pm, Sat 9am–2pm; Nov–March Tues–Fri 9am–2pm, Sat 9am–1pm; €2), located opposite the furnace in the **Plavec house**, dating from 1637 and named after the former owner of the furnace. Despite the absence of English captions, the museum is an enjoyable affair, and includes a lovely collection of lace work from Železniki, considered to be the second largest lace centre in Slovenia after Idrija. If you want to see what all the fuss is about, visit the town in mid-July during the **Days of Lace Fair** (Čipkarski Dnevi v Železnikih), a week-long series of lace-related events.

Buses drop passengers off in the centre of town by the church. The only **place to stay** in Železniki is the homely *Kemperle*, just beyond the public swimming pool in the eastern part of town at Otoki 3 (℡04/514-6084, ✆kemperle@siol.net; ➍). There's nowhere decent to eat in town, but if you've got your own transport, it's worth stopping off at the *Pri Slavcu* (Thurs–Mon) in **Zali Log**, the next village along.

Dražgoše and Jamnik

If you have your own transport, a delightfully scenic ride from Železniki – and a good short cut to Kropa (see p.110) – is up and over the **Jelovica Plateau**, a thickly forested highland plain that offered refuge to Partisans during World War II. That didn't, however, stop several ferocious battles taking place here, in particular in the hamlet of **DRAŽGOŠE**, 8km beyond Železniki on the plateau's southern fringe. Forty-one villagers were shot dead and the rest expelled as the village was razed by German troops in January 1942, an event belatedly commemorated by the erection of a brutal-looking concrete monument – though this can't detract from the superlative views of the surrounding lush countryside. Some 10km further on, the diminutive fifteenth-century Church of St Primoz, perched on a slender ridge just outside the village of **Jamnik**, hoves into view. On a clear day, you can easily identify a number of sights spread out below – including Kropa, Radovljica, and the Basilica in Brezje. From Jamnik, it's just 4km down to Kropa by which time you're out of the valley.

Sorica

Nine kilometres west of Železniki, the road branches off to the right and winds steeply up to the extraordinarily picturesque alpine village of **SORICA**, its smooth undulating pastures spotted with small clusters of houses and dozens of hayracks. Sorica's most famous son is the great Slovene Impressionist painter Ivan Grohar, a sculpture of whom – palette in hand – greets visitors at the entrance to the village; his **birthplace** (Groharjeva hiša; July & Aug Sat & Sun 2–5pm; Sept–June Mon–Fri 10am–2pm, Sat & Sun 2–5pm; €2) is located beyond the church at Spodnja Sorica 18, and contains a limited collection of his paintings and belongings. **Accommodation** possibilities include the *Pintar* apartment just a few paces down from Grohar's house at no. 13 (℡04/519-7055; ❸), and the *Pri Jurju* tourist farm next door at no. 14 (℡04/519-7018; ❸). The road continues onwards and upwards to the Soriška Planina ski resort and beyond to Bohinj. The only buses from Sorica to Železniki (and vice versa) are the school (term-time) ones, with four or five per day in both directions.

The Poljanska Valley

Flanked by the Škofja Loka Hills to the north and the slightly lower Polhov Gradec Hills to the south, the **Poljanska Valley** extends for some 35km between Škofja Loka and the small town of Žiri. Eleven kilometres southwest of Škofja Loka, in the tiny settlement of **LOG**, is the *Gostišče Premetovc*, a magnificent roadside inn accommodating one of the most distinguished restaurants in

---

Rupnik Line

Sequenced in an almost vertical chain between Soriška Planina in the north and the small town of Žiri some 50km further south are dozens of bunkers, tunnels, casemates and observation posts built by the Yugoslavs in response to border fortifications constructed by the Italians following the **Treaty of Rapallo in 1920** (see p.324). Although proposals to fortify the border were initially submitted in the mid-1920s, construction work didn't begin until 1937, under the command of its chief architect **Leon Rupnik**, a Yugoslav army general who was later tried and shot in Ljubljana for treason. In the event, the line was neither fully completed – due to the onset of World War II – nor were its existing defences pressed into service.

Many of the fortifications have recently been cleaned up and it's now possible (with a guide) to visit some of them, an opportunity that will almost certainly appeal to adrenaline junkies; the descent into the bunkers and tunnels – some nearly forty metres deep – is exhilarating. Moreover, the **hiking** in this region is terrific. The line has been divided into three stages (each stage is roughly a 6–7hr hike, the first is also accessible to cyclists), with a number of different excursions organized by the tourist office in Škofja Loka (℡04/517-0600; see p.94). These range from short two-hour tours (€6), to day-long hikes (€17 per person), though tours can be tailored to suit individual or group needs. The Rupnik Line Trail **map** (Po Sledeh Rupnikove Linije; €2), available from the tourist office in Škofja Loka, outlines all three stages.

the region (Tues–Sat 4–9pm, Sun noon–6pm; ☎04/510-9600, ⓔpremetovc @siol.net). The inn also has two immaculately furnished suites (❽).

Five hundred metres beyond the inn, across the bridge on the left, and then along the road to the right, is the **Visoko Mansion**, once the property of the celebrated writer Ivan Tavčar (1851–1923). The mansion (also known as the Tavčar Manor) is now sadly derelict and all there is to see is an enormous bronze sculpture – completed in 1957 by Jakob Savinšek – of a cross-legged Tavčar gazing across the field. Born in **Poljane**, the next village along, Tavčar, erstwhile Ljubljana mayor and politician, was considered one of the country's foremost prose writers, basing much of his work on his experiences of life in the valley. His most famous novel, *Visoška Kronika* (*Visoko Chronicle*), charted the lives of the Kalan family who lived in the same house some two hundred years before Tavčar.

Žiri

Twelve kilometres south of Gorenja Vas is **ŽIRI**, a small, quiet town renowned for its lace and shoemaking industries, both of which are well covered in the **Žiri Museum** (Muzej Žiri; May–Oct Sat & Sun 2–4pm; other times by appointment, contact the tourist office; €2). This is located 1km south of the centre at Tabor 2 in the dilapidated former mansion of the Freising bishops. Following World War II the town's various shoemaking industries morphed into the Alpina factory, which now employs around eight hundred people who manufacture ski boots and a range of other sports footwear for some of the world's top climbers and athletes. Although Žiri is not as large a lace centre as either Idrija or Železniki, the museum's bobbin-lace collection attests to its importance in the town during the first part of the twentieth century. If you wish to have a look at, or buy, some lace items, pop into the small **Lace Gallery** at Jobstova 29 (Mon–Fri 4.30–7pm, Sat 9am–noon).

Buses drop passengers off in the centre of town, from where it's a two-minute walk to the **tourist information** booth on the main square, Trg Svobode (June–Sept daily 9am–5pm; Oct–May Sat & Sun 9am–1pm), where you can book **accommodation** on local tourist farms (❸). The *Gostilna Županu*, at Loška 78 (☎04/505-0000; ❹) in the northern part of town, is the sole central source of accommodation here, with a handful of neat, fresh-looking rooms. This is also the best place in town to **eat**, with pizzas, salads and meat dishes constituting the bulk of the menu. For **drinking**, most townsfolk congregate at the pubby *Na Voleriji* on Trg Svobode.

Kranj and around

Despite its reputation as a hard-nosed and gritty industrial centre, **KRANJ**, 10km from Škofja Loka and Slovenia's fourth-largest city, possesses an attractive old city centre severely at odds with its drab surrounds. Positioned on a steep, rocky promontory above the confluence of the Sava and Kokra rivers, between the foothills of the Julian Alps and the western spur of the Kamniške-Savinja Alps, Kranj has been the country's most important industrial city since the end of World War I. It is home to several of Slovenia's major manufacturing industries, including textiles, leather and electronics, which in total employ almost half of the city's population. However, beyond the grimescape of smoking chimneys, the old town possesses a clutch of fine late-Gothic buildings, and the city's strong associations with the poet France Prešeren – he lived, worked and

KRANJ

▲ Brdo Castle

Bus Station

Prešeren Grove

BLEIWEISOVA CESTA
MLADINSKA ULICA
GREGORČIČEVA ULICA
PARTIZANSKA CESTA
STRITARJEVA ULICA
KOROŠKA CESTA

SLOVENSKI TRG

N

KOKRŠKI BREG

MAISTROV TRG

REGINČEVA

PREŠERNOVA ULICA
TAVČARJEVA

Prešeren's House

TOVŠTIČEVA ULICA
JENKO ULICA

Train Station

GORENJSAVSKA CESTA

Sava

LJUBLJANSKA CESTA

Gorenjska Museum

Town Hall

GLAVNI TRG

POŠTNA ULICA

HUJE

CESTA 1 MAJA

Kieselstein Castle

Parish Church of St Cantianus

Prešeren Monument

VODPIVČEVA ULICA

Church of the Holy Rosary

Prešeren Theatre

Kokra River

LJUBLJANSKA CESTA

SAVSKA CESTA

S-E-IMIŠČE

Succursal Church

Spital (Defensive Tower)

0   200 m

EATING & DRINKING	
Carniola	3
Cukrarna	6
Klub Bar	2
Kot	5
Pr' Matičku	1
Stara Pošta	4
Stari Mayr	7

ACCOMMODATION	
Hotel Creina	A

▼ Šmarjetna Gora & Sv Jošt

died here – are manifest in an excellent **museum**. The city's two key events are **Festival Carniola**, a month of street theatre, concerts and workshops at several locations throughout the Old Town from mid-June to mid-July, and **Kranjfest**, a series of evening concerts at the end of August.

Kranj's environs present some good opportunities for more solitudinous excursions, the best of which is **Brdo Castle**, while the modest peaks of **Šmarjetna Gora** and **Sv Jošt** offer good walking for those with slightly more energy to expend.

Arrival, information and accommodation

The **train station** is on the west bank of the River Sava, a ten-minute walk from town (or bus #2), and the **bus station** lies 500m north of the old town on Stošičeva ulica. The **tourist office**, at Glavni trg 2 (Mon–Sat 8am–7pm, Sun 9am–6pm; ☎04/238-0450, ⓦwww.tourism-kranj.si), has **internet** access and

bikes for rent (€2 for 2hr, €5 per day), and can also arrange **accommodation** on tourist farms (②) in the villages of **Preddvor**, **Naklo** and **Jezersko**, all a short way north of Kranj. The town's only hotel is the business-like *Creina*, a hideous-looking brick building midway between the bus station and the old town at Koroška cesta 5 (☎04/281-7500, ⓦwww.hotelcreina.si; ⑦) – the rooms, though, are fresh-looking and perfectly agreeable. The **post office** is at Poštna ulica 4 (Mon–Fri 8am–7pm, Sat 8am–noon).

The Town

The town's attractive medieval centre begins at **Maistrov trg**, formerly the site of the upper town gate and once enclosed by the northern section of the city walls. The most obvious legacy of the walls is the **Spital Tower** – one of seven defensive towers incorporated within the walls – and which now forms part of the shop at no. 3. The square, liberally sprinkled with cafés and the hub of all social activity, segues into Prešernova ulica. At no. 7, a memorial plaque above the entrance denotes **Prešeren's House** (Prešerenova hiša; Tues–Sun 10am–6pm; €3). The two-storey building where Prešeren spent the last three years of his life is a fine example of a late-Gothic town house, its arcaded gallery uniting what were once two separate dwellings. The first floor has been turned into a superb memorial museum, chronologically presenting phases of Prešeren's life, with manuscripts, diaries and letters, accompanied by excellent explanatory notes. There is also much original furniture to admire, including the bed he died in and the desk and chair he used while working as a lawyer (see box, p.121). Prešeren is buried in **Prešeren Grove** (Prešernov Gaj), a small cemetery 500m north of town, which has only one other grave, that of another local poet, Simon Jenko.

Glavni trg

Prešernova ulica opens up into **Glavni trg** (Main Square), an elongated square framed by delightful Gothic and Renaissance buildings, the most

▲ Kranj Old Town

prominent of which is the **town hall** (Mestna hiša) on the corner of Poštna ulica, and which now accommodates the enjoyable **Gorenjska Museum** (Muzej Gorenjski; Tues–Sun 10am–6pm; €3). Its trio of exhibitions kicks off with an above-average collection of archeological finds, notably some outstanding grave goods including ceramic jugs and vessels, and finely cut jewellery and figurines. The most recent find is a valuable hoard of Roman tools – probably from a carpenter's workshop and thought to date from 4 AD – discovered in 1996 near Radomlje. The remainder of the museum's collection comprises an interesting assortment of sculptures by Lojze Dolinar (a student of the eminent Croatian sculptor Ivan Mestrovič), and an ethnological exhibition of folk art from Gorenjska, including beautifully crafted chests and cupboards, fifteenth-century frescoes, and a selection of Slovenia's famous beehive panels (see p.109). Have a look, too, at the magnificent Renaissance Hall, sporting a coffered ceiling and two inlaid wooden portals, which is now used as a venue for wedding ceremonies.

Dominating the square – indeed the city skyline – is the glowering **Parish Church of St Cantianus** (Cerkev Sv Kancijan), the most outstanding example of a Gothic hall-church in Slovenia; supported by four immense octagonal columns, its stellar-vaulted central nave is decorated with the *Star of Beautiful Angels* fresco, attributed to the workshop of Janez Ljubljanski, while numerous detailed keystones adorn the arches, most notably Mary and infant Jesus in front of the Triumphal Arch. Other highlights are the modestly fashioned high altar by the church architect Ivan Vurnik, and the neo-Gothic stained-glass windows by Kregar. The tympanum above the main entrance incorporates a fine relief of Christ on the Mount of Olives.

Outside the north side of the church is an early Slavonic **ossuary**, containing thousands of neatly stacked bones and skulls of Kranj citizens, thought to have been buried here between the fourteenth and sixteenth centuries but which were only discovered in the early 1970s (you need to ask at the town hall if you want to have a look). On the church's exterior south wall is a small **lapidary** of Roman and medieval tombstones and, beneath, a **fountain** bearing a statue of St John Nepomuk, somewhat bizarrely entangled in an octopus.

South to Pungert

From here the square narrows into Cankarjeva ulica; halfway down is the **Church of the Holy Rosary** (Cerkev Roženvesnka), a bland Gothic structure entirely reconstructed in 1892, which once served as a Protestant sanctuary during the Reformation. Beside the church is a Plečnik-designed **staircase**; on one side is a characteristic arcade, and in the middle, an unattractive looking fountain, also both by Plečnik. Walking down the stairs brings you to Vodopivčeva ulica (Mohor's Slope), where the lower town gate once stood, and beyond to the Sava River.

Cankarjeva ulica winds up at Trubarjev trg and the southern tip of the promontory known as **Pungert**, which rises up over the confluence of the Sava and Kokra rivers; unfortunately, the **Kokra Gorge**, an inaccessible thirty-metre-deep canyon, is largely obscured by trees, though there are some much better views from the Poštna ulica bridge, east of Glavni trg. The three-storey **Defensive Tower**, right on the tip, is the only entirely preserved tower within the ancient city walls; at one stage it was adapted for use as a prison and as lodgings. Next to the tower, the late fifteenth-century **Succursal Church** (also called the Plague Church) is dedicated to Sts Rok, Fabian and Sebastian in thanks for their intervention against the plague. The church is now used for services by the local Serbian Orthodox community.

Retracing your steps back to the Church of the Holy Rosary, head north along Tomšičeva ulica, where you'll pass a restored section of the **city walls**, beyond which is the **Kieselstein Castle** (Grad Kieselstein), formerly a fifteenth-century stronghold, later a manor house and now home to several cultural organizations – it's currently undergoing extensive restoration work. Continuing along the street, past a series of decaying buildings, you'll eventually end up back at Maistrov trg.

Eating and drinking

The best of a largely disappointing bunch of **restaurants** is *Pr' Matičku*, albeit inconveniently situated in a residential area 1km northeast of town at Jezerska cesta 41; it's in a building aping a hunter's lodge, and the menu features a good selection of game dishes (such as medallions of bear, deer and pheasant), alongside the more prosaic pizzas and salads. Of those places in the old town, *Kot*, tucked away in the eastern corner of Maistrov trg, is the most agreeable, serving up very reasonably priced home specials; and *Stari Mayr*, down by the parish church, which, though it may not look like much, has good Slovene food, including cheap daily set menus. Note that all these restaurants close on Sundays.

Kranj's **nightlife** is similarly restrained, though the loud and lively *Klub Bar*, at Slovenski trg 7, features DJ nights at weekends. Otherwise, the area in and around Maistrov trg has a few watering holes, the best being the classy and comfortable *Stara Pošta*, up on the fourth floor of the old post office building and sporting a groovy semicircular terrace bar that overlooks the square.

For coffee, there's the appealing *Cukrarna*, a funky, designer-furnished café at Tavčarjeva ulica 9, with an open terrace offering fine views over the Kokra River; while *Carniola*, at Gregorčičeva 2, is especially good for ice creams.

Brdo Castle

Four kilometres northeast of Kranj, near the village of **Predoslje**, is **Brdo Castle** (Grad Brdo), Slovenia's most elite presidential residence. Surrounded by 11km of fencing, the estate is no longer reserved exclusively for visits by high-ranking politicians and statesmen – among others, its more distinguished guests have included George W. Bush, Vladimir Putin, and Queen Elizabeth II – and now anyone can nose around the castle's stately rooms (groups only), ramble through the expansive parklands, or even partake in some sporting activities.

As early as 1446, a manor house – under the proprietary of the noble Egkh family (Egkh is German for "brdo" which in English means "hillock") – existed close to, or on the site of, the present castle, though it didn't assume its present form until the sixteenth century. In the mid-eighteenth century, ownership was transferred to the munificent Zois family, who remained in custody of the estate until 1929, after which time it was owned for a short period by the Karadjordjevič Yugoslav royal family. At the end of World War II the estate was nationalized and became one of Tito's many summer retreats – he was particularly enamoured with the place as it afforded him ample opportunity to indulge in his favoured activity of hunting. During this period security was such that a soldier was positioned every 100m, whether the great man was in residence or not. In 1961 Tito issued a decree declaring the estate to the Republic of Slovenia, though this hasn't stopped various members of the Karadjordjevič clan from recently trying to reclaim the property; unsurprisingly, the Slovene authorities have rejected this out of hand.

Even if you don't visit the castle itself (€8) – essentially a brief tour around a handful of rooms, including the magnificent dining room and Tito's trophy room – the grounds (€2.50) are most definitely worth the short trip from Kranj. Furthermore, you can participate in some horseriding (€20 for a 45min lesson; €22 for a 2hr jaunt around the estate) or fishing (€85 per day).Visits to the castle must be booked several days in advance, as must bookings to the sumptuous *Zois* **restaurant** – the catch being that only groups (ten or more) are admitted to both. If you require **information** regarding any aspect of visiting the estate, contact the reception desk at the *Hotel Kokra*, at the park entrance (℡04/260-1000, ⊛www.brdo.com; ❾); this smooth and expensive place is almost entirely geared up for conference guests and business groups flying into nearby Brnik airport. Buses #5 and #6 run daily from the bus station in Kranj to the estate every forty minutes or so.

Šmarjetna Gora and Sv Jošt

From Kranj's western suburb of Stražišče, several paths wend their way up to **Šmarjetna Gora** (St Margaret's Hill), a popular forty-minute walk also accessible by car. At the summit is **St Margaret's Church** (Cerkev Sv Marjete), originally dating from 1342, but heavily renovated in 1989; though there's little to see inside, if you want to have a look the key can be obtained from the *Hotel Bellevue* (℡04/270-0000, ⊛www.bellevue.si; ❻), across the car park; this lovely place possesses large, designer-furnished rooms, some with water beds and all with a balcony, plus a good **restaurant** with a pleasant outdoor terrace. There are marvellous views of Kranj, the Alps, and west across to **Sv Jošt**, a higher peak at 847m, and reachable from Stražišče – it's around a two-hour hike from Pot na Jošt. At the summit is the Baroque **Church of St Jošt** (Cerkev Sv Joštu), built between 1735 and 1740 on the site of a former Gothic church. Snacks and drinks are available from the hut a few paces away (closed Mon).

Tržič

From Kranj, hourly buses make the twenty-minute trip north to **TRŽIČ**, a small, somnolent market town holding a handful of satisfying museums and just a stone's throw away from a delightful gorge. Although the town has a strong tradition in a number of trades and crafts dating back to the Middle Ages, it was shoemaking that put Tržič on the map, an industry which forms the centrepiece of the **Tržič Museum**, located in the upper reaches of town at Muzejska 11 (Tržiški Muzej; July & Aug Tues–Sun 9am–5pm; Sept–June Mon–Fri 9am–3pm, Wed till 5pm; €2). At the end of the nineteenth century, almost every second house in town accommodated a shoemakers' workshop, though the trade slowly became more industrialized, culminating in the Peko factory – once, one of the most modern footwear factories in Europe, but now a dying industry employing around just two hundred people. Other important town crafts represented in the museum include tanners, wheelwrights, dyers and charcoal-burners.

One hundred and fifty metres south of the Tržič Museum, housed in the former Peko factory building at Koroška 9, is the entertaining **Homogea Museum** (July & Aug Tues–Sun 9am–1pm; rest of year by appointment, contact the tourist office; €2). Its permanent exhibition, entitled "Mammoth Hunters", traces the evolution of man and his environment from four million years ago to the end of the early Stone Age in the form of fossil remains, archeological finds and life-size models. Two hundred metres southeast of the museum at Kurnikova pot 2 – walk south to the church, then along Partizanska ulica and across the bridge – is the **Kurnik House** (Kurnikova hiša; Mon–Fri 11am–noon; other times by appointment, contact the tourist office; €2), a neatly preserved eighteenth-century Gorenjska peasant house named after its original owner, Vojteh Kurnik, who was born here in 1826. Although a wheel-wright by profession, Kurnik's true passion was poetry, and in the memorial room dedicated to him, you can see a handful of wood shavings on which he wrote verses while working.

A forty-five-minute walk northeast of Tržič, beyond the tiny settlement of **Čadovlje**, is the fabulous **Dovžan Gorge** (Dovžanova soteska), a protected natural monument owing to its rich deposits of Palaeozoic fossils. Its most distinguishing features are the pyramidal limestone columns on the eastern slopes, and Borova Peč (Pine's bluff) on the western side, though the thrashing Tržiška Bistrica River, bisecting the gorge's steeply pitched sides, is no less impressive. At the gorge entrance you'll pass through a remarkable road tunnel, built at the end of the nineteenth century by Julij Born.

There are no trains to Tržič, but the **bus station** is handily located south of town on Cankarjeva Cesta, from where it's a couple of minutes' walk north to the **tourist office** at Trg svobode 18 (June–Aug Mon–Fri 8am–7pm, Sat 9am–2pm; Sept–May Mon–Fri 9am–5pm; ☏04/597-1536, ⓦwww.trzic.si). There's nowhere to sleep in town but the tourist office can book **accommodation** on local tourist farms (❷). The only place of note to **eat** here is the *Pizzeria Pod Gradom*, just up from the Homogea Museum at Koroška 26 (closed Mon), while *Café Špela*, through the passageway next to the tourist office, is the place to head to for a coffee.

Radovljica and around

The initial urge for most travellers on reaching **RADOVLJICA**, a likeable little town 21km north of Kranj, is to push straight on to Bled. This is a pity, as it boasts a beautiful square stuffed with some superb Gothic and Renaissance architecture, and one of Slovenia's most surprisingly engaging museums. Built on a 75-metre-high outcrop above the River Sava, the town came into its golden period during the early Middle Ages when feudal lords, most impor-tantly the Ortenburgs, settled here, building their vast estates. Although Radovljica suffered a lengthy period of stagnation in the eighteenth and nineteenth centuries, the subsequent development of both the highway and railway kick-started the town back into life, and today, despite a population of little more than six thousand, it's a significant administrative and educational centre. With buses every thirty minutes from Bled, just 6km north, it makes for a simple and satisfying half-day trip.

For two weeks in mid-August Radovljica stages the **Festival Radovljica** (ⓦwww.festival-radovljica.si), one of Europe's foremost festivals of ancient classical music, featuring an international crop of artists – tickets (€10–15) can be bought online or from the tourist office.

Arrival, information and accommodation

The **bus station** is smack bang in the centre of town on Kranjska cesta, and the **train station** a couple of minutes south of the centre on Cesta svobode – from here head up Kolodvorska ulica, at the top of which is the **tourist office** (June–Sept Mon–Fri 9am–7pm, Oct–May till 6pm, Sat 9am–1pm; ☏04/531-5300).

With Bled so close you'll probably not need to stay over, but if you do the wonderful ⚒ *Pension Lectar*, Linhartov trg 2 (☏04/537-4800, ⓦwww.lectar .com; ❻), has eight homely rooms, each containing folksy, hand-painted furniture – gingerbread making has been an ongoing activity in the house for over 250 years, hence the gingerbread signs outside each room represent various trades and crafts. Alternatively there's the restful *Sport Penzion Manca*, 1.5km north of the centre at Gradnikova cesta 2 (☎04/531-4051, ⓦwww.manca-sp .si; ⓪), which also has a pool and tennis court; to get here, head north along Gorenjska cesta (direction Bled), turn right at the traffic lights and walk to the end of Ulica Staneta šagarja, which joins up with Gradnikova cesta. There's a small **campsite** just south of the *Manca* at Obla gorica (☎04/531-5770; June to mid-Sept). Use of the adjoining, championship-standard swimming pool is free for campers.

The Town

Everything of interest in town is centred on quiet **Linhartov trg** (Linhart Square), the old medieval core framed by a raft of fine Gothic and Renaissance buildings. The square was named in honour of the Slovene dramatist-historian Anton Tomaž Linhart (1756–95), whose **birthplace** at no. 7 bears a commemorative plaque and bas-relief of people at work and play. Linhart was regarded as Slovenia's most important enlightener, a position reinforced following the publication (in German) in 1791 of his seminal works on the history of Slovenes; moreover, he was credited with writing the first Slovene plays – *Županova Micka* (Mayor's Maid Micka) in 1789, and *Matiček se ženi* (Matiček Gets Married) in 1790.

The Thurn Mansion and Beekeeping Museum

Continuing eastwards you'll pass several more exceptional buildings – notably the **Vidic House** (Vidičeva hiša) at no. 3 – now a splendid café and confectioners (see p.110) – before hitting the **Thurn Mansion** (Thurnov Grad), clearly recognizable by its thickly stuccoed facade and vast spread of coats of arms. Built by the Ortenburg counts in the early Middle Ages, the mansion underwent several reincarnations before it acquired its current Baroque appearance in the eighteenth century. Inside, a magnificent double stairway leads up to the first floor and the quite splendid **Beekeeping Museum** (Čebelarski Muzej; May–Oct Tues–Sun 10am–6pm; March–April & Nov–Dec Tues, Thurs, Fri 8am–3pm, Wed, Sat & Sun 10am–noon & 3–5pm; Jan & Feb Tues–Fri 8am–3pm; €3). Comprising a handful of slickly arranged rooms, the museum presents the development and tradition of Slovenian apiculture from the eighteenth century to the present day. It begins with a collection of hives and wax presses, and by acknowledging the debt owed to the pioneers of beekeeping, such as master apiarists Anton Janša (1734–73), who published the first treatise on beekeeping, and Michael Ambrošič (1846–1904), the first Slovene to trade in the indigenous Grey Carniolan bee. Next up, and the undoubted high point of the museum, is its collection of over two hundred **beehive panels** – wooden end panels painted with religious, satirical or humorous motifs and scenes – illustrated here in individually themed cabinets (deserters, bandits, religion and so on). Elsewhere, there is an exposition on the **biology** of the aforementioned Carniolan bee, including a live hive and a reconstructed **apiary**. The mansion also houses the **Linhart Memorial Room** (same times; €2.50), which keeps a few facsimiles of his works in addition to some costumes used in performances of his plays in Ljubljana and elsewhere.

Parish Church of St Peter and the Šiveč House

A few paces east of the mansion, in a pretty, irregularly shaped courtyard, stands the **Parish Church of St Peter** (Cerkev Sv Petra), another fine Gothic hall-church, modelled on the parish church in Kranj. The oldest part of the church,

A nation of beekeepers

Beekeeping is one of Slovenia's oldest and most celebrated traditions, originating during the sixteenth century when honey was the principal sweetening agent available and wax an indispensable material for making candles. Bees, in particular the Grey Carniolan – affectionately known as the "Grizzly" owing to the lining of bright grey hair along its abdomen – have thrived in Slovenia for centuries, attracted to the rich forage in the country's abundant fields and forests. At the tail end of the nineteenth century **bee trading** became a hugely lucrative business, with the export of bees and their products of honey, wax and royal jelly to numerous European countries; today, the country's seven thousand beekeepers produce around two thousand tonnes of honey annually, just about sufficient for domestic requirements.

Bees were traditionally kept in wooden, oblong **hives** called *kranjiči* (Carniolans), neatly stacked together in rows which could be mounted onto carts and transported; the hives were particularly well known for their painted **front panels** (*panjske končnice*), a Slovenian folk art which emerged during the mid-eighteenth century, reaching its acme a century later. Panels were illustrated with colourfully crafted motifs; older motifs typically portrayed biblical or historical happenings, while later paintings depicted moral or satirical, and occasionally profane, images, usually pertaining to peasant life. Many of these were deliciously humorous – such as the local gossip having her tongue sharpened on a grindstone by villagers, or the hunter being pursued by a gun-toting bear – many other panels feature Job, the patron of beekeepers. Panels had practical functions, too, their bright colours supposedly making orientation easier for bees, as well as enabling the beekeeper to distinguish between his many swarms.

the presbytery, dates from the fifteenth century, while the church's Romanesque nave was replaced with its present, late-Gothic one in 1495. The Baroque high altar, from 1713, incorporates beautiful sculptural decoration by Angelo Pozzo, as does the white marble altar of St Mary, its sculptures completed by local stonemason Janez Vurnik. Next to the church is the **Priest's House**, assimilated within a neat, recently renovated, late-Gothic arched courtyard (if the church is closed you can obtain the key from here).

The most outstanding building on the square is the muralled **Šiveč House** (Šivčeva hiša) at no. 22, an exceptional example of a Gothic-Renaissance house, and especially noteworthy for its vaulted ground-floor hall and first-floor wood-panelled drawing room – the latter was once the living quarters of a Radovljica burgher family but is now used for weddings. The building also hosts an **art gallery** with rotating exhibitions (daily 10am–1pm & 4–8pm; €2). Leaving town en route to Bled, keep an eye out for the former **Savings Bank Building**, on your right at Gorenjska 17, an Art Nouveau edifice notable for its Secessionist-style mosaic of a flowering tree surrounding the entrance.

Eating and drinking

The town is blessed with a trio of first-rate **restaurants**: located within the pension of the same name, *Gostilna Lectar* – which has functioned as a restaurant for some two hundred years – offers an upscale take on traditional Slovenian meat dishes, as well as buckwheat, mushrooms and dumplings for vegetarians, while *Gostilna Avguštin*, at no. 15, serves cheaper standards as well as a more discerning menu of beef, lamb and fish; the seating towards the rear of the restaurant is more comfortable, as is the lovely garden terrace with marvellous views across to Jelovica. A few paces west of Linhartov trg at Gorenjska cesta 9, the homely, low-key *Gostilna Kunstelj* offers superbly prepared Slovene-oriented food, plus some top-notch wines too (closed Thurs). For **coffee** and all things sweet pop into the *Vidic House*, at no. 3, and if you want to buy some Slovenian wine, head to *Vinoteka Sodček* at Linhartov trg 8 (Mon–Fri 9am–9pm, Sat 8am–9pm).

Kropa

Settled in a narrow valley below the Jelovica plateau, and flanked by precipitously slanting hills, **KROPA**, 10km southwest of Radovljica, is the place to aim for if you've only time for one excursion. This comely single-street village is renowned for its iron-mining and forging industries, which reached their peak here during the early to mid-nineteenth century, and whose history is relayed in the **Iron Forging Museum**, part of the **Klinar House** – owned by the eponymous iron baron – at no. 10 (Kovaški Muzej; May–Oct Tues–Sun 10am–6pm; March–April & Nov–Dec Tues, Thurs, Fri 8am–3pm, Wed, Sat & Sun 10am–noon & 3–5pm; Jan & Feb Tues–Fri 8am–3pm; €3). As impressive as the assemblage of models, bellows and spikes is (there are, incredibly, over one hundred varieties of spike), it's the work of master forger Joža Bertoncelj (1901–76) which trumps all else here; already forging nails at the age of 11, Bertoncelj soon graduated to the village's Plamen factory before settling on a career as an artistic forger, resulting in a quite marvellous collection of wrought-iron gratings, chandeliers and sepulchral monuments. The second floor illustrates the economic and social conditions under which a blacksmith lived and worked; typically, the smiths and their families would squeeze into the attic, while the first floor was given over to the owner of the foundry. Judging by the salon and its coffered ceiling in the Klinar house, it's possible to appreciate just how wealthy some of these owners were.

A few paces north of the museum, at no. 7a, is the **UKO workshop** (Umetnokovaška Obrt; July & Aug Mon–Fri 7am–6pm, Sat 9am–noon; Sept–June Mon–Fri 7am–noon, Sat 9am–noon; ⓦ www.uko.si), a decorative ironwork company set up in 1956 in order to preserve the tradition of manual forging; you can view the masters at work here and buy ironwork products from the neighbouring shop. Heading south towards **Plac**, the very small main square, have a look at the **partisan monument**, comprising iron figures made at the aforementioned workshop, before crossing the **Kroparica**, a rapid, thrashing mountain stream that once propelled over fifty water wheels for the bellows and sledgehammers of the foundries, most of which were decommissioned after World War I. A short way south of the bridge is the **Vice Forge** (Vigenjc), the only preserved and operative workshop in Kropa; to view a (free) demonstration, contact the Iron Forging Museum a day or two in advance (☎04/533-7200). Just north of the forge, up the slope, is the Gothic **Parish Church of St Leonard** (Cerkev Sv Lenarta), whose cemetery contains some beautifully crafted iron headstones, including the grave of Bertoncelj; there are some lovely views of the village from the terrace. One and a half kilometres south of the village, up on the road to Železniki, stands a fourteenth-century **smelting furnace**, discovered as recently as 1953 when the mountain road to Jamnik was built. Nicknamed the "wolf", it could produce 200kg of iron in one day.

The village has two very welcoming **restaurants**: fifty metres south of Plac at Kropa 30, is the cosy *Pri Kovač* (closed Mon), which knocks up some superb local specialities such as Blacksmith's Plate (an assortment of meats) and sour milk and bean soup – they have some excellent wines too; while at the extreme northern end of the village, at Kropa 2, is the *Gostilna Pri Jarmu* pizzeria (closed Wed & Thurs). The main **bus stop** is near the post office, 200m south of the *Pri Jarmu*.

Brezje

A cluster of souvenir stalls, snack bars and an enormous car park (€2) welcome you to the small village of **BREZJE**, setting for Slovenia's most important place of pilgrimage, the **Basilica of the Virgin** (Marija pomagaj). Attracting some 300,000 visitors each year, the church began life in 1800 as a chapel, built as an extension to the fifteenth-century **St Vitus' Church**. It first became a site of prayer during Napoleon's occupation of northern Slovenia at the beginning of the nineteenth century, but it wasn't until the French departed that rumours of miracles occurring at Brezje began to spread, fuelling the arrival of tens of thousands of pilgrims from all over Europe. So great was the influx that, in 1900, it was necessary to construct a larger church, the results of which you see today. Around the same time, the Franciscans pitched up and proceeded to build an adjoining **monastery** and have remained the guardians of the church ever since.

Save for Janez Vurnik's stunning **high altar** – adorned with smoothly sculpted cherubs and instrument-playing angels – the interior is actually rather plain; still, this doesn't bother the majority of visitors, most of whom come here to pray at the **altar** of the Blessed Virgin of Help. This much reworked altar – in the fourth chapel on the right – contains the church's most renowned piece of work, Leopold Layer's painting *Mary Help*, framed by a dazzling gold mount designed by Tone Bitenc in 1977. There's also a contribution from Ivan Grohar, who completed the paintings in the third altars on the left and right. In the niche above the southern door is a statue by Boris Kalin, which previously stood at the nearby Otoče train station, and just across the way is a statue of Pope John Paul II, built to commemorate his visit here in 1996.

The easiest way to get to Brezje is by bus from Bled (Mon–Fri 7.20am, 9.20am, 3.20pm & 5.20pm) to the small village of Črnivec, from where it's a ten-minute walk to the village – four buses also make the return trip (at 8.50am, 10.50am, 12.50pm & 4.55pm).

Begunje

In the tidy little village of **BEGUNJE**, 5km north of Radovljica, thousands of people – including many women and children – were detained, beaten and executed during the German occupation of Gorenjska (1941–45). During World War II the village's seventeenth-century **Katzenstein Castle** was used as a Gestapo prison; the bare statistics reveal that 849 prisoners were either executed or died here, while a further five thousand were sent away to concentration camps in Austria, Germany and Poland. This grim episode in Slovenian history is vividly documented in the moving **Museum of Hostages** (Muzej talcev; July & Aug Tues–Sun 1–6pm; May–June & Sept–Oct Tues–Fri 9am–1pm, Sat & Sun 1–6pm; March–April & Nov–Dec Wed & Sat 9am–1pm, Sun 1–5pm; €2), housed in a wing of the castle, 200m north of the main bus stop.

Ten preserved cells illustrate the brutal experiences of the hostages confined here for months and years on end, most harrowingly in the form of farewell messages, which the Germans tried unsuccessfully to erase, etched into the walls as they awaited impending death. In one cell there are stakes onto which prisoners were tied before being shot, and in another, objects from Dachau, such as books belonging to the murdered and keys of the guards, as well as more sobering items such as a gas sprinkler and a branch from which prisoners were hung. In the park just across from the museum is a **graveyard** where many of those executed are buried, while just up beyond the graveyard stands a small **chapel**, unmistakably the work of Jože Plečnik (see box, p.60).

Two kilometres north of the village lie the impressive ruins of **Kamen Castle** (Grad Kamen; dawn to dusk – if you want a guide call ☎041/368-940; free), established by the Ortenburg counts in the twelfth century as a means of defending the Radovljica Plain. Its most extensive period of development, however, came in the fifteenth century, when the still remarkably well-preserved tower and residential palace were constructed. In the early eighteenth century, its function of protecting trade routes, warding off Turkish invaders and quelling peasant revolts was rendered obsolete and it was abandoned. The castle remained in a state of decay until 1959, when work finally began to restore it.

Directly across the road from the main **bus stop** in the centre of the village, the **Avsenik Gallery** (Tues–Sun: summer 10am–6pm; winter 11am–5pm; €2) contains an arsenal of awards dedicated to local folk musician and celebrity Slavko Avsenik – a bigger star in Germany than in Slovenia, apparently; you can also get some basic tourist information here. If you'd like to eat in Begunje, head to the reasonable *Avsenik* **restaurant** next to the gallery, though it's all rather hammed up for the tourists (closed Mon). There are hourly **buses** to and from Bled and Radovljica.

Bled and around

One thousand years old in 2004, **BLED** is by far the country's most popular destination, thanks to its placid fairytale lake and island, dramatically sited castle and snow-tipped mountains. The town itself, which is most densely concentrated to the east of the lake, is thoroughly unspectacular, and there's nothing specific to see. In contrast, the lake – created some 14,000 years ago when water flooded the depression left by a receding glacier – is a natural playground, deluged with skaters during the winter and bristling with row-boats, gondolas and swimmers during the spring and summer months.

The town dates from 1004, when the German emperor Henry II bestowed the castle, and the land between the two Sava rivers, to the bishops of Brixen – who would subsequently rule for the next eight hundred years. The first visitors to Bled were medieval pilgrims from Carniola and Carinthia, who came to pray at the island church, although mass tourism didn't take long to find its feet. This was in large part thanks to Arnold Rikli, a Swiss-born physician who opened a bathing resort and lodgings at Bled in 1855. Between the two World Wars the resort became a popular hideaway for politicians and royalty, with both the Yugoslav royal family, and later, Tito, spending much time here during the summer; even today, Bled is the one place high-ranking officials and diplomats are ushered to when visiting Slovenia.

Despite its status as the country's star turn, Bled rarely feels overwhelmed – indeed it can even feel a little bleak outside summer and winter – but if you do fancy a change of pace and a bit of solitude, there are some terrific attractions close by, each of which can be comfortably accomplished within three to four hours; the hugely popular **Vintgar Gorge**, the lesser visited, but no less impressive **Pokljuka Plateau**, and the fascinating **Babji Zob Caves**. To the northwest, in the village of **Vrba**, you can visit the birthplace of France Prešeren, Slovenia's greatest poet. Furthermore, it's a good place to base yourself for hikes into the eastern tranche of the Julian Alps.

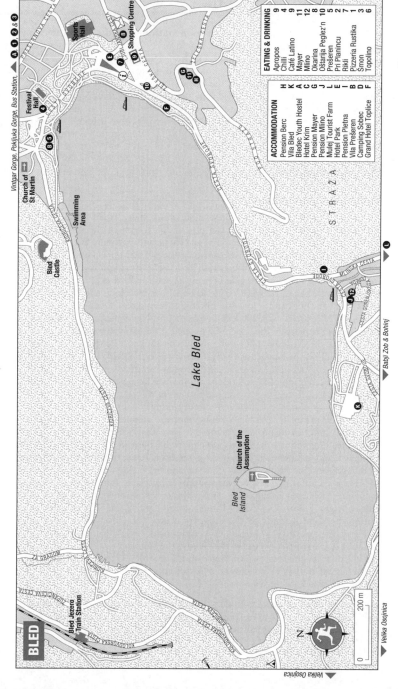

www.roughguides.com

113

BLED

Lake Bled

Bled Island

Church of the Assumption

Bled Castle

Church of St Martin

Swimming Area

Festival Hall

Sports Hall

Shopping Centre

STRAŽA

Bled Jezero Train Station

N

0   200 m

Lesce, C, D & 6

Vintgar Gorge, Pokljuka Gorge, Bus Station,

C, 1, 2 & 3

Velika Osojnica

Velika Osojnica

Babji Zob & Bohinj

ACCOMMODATION

Pension Berc	H
Vila Bled	K
Bledec Youth Hostel	A
Hotel Krim	C
Pension Mayer	G
Pension Mlino	J
Mulej Tourist Farm	L
Hotel Park	E
Pension Pletna	I
Vila Prešeren	B
Camping Sobec	D
Grand Hotel Toplice	F

EATING & DRINKING

Apropos	9
Chilli	4
Café Latino	9
Mayer	11
Mlino	12
Okarina	8
Oštarija Peglez'n	10
Prešeren	5
Pri Planincu	2
Rikli	7
Pizzeria Rustika	1
Šmon	3
Topolino	6

Arrival and information

Bled's **bus station** is five minutes northeast of the lake at the junction of Cesta svobode and Grajska cesta. The nearest **train station** to Bled is Bled Jezero (on the Jesenice–Nova Gorica line), on Kolodvorska cesta, a ten-minute walk northwest of the lake. However, if coming from Ljubljana, you'll alight at Bled-Lesce, 4km southeast of Bled and connected to the town by half-hourly buses.

The **tourist office** is located on the lakefront opposite the *Hotel Park* at Cesta Svobode 10 (July & Aug Mon–Sat 8am–9pm, Sun 9am–5pm; March–June & Sept–Oct Mon–Sat 8am–7pm, Sun 10am–5pm; Nov–Feb Mon–Sat 8am–6pm, Sun 8am–1pm; ℡04/574-1122, Ⓦwww.bled.si); they have **internet** access as well as **bikes** for rent (€6 for 5hr, €11 per day). If you require information on any aspect of Triglav National Park, contact the park's information office at Ljubljanska cesta 27 (Tues–Sun 10am–6pm; ℡04/578-0200, Ⓦwww.tnp.si). The **post office** is at Ljubljanska 14 (Mon–Fri 8am–7pm, Sat 8am–noon).

Accommodation

As befits Slovenia's premier tourist destination, there is an abundance of **accommodation** in town, from top-class hotels to run-of-the-mill package-type places and homely pensions. The excellent and well-run **Bledec Youth Hostel**, a couple of minutes' walk north of the bus station at Grajska cesta 17 (℡04/574-5250, Ⓦwww.youth-hostel-bledec.si), has spotless multi-bedded rooms (sleeping between three and seven), all with bathrooms (€20 per person including breakfast) – reservations are essential between June and August; there are laundry facilities and it also has a pretty good restaurant.

Camping Bled (℡04/575-2000, Ⓦwww.camping-bled.com; April to mid-Oct) – the only **campsite** in Bled itself – is located at the far western end of the lake in a lovely pine-sheltered valley (take any bus heading towards Bohinj and alight at the beginning of Kidričeva cesta). *Camping Šobec* (℡04/535-3700, Ⓦwww.sobec.si; mid-April to Sept) – Slovenia's largest campsite – is 2km from Bled-Lesce in the direction of Bled. The site also has ten bungalows, with heating and showers, and each sleeping two to six people (❼–❽). With no public transport to the site it's a rather convoluted twenty-minute walk: exiting Bled-Lesce station, walk north towards the crossing, take the second left down Finžgareva ulica for 100m, left again and continue behind the industrial zone for 400m before heading down a gravel track to the right. Both sites are extremely well equipped and maintained, each with a restaurant, supermarket and sporting facilities; *Šobec* also has its own lake for swimming.

There is plentiful **private accommodation**, available from several agencies, including Mtours at Ljubljanska cesta 7 (June–Sept Mon–Sat 8am–8pm, Sun 8am–noon & 4–8pm; Oct–May Mon–Sat 10am–4pm; ℡04/575-3300, Ⓦwww.mtours.net) and Kompas, in the shopping centre at Ljubljanska cesta 4 (same times as Mtours; ℡04/574-1515, Ⓦwww.kompas-bled.si). Furthermore, there are quite a few **tourist farms** in the vicinity, the largest concentration of which are located in the villages of **Selo** and **Zgornje Gorje**, southwest and northwest of the lake respectively; you can approach farms directly or book through the above agencies.

Pension Berc Želeška cesta 15 ℡04/574-1838, Ⓦwww.berc-sp.si. Lovely, family-run place in a renovated nineteenth-century farmhouse, with spacious, cosily furnished rooms – the most restful, and best value, option in town. In much the same vein, they've also got some splendid, and only marginally more expensive, rooms in their new, hotel-style building opposite. ❺–❻

Vila Bled Cesta svobode 26 ℡04/575-3710, Ⓦwww.vila-bled.com. Set in its own extensive grounds on the lake's western shore, this is Bled's most characterful establishment. Rebuilt as yet another country retreat for Tito in 1947, the extraordinary socialist-era rooms have remained largely untouched since the president entertained world leaders here. The hotel also has a spa facility, its own private beach and boats. ⑨

Hotel Krim Ljubljanska cesta 7 ☏04/579-7000, ⓦwww.hotel-krim.si. Firmly in the category of package-tourist hotel, the modestly sized rooms are neat and bright, if functional, and it's one of the cheaper hotel options in town. ⑦

Pension Mayer Želeška cesta 7 ☏04/576-5740, ⓦwww.mayer-sp.si. Located next to the *Berc*, and in a similar style, this fine nineteenth-century building has stylish, parquet-floored rooms with large comfy beds and spankingly clean bathrooms. Bikes for rent too. Good value. ⑥

Pension Mlino Cesta svobode 45 ☏04/574-1404, ⓦwww.mlino.si. A short walk west of *Vila Bled*, this popular and fairly priced lakeside place has a convivial atmosphere despite the rooms being somewhat dated and a little cramped. Reservations advised. ⑥

Mulej Tourist Farm Selo pri Bledu 42a ☏04/574-4617, ⓦwww.mulej-bled.si. 1km south of the lake in the village of Selo, this large, friendly and popular tourist farm has eight simply furnished but very comfortable en-suite rooms, as well as four apartments. There's superb home cooking, while the farm animals and pets will go down a treat with kids; free bike rental too. ⑤

Hotel Park Cesta svobode 15 ☏04/579-3000, ⓦwww.hotel-park-bled.com. This horrible construction blotting the southeastern corner of the lake is Bled's largest hotel; the rooms are smart though somewhat uniform, with those facing the lake having a/c. ⑧–⑨

Pension Pletna Cesta svobode 37 ☏04/574-3702, ✉pletna@bled.net. Despite all five rooms in this good value pension, just 100m east of the *Mlino*, facing the noisy main road, each has a balcony with superb lake views. Bikes, rowing boats and kayaks for rent too. ⑤

🎿 **Vila Prešeren** Veslaška promenada 14 ☏04/575-2510, ⓦwww.vilapreseren.si. Graceful nineteenth-century villa concealing six immaculate and supremely stylish rooms, decorated in cool pinks, greys and blacks, with wrought-iron furnishings, elegant bedside lamps, wood-framed mirrors, and a host of other neat touches. Wonderful terrace café and restaurant to boot (see p.118). ⑧

Grand Hotel Toplice Cesta svobode 12 ☏04/579-1000, ⓦwww.hotel-toplice.si. Bled's most opulent hotel has magnificently appointed rooms, with antique furniture, large, handsome beds and gold-plated trimmings; the more expensive lakeside rooms have a/c and bed pumps, for that little extra firmness. Houses a thermal pool, jacuzzi and Finnish and Turkish saunas, all free to guests. ⑨

Lake Bled

From a visitor's perspective, Bled is essentially the **lake** and all that happens on or around it. The best way to get your bearings is to engage in a circular walk, beginning at the *Hotel Park* and working your way round clockwise, which should take no more than two and half hours. If you don't fancy walking around the lake, you can take the **tourist train**, a jump-on, jump-off vehicle that crawls around the lake clogging up the traffic; its starting point is the sports hall on the lake's east shore (April–Nov; €3 for a day-ticket). Alternatively you can take a ride on one of the **horse-drawn carriages** (*fijaker*), which are parked near the Festival Hall (a thirty-minute jaunt around the lake costs €30 for five people) – longer trips are available too.

Bled Castle

Perched high up on a craggy bluff on the north shore is **Bled Castle** (Blejski Grad; daily 8am–8pm, till 5pm in winter; €7), enclosed by a Romanesque wall and spotted with stout-looking parapets, towers and ramparts, just as a castle should be. Originally an eleventh-century fortification, the castle's present appearance dates from the seventeenth century (albeit with further renovations in the 1950s), and is characterized by a lower and upper courtyard. The outstanding feature of the neat upper courtyard is the lovely sixteenth-century **chapel**, decorated with frescoes from around 1700, and containing a fine painting of Henry II conferring the property of Bled on Bishop Albuin.

Adjacent to the chapel is the **museum**, a neat and well-presented affair, primarily featuring a collection of local archeological finds from the region, including Iron Age whorls and vessels, stone mortars and axes, bone harpoons and the like. From the castle terrace there are peerless views – and great photo opportunities – of the lake and island below.

Several paths (marked "Grad") wind up to the castle, each a reasonably stiff fifteen-minute climb; one from behind the swimming area (Grajsko Kopališče) on Kidričeva Cesta, another from the youth hostel on Grajska cesta, and a third from Rikljeva ulica, near the **Parish Church of St Martin** (Cerkev Sv Martina), a neo-Gothic structure built in 1905 on the site of a previous Gothic church; it has sculptures by the ubiquitous Vurnik and frescoes by Slavko Pengov.

Bled Island

During the day, a continual relay of stretch gondolas (*pletnas*) glides back and forth across the water between the shore and **Bled Island** (Blejski Otok), a magically picturesque islet crowned by the exquisite **Church of the Assumption** (Cerkev Sv Marija Božja; daily 8am–dusk). Findings support the theory that there was a settlement here in prehistoric times, while further excavations have revealed the remains of a pre-Romanesque chapel, as well as a large Slavic cemetery dating from around 9 AD. The present Baroque church dates from 1698, though its most outstanding features are from the preceding Gothic church, namely the remarkably well-preserved **frescoes** on the north and south presbytery walls, depicting scenes from the life of the Virgin, and a wooden statue of the Virgin with Child. The porch on the west side of the church holds more Gothic fresco remains, discovered during the most recent excavations in 1965. The wishing bell, which keeps most visitors amused, was installed in 1534, though a larger bell hangs in the enormous free-standing belfry, itself a hybrid of Gothic and Baroque elements. As well as providing a home to the provost, the **Provost's House** next to the church also functioned as a guesthouse, as did the **hermitage**, the smaller building behind the church.

Predictably enough, a café and souvenir stall have been squeezed onto the island, not that you'll have much time to enjoy them if you come across on a *pletna*. They depart from three locations: down below the *Hotel Park*, near the *Vila Prešeren* (both 30min to the lake) and opposite *Pension Mlino* (15min), though the price is the same whichever location you leave from (€12 per person); departing only when they are full – which means you may have to sit idly for a bit while the *pletnar* solicits custom – you then have thirty minutes on the island to nose around before returning. The alternative is to make your own way across: **rowing boats** can be rented from several points at the western end of the lake (€10 per hour for a four-person boat); it may be harder going, but you won't feel rushed once on the island. Both the *pletnas* and rowing boats operate year-round, depending on the weather.

Eating and drinking

Bled can count on a number of superb and characterful **restaurants**, a few of which are located within some of the lake's better pensions. Conversely, Bled **nightlife** is fairly tame and you'll be hard pushed to avoid drinking in the same venues if you're here for any length of time. Bled's most enduring **café**, thanks to its prodigious selection of home-made pastries (notably the very creamy Bled speciality *Kremna Rezina*), is *Šmon* (The Bear), just up from the bus station at Grajski cesta 3. Rather dispiritingly, most of Bled's **bars** are scattered around the sprawling, incoherent shopping centre on Ljubljanska cesta; take your pick from

Activities in and around Bled

Although far more challenging hikes can be had in Triglav National Park (see box, p.122), there are some very enjoyable walks in the immediate vicinity of the lake. Velika Osojnica, a 756-metre-high peak at the southwestern corner of the lake, offers the stiffest walk but also the most superlative views; take either the path from Bled campsite (via Ojstrica), or from the main road, Kidričeva cesta (via Mala Osojnica) and allow three hours for a round-trip. A more gentle alternative is a walk up to Straža, a 638-metre-high hill southwest of the *Grand Hotel Toplice*; this is also Bled's very modest **ski slope**, suitable for beginners only. Between December and February a chairlift operates from Pod Stražo, the road above Cesta svobode, to the summit while, between April and September, the same hill becomes a 520-metre **sled run** (€6 for one run, €13 for three runs).

Although **swimming** is permitted at various points around the lake (Mlino, Velika Zaka and Mala Zaka, all at the western end), you're better off sticking to the designated, roped-off, area on the north shore underneath the castle, which also has a grassy beach (Grajsko Kopališče; daily mid-June to Sept 8am–7pm; €7 for a daily ticket, €5 after noon). During winter, the lake often freezes over, tempting skaters out onto the ice, though caution should be exercised if you decide to have a go yourself. Although not quite as romantic, there's an indoor rink at the sports centre (Športna Dvorana) just to the east of the *Hotel Park* (Oct–March Mon–Sat 9.30–11am & 4.30–6pm, Sun 4.30–6pm; €4, plus €3.50 for skate rental).

Licences for **fishing**, permitted on the lake between April and December, can be purchased from the tourist office (€25 per day). There is **horse riding** at the Hippodrome in Lesce (☎041/675-482), with a half-hour lesson, or a one-hour ride (either cross-country or around the track), costing around €20. Also in Lesce, the Alpine Flying Centre at Begunjska cesta 10 (☎04/532-0100, ⊛www.alc-lesce.si) offers **panoramic flights** around Bled for €75, and Bohinj for €135. Slovenia's premier **golf** course, the Bled Golf and Country Club (☎04/537-7711, ⊛www.golfbled.com), is 2km east of town on the Bled–Lesce road, and comprises the eighteen-hole King's course (€60), and the nine-hole Lake course (€40). **Bikes** (€5 for 2hr, €8 for half a day and €12 per day) can be rented from both the Mtours and Kompas agencies, and 3glav Adventures.

Humanfish (☎051/321-383, ⊛www.humanfish.com) offers an excellent programme of **hikes** in the Julian Alps and Karavanke mountains, including two-day trips to Triglav (€180), as well as a number of easy/moderate (Meadows of Bohinj, Debela Peč; €40) and difficult (Mojstrovka, Prisojnik; €70) day hikes; it also offers biking and tailor-made tours, as well as a comprehensive winter ski and snowboarding programme. Located in huts next door to each other opposite the *Hotel Lovec* at Ljubljanska 1, both Lifetrek (☎04/578-0662, ⊛www.lifetrek-slovenia.com) and 3glav Adventures (☎041/683-184, ⊛www.3glav-adventures.com), organize similar hikes, in addition to a number of **river-bound activities** on the Soča and Sava Rivers – principally rafting (€25), hydrospeed (€30), canyoning (€50) and kayaking (€45). Lifetrek also organizes winter sports, such as tobogganing (€40), ice climbing (€55) and snowshoeing (€40).

Apropos, a small cocktail bar and ice-cream parlour, or *Café Latino* just across the way, a slightly classier affair which is good for beer and wine. The best pub-style place is actually the cosy *Pri Planincu* (see restaurants). The town's principal **club** is *Club Stop*, an ear-bursting place down by the steps opposite the shopping centre at Cesta Svobode 15.

Restaurants

Chilli Cesta Svobode 9. Fun, contemporary establishment serving up a stack of colourful Mexican dishes, crisp salad platters (chilli, seafood, Greek), fresh fish (grilled trout, octopus, stuffed squid) and grilled meats. Its large wood-decked terrace is the ideal place for a beer or cocktail at sundown.

Mayer Želeška cesta. Refined and extremely well-regarded restaurant in the pension of the same name with a moderate to expensive menu featuring some good starters (buckwheat, fried cheese) and impressive mains, in particular game and trout. Closed Mon.

Mlino Cesta svobode 45. Atmospheric terrace restaurant in the *Mlino* pension, with a commendably adventurous menu featuring horse, shark cutlets and, more teasingly, ox testicles – it also has good veggie options. Also has an a/c indoor restaurant.

Okarina Ljubljanska cesta 8. Beautifully appointed restaurant which, in addition to its signature Tandoori dishes, has an exhaustive and enticing menu of seafood (Bouillabaisse fish stew, scorpion) and game (chamois ragout, roe deer), as well as a dozen or so imaginative vegetarian dishes (spinach pancakes, tofu and vegetables, soya steak). Expensive.

Oštarija Peglez'n Cesta Svobode 19. Warm, homely restaurant whose seafood menu is the best in town, with smoked tuna, shark chops and cuttlefish risotto the pick of the wet stuff on offer. The sunny yellow and blue interior, with its wicker blinds and walls happily cluttered with ceramics and household implements looks great.

Prešeren Kidričeva cesta 1. Take your pick from the sumptuously elegant inside restaurant or the beautiful lakeside terrace to indulge in fresh fish from the Adriatic or some of the splendid house delicacies, such as mushrooms and ostrich – a fairly expensive, but hugely enjoyable, dining experience.

Pri Planincu Grajska cesta 8. Hugely popular and frenetic Alpine inn-style place, serving hearty meat-heavy dishes, notably the juicy Serbian specialities *pljeskavica* (oversized hamburger) and *čevapčiči* (rissoles of spiced minced meat); a great spot for a beer too.

Rikli Cesta svobode 15. Positioned alongside the *Hotel Park*, this seductive-looking place offers a top-class à la carte menu, with heavy emphasis on fish. More modestly, their bright little pizzeria next door serves pasta, noodles and gnocchi.

Pizzeria Rustika Riklijeva 13. As the name suggests, plenty of rustic trappings, such as dark wooden tables and thick bench seating, in this simple but warm and pleasant pizzeria a short walk down from the youth hostel.

Topolino Ljubljanska cesta 26. This low-key, slow-food restaurant is Bled's most sophisticated outfit, gorgeously decorated throughout, with food and wine of the highest quality and prices to match. Closed Tues.

Entertainment and festivals

Bled's big event is **Bled Days** (Blejski Dnevi) on the fourth weekend of July, when three days of fairs and concerts take place along the promenade at the eastern end of the lake; the event culminates in the lighting of thousands of candles on the lake – a memorable sight – and fireworks. Otherwise, there are two prestigious musical events; the **International Music Festival** (Ⓦwww.festivalbled.com), at the beginning of July, is a two-week run of classical concerts staged at various venues around the lake, but principally the Festival Hall and

---

Competitive rowing on Lake Bled

When the rowers Iztok Čop and Luka Špik claimed Slovenia's first-ever **Olympic Gold medal** at the Sydney 2000 games (Čop also bagged Slovenia's first-ever Olympic medal (bronze) at the 1992 Barcelona games), Slovenian sport, and particularly rowing, at last gained the recognition it had craved since independence in 1991. Rowing has a long and distinguished history in Slovenia, with many of its rowers having formed the core of ex-Yugoslav teams before each republic went their separate ways. Since then rowing has been a byword for Slovenian sporting achievement; its most successful rowers having been trained at the **Bled Rowing Club**, formed in 1949 and based at the western end of the lake, at Mala Zaka.

The lake is hugely popular as a practice arena with both Slovenian and international rowers, while its standing as a top-class international venue is manifest in the staging of three World Rowing Championships, in 1966, 1979 and 1986, with another scheduled for 2011. Although several domestic regattas take place in Bled during spring and autumn, the best time to be here is in mid-June when the **Bled International Regatta** draws a world-class field.

St Martin's Church; and the **Okarina Ethno Festival**, featuring performances by an eclectic group of world musicians and taking place across the first three weekends of August.

Vintgar Gorge

The major attraction in Bled's immediate environs is the **Vintgar Gorge** (Soteska Vintgar; daily April–Oct 8am–7pm; €4), an impressive 1600-metre-long and 150-metre-high defile 4km north of town. The most enjoyable way to get here is to walk, an easy and pleasant stroll along country roads and through a handful of pretty villages: from the bus station join the main road, Prešernova ulica, and head north until you come to Partizanska cesta; continue north along here and after crossing the stream take the left fork (Cesta v Vintgar), continuing towards the village of **Podhom**, from where the gorge is signposted. If the walk is beyond you, there is a daily bus to (10am) and from (12.30pm) the gorge between June and September, leaving from the bus station.

The gorge was actually chanced upon by a local mayor and his cartographer colleague in 1891. So thrilled were they with their discovery that they set up a construction committee in order to seek ways of opening the gorge up to the public, an event that duly occurred two years later. It's since been accessible via a continuous chain of wooden gantries and bridges, suspended from the precipitous rock face, and running the entire length of the gorge to the **Šum Waterfall** (Slap šum) at its northern end; from here you can either retrace your steps and return the way you came, or take the path on the right, returning to Bled via the pilgrimage **Church of St Catherine** and the village of **Zasip**. It can get very damp in the gorge, and if it's been raining, very slippery, so you'd do well to bring some waterproofs and good walking boots. There's a decent *gostilna* near the car park.

Pokljuka Gorge

As an antidote to the hordes that pile up to the Vintgar Gorge, the **Pokljuka Gorge** (Pokljuška soteska), a magnificent fossilized ravine 7km west of Bled, is perfect for those seeking some solitude. Located on the northeastern margins of the **Pokljuka Plateau** – a thickly forested plain at the eastern extremes of the Julian Alps and a world-class venue for cross-country skiing – this dry and narrow trough-like ravine was hollowed out by the former course of the Ribščica River some ten thousand years ago, the retreating glaciers leaving behind the largest fossilized gorge in the country. It's characterized by peculiar dilations – known as *vrtci* (garden plots) – and a series of natural arches, although its most spectacular feature is the **Pokljuka Luknja** (Pokljuka Window), a fifteen-metre-high subterranean hall with three natural windows hollowed out of its ceiling. To get here take one of the regular buses from Bled to the village of **Krnica**, from where it's a two-kilometre walk (follow the signs) to the gorge entrance. If you have your own transport, it's possible to drive right to the entrance.

Babji Zob Caves

Completing this trio of natural wonders are the **Babji Zob Caves** (Jama Pod Babjim Zobom), near the village of **BOHINJSKA BELA**, 4km west of Bled. Located beneath **Babji Zob** (Hags Tooth), a formidable-looking, tooth-shaped pillar poised atop a 1128-metre peak, it couldn't be more different from your conventional cave visit – as with Postojna or Škocjan for example. The caves can only be visited on a guided tour, which entails a not inconsiderable one-hour hike up to the cave entrance; thereafter it's a further hour's trek through the complex, before the steep descent back down the hill (approximately three hours in total).

At just 300m long it's not an expansive cave system, but it does possess some unique features, not least several groupings of rarely seen helictites – contorted, sometimes horizontal, calcite deposits, which grow in random directions seemingly defying gravity. Their existence has long confounded experts and remains one of the most vexing speleological questions, though one theory suggests that their form is caused by airflow within the cave. Run by the Bled Caving Association, at Ljubljanska 1 (T031/457-509), **tours**, which cost €15, take place at 10am on Sundays in July and August; the meeting point is in front of the caves. For the visit, take some warm clothing, waterproofs and a pair of older shoes, as it can get quite muddy.

About 3km on from Bohinjska Bela, on the Bohinj road and beside the Bohinjska Sava river (just outside the village of Obrne), the *Reka Hiša* (T04/576-0340, W www.actionslovenia.com) is a delightfully welcoming guest house, offering simple but cosily furnished rooms (●; price includes evening meal). The owners also organize a range of activities (including kayaking and, in winter, skiing) and are able to arrange transfers from Bled or Bohinj; otherwise, take any Bohinj-bound bus and alight by the bridge after the second exit for Bohinjska Bela, from where it's a ten-minute walk.

Vrba

VRBA, a tiny village 4km northeast of Bled just off the main road to Kranjska Gora, is famed as the birthplace of France Prešeren, Slovenia's most celebrated poet. Prešeren was sufficiently enamoured with his home village to write:

Vrba, happy village, my old home
My father's cottage stands there to this day
The lure of learning beckoned me away
Its serpent wiles enticing me to roam

The solid whitewashed **house** (Rojstna Hiša Prešerna hiša; Tues–Fri 9am–4pm, Sat & Sun 10am–5pm; €3), located on the right-hand side of the village as you enter (no. 2), was originally built in the sixteenth century, but partly destroyed by a village fire in 1856. It contains a few original items of furniture, including the poet's cradle, as well as translations of some of his work, but the house is actually more interesting as an architectural monument – most impressive is the traditional "Black Kitchen" (see p.129) preserved in its entirety. As interesting as the exhibition is, you'll learn more about the man and his work at the memorial house in Kranj (see p.103), where he lived and worked for the last few years of his life.

Just up behind the birthplace on a small grassy hill, the Gothic **Church of St Mark** (Cerkev Sv Marko) is worth a look for its sixteenth-century frescoes by the prolific Jernej of Loka – including Christ's Passion and traces of St George doing battle with the dragon – and murals by Friulian masters. The wooden ceiling dates from 1991 when the latest renovation took place. A five-minute walk to the western edge of the village brings you to a sturdy two-hundred-year-old linden tree encircled by sixteen large stones, one for each of the farmhouses that originally stood in the village – it was supposedly also the place where debates between the village representatives would take place. To get here take one of the hourly buses from Bled to Jesenice, which takes a rather convoluted route via Radovljica.

France Prešeren

One of Slovenia's greatest nineteenth-century heroes and indisputably the country's greatest romantic poet, **France Prešeren** did more to advance the cause of the Slovene national consciousness in the nineteenth century than just about any other figure. Born in Vrba in 1800, Prešeren was educated in Ribnica and Ljubljana, before obtaining his law degree in Vienna. Although a lawyer by profession, Prešeren's true vocation was poetry. Underpinned by themes of unrequited love, homeland, friendships and other existential laments, Prešeren's poems combined classical, Renaissance and Romantic elements with traditional Slovene folk customs, resulting in a body of work considered to be the apotheosis of nineteenth-century Slovene language and culture. His most recognized piece of work was the epic *Krst pri Savici* (*Baptism at the Savica*), which explores themes of Christianization in Slovenia, though only one volume of his work, *Poezije doktorja Franceta Prešerna* (*Poems of Doctor France Prešeren*), was published during his lifetime, in 1845.

Through his writing, the liberal-minded Prešeren – along with his peers, in particular his mentor Matija Čop – attempted to create an **independent Slovene culture** oriented towards classical Western traditions, while he also sought to stimulate national awareness among the emerging Slovene middle class. However, he frequently clashed with the government in Vienna over his anti-German sentiments, as well as the Catholic Church, which considered his work immoral.

Prešeren's **personal life** was deeply unhappy: he was a melancholy character, a drunkard and philanderer and had three children out of wedlock. He was particularly depressed by an unrequited love affair with Julija Primič, whom he first met at the Church of St John in Trnovo, Ljubljana, and by the untimely death of the aforementioned Matija Čop.

From 1846 until his death, from cirrhosis of the liver, on February 8, 1849, Prešeren spent the last three years of his life working in Kranj, the city in which he is also buried. His writing aside, Prešeren's legacy is very much alive in other forms – the public holiday on February 8 is celebrated as Prešeren Day (the Day of Slovene Culture), while the seventh stanza of *Zdravljica* (*A Toast*), set to music by composer Stanko Premrl, was adopted as the national anthem of the republic in 1991.

Bohinj and around

Some 20km long and 5km wide, **Bohinj** is the name given to the entire Sava Bohinjka basin southwest of Bled, a region of immense charm and beauty, embracing rugged valleys and mountains, alluring rustic idylls and, best of all, a magical **lake**.

Archeological finds have determined that Bohinj was settled in the late seventh century, a theory given further credence following the discovery of a handful of forges and foundries in the area. Indeed, for many centuries, the smelting of iron was the mainstay of the economy in the region, although eventually, as elsewhere in Gorenjska, competition from more sophisticated European foundries signalled an end to production. As a result, the natives turned to alpine dairy farming, and in particular the mass production of cheese, the quality of which was highly regarded throughout Central Europe. Although alpine farming is still practised by small pockets of the community, many more villagers are now becoming engaged in tourism as a means of subsistence.

Bohinj's two key settlements, **Bohinjska Bistrica** and **Ribčev Laz**, suffice for all things of a practical nature, including the main rail and bus connection points, and the tourist offices. By way of contrast, the group of villages northeast of the lake in the upper valley – **Stara Fužina**, **Studor** and **Srednja Vas** – are not only a restful antidote to the often crowded lakeside, but also boast some fabulous indigenous rural architecture. More excitingly, there are some wonderful excursions close at hand, such as the immensely popular **Savica Waterfall** and the beautiful **Mostnica Gorge** and **Voje Valley**, both a short way north of the aforementioned villages. Although a fair proportion of visitors come to Bohinj to partake in water-bound activities – on both the lake and the Sava Bohinjka River – many more come to trek the mountains, with the major southerly approach to Triglav via the stunning **Valley of the Triglav Lakes (Valley of the Seven Lakes)** starting here. Bohinj can also count on two spectacularly sited ski resorts, Kobla and Vogel.

Bohinjska Bistrica

Routinely given the cold shoulder by travellers keen to reach the star attraction a few kilometres further on, **BOHINJSKA BISTRICA** – 20km southwest of Bled – is Bohinj's main settlement. It is a rather nondescript place, though there's a modest aquapark, as well as a mildly diverting museum and a sprinkling of accommodation including one of Bohinj's two campsites. Furthermore, its **train station** is the closest to the mountains on this side of the Alps, while the **car-train** runs from here to Most na Soči further south (see box, p.125). Buses meet trains arriving at the station, which is ten minutes east of the centre, and link up to Ribčev Laz (see p.125), while the main **bus stop** is located a few paces north of the post office on Triglavska cesta. The **tourist office** is at Triglavska cesta 50 (mid-June to mid-Sept Mon–Fri 7am–8pm, Sat 9am–3pm, Sun 9am–noon; rest of year Mon–Fri 7am–3pm; ☏04/574-7590, ⓦwww.bohinj.si).

Close by, at Triglavska cesta 17, is the super classy *Bohinj Park* **hotel** (☏04/577-0210, ⓦwww.bohinj-park-hotel.si; ⑨), a self-styled eco-hotel which also houses

Triglav National Park

Abutting the Italian border to the west, within touching distance of the Austrian border to the north, and embracing almost the entire Slovene part of the Julian Alps, **Triglav National Park** (Triglavski Narodni Park) attracts some two million visitors each year. The park comprises three distinct sectors: the Bohinj district – which incorporates Bohinj Lake and the greatest concentration of settlements; the Sava Dolinka district to the north, characterized by a series of glaciated valleys; and the Soča district in the west, extending southwards to Bovec and the Soča Valley (see chapter 3), and which accommodates the only road passing directly through the park.

The park is home to a wonderful array of **flora and fauna**; its most revered creature is the elusive **chamois**, of which some two thousand are believed to roam the grassy slopes. Other significant species include the recently reintroduced **marmot** and **ibex**, while sightings of the **golden eagle**, and encounters with **brown bear** – who stray up from the southern forests – are not unknown. However, the possibility of sighting any of the above is slim, as they are all apt to steer well clear of humans. Many of the park's plant species are endemic to the mountains, such as the **Julian poppy** (*Papaver julicum*) and the purple **Zois' bellflower** (*Campanula zoysii*), named after the Slovene botanist Karl Zois – be warned that most alpine flora here is protected and picking them is an offence.

The park is administered by rangers, who are on hand to provide assistance, though there are also information boards haphazardly scattered throughout the park. Otherwise, information can be obtained from the **Triglav National Park Information Centre**, in the village of Trenta in the Trenta Valley (see p.143), and the park's headquarters in Bled (see p.114).

a fantastic bowling alley and is linked to an **Aquapark** (Vodni park; daily 9am–9pm; ☎04/577–0210, ⓦwww.vodni-park-bohinj.si) incorporating an indoor pool (€12 day-ticket, €10 for 3hr), climbing wall, steambath, sauna and gym. Somewhat more low-key, but very commendable, is the *Pension Tripič*, just across the road at Triglavska 13 (☎04/572-1282, ⓦwww.bohinj.si/tripic; ❼). On the western fringe of the village, heading towards the lake, is the *Danica* **campsite** (☎04/572-1055, ⓦwww.camp-danica.si; May–Sept), a well-shaded site backing onto the Sava River, with restaurant and sports facilities.

If you have a bit of time to spare, pop into the **Tomaž Godec Museum** (Muzej Tomaža Godca; May–Oct Tues–Sun 10am–noon & 4–6pm; Jan–April Wed, Sat & Sun, same hours; €2) at Zoisova 15 – it's located five minutes west of the post office, down Vodnikova cesta and across the stream. Trained as a leather tanner, Godec was also a champion skier and mountaineer. However, he was best known for his role as one of the founder members of the Slovene National Liberation Movement and as organizer of the 1941 Bohinj uprising. In 1942 he was captured by the Germans and carted off to Begunje (see p.111), before being transferred to Mauthausen where he was executed. The museum was also party to a rather significant piece of history: between March 15 and 18, 1939, in the modest room now dedicated to Godec, the **Central Committee of the Communist Party of Yugoslavia** (CKKPJ) was formed. Fittingly, Tito, who was present at the meeting, returned to open the museum some forty years later. The remainder of the museum is given over to a reconstructed leather-tanning workshop – the only one of its kind in the country – with a display of brutal-looking World War I weapons recovered from the Southern Bohinj mountains.

Lake Bohinj

The largest permanent body of water in Slovenia, **Lake Bohinj** (Bohinjsko Jezero) is utterly different from Lake Bled; its brooding, unerringly calm waters provide perfect theatre to the majestic, steeply pitched mountain faces which frame it. In his epic poem, *Baptism of the Savica*, France Prešeren eloquently described it thus:

The lake of Bohinj calm in stillness lies,
No sign of strife remains to outward sight;
Yet in the lake the fierce pike never sleep,
Nor other fell marauders of the deep.

Over 4km long, 1km wide, and reaching depths of 45m, the lake is fed by water from the Savica falls, which, in turn, feeds the Sava Bohinjka River at the southeastern corner of the lake. Mercifully, and unlike Bled, building has been forbidden along the entire lake shore, resulting in a virtually unbroken sequence of trees and grassy banks. Nevertheless, and even more so than Bled, the lake is well geared up for a number of activities, with canoeing, kayaking and windsurfing supplementing the more traditional pursuits of swimming and fishing. Moreover, it's far more likely to freeze over during winter, meaning better opportunities for skating.

Bohinj is also the location for two of the country's most colourful alpine festivals; taking place throughout the last week of May and first week of June, the **International Wildflower Festival** showcases the region's wonderful flora in the form of exhibitions, workshops, and guided botanical tours, while, in the second or third weekend of September, the **Kravji Bal**, or "Cows Ball", celebrates the return of the cattle from alpine pastures in the form of folklore events, live bands and much boozing.

▲ Lake Bohinj

Arrival and information

Buses set passengers down just before the lake by the *Hotel Jezero* in Ribčev Laz, from where it's a few steps to the busy **tourist office**, housed in the small complex at no. 48 (July & Aug daily 8am–8pm; rest of the year Mon–Sat 8am–6pm, Sun 9am–3pm; ☎04/572-3370, ⓦwww.bohinj.si), which has **internet** access. The **Bohinj Guest Card** (€10), available to anyone staying in one of Bohinj's hotels, rooms or apartments, offers a number of good discounts on local attractions, activities and restaurants – it can be purchased from either the tourist office or any of the hotels. The **post office** is next door (Mon–Fri 8am–9.30am, 10am–3.30pm & 4–6pm, Sat 8am–noon).

Accommodation

Lake Bohinj can count on just a handful of **hotels**, and although they generally represent poor value for money during the summer period, prices do drop considerably out of season. Fortunately, there is plentiful **private accommodation** around the lake, particularly in Ribčev Laz and in the villages along the upper valley (Stara Fužina, Studor and Srednja Vas). Be warned, though, that during July and August rooms get snapped up very quickly, so it's best to book in advance, or pitch up early in the morning to be sure of finding somewhere. During the summer expect to pay around €17 per person per night for a room with bathroom, and an additional €6 should you require breakfast; note that for stays of less than three nights you'll have to pay thirty percent more than this; outside peak season, prices are around twenty percent less. An apartment for two people costs around €40–45 per night. Bookings can be made through the tourist office.

Located on the road midway between Ribčev Laz and Ukanc is the **hostel** *Pod Voglom* (☎04/572-3461, ⓦwww.hostel-podvoglom.com), which has basic two- three- and four-bedded rooms, some with shower (€19–26 including breakfast). Up in the village of Studor, the *Backpackers hostel* at no. 13 (☎031/466-707, ⓦwww.studor13.si; €23) is a delightful, family-run place accommodating two six-bed dorms and a double room. The *Zlatorog* **campsite** is located at the southwestern corner of the lake in Ukanc (☎04/572-3482; May–Sept).

Hotel Bellevue Ribčev Laz 65 ☎04/572-3331, ⓦ www.hotelbohinj.si. Perched on a hill 800m north of the *Hotel Jezero*, the secluded Bellevue is where Agatha Christie once stayed, the grand old lady commenting that "the lake is far too beautiful for a murder". The hotel retains a pleasant old-style atmosphere, despite the rooms being a little frayed around the edges. If you're walking, take the rocky footpath through the wood (5min) instead of the road, which is a gruelling twenty-minute walk. ❻

Hotel Bohinj Ribčev Laz 45 ☎04/572-6000, ⓦ www.hotelbohinj.si. Pitched on a small rise across from the tourist office, this alpine-style building offers large and attractive pine–furnished rooms, some of which have glorious views overlooking the lake and across to Mount Triglav. Tennis courts, sauna and bike rental. ❽

Hotel Center Ribčev Laz 50 ☎04/572-3170, ⓦ www.bohinj.si/center. Modern and shiny hotel a few paces along from the tourist office, some of whose rooms have a little lounge area and balcony or terrace. Decent pizzeria attached. ❼

Hotel Jezero Ribčev Laz 51 ☎04/572-9100, ⓦ www.bohinj.si/alpinum/jezero. Just 50m from the water, this is the lake's most prominent hotel, a slickly run place accommodating bright, smartly furnished rooms. Pool and fitness suite free to guests; sauna facilities too. ❽

Hotel Kristal Ribčev Laz 4 ☎04/577-8200, ⓦ www.hotel-kristal-slovenia.com. Located at the entrance to the village, this popular and welcoming family-run pension provides simple but smartly furnished rooms. Triples and quads, plus two rooms for disabled persons. ❻

Pension Rožič Ribčev Laz 42 ☎04/572-3393, ⓦ www.pension-rozic.com. Situated 100m east of the tourist office, this quiet pension offers rustically styled rooms that are somewhat old-fashioned and boxy, but comfortable enough. Has a reasonable restaurant too (see p.129). ❺

Ribčev Laz and the Church of St John the Baptist

As well as containing all things of a practical nature, **RIBČEV LAZ** is the location for the lake's outstanding monument, the tiny **Church of St John the Baptist** (Cerkev Sv Janez Krstnik; July & Aug daily 9am–noon & 5–8pm; other times contact the tourist office; €1), one of the most brilliantly frescoed churches in all Slovenia. Located opposite the stone bridge – invariably clogged with walkers and traffic, but offering glorious head-on views of the lake – this chunky, evocative structure has origins dating back to the thirteenth century. Its exterior features a striking **wooden porch**, paved with round river stones in rhomboid style, the middle stones arranged to form the date – 1639 – when it was laid out. Most of the exterior's sixteenth-century frescoes are barely discernible, save for those to the right of the entrance, one of which depicts St John, book in hand, baptizing kneeling people, and another of St Florian doing what he does best, dousing fires. The south exterior wall bears

---

The Bohinj Tunnel

Built between 1901 and 1906, the **Bohinj Tunnel** extends for some 6327m (6.3km) between Bohinjska Bistrica and Podbrdo, making it Slovenia's longest railway tunnel. Introduced in 1999, the **car-train** transports vehicles (car, van or mobile home) through the mountains in a mere ten minutes – as opposed to the one hour it takes to drive across the tortuous road between Bohinj and Baška Grapa, via the village of Sorica. There are six daily trains between Bohinjska Bistrica and Podbrdo, three of which continue to Most na Soči, thirty minutes further on at the southernmost tip of the park – the same number of trains run in the reverse direction (six daily trains from Podbrdo to Bohinjska Bistrica, three of which originate in Most na Soči). From Bohinjska Bistrica to Podbrdo the cost (car and passengers) is €8 one-way and €12 return. The full journey (Bistrica to Most na Soči) is €12 one-way, €20 return – for bicycles the cost is €2 and €3 respectively.

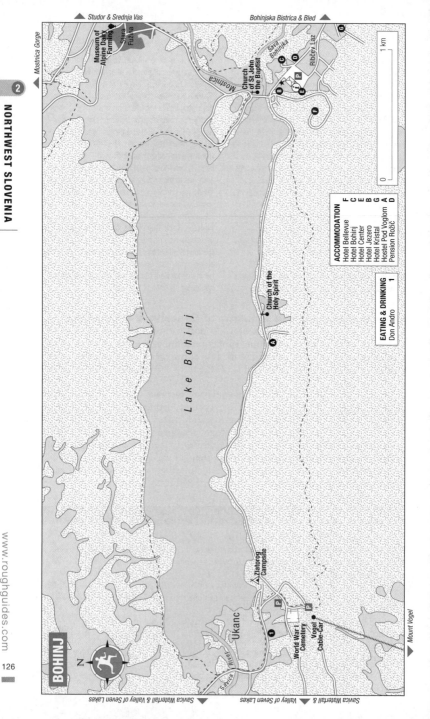

BOHINJ

N

Lake Bohinj

▲ Studor & Srednja Vas   Bohinjska Bistrica & Bled ▲

◄ Mostnica Gorge

Museum of Alpine Dairy Farming

Stara Fužina

Sava Bohinjka

Church of St John the Baptist

Mostnica

Ribčev Laz

G

C
B   D
P
E
B

F

Church of the Holy Spirit

A

ACCOMMODATION
Hotel Bellevue   F
Hotel Bohinj   C
Hotel Center   E
Hotel Jezero   B
Hotel Kristal   G
Hostel Pod Voglom   A
Pension Rožič   D

EATING & DRINKING
Don Andro   1

1 km

0

Ukanc

Zlatorog Campsite

World War I Cemetery

Vogel Cable-Car

P

P

1

Sava Pisca River

▼ Mount Vogel

▼ Savica Waterfall & Valley of Seven Lakes

▼ Valley of Seven Lakes

▼ Savica Waterfall & Valley of Seven Lakes

an oversized St Christopher with the Christ Child on his shoulder. Its Baroque **bell tower**, renovated several times over, features double windows framed with green stone from the Piračica stream, a material common to many church bell towers in the region.

Such is the sheer mass of interior **frescoes** – most of which were painted by the Master of Bohinj – that you may desire a repeat visit just to take them all in, particularly if it's crowded. The Gothic presbytery, dating from around 1440, contains the densest concentration of frescoes; working upwards, the lower walls are painted with singing angels holding up patterned curtains, while the next belt depicts bust-length pictures of holy figures in niches bearing a random selection of items (a lamb, a dragon, a pair of breasts); next up are the Apostles, standing against a background of stage scenery carrying various items of weaponry, above which, in the vaulted compartments, are angels playing instruments. The oldest layer of frescoes – dating from the fourteenth century – are those on the north wall of the nave, featuring just about detectable fragments of scenes of St George and the Dragon, as well as St John the Evangelist blessing the poison (before drinking it and staying alive); adjacent to this, on the north exterior of the arch, are some grisly scenes entitled *St John's Head to Herodius* and *Beheading of a Saint*, the latter featuring St John's headless corpse spewing blood.

The lakeshore walk

The best way to enjoy the lake is to take a leisurely, circular walk around it, which can be completed in around four and a half hours – the route outlined here follows a clockwise fashion. Generally speaking, the **south shore** – alongside which the road to the hamlet of **Ukanc** runs – contains all the historical points of interest, but it's a bit of a grind, and the path is situated away

Activities in Bohinj

Bohinj presents some excellent opportunities for a whole raft of activities. Pac Sports (☎04/572-3461, ⓦwww.pac-sports.com), based at the *Pod Voglom hostel* (but also with a hut just below *Pension Rožič*), offers **rafting** (€25), **canyoning** (€45), **hydrospeed** (€35) and **tandem paragliding** (€85 for a 15min flight). It also rents out **canoes and kayaks** (€4 per hour, €14 per day), as does Alpin Sports by the bridge (☎04/572-3486, ⓦwww.alpinsport.si). Both these places also rent out **bikes** (1hr €4, half a day €11, full day €15).

The **Bohinj Horse Centre** (Mrcina Ranč) in Studor, with its stable of Icelandic ponies, offers a varied programme of treks, with one-hour rides from around €20, half-day trips around €70 and full day-trips around €100 (☎041/790-297, ⓦwww .ranc-mrcina.com). For something more relaxing take the **excursion boat** (Turistična Ladja; June to mid-Sept daily 10am–6pm, every 40min; departures during rest of year dependent on weather; €9 one-way, €12 return) which shuttles up and down the lake between Ribčev Laz and the *Hotel Zlatorog*.

It's also possible to **fish** on the lake (March–Oct) and in the Sava Bohinjka river (April–Oct), the latter well stocked with brown trout; permits begin at €25 per day up to €115 for a week for the lake, and €40 (€240) for the river; these can be obtained from the tourist office. **Swimming** is better here than in Bled due to the shallower waters close to the shore – the best areas are at the extreme western end of the lake and the bay-like area to the northeast. Bohinj has two major **ski resorts**, both of which offer easy to moderate skiing: **Kobla** (ⓦwww.bohinj.si/kobla), accessible from the southern part of Bohinjska Bistrica, and the larger **Vogel** ski resort (ⓦwww.bohinj .si/vogel), high above the lake's southwestern corner.

from the lake, elevated above the busy main road. By way of contrast, the rocky, undisturbed **north shore** – accessible only by foot – is uplifting and possesses superior **views** of the lake – if you're short of time take a bus to the *Hotel Zlatorog* and walk the north shore back to Ribčev Laz.

Two kilometres along the road from the stone bridge in Ribčev Laz, just beyond the *Hostel Pod Voglom*, is the **Church of the Holy Spirit** (Cerkev Sv Duh), a compact Baroque structure enclosed within a shallow wall and distinguished by its neat shingle-topped roof. On its north-facing exterior is a large fresco of *St Christopher with Infant Child*, completed by Matija Koželj, who also executed the interior side-altar paintings. Its pretty interior also holds some interesting decoration, including a dazzling crystal chandelier from 1743, and stucco ornaments on the nave and presbytery vaults. If the church is closed the key can be obtained from no. 62, just up the path.

Hereafter, the road continues unexcitingly towards Ukanc, the setting for one of Slovenia's more bizarre alpine festivals (see p.123). Just short of here is the turn-off for the **Vogel cable car** (daily 8am–6pm: May to mid-Oct every half-hour; rest of year hourly; €9 one-way, €13 return), which can accommodate up to eighty people. Cruising up to the *Ski Hotel* (1537m) in a speedy five minutes, the panorama gradually reveals itself, culminating in memorable views of the lake below and the serried peaks opposite – on cloudless days Triglav is visible. If you fancy an easy to moderate walk, then you can always hike up; one route starts from the *Hotel Bellevue* in Ribčev Laz, and another from Ukanc (both take around 2hr).

One hundred metres beyond the turn-off for the cable car is the Austro-Hungarian **World War I Cemetery**, containing the graves of some three hundred soldiers buried here between 1915 and 1917 following ferocious battles on nearby Mount Krn. From here, the road continues uphill for 4km towards the Savica Waterfall (see p.130); retracing your steps back to the main road, follow it round to the left, past the campsite and the *Hotel Zlatorog*, and continue across the bridge spanning the Savica River. Here, the path splits – the left track heads towards the Savica Waterfall, while the other turns back towards the shore, opening up onto a pleasant grassy expanse popular with bathers and picnickers – and the views across to the eastern end of the lake from here are splendid. The initial part of the walk along the north shore is characterized by steep slopes of scree, a dry, boulder-strewn channel and densely forested woodland, which, for the most part, meanders tightly along the course of the shoreline. It then opens up into meadowland and a curving shallow bay, one of the best locations around the lake for **bathing** – if you can find a spot. Continuing along the path will bring you back to the bridge and the Church of St John the Baptist.

Stara Fužina, Studor and Srednja Vas

One kilometre north of Ribčev Laz is **STARA FUŽINA**, the largest of the upper valley villages. Here, just by the bridge in the centre of the village, you'll find a small **tourist office** (July & Aug only Mon–Fri 9am–noon & 5–7pm, Sat & Sun 9am–noon & 1–7pm; ☎04/572-3326). Just across the bridge, thirty metres up from the *Gostilna Mihovc*, is the enjoyable **Museum of Alpine Dairy Farming** (Planšarski Muzej; Tues–Sun: July & Aug 11am–7pm, Jan–June & Sept–Oct 10am–noon & 4–6pm; €2), which, as its name suggests, relays the story of the valley's rich dairy-farming heritage. Thanks to its dense concentration of high-altitude meadows, Bohinj was for centuries the centre of alpine dairy farming in Slovenia, reaching its high point in the late nineteenth century when the introduction of cheese cooperatives substantially increased the lot of farmers and their families. The industry continued to prosper until the 1970s, but following the opening of a modern dairy in Srednja Vas, and the exodus of younger generations to the towns and cities, dairy farming slipped into decline and today it's barely sustained by a handful of older villagers.

Among the more interesting exhibits on display in this abandoned cheese dairy are two huge copper rennet vats, a herdsman's backpack from 1961, containing all the essential items required for a season up in the mountains, and a reconstructed herder's hut. At the eastern end of the village, the **Church of St Paul** (Cerkev Sv Pavel) manifests similar external characteristics to the Church of St John, notably its paved porch, bell tower with stone windows and onion dome, and a more complete fresco of St Christopher – sadly, the frescoes by the main entrance have all but disappeared.

One and a half kilometres beyond the church is the village of **STUDOR**, well known for its splendid double **hayracks**, called *toplars*. While the single stretch type of hayrack (*kozolec*) is more common – and can be found elsewhere in Europe – the double hayrack, consisting of two parallel single hayracks connected by a double-gabled roof (used for storage), is unique to Slovenia; the ones here, dating from the eighteenth and nineteenth centuries, are perhaps the most picturesque grouping of hayracks to be seen anywhere in the country. Heading up into the village you'll pass the Bohinj Horse Centre (see box, p.127), beyond which, at no. 16, is the **Oplen House** (Oplenova hiša; same hours as Alpine Museum; €2), a typical nineteenth-century Bohinj farmhouse, also known as a longhouse because of its unusual arrangement, whereby the living quarters and barn are conjoined under one roof; aside from the typical living room (*hiša*) and "black" kitchen – the latter so-called because of its blackened walls from the open cooking area – the dwelling area consists of a chamber – used primarily as a bedroom, as evidenced by the two impossibly small beds – and an attic. If the house is closed you can get the key from no. 14a next door. **Srednja Vas**, 1km further on, is the upper valley's central settlement, and though there's nothing specific to see, it's a pleasant enough place to stroll around, and there are some good restaurants here (see below).

Eating and drinking

Aside from the hotel **restaurants**, of which the one in the *Jezero* is the best, there are precious few choices when it comes to eating in the vicinity of the lake, though the best places are up in the villages. For **drinking**, the *Hotel Jezero*, and the convivial open-air *Paviljon* café opposite, is where most people congregate by day and night.

Restaurants

Don Andro Ukanc 20. Bright and tidy spaghetteria 200m along from the *Zlatorog* campsite, with a long list of salads and pasta dishes (Karst ham, truffles, blue cheese); the terrace is a lovely spot from which to enjoy the mountain views.

Pizzeria Ema Srednja Vas 73. This large, colourful and popular pizzeria is an enjoyable establishment serving better than average pizza and pasta, while the views from the gravel terrace are terrific.

Gostilna Mihovc Stara Fužina 118. Just down from the Museum of Alpine Dairy Farming, this basic but friendly restaurant offers good quality home-style cooking such as bean soup, goulash and Bohinj sausage in minced lard.

Rožič Ribčev Laz 42. In the pension of the same name, the very agreeable restaurant has a daily menu chalked up on a board featuring such delicious staples as deer steak, smoked sausages and Bohinj trout.

Gostilna Rupa Srednja Vas 87. Just across the road from *Pizzeria Ema*, the emphasis at this rustically styled, and rather touristy, place is firmly on pork and fish, while every Thursday during the summer there's roast suckling pig to feast on, usually accompanied by live music. Closed Mon.

Hikes and excursions around Bohinj

Beyond the confines of the lake, Bohinj has much to offer walkers of all abilities. The easiest short trek – and the only one accessible by public transport – is the **Savica Waterfall** near the western end of the lake; from here paths break off towards the **Valley of the Triglav Lakes**, an ideal destination for those seeking slightly more physical exertion. To the north of the lake, and accessible from Stara Fužina, is **Mostnica Gorge**, a masterpiece of nature.

Savica Waterfall

Unequivocally the number-one attraction around these parts is the majestic sixty-metre-high **Savica Waterfall** (Slap Savica; April–Oct 8am–6pm), a 45-minute walk along the path (signposted) west of the *Hotel Zlatorog* (this hike can also be done as an extension of the circular walk – see p.127). You can also drive here or, between June and September, take one of the three daily buses from the *Hotel Jezero*. Once you've reached the entrance and paid the path maintenance fee (€3), it's a heavy-going twenty-minute climb up a series of zigzagging steps to the top of the gorge and a small observation hut, invariably crammed with people angling to get a photo in. The falls themselves are spectacular: smooth photogenic ribbons of water tumbling into the circular pool below, before falling away to begin the long journey as the Sava River. To the left,

Hiking in the Julian Alps

The Julian Alps are a hiker's wonderland, its meadows, valleys and mountains carved up by a well-worn nexus of waymarked paths and trails. There are several key **starting points: Bled**, furthest from the park's mountainous heart, offers easy to moderate hikes around the eastern spur of the Alps, though there are more demanding walks to be had in the heavily forested **Karavanke** chain bordering Austria to the north. From **Kranjska Gora**, trails head off up into the **Planica** and **Tamar Valleys**, as well as up the **Vršič Pass**, from where further tracks fan out in several directions. A short way east of Kranjska Gora, a trio of valleys – the most prominent being the **Vrata Valley** – provide the starting point for ascents towards Triglav itself (see box, p.134). The greatest choice of hikes, however, emanate from **Bohinj** in the southeastern corner of Triglav National Park: the lush pastures of the **Fužine highlands** and the **Voje Valley** north of the lake; the **Lower Bohinj** mountains on the south side; the **Komna Plateau** to the west; and up through the **Valley of the Triglav Lakes** to the northwest (which continues towards Triglav), arguably the park's most scenic trek. All paths in Slovenia are marked by a "target", that is, a red circle with a white centre, with intersections and forks indicated by arrows; however, some of the markings are a little inconclusive in places.

The best hiking months are May, June and September, when the weather is at its most dependable and the crowds are somewhat thinner; bear in mind that the weather in the mountains can change with alarming rapidity and so the usual provisos apply – sufficient provisions and appropriate clothing and equipment – particularly if you plan to do any high-altitude hiking. If you fancy hooking up with other walkers, a number of **agencies** in Bled and Bohinj (see p.117 & p.127) offer a full range of hikes, from easy to moderate half- or full-day trips such as Debela Peč and the meadows of Bohinj, to more difficult two-day trips up to Triglav (with an overnight stay in a hut). The best up-to-date **maps** are the 1:50,000 editions of *Triglavski Narodni Park* and *Julijske Alps*, published by the Alpine Association of Slovenia (Planinska Zveza Slovenije or PZS; ⓦwww.pzs.si). There's also Roy Clark's pocket handbook *The Julian Alps of Slovenia* (see p.333), which outlines key hikes from Bled, Bohinj, Kranjska Gora, Bovec and Kobarid.

▲ Mostnica Gorge

emerging from the same fault, is the subsidiary fall, known as **Mali Savica** (Little Savica). Savica can get murderously busy on a summer's day, so to get the most out of it you're best off making an early start. The *Koča pri Savici* hut (☎040/695-787; April–Oct daily; Nov–March Sat & Sun), by the car park at the entrance to the Savica Waterfall, offers dorm accommodation and refreshments.

Valley of the Triglav Lakes

The car park also marks the starting point for several superb hikes into the heart of the Triglav National Park – and, if desired, an assault on Triglav itself (see box, p.134). One track forges westwards to the large *Dom na Komni* hut (1520m; 2hr 30min), open year-round (☎040/695-783), while another spears northwards via the formidable Komarča cliff, a tough and very steep route, aided by iron pegs and rungs. Both then carry on northwards, meeting at the *Koča pri Triglavskih Jezerih* (1685m; ☎040/620-783; mid-June to mid-Oct), which marks the beginning of the magical **Valley of the Triglav Lakes** (Dolina Triglavskih jezer), also known as the **Valley of the Seven Lakes**.

Lined with white limestone cliffs, and rich in alpine and karstic flora, the valley is famed for its beautiful tarns, the lowest and warmest of which is the **Black Lake** (Črno jezero), just above Komarča, while the highest, the **Lake below Vršac** (Jezero pod Vršacem), lies at an altitude of 2000m. The largest and deepest of the seven lakes, the **Great Lake** (Veliko jezero), is approximately midway between these two. The valley is also home to Zlatorog, the mythical chamois with golden horns.

Mostnica Gorge and the Voje Valley

Another superb outing is the hike up through the **Mostnica Gorge** (Mostnice Korita), 1km north of Stara Fužina. Two trails – one just before the bridge and one by St Paul's Church – head towards the gorge entrance, before which you cross the stone **Devil's Bridge** (Hudičev Most); follow the path to the right for 400m, pay at the kiosk (€2), then take the path to the right. The ravine, 1km long and 20m deep in places, has been smoothly sculpted into all

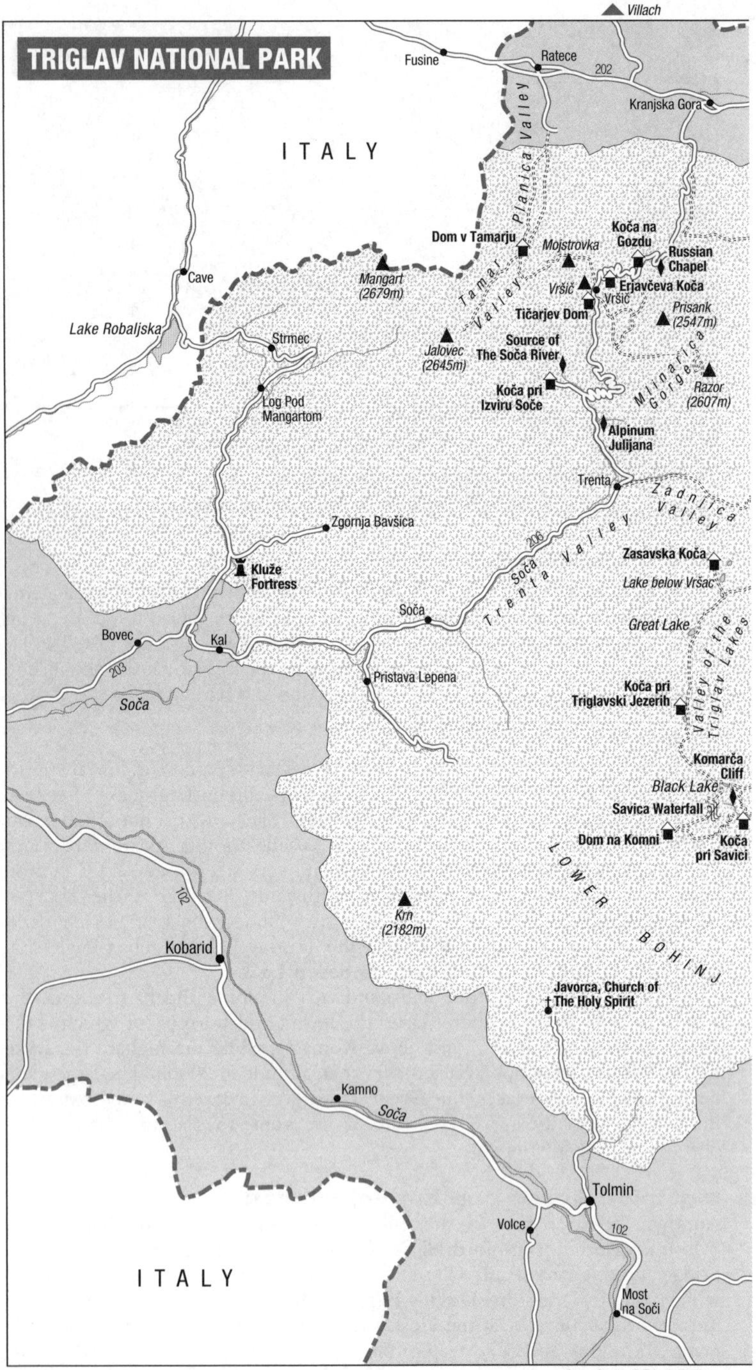

TRIGLAV NATIONAL PARK
Villach
Fusine
Ratece
202
Kranjska Gora
ITALY
Planica Valley
Dom v Tamarju
Mojstrovka
Koča na Gozdu
Russian Chapel
Erjavčeva Koča
Vršič
Vršič
Tamar Valley
Mangart (2679m)
Cave
Lake Robaljska
Tičarjev Dom
Prisank (2547m)
Strmec
Jalovec (2645m)
Source of The Soča River
Mlinarica Gorge
Razor (2607m)
Log Pod Mangartom
Koča pri Izviru Soče
Alpinum Julijana
Trenta
Zadnjica Valley
Zgornja Bavšica
206
Trenta Valley
Soča
Kluže Fortress
Zasavska Koča
Lake below Vršac
Soča
Bovec
Kal
Great Lake
203
Pristava Lepena
Soča
Valley of the Triglav Lakes
Koča pri Triglavski Jezerih
Komarča Cliff
Black Lake
Savica Waterfall
Dom na Komni
Koča pri Savici
LOWER BOHINJ
102
Krn (2182m)
Kobarid
Javorca, Church of The Holy Spirit
Kamno
Soča
Tolmin
Volce
102
ITALY
Most na Soči
Nova Gorica & Trieste

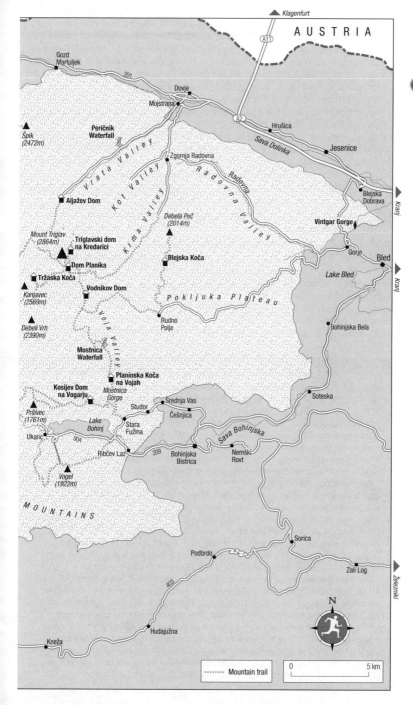

Klagenfurt

AUSTRIA

A11

Gozd
Martuljek

201

Dovje

Mojstrana

A2

Hrušica

Jesenice

Sava Dolinka

Špik
(2472m)

Peričnik
Waterfall

Zgornja Radovna

Vrata Valley

Kot Valley

Krma Valley

Radovna

Radovna Valley

Blejska
Dobrava

Vintgar Gorge

Aljažev Dom

Debela Peč
(2014m)

Gorje

Bled

Mount Triglav
(2864m)

Triglavski dom
na Kredarici

Blejska Koča

Dom Planika

Lake Bled

Tržaska Koča

Kanjavec
(2569m)

Vodnikov Dom

Pokljuka Plateau

Bohinjska Bela

Debeli Vrh
(2390m)

Vola Valley

Rudno
Polje

Mostnica
Waterfall

Planinska Koča
na Vojah

Kosijev Dom
na Vogarju

Mostnica
Gorge

Studor

Srednja Vas

Soteska

Pršivec
(1761m)

Lake
Bohinj

Stara
Fužina

Češnjica

Sava Bohinjska

Ukanc

904

Ribčev Laz

209

Bohinjska
Bistrica

Nemški
Rovt

Vogel
(1922m)

MOUNTAINS

Sorica

Podbrdo

Zali Log

403

N

Kneža

Hudajužna

Kranj

Kranj

Železniki

.... Mountain trail

0   5 km

manner of extraordinary shapes, while hundreds of circular hollows, known as river mills, have been eroded into the riverbed, the result of stones spun by whirlpools in the stream; close inspection of the river is possible, as regular paths divert away from the main track, but be particularly careful if it has been raining. At the end of the gorge (by the bridge), you can either return (via the other side), or continue northwards towards the **Voje Valley** – scramble upwards through the trees for twenty minutes before arriving at the *Koča na Vojah* hut (℡04/572-3213; May–Sept), a good place to stop for refreshments; thereafter, it's a pleasant forty-minute walk through open fields and meadows to the precipitous valley headwall and the modest 21-metre-high **Mostnica Waterfall** (Slap Mostnice). From here, you can continue to Velo Polje and the *Vodnikov dom na Velem polje* hut (℡051/607-211; June–Sept) at 1817m (3hr 30min), or return the way you came.

Kranjska Gora and around

Tucked away in the extreme northwestern corner of the country, on the doorstep of Triglav National Park, the small town of **KRANJSKA GORA** is Slovenia's number-one winter playground. A remote settlement since the fourteenth century, the town merited little attention and was strategically unimportant until World War I when the nearby Vršič Pass was built to enable supplies to reach the Austrian army fighting along the Soča front. Kranjska Gora then developed into a major winter sports venue, with Slovenia's first ski jump and ski lifts constructed here in 1934 and 1950 respectively. Although its skiing

---

Climbing Triglav

It's said that every Slovene has to climb **Mount Triglav** at least once in their lifetime, but this in no sense means that it's an easy outing. In fact it remained unclimbed until 1778, when a German doctor and three local guides made it to the 2864m summit. The mountain can be approached via several routes.

The **most dramatic approach** – and one not for the inexperienced or fainthearted – is from the **north**, as Triglav's north face is no less than 1200m high; its central part is for climbers only, but there are fairly tough hiking routes to either side, involving the use of fixed cables. From the *Aljažev Dom* hut (1015m; ℡04/589-1030) at the end of the Vrata valley, continue past a monument to the partisans, and after 45 minutes take the Prag path to the left. At the foot of the north face the Prag, or threshold (a rock cliff), is scaled with the help of metal steps and pegs; thereafter the path winds on up to a small spring, after which you fork right to reach the *Triglavski dom na Kredarici* (2515m; ℡04/531-2864), four or five hours from the *Aljažev Dom*. From the saddle above the hut, a huge painted marker denotes the start of the final ascent; with the aid of steel cables and pegs you should reach the summit in an hour or so. Here you'll find the Aljažev Stolp, or turret, a tiny refuge erected in 1865 that looks like a small space rocket.

The **shortest ascent** is from the **east**, from Rudno Polje (1340m); from here it's about two hours' hike to the Studorski preval (1892m), and another hour to the *Vodnikov dom na Velem polju* (1817m; ℡051/607-211), from where you continue to *Dom Planika pod Triglavom* (2401m; ℡04/574-4069) and beyond to the summit.

The **most popular route** is from the **south**; from the *Hotel Zlatorog* at the western end of Lake Bohinj, it's a forty-minute walk to the Savica Waterfall, where a path to the right begins the ascent of the formidable-looking Komarča Cliff, a tough climb of seven hundred metres but fitted with cables. At the top, continue gently uphill in beech trees before arriving at the Black Lake (Črno Jezero; 1294m) on your left.

is undoubtedly the main draw, during the summer it's an excellent base from which to embark on any number of hikes, while cyclists will appreciate the extensive network of well-marked cycle paths.

Arrival and information

The basic **bus station** is just five minutes' walk north of the centre on Koroška ulica – head down Kolodvorska ulica to Borovška cesta, the town's main street. The **tourist office** is in the centre of town at Tičarjeva 2 (Jan–March & June–Sept Mon–Sat 8am–7pm, Sun 9am–6pm; other times Mon–Fri 8am–3pm, Sat 9am–6pm; ℡04/588-1768, Ⓦwww.kranjska-gora.si), 100m west of which is the **post office** (Mon–Fri 8am–7pm, Sat 8am–noon).

Accommodation

As you'd expect from Slovenia's largest ski resort, there's a healthy stock of **hotels** in town, though the **pensions** here generally offer better value for money. Note that prices in most places rise during the peak winter ski months (Dec–March). There is plentiful accommodation in **private rooms** (❷) or **apartments** (❹–❼) in the town centre and surrounding villages, which can be arranged through the tourist office. There are also numerous apartments advertised in the streets east of the bus station.

There's cheap **hostel** accommodation at the *Penzion Porentov Dom*, just outside town overlooking the golf course at Čičare 2 (℡04/588-1000, Ⓔvila .tatjana@telemach.si), which has very basic but clean multi-bed dorms (€15); while **Podkoren**, 2km west of Kranjska Gora, is home to the *Pr' Tatko* hostel,

Soon after, turn left to pass around the lake to the north; after a couple of minutes go straight ahead at a junction, continuing on a slightly rocky path in pine trees, level and then rising for an hour in all. From the top of the White Cliff (Bela Skala) it's an easy fifteen-minute walk through limestone dykes to the *Koča pri Triglavskih Jezerih* (1685m; ℡040/620-783), three to four hours from the *Hotel Zlatorog*. From the hut continue north up the valley and past the Great Lake (Veliko Triglavskih Jezero), reaching the foot of an escarpment after an hour; the route leads steeply up to the right (following a red arrow to Hribarice), reaching the ridge in twenty minutes and the Yellow Lake (Želeno Jezero; 1988m) soon after. Continuing up to the right, you'll pass a turning to the Prehodavci hut (visible not too far to the left), and climb up, partly on scree, for half an hour. In another thirty minutes you reach the Hribarice saddle (2358m), from where the path is reasonably marked for a while; it descends and kinks to the left after about five minutes, then rises a little to reach the Dolič saddle (2164m) in another twenty minutes; from here the *Tržaška Koča na Doliču* (2151m; ℡04/574-4069) is also visible just to the left. The path swings sharply to the right here, and after an hour you'll reach the start of a fairly steep section, after which it takes just five minutes to reach the *Dom Planika pod Triglavom* (2401m), a good place to spend the night. From here the route brings you, in thirty minutes, to the foot of a cliff, where a big red and white dot marks the start of the final climb. With the aid of pegs and cables you soon reach a shoulder, where a path leads left and down to the *Dolič* hut. The route to the summit turns right and climbs onwards, reaching the top after another forty minutes.

More detailed information on the various routes can be found in *The Julian Alps of Slovenia* (see p.333); alternatively, any of the park's tourist offices can supply you with in-depth information and maps on Triglav.

an easy-going place with four- and eight-bed dorms (€18) in the centre of the village at no. 72 (T031/479-087, Wwww.prtatko.com). The only **campsite** is the small *Camping Kamne* (T04/589-1105, Wwww.campingkamne.com), some 14km east of Kranjska Gora in **Dovje**, situated just above the main road heading down to Mojstrana (buses stop on the road just outside the site) – it also has two- to five-bed bungalows (❸–❺).

Hotel Alpina Vitranška 12 T04/589-3100, Wwww.hit.si. Ignore the portentous exterior, the rooms are tastefully decorated, albeit somewhat lacking in character. It's well worth paying the minimal extra for the renovated rooms. Free use of pools in the *Kompas* hotel. ❽

Hotel Kompas Borovška cesta 100 T04/589-2100, Wwww.hit.si. Rooms in this sprawling complex on the western edge of town are bright and well furnished, all with large flat screen TVs and good-sized balconies. There's also a smart indoor pool. ❾

Hotel Kotnik Borovška cesta 75 T04/588-1564, Wwww.hotel-kotnik.si. Housed in a luminous yellow building, this classy, family-run hotel offers fifteen large and beautifully designed rooms, including triples and quads – the best-value place in town. ❻

Hotel Lek Vršiška 38 T04/588-1520, Wwww .hotel-lek.si. South of town on the road to Vršič, this polished hotel has all the requisite four-star facilities, including supremely comfy rooms, a beautiful indoor pool, gym and sauna. ❾

🎿 **Pension Lipa** Koroška cesta 14 T04/582-0000, Wwww.penzion-lipa.si. Attractive, comfortable pension right next to the bus station, with warm, softly coloured rooms; also has a lovely restaurant (see p.138). ❼

Skiing in northwest Slovenia

Given its predominantly mountainous terrain, it's not surprising that northwest Slovenia contains the greatest concentration of the country's **ski resorts**, and although you won't find the range of slopes that you would in Italy or France, the spectacular alpine scenery, thinner crowds and considerably lower prices are ample compensation. Moreover, Slovenia's ski resorts are uniformly well equipped and extremely safe, although most suffer from a lack of decent après-ski facilities.

Slovenia's largest and best-known ski resort is **Kranjska Gora**; however, the skiing here is not particularly exciting, its slopes best suited to beginners and intermediate skiers, which makes it a great base for families – it is, however, one of only two resorts in the country to host international ski (and ski-jumping) competitions. Rated as one of the most fashionable centres in Slovenia – and the most popular resort among weekending *Ljubljančani* – is **Krvavec**, some 25km due north of the capital; located at a relatively high altitude, its extensive range of slopes is suitable for skiers of all abilities, moreover, it has a snowboard school, speed-skiing track and a freestyle mogul course. The country's highest-altitude skiing (over 2000m) is at **Kanin**, near Bovec in the Soča Valley. Both this and the centres in Bohinj – **Kobla** and **Vogel** – offer the most dramatic skiing in terms of scenery; the former is the only ski resort in Slovenia accessible by train while the latter has the most modern cable car in the country. An increasingly popular centre is **Cerkno**, a well-developed and sophisticated resort with some of the most challenging pistes in the country.

The **season** typically lasts from December to March, though skiing on the higher pistes, such as Kanin, is often possible until the end of April. Expect to **pay** in the region of €25–30 for a day ski pass and €120–160 for a weekly pass, the latter figure representing the sort of price you'd expect to pay at the more developed resorts. The **Ski Pass Julijske Alps** (€48 for two days, up to €140 for a week) covers all the ski centres located within the Julian Alps. Most centres have **ski schools** with English instruction (around €30 for a two-hour individual lesson, and €70 for five two-hour lessons as part of a group), and you can **rent equipment** (around €20 for skis, boots and poles). For more **information** on skiing (and other winter sports) in Slovenia check out the website Wwww.sloveniaholidays.com/end/winter-activities/skiing, which provides details on resorts, ski trails, ski schools, ticket prices, weather forecasts and so on. Latest ski conditions can be obtained from the Snow Hotline (T041/182-500).

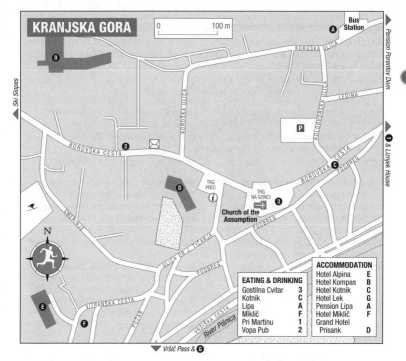

KRANJSKA GORA

0   100 m

Bus Station

Pension Porentov Dom

Ski Slopes

KOROŠKA ULICA

KOROŠKA ULICA

KOLODVORSKA ULICA

LEDINA

BOROVŠKA CESTA

BOROVŠKA CESTA

PODBREG

& Liznjek House

P

TRG PRED

TRG NA GORICI

Church of the Assumption

PODBREG

SMERINJE

ULICA DR. J. TIČARJA

PODBREG

N

VITRANSKA CESTA

POŽAR

VRŠIŠKA CESTA

River Pišnica

Vršič Pass & **G**

EATING & DRINKING	
Gostilna Cvitar	3
Kotnik	C
Lipa	A
Miklič	F
Pri Martinu	1
Vopa Pub	2

ACCOMMODATION	
Hotel Alpina	E
Hotel Kompas	B
Hotel Kotnik	C
Hotel Lek	G
Pension Lipa	A
Hotel Miklič	F
Grand Hotel Prisank	D

Hotel Miklič Vitranška 13 ☎04/588-1635, ⓦwww.hotelmiklic.com. Surrounded by baize-like lawns and neatly arranged flowerbeds, this pristine pension, just below the *Alpina* hotel, has decently sized, well turned out rooms and a terrific restaurant too (see p.138). ❼

Grand Hotel Prisank Borovška cesta 93 ☎04/588-4820, ⓦwww.hit.si. In a central location a few steps west of the tourist office, this big, pink hotel – complete with ultra-modern rooms – is as luxurious as it gets in town. There's also a good little pizzeria, tearoom and pub. ❾

The Town

The one key site in town is the **Liznjek House** (Liznjekova hiša; Tues–Sat 10am–6pm, Sun till 5pm; €3), 200m east of the *Hotel Kotnik* at Borovška cesta 63. This superbly preserved alpine homestead – once the property of a wealthy local farmer and the largest farm in the village – mostly dates from the late eighteenth century, though its stone ground floor is of seventeenth-century origin. Its interior furnishings are particularly outstanding; in one of the rooms sits a lovely selection of folk-painted trousseau chests, while in the main living room there is a beautiful corner stove and a handsome, slender grandfather clock. Upstairs is a typically modest bedroom, and a vast attic, once used as storage space and still chock-full with farmers' tools. Opposite the house is the capacious barn, built in 1796 and originally used for storing food and housing livestock; it's now mostly empty, save for some battered old horse carts and grand-looking sleds. Downstairs in the small one-room basement is an exhibition dedicated to the Slovene writer Josip Vandot (1884–1944), whose many stories about the clever shepherd boy Kekec endure to this day – many of these were made into films (see p.336).

Three hundred metres west of the Liznjek House, sited on the attractive, square-like portion of Borovška cesta, is the squat, late-Gothic **Church of the Assumption** (Cerkev Sv vnebovzetje). The only surviving part of the original church is the stocky, Romanesque bell tower, while the church you see today dates from 1510. There's not an awful lot to see inside, though its exquisite interior does contain one of the most impressive vaulted ceilings in the region and a particularly fine organ, one of the oldest in Gorenjska.

Eating and drinking

The town is blessed with a handful of first-rate **restaurants**, the best of which are located within several of the pensions and hotels. Given the town's prominence as a ski resort, most **bars** are out towards the slopes and are seasonal.

Gostilna Cvitar Borovška cesta 83. Tucked away in a delightful 200-year-old building next to the church, this characterful tavern has the best Slovene food in town, not least some terrific roasted meats. The stylish interior is an enjoyable place to eat, though not as much fun as the informal stone terrace; reasonably priced and top-class service to boot.

Kotnik Borovška cesta 15. Warm, elegantly styled place in the *Hotel Kotnik*, with a highly creditable menu featuring lots of grilled meats (including lamb) and fish. There's also a small, rather frenetic, pizzeria.

Lipa Koroška cesta 14. The downstairs restaurant in the Pension Lipa serves up outstanding international

and Slovene food, while there are tasty pizzas to be had in the hugely popular winter garden.

Miklič Vitranška 13. As accomplished as the hotel it's part of, this beautiful and classy restaurant offers an upscale international menu, with an outstanding selection of vegetarian dishes, as well as a colourful salad bar.

Pri Martinu Borovška cesta 61. Enjoyable, vaguely medieval themed restaurant next to the Liznjek House, rustling up healthy portions of solid meat dishes – such as veal stew with buckwheat mush – and some sound veggie options, including dumplings and polenta.

Nightlife

The town's central watering hole is the energetic *Vopa Pub*, just along from the post office at Borovška cesta 99a, while the terrace of the *Gostilna Cvitar* is an enjoyable spot to sup a beer or two. If you fancy chancing your luck, as many neighbouring Italians do each night, then head to the 24-hour casino adjoining the *Hotel Korona*, located to the south of town at Vršiška cesta 23. Entrance is €8 (but you get chips to the value of that), and you'll need some ID, ideally your passport.

Zelenci Nature Reserve

Three kilometres west of Kranjska Gora, sandwiched between the ski slopes of Podkoren and the main road to Italy, is the **Zelenci Nature Reserve**, home to an exceptional range of flora and fauna. Located within the reserve is a marsh, which consists of a brilliant emerald-blue, crystal-clear lake, below which cool springs spurt, volcano-like, from limestone sediment called *kreda* – a phenomenon unique to Slovenia. The lake – which is also the source of the Sava Dolinka River, though technically this begins at the Nadiša karst spring up in the Tamar Valley (see opposite) – can be accessed via a series of carefully constructed walkways from either side of the reserve, while the observation tower provides some lovely overhead views.

As well as a dense concentration of vegetation – including pygmy willows, alder trees and common cottongrass – the reserve supports some unusual fauna, such as the whiskered bat, sand lizard, common viper snake and a rare bird species, the scarlet grosbeak, all of which have been placed on the "Red List" – a list of Slovenia's most endangered species.

Activities around Kranjska Gora

The area around Kranjska Gora offers some of the best **cycling** in the region. The excellent cycling map (*Kolesarski izleti*), available from the tourist office, details some twelve excursions, ranging from gentle (Rateče), to very demanding (Vršič Pass, Belca) routes; paths are clearly signposted at regular intervals, each one indicating relevant turn-off points, distances and length of time to the next destination.

Bikes (€4 for one hour, €7 for half a day and €12 for a full day) can be rented from the Julijana agency (℡04/588-1325, ⓦwww.sednjek.si), just west of the *Hotel Prisank*; Intersport Bernik, at Borovška 88a (℡04/588-1470, ⓦwww.intersport-bernik.com); and Sport Point (℡04/588-4883, ⓦwww.sport-point.si) next to the *Hotel Prisank*. Julijana also organizes **whitewater rafting** (€30) on the Sava and Soča rivers, and **hiking** (€20), so long as there are at least four people.

The slopes of **Vitranc** and **Podkoren**, just west of the town centre, offer some 20km of **ski runs** (with five chairlifts and numerous towbars). These are suitable for skiers of all abilities, though the proliferation of easy slopes makes it a popular destination for **families and beginners**. Kranjska Gora also has night-time skiing, and between late December and early January, the town welcomes international skiers for the men's World Cup Slalom and Giant Slalom races. **Ski passes** (Vozovnice; around €30 for a day pass, and €160 for a weekly pass) are available from the ticket office at the Alpine Ski Club (Alpski Smučarski Klub), Borovška 99 (daily in winter 9am–4pm; ℡04/588-5300, ⓦwww.ask-kg.com). The club's school gives **ski lessons** (around €30 for a 1hr individual lesson, and around €70 for five two-hour lessons as part of a group); and **snowboarding** lessons (€25 1hr). Both the Alpine Ski Club and Intersport Bernik have **ski rental** (skis €15 for one day, boots €8, snowboard €20). Between December and April the Julijana agency offers **tobogganing** (€15).

The Planica and Tamar valleys

The most enjoyable hike from Kranjska Gora is up the **Planica Valley**, and beyond to the **Tamar Valley** (route no. 3 on the cycling map – see above). Just under 1km beyond the Zelenci Nature Reserve, you come to the grassy lower part of the Planica Valley, the most westerly access point into the Alps. From here, the road ascends steeply up towards the extraordinary **Planica ski jumps** (see box, p.140); a short way north of the last ski jump, you re-enter the National Park, at which point the road gives way to an untidy mess of gravel workings, before continuing as a stony, gently inclining track (used as a cross-country ski track in winter) for about 3.5km up to a lush grassy glade and the *Dom v Tamarju* mountain hut at 1108m (℡04/587-6055; open all year), which offers beds and good food. The walk up to this point is tremendous, largely for the views of the mighty, razor-sharp peak of **Jalovec** (2645m), due south, and **Mojstrovka** (2366m) to the east. A ten-minute walk west of the hut is the **source of the Nadiža stream**, a powerful karstic spring which squirts through a small fissure in the rock face before disappearing into underground channels and re-emerging in Zelenci at the base of the valley (see opposite). From the hut, one path heads south up the Tamar Valley to **Jalovec** (2645m; 6hr), and another east to **Vršič** (1611m; 3hr); both contain some very exposed and difficult sections.

Mojstrana and the Vrata Valley

The small village of **Gozd-Martuljek**, 3km east of Kranjska Gora, is the starting point for hikes into the **Martuljek** group of mountains, a fierce, spectacular range which counts the imperious **Mount Špik** (2472m) among its number, regarded as one of the toughest climbs in the Alps. From the village of

The incredible flying men

Situated at the mouth of the picturesque Planica Valley, 2km west of Kranjska Gora, are the world-renowned **Planica ski jumps**, site of the world's largest ski jump and venue for the longest jump in history. The first of the three jumps located here was built in 1934, on the initiative of **Stanko Bloudek**, engineer, figure-skating champion and the man widely credited with bringing winter sports to a wider Slovenian audience. Not long after its construction (a mere 90m, the longest is a breathtaking 190m), the first record at Planica fell, as the Austrian, **Sepp Bradl**, became the first man to jump beyond the magical one-hundred-metre mark, in 1936. To this day, Planica proudly boasts of holding more ski-jump records than any other venue in the world, not least the current **world record**, held by the Norwegian **Björn Romören**, who jumped an astonishing 239m here in 2005.

Slovenes too have a fine pedigree in the sport, gaining their first Olympic medal (a team bronze) in the 2002 Salt Lake City games, while their record-holder is **Rok Benkovič**, who leapt 226m at Planica in 2005. If you've got the energy, take a hike up the stairs located to the side of the jumps and enjoy the extraordinary views. Better still, if you're around at the end of March, then you shouldn't miss the annual World Cup event – celebrated as much for its drinking and music as for its sporting theatrics.

Mojstrana, a further 10km east, three parallel valleys fan out southwards into the core of the Park, each furrowed with mountain paths heading towards Triglav itself. Thirteen kilometres east of Kranjska Gora, just off the main road towards Jesenice, is the village of **MOJSTRANA**, the starting point for hikers attempting Triglav's north face (see box, p.134). The most direct road from the village heads southwest up into the **Vrata Valley** (Gateway Valley), the largest glacial valley in the northern tract of the Julian Alps and the most direct route to Triglav – consequently, it's often overflowing with hikers and motorists.

In the centre of the village, at Triglavska cesta 50, the **Triglav Museum Collection** (Triglavska Muzejska Zbirka; May–Oct Tues–Sun 10am–4pm; €3) has some illuminating exhibits pertaining to the National Park and those who have shaped it. One of the park's foremost pioneers was Jakob Aljaž (1845–1927) – parish priest, composer and mountaineer – after whom both the hut at the end of the valley and the rocket-shaped turret (Aljažev stolp) at the top of Triglav are named. In 1895, as competing claims from Germany and Austria for Triglav intensified, Aljaš, a staunch Slovene patriot, purchased the peak for the sum of 1 florin, thus ensuring the mountain remained Slovene property. Other rooms document the work of the Slovenian Mountain Association, the Mountain Rescue Service and the first mountain guides.

Four kilometres beyond the village, two paths branch off up a forest slope (10min) to the **Peričnik Waterfall** (Slap Peričnik), which actually comprises an upper (16m) and lower (52m) fall. Unusually, the falls can be circled – via the narrow, sandy ledge – but wherever you view it from you're likely to get a good soaking from the itinerant spray. The best time to see the falls is in winter when the water freezes into thick curtains of ice.

Six kilometres further north, up an increasingly steep and rugged track (accessible by car), is *Aljažev Dom* (℡04/589-1030; May–Oct), named after the eponymous mountaineer, and the key lodge for hikers en route to Triglav. Ten minutes' walk north of the hut is a **memorial to World War II Partisan fighters**, which takes the form of climbing equipment (a carabiner and piton). From here, a couple of paths lead towards the summit. On a clear day, the views of Triglav's indomitable 1200-metre-high and 3km-wide north face are nothing short of spectacular.

Kot and Krma valleys and Zgornja Radovna

From Mojstrana another road cuts south towards the second and third of the glens which forge into the belly of the National Park. Three kilometres beyond the Kosma Pass (847m), one road branches off into the secluded **Kot Valley**, while the main road continues through the hamlet of **ZGORNJA RADOVNA** and on to the **Krma Valley** which, at 7km in length, is the longest of the glacial valleys in the Julian Alps. In Zgornja Radovna, at no. 25, is the **Pocar Farmhouse** (Pocarjeva Domačija; Fri–Sun 10am–5pm; €2), one of six farms believed to have existed in the hamlet during feudal times. This unusually large seventeenth-century farmhouse consists of a main living area, bedroom – note the date, 1775, inscribed onto the ceiling beam – a "black" kitchen (see p.129) and, upstairs, the attic and granary room. The entire furnishings and contents of the house are all original. The two-storey, part-stone, part-wooden **outbuilding**, previously used for housing livestock and storing hay, now displays farmers' implements and long wooden carts. From the farmhouse, the road east continues down through the **Radovna Valley** towards Bled, some 15km away. For cyclists there is a fairly sedate but attractive path (3hr) from the farmhouse to Krnica near Bled – regular information boards detail local points of interest. At roughly the midway point between Radovna and Bled, in the hamlet of Srednja Radovna, you'll come across the ruins of the Smolej farmhouse – the only building that remained following an attack on the village by Germans in September 1944, in retaliation for the ambush of two of their soldiers. At the road junction is a **monument to Jakob Aljaž**, which has the local hero pointing towards Triglav.

South to the Soča Valley

Linking the Upper Sava and Soča Valleys, the **Vršič Pass** – the highest mountain pass in Slovenia – is one of the most spectacular and scenically rewarding trips in the country. Constituting the stretch of road between Kranjska Gora and Trenta – a total of some 25km – the pass is defined by fifty hairpin bends, twenty-four on the Kranjska Gora side, twenty-six on the Trenta side (each bend is numbered and the altitude recorded). Between June and September, four daily buses haul themselves up and over the pass and down to Bovec (44km south of Kranjska Gora), and while there are regular stops at all the huts and villages along the way, this limited service makes it extremely difficult to see much in one day. It's really only feasible to see many of the places described here if you have your own transport (the road is not suitable for caravans or trailers). The other alternative, of course, is to hike to or between various points. Due to snow drifts and the threat of avalanches, the pass is periodically closed between November and April.

From Kranjska Gora to Vršič

Two kilometres south of Kranjska Gora, in the centre of a large gravel flood plain, is the artificial **Lake Jasna**. The road then climbs steadily up past the 1000-metre point, reaching, at turn eight (1129m), the **Russian Chapel** (Ruska kapelica), probably the most poignant sight along the pass. Set back 100m from the road, the tiny wood-latticed chapel (which cannot be entered) was built between 1916 and 1917 to commemorate the deaths of over three hundred Russian prisoners of war buried by an avalanche as they constructed the road; thousands more prisoners died from fatigue, starvation and torture

Mountain huts

Nearly a third of Slovenia's 169 **mountain huts** (Planinarski Domovi) lie within the National Park's boundaries, all managed and maintained by the **Alpine Association of Slovenia** (Planinska Zveza Slovenije or PZS). Huts range from the most basic of refuges (*zavetišče*), often without accommodation or with very few beds and sometimes no running water, to more comfortable places, namely **huts** (*koča*) or **houses** (*dom*), which vary considerably in size, quality and sleeping capacity; expect to pay around €15 for a dorm bed, €20 in a five- to eight-bed room, and €25 in a twin-bed room – these are the maximum prices for category I huts (classified as a hut more than one hour's walk away from motorized transport) – and typically those around Triglav. A thirty-percent discount is available to UIAA-affiliated members (International Mountaineering and Climbing Federation).

Food, available at just about all huts, is usually wholesome, filling and cheap; typical staples include vegetable soup (*zelenjavna juha*; €3), goulash (*golaž*; €5) and tea with lemon (*čaj z limono*; €1.50). Owing to their high-altitude location, the majority of the park's huts are only **open** between June and September, though most of those along the Vršič Pass are open year-round. However, these dates aren't fixed and may deviate by a month either side depending on the weather. All huts take bookings.

during its construction, a few of whom are buried in the small **military cemetery**, set back forty metres from the road just after turn 21.

Beyond this point the road becomes ever more sinuous, passing a couple of mountain huts – *Koča na Gozdu* (☎050/626-641; daily May–Sept, Sat & Sun Oct–April) and *Erjavčeva koča* (☎051/399-226; all year) – before arriving at **Vršič**, the highest point along the pass at 1611m; if you wish to park, you'll have to pay (€3). There's another hut here – *Tičarjev Dom* (☎050/634-571; May to mid-Oct) – and it's a good starting point for hikes into the surrounding mountains, including **Tamar**, via Vratca (1108m; 3hr 30min), and **Prisank** (2547m; 4hr 30min), though both are hikes of some difficulty.

From Vršič to Trenta

The descent from Vršič to the Trenta Valley is every bit as dramatic as the ascent, with many an unscheduled diversion almost guaranteed – if you have wheels that is. Stationed on an exposed ledge just after turn 48 is a fine-looking **monument** to Julius Kugy, the esteemed mountaineer and botanist who pioneered many new routes across the Alps, and whose biography *Alpine Pilgrimage* extolled the virtues of both the mountains and those who climbed them. At the next bend, a road branches off towards the *Koča pri Izviru Soče* hut (which has dorm beds) (☎04/586-6070; May–Oct), 2km away, and the source of the Soča River (Izvir Soče). From the hut, it's a short, twenty-minute climb up a very rocky and partially secured path to the source – care should be taken on approaching the latter part as it can get slippery; fed by an underground lake, the water emerges from a dark cave before streaking away on its long and eventful journey to the Adriatic, some 136km downstream. If you don't fancy walking that far, you might like to tackle the 20km long Soča Trail (Soča Pot), a carefully tailored path (no bicycles) that follows the course of the river from its source down to Bovec – regular information boards (marked "TNP") line the route indicating various points of interest. At 9am every Thursday in July and August there are **guided tours** (2hr; €10) from the source down to the lodge in Trenta (see opposite).

Secreted away in perfect rural isolation just ten minutes' walk west of the hut (signposted) is the wonderful *Kekčeva domačija* pension (☎041/413-087,

@kekec.trenta@siol.net; **❽**), named after the legendary Slovenian children's character *Kekec*, the clever shepherd boy, created by the Kranjska Gora-born writer Josip Vandot (see p.137) – the film *Good luck, Kekec* was shot here in 1963. The pension has nine beautifully appointed apartments, each with an upstairs bedroom and a downstairs living area and bathroom.

Back on the main road, 400m south of the junction, is the **Mlinarica Gorge**, another magical masterpiece of nature, which takes the form of immense, overhanging rock faces and an impenetrable ravine, at the head of which is another waterfall; to get here, cross the suspension bridge and follow the footpath to the right around to the gorge entrance. Grafted onto a picturesque hillside 2km south of the gorge is the **Alpinum Juliana** (Alpski botanični vrt; daily May–Sept 8.30am–6.30pm; €3), Slovenia's only alpine botanical garden. Founded in 1926 by Albert Bois de Chesne, a Trieste merchant and close colleague of the botanist Kugy, the garden has a fine collection of flora from the country's various alpine regions, as well as samples from the Pyrenees and Caucasus. The best time to visit is in May following the winter thaws.

Two kilometres further down the road is *Camping Trenta* (☎031/615-966), which also has bungalows sleeping three (**❸**), and five double rooms (**❹**) – this is the first of four campsites between here and Bovec, all of which are open between May and October. The road continues down the narrow valley and into the village of **TRENTA**, which marks the border of the upper part of the Trenta Valley. The major point of interest here is the **Trenta Lodge** (Dom Trenta), at no. 34, which houses both the **Triglav National Park Information Centre** (daily: May–Oct 10am–6pm, Nov–April 10am–2pm; ☎05/388-9330, ⓦwww.tnp.si) and the **Trenta Museum** (same times; €4). Beginning with an insightful fifteen-minute multi visual presentation on the National Park, the museum goes on to explore, in excellent and detailed fashion, the geology and geomorphology of the park, together with displays on its indigenous flora and fauna. The exhibition then peters out somewhat with a rather flat ethnological collection, though there's a reasonably faithful attempt at a mock-up of a Trenta homestead and shepherd's dwelling. The lodge also has a handful of apartments, each sleeping up to five people, with a kitchen and living space downstairs and a bedroom upstairs (**❻**); they can also arrange private rooms in a house some 300m away (**❷**). Trenta is also the starting-off point for assaults on Triglav's massive west face, via the **Zadnjica Valley**.

From Trenta to Bovec

Ten kilometres on from Trenta is the long, straggling village of **SOČA**, consisting of little more than a string of roadside houses and the **Church of St Joseph** (Cerkev Sv Jozef), renowned for Tone Kralj's 1944 painting of the devil, which here bears an uncanny resemblance to Mussolini. At the entrance to the village is the *Korita* **campsite** (☎05/388-9322), adjoining which is an **eco-camp**, a fabulous little set-up comprising around a dozen wood cabins (called lean-tos – each sleeps two people and comes equipped with bedding), as well as hammocks, complete with sleeping bag. Back on the main road, and a little further down, is the decent *Gostišče Andrejc* at no. 31 (☎05/388-9530; **❹**). Below the village, the powerful current of the Soča river has hollowed out spectacular erosion and abrasion potholes in the limestone rock, creating the fantastic 750-metre-long, fifteen-metre-deep **Velika Korita Gorge** (also called the Soča Ravine), the best views of which can be had from the swing bridge at its upper end. Here, a road branches off left towards the *Klin* campsite (☎05/388-9513) and the **Lepena Valley**; the road winds up to *Pristava Lepena* (mid-April to Oct; ☎05/388-9900, ⓦwww.pristava-lepena.com), a self-contained complex incorporating some ten wooden, cottage-style apartments (**❽**; no kitchen facilities) at the edge of the forest, a **riding school** (€18 for 50min in riding ring, €24 for 50min trail ride on Lipizzaners), and a first-rate **restaurant**; guests receive discounted rates for the riding school and free use of the swimming pool and tennis court.

The last point of interest before exiting the park is the **Golobar Telpher Line** (Žicnica Golobar), an odd-looking, but immensely powerful, roadside contraption which was once used to transport heavy goods via overhead cables. Although this one was built in 1931 – one of the few remaining in Slovenia – telpher lines first appeared throughout the region during World War I as a means of supplying the front lines. They were later put to good use by farmers and foresters who used them to transport timber back and forth across the valley. The road descends through the lower Trenta valley and exits the park just prior to Bovec, covered in the next chapter.

Travel details

Trains

Bled Jezero to: Bohinjska Bistrica (Mon–Fri 6 daily, Sat & Sun 4 daily; 20min); Most na Soči (Mon–Fri 6 daily, Sat & Sun 4 daily; 55min); Nova Gorica (Mon–Fri 6 daily, Sat & Sun 4 daily; 1hr 45min).

Bled Lesce to: Jesenice (every 1–3hr; 15min); Kranj (every 1–3hr; 25min); Ljubljana (every 1–3hr; 1hr); Radovljica (every 1–3hr; 5min); Škofja Loka (every 1–3hr; 35min).

Bohinjska Bistrica to: Bled Jezero (Mon–Fri 7 daily, Sat & Sun 4 daily; 20min); Most na Soči (Mon–Fri 8 daily, Sat & Sun 5 daily; 35min); Nova Gorica (Mon–Fri 8 daily, Sat & Sun 5 daily; 1hr 20min).

Kamnik to: Ljubljana (hourly; 50min).

Kranj to: Bled Lesce (every 1–3hr; 25min); Ljubljana (every 1–3hr; 35min); Radovljica (every 1–3hr; 20min); Škofja Loka (every 1–3hr; 10min).

Radovljica to: Bled Lesce (every 1–3hr; 5min); Kranj (every 1–3hr; 20min); Ljubljana (every 1–3hr; 55min); Škofja Loka (every 1–3hr; 30min).

Škofja Loka to: Bled Lesce (every 1–3hr; 35min); Kranj (every 1–3hr; 10min); Ljubljana (every 1–3hr; 25min); Radovljica (every 1–3hr; 30min).

Buses

Bled to: Kranj (hourly; 40min); Kranjska Gora (7 daily; 1hr 15min); Ljubljana (hourly; 1hr 15min); Radovljica (every 30min; 15min); Ribčev Laz for Lake Bohinj (hourly; 40min).

Bohinjska Bistrica to: Bled (hourly; 25min); Ribčev Laz, for Lake Bohinj (hourly; 15min).

Kamnik to: Ljubljana (Mon–Fri every 20–30min, Sat & Sun every 45min–hourly; 40–50min).

Kranj to: Bled (hourly; 40min); Ljubljana (every 20–30min; 50min); Radovljica (every 30min; 30min); Škofja Loka (hourly; 20min); Tržič (hourly; 20min).

Kranjska Gora to: Bled (every 1–2hr; 1hr 15min); Bovec (July & Aug 4 daily; 1hr 45min); Ljubljana (every 1–2hr; 2hr 30min) Radovljica (every 1–2hr; 1hr 25min).

Kropa to: Radovljica (Mon–Fri 8 daily; 20min).

Radovljica to: Begunje (hourly; 25min); Bled (every 30min; 15min); Kranj (every 30min; 30min); Kranjska Gora (hourly; 1hr 25min); Kropa (6 daily Mon–Fri; 20min); Ljubljana (every 30min; 1hr 15min); Ribčev Laz, for Lake Bohinj (hourly; 45min).

Ribčev Laz (Lake Bohinj) to: Bled (hourly; 40min); Bohinjska Bistrica (hourly; 15min); Ljubljana (hourly; 1hr 45min); Stara Fužina (Mon–Fri 5 daily; 10min); Studor (Mon–Fri 5 daily; 10min).

Selca to: Škofja Loka (7 daily; 20min); Železniki (9 daily; 10min).

Škofja Loka to: Kranj (hourly; 20min); Ljubljana (hourly; 30min); Selca (Mon–Fri 6 daily, Sat & Sun 3 daily; 20min); Železniki (Mon–Fri 6 daily, Sat & Sun 3 daily; 30min); Žiri (Mon–Fri 10 daily, Sat 5, Sun 3; 45min).

Stara Fužina to: Bohinjska Bistrica (Mon–Fri 5 daily; 15min); Ribčev Laz, for Lake Bohinj (Mon–Fri 5 daily; 10min).

Tržič to: Kranj (hourly; 20min); Radovljica (Mon–Fri 7 daily, Sat & Sun 2 daily; 30min).

Železniki to: Škofja Loka (Mon–Fri 6 daily, Sat & Sun 3 daily; 30min).

The Great Outdoors

There are few more active nations in Europe than Slovenia, where abundant mountains, forests, hills, rivers and lakes offer unlimited potential to indulge in a wide range of outdoor pursuits: from hiking the lush meadows and valleys of the Julian Alps, cycling amid the rolling hills and forests of Dolenjska, rafting and kayaking the thrashing Soča River, or climbing Mount Triglav, Slovenia's highest mountain – the permutations for adventure are endless.

Hitting the slopes

First popularized in Slovenia in the seventeenth century, skiing unequivocally remains the nation's number one sport. Uniformly well-equipped, efficient and safe, the country counts more than fifteen major resorts (and many smaller ones), the best and most popular of which are Kranjska Gora, a good family resort and international competition venue near the Austrian border, Krvavec, near Kranj (very popular with weekending Ljubljančani), Kanin, near Bovec, and Pohorje, on the outskirts of Maribor – this the country's largest skiing area. A number of resorts (such as Krvavec, and Vogel, near Lake Bohinj) also offer good snowboarding facilities, while cross-country skiing is another Slovene institution, the main venue here being the Pokljuka Plateau near Bled.

Skiing at Vogel ▲

Climbing in the Julian Alps ▼

Scaling the peaks

Slovenia is traversed by over seven thousand kilometres of marked paths and for the majority of climbers and hikers, the main destination is the Julian Alps, at the heart of which is Mount Triglav (2864m), the country's highest peak. Along with the Julians, the Karavanke Mountains and the Kamniške-Savinja Alps (both of which count numerous peaks topping the 2500m mark) offer the country's most varied and challenging climbs and hikes. For the less energetic, there's more moderate walking in the non-alpine tracts of the Pohorje Massif near Maribor, and the Snežnik hills south of Postojna along the Croatian border. There's also gentler rambling territory south of Triglav National Park in the sub-alpine hills of Cerkno and Idrija, and in the deep forests of Dolenjska.

Horsing around

As the home of the Lipizzaner it's perhaps not surprising that Slovenia displays a deep-rooted attachment to all things equine. While the most obvious destination for equestrians is Lipica (see p.185), there are dozens more **horseriding centres** throughout the country, many sited in fabulously scenic locations. Most offer some form of recreational (trail) and arena riding, a range of classes and courses – and sometimes carriage rides, too; three of the most established centres are Pristava Lepena in the gorgeous Trenta Valley (there are Lipizzaner here too), the Kaval Centre at Prestranek near Postojna, and the Brdo estate just outside Kranj.

Casting a line

Slovenia offers some of the finest freshwater **fishing** in Europe, its abundant rivers, streams and lakes richly stocked with many different species of fish – indeed more than ninety species have been catalogued, many of which are under permanent protection. The Soča river is renowned for its bountiful reserves of grayling and trout – brown trout, rainbow trout, and, above all, the highly prized marble trout (*Salmo trutta marmoratus*). Elsewhere, the Kolpa, Krka, Sava Bohinjka and Unica rivers have healthy stocks of pike, perch, chub and eelpout. Of the lakes, fishing from boats is permitted at Lake Bohinj and the intermittent Lake Cerknica. The main fishing season lasts approximately from April to October, although this can vary slightly depending upon the water levels. Permits are required (around €25–40 for a daily permit), details of which are listed throughout the guide.

▲ Horseriding in Pristava Lepena

▼ Fishing on the Krka River

Kayaking near Kobarid ▲

Canyoning near Kobarid ▼

Daredevil Slovenes

Slovene alpinists have gained a world-class reputation, thanks to the daredevil deeds of several **extreme athletes**; the climber Tomaz Humar made over 1500 ascents until his death in 2009 while climbing in Nepal, and extreme skier Davo Karničar has skied down the highest mountain of every continent, including, in 2000, Mount Everest – the first person to do so. Equally remarkable is the ultra-marathon swimmer Martin Strel whose many world records include a two-month swim of the Amazon in 2007. Ironically, the name of his home town, Mokronog, translates as "Wet Feet".

Slovenia's top five adrenaline rushes

Slovenia is geared up in a big way for **adventure sports and activities**, in particular around its rivers, which attract enthusiasts from all over Europe each summer.

▸▸ **Whitewater rafting** Whether on the fast, foaming waters of the Soča River, or the calmer, warmer stretches of the Kolpa, this is the country's most popular adventure sport.

▸▸ **Canyoning** The ultimate adrenaline experience, involving abseiling down ravines and waterfalls, jumping into pools and sliding through mountainous rivers.

▸▸ **Hydrospeed** Descending the rapids face down on a small polyurethane raft, this pursuit is the most extreme of all water activities.

▸▸ **Kayaking** Paddling solo or in a pair, Slovenia's rivers allow for thrilling white-water kayaking experiences.

▸▸ **Tandem paragliding** A head for heights is all that's required for spectac-ular bird's-eye views of Slovenia's phenomenal natural scenery.

3

The Soča Valley to the Istrian coast

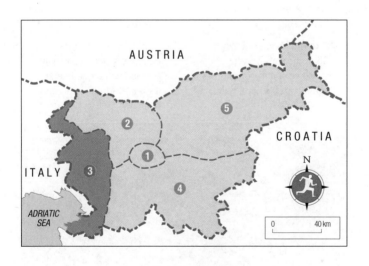

CHAPTER 3 # Highlights

✱ **White water rafting on the Soča** This magical alpine river provides some of the best whitewater rafting, kayaking and canoeing in Europe. See p.151

✱ **Hiša Franko, Kobarid** Enjoy top-rank comfort and food in this sublime pension/restaurant. See p.155

✱ **Kobarid Museum** Compelling and moving museum documenting the region's World War I mountain battles. See p.156

✱ **Oldtimer Museum Train** Chug through wonderful alpine countryside from the comfort of the Oldtimer. See p.163

✱ **Goriška Brda** Trek down the cellars of these gorgeous, vineyard-clad hills, which touch the Italian border. See p.169

✱ **Škocjan Caves** Take a trip through this breathtaking cave system, which features the world's largest subterranean canyon. See p.188

✱ **Church of the Holy Trinity, Hrastovlje** A Romanesque monument, smothered with exceptional fifteenth-century frescoes including the famous *Dance of Death*. See p.189

✱ **Piran** The coast's most beautiful resort has Venetian Gothic-inspired architecture, Italianate squares and pretty churches. See p.199

▲ *Dance of Death* fresco, Church of the Holy Trinity, Hrastovlje

The Soča Valley to the Istrian coast

W hile northwest Slovenia may possess the lion's share of the country's primary attractions, the thin wedge of land skirting the Italian border – known as Primorska – is unquestionably the country's most diverse region, constituting four geographically distinct areas, namely, from north to south, the Soča Valley, Central Primorska, the Karst and the Coast.

Crossing over from the Julian Alps or Triglav National Park, your first encounter with this region is likely to be the magisterial **Soča Valley**, whose rugged peaks were the setting for a sustained period of crushing mountain warfare between Italian forces and the Central Powers during World War I – events that are superbly relayed in the museum in **Kobarid**, itself situated close to many of the battle sites. The valley now ranks as the country's premier adventure-sports centre, thanks both to its mountains, which embrace a continuous stream of hikers and skiers, and the amazing **Soča River**, one of Europe's most scenic, chock-full of rafters, canoeists and kayakers during the warmer months.

The valley's alpine peaks eventually give way to the more uniform topography of **Central Primorska**, a region defined primarily by its fertile wine and fruit-growing regions – specifically the **Vipava** and **Brda** hills, located east and west respectively of the bland, modern town of **Nova Gorica**. Central Primorska also incorporates an attractive belt of subalpine countryside (but with peaks still exceeding 1200m), sheltering the relatively little-known and under-visited towns of **Idrija** and **Cerkno**, themselves handy bases from which to take in any number of local sights. Nature asserts itself in spectacular fashion a short way south of here with the **Karst** region, whose star attractions are the jaw-dropping **Škocjan Caves** and the world-famous **Lipica Stud Farm**.

Although the **Slovene coast** (all 46km of it) might lack some of the glamour of its more well-heeled Croatian cousin to the south – its beaches are, for the most part, rocky, concrete or grass affairs – there is still much to enjoy. Nearly five centuries of Venetian rule have endowed its towns with some fabulous architecture, not least in its prettiest and most popular resort, **Piran**, although both **Izola** and the coast's largest town and major port, **Koper**, possess a fine kernel of medieval buildings. Those seeking more self-indulgent fare should find **Portorož**, a stone's throw from Piran and the coast's brashest resort, more

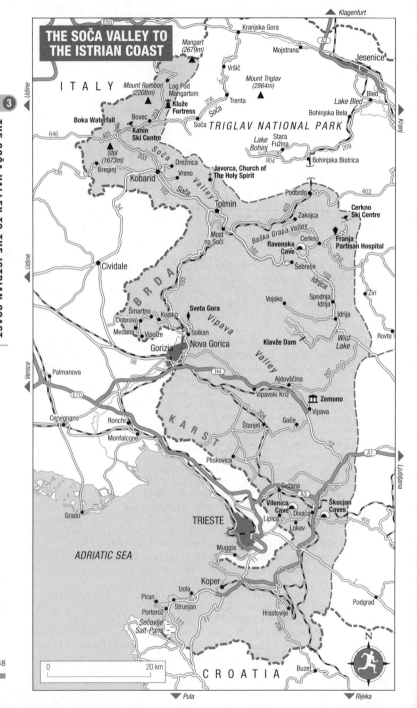

THE SOČA VALLEY TO THE ISTRIAN COAST

Klagenfurt ▲

Kranjska Gora

Mojstrana

Jesenice

E55

ITALY

Mangart (2679m) ▲

Vršič

Mount Triglav (2864m) ▲

Lake Bled
Bled

Mount Rombon (2208m) ▲
Log Pod Mangartom
Kluže Fortress

206
Trenta

Soča

Bohinjska Bela

Boka Waterfall
Bovec

Soča *TRIGLAV NATIONAL PARK*

Kanin Ski Centre

646

Stol (1673m) ▲

Lake Bohinj
Stara Fužina

Bohinjska Bistrica

209

Breginj

203
Drežnica

904

Vrsno
Javorca, Church of † The Holy Spirit

Kobarid

54

102

Soča

Tolmin

Podbrdo

403

Zakojca
Cerkno Ski Centre

Most na Soči

Baška Grapa Valley
Cerkno
Ravenska Cave ○
Franja Partisan Hospital

102

Šebrelje

210

B R D A

103

Cividale

Idrijca

Vojsko

Spodnja Idrija

Žiri

Idrija

Vipava Valley

Sveta Gora ◆

Rovte

Šmartno
Kojsko

Dobrovo

Medana
Vipolže

Solkan

Klavže Dam

Wild Lake

Gorizia

Nova Gorica

56

Vipava Valley

207

Palmanova

H4

Ajdovščina

E70

K A R S T

Vipavski Križ

Goče
Vipava

Zemono 🏛

Cervignano

Ronchi

Štanjel

204

Monfalcone

Pliskovica

12

A1

TRIESTE

Sežana

A3

Vilenica Cave ○

Divača

Škocjan Caves ○

405

Grado

Lipica
Lokev

Muggia

111

ADRIATIC SEA

Ljubljana ▶

Koper

Izola

Piran

Strunjan

Portorož

Sečovlje Salt-Pans

Hrastovlje

Podgrad

111

208

N

0 ——————— 20 km

C R O A T I A

Buzet

▼ *Pula*

▼ *Rijeka*

to their liking. Crowds in this part of Slovenia are rarely an inconvenience, although the major coastal spots can get uncomfortably congested during August; even then, as in other parts of the region, finding accommodation should present few problems.

Getting around the Karst and coastal areas is simple enough, with a healthy stream of **trains** and **buses** serving both. However, access up and down the Soča Valley is patchy, the rail line going no further than Most na Soči (midway between Nova Gorica and Kobarid), and bus services are sporadic.

The Soča Valley

Richly textured by history and nature, the **Soča Valley**, skirting Triglav National Park's western boundary and extending all the way down to the flatlands of Nova Gorica, is one of Slovenia's most captivating regions. Although not an immediately obvious destination, the valley has few peers when it comes to sheer, stark beauty; moreover, it boasts one of Europe's most dramatic alpine rivers, the **Soča**, which commands thousands of watersport enthusiasts to its milky blue-green waters.

During World War I the valley marked the front line – known as the **Soča Front** (or Isonzo Front) – between the Italian and Austro-Hungarian armies who engaged in some of the most savage and relentless fighting in the history of mountain warfare. Consequently, the valley is strewn with memorial chapels, abandoned fortifications and dignified military cemeteries.

There are several key settlements sequenced in vertical fashion down the valley's spine: both **Bovec** and **Kobarid**, in the upper part of the valley (Gornje Posočje), are important tourist hubs, the former, one of the major adventure-sports centres in the country, the latter replete with poignant reminders from the battle front, as attested to in its memorable museum. Further down the valley, the small town of **Tolmin** is worth investigating, not least because of its proximity to the fantastic **Tolminska Gorge** and stunningly situated **Church of the Holy Spirit** in Javorca, while a few kilometres further south, **Most na Soči** holds some of Slovenia's most significant archeological sites.

Bovec and around

Lying in a broad basin in the shadow of the Kanin mountain range and the mighty Mount Rombon, the small alpine town of **BOVEC** is one of Slovenia's premier watersports centres due to its proximity to the Soča River. For centuries, however, the town and its surrounds were an important centre for animal husbandry, the lofty alpine plateaus ideally suited for high-level pasturing, while the broad valley floor was used for growing hay. The last century was particularly unkind to Bovec: it was burnt down in 1903; massive destruction followed during World War I, when the town was razed and much of the population deported; and more recently Bovec was struck by three earth-quakes – two extremely powerful ones in 1976 and 1998, and a third, less destructive one, in 2004.

There are several worthwhile attractions within close proximity to Bovec, including the magnificent **Boka Waterfall**, the **Kluže Fortress**, and, right up towards the Italian border, the pretty village of **Log pod Mangartom**.

Arrival, information and accommodation

All **buses** terminate outside the *Letni Vrt* restaurant on the main square, Trg Golobarskih Žrtev. Just across the square, at no. 22, the **tourist office** (June–Aug daily 9am–8pm; rest of year Mon–Fri 9am–5pm, Sat & Sun 9am–1pm; ☎05/384-1919, ⒲www.bovec.si) has a good stock of information and maps on the Soča Valley. The **post office** is just up from the tourist office at Slomškov trg 10 (Mon–Fri 8–9.30am, 10am–3.30pm & 4–6pm, Sat 8am–noon).

For private **accommodation** (❷) head to GoTour, located through the passageway next to the Mercator supermarket on the square (Mon–Fri 9am–1pm & 2–5pm, Sat 9am–1pm; ☎05/389-6366, ⒲www.gotourbovec .com). The town's most upmarket **hotel** is the *Dobra Vila*, on the eastern edge of town at Mala Vas 112 (☎05/389-6400, ⒲www.dobra-vila-bovec.com; ❼); its twelve beautifully appointed, and very spacious, rooms are handsomely furnished with big lush beds, televisions with DVD player, and air-conditioning. The town's two other hotels are the very ordinary *Hotel Alp* (☎05/388-4000, ⒲www .alp-hotel.si; ❼), prominently positioned on the south side of the main square, and the marginally more appealing *Hotel Kanin* (☎05/389-6880, ⒲www.hotel -kanin.com; ❽), just behind the *Alp*, which also has a pool. Another option is the *Stari Kovač*, a few paces down from the *Hotel Alp* at Rupa 3 (☎05/388-6699, ⒲www.starikovac.com; ❺–❽), which has comfortable and well-furnished rooms and apartments, some sleeping up to eight people.

There are four **campsites** on the southern edge of town, all of which are open between April and October. The closest, and smallest, is the *Polovnik* (☎05/389-6007, ⒲www.kamp-polovnik.com), 500m southwest of the *Hotel Kanin*. Two kilometres further south (follow the sign for Čezsoča), there are three sites bunched together: the first is *Vodenca* (☎041/620-885, ⒲www .camp-vodenca.com); 200m down the hill is *Kajak Kamp Toni* (☎05/388-6454, ⒲www.kajakkamptoni.com), the best equipped of the sites and frequented almost exclusively by kayakers due to its proximity to the water; and behind there is the smaller *Liza* site (☎05/389-6370).

The Town

As a result of the 1998 earthquake over sixty percent of the buildings in town were seriously damaged, most of which have now been repaired or rebuilt. One of the most affected buildings, and among the first to be repaired, was the **Parish Church of St Ulric** (Cerkev Sv Urh), situated 200m up the hill from the main square. Originally a Gothic construction, the present church was rebuilt in neo-Romanesque style in 1734, but underwent substantial reconstruction following heavy World War I damage. Although the interior retains the odd Gothic flourish, notably the portals and triumphal arch, the highlight is the reddish-brown Baroque high altar, made from marble hewn from Mount Rombon, and framed either side by sculptures of St John Nepomuk and St Paul. Unusual features of the church are the niches on the front exterior, containing statues of Sts Peter, Paul and Ulric, and the headstones in the surrounding walls, which would indicate that this used to be a cemetery.

For those keen to learn more about the Soča Front (see box, p.156), it's possible to view a **private collection** of World War I weaponry and other objects retrieved from the battle sites. Amassed by a member of the **1313**

Sports and activities on the Soča River

Between April and October, the **Soča River** draws watersports enthusiasts from many countries keen to test out one of the most challenging white water rivers in Europe. Sections of the river are graded according to the level of difficulty – from one, the easiest, up to six, the most difficult (which is open only to experienced competition rafters); most trips depart from Boka, 6km west of Bovec, and finish at Trnovo ob Soči, 10km further downriver. A number of agencies in Bovec and Kobarid offer rafting and a plethora of other river activities. The best options in Bovec are: Bovec Rafting Team, based in a small hut a few paces west of the main square (☎05/388-6128, ⊚www .bovec-rafting-team.com), Alpe Sport Vančar, Trg Golobarskih Žrtev 20 (☎05/389-6350, ⊚www.bovecsport.com) and Top Extreme (☎041-620-636, ⊚www.top.si) – actually 6km south of Bovec in Žaga. In Kobarid there's X-Point at Stresova 1 (☎05/388-5308, ⊚www.xpoint.si). Each raft can take up to ten people including one instructor; whoever you go with, expect to pay around €30 per person, which also covers transfers to and from the river and all equipment – just make sure you have swimming gear and a towel. Most of the agencies also run **kayak** and **canoe** courses (around €60 for one day), as well as kayaks (€25 full-day) and Canadian canoes, which seat two (€30 full-day), to rent, in addition to **hydrospeed** (€35) and **canyoning** (€40). All agencies have similar opening times (July–Sept daily 9am–7/8pm; April, May & Oct weekends only, same times).

Between April and October, the river becomes prime **fishing** territory, richly sourced with brown trout, rainbow trout, the famous marble trout (*Salmo trutta marmoratus*) and grayling. There are two types of licence: the regular one (1 day €65, 3 days €180, 1 week €270), valid for the upper section of the Soča and its tributaries; and the Trophy licence (€70, €180, €360), which covers a three-kilometre stretch of the river in the middle part. Contact the tourist office in Bovec (see opposite) for information with regard to obtaining permits.

At weekends between April and October, Top Extreme offers **bungee-jumping** over the Soča (€45), although this takes place in Nova Gorica, some 70km away, as well as Extreme Days, typically a combination of rafting with one other activity (around €75). Depending on where you fly, a twenty-minute **tandem paragliding** flight with Bovec Rafting Team or Top Extreme will cost around €85. **Bikes** (€5 1hr, €15 half-day, €20 full-day) can be rented from Bovec Rafting Team.

Association (Društvo 1313) – an ardent group of local historians committed to honouring the men who fought on the Front – this extraordinary collection consists of a stash of weapons (grenades, shells, knives and so on), personal belongings (flasks, combs and toothbrushes), and illuminating photographs of some of the battle scenes; to arrange a visit either call directly (☎041/821–269) or contact the tourist office. If you want to see where part of the action took place, follow a signposted path 1km south of Bovec (500m before the turning towards Trenta) towards **Ravelnik**, the name given to an area containing a string of huts, caverns and trenches, abandoned following the cessation of fighting; many have been cleaned up and partly reconstructed but are, nevertheless, fascinating to look around. Two kilometres east of Bovec, at the crossroads of the Predel and Vršič roads, is the **Bovec military cemetery** (Vojaško Pokopališče), containing over five hundred headstones of Austrian soldiers killed near Bovec and on Mount Rombon between 1915 and 1917.

Eating and drinking

Bovec can rate three extremely commendable **restaurants**, all of which lean heavily on local food and ingredients; the popular *Letni Vrt* gostilna on the main square, with its huge terrace, has a reputation as a fantastic pizzeria, but this doesn't do justice to its exhaustive menu of fish, game, lamb and local cheeses (closed Tues). More expensive is the warm and classy *Martinov Hram*, 50m west of the square at no. 27, whose grilled Balkan meat and fish dishes are the pick of an outstandingly long and varied menu, which also includes superb vegetarian options. More basic, but no less enjoyable, *Stari Kovač*, at Rupa 3, has cracking oven-baked pizzas (closed Mon).

There are disappointingly few **drinking** venues in town, though the *Pink Panter*, up the hill from the church at Kaninska Vas 7, is an enjoyable place to relax with a beer, as is *Café Plec*, opposite the post office. The *Dobra Vila*'s cosy conservatory café/bar serves up the best coffee (and views) in town, while the *Hotel Alp's* terrace café and delicious ice-cream parlour is also worth stopping off at. If you don't mind a little trek, there's the raucous *Skripi* pub out by the ski centre in Dvor.

Boka Waterfall

The most popular local attraction is the thundering 106-metre-high and thirty-metre-wide **Boka Waterfall** (Slap Boka), located 6km southwest of Bovec just before the village of **Žaga** – indeed, Žaga itself was recently in the spotlight, as it was here that a large amount of filming took place for the 2008 Disney film, *The Chronicles of Narnia: Prince Caspian*. It's possible to see the waterfall from the main road (albeit at quite some distance), and close-up views can be obtained by scrambling along two trails by the **Boka Bridge** (Most Boka), each offering very different perspectives of Slovenia's highest permanent waterfall: the trail beginning at the west side of the bridge – which

Skiing and hiking around Bovec

Ranged high above Bovec to the west, the Kanin mountains offer the highest-altitude skiing in Slovenia (around 2300m), with slopes here for skiers of all abilities. The **Kanin ski centre** (☏05/389-6310, ⊛www.boveckanin.si) is based in the hamlet of **Dvor**, 1km southwest of Bovec, and is directly connected to the resort of Sella Nevea across the border in Italy (€26 for a day pass, €130 for a week). The modern, four-seater **cable cars** transport passengers to the upper station (station D; 2200m) in thirty minutes (winter daily 8am–4pm nonstop; July & Aug daily 7am–5pm hourly; June & Sept Fri–Sun 8am–4pm hourly; €14 return), but be warned, this ride is not for the jittery. In summer, the sun-bleached rocks and boulders make for a rather bleak scene, but the views on a cloudless day are sensational – there's a basic restaurant at the top too.

If you're not here to ski, or have just come up to have a look around, then there are a number of excellent **hikes** to consider; one of the easiest, though not particularly well-marked, paths is to **Prestreljenik** (2499m; 1hr 30min), with more demanding paths to **Visoki Kanin** (2587m; 3hr 30min) – on a clear day it's possible to see the Adriatic from here – and **Rombon** (2208m; 5hr). The one hut in these mountains is the *Dom Petra Skalarja na Kaninu* (July–Aug daily; June & Sept weekends only; ☏040/829-701), a 45-minute walk south of the upper station. All the above hikes are doable from Bovec itself but, with the exception of Rombon (5hr from Bovec), you should count on an additional four hours at least for each. The excellent 1:50,000 map *Posočje*, available from the tourist office, will help you get your bearings. Bovec Rafting Team (see box, p.151) organizes a number of guided hikes and walks, such as a full-day trek (8hr) to Krn Lake, which costs around €30 (including transfers).

provides a head-on view – is the shorter and easier of the two paths, but does involve a fair amount of clambering over boulders; the far more difficult second route, beginning at the east side of the bridge, ascends to a spot above the head of the falls. Emanating from a deep karst spring in the Kanin mountains, the Boka is a stupendous sight, highly dependent on rain and snow-melt from the Kanin plateaus for its massive volume of water – so the best time to view it is in late spring.

Kluže Fortress

Four kilometres north of Bovec, back inside Triglav National Park on the road towards Log pod Mangartom and the Predel Pass, stands the formidable-looking **Kluže Fortress** (Trdnjava Kluže; July & Aug daily 9am–8pm; May, June, Sept & Oct Mon–Fri 10am–5pm, Sat & Sun till 6pm; €3). Strategically positioned on a steep rock face overlooking the impressive sixty-metre-deep Koritnica gorge, this heavily restored chunky grey fortress has seen more than its fair share of action over the years.

Although a wooden fortification was built here in the fifteenth century, it's believed that some kind of fortress existed on this site during Roman times, a theory based on the fact that a Roman road ran through the nearby Predel Pass, connecting the northern and southern parts of the Empire. The wooden fortification was supplanted by a stone construction in 1613, during which time it successfully repelled repeated Turkish attacks, before Napoleon's French marauders razed it in 1797. Its current appearance dates from 1882, though the upper part – named Fort Hermann after the hero of the 1809 Battle of Predel – was demolished by heavy and sustained shelling during World War I. The interior rooms now display enlightening exhibitions on the Soča Front and the fortress itself while, during July and August, the courtyard makes a fitting venue for re-enactments of battle scenes performed by the 1313 Association. It's also the setting for the **Kluže Festival**, a two-part event taking place in the first week of July and August, and comprising theatre, music and dance in addition to performances for children.

Log pod Mangartom and Mount Mangart

Nestling under the Mangart mountain range 6km north of Kluže is the pretty village of **LOG POD MANGARTOM**, which actually comprises the two adjoining settlements of **Spodnji Log** (Lower Log) and **Gorenji Log** (Upper Log). As if the 1998 earthquake wasn't enough, the village had to contend with an even greater catastrophe during the night of November 16–17, 2000, when a crushing **landslide** – believed to have been caused by a combination of torrential rainfall and significant seismological activity in the area – struck. The landslide began some 1000m further up in the Mangartski mountains and coursed down the valley slopes and along the bed of the Predelica River in a matter of seconds, before smashing into the upper settlement. The impact was such that seven people lost their lives – one person was never found – and a number of houses and farm buildings were wiped out or irreparably damaged.

At the reconstructed stone bridge in Gorenji Log, a board with photographs documenting the history of the village illustrates the aftermath of the landslide, while the wide open spaces around are testament to the devastation wrought. If you have your own transport, you can drive up to the top of the pass, and another reconstructed bridge, to see where the slide began. Just beyond the bridge, the main road continues onwards to Italy, while another – the country's highest mountain road – branches off towards the **Mangart Saddle** (2072m), below which is the *Koča na Mangrtskem sedlu* (☎041/954-761; mid-June to Sept), the only hut in this group of mountains. Two hours' walk from the hut is the magnificent **Mount Mangart** (2679m), Slovenia's third highest peak and known for its reddish-coloured sandstone.

Back in Gorenji Log, the **Parish Church of St Stephen** contains a ceiling fresco by Ivan Grohar, entitled *The Stoning of St Stephen*, and a wooden Gothic statue of Queen Mary dating from the end of the fifteenth century. Midway between the two settlements, just behind the small civilian cemetery, lies a **World War I military cemetery** – one of the few in the region preserved in its original form. It has neat rows of black iron crosses on mounds denoting the final resting places of nearly nine hundred Austrian soldiers killed on Mount Rombon and Mount Čuklja. The monument in the centre of the cemetery features two soldiers, one an Austrian, the other a Bosnian, gazing up to the summit of Rombon. A few paces along from the church a path leads up to the entrance of the now disused **Rabelj mining tunnel**, alongside which is an informative outdoor exhibition documenting the tunnel's history from its opening in 1905 to its closure in 1991. Villagers used to travel through the 4km-long tunnel in order to reach the lead and zinc mines at Cave del Predil in Italy, while it was also used to supply the army with troops and materials during World Wars I and II.

There are a few **places to stay** in the village: in the lower settlement, the *Motel Encijan* at no. 31 (☎05/384-5130, ⓦwww.encijan.com) has basic but pleasant rooms (❹) and apartments (❻), as well as a small pool; in the upper settlement, the *Gostišče Mangrt* at no. 57 has three simple rooms (☎05/388-5140; ❸) – its comely little **restaurant** serves excellent home-style Slovenian cooking, such as the local speciality *Čompe*, a delicious combination of potato, hard cheese and cottage cheese. Unfortunately, there is no public transport from Bovec to Log pod Mangartom, so if you don't have your own wheels you'll have to hitch or walk.

Kobarid and around

"A little white town with a campanile in a valley" was how American writer Ernest Hemingway described **KOBARID** in *A Farewell to Arms* in 1929, and though it has retained its pleasantly relaxed air, this handsome town 21km south of Bovec has had a pretty rum time of it over the years. In October 1917, the nearby Krn mountain range was the chief battleground for one of the war's most decisive military engagements – otherwise known as the Twelfth Offensive – in which the Italians were routed by the combined Central Powers of Germany and Austria, an event superbly documented in the town's gripping museum. The interwar years were defined by nationalist struggles on both sides, but Kobarid (then Caporetto) remained, as did much of the region, under Italian control until the end of World War II. Along with its museum, and a superb selection of restaurants, Kobarid's proximity to the Soča River and a stack of other historical and natural sights could quite easily detain you for a day or two. Moreover, the nearby lovely mountain villages of Drežnica, Vrsno and Breginj all have worthwhile attractions, though without your own transport they're all fairly difficult to reach.

Arrival, information and accommodation

All **buses** stop opposite the church on the main square, Trg svobode, which is also the location for the **tourist office** at no. 16 (July & Aug daily 9am–8pm;

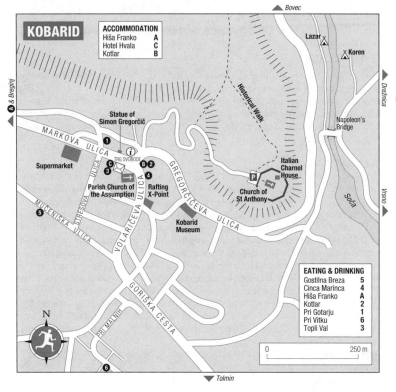

April–June & Sept–Dec Mon–Fri 9am–1pm & 2–7pm, Sat & Sun 9am–1pm & 3–7pm; Jan–March Mon–Fri 10am–12.30pm & 1.30–3pm, Sat 10am–1pm; ℡05/389-0000, Ⓦwww.lto-sotocje.si) – it can provide a good range of literature and maps on the Soča Front – and the **post office** opposite (Mon–Fri 8–9.30am, 10am–3.30pm & 4–6pm, Sat 8am–noon). The tourist office can book **rooms** (❷) both in the town and in the villages of Drežnica and Trnovo ob Soči, 5km north.

The town's single **hotel** is the warm, family-run *Hotel Hvala*, on the main square (℡05/389-9300, Ⓦwww.hotel-hvala.si; ❼), whose cosy, if somewhat small, rooms are reasonably good value. Much better are two first-class pension-style places; on the east side of the square at no. 11, the *Kotlar* (℡05/389-1110, Ⓦwww.kotlar.si; ❼) has six simple, but exquisitely furnished, rooms, each with sumptuous designer beds – its top-floor pool is free to guests. Located 3km west of town in the settlement of **Staro Selo**, at no. 1, ⚑ *Hiša Franko* (℡05/389-4120, Ⓦwww.hisafranko.com; ❽) simply oozes class; the highly original and idiosyncratic rooms (one with massage bath) are gorgeously furnished with finely cut drapes, bamboo and other such exotic materials, and each has a stereo (TV if desired); there's also a handful of more modest rooms in the building opposite (❺).

The town's two excellent **campsites** are down by the Soča River, 500m east of town on the road towards Drežnica; *Camp Lazar* (℡05/388-5333, Ⓦwww.lazar-sp.si; April–Oct), on the west bank, is a small site with good, clean facilities and a fun, ranch-style bar, while the larger *Camp Koren* (℡05/389-1311,

Ⓦ www.kamp-koren.si; open all year), across Napoleon's Bridge on the opposite bank, also has six large log cabins each sleeping up to six people (❼).

The Town

Although it retains a strong Italianate flavour – the border is just 9km to the west – much of Kobarid's present appearance dates from 1976 following the massive earthquake. The centre of town is essentially the small main square, where the main roads from Bovec and Tolmin, and the road from Italy, converge. From the square, it's no more than ten minutes' walk to any of the town's attractions or facilities.

Kobarid Museum

Situated in the lovely two-storey Baroque house at Gregorčičeva 10 (once owned by the naval commander Sergej Mašera), the **Kobarid Museum** (Kobariški Muzej; April–Sept Mon–Fri 9am–6pm, Sat & Sun 9am–7pm, Oct–March Mon–Fri 10am–5pm, Sat & Sun 9am–6pm; €5; Ⓦ www.kobariski-muzej .si), memorably evokes the horrors of the Soča Front (see box below). First off you'll get to see a twenty-minute **multimedia presentation**, containing superbly shot footage of the battles along the Soča Front, and in particular the decisive Twelfth Offensive. The museum's rooms are thematically arranged: up on the first floor, the **Krn Range Room** is represented by a vast map-relief of the Krn mountain range, which illustrates the complex arrangements of the military positions confronting the warring sides. The photographs here, as in most of the rooms, provide an exceptional supplement to the main exhibits. The next room along – the **Black Room** – reflects upon the suffering of the combatant, as

---

The Soča Front (Izonso Front)

When the Italians declared war on the Central Powers in May 1915, the Great War assumed a new and altogether more brutal dimension. This fresh battlefield, part of which extended for some 90km from Mount Rombon, north of Bovec, through Kobarid to a position a short way north of Trieste (Trst) on the Adriatic coast, was known as the **Soča Front** (Izonso Front).

Although the Austro-Hungarians, under the command of the "Soča Lion", General Svetozar Borojevič von Bojna, had already fortified the front, the Italians secured immediate success, capturing Kobarid and the nearby Krn range. More than two years and eleven debilitating and futile offensives later, the two heavily entrenched sides prepared for the denouement. With severely depleted troop numbers, Austrian Emperor Charles I approached the German Kaiser Wilhelm II for reinforcements, and together, they formed the fourteenth Austro-German army. Their breakthrough plan, "Faith in Arms", was based on swiftly coordinated lightning strikes and the element of surprise; in this case, thousands of troops and armoury were quickly repositioned between Bovec and Tolmin.

Effected on October 24, 1917, this **twelfth offensive** – the first counteroffensive by the Central Powers – resulted in the Italian army being pressed all the way back to the Friulian Plain and the Piave River, an episode acknowledged as the greatest single breakthrough of the war and the first successful "blitzkrieg" in the history of European warfare. Fighting continued around the Piave River for another year, the outcome of which was victory for the Italians. With an estimated million fatalities on all sides, a significant number of whom were women and children, the human cost was catastrophic; moreover many thousands more were forced to flee the region, only a fraction of whom returned at the war's end.

graphically illustrated by the pictures of hideously disfigured soldiers; there is also a graffitied door from the military prison in Smast village near Kobarid. The other two rooms on this floor – the **White Room** and **Rear Room** – are given over to themes of mobilization and civilian displacement, and the nightmarish struggle for survival in the mountains during the ferociously cold winter months. As an interesting aside, the two rooms behind the Krn room hold a collection of local archeological finds, the most fascinating exhibits being some delicate bronze statuettes unearthed from Gradič Hill.

On the second floor, the room with the **map-relief** of the Upper Soča region clearly identifies both the positions of the warring troops throughout the valley prior to the Twelfth Offensive, and the awesome volume of military machinery required for this attack; this room leads through to a mock-up **cavern**, in which a wistful young soldier pens one last letter to his father. The central **Breakthrough Room** considers the events pertaining to the critical breakthrough operation of October 24–27, 1917, featuring a hoard of hellish-looking weaponry.

Parish Church of the Assumption

On the south side of Trg Svobode, the ordered **Parish Church of the Assumption** (Cerkev Marijino vnebovzetje) is bestowed with some terrific artwork. The striking red and white marble high altar, designed by Lazzarini in 1716, features a handful of sculpted saints and angels, but is more interesting for what you can't see. Concealed behind the altar picture is a late fifteenth-century statue of the Holy Mother, which is only revealed on special religious occasions or, if you're lucky, upon request; ask at the priest's house opposite the church entrance. To commemorate Pope John Paul II's visit to Slovenia in 1996 (although he didn't actually visit Kobarid) the balcony was blanketed with a beautiful canvas, and is notable for its paintings of several eminent historical characters, including the pope himself. The stained-glass windows were installed in 1995 in order to lighten the church interior. Opposite the church is an oversized **sculpture of Simon Gregorčič** (1844–1906), the beloved Slovenian priest and poet who hailed from nearby **Vrsno** (see p.160).

The Kobarid Historical Walk

For a real flavour of Kobarid's historical, cultural and natural heritage, you should participate in the **Kobarid Historical Walk** (Kobariška Zgodovinska Pot), an enjoyable five-kilometre stroll taking in wartime monuments, abandoned fortifications, bridges and waterfalls. A free leaflet outlining the route, and the key sights along the way, is available from the museum – a gently paced walk, including stops for viewing, should take between three and four hours.

Beginning on the north side of the main square, Trg svobode, a winding road lined with the stations of the cross ascends to Gradič Hill and the **Italian Charnel House**, perhaps the valley's most evocative monument, especially when viewed from afar (it's possible to drive up to this point, but no further). The Charnel House – opened in 1938 with Mussolini in attendance – consists of three-tiered octagons tapering upwards towards the **Church of St Anthony**, in itself nothing outstanding. Inside the huge ossuary lie the remains of more than seven thousand Italian soldiers killed during fighting on the Soča Front, the names of whom are engraved onto the slabs of greenish serpentine inside the large niches. From the Charnel House, take the path to the left which forks off into the woods – hereafter, the route is marked with red arrows and the museum logo – and onwards to the remains of the ancient fort of **Tonočov**

Grad, unique in that it was occupied continuously from the middle Stone Age, through Antiquity to the Middle Ages.

From the fort, the path continues down towards the main road, which you should cross carefully, before a knee-jarring descent down to the Soča River – en route you'll pass a section of the **Italian Line of Defence**, one of three constructed by the Italians on the Soča Front during World War I; the trail then continues along a track in the direction of the *Koren* campsite, but you should take the path to the left which opens up into the **Soča Gorge** and a sturdy swing bridge, this one having replaced the original from World War I. From the bridge – where there are terrific views of the gorge and river – it's a twenty-minute walk to most people's favourite part of the circuit, the **Kozjak waterfall** (Slap Kozjak), a graceful, fifteen-metre-high waterfall less impressive for its height than for its atmospheric cave-like hall carved out of the surrounding rock. From here, retrace your steps and take the path that forks left up to a **small fortress** and another **line of defence**, scattered with yet more caverns, shelters and observation posts.

The path then cuts inland, passing the campsite and winding up at the **Napoleon Bridge** (Napoleonov Most), an elegant, stone-arched structure connecting the two banks of the river at one of the narrowest and most

▲ Napoleon Bridge, Kobarid

spectacular points of the gorge. The original bridge was built in 1750 and later named for the eponymous French leader after he marched across it en route to the Predel Pass. The day after World War I was declared, the bridge was blown up by retreating Austrians, though this didn't deter the Italians who first replaced it with a wooden, then an iron bridge, while this one was completed after the war. For the really keen, staff at the Kobarid museum (see p.156) organize a number of excellent **guided tours** – ranging from easy to medium three-hour walks to demanding day-long hikes. This includes sections of the **Walk of Peace** (Pot Miru), a 100km long trek (varying degrees of difficulty) starting in Log pod Mangartom and ending on Mengore Hill near Tolmin. For all tours (around €25 per hour) call at least one day, but preferably two or three, in advance. Whether on a guided tour or hiking alone, the 1:50,000 *Isonzo Front* (*From Mount Rombon to Mengore Hill*) map (€7) details all the major battle sites and areas of interest throughout the Soča Valley.

Eating and drinking

Few places in the country can boast such a surfeit of distinguished **restaurants** as Kobarid, which may explain why the town is so popular with neighbouring Italians. The restaurants listed here offer first-class cuisine, exemplary service and an enjoyable atmosphere, though they don't come cheap, apart from one budget option, *Pri Vitku*. Wherever you eat, it'd be remiss not to try the delicious local speciality, *Kobariški Štruklji*, a sweet dumpling with nut and raisin filling.

More predictably, the **drinking** options in such a small place are very limited, though there are one or two pleasant cafés, such as *Cinca Marinca*, on the west side of the square next to *Kotlar*, and *Pri Gotarju* on Markova Ulica, whose flowery garden with wooden bench seating makes for a pleasant summer venue. If you don't mind a little walk, you could always head down to the lively bar at *Camp Lazar* (see p.155).

Restaurants

Gostilna Breza Mučeniška ulica 17. Secreted away 300m south of the main square, this restful, homely place serves up the most traditional Slovene food in town, including lamb and game; the interior's subtle green colour scheme, wood-beamed ceiling and ceramic stove is complemented by the smart summery terrace. Fri–Tues 11am–3pm & 6–10pm.

Hiša Franko Staro Selo 1 A breathtakingly imaginative menu features dishes such as toasted scallops in red wine and sun-dried plum sauce, and roe buck fillet with chocolate and sage sauce and rhubarb. The bright orange restaurant looks fantastic, while the charming staff and extensive wine list (with some 350 bottles) ensure an exquisite dining experience. Wed–Sun noon–3pm & 7–11pm, plus Tues in summer.

Kotlar Trg svobode 11. Along with the *Topli Val*, this is one of the country's finest fish restaurants, with a menu almost exclusively devoted to seafood from the Adriatic as well as a marvellous wine list. The beautifully lit interior and curvaceous, nautically themed bar with blue drapings are superb. Closed Tues & Wed.

Pri Vitku Pri Malnih 41. For those on a somewhat tighter budget, this small and welcoming place, located in a residential area a ten-minute walk south of town (follow the signs), suffices for the simplest of pizza, pasta and grilled meat dishes.

Topli Val Trg svobode 1. Despite now having a serious rival in the *Kotlar*, the classy "Warm Wave" restaurant (in the *Hotel Hvala*) is the town's most established place, with a freshwater and sea fish menu regarded as one of the country's finest – crayfish cocktail, trout salami, mussels and lobster are just some of its specialities.

Drežnica, Vrsno and Breginj

Dramatically situated under the sunny slopes of the Krn mountain range 6km north of Kobarid, the peaceful little village of **DREŽNICA** is renowned for its **Shrovetide Carnival**, one of the most enjoyable local events in Slovenia. Taking place at the end of February, it's a kind of mini-Kurent (see box, p.304), starring a procession of masked figures (known as *psti*), who cut a dash through town, visiting houses and causing good-natured mayhem; the day concludes with much drinking and dancing.

Towering over the village is the oversized neo-Romanesque **Church of the Sacred Heart**, which, despite its prominent position, survived remarkably unscathed amidst the fighting in these parts during World War I. Dating from 1911, this church replaced one pulled down a few years earlier and features a capacious, pastel-coloured tripartite nave smothered in frescoes, the most celebrated of which is *The Sacred Heart*, a dual effort by Avgust Černigoj and Zoran Mušič. Note too, above the main entrance, the mosaic representing the Good Shepherd, completed by Kokalj in 1981. The village has some good **accommodation**, particularly the *Gostišče Jelkin Hram* at no. 30 (☎05/384-8610, ⊛www.jelkin-hram.com; ❸), which has simple, but colourful, homely rooms, as well as a super little restaurant – the wild meat dishes prepared at weekends are a treat (closed Mon & Tues); otherwise, enquire at the tourist office in Kobarid (see p.154) about private rooms. From the village it's a four-hour hike up to **Mount Krn** (2244m), the valley's most exalted peak and scene of some of the most ferocious battles during World War I.

While one road snakes up to Drežnica the other winds steeply uphill for 7km to the village of **VRSNO**, known as the birthplace of nineteenth-century priest, poet and national revivalist Simon Gregorčič. His **birthplace** (daily: May–Oct 9am–4pm; Nov–April 10am–3pm; €2) at no. 27 holds his cradle, other original furnishings and some of his works, as well as a small museum downstairs. His descendants still live next door and will be happy to show you around; you can get refreshments in the adjoining café. Gregorčič is actually buried in the village of Smast, back down on the road towards Kobarid. To get to either Drežnica or Vrsno from Kobarid, you'll have to walk or hitch if you're not using your own transport.

Until the earthquake in 1976, the village of **BREGINJ**, 15km west of Kobarid, was unique for its highly unorthodox street layout, whereby houses were conjoined in oval fashion, joined to a stable and hayloft and connected by wooden galleries known as *gank*. The one building left standing, or at least not so badly damaged that it couldn't be reconstructed, has been converted into a **museum** (no set times; contact the tourist office in Kobarid; €2), located in the centre of the village and signposted from the main road. This building, fairly representative of most of the village before the earthquake, comprises three separate, but interconnected, dwellings, each with four, almost identically sized rooms. Although it's not clear when these buildings date from exactly, it's believed that they were first inhabited around the beginning of the eighteenth century. The exhibition room has some superb aerial photos, depicting the village as it was both before and after the earthquake – you could easily be forgiven for thinking that these were two different places. From Kobarid there are just three **buses** (Mon, Wed & Fri at 7.40am, 11.20am & 3.45pm), though these only run on school days, and just one return bus on the same days (12.20pm), while there is nowhere to stay in the village.

Tolmin and around

Travelling south from Kobarid, the valley flattens out markedly before reaching **TOLMIN** some 14km further on. As the area's administrative centre it's not an especially appealing place, but it does conceal a handful of worthwhile sights, and also serves as an excellent jumping-off point for a couple of attractions just inside Triglav National Park a short way north, namely the fabulous **Tolmin Gorge**, and the **Church of the Holy Spirit** in Javorca. Furthermore, it's home to two of the country's foremost music festivals: **Metalcamp** in the first week of July, and the four-day **Reggae Riversplash** in mid-July, both of which take place down by the banks of the Soča, 3km south of town.

Arrival, information and accommodation

The **bus station** is right in the centre of town on the main through road, Trg maršala Tita. Three hundred metres southwest of here, just beyond Mestni trg at Petra Skalarja 4, is the **tourist office** (July & Aug Mon–Fri 9am–12.30pm & 1.30–8pm, Sat & Sun 9am–1.30pm & 3.30–8pm; Sept–June Mon–Fri 9am–12.30pm & 1.30–4pm, Sat 9am–1pm; ☎05/380-0480, Ⓦwww.lto-sotocje .si), which has free **internet** access and can book **private accommodation** (❷) in town and the surrounding villages. They also sell the excellent 1:50,000 *Turistični Zemljevid Kobarid Tolmin* regional map (€9). The **post office** is 100m west of the bus station (Mon–Fri 8am–7pm, Sat 8am–noon).

The Maya sports agency, 100m west of Mestni trg at Ulica Padlih borcev 1 (daily: July & Aug 8am–8pm; April–June & Sept–Oct 9am–3pm; ☎05/380-0530, Ⓦwww.maya.si), runs a welter of **activities**, including the usual water sports plus mountain-bike trips (€35 for one day), adrenaline park (€39 for three hours) and excursions to Dante's Cave (€30; see p.162) – for waterbound activities, expect to pay the same prices as you would do at those agencies in Bovec (see box, p.151); they've also got **bikes** for rent (€10 for half a day, €17 for day).

The two places to **stay** are opposite each other on Mestni trg; the very agreeable, lime-green *Pension Rutar* (☎05/380-0500, Ⓦwww.pension-rutar.si; ❻), whose nine supremely comfortable rooms have air-conditioning and wi-fi; and the dour looking but friendly *Hotel Krn* (☎05/382-1100, Ⓦwww.hotel-krn.com; ❺), which conceals tidy, fairly modern rooms.

The Town

Wedged between the *Hotel Krn* and *Pension Rutar* on Mestni trg is the **Tolmin Museum** (Tolminski Muzej; Tues–Fri 10am–4pm, Sat & Sun 1–5pm; €3; Ⓦwww.tol-muzej.si), housed in the Coronini Mansion, formerly the home of the noble sixteenth-century Coronini family. The centrepiece of the museum's rich and beautifully presented collection is its treasure-trove of **archeological finds**, excavated from a grave in Most na Soči between 1999 and 2001 (see p.163); the most extraordinary discovery was a clay skyphos (a drinking cup) from Attica in Greece, an exquisite piece featuring one horizontal and one vertical handle, to the side of which is a painted owl. Look out too for the bronze handle of a patera in the form of a ram's head, the ornamented clay pithos (a pottery urn) – which, when discovered, contained charred human remains – and the group of bronze fibulas (a type of clasp), the kind worn by females in the Soča and Bohinj regions. No less impressive is the **ethnological collection**, relating to life in Tolmin from the time of the peasant uprisings of 1713, through to the region's various struggles for identity during the twentieth century. Rounding things off is a collection of valuable fifteenth- to eighteenth-century sacral art, comprising wooden sculptures, paintings, religious relics and the wall painting *Our Lady of Mercy* (1886), rescued from a house in Breginj following the earthquake in 1976 (see opposite).

Two kilometres south of town, down by the Soča River, is the tiny and undistinguished-looking **German Charnel House** (Nemška kostnica), completed in 1936 from German materials and containing the remains of nearly one thousand German soldiers killed during the Twelfth Offensive (see box, p.156). Beyond the forged grill that divides the space inside, the names of the dead are beautifully engraved mosaic-style on three walls – the key to the house can be obtained from the tourist office or the museum. To get here walk past the tourist office and follow the tarmac road to the end, then take a right turn along the asphalt track.

If you've got further energy to expend, then you might consider tackling **Kozlov Rob**, a 426-metre-high hill one kilometre northwest of town, atop which are the substantial remains of a Middle Ages fort. To get to the base of the hill it's a fifteen-minute walk along Brunov drevored, the road which forks left by the Church of St Ulric, itself located a short way north of Mestni trg; from here it's a pleasantly exhausting forty-minute, zigzagging climb to the top, and, despite the thicket of shrubs and weeds smothering the fort, there are some tremendous views. Once fortified by four gigantic towers, Kozlov Rob (Goat's Edge) is believed to have originated around the twelfth century, when it was fought over by various factions, including the Venetian and then the Habsburg monarchies. The fort underwent several restoration projects thereafter, the last of which occurred under the auspices of the Dornberg family at the beginning of the seventeenth century, after which time the Coronini family took control and the fort fell into a long-term state of dilapidation; despite periodic excavation works, it has pretty much remained that way ever since.

Eating and drinking

The *Pension Rutar* houses the only decent **restaurant** in town, offering fresh Italian cuisine and first-class service, all at very affordable prices; alternatively, there's *Ostarija no. 1*, a popular local pizzeria just across from *Rutar* on the main crossroads. **Drinking** options are limited to the occasionally lively *Paradiso*, next to the post office, and the more restful *M Bar*, opposite the tourist office.

Tolminska Gorge, Church of the Holy Spirit and Čadrg

There are two wonderful excursions to consider in the vicinity of Tolmin, both of which are easily reached by car or foot. Forty-five minutes' walk north of town (it's all signposted), the **Tolminska Gorge** (Tolminska Korita; €3) – the lowest point of Triglav National Park (180m) and its southernmost entry point – is as wild and spectacular as anything the park has to offer. From the entrance, just up from the snack bar, there are several rather confusing signs pointing to various sections of the gorge. However, the best way forward is to head straight along the road and through the tunnel to the vertiginous **Hudičev Most** (Devil's Bridge), looming some 60m above the magnificent ravine. Approximately 500m on from the bridge, just after the bend in the road, is the **Zadlaška Cave**, also known as **Dante's Cave**, for it was here that the poet supposedly found the inspiration for his terrifying inferno images in the *Divine Comedy* – the caves can only be visited on a guided tour (contact the Maya agency in Tolmin – see p.161).

Backtracking 200m or so down the road, steps lead down to a couple of paths which fork – take the left path down the **Zadlaščica gorge** and after 400m, where the path ends, you'll chance upon the gorge's most bizarre feature, **Medvedova Glava** (Bear's Head), a huge triangular-shaped boulder wedged between two rock faces. Caution should be exercised here as the paths can get very slippery. Retracing your steps back to the fork, a couple of paths head down to the river; at this point you'll probably get lost among the twisting paths, secret tunnels and swing bridges, but it's all good fun and you're never far from the nearest path out.

From the gorge it's a twenty-minute drive (or a two-hour walk) up a mainly asphalt track that ascends to **Javorca** (571m) – coming by car, you'll have to walk the last 500m or so, as the road is too steep and narrow to continue up. Perched on a panoramic terrace, with resplendent views across the Tolmin Valley, the half-stone, half-wooden **Church of the Holy Spirit** (Cerkev Sv Duha; July & Aug Tues–Sun 10am–5pm; May, June & Sept Sat & Sun 10am–5pm; €2) was built in 1916 by soldiers of the Austro-Hungarian army. Approaching via the stone staircase – which replaced the previous one damaged in the 1998 earthquake – the first thing you'll notice is the remarkably well-preserved coats of arms (22 in all) representing the various regions of the Austro-Hungarian Empire. The interior, meanwhile, is striking for its bold Secessionist-style decoration, painted in just four colours, black, blue, white and gold, and the wall-covered wooden panels, onto which the names of nearly three thousand soldiers have been scorched. There is also, somewhat oddly, a small collection of rusting World War I weaponry just inside the church entrance.

From Javorca it's a ninety-minute walk across to the elevated village of **Čadrg** (700m), a unique place in so much as each of the settlement's five houses is a designated ecological (or organic) farm – hence its status as Slovenia's first **ecological village**. The villagers produce large quantities of cheese and other dairy products - made within their small cheese factory – as well as nuts, vegetables and brandy, all of which you can buy. You can stay here, too, at the *Pri Lovrču* tourist farm, at no. 8 (☎05/381-1154, ✉marija.cadrg@gmail.com; ❹), which has two apartments, both sleeping four. To get here by car or bike, continue up the road that passes through the Tolmin Gorge, though be warned, it's very narrow and not particularly well surfaced in places.

Most na Soči

Located on a rocky ledge at the confluence of the Soča and Idrijca rivers 5km south of Tolmin, **MOST NA SOČI** (formerly St Lucija) was one of the most important prehistoric settlements in Slovenia, as evidenced by its exceptional hoard of archeological finds from the Bronze and Iron Ages through to the early Middle Ages. Since the former rector of St Lucija, Tomaž Rutar, began excavations in the mid-nineteenth century, some seven thousand graves and architectural remains including 35 Hallstatt dwellings have been discovered in the surrounding area; further recent digs have unearthed yet more finds, such as, in 2002, some one hundred Iron Age and Roman graves (5 BC to 2 AD).

The Oldtimer Museum Train

On select days between mid-May and mid-October, the marvellous **Oldtimer Museum Train** (Muzej Vlak) puffs its way between Jesenice, some 12km north of Bled, to Nova Gorica, stopping off at Bled, Bohinjska Bistrica and Most na Soči along the way – the total journey time is one hour thirty minutes. It's a fantastic ride, but not cheap; a return fare costs €35, while, for an additional €30, you can partake in a full-day programme, which includes a tour of the wine-growing region, Goriška Brda, and lunch – bicycles can be taken on the train for no extra charge. Tickets can be booked through the ABC Rent-a-Car office in Ljubljana (☎01/510-4320, ⊛www.abc-tourism.si), and some of the agencies in Bled or Bohinj.

You can see a selection of these treasures on display at the Tolmin Museum (see p.161), while other items are kept in Ljubljana, Trieste and Vienna. During the 1970s and 1980s several Hallstatt dwellings were also discovered here, one of which has been partially reconstructed and is now displayed in the small **Archeological Museum** (Halštatska hiša; call the tourist office in Tolmin to arrange a visit; €2), at the school at no. 18, in the centre of town. Disappointingly, neither this nor the remainder of the exhibits has English labelling. For those with a bit more time, the **Cultural and Historical Trail** is a most enjoyable stroll, marking the town's surprisingly rich tapestry of natural and cultural sights, such as burial grounds and settlements, and the extraordinary turquoise-coloured lake. The trail begins at the information point (Plac) next to the petrol station; thereafter all points are marked by information boards, denoted by an owl symbol after the clay skyphos discovered here in 2001.

Next to the museum, the former Gothic, but now Baroque, **Parish Church of St Lucy** (Cerkev Sv Lucija) is worth a glimpse for its exceptional range of artwork by Tone Kralj. He painted the allegory of St Lucy and the Apostles on the ceiling, but also the eight paintings in the presbytery representing the life and martyrdom of the same saint and the fantastically colourful oil pictures of the Way of the Cross in the nave. For good measure he completed the four wall statues. Much like the private collection in Bovec (see p.150), the **Soča Front Museum** (Muzej Soške Fronte), a few paces west of the petrol station at no. 53, harbours a comprehensive stash of weaponry from both the Italian and Austrian armies – these items were retrieved from the Tolmin region. To arrange a visit call ℡031/699-968, or contact the tourist office in Tolmin (see p.161). Should you wish to **stay** here, try the *Hotel Lucija*, in the centre at no. 57 (℡05/381-3292, ⓦwww.hotel-lucija.com; ❻), an accomplished, if unspectacular, place, or there's the cosy *Pension Sterk* (℡05/388-7065, ⓦwww.penzion-sterk.si; ❺), across the bridge from the *Lucija*, and with views overlooking the lake.

Most na Soči is on the rail line between Jesenice and Nova Gorica, and is also the last stop for the **car-train** (see box, p.125) from Bohinjska Bistrica; the **train station** is across the river 1.5km southeast of town on the road to Idrija – there are sporadic buses from town, which then continue to Tolmin.

Baška Grapa Valley

If you have your own transport, and an hour or two to spare, take a ride through the lovely **Baška Grapa Valley**, which meanders eastwards from Most na Soči joining up with the **Selščica Valley** some 30km distant. Incised with deeply cut slopes onto which dozens of picturesque hamlets and lush vegetation have been neatly grafted, the road snakes along the valley floor in tow with the Bača stream and the scenic rail line.

At the narrow upper end of the valley, the village of **PODBRDO** was once an important frontier post, but is now significant as the southern entrance of the Bohinj tunnel and one of the stopping stations for the car-train (see box, p.125). A few kilometres east of Podbrdo is **PETROVO BRDO**, a tiny hamlet on the mountain-top pass linking the two valleys. The owner of the roadside hut *Planinski Dom na Petrovem Brdu* (℡05/380-8101), which serves limited refreshments and has a few beds, organizes local excursions along the **Rapallo Border Trail**, the one-time border between Yugoslavia and Italy. Established in 1918, and confirmed by the Treaty of Rapallo in 1920 – which effectively annexed the Primorska region to Italy – the border is riddled with deserted fortifications, overgrown bunkers (there's one just yards from the hut) and bomb shelters constructed by the Italians between the two World

Wars. Walks, which take in a number of these extraordinary defences (many of which are in the process of being cleaned up), can be improvised to suit whatever time you have, from a short two-hour trip (€9) to a full-day excursion (€20). If you want to know more about visiting the trail, contact the hut or the tourist office in Tolmin (see p.161). Petrovo Brdo is also an excellent starting point for ascents up into the Lower Bohinj mountains; trails lead to **Kobla** (1498m; 90min) and **Črna Prst** (1844m; 4hr), where there's the *Dom Zorka Jelinčiča na Črni prsti* hut (☏05/380-8609; mid-June to mid-Sept), and **Porezen** (1630m; 2hr 30min) and the *Dom Andreja Žvana-Borisa na Poreznu* hut (☏051/615-245; July & Aug).

Central Primorska

Central Primorska – which roughly covers the block of territory between the southern reaches of the Soča Valley and the Karst region, and the area inland from here – provides a number of exciting and wide-ranging attractions and activities. The one exception is the modern casino town of **Nova Gorica**, which offers little more than the opportunity to make or lose a quick buck, though it does serve as a handy base from which to explore the lovely wine regions of **Goriška Brda** and the **Vipava Valley**. Northeast of here, sheltered amid the deep-sided valleys of the Idrija and Cerklje Hills, the towns of **Idrija** – famed nationwide for its mining and lace – and **Cerkno** – a popular ski town – can both count on enough attractions and activities, particularly in their outlying areas, to make a visit worthwhile.

Nova Gorica and around

Thirty-nine kilometres south of Tolmin, **NOVA GORICA** was built little more than sixty years ago following Gorica's (Gorizia) annexation to Italy at the end of World War II. Until this point in time, and despite having been placed under Italian jurisdiction as part of the 1920 Treaty of Rapallo, it had been a predominantly Slovene-speaking community, but following the Paris Peace Treaty of 1947, the city was assigned to Italy leaving the Slovenes without a centre of their own. Undeterred, the local authorities pressed on with the construction of a nascent Slovene Gorica, based on plans drawn up by the prominent Slovene architect Edo Ravnikar, a keen disciple of Le Corbusier.

Although vestiges of antiquity remain, most notably in the northern suburb of Solkan, as well as in the form of one or two other historic structures, its central hub is ultimately too modern to be anything other than charmless. With only its casinos (owned by the ubiquitous HIT group) – on which the local economy is almost entirely dependent – and the odd splash of greenery to possibly detain you, it's not a place to linger. That said, there are some wonderful diversions close by, most obviously the enchanting **Goriška Brda** wine region northwest of town, the twin attractions of **Sveta Gora** and

Nova Gorica's casinos

As Slovenia's gaming capital, Nova Gorica panders unashamedly to the pretensions of its Italian neighbours, with both the **Perla** and **Park** hotels offering the stock American and French Roulette, Black Jack and Draw Poker games, not to mention a combined total of over one thousand slot machines. Open round the clock, **admission** (you must be 18 or older) to either casino is €5 Friday to Sunday, and free all other days; you should hold on to the admission ticket until you leave the gaming floor. Once inside, you play with tokens (chips) – which can be obtained from the cashier or from automated machines – or cash. If you fancy something a little more relaxing, there's bingo twice a night, each card costing €5. The only regulation as regards dress code is no shorts.

Kostanjevica Monastery, both of which should satisfy those in search of ecclesiastical excitement, and **Kromberk Castle**, out in the suburbs.

As well as being an important **transport** hub for destinations north into the Soča Valley and south towards the Karst and coast, Nova Gorica is also a key crossing point into Italy, so there's a good chance you'll wind up here at some point.

Arrival and information

The **train station**, a lovely Secessionist pile built in 1906, is located 1.5km west of town on Kolodvorska ulica right on the Italian border; on exiting the station turn left towards Erjavčeva, from where it's a further fifteen minutes' walk into the centre. The **bus station** is smack bang in the centre of town on Kidričeva ulica, from where it's a five-minute walk north to the **tourist office**, housed in the Cultural Centre on Bevkov trg (Mon–Fri 8am–6pm, Sat & Sun 9am–1pm; ☎05/330-4600, ⓦwww.novagorica-turizem.com). The **post office** is across the road from the bus station at Kidričeva ulica 19 (Mon–Fri 8am–7pm, Sat 8am–1pm). There's free **internet access** at the student club, *Klub Goriških* (*KGS*), located in the town hall on Trg Edvarda Kardelija (Mon–Fri 9am–8pm, Sat 11am–3pm).

Accommodation

There's cheap, clean accommodation in the form of the *Dijaški Dom Nova Gorica*, ten minutes' walk south of the bus station at Streliška pot 7 (☎04/335-4800, ⓦwww.hostel-ng.si; ❶–❷); this enormous **hostel**, with single, double and triple rooms, is open daily in July and August and at weekends throughout the rest of the year. There's not much in the way of **private accommodation**, but the Lastovka agency (Mon–Fri 1–5pm, Sat 9am–noon; ☎04/333-4400, ⓔlastovka @siol.net), inside the train station, or the tourist office, can organize rooms.

The town's premier **hotel** is the *HIT Perla* (☎05/336-3000, ⓦwww.hit.si; ❾), a flash glass and steel behemoth at Kidričeva 7; concealing extremely plush, generously sized rooms, it's mainly used by business people, as is its less glamorous sister hotel, the *HIT Park*, 100m west of the bus station at Delpinova 5 (☎05/336-2000, same website; ❾). More affordable is the *HIT Sabotin*, a comfortable and decently furnished hotel 2km north of town in the suburb of Solkan at Cesta IX korpusa 35 (☎05/336-5000, same website; ❾); guests of all three hotels receive free entrance to the casinos.

If you have your own transport and don't mind staying out of town, the *Pri Martinovih* **tourist farm** (☎05/395-3190, ⓦwww.binst.si; ❹), 11km north of Nova Gorica in the hamlet of Zagora, is a terrific possibility. This tranquil homestead – signposted from the main road and right at the top of a steep winding road – has five elegantly furnished rooms, some with a balcony terrace.

Kostanjevica Monastery

Fifteen minutes' walk south of town (walk down Erjavčeva ulica and follow the signs), situated atop a small, green hill overlooking Gorizia is **Kostanjevica Monastery** (Kostanjevica Samostan; Mon–Sat 9am–noon & 3–5pm, Sun 3–5pm; €2). Built in 1624, its first custodians were the Carmelites, but following their expulsion in 1781 and a brief period of closure, the monastery was entrusted to the Franciscans, who have remained its guardians ever since.

Most visitors come here to view the tombs of the **French Bourbons**. Exiled from France following the 1830 Revolution in Paris, Charles X sought refuge in various countries, before eventually finding sanctuary in Gorizia under the protection of Count Coronini. His stay, however, was a short-lived one, for barely three weeks after his arrival he died of cholera. The **crypt**, located along a narrow whitewashed passageway under the central aisle of the church, holds the sarcophagi of Charles X and five other members of the Bourbons, including Marie Thérèse Charlotte, daughter of Marie-Antoinette (who was the grand-daughter of Austrian Empress Maria Theresa).

NOVA GORICA

▲ Sveta Gora & Goriška Brda

SOLKAN

ITALY

EATING & DRINKING
Grad Kromberk	4
Pecivo	3
Pri Hrastu	1
Vrtnica	2

ACCOMMODATION
Dijaški Dom	D
Hotel Park	C
Hotel Perla	B
Hotel Sabotin	A

Train Station

Cultural Centre

BEVKOV TRG

Bus Station

GORIZIA

Koren

Kanal Koren

▶ Kromberk Castle & ❹

🏛 Kostanjevica Monastery

0   500 m

Although usually only open to groups, it's worth enquiring about visits to the monastery's beautiful, sixteenth-century, completely renovated **library**, named after Stanislav Škrabec, one of Slovenia's greatest linguists and grammarians, who lived here for more than forty years. The library's most priceless work is Adam Bohorič's delightful pocket-sized book, *Arcticae horulae* (*Winter Hours*), the first Slovene grammar book, written in 1584. Try, too, to catch a glimpse of the fabulous stuccowork in the monastery's small, single-nave **church**, which was almost completely destroyed during World War II.

Kromberk Castle

Three kilometres east of town in the suburban village of **KROMBERK** is **Kromberk Castle** (Mon–Fri 8am–3pm, Sun 1–5pm; €2), a northern-Italian-inspired construction that replaced the original thirteenth-century castle in the early seventeenth century. Despite several reincarnations since – most markedly an almost complete reconstruction following the 1976 earthquake, and a thorough restoration of the interior in the 1990s – the castle has retained its Renaissance appearance. The most inspiring part of its **museum collection** is the ethnographic section on the second floor, which puts on temporary thematic exhibitions related to the Goriško region; there's also a small lapidarium on the ground floor.

A much better reason for coming to the castle is to dine in the elegant *Grad Kromberk* **restaurant** on the ground floor (see opposite). If you don't fancy the hike, take one of the three buses (Mon–Fri 8.30am, 1.45pm & 3.25pm) which stop off en route to Ajdovščina, with just one return bus (Mon–Fri 3.54pm).

Sveta Gora

Positioned atop the 681-metre-high **Sveta Gora** (Holy Mountain), just over 5km north of Nova Gorica, the **Basilica of the Assumption** has been an important place of pilgrimage for centuries. Local legend has it that in 1539 a shepherd girl, Urška Ferligoj, was visited on several occasions by apparitions of the Virgin Mary, an occurrence that precipitated the building of the basilica two years later. A stone slab unearthed during its construction indicated that some form of religious centre has been present on this site since possibly as early as the eleventh century; however, it was most likely destroyed by the Turks in the late fifteenth century.

When the church was reduced to a pile of rubble during World War I, authorities initially considered employing Jože Plečnik to undertake a redesign, though, ultimately, the project was taken up by Silvano Barich from Gorizia, as it was ostensibly an Italian concern. The stained-glass windows aside, the church's high, dark and capacious interior betrays little in the way of ornamentation or colour. The high altar, too, is very simple, its only distinguishing feature a picture of the Virgin Mary; originally donated to the church in 1544, the painting (believed to be of Venetian origin) was taken to Gorizia during World War II, later found at the Vatican and returned to the basilica in 1951. Miraculously, the **Chapel of Appearance** – located to the rear of the high altar and containing the original gold wooden statue dating from 1541 – survived the bombing almost completely unscathed. The basilica's **museum** (visits by appointment only) holds fragments from the bombed-out church, and the usual stock of church reliquaries.

Unfortunately, there are no buses to Sveta Gora so, unless you have your own transport, it's a very steep and exacting walk (roughly 1hr): after passing through Solkan, take the road marked Trnovo/Čepovan (it's a sharp right – the road straight ahead is the Tolmin road) for about 3km, before branching off up the steep and twisting road towards Sveta Gora. From the summit, there are superlative views south across to the Gulf of Trieste and the snow-tipped mountains of the Soča Valley to the north. On the way from Nova Gorica, you'll see the magnificent **Solkan Railway Bridge**, which was, at the time of its construction in 1906, the largest stone arch bridge in Europe, some 85m high.

Eating and drinking

There are depressingly few **restaurants** in town, but there are a couple of terrific places on the outskirts. Located 3km east of town, on the ground floor of Kromberk Castle, is the outstanding ⌘ *Grad Kromberk* (Fri–Tues): tall-backed wooden chairs, lush red carpets and cast-iron chandeliers provide a classy setting for a distinguished and unusual menu, typically featuring *mešani narezek* (cold cuts of ham), *jota* (a local vegetable soup) and *oves s'rno trobento* (oatgrain with black trumpet mushrooms); there's a fine wine selection too. Not quite in the same league, but very enjoyable and a good deal cheaper, is *Pri Hrastu*, a one-hundred-year-old inn at Kromberška cesta 2, just fifteen minutes' walk from the centre on the main road towards Kromberk Castle. For those on a somewhat tighter budget, try *Pecivo*, opposite the *Hotel Park* at Delpinova 16, which doubles up nicely as a café and simple restaurant, or the *Vrtnica* self-service restaurant at Kidričeva 11 (Mon–Fri 9.45am–4pm).

Casinos aside, nightlife in town is very low-key, the most interesting places to **drink** being the clutch of cafés on Bevkov trg, such as *Splendid* and *Tokio*'s, both of which are good spots for a daytime coffee or evening beer.

Goriška Brda

Goriška Brda (often just referred to as Brda, which means hill), a small nub of land around 5km northwest of Nova Gorica, is a beautiful region of low, smoothly rounded hills, scattered villages and little white churches, best known for producing some of the country's finest wines. The hills are perfect for fruit growing, too, with the harvesting of cherries, peaches and apricots a major seasonal activity. From the wine aficionado's point of view, the most interesting villages are concentrated in the southernmost part of Brda, namely **Dobrovo** and **Medana**, while the villages of **Šmartno** and **Vipolže** attest to the region's position as an important frontier zone during the Venetian-Habsburg wars.

Whether you're here for the wine or not, Goriška Brda is a wonderful place to explore and, should you choose to stay longer, there's a smattering of accommodation available in several villages. However long you decide to stay, you'll get a lot more out of the region with your own transport, as there is only a very limited, and poorly coordinated, bus service between Nova Gorica and Dobrovo (Mon–Fri school term-time – roughly Sept–June) at 12.20pm & 3.25pm, returning at 12.10pm & 1.40pm.

Kojsko and Šmartno

The first major stop travelling from Nova Gorica is **KOJSKO**, a comely little wayside settlement worth a brief stop to view the **Church of the Holy Cross on Tabor** (Sveta Križna Taboru), stationed just above the village. One of the four watchtowers (the other three were burnt down) which once formed part of an ancient fortification here was later rearranged into the church bell tower,

▲ Šmartno

a feature common to many churches in these parts. The interior stars a beautifully preserved late-Gothic winged high altar from around 1500.

A couple of kilometres west of Kojsko, a monumentally ugly 23-metre-high **viewing tower** provides a commanding sweep of the surrounding hills, including splendid views of **ŠMARTNO**, a superb-looking, fortified village some 2km away. Girdled by partially preserved white-stone walls and watchtowers erected during the sixteenth century, the village is an attractive jumble of crooked, unevenly paved streets lined with crumbling stone houses. In the centre stands the **Church of St Martin** whose fourteenth-century bell tower is another that was converted from a watchtower; take a look inside at the contemporary, and very colourful, frescoes by Tone Kralj. There are light refreshments available at the nearby *Turn* restaurant (Thurs–Sun).

Dobrovo

Three kilometres west of Šmartno, **DOBROVO** is Goriška Brda's largest and most heavily populated town, as well as the region's principal wine centre. Here, too, you will find Goriška Brda's only **tourist office**, in the courtyard of Dobrovo Castle on Grajska cesta (April–Oct Mon–Fri 9am–4pm, Sat & Sun 10am–6pm; Nov–March Mon–Fri 9am–4pm; ☎05/395-9594, ⊛www.brda.si); the office can assist with enquiries on any aspect of the Brda region, from wine tours and tasting to private accommodation; they've got free **internet** too.

Dobrovo Castle (Grad Dobrovo; Tues–Fri 8am–4pm, Sat & Sun noon–4pm; €2) is a Renaissance-style structure erected around 1600 on the site of an older castle, and not dissimilar from Kromberk near Nova Gorica (see p.168); its cultural history collection is not particularly stimulating, though the gallery of graphic prints up on the second floor by internationally renowned local artist Zoran Mušič (1909–2005) is worth a look. In any case, chances are you'll soon end up sampling wine in the Vinoteka (Wed–Sun 11.30am–9pm), a magnificent stone-vault cellar in the castle's handsome courtyard. **Bikes** can also be rented from the castle courtyard (€3 for 1hr, €14 for the day).

A short way north of the castle at Zadružna cesta 9 (in the direction of Neblo), the **Goriška Brda** winery (Ⓦ www.klet-brda.com) is one of the largest wine production cellars in Slovenia. A visit includes some informative spiel about the region's wines, a tour of the cellar – where you'll get the chance to see stunning four-hundred-year-old oak barrels from Bosnia – and a tasting session with snacks (€10 per person for five wines). Wines can be purchased from their on-site shop (Jan–April Mon–Fri 8am–5pm, Sat 8am–1pm; April–Dec Mon–Fri 8am–7pm, Sat 8am–5pm).

Medana and Vipolže

Two further villages worth checking out are **MEDANA** and **VIPOLŽE**, 1.5km and 3.5km south of Dobrovo respectively, the former one of Brda's most prolific winegrowing villages. One of the most highly regarded wineries here is the **Klinec** tourist farm at no. 20 (Ⓣ 05/304-5092, Ⓦ www.klinec.si), which has been producing vintages since 1918; the **accommodation** (⓺) comes in the shape of five modern and artfully styled rooms, which are actually located in another building just down the road. The owners of the farm also organize the **Days of Poetry and Wine Festival** in late August, an international gathering of poets complemented by the requisite quantities of wine. A short walk up the road, at no. 32, the *Belica* tourist farm (Ⓣ 05/304-2104, Ⓦ www.belica.net; ⓺–Ⓕ) is an upmarket establishment with eight decadently furnished, air-conditioned rooms overlooking a gorgeous lawn terrace and with views across to the Friulian hills; they also have tastings, as well as a fabulously classy restaurant

The wines of Goriška Brda

Goriška Brda is the northernmost of the four wine-growing districts that constitute Slovenia's **Primorje** (coastal) region. Thanks to its favourable geographical location and Mediterranean climate and soil, Goriška Brda consistently yields a superlative range of both **red** and **white wines** – one of the few regions in Slovenia to harvest both, though whites account for roughly seventy percent here. Among the former, Cabernet Sauvignon and the lighter Merlot are pre-eminent, while of the latter, the ubiquitous Chardonnay (produced all over Slovenia), Beli Pinot, Sivi Pinot and the dry Briški Točaj (as opposed to the famous sweet Hungarian variety) prevail. The most distinctive white, though, is the golden-yellow Rebula, a widely cultivated, indigenous grape used in the production of *slamno vino* (straw wine). Local **vintners** to look out for include Simčič (Ⓣ 05/395-9200) and Movia (Ⓣ 05/395-9510), both in Ceglo, and Prinčič (Ⓣ 05/304-1272), in Kozana.

If you fancy a spot of **tasting**, there are dozens of cellars in a number of villages to choose from, all well signposted; expect to pay around €6–10 per person for four or five wines, with bread and cheese or *pršut*. You can either contact the cellars directly (a few hours' notice is usually appreciated), or call the tourist office in Dobrovo for further information (see opposite).

The most important of several wine-related events occurring throughout Brda during the year is **Martinmas (St Martin's Day)** on November 11, which is celebrated in grand style throughout the region, topped off with a day of concerts and tasting aplenty within the grounds of Vipolže Castle (see p.172). Otherwise, the biggest and brashest festival in Brda is the **Cherry Fest**, which takes place in Dobrovo during the second weekend of June. Marking the beginning of the cherry season this lively spectacle entails concerts, tastings and much general merriment, climaxing with the parade of the "Cherry Girl". On the first weekend of May, the **Rebula and Olive Oil Festival** in the village of Višnjevik celebrates both the eponymous local grape and oil with lots of music and dancing.

(closed Mon), with the pick of the menu a delicious range of home-made salamis, sausages and ribs.

From Medana, the road continues south towards the Italian border; after passing through the village of Ceglo veer eastwards (continuing south will bring you to the border crossing) and continue up the hill towards **VIPOLZE**. Located in the upper reaches of this quaint little village is **Vipolže Castle**, originally an eleventh-century fortification, but later transformed into a handsome Renaissance-style manor house following its appropriation by the Venetians in the seventeenth century. The oaks and cypresses of this once lovely park still flourish, but otherwise it's a wretched site, the castle's bricked-up windows and tumbledown walls the result of heavy bomb damage during World War I, when it was used as a military hospital, and years of subsequent neglect. As some compensation, there are marvellous **views** across the Friulian Plain. From Vipolže, you can return to Dobrovo via the road running parallel to Medana, or take the northeasterly road towards Šmartno.

The Vipava Valley

If the Brda region hasn't sated your thirst for wine, you might like to venture in the opposite direction towards the **Vipava Valley** (Vipavska dolina), the second and largest of Primorje's wine-growing regions. Sandwiched between the thickly forested Trnovo Plateau to the north and the low-lying Karst region to the south, this flat-bottomed valley is raked by lush rolling vineyards which, like Goriška Brda, yield a superb quota of both reds, notably Cabernet Sauvignon, Merlot and the indigenous Barbera; and whites, particularly the indigenous varieties, Zelen and Pinela.

The valley's continental climate is epitomized by the **burja** (bora), a fiendishly cold and dry wind that whips down from the northern mountain peaks and batters its way through the valley, across the Karst, and down towards the Adriatic. For this reason many of the two dozen or so **wine villages** dispersed throughout the Vipava hills were built in relatively sheltered, south-facing locations, with neither windows nor doors positioned on sides exposed to the wind. The small, rather unspectacular, towns of **Ajdovščina** and **Vipava** are both useful as jumping-off points if the villages are your intended target. The handy little *Vipava Wine Road* leaflet (available from the tourist office in Ajdovščina – see opposite) outlines a number of villages and cellars you can visit. However, having your own **transport** is pretty much essential here, as public transport is virtually nonexistent.

Ajdovščina

The only centre of any significant size in the Vipava Valley is **AJDOVŠČINA**, a small, plain sort of town, with little to hold your attention save for some extant Roman remains. The compact ancient core of present-day Ajdovščina was once a military encampment called **Castra ad Fluvium Frigidum** (Fortress by the Cold River), built by the Romans around 270 AD as an important link in the defence line of the Empire. Its four-metre-thick defence walls were perforated with fourteen circular towers, of which seven, either whole or partial, remain; the most tangible remnants, including an almost complete tower, lie east of the main square Lavričev trg – other portions of the wall can be detected on the western side of the ancient quarter. There are further exhibits relating to the town's ancient past in the small town **museum** (Sat & Sun 1–6pm; €2), five minutes' walk east of the tourist office at Prešernova ulica 24.

More stimulating is the **Pilon Gallery** (Pilonova Galerija; Tues–Fri 10am–4pm; free; ⓦwww.venopilon.com), just across the road from the tourist office at Prešernova ulica 3. A fantastically prolific and versatile artist, Pilon (1896–1970) was among Slovenia's foremost expressionist painters, though his repertoire also extended to graphic art and photography. Among the most interesting works on display here are sketches completed during his time incarcerated as a prisoner of war in Russia during World War I, and his landscape paintings – mostly motifs from the Vipava Valley – which represented the high point of Slovene modernism in the 1920s. As if that wasn't enough he also starred in Slovenia's first feature film, *Na Svoji Zemlji* (*On Our Own Land*), and translated a great deal of Slovenian poetry into French.

Arriving at the **bus** or **train** station, located opposite each other on Goriška cesta, it's a five-minute walk northeast to the centre of town and the **tourist office**, housed in a section of a Roman tower at Lokarjev drevored 8 (April–Oct Mon–Fri 10am–6pm, Sat 10am–noon; Nov–March Mon–Fri 8am–4pm; ⓣ05/365-9140, ⓦwww.tic-ajdovscina.si); they can arrange accommodation on local tourist farms and visits to local wine cellars. Should you desire to stay in town, there's the *Hotel Gold Club* 200m east of the stations at Goriška cesta 25 (ⓣ05/364-4700, ⓦwww.hotelgoldclub.eu; ❻), a dreary-looking hotel which conceals cool, brown-coloured minimalist rooms. There's also the oddly named *Police* **campsite**, 500m north of the station on Cesta 5 maja (ⓣ05/364-4724; July–Sept).

Vipava and Zemono

From Ajdovščina, hourly buses continue southeast to **VIPAVA**, the valley's second centre some 6km distant. This somnolent little market town, lying under the towering slopes of the Nanos Plateau, somewhat misguidedly styles itself as the Slovene Venice – for no good reason other than that it developed alongside the many karstic springs of the Vipava River. Of course, it's nothing like Venice and, though endowed with a modicum of charm thanks to its generous spread of Baroque architecture and picturesque stone-block bridges, you're unlikely to stay long, if you stop at all.

That said, the **Vipava Winery** at Vinarska cesta 5 (ⓣ05/367-1200, ⓦwww .vipava1894.si), 800m east of the main square where buses drop passengers off, is one of Primorje's major wine cooperatives, and is worth considering if you're unable to reach any of the villages. Its barrique (harvested in barrels) red wines – in particular Merlot and Cabernet Sauvignon – are rated as some of the best in the country. Guided tours and tastings (€5 for five wines) are possible, and there's also a good restaurant, the *Viparski Hram* (Tues–Sat noon–10pm), and wine shop on site. Otherwise, the friendly little **tourist office**, on the main square at Glavni trg 1 (July–Sept daily 9am–7pm; Oct–June Mon–Fri 9am–5pm, Sat 9am–2pm; ⓣ05/368-7041, ⓦwww.vipavska.dolina.si), can help arrange visits to a number of the local wine cellars. Just next door to the tourist office, there's accommodation at the *Apartmaji Koren* (ⓣ040/217-213, ⓦwww.apartmaji-koren.com; ❺), which offers excellent, modern rooms and apartments, while, 2km north of town in Vrhpolje, there's the welcoming little *Vrhpolje* **campsite** (ⓣ05/366-5305, ⓔkampvrhpolje@gmail.com; mid-April to mid-Oct).

Occupying a solitary location less than 2km west of Vipava (just off the main road), the Palladian-style **Zemono Mansion** (Grad Zemono; Mon & Tues 9am–4pm, Wed–Fri noon–7pm, Sat 9am–1pm; free) is one of Slovenia's best-preserved Renaissance buildings. Formerly a seventeenth-century hunting lodge, the cross-shaped ground floor, whose walls are blanketed with pastel-coloured landscape murals, is now used principally as a concert venue, and occasionally for weddings. The upper floor, meanwhile, has been rather crudely turned into a home furnishings showroom. More appropriately, the cellar has been converted into the high-class and very expensive *Gostilna Pri Lojzetu* **restaurant**, one of the country's most celebrated slow-food establishments, featuring an innovative menu using specially prepared vegetables, mushrooms and the freshest seafood (℡05/368-7007; Wed–Sun noon–10pm).

Vipavski Križ and Goče

Rising out of the flat plain just 2km west of Ajdovščina, the scenic fortified medieval village of **VIPAVSKI KRIŽ** is one of the few settlements in the valley whose historical importance is greater than its viticultural significance. Its focal point is the **Capuchin Monastery**, built in 1637 and whose **Church of the Holy Cross** displays a beautifully carved dark-wooden high altar, together with a sublime painting of the Holy Trinity, one of the largest Baroque canvases in the country and dating from 1668. Its **library** contains an extensive assortment of books from the fifteenth century onwards. Visits to the monastery are best arranged through the tourist office in Ajdovščina (see p.173). Adjacent to the monastery, on the eastern tip of the village, is the magnificent shell of the ruined fifteenth-century **castle**, erected on the orders of the bishop of Gorica so as to protect the village from Turkish and Venetian raids.

If just one wine village is your limit then make a beeline for **GOČE**, some 5km west of the main trunk road in the southeastern Vipava hills. With streets barely wide enough to squeeze a car through, the village is distinguished by its knot of tightly clustered eighteenth-century sandstone houses, ornamented with Karst-style courtyards and hewn stone portals. You'll have little difficulty tracking down somewhere to sample some wine; there are over sixty **cellars** here, which amounts to one for almost every house. A couple of good ones are Fajdiga at no. 4a and Ferjančič at no. 9.

Idrija and around

The history and development of **IDRIJA**, a town of some seven thousand inhabitants 36km north of Vipava, has been inextricably linked to its mines ever since the discovery of mercury here in 1490. During the eighteenth century, the growth and success of the **mines** – which are now in the process of being closed down for good – spawned a number of other local industries, most importantly forestry and medicine; during this period, the town could justifiably claim to rival Ljubljana as a centre of scientific and technological advancement. **Lace-making** has also played a significant part in shaping the town's identity; originally a seventeenth-century cottage industry, the craft grew to such an extent that Slovenia's first lace school was established here in the late nineteenth century, an institution that still functions today. Indeed, Idrija's major annual event is the **Lace Festival** (Čipkarski Festival) in mid-June, entailing lace-making competitions, arts and crafts exhibitions and evening entertainment.

Despite its modest size, Idrija can comfortably summon up enough attractions to rate a full day's sightseeing, more if you're looking to explore the surrounding countryside. Within walking distance of town is the mysterious **Wild Lake**, while further afield, the immense **Klavže** water barriers and the fascinating **Partisan Printworks** are no less deserving of a visit.

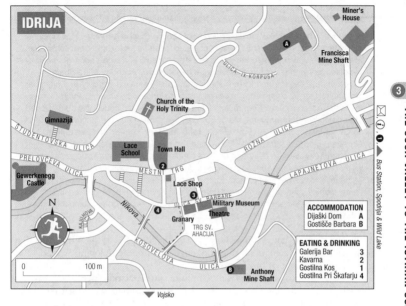

Map labels:

IDRIJA

Miner's House
Francisca Mine Shaft
ULICA IX KORPUSA
Church of the Holy Trinity
Gimnazija
ŠTUDENTOVSKA ULICA
ROZNA ULICA
Lace School
Town Hall
LAPAJNETOVA ULICA
PRELOVČEVA ULICA
MESTNI TRG
Gewerkenegg Castle
Lace Shop
Nikova
ULICA SV. BARBARE
Military Museum
Theatre
Granary
TRG SV. AHACIJA
KOSOVELOVA
N
ULICA
Anthony Mine Shaft
0   100 m

Bus Station, Spodnja & Wild Lake

ACCOMMODATION
Dijaški Dom   A
Gostišče Barbara   B

EATING & DRINKING
Galerija Bar   3
Kavarna   2
Gostilna Kos   1
Gostilna Pri Škafarju   4

▼ Vojsko

Arrival, information and accommodation

The **bus station** is centrally situated on Vodnikova ulica, from where it's just a few paces to both the **tourist office** (July–Aug Mon–Fri 9am–6pm, Sat & Sun 10am–4pm; Sept–June Mon–Fri 9am–4pm; ☏05/374-3916, ⓦwww.idrija-turizem.si), which has free **internet** access, and the **post office** (Mon–Fri 8am–7pm, Sat 8am–noon).

There's precious little **accommodation** in town: the small *Dijaški Dom*, up on the hill at Ulica IX Korpusa 17 (just behind the Francisca Mine Shaft), has beds available in summer for around €13 (☏05/373-4070, ⓔinfo@ciu-np.si). Otherwise, the only other place to sleep is at the *Gostišče Barbara*, which occupies the second floor of the Anthony Mine Shaft building at Kosovelova ulica 3 (☏05/377-1162, ⓦwww.barbara-idrija.si); it has two categories of room – four en-suite double/triple rooms with TV (⑤), and two hostel-style rooms sleeping four people, with shared wash/shower facilities (②). Another option, albeit a very expensive one, is the five-star *Hotel Kendov Dvorec*, a splendidly renovated fourteenth-century manor house 4km north of town in **Spodnja Idrija**, at Na griču 2 (☏05/372-5100, ⓦwww.kendov-dvorec.com;⑨); the immaculate rooms come with antique furniture and linen made from Idrija lace.

The Town

Idrija's handful of terrific sites – all more or less associated with the mining and lace industries, such as the **Mine Shaft**, **Gewerkenegg Castle** and **Lace School** – are broadly contained within the attractive and compact old core on the western side of town, and all within comfortable walking distance of each other.

Anthony Mine Shaft

The town's star attraction is undoubtedly the **Anthony Mine Shaft** (Antonijev Rov) whose main entrance building (Šelštev) is at Kosovelova ulica 3. Sunk in

Mining in Idrija

In 1490, a local tub-maker, busy soaking his wooden vessel in a spring on the present-day site of the Holy Trinity Church, chanced on a hitherto unknown substance, **mercury**. He was unable to keep this secret to himself, and locals soon got wind of the discovery; some eight years later work began on the **Anthony Mine Shaft**.

Mercury appeared in the Idrija mine in two forms: as native mercury and cinnabar ore, the former as shimmering silver-grey drops dripping down on to the rock face, the latter a deep red-coloured material, from which the liquid could only be extracted after being burnt at temperatures of 800 degrees. At its peak the Idrija mine yielded some thirteen percent of the world's total mercury output, second only to the Almaden mine in Spain. Working conditions were notoriously bad and, with prolonged exposure to this most toxic of substances, a miner could be expected to work for no more than six or seven years before becoming too ill to continue.

The mine has now been closed down completely, with several factors contributing to its demise, namely the lack of rich ore, almost negligible prices on the world market and the increasing use of alternative, environmentally friendly substances.

1500, the tunnel shaft (1.5km long and 400m deep) was, after the Almadén mercury mine in Spain, the most productive in Europe, employing around 1300 miners at the height of production.

The visit begins with a twenty-minute **audiovisual presentation** (in English) in the checking room – the place where miners would gather in the early morning hours to be allocated their duties by the Obergutman (a kind of foreman) before heading down into the mine. On the wall at the back of the room is the so-called death clock: before descending into the pit, each miner was obliged to take a number plate which, if not replaced at the end of the shift, indicated that he'd got lost or was in some sort of trouble. Having donned jacket and helmet, you're led along a series of lit galleries and laddered passageways, part of the Main Road which served as the main mine entrance for over two hundred years. Descending to a depth of 100m, you'll pass by several small alcoves in which benches were placed for the miners to take their lunch; now displaying items of equipment used to bore through the rock, and a number of life-size puppets of miners – including one of **Berkmandlc**, the pit dwarf, who in return for parcels of food, would tap the walls to indicate to the miners where the richest sources of mercury lay.

The tour winds up at the tiny underground **Chapel of the Holy Trinity**, where miners would pray before the statues of Sts Barbara and Acacius (patron saints of miners) for a safe return from their day's work. Scheduled tours, which last around one hour thirty minutes, take place daily at 10am and 3pm (and at noon in July & Aug), with an extra tour at 4pm on weekends (€6).

Gewerkenegg Castle and the Town Museum

Sited atop a small hill on the western fringe of town, and discernible from some distance thanks to its two cylindrical corner towers and an oddly protruding central clock tower, **Gewerkenegg Castle** (Grad Gewerkenegg) was built by the Acacius Society of Mining Entrepreneurs around 1530 to house the mine administration and other official bodies. Though prevailingly Renaissance in form, the castle was embellished with Baroque appendages in the eighteenth century – including the arcaded courtyard and its rather lurid foliage-style frescoes.

It now plays host to the **town museum** (Mestni muzej; daily 9am–6pm; €3) which, not surprisingly, dotes heavily on the town's **mining** heritage. An absorbing exhibition begins with an introduction to the Idrija mine, including a depiction of the local tub-maker who kick-started the whole thing. The next three rooms are devoted to all matters geological, and while most people are drawn to the steel ball floating in a bowl of mercury, don't let that detract you from the fine assemblage of fossils, minerals and cinnabar ore deposits on display. Similarly enlightening is the collection of mine maps, land registers, flasks and other objects gathered in the northern Rondel Tower, while the staircase in the southern Mercury Tower has been designed to symbolize the descent down the pit. At the bottom is a Plexiglas cube filled with droplets of mercury.

No less engaging is the exhibition charting Idrija's development in the twentieth century. Aided by some fascinating photographs, there is superb coverage of the town's involvement during the two World Wars, including the first Italian occupation in 1918, which culminated in the Rapallo Treaty (see p.324), thereby annexing part of Slovenia and turning Idrija into a border town; while World War II focuses on the German occupation between September 1943 and April 1945, and its attendant Fascist denationalization policies – the most sobering exhibit is a tree stump upon which two Partisans were beheaded. The last section covers local industry in Idrija and, despite the closure of the mines – you can't fail to miss the enormous hammer and sickle that used to adorn the entrance to the Francisca Mine Shaft (see p.178) – unemployment is less than one percent here, the lowest in the country.

Inevitably, the town's rich **lace** tradition is well documented with, among other exhibits, a display of work by the winners of the annual bobbin lace competition; the most interesting piece is a sprawling tablecloth, originally made for President Tito's wife, Jovanka Broz, but retained by the museum following his death, and her banishment from political life, in 1980.

The Military Museum and the Lace School

Just below the castle, the old town core showcases a couple of significant buildings including the former mine **Granary** on Trg Svetega Ahacija, part of which is now a **Military Museum** (Tues–Sun 10am–noon & 3–6pm; €2.50); this absorbing, privately run collection features a welter of paraphernalia (uniforms, weapons, shells and the like) from World War I onwards, concluding

Lace-making in Idrija

The art of bobbin **lace-making** first took off in Slovenia in the seventeenth century and, despite having been practised in many towns and rural areas throughout the country, its roots have remained strongest in Idrija, where the craft has been taught in the town's **Lace School** since 1876.

Traditionally, lace-making was practised by most women as a means of supplementing a miner's often very meagre wage – a state of affairs that became even more pressing following the decline of this and other traditional industries (such as iron smelting) in the late nineteenth and early twentieth centuries. The lace-making industry continued apace, with its products sold mainly to the Church, until World War II. After this, however, its popularity waned, only to be revived in the 1980s. Today's lace products are primarily made as gifts and souvenirs.

Idrija Lace (*Idrijska čipka*) takes many forms, from simple flower-based patterns to intricately woven cloths featuring folk or peasant motifs, many of which are technically superb; you can view, and purchase, many such specimens in several of the region's museums and shops. Moreover, the **Lace Festival** in Idrija, and the **Days of Lace Fair** in Železniki (another important regional lace centre), attest to this exquisite handicraft's ongoing importance and enduring popularity.

with memorabilia from the 1991 Ten-Day war; next to the granary stands the oldest **theatre** in Slovenia, built in 1769 and now a cinema.

The most impressive building, however, is the lovely Neoclassical Old School (Stara šola) at Prelovčeva ulica 2, which has been home to the town's **Lace School** (Čipkarska šola; Mon–Fri 10am–1pm, plus 3–6pm in July & Aug; Ⓦwww.cipkarskasola.si; €3) since 1876 (see box, p.177). The items on display here were completed by students of the school, all of whom attend voluntarily and are mostly aged between 6 and 14; if you ask, you may be allowed to see a lesson in progress. You can also buy lace here, or at one of several **lace shops** dotted around town; the best of these is the Galerija Idrijske Čipke, opposite the town hall at Mestni trg 16 (Mon–Fri 10am–noon & 4–7pm, Sat 10am–noon).

The Francisca Mine Shaft and the Kamšt

Up the hill on Bazoviška ulica is the **Francisca Mine Shaft** (Jašek Frančiške; no set opening times – contact the town museum in the castle; €2), whose former workshops now house a marvellous collection of carefully restored, nineteenth-century steam-driven pumps, boilers and compressors, most of which were taken out of operation in the 1950s following the introduction of more modern working practices.

Set against a gentle slope just behind the mine shaft is a typically striking, albeit heavily renovated, example of an eighteenth-century **miner's house** (Rudarska hiša). Defined by a high, slender frontage, a sharply pointed roof and neat rows of small, square windows, these houses were traditionally constructed from wood and stone, the external walls made of thick boards daubed with lime-wash, and the rooftops protected with wooden shingles. A miner's house usually comprised three or four floors, in order that several families could be accommodated in the same building – an important consideration during times of overpopulation; moreover, miners could rarely afford their own houses.

There's yet another reminder of Idrija's industrial pedigree 1km southeast of the bus station at the end of Vodnikova ulica. Concealed within the chunky stone-block building is the well-preserved **Kamšt** (no set opening times – contact the town museum in the castle; €2), held to be the largest wooden waterwheel in Europe, measuring 13.6m in diameter. For more than 150 years, it pumped pit water from a depth of over 200m from the Joseph Shaft.

Eating and drinking

Idrija is bereft of decent places to **eat**, though there are two very agreeable *gostilna* here, both of which serve up the Idrija speciality, *Žlikrofi* – spiced potato balls wrapped in thin pastry. *Gostilna Pri Škafarju*, 50m east of the former granary at Ulica Svete Barbare 9 (closed Tues), is fairly plain-looking, but there's a decent menu to choose from, including a handful of horse-meat dishes (including, somewhat disconcertingly, grilled colt); while *Gostilna Kos*, 200m east of the bus station at Tomšičeva ulica 4, veers more towards Italian fare (closed Sun). Two good spots for a **drink** are *Kavarna*, on the ground floor of the town hall, and the *Galerija Bar* next to the granary.

The Wild Lake and Klavže dams

From the Kamšt a three-kilometre-long trail (Pot ob Rakah) leads south to the brilliant blue-green **Wild Lake** (Divje Jezero), an apposite name for this small body of water that has claimed the lives of several divers attempting to locate the lake's as yet undiscovered source – to date 156m is the deepest anyone has got. What is known is that water flows into the lake from an underground passage, or siphon, reckoned to measure approximately 200m long. The lake itself measures about 65m in length and 30m in width, taking barely fifteen minutes to circle, unless, that is, you happen to be here following snow melt or extremely heavy rainfall, when massive volumes of water are discharged from its depths, flooding the lake to 3m above its normal level. Emanating from the lake is Slovenia's shortest river, the Jezernica, which discharges into the Idrijca after only 55m.

Just as impressive are the precipitous, hundred-metre-high cliffs encircling the lake, whose crevices and ledges shelter a galaxy of alpine **flora**, including several endemic species, such as the Carniolan primrose and hacquetia, the latter named after eminent local surgeon Baltazar Hacquet. Lurking in the lake's depths, and something you won't see, is Proteus Anguinus, the human-fish (see *Subterranean Slovenia* colour section). If you have your own car, take the Ljubljana road south from Idrija and the lake is signposted after about 1.5km.

Twelve kilometres upstream from the Wild Lake on the Belca River (accessible via an increasingly rutted forest road) is the first of four remaining **dams** (Klavže) in the area. Known locally as the Slovene Pyramids, these superb technical monuments were originally constructed from wood in the sixteenth century, but were replaced by sturdier stone structures in 1770. Their function was to accumulate enough water to enable vast quantities of timber to be floated downriver to Idrija, whereupon the logs would gather in front of a 412-metre-long dam (rake), at which point they would be carted off to the mines (where they were used as supporting structures for the galleries) and smelting plants (for fuel for burning iron ore). The rake remained operational until 1926, when road transportation was deemed more efficient, while the Klavže gradually fell into a state of disrepair. Restored in the 1980s, they now stand as a fitting memorial to a bygone era. There's another dam about 1.5km further upstream and another, also accessible by road, on the Idrijca River, which runs roughly parallel to the Belca.

The most impressive of the renovated dams – completed in 2005 – is located on the Klavžarica river, 8km west of Spodnja Idrija beyond the village of Kanomlja; some 34m long and 8m wide, and constructed from sculpted lime rocks, the **Kanomeljske Klavže** was built in 1813 and served the needs of the Idrija mine until 1912. To get here, take a left turn at the village of Spodnji Kanomlja and follow the signs – the final kilometre is not suited for cars, but it's a pleasant enough walk anyway.

Partisan Printing Works

Secreted away in an almost impenetrable forest ravine below the Vojsko plateau, 2km north of the tiny hamlet of **Planina** (itself 14km west of Idrija), are several modest wooden cabins which, for a brief period during World War II, functioned as the **Partisan Printing Works** (Partizanska tiskarna; mid-April to mid-Oct 9am–4pm; €2). Operational between September 1944 and May 1945, and with some forty employees, the clandestinely run printworks rolled out between four thousand and seven thousand copies of *Partizanski Dnevnik* (*Partisan Daily*) per day, the only daily newspaper to be published by a resistance movement in occupied Europe during the war; over the eight months more than a million copies of the paper were published, as well as stacks of other printed matter.

During the visit, you'll get to see the typesetting room (complete with printing moulds and dozens of original papers), the bindery, kitchen and dining room, the power plant, and the printing room. Purchased for a million lire, the still-functioning printing press was smuggled across from Milan, via Gorica, before being transported, piece by piece, to Vojsko; a printing demonstration is usually given. Despite numerous German offensives in the vicinity – including one final major assault during the Spring of 1945 in which over three hundred Partisans were killed – the printworks was never rumbled. Owing to its extremely remote location, a visit requires a little organization and a degree of physical exertion; in the first instance, you should contact the tourist office in Idrija or the Town Museum at Gewerkenegg Castle (see p.176).

Cerkno and around

Located somewhat out on a limb 19km north of Idrija (and 4km off the main Idrija–Tolmin road), the anonymous little town of **CERKNO** was a key centre of Partisan activity during World War II, when a number of military and political bodies, workshops and schools were stationed hereabouts. Life in Cerkno today is played out at a rather more languid pace, and there's little inducement to linger. That said, there's good **skiing** close by (see box, p.136), the **Laufarija carnival** in February (see box opposite), and the annual **Jazz Festival** (ⓦwww.jazzcerkno.si), a three-day event in mid-May featuring a surprisingly impressive, and refreshingly diverse, roster of both domestic and international jazz and folk artists.

The **Cerkno Museum** (Cerkljanski muzej; Tues–Fri 9am–3pm, Sat & Sun 10am–1pm & 2–6pm; €2), a five-minute walk from Glavni trg at Bevkova 12 is also worth a browse. This engaging exhibition documents the history of the Cerkljansko region from the nineteenth century onwards, with a particularly interesting resumé of events hereabouts during World War II – exhibits include the wedding blouse of Franja Bidovec, founder of the Partisan Hospital (see opposite), and items belonging to writer France Bevk (see p.182) who served with the Partisans. There's also a display of the masks used during the Laufarija Carnival

If there's little to excite in Cerkno itself, then the surrounding countryside is invested with some terrific sites, although unless you have your own wheels or aren't disposed to a reasonable amount of walking, reaching them will prove problematic. Sadly, the best of these, the superbly evocative **Franja Partisan Hospital**, is currently closed for restoration. The other, less well-known, and hence rarely visited, sites are the **Divje Babe** and **Ravenska Caves**, both a little way southwest of town; and in **Zakojca** to the north, the writer France Bevk's house. Embracing most of the above, the **Cerkno hills** themselves offer some good hikes.

Practicalities

Buses arrive and depart from Glavni trg, the small main square around which everything in town revolves. The **tourist office** is right by the square at Močnikova 2 (Mon–Fri 8am–4pm, Sat 8am–1pm, Sun 8am–noon; ☎05/373-4645, ⓦwww.cerkno.si); they have free **internet** access and can help to arrange visits to some of the outlying attractions. The **post office** is 100m west of Glavni trg at Bevkova 9 (Mon–Fri 8am–6pm, Sat 8am–noon). The only **accommodation** in town is the *Hotel Cerkno*, a comfortable, clean and roomy place just off the main square at Sedejev trg 8 (☎05/374-3400, ⓦwww.hotel-cerkno.si; ❻); its large pool is free to guests.

If you don't mind staying a little way outside town, there are two very welcoming possibilities: back out on the Idrija–Tolmin road (at the junction of the Cerkno turn-off) in **Straža**, the *Želinc* tourist farm (℡05/372-4020, ⓦ www.zelinc.com; ❹) offers very comfortable rooms, a small spa facility, good food and bikes for rent; in the other direction, 6km along the road towards the ski centre in the wayside hamlet of **Log**, the decent-value *Gostilna Gačnk v Logu* (℡05/372-4005, Ⓔgacnk@cerkno.com; ❹) is a roadside, family-run tavern with nine cosy, wood-furnished rooms; its modern **restaurant** features a wide choice of exotic game (stag's back, chamois, boar and the like), Serbian meats (*Čevapi* and *Sarma*), and the local Idrijan ravioli-style speciality (*Žlikrofi*). In Cerkno itself, the restaurant in the *Hotel Cerkno* is just about the only worth-while place to dine. For a **drink**, pop along to the pretty lively *Pri Gabrielju*, just off the square at Prekomorskih brigad 1.

Franja Partisan Hospital

Dramatically sited in the heart of the spectacular **Pasica gorge** 7km northeast of Cerkno, the **Franja Partisan Hospital** (Partizanska Bolnišnica Franja; contact the tourist office in Cerkno) was built in December 1943 for wounded soldiers of the Ninth Corps of the Slovene Partisan Army. Named after its chief physician Franja Bojc-Bidovec, the hospital remained operational until May 1945, a period during which it treated more than five hundred Partisans, as well as soldiers from Italy, Russia and America. Sadly, in September 2007, much of the hospital was swept away under torrential floods, though it is currently being reconstructed.

The original hospital comprised thirteen camouflaged **wooden cabins** housing an operating room, isolation ward, kitchen, X-ray room and several recovery rooms, with the entire complex protected by bunkers, minefields and machine gun nests pressed into the cliffs above. However, despite the area being shelled by Germans on several occasions, it was never captured. Indeed, its secrecy was such that the wounded were blindfolded before being admitted, food was lowered down the cliff face by neighbouring farmers, and medical supplies were air-dropped in by Allied forces. Supplies notwithstanding, the hospital was remarkably self-reliant throughout the period of its operation, making its own orthopedic accessories, organizing cultural and educational activities for the wounded and even managing to publish its own bulletin, *Bolniški list* (*Patient's Bulletin*).

The Laufarija

One of Slovenia's more enjoyable *Pust* (Shrovetide) festivals is the **Laufarija**, staged each year on the Sunday before Ash Wednesday and on Shrove Tuesday in Cerkno's small town square. The central character is the horned **Pust**, made up of a weighty costume of straw, moss and pine branches; as the personification of winter, the Pust is hauled up in front of a court and charged with a litany of barmy crimes – a poor harvest, inclement weather, dodgy roads and so on – before being found guilty and sentenced to summary execution.

The two dozen or so other members of the Laufarija family – each of whom wears one of the distinctive **masks** (*larfe*) carved from soft lime-tree wood – represent either a local trade or craft (baker, butcher, cobbler, and so on), or display certain character traits or afflictions, such as the drunk and his wife, the scabby one, and the sick man with his accordion.

To be honest it's debatable whether even the locals know what's going on, but it's a great deal of fun all the same. If you don't manage to get here for the festival, there's a fine display of the masks worn in the Cerkno Museum (see opposite).

Due to its relatively remote location, you really need your own transport to get to the hospital; the only buses that pass this way are the ski buses from Cerkno in the winter. Seven kilometres along the road east of Cerkno, a road branches north just beyond the tiny hamlet of **Log**; 1km on you come to a car park. From here, a trail (10min) inclines up the forested gorge, bisected by the babbling Čerinščica stream and hemmed in by overhanging boulders.

The Divje Babe and Ravenska Caves

Two hundred metres above the Idrija–Tolmin road and the Idrijca river, near the village of **Šebrelje**, some 12km west of Cerkno, is **Divje Babe Cave**, one of the most important Palaeolithic sites in Slovenia. While digging near the cave entrance in 1995, excavators stumbled across the femur of a young cave bear – nothing particularly revelatory in itself – but this one had been perforated with four holes (two complete, two partially worn away), giving it a flute-like appearance. Researchers in Canada calculated the four-inch bone to be around 45,000 years old, possibly more, thus dating from the Mousterian period, time of Neanderthal man. On the assumption that the holes were made by human hands – the most plausible explanation given that no teeth marks were detected on the bone – it can lay fair claim to being the oldest known **musical instrument** in Europe. The flute currently resides in the National Museum in Ljubljana. Getting here really does entail having your own transport; otherwise, you can take a Cerkno–Tolmin bus and alight at the roadside hamlet of Stopnik; however, from there, you've still got a long (about 3km) and steep walk along the road up to Šebrelje.

Chanced upon by a local farmer in 1832, the **Ravenska Cave** (Ravenska jama), high up in the village of **Ravne Pri Cerkne**, 7km southwest of Cerkno, is known for its clusters of brilliant white aragonite crystals, spidery-like formations that owe their shape and colour to the high levels of magnesium present in the soil. The crystals here are among some of the finest specimens of aragonite to be found anywhere in Europe. The cave itself is something of a minnow in Slovene terms, measuring just over 350m in length, of which you'll get to see about 100m; there's no need for sensible shoes, as walkways have been constructed, but bring a jumper as the temperature is around just eight or nine degrees.

To arrange a visit to either cave, contact the tourist office in Cerkno (see p.180). If you don't have transport and are considering walking, there's a very satisfying circular hike from Cerkno to the cave, via the village of **Zakriž** (4hr).

Zakojca and the Cerkno Hills

Approximately 20km north of the Ravenska Cave, and rather more difficult to reach (but still accessible by road or several marked paths), is the tiny village of **ZAKOJCA**, birthplace of children's novelist France Bevk (1890–1970). The immaculately restored **homestead** (Domačija Franceta Bevka; no set times; €2) where Bevk also spent much of his youth is a fairly simple dwelling; the downstairs space comprises a living room (*hiša*), two small bedrooms, a "black" kitchen (see p.129) and a small stable for livestock, while the first floor attic, where he wrote his earliest works, has been transformed into an exhibition space, with family photos, books and personal effects.

The house is a ten-minute walk from the *Pri Flandru* tourist farm (where you'll have to go first to get the key) in the centre of the village at no. 1 (☎05/377-9800, ⓦ www.kmetija-flander.si; ❹) – this is a good place to **stay** if you're planning to spend a day or two hiking in the surrounding hills, and there's terrific home cooking on offer too. From Zakojca, you could tackle the highland area's highest peak, **Porezen**, which tops a very respectable 1630m (2hr); just below the summit is the *Koča na Poreznu* mountain hut (☎05/377-6275; June to mid-Sept). Porezen can also be attempted from the Franja Partisan Hospital (3hr). If you're considering any sort of hiking in the hills, consider buying the 1:50,000 *Idrijsko In Cerkljansko* map.

The Karst

A dry, rocky, and thickly forested limestone plateau, scattered with ancient stone villages, the Karst is famed for its subterranean wonderland of rivers and streams, hollows, depressions and caves, which have fired the imagination of travellers for centuries – none more so than those at **Škocjan**. Just a few kilometres west of Škocjan is the Karst's second major draw, the world-famous **Lipica Stud Farm**, home of the magnificent Lipizzaner horses, and another fine cave at **Vilenica**. Of the villages, the obvious draw is **Štanjel**, whose bleached-white stone houses and wonderfully disparate range of sights are a delight.

While here take the opportunity to sample the local culinary delights, in particular the delicious air-dried *pršut* ham, which complements perfectly a glass of **Kraški Teran**, a spiky, cherry-red wine that acquires its deep aroma and colour from the iron-rich *terra rosa* soil peculiar to this region.

Štanjel and around

Contender for most picturesque village in the Karst, if not Slovenia, the medieval hilltop settlement of **ŠTANJEL**, situated 28km southeast of Nova Gorica, is the archetypal Karst village. Most likely the site of a Halstatt settlement, the prominent limestone hill was fortified around the twelfth century, gradually evolving across several gently curving, south-facing terraces, a layout modelled on the plans of the ancient Etruscan towns. Its textbook stone houses are delightful, and there's more than enough to warrant a few hours' exploration. For **guided tours** of the village (April–Oct at 3.30pm; Nov–March at 2.30pm; €4) contact the tourist office (see p.184).

The best place to start is the **Castle** (Grad Štanjel), located through the main **entrance tower**. Erected by the counts of Koblenz in the sixteenth century, on the foundations of an older, medieval castle, there is now little to see except for a battered shell, the result of heavy pounding during World War II. There's redemption, however, in the renovated residential wing of the castle, which houses the **Lojze Spacal Gallery** (Galerija Lojzeta Spacala; April–Oct Tues–Fri 10am–2pm, Sat & Sun 10am–6pm; Nov–March Tues–Fri 11am–2pm, Sat & Sun 11am–5pm; €2.50, including entry to the Karst House – see p.184), a brilliant collection of abstract paintings, prints, woodcuts and tapestries by the eponymous, Trieste-born artist. Spacal was profoundly influenced by the surrounding landscape, as is evident in his extensive use of Karst motifs and colours – greys and whites representing stone, and reds representing the soil.

Štanjel's most visible symbol, courtesy of its smooth steeple shaped like a bishop's hat, is the **Church of St Daniel**. Its most interesting interior features are a marble tomb etched with a relief of Daniel and the lions, a relief of the castle as it once supposedly looked, and paintings of interlocking crosses on the presbytery walls; the church is usually closed, so contact the gallery if you want to visit.

From the church it's a few paces east to the six-hundred-year-old **Karst House** (Kraška Hiša; same times as gallery; €1.50), a superb example of vernacular architecture, constructed entirely from stone, including the roof and gutters. The downstairs space would have been used for keeping livestock, with a family of typically five or six members squeezed into the living quarters upstairs; both floors now hold a modest ethnological collection. To visit, contact the gallery.

In the southeastern corner of the village, a few hundred metres and a couple of terraces below the Karst house, is the **Ferrari Garden**, designed by internationally renowned architect and town planner (and former mayor of Štanjel) Max Fabiani, but named after his brother-in-law, Enrico Ferrari. This winsome little park was designed as an adjunct to the now abandoned Ferrari Villa (which rises above the eastern edge of the park), incorporating traditional Karst features – terraces, stone retaining walls and stairways – and foreign elements, such as a pavilion, oval pool and a delicate, balustraded stone bridge, the inspiration for which was undoubtedly the author's earlier work in Vienna. The park had a more utilitarian function, however; in order to counter the chronic water shortages in the Karst region, Fabiani designed a water supply system using a series of ditches, storage tanks, pipes and irrigation channels, all integrated within a complex system, thus providing the villa and surrounding buildings with their own source of running water.

From the garden there are expansive views across the Karst towards Italy and the hills of the Vipava Valley. You can also follow a marked footpath (Fabiani Path) south towards the village of **Kobdilj**, Fabiani's birthplace.

Practicalities

Trains actually stop in Kobdilj, the next village along, though it's only a fifteen-minute walk into Štanjel itself; **buses** stop on the main road opposite the main entrance to the village. The **tourist office** (mid-May to mid-Oct Tues–Sun 10am–6pm; rest of year Tues–Sat 11am–4pm, Sun 2–5pm; ☎05/769-0056, http://vodnik.kras-carso.com), in the modern block of buildings just a few steps from the bus stop, can arrange **private accommodation** in rooms and apartments (❷–❸) in Štanjel. There's good food to be had in the simple but elegant **restaurant** in the castle courtyard (Tues–Sun 10am–9pm).

There are several further accommodation possibilities between Štanjel and Sežana. About 10km southwest of Štanjel, in the small isolated village of **Pliskovica**, is the terrific ⚐ *Pliskovica* **youth hostel** at no. 11 (☎05/764-0250, ✉info@hostelkras.com; €16–18). A preserved heritage site, this beautifully restored four-hundred-year-old farmstead has six- to fourteen-bed dorms, all with shared bathroom facilities, as well as double rooms; they've also got bike rental, laundry and internet – and it's possible to camp here. Also in the village, at no. 93, is the charming Petelin-Durcik tourist farm (☎05/764-0028, ✉petelin.durcik@siol.com; ❸), which has four small, tidy rooms and first-rate home cooking. However, without a car or bike, you'll struggle to get here, as there are only two buses from Sežana (Mon–Fri 10.40am & 3.30pm). Easier to reach is the *Škerlj* **tourist farm**, 12km south of Štanjel on the main road towards Sežana, in **Tomaj**, at no. 53a (☎05/764-0673, ✉skerlj.tomaj@gmail .com; ❸); comfortable rooms are complemented by good food and hospitality – they've also got bikes for rent.

Sežana and Divača

If you're heading to Lipica or the Škocjan Caves, there's a good chance you'll pass through either **Sežana** or **Divača** at some point, as both towns are on the rail line from Ljubljana and the bus route to the coast or Trieste. Although there are a couple of mildly diverting things to see in these small towns, they're more useful from a practical point of view, with information, accommodation and refreshments available. If you do find yourself waiting for a connection in **SEŽANA** (5km north of Lipica), you could make the fifteen-minute walk north along Partizanska ulica – the town's main through road – to view the well-turned-out **Botanical Gardens** (Botanični Park; Mon–Fri 7am–3pm; €2). Alongside the gardens (behind the civilian cemetery) is a World War I **cemetery**, holding some fifty neatly tended graves.

The **train** and **bus** stations are situated just 200m apart on Kolodvorska ulica; inside the bus station building the small and helpful **tourist office** (Mon–Fri 8am–4pm, Sat 8am–6pm, Sun 9am–2pm; ☎05/731-0128, ✉tic.sezana@siol .net) can advise on private **accommodation** and other aspects of visits to Lipica or the Škocjan caves. Conveniently situated between the two stations is the bright and clean *Hotel Tabor*, at Kolodvorska 4 (☎05/734-1551, ⓦwww .hotelitabor-kozina.com; ❺). You can **eat** well at the *Carvallino* pizzeria and spaghetteria, Partizanska ulica 25.

DIVAČA, 6km east of Lipica, is an even less enticing option but there is a worthwhile diversion here, as well as a couple of cheap accommodation possibilities. In the centre of town, at Kraška cesta 26, the **Škrateljnova House** (Škrateljnova domačija; Sat 10am–noon & 3–5pm, Sun 10am–1pm; €1.50) hosts a small exhibition on Slovenia's first major female film star, **Ita Rina** (1907–79), but is actually far more interesting from an architectural point of view; a marvellous example of vernacular architecture, this seventeenth-century homestead claims to be one of the oldest houses in the Karst region. On the first weekend of July a selection of old Slovene films are staged in the back yard.

Both the **train** station (with a handful of left-luggage lockers) and the main **bus** stop are on Trg 15 Aprila from where it's a five-minute walk up the road to the perfectly acceptable *Pension Risnik* (☎05/763-0008; ❸) opposite the petrol station, though a better option is the bright *Malovec*, 200m north of the *Risnik* at Kraška cesta 30a (☎05/763-1225; ❸). The *Orient Express*, just across the road at Kraška 67, is a lively and colourful **restaurant/bar**, serving up salads, grills and meat platters alongside a great selection of light and dark beers brewed on site. If you are planning to visit the Škocjan Caves from Divača, and don't fancy walking, there are free **buses** from the train station (May–Sept 10am, 11.05am, 2pm & 3.35pm; Oct–April 11.05am & 14.35pm).

Lipica

After Postojna and Lake Bled, Slovenia's most emblematic tourist draw is **Lipica** (ⓦwww.lipica.org), birthplace of the famous white Lipizzaner horse. Located 6km south of Sežana and just 2km from the Italian border, the Lipica estates were acquired by the Austrian Archduke Karl (son of Emperor Ferdinand I) in 1580. He established the stud in order to breed horses for the Spanish Riding School in Vienna, as well as the Royal Court stables in Graz. That the Lipizzaner has survived at all is remarkable; the breed was evacuated to southern Hungary during Napoleon's occupation in the late eighteenth century, divided by the Italians and Austrians during World War I and seized by the Germans during World War II. Today the horse is bred at half a dozen European stud farms and widely throughout the United States. Here at

The Lipizzaner

Despite competing claims from Austria and Italy over the geographical origin and lineage of the **Lipizzaner** (Lipicanec), the original stud was established at Lipica in 1580 by the then governor of the Slovene territories, Habsburg Archduke Karl. Horses of Spanish, Arabian and Berber stock were bred with the tough and muscular local Karst horse, thus creating the Lipizzaner strain. As a result of such fastidious breeding, Lipizzaner are comparatively small in stature – 14.3 to 15.2 hands – with a long back, short, thick neck, and a powerful build. Born dark or bay coloured they do not turn white until the age of 5 or 6, though their coat is in fact grey, a colour that only manifests itself when the horse sweats. These distinctive physical traits are complemented by a beautiful sense of balance and rhythm, a lively, high-stepping gait and an even temperament. With such qualities, it's little wonder that the Lipizzaner have for centuries excelled at **carriage driving** and as **show horses** – performing the bows, pirouettes and other manoeuvres that delight dressage cognoscenti as well as the average punter.

Lipica there are around four hundred horses divided between show, competition and riding horses, and some three hundred more around Slovenia in private hands – thus it is estimated that Slovenia is home to around one-fifth of the world's Lipizzaner.

A tour of the **stud farm**, which entails a visit to the stables, riding halls and carriage museum, is not in itself that enthralling, though you do get the opportunity to see these magnificent creatures close up. **Tours** take place throughout the year (daily: Jan–March & Nov–Dec hourly 10am–3pm, except noon; April–June & Sept–Oct hourly 9am–5pm, except noon, plus an extra tour at 6pm on Sat & Sun; July & Aug hourly 9am–6pm, except noon; €10). To really make your visit worthwhile, try and coordinate it with a presentation of the **Classical Riding School** (April–Oct Tues, Fri & Sun at 3pm; €17); while nothing as grand as the shows put on at the Spanish Riding School in Vienna, it's still quite something to see, the riders all toffed up in period costume while the horses go about performing their well-crafted exercises.

The school runs a number of **riding** programmes (all 50min long), from rides out in a guided group (€20), to group or individual classes with an instructor (€25/€40), and dressage (€45). For real enthusiasts, there are a host of week-long riding courses. Reservations are required for all lessons. Between April and October it's also possible to go **carriage riding** (Tues–Sun 10am–2pm & 4–6pm; €40 per carriage for 1hr, maximum 4 people).

Practicalities

If you don't have your own **transport**, getting here will be difficult; the only buses which head this way are the school ones, during term-time only (Mon–Fri at 11.45am, 12.25pm, 1.30pm & 3.50pm, with return buses at 8.30am and 2.50pm) – otherwise you'll have to hitch or take a taxi (€10), which can be booked through the tourist office in Sežana (see p.185).

For **accommodation** in the area, you're best off staying in Sežana or Divača (see p.185), although it is possible to stay within the Lipica estate; rooms at the *Maestro* (☎05/739-1580, ⓦwww.lipica.org; ❻) are spacious and comfortable. There are several sporting and leisure amenities available here too, including a casino, swimming pool (€6), tennis (€8 per hour; free to hotel guests) and a nine-hole golf course, Slovenia's only year-round course (☎05/734-6373; €23 for nine holes/€30 for eighteen).

Vilenica Cave and Lokev

Two kilometres east of Lipica is the **Vilenica Cave** (Jama Vilenica), a relative minnow in comparison to Slovenia's better known and more glamorous showcaves, but certainly no less attractive for it. Reputedly the first cave in the country open to the public, way back in 1633, it wasn't until 1963, when the local caving club took it upon themselves to clean up the galleries and install electric lighting, that tourism really made its mark here. The walk of some four hundred metres takes in numerous galleries, home to a wondrous array of weird and fantastically shaped stalagmites and stalactites, many stained a rich rust-red colour owing to the surrounding Karst soil. Tours (€8), which last one hour, take place on Sundays throughout the year (May–Sept 3pm & 5pm; Oct–April 3pm). Each year, the largest hall in the system hosts the **Vilenica Festival**, a prestigious international literary gathering each September.

Just two kilometres on from Vilenica, in the village of **LOKEV**, there's yet more delightful Karst architecture on view; the most outstanding building here is the **Tabor Tower**, a cylindrical stone edifice built in 1485 by the Venetians as a defence against the Turks and which later served as the town granary. Its three floors now accommodate a **war museum** (Vojaški muzej; Wed–Sun 10am–noon & 2–6pm; €3), with memorabilia from both World Wars. Crammed into every conceivable space, there's a wealth of stuff on display, including the uniform of the commander of the Austrian forces on the Soča Front, Svetozar Borojevič (the Soča Lion), and stacks more accoutrements from the various warring sides; there's a fine display of photos too, including one of Mussolini during his visit to the Postojna Caves in 1938.

Škocjan Regional Park

Located 5km south of Divača in the belly of the **Škocjan Regional Park**, the **Škocjan Caves** are the country's most memorable natural attraction, a breathtaking complex of passages, chambers, collapsed valleys and, reputedly, the world's largest subterranean canyon. Measuring around 5800m in length, the caves were formed by the **Reka River** (River River), which begins its journey from springs deep below Snežnik mountain 50km southeast of the cave near the Croatian border. At the village of Škocjan, not far from the cave entrance, the river sinks underground for the first time, briefly reappearing at the bottom of two collapsed sinkholes, before vanishing again into the mouth of the cave. It re-emerges some 40km later at the Timavo springs north of Trieste. The park also contains three tiny villages, **Škocjan**, **Betanja** and **Matavun**.

Little was known about the caves until the sixteenth century, when the first maps of the system were printed. After that, more thorough accounts were presented in several seminal seventeenth- and eighteenth-century works, most notably Valvasor's *Glory of the Duchy of Carniola* and Gruber's *Hydrological Letters from the Carniola*.

Although parts of the cave had already been discovered, and several paths cut, during the early nineteenth century, it wasn't until around 1840 that the first systematic explorations of the main cave took place, when Giovanni Svetina from Trieste managed to penetrate some 150m downstream. Other pioneering explorers followed, but the most important explorations were left to **Anton Hanke**, a Czech mining engineer, and two colleagues who, between 1884 and 1890, progressed to the fourteenth waterfall along what is now known as the Hanke Canal – in the process stumbling upon several more

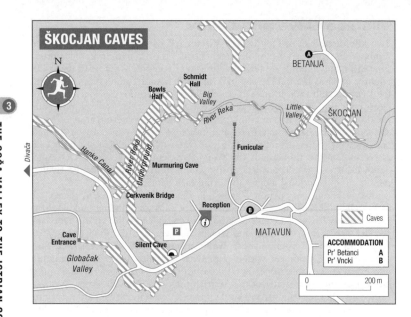

chambers. A few years later four locals entered the cave proper for the first time. Electricity was installed in 1959 and the caves were given UNESCO World Heritage status in 1986.

The Caves

After purchasing your ticket from the booth in the reception area in Matavun (tours daily: June–Sept hourly 10am–5pm; April, May & Oct 10am, 1pm & 3.30pm; Jan–March & Nov–Dec 10am & 1pm, plus 3pm on Sundays; €15, tours last approx 1hr 30min; Ⓦwww.park-skocjanske-jame.si), join the crowd milling around by the tables and wait for the guides to appear. From here, you'll be escorted to the cave entrance down in the **Globočak Valley** (Dolina Globočak), some ten minutes' walk away. Heading along the 130-metre-long, artificially created tunnel, you enter the cave proper, the first part of which is called the **Silent Cave** (Tiha jama); at this point, you'll break off into different groups, depending on which language you speak.

Discovered in around 1904, and totalling some 500m, the Silent Cave comprises several smaller chambers, each modestly decorated with stalagmites and stalactites, though neither the first, the **Paradise Cave**, nor the second, the **Calvary**, is particularly well endowed, having been subjected to earthquakes and floods aeons ago. More impressive is the 130-metre-long and thirty-metre-high **Great Hall** (Velika dvorana), whose most celebrated formations are the 250,000-year-old Giant stalagmite, and a ribbed dripstone stalactite dubbed the Organ, because of its resemblance to a pipe organ and the sounds it emits when tapped.

Beyond here the cave widens, the temperature drops and the low rumbling of the **Reka River** can be heard; this marks your entry into the magnificent **Murmuring Cave** (Šumeča jama), a three-hundred-metre-long, sixty-metre-wide and one-hundred-metre-high subterranean gorge carved out by the Reka

– it is, quite simply, the most fantastic creation imaginable. From here you walk along a narrow ledge incised into the great shafts of limestone rock, towards the vertiginous 45-metre-high **Cerkvenik Bridge** (Cerkvenikov most), under which the Reka flows before continuing its course along the **Hanke Canal** towards further, larger chambers (accessible only to speleologists). The bridge was rebuilt in 2003, replacing the original Hanke Bridge – dating from 1933 – which itself replaced the **Cat's Footbridge**, the remains of which can be detected 20m higher, just below the ceiling.

From the bridge, the path continues upstream along the side of the gorge for several hundred metres, through the **Bowls Hall** – so-named because of its circular limestone troughs – and towards the **Schmidt Hall** (Schmidlova dvorana), the yawning, natural cave entrance which emerges into the collapsed **Velika Dolina** (Big Valley); from here it's a short walk to the funicular, which transports you the 150m back to the top.

The Park

If you've still got time, you might want to trek the **Educational Trail** (Učna pot), a scenic two-kilometre-long footpath, which more or less circles the two collapsed valleys, **Velika Dolina** (Big Valley) and **Mala Dolina** (Little Valley); you can pick up a leaflet from the reception area, from where the trail begins and ends. Alternatively, you could just do part of the walk taking you as far as the tiny Karst hamlet of **Škocjan**, a ten-minute walk from the reception area, where three renovated stone barns house a modest collection of implements and archeological, geological and ethnological artefacts (daily June–Sept 11am–5pm, at other times enquire at the information booth; €3, free if visiting the cave). The most interesting collection is that devoted to cave exploration, with maps and sketches illustrating the discovery of the cave, one of which was drawn by Valvasor, a rudimentary-looking wooden boat, and an old ladder used for lowering cavers down into the depths. The 1:6000 *Regijski park Škocjanske jame* map outlines further walks in the park.

Practicalities

The nearest **train station** is in Divača, some 5km to the northwest by road (see p.185), from where there are free buses to (May–Sept 10am, 11.05am, 2pm & 3.35pm; Oct–April 11.05am & 14.35pm) and from (May–Sept 10.10am, 11.15am, 2.15pm & 3.45pm; Oct–April 11.25am & 15.05pm) the caves. Otherwise it's a one-hour walk; the caves are signposted from the station. If travelling by **bus**, you may be able to get the driver to set you down by the access road (just off the Ljubljana–Koper highway), from where it's a more manageable 1.5km to the caves.

If you wish to stick around, there are two excellent **tourist farms** close by: *Pr' Vncki* is a lovely renovated farmstead just behind the cave entrance at Matavun 10 (☎05/763-3073, ✉pr.vncki.tamara@gmail.com; ➍), with cosy rooms and an original black kitchen; and *Pr' Betanci*, in Betanja at no. 2 (☎05/763-3006, ⊕www.prbetanci.si; ➍), whose rooms overlook the Big Valley. Next to the ticket booth is a **café**, where you can get drinks and simple meals.

Church of the Holy Trinity, Hrastovlje

Thirty-one kilometres south of Divača, in the upper Rižana River Valley – which roughly separates the Karst plateau from the coastal hinterland – **HRASTOVLJE** would be just another pretty, yet inconsequential, Istrian village, were it not for the Romanesque **Church of the Holy Trinity** (Sveta

The Dance of Death

The **Dance of Death** is not unique to Hrastovlje and can be found in many countries throughout Europe, from England to Estonia, although the only other one in Istria is in the village of Beram, in Croatia. Thought to have derived from a thirteenth-century literary genre called Vado Mori ("I prepare myself to die"), the artistic genre of the Dance of Death originated as **La Danse Macabre** at the Cemetery of the Innocents in Paris around 1424. More often than not painted (or carved) on the outside walls of cloisters and ossuaries, or church interiors, the composition of the dance, and the number of characters involved, varied from place to place.

In this one in Hrastovlje, a cast of eleven characters – which include the pope, a king and queen, bishop, burgher, cripple and child – are escorted by skeletons towards the narrator (the twelfth skeleton), who sits on a stone throne, waiting with shovel and pick at his feet, and hand poised on the coffin lid. There's some wonderful detail to admire, such as the painting of the usurer who – deciding it's not his time to go – tries to bribe the skeleton by offering a purse, seemingly impervious to the idea that not even the rich can circumvent a fate that awaits us all.

Trojica), whose exceptional spread of late-medieval frescoes mark it out as a cultural monument of the highest rank.

Sited on an exposed, shallow rise and concealed within a thick, ten-metre-high, grey-stone wall, the church (daily 9am–noon & 1–6pm; €2) was built sometime between the twelfth and fourteenth centuries, although the wall was a sixteenth-century addition, erected to provide a place of refuge for the locals against marauding Turks. Constructed from stone-cut square blocks, with a typical stone-slab roof, this charmingly compact church is even smaller than you might have imagined from outside the wall. The inside, comprising a simple tripartite nave, is completely unfurnished.

Taking almost ten years to complete, the **frescoes** were executed by the master Istrian painter Johannes de Castua (Janez Kastav) at the end of the fifteenth century, although they weren't discovered until the 1950s, concealed under several layers of whitewash. Far and away the most celebrated and complete painting is the *Dance of Death*, or *Danse Macabre* (see box above), on the lower half of the south wall; with its powerful images alluding to the inevitability of death, this fresco pretty much surpasses any other specimen of medieval iconography in Slovenia. Cast your eye downwards and you'll see some decorative **Glagolitic inscriptions**, an ancient Slav script which originated in the ninth century as a means of converting Slavs to Christianity.

The remaining frescoes depicting numerous biblical scenes take some digesting, so it's worth focusing your attention on a select few: represented in fifteen scenes immediately above the *Dance of Death* is the cycle of Christ's Passion, while, on the opposite, north wall, the Three Kings come bearing gifts for Mary, who is seated on a gold throne with Infant Child. On the ceilings of the north and south aisles, the calendar year is represented by scenes (note there are fourteen) of seasonal activities – hunting, harvesting and so on – and local customs, and is unique in that it is believed to be the only case of a secular cycle in a Slovene Gothic church. The apses are decorated with portraits of the Apostles, and scenes from the Crucifixion and the crowning of Mary. To help you negotiate your way around this tangle of paintings, there's a taped commentary available in English.

Practicalities

Getting to Hrastovlje is not easy. The closest that **buses** get is 6km north, in the village of **Črni Val** just off the main highway to Koper. A return trip by **taxi** from Koper will cost around €35. Just down from the church the super *Gostilna Švab* serves terrific home-cooked **food** (closed Mon & Tues).

The Istrian Coast

Sandwiched between the Gulf of Trieste and the Croatian coast, the Slovenian seaboard packs a surprisingly large amount into its short 46km stretch, with a rich complement of historical sights among the more traditional beach-related pursuits. While its proximity to Italy ensures that it receives a healthy number of vacationing Italians, this also means that certain places can get a little mobbed at the height of summer. By way of contrast it's largely avoided by Slovenes, most of whom prefer to holiday along Croatia's Dalmatian coast. That said, in places, it possesses an abundance of charm, not least in **Piran**, a protected cultural monument and the coast's most seductive spot. **Koper**, too, possesses a fabulously appealing old town, much at odds with its prevailingly industrial backdrop; edging down the coast, the pretty little fishing town of **Izola** is worth a minor diversion, while **Portorož** – the coast's main beach resort, just a stone's throw from Piran – will appeal to those seeking more hedonistic fare. More generally, the beaches along the coast, such as they are, are invariably rocky or concrete affairs, though you might find the odd sandy spot if you're lucky.

▲ The Istrian Coast

The basis for much of the coast's fabulous cultural legacy is overwhelmingly Italian – indeed, its handful of towns wouldn't look out of place on the other side of the Adriatic – thanks to nearly five hundred years of **Venetian rule** that preceded the region's incorporation into the Austro-Hungarian Empire, and, eventually, the Yugoslav Federation.

This northern part of Istria didn't actually become a part of Yugoslavia until the **1954 London Agreement**, which finally resolved the problem of post-World War II territorial boundaries between Italy and Yugoslavia. Until then, this bitterly disputed area of the Adriatic had been divided into two zones, known as the Free Territory of Trieste – Zone A (which included Trieste), and Zone B (which included Koper); the agreement subsequently assigned Zone A to Italy and Zone B to Yugoslavia. However, neither side was entirely appeased, as both lost what they considered to be historic pieces of territory, a fact recognized by the Italians who refused to ratify the agreement, at least until the 1975 Treaty of Osimo, which did little more than review and reaffirm the original agreement. Although many Italians resettled in their homeland following the 1954 Agreement, many towns have retained significant communities.

Getting around is simple enough, with buses and ferries shuttling up and down the coast, and, if you're looking to push on to Trieste or the Croatian Istrian towns, there are frequent bus connections.

Koper

Easily reached by train from Ljubljana, and just 20km from Trieste, **KOPER** (Capodistria in Italian) is the first major stop along the coast. At first glance it's an unenticing spectacle, little more than a messy jumble of cranes, tower blocks and wasteland. However, within this gritty outer shell lies a beautifully preserved medieval core, embracing an attractive lattice of paved alleys, Italianate squares and a stack of fine cultural monuments.

Believed to have originated as Aegida in around 3 BC, the town – at that time an island – acquired several identities before the Venetians assumed control in the late thirteenth century. Thanks to its maritime industries, the town's economy remained in rude health until the beginning of the eighteenth century, when both Trieste and Rijeka (in Croatia) were proclaimed free ports and an already bleak situation was further compounded by the opening of the Vienna–Trieste rail line in 1857. Following the 1954 London Agreement, the town experienced a surge of development, with the advancement of a new port and an extension of the rail line to Koper, thus reaffirming the town's status as the coast's most important economic and political centre. Today, not only is it Slovenia's largest coastal town and chief maritime port, but it also services the shipping needs of Austria and Hungary.

The town's premier annual happening is the **Primorsko Summer Festival**, a series of open-air theatrical performances (and occasionally dance and music) taking place throughout July and August in several towns along the coast, but principally here and in Izola and Portorož. Some of the more unusual venues include a catamaran, a disused railway tunnel and the Sečovlje saltpans (see p.207). Otherwise, the main summer event is **Festiko** during the last week of July, featuring theatrical and musical performances and an epic fireworks display. The town's small but tidy pebble and grass **beach** is located between the pier and the Marina on Kopališko Nabrežje (daily 8am–8pm), while further fun can

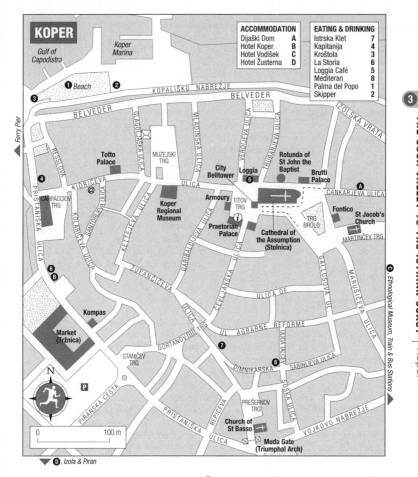

be had at the **Aquapark**, next to the *Žusterna* (see p.194); it has seven indoor and outdoor pools (daily 9am–9pm; weekdays €7 for 2hr, €13 all day; weekends €9 for 2hr, €17 all day).

Arrival and information

The **train** and **bus** stations are located next to each other in a wasteland 1.5km southeast of town, from where it's a dull walk along Kolodvorska Cesta to the centre; alternatively, regular buses shuttle passengers into town, and then onwards to Izola, Portorož and Piran. The **tourist office** is inside the Praetorian Palace on Titov trg (June–Sept Mon–Sat 9am–8pm, Sun 10am–8pm; Oct–May daily 9am–5pm; ☏05/664-6403, ✆tic@koper.si). The **post office** is in the old town on Muzejski trg (Mon–Fri 8am–6pm, Sat 8am–noon), and there's **internet access** at the *Pina Bar*, Kidričeva ulica 43 (Tues–Fri noon–10pm, Sat & Sun 4–10pm).

Accommodation

The Kompas agency, at Pristaniška ulica 17 (Mon–Fri 8am–7pm, Sat 8am–1pm; ☏ 05/663-0582, ℮ kompas.koper@siol.net), has a good stock of **private accommodation**, including rooms (❶) and apartments (❸–❺) – note that there is a surcharge for stays of less than three nights.

Those on a budget should head to the student **hostel** *Dijaški Dom Koper* at Cankarjeva 5 (☏ 05/662-6250, ℮ ddkoper-recepcija@guest.arnes.si; ❶), 100m east of the cathedral; it has one-, two- and three-bed rooms (all with shared wash and shower facilities) available during July and August, and a handful at weekends during the rest of the year.

The town has extremely limited **hotel** possibilities; the most central is the *Hotel Koper* at Pristaniška 3 (☏ 05/610-0500, ⓦ www.terme-catez.si; ❽), a stylish place with big, airy rooms, frequented in the main by busloads of package tourists; part of the same hotel group is the *Žusterna*, located out on the road to Portorož at Istrska 67 (☏ 05/663-8000, same website; ❼) – this colourful, frenetic place has cool, air-conditioned rooms, some of which have a balcony, while guests at both places receive free entry to the adjoining aquapark. Buses stop by the swimming pool opposite. The *Vodišek*, situated in a small shopping complex midway between the stations and the town centre at Kolodvorska 2 (☏ 05/639-2468, ⓦ www.hotel-vodisek.com; ❼), has neat, bright rooms, all with air-conditioning and wi-fi.

The Town

As good a place as any to start your exploration of the old town is **Carpaccio trg**, just behind the old **salt warehouse**. In the centre of this peaceful little square, named after the Venetian painter, is the spindly **Column of St Justin**, erected to commemorate the famous naval victory against the Turks at Lepanto in 1571, in which a Koper galley participated. From here, Kidričeva ulica inclines gently eastwards past the redundant churches of **St Nicholas** (1594) and the **Holy Trinity** (1735). A little further up on the right is a splendid **Venetian-Gothic town house** – one of several such buildings in town – sporting a protruding upper floor and check-painted facade. Opposite here is the **Totto Palace**, whose tatty facade bears a fine relief of a lion with an open book; traditionally, this was meant to symbolize peace, as opposed to a closed book which symbolized war; similar reliefs adorn many other prominent buildings along the coast.

A few paces along at no. 19 is the fine, sixteenth-century Mannerist-Baroque **Belgramoni–Tacco Palace**, whose interior is palpably more interesting than the **Regional Museum** housed within (Pokrajinski Muzej; July & Aug Tues–Sun 9am–1pm & 6–9pm; Sept–June Tues–Fri 8am–3pm, Sat & Sun 9am–1pm; €2.50). The highlight is a decent archeological collection, which includes a collection of animal reliefs, and a copy of the *Dance of Death* fresco from Hrastovlje (see p.190). The exhibition of contemporary history, describing Slovene Istria's role before, during and after the two World Wars, is marginally more interesting. The most illuminating aspect of this exhibition, however, is Tone Kralj's gruesome painting, *Rapallo*, in which a woman is savaged by hideous-looking creatures.

Titov trg and around

Continuing eastwards, Kidričeva ulica opens up into **Titov trg** (Tito Square), laid out in the fifteenth century and once the fulcrum of the old city. The square's stunning synthesis of Gothic, Renaissance and Baroque styles is superbly encapsulated in the **Praetorian Palace** (Pretorska palača), Koper's most enduring symbol, whose battlements look like a stage backdrop for a Renaissance drama. Equally as impressive is its facade, randomly plastered with reliefs and busts – the most striking of which is the black bust of Nicola Donato, praetor of Koper between 1579 and 1580. Although there was a building here in the thirteenth century (which was subsequently destroyed), the foundations for the current palace were laid down in the fifteenth century, when the Gothic left wing and the Renaissance right wing were constructed; its Baroque elements were added during further seventeenth-century renovations. Following the 1797 downfall of the Venetian Republic, whose governors had used the palace as their main headquarters, the palace fell into a state of long-term decline; first the Austrians moved into the adjacent **Armoury building** (previously an arms dump, but which has been restored to accommodate part of the new University of Primorska), then successive town authorities snubbed it in favour of alternative buildings.

Opposite the palace, the fifteenth-century **Loggia** (Loža), with its striking Gothic-style lancet arches, has been the town's most popular meeting place ever since philosophers and artists gathered here for chinwags in the seventeenth century – its first coffee house, *Caffe della Loggia*, established in 1846, is now the *Loggia*, which remains the most swish **café** in town; the statue of the Madonna in the corner pillar was placed there to commemorate the 1554 plague.

The **Cathedral of the Assumption** (Stolnica Marija vnebovzetja; 7am–noon & 3–7pm) on the east side of the square is believed to be the fifth or sixth church on this site, though much of this present one has eighteenth-century origins. Its exterior is an odd amalgam of Gothic lower storey and Lombardy-style upper storey, the latter part completed a century later than the lower part. By way of contrast, its vast interior, endowed with some glorious works of art and furnishings, is mostly of Baroque appearance; particularly worth paying attention to is the central nave's magnificent Rococo pulpit, designed by Lorenzo Ferolli in 1758, and, in the presbytery, the finely carved olive-wood choir pews and the gold-plate-encrusted bishop's throne, dating from 1730. The major works of art were completed by Vittore Carpaccio, the most outstanding of which is *The Enthroned Madonna with Child and Saints* from 1516. Pressed into the cathedral's south side is the formidable **city bell tower** (daily 10am–1pm & 3–5pm; €2), a fifteenth-century structure which once doubled as a lookout; climb the 43m to the top and you'll understand why – the views of the town, coast and hinterland are tremendous. Situated on the cathedral's north side is one of the coast's oldest sacral monuments, the twelfth-century Romanesque **Rotunda of John the Baptist**.

Trg Brolo, a leafy, triangular square just east of the cathedral, showcases some terrific Venetian-Baroque architecture, the most eye-catching of which is the **Brutti Palace** on the north side, whose facade is attractively ornamented with relief images from the Old Testament – the building now functions as the town library. On the east side of the square at no. 4 is the several-times rebuilt **Fontico**, a former grain warehouse studded with rich heraldic decoration completed by Lombardian stonemasons.

South and east of Titov trg

Back on Titov trg, pass through the portico under the Praetorian Palace and take a stroll down Čevljarska ulica (Shoemaker's Street), which took its name from the profession which was practised here for several centuries. Probably the single prettiest street in the town, Čevljarska ulica preserves a happy ensemble of two- and three-storey shuttered tenements, shops and galleries. At the end of the street cross Župančičeva ulica, and continue down the steps passing the pink-chequered façade of the Almerigogna Palace into Gortanov trg. This square segues into Staničev trg, which in turn brings you out to the main road ringing the old town, a rather sobering return to the twenty-first century.

By taking a left turn at the junction of Čevljarska ulica and Župančičeva ulica, you'll wind up at Prešernov trg (Prešeren Square), a pleasant, elongated space, in the centre of which stands Ponte's Fountain; built in 1666, the fountain is furnished with a small, Plečnik-style bridge – *ponte* is Italian for bridge – and, at the bottom, four masks which until 1898 spouted water. South of the fountain is the triumphal arch-style Muda Gate (Vrata Muda), built in 1516 and the last of the city's twelve town gates; note, on the inner arches, two reliefs of a blazing sun with the shape of a face, which is the city coat of arms.

Housed in another exceptional Venetian-Gothic building east of town at Gramšijev trg 4 is the **Ethnological Museum** (Etnološki Muzej; July & Aug Tues–Sat 9am–1pm & 6–9pm; Sept–June Tues–Fri 9am–3pm, Sat 9am–1pm; €2), one of the most enjoyable museums on the coast, though it's little visited due to its rather isolated location. For the most part, the collection focuses on the Istrian cultural landscape, with particular emphasis on the art of stonecutting and stonedressing, industries which first took wing in the region during the seventeenth century. The pick of the museum's collection is its assemblage of skilfully hewn stone-cut **portals**, commonly found at entrances to courtyards and houses; many portals were traditionally ornamented with floral patterns, sacral symbols and other motifs and reliefs, though few have been preserved. More superb stonemasonry can be seen in a partial reconstruction of a **shepherd's hut**, typically used to store farming tools and arable crops but also useful as a form of shelter during extremes in temperature; and a portion of a **dry-stone wall**, a prevalent feature of the Istrian landscape. To round off this engaging collection, there is a presentation of a Koper **kitchen**, at the centre of which is a hearth, surrounded by some exquisite copper, glass and china food-preparation items garnered from the Veneto and Friuli regions, and which date from the nineteenth and twentieth centuries.

Eating and drinking

Disappointingly, Koper has a meagre selection of **restaurants**; the best is *La Storia*, a friendly trattoria next to the *Hotel Koper* – the large covered terrace is a congenial place from which to take your pick from a generous and inexpensive menu featuring pasta, risotto, gnocchi and fish. Another convivial place is *Mediteran*, a small hideaway located a short walk northeast of Prešernov trg at Ulica Talcev 8, which serves up salads, pasta, meat and fish, as well as a strong veggie menu (closed Sun). Although rather staid, *Skipper*, next to the beach at Kopališko Nabrežje 3, does have the best fish and wine in town, as well as lovely views overlooking the water. Then there's the very basic *Istrska Klet* at Župančičeva ulica 39, which has filling domestic fare and wines straight from the barrel (closed Sat). Otherwise, you can pick up goods from the lively **market** by the shopping centre (Tržnica) on Pristaniška, which also has a couple of very tempting ice-cream parlours.

There are some good **cafés** around, the coolest place being *Kapitanija* at Ukmarjev trg 8, whose lounge-style seating and vine-covered terrace is a most enjoyable spot to indulge in beer, coffee, cakes and ices. During the summer the cosy little beachfront cafés, *Palma del Popo* and *Kroštola*, are popular hangouts, while the well-established and classy *Loggia Café* on Titov trg has the best coffee in town.

Izola and around

Jutting out to sea on a rounded promontory 6km south of Koper, **IZOLA** is a busy little fishing town and one of the country's fastest-growing tourist destinations. Though most visitors come here for the beaches, Izola possesses an endearing old town core, whose narrow, sloping streets and pastel-coloured tenements delight in all their crumbling charm.

Numerous local ruins bear testament to the long-standing presence of the Romans hereabouts, not least in Simon's Bay, where the ancient port of Heliaetum was located – it's said that, at very low tide, parts of the ancient pier are still visible. First mentioned in historical sources in 972 AD as Insula, the town enjoyed a brief period of autonomy before becoming a satellite of Venice in 1280, which it remained until the Republic's downfall in 1797; around the same time, both the town wall and its two gates were pulled down, and the town (hitherto an island) was finally connected to the mainland. Thereafter, the town acquired the northern Adriatic's largest fishing fleet, as well as a number of fish canneries, the first of which opened in 1879. While tourism has since supplanted the industry as the main source of income, the town's fishing tradition remains alive and kicking.

One of the best events along the coast is the **Izola Film Festival** in mid-September, a five-day run of colourful and wide-ranging world films, some of which are screened in the open-air on Manzioli trg.

Arrival and information

The town's main **bus stop** is on Trg Republike, from where it's a 50m walk west to the **tourist office** at Sončno nabrežje 4 (June–Sept Mon–Sat 9am–9pm, Sun 10am–5pm; Oct–May Mon–Fri 9am–7pm, Sat 9am–5pm; ℡05/640-1050, ⓦwww.izola.eu). Between April and October, day-trips on the *Prince of Venice* catamaran to Venice and back depart from the pier by the fishing port, opposite Veliki trg; tickets (the schedule changes monthly; around €65) can be purchased from the Bele Skale and Laguna agencies (see below). You can also find the **post office** on Trg Republike (Mon–Fri 8am–7pm, Sat 8am–noon).

Accommodation

For **private accommodation**, head to either the Bele Skale agency (July–Aug Mon–Sat 9am–6pm, Sun 9am–noon; Sept–June Mon–Fri 9am–5pm, Sat 9am–noon; ℡05/640-3555, ⓦwww.beleskale.si), right next to the bus stop, or the Laguna agency, towards the marina at Istrska vrata 7 (Mon–Sat 9am–1pm & 4–7pm, Sun 9am–1pm; ℡05/640-0278, ⓦwww.laguna-sp.si).

The cheapest place to **stay** in town is the *Hotel Riviera* (℡05/641-7159; ❷), a somewhat misleading name for this large student dorm situated on the waterfront, 200m south of the tourist office at Prekmorskih brigad 7; the rooms, available between June and August and at weekends during the rest of the year, come with or without shower facilities. The *Hotel Marina*, in the centre of town on Veliki trg (℡06/660-4100, ⓦwww.hotelmarina.si; ❼–❽), is a considerable step up in class, with variously sized, well-turned-out rooms, some of which have balconies with sea views. Nestled amid a pine grove atop a bluff 2.5km west of town is the *Belvedere Hotel* (℡05/660-5100, ⓦwww.belvedere.si), which has good-looking rooms (❼) and apartments (❻–❽) housed within several brightly coloured villas. There is also a **campsite** (April–Sept) within the grounds; buses doing the Koper–Portorož route stop outside the entrance. These same buses also stop outside Izola's other campsite, the *Jadranka*, which is wedged between the noisy main road and its own bit of beach 1km east of town at Polje 8 (☎05/640-2300; April–Oct).

The Town

Everything of interest in Izola is located within the confines of the old town. From **Trg Republike** head north to Kristinov trg, past the small market, and then left up Smrekarjeva ulica for about 100m before taking a right turn down Alme Vivoda. Just before the church, a passageway leads to the **Parenzana Museum** (Muzej Parenzana; Tues–Sun 9am–3pm; €2.50), which contains a staggering assortment of model trains assembled from all over the world. Its chief exhibit, however, is a model replica of the Parenzana Line, once the most important transport link between Central Europe and Istria; built in 1902 by the Austrians, the line ran between Trieste and Poreč (in Croatia), passing through Koper, Izola and Portorož along the way, until 1937 when Mussolini pulled the plug and closed it. The locomotive that used to chug up and down the line is stationed at the town's eastern entrance by the *Jadranka* campsite. Meanwhile, the line – passing through settlements, hills, vineyards and all the old tunnels – has been transformed into a **recreational cycle track**; ask at the tourist office for more information.

From the church, take a left, and then another left, onto Gregorčičeva ulica; after about 300m you come to the town's most important architectural set piece, the **Besenghi degli Ughi Palace**, distinguished by its pale blue, stucco-ornamented wrought-iron grilles. Its interior, too, is festooned with stuccowork, but is especially worth viewing for its first-floor salon, furnished with a fine wooden balcony and illusionist ceiling piece – the palace is now home to a music school. The street to the side of the building, Bruna ulica, slopes upwards to the much remodelled sixteenth-century **Church of St Maurus** (Cerkev Sv Mavricij), notable for its clutch of dark yet impressive paintings; the mighty **bell tower**, visible from all over town, was built in 1585.

From the church, head down Garibaldjeva, then Krpanova, which brings you to Veliki trg and the waterfront. From Veliki trg walk south past the **Municipal Palace**, whose Gothic frontage bears another relief of a lion with an open book, and round to Manzioli trg, a bright little square on which stands the **Church of St Mary** (Cerkev Sv Marija), whose oldest parts date from the ninth century. Directly opposite the church is the recently restored Venetian late-Gothic **Manzioli Palace**, now the town's Italian centre. Walking down Koprska ulica and Ljubljanska ulica, two pleasant streets that curl southwards towards Trg Republike, you'll notice a disproportionate number of **artists' workshops and galleries**; these were set up a few years ago on the initiative of the town authorities, who decided to rent out these previously empty buildings for free in the hope of rejuvenating the area – evidently, this was a highly successful strategy.

One of the coast's best beaches is at **Simon's Bay** 1.5km west of the centre; backed by pine trees and a large expanse of grass, this blue flag pebble beach (€2.50, €1.50 after 2pm) has good facilities including water slides and a play area for kids, as well as sports activities (pedaloes €8 for 30min, tubes €20 for 15min, water scooters €80 for 30min). There's another, much less developed, rocky and grassy beach north of Veliki trg.

Eating and drinking

The most convivial **place to eat** is *Gušt*, just south of Trg Republike at Drevored 1 Maja, serving up over thirty varieties of pizza, steaming plates of pasta and spaghetti, soups and salads – it's also a good place to **drink**. Of those restaurants along the waterfront, the best is *Parangal* at Sončno nabrežje 20, a refined, beautifully decorated place with a large vine-covered terrace to escape the heat, and a spot-on fish menu. Next door, the *Wall Pub* is the liveliest spot for a beer, while the *KT1* cybercafé, opposite the market on Kristinov trg, is a chilled-out place with **internet access**. The classy little *Manzioli* **wine bar** on the square of the same name is a delightful spot to sample wines from the Koper hinterland.

Izola can boast two of the coast's better **clubs**: *Ambasada Gavioli* (Fri & Sat; around €15) out in the industrial zone east of town at Industrijska cesta 10, which stages really top-class DJ nights, and *Club Belvedere* (daily) in the grounds of the *Hotel Belvedere*.

Strunjan

A few kilometres along the coast from Izola is **STRUNJAN**, a small, yet widely dispersed settlement, part of which has been turned into a **nature reserve**. All Koper–Piran buses stop just off the main road, from where it's a three-hundred-metre walk west towards the pleasant year-round Strunjan **campsite** (☏05/678-2076). Five hundred metres further on, in a wonderfully secluded spot facing the bay, is the *Salinera* complex (☏05/676-2502, Ⓦ www.salinera.si; April–Sept), which has **accommodation** in the form of a very comfortable hotel (❼) and some lovely, well-furnished apartments, sleeping three to six people (❻–❽); there's also a decent bathing area here (€4). Retracing your steps back to the abandoned saltpans, where the brackish water now supports a wide range of fauna, walk north along the narrow path to another, busier, beach (€3), to the west of which is **Giuseppe Tartini's Villa**, once the Tartini family home (see p.202) but now off-limits to visitors.

North of the large **Stjuža lagoon**, which backs onto the beach, a cobbled road trundles up to the top of the cliffs, passing the Church of St Mary and a small snack bar along the way. Unique along the Adriatic for its distinctive layers of Flysch sediment – composed of sandstone, marl and turbidite – the most prominent feature of this stretch of coastline is **Cape Ronek** (Rtič Ronek) at its northernmost point, home to what few sub-Mediterranean species exist in the region, such as myrtle and strawberry trees. Below, in the **Bay of St Cross** (Zaliv Sv Križa), the large bed of seaweed shelters fan-mussels, sea dates and crabs. From the cliff top several paths wind down to the rocky beaches below, popular with naturists.

Piran

Located on the tip of a long, tapering peninsula that projects like a lizard's tail into the Adriatic, **PIRAN** – the most Italianate of the coastal towns – is simply delightful. Having retained its compact medieval shape and character, the town is a tangle of arched alleys and tightly packed ranks of houses, fantastic Venetian-inspired architecture and exquisite little churches.

Major urban development first occurred during the seventh century following the fall of the Roman Empire, when Piran became a heavily fortified "castrum". Under Venetian rule, which began here in 1283, the town's physical appearance changed considerably, as further town walls were erected to supplement the existing ones – which at that time encompassed the western Punta district at the end of the promontory. Economically, too,

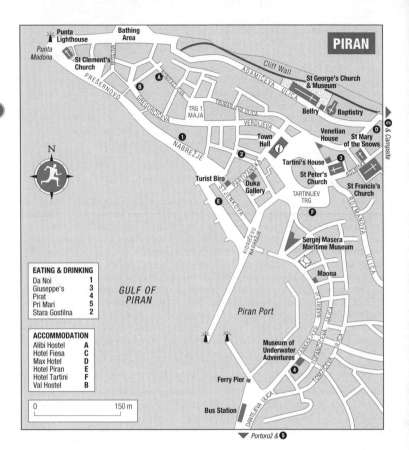

PIRAN

Punta Lighthouse
Bathing Area
Punta Madona
St Clement's Church
Cliff Wall
PREŠERNOVO
ADAMIČEVA ULICA
PREŠERNOVO
GREGORČIČEVA
ROŽNA ULICA
A
B
St George's Church & Museum
TRUBARJEVA ULICA
TRG 1 MAJA
Belfry
Baptistry
VERDIJEVA
NABREŽJE
Town Hall
i
Venetian House
St Mary of the Snows
D
& Campsite
1
2
PARTIZANSKA
3
Turist Biro
Duka Gallery
Tartini's House
St Peter's Church
St Francis's Church
ROMANOVA ULICA
ST JENKOVA
E
TARTINIJEV TRG
F
KIDRIČEVO NABREŽJE
Sergej Masera Maritime Museum
GULF OF PIRAN
Maona
EATING & DRINKING

Da Noi	1
Giuseppe's	3
Pirat	4
Pri Mari	5
Stara Gostilna	2

Piran Port

Museum of Underwater Adventures

CANKARJEVO NABREŽJE
ŽUPANČIČEVA ULICA
TOMŠIČEVA

4

ACCOMMODATION

Alibi Hostel	A
Hotel Fiesa	C
Max Hotel	D
Hotel Piran	E
Hotel Tartini	F
Val Hostel	B

Ferry Pier

0   150 m

Bus Station

DANTEJEVA ULICA

▼ Portorož & 5

the town was in good shape, thanks in no small measure to its three **saltworks** – in Sečovlje, Strunjan and Lucija, of which only the first is still operational. A prolonged period of decline ensued thereafter, first under the Habsburgs, and then, between the two World Wars, the Italians. However, the development of nearby Portorož as a popular health resort, and the construction of the Lucija–Piran rail line, last operational in 1956, led to an increase in visitors to the town. While relations with Italy are today on a somewhat better footing, it remains to be seen whether or not the recent agreement with Croatia over fishing rights in the Bay of Piran will result in better relations between the two countries. The town's major annual event is the week long **Tartini Festival** at the end of August/beginning of September, incorporating a highly impressive run of classical music concerts.

Arrival and information

The **bus station** is on Dantejeva ulica, from where it's a pleasant 400m walk past the bustling little fishing harbour to Tartinijev trg, the main square. Located on the square's west side, by the town hall, is the **tourist office** (July–Sept daily 8am–8pm; Oct–May Mon–Sat 9am–5pm, Fri 10am–2pm; ℡05/673-0220, ⓦwww.portoroz.si). The **post office** is on Cankarjevo nabrežje (Mon–Fri 8am–7pm, Sat 8am–noon). **Bikes** can be rented from Artus, Vidalijeva 6 (Mon–Fri 9.30am–1pm, Sat 10am–1pm; €10 for half a day, €15 for the day), particularly useful if you're thinking of heading to the saltpans in Sečovlje. There are a few companies around the harbour offering **boat trips** up and down the coast, including to Trieste (around €15 return), and Poreč (€25) and Rovinj (€35) in Croatia – tickets can be purchased at the tourist office or one of the agencies such as Maona.

Accommodation

Piran has a limited selection of **hotels**, though there are some decent budget possibilities. Moreover, there's plenty of **private accommodation** to go around, bookable through Maona, midway between the bus station and the main square at Cankarjevo nabrežje 7 (July & Aug Mon–Sat 9am–8pm, Sun 10am–noon & 5–8pm; April–June & Sept–Oct Mon–Fri 9am–5pm; ☎05/673-4520, ⓦ www.maona.si), or Turist Biro opposite the *Hotel Piran* (June–Sept daily 9am–1pm & 4–7pm; Oct–May Mon–Fri 10am–1pm & 4–6pm; ☎05/673-2509, ⓦ www.turistbiro-ag.si). The only **campsite** (☎05/674-6230; May–Sept) hereabouts is the one adjoining the *Fiesa* hotel – the quickest way to get here by foot is to follow the coastal path that runs east from the Church of St George.

Alibi Hostel Bonifacijeva 14 ☎031/363-666, ⓦ www.alibi.si. A busy little hostel with rooms in two buildings opposite each other, comprising a mix of clean and simple doubles (some with shower) and four-bed rooms. They've also got another hostel at Trubarjeva 60 (same reception). No kitchen facilities available. May–Sept. **❶–❷**

Hotel Fiesa Fiesa 57 ☎05/671-2200, ⓦ www .hotelfiesa.com. Located 1km east of town this large hotel is a comfortable place with good facilities, though it's not a quiet area with the beach below and a noisy games room next door. **❽**

Max Hotel Ulica IX korpusa 26 ☎05/673-3436, ⓦ www.maxpiran.com. Characterful, welcoming guesthouse in an eighteenth-century town house up by St George's Church, with six colourful, intimate rooms and a cosy little breakfast area. Reservations essential. **❺**

Hotel Piran Stjenkova 1 ☎05/676-2100, ⓦ www .hoteli-piran.si. Popular hotel with a fabulous waterfront location, though the rooms are nothing out of the ordinary and the balconies are very small (avoid those on the ground floor). Only the sea-facing rooms have wi-fi. **❼–❾**

Hotel Tartini Tartinijev trg 15 ☎05/671-1000, ⓦ www.hotel-tartini-piran.com. One of the coast's most elegant hotels, featuring stylish air-conditioned rooms with ultra modern fittings – it's worth paying the minimal extra for sea- or square-facing rooms. Charmingly staffed too. **❽**

Val Hostel Gregorčičeva 38a ☎05/673-2555, ⓦ www.hostel-val.com. Secreted away among an atmospheric warren of alleys, this quiet place has spotless two-, three- and four-bedded rooms with shared shower facilities; laundry and internet access too. **❷**

The Town

From the lovely main square, Tartinijev trg, it's no more than a five-minute walk to any of the town's churches and museums, while the beach area is sited over towards the northwestern tip of the peninsula.

Tartinijev trg

The town's most obvious point of reference is **Tartinijev trg** (Tartini Square), whose striking, marble-surfaced oval interior features a bronze statue of the acclaimed violinist Giuseppe Tartini (1692–1770), after whom the square is named. At its entrance, on the southeastern corner, are two fifteenth-century **stone flagpoles** bearing several Latin inscriptions and reliefs of St Mark with the lion symbol, and St George, the town patron.

The building on the square's west side is the old **court house**, adjacent to which is the **town hall**, dating from the late nineteenth century and distinguished by four graceful pillars, the lower parts of which are beautifully ornamented; in the central axis is the ubiquitous lion relief with an open book (see p.194). Continuing in a clockwise fashion, the stunning ruby-red Gothic **Venetian House** (Benečanke hiša) at no. 10 is the oldest preserved building on the square, a fifteenth-century edifice showcasing some outstanding stonemasonry, exemplified by its superb corner balcony. The relief under the windows on the second floor bears the inscription "Lassa pur dir" ("Let them talk"), a retort to gossiping townsfolk disapproving of a wealthy merchant's romantic liaisons with a local girl. About 50m further south, up the small flight of steps, is **Tartini's House** (Tartinijeva Hiša; daily: June–Aug 9am–noon & 6–9pm; Sept–May 11am–noon & 5–6pm; €2), where the musician was born in 1692. After being schooled in Koper, Tartini left Piran for Padua, in Italy, and remained there for the greater part of his life, composing, teaching and performing, before later devoting himself to theoretical and pedagogical issues. He is buried alongside his wife in Padua. One room of the birthplace has been converted into a small memorial space containing one of his four violins – the whereabouts of the other three are unknown – his death mask, and scores of books, diaries and letters.

Opposite Tartini's house is **St Peter's Church** (Cerkev Sv Petra), unremarkable save for the **Crucifix from Piran**, one of three such medieval masterpieces on the eastern Adriatic (the others are in Split, in Croatia, and Kotor, in Montenegro). This much-restored polychrome sculpture, a beautifully mournful Christ nailed to a tree-shaped cross, is believed to have been completed some time in the fourteenth century, though its creator is unknown. Unfortunately, owing to previous incidents of theft and vandalism, most of Piran's churches can only be viewed through metal grilles.

West of Tartinijev trg

Heading west from Tartinijev trg through the dense lattice of arched alleys, you'll wind up at **Trg 1 Maja** (First of May Square), once the heart of the town but now a pleasantly scruffy space framed by peeling Baroque edifices. Located under the square's vast elevated deck and guarded by allegorical stone statues of law and justice is a stone rainwater cistern, built in 1776 following a drought in order to conserve water; at the rear, the two statues of babies – one holding a pot, the other a fish – once connected surrounding gutters with the cistern. Classical concerts are regularly held here during the summer.

Picking your way west through the maze of streets will eventually bring you out at the very tip of the peninsula and the **Punta lighthouse**, behind which is the sadly decrepit **Church of St Clement** (Cerkev Sv Zdravja), also known as the Church of Our Lady of Health on account of the role it played during the plague which swept across Istria in the seventeenth century. The lively promenade east of here is the location for the town's main (concrete) **bathing area** and a handful of places to eat and drink. Being a protected reef, it's also one of the coast's best **diving** areas – if you fancy a spot of diving, Sub-net, along the promenade at no. 24 (☎05/673-2218, ⊛www.sub-net.si), offers a comprehensive programme; expect to pay around €30 for one dive (approx 90min). En route back to the square take a look at the fine Gothic **Dolphin Gate** (Dolfinova vrata) in Savudrijska ulica, and, if you've time, pop into the **Duka Gallery**, close by at Partizanska 2 (Atelje Duka; Mon–Sat: June–Aug 9am–1pm & 6–10pm; Sept–May 8am–5pm), which has a marvellous display of pottery and ceramic art; you can even see items being made, many of which are for sale.

Church of St George and around

Crowning a commanding spot on a steep rise to the north of town is the temple-like **Church of St George** (Cerkev Sv Jurija), originally built some time around the twelfth century, but whose present appearance dates from 1637. It's a classic example of a simple Baroque hall-church, lined with seven mighty altars, each laden with paintings by Venetian and Dutch artists; the second altar on the left also incorporates a large sculpture of St George slaying the dragon. Take a look too at the cream and gold church organ, a magnificent specimen designed in 1746 by the Venetian master organ builder Peter Nakič. The unusually long and deep presbytery boasts the largest oil on canvas painting in the country, a colourful depiction of the martyrdom of St George (1844).

Displayed within the small **church museum** (Župnijski Muzej; daily 11am–5pm; €1.50), which is actually more interesting than it sounds, is a glittering hoard of church treasures, including bejewelled chalices, reliquaries and staffs, though the most memorable piece is a marvellous silver-coated sculpture of St George and the dragon. One floor below are some well-preserved archeological remains from an eighth-century Roman temple and a section of the church as it was in the fourteenth century; look out for the protruding bones in the corner. The sacristy, held in the basement, is especially interesting for its superb pictures illustrating the restoration process of the Crucifix from Piran, now in St Peter's Church (see opposite), and a four-hundred-year-old wooden model of St George's Church thought to be the oldest of its type in the country. Between the church and **Baptistry** − where a large Roman sarcophagus can be viewed − is the monumental **belfry** (same times as museum; €1), a fine-looking structure built in 1609 and modelled on the campanile in St Mark's Square, Venice. If you thought the views from the church terrace were impressive, then you'll be wowed by the sensational vista of the Adriatic from atop the 46-metre-high tower.

South of here, among the tightly knit web of streets, are a cluster of beautiful little churches. At the corner of Istrska and Bolniška, the delightfully named **Church of St Mary of the Snows** (Cerkev Marije Snežne) features a marvellous Baroque altar and two broad canvases depicting the Annunciation and other scenes from the life of the Virgin Mary. Opposite here is the fourteenth-century, but much remodelled, **Church of St Francis** (Cerkev Sv Frančiška), whose impressive gallery of paintings would be even more valuable had the most important one − *Mary with all the Saints* by Vittore Carpaccio − not been taken to Italy in 1940. It's an issue that still rankles with Slovenes, many of whom insist that this and other valuable Renaissance works be returned to Slovenia (these are collectively known as "Istria's Jewels", some of which are currently on display in Rome); not surprisingly, the Italians have steadfastly resolved to keep them. The adjoining **Minorite Monastery** incorporates a bright atrium (*Križni Hodnik*, or *Passage of the Cross*), entered via a lovely stone-carved portal; the acoustics in the atrium are splendid, so try and catch a concert here if you can.

From Korpusa ulica (back up by St George's Church), one path heads down towards a rocky beach and onwards to the small bay at **Fiesa** 1km away, the other uphill towards Mogorn Hill − which is also accessible from Tartinijev trg via Rožmanova ulica. Ranged across the top of the hill is a two-hundred-metre stretch of the old **town walls**, completed between the late fifteenth and early sixteenth centuries and perforated with seven inspiring-looking towers; at the southern end of the wall stands the Gothic **Rašpor Gate** (Rašporska vrata). The walls, now connected by specially constructed walkways and stairs, give the best photo opportunities in town.

South of Tartinjev trg

Occupying the splendid nineteenth-century **Gabrielli Palace**, a short walk south of Tartinijev square, is the **Sergej Mašera Maritime Museum** (Pomorski Muzej Sergej Mašera; Tues–Sun: July & Aug 9am–noon & 6–9pm; Sept–June 9am–noon & 3–6pm; €3), named after the naval commander, whose destroyer, *Zagreb*, was blown up off the Croatian coast during World War II. The highlight of this eminently enjoyable collection, which charts Slovenia's seafaring exploits, is its outstanding ensemble of eighteenth-century model ships – originally built as teaching aids for future naval officers and nautical engineers – made in the Gruber workshop in Ljubljana; one model in particular to look out for is the Austrian warship, *Emperor Charles VI*. On the ground floor there is a fine, and cleverly presented, display of underwater archeological finds from the Slovene Istrian coast, consisting mainly of Roman amphorae, fragments of earthen vessels and lead tiles and hoops; there's also an informative ethnological saltworks collection, which will especially appeal if you're thinking of visiting the saltpans in Sečovlje (see p.207).

The nautical theme is continued 200m further on in the enthusiastically titled **Museum of Underwater Adventures** (Muzej podvodnih dejavostni; July & Aug daily 10am–9pm; Sept–June Fri–Sun 10am–6pm; €3), at Zupančičeva 24, charting the region's considerable contribution to underwater discovery with a wealth of military, sporting and caving paraphernalia.

Eating and drinking

Most people are drawn to the row of uninspiring, rather samey and quite expensive seafood **restaurants** lining the waterfront promenade, Prešernovo nabrežje. There are much better value establishments elsewhere, notably *Pri Mari* just beyond the bus station at Dantejeva ulica 17; this homely, gostilna-style place offers lots of great fish and pasta dishes, risottos and Mediterranean salads. Heading back towards Tartinijev trg, *Pirat*, at Zupančičeva 24, is another pleasant antidote to the town's touristy restaurants, with no-frills seafood served in copper bowls and a good-value daily tourist menu (soup, salad and main dish) for €10. Otherwise, there's *Stara Gostilna*, 50m north of the *Hotel Piran* at Savudrijska 2, a secluded place with a pleasant little conservatory restaurant and pavement dining; and *Giuseppe's*, next to Tartini's house, which is a more traditional *gostilna* doing a good line in moderately priced meats and grills.

The town's best **drinking** spot is *Da Noi* on Prešernovo nabrežje, whose neat outdoor drinking terrace is complemented by a cool, indoor cellar-style bar. Otherwise, take your pick from the stack of open-air cafés lining the eastern and southern sides of Tartinijev trg.

Portorož and around

Situated in its own sunny sheltered bay just 2km south of Piran, **PORTOROŽ** (Port of Roses) is Slovenia's major beach resort. While it may feel like stepping into a cold shower after Piran's charm, it's a likeable enough place, and despite possessing all the customary trappings of your average seaside resort, it's by no means a brash place; moreover, the beaches are clean, safe and well maintained, and there's enough going on here to keep activity-seekers happy.

The town's modern appearance belies a history dating back to the thirteenth century, when Benedictine monks from the nearby monastery of St Lawrence

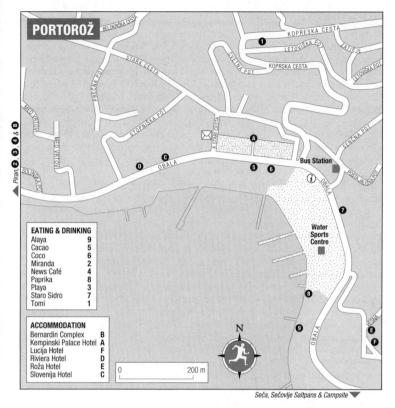

PORTOROŽ

KOPRESKA CESTA
LETOVIŠKA POT
ZATIŠJE
KOPRSKA CESTA
BELOKRIŠKA CESTA
CVETNA POT
STARA CESTA
PREČNA POT
STOPNIŠKA POT
SENČNA POT
LETOVIŠKA POT
MEDVRTOV
K STARI CESTA
POSTA MILISKA POT
MED VRTOV
OBALA
Bus Station
(i)
OBALA
SOLINSKA POT
Piran, 2, 3, 4 & B

EATING & DRINKING

Alaya	9
Cacao	5
Coco	6
Miranda	2
News Café	4
Paprika	8
Playa	3
Staro Sidro	7
Tomi	1

Water
Sports
Centre

ACCOMMODATION

Bernardin Complex	B
Kempinski Palace Hotel	A
Lucija Hotel	F
Riviera Hotel	D
Roža Hotel	E
Slovenija Hotel	C

N

0   200 m

OBALA

Seča, Sečovlje Saltpans & Campsite ▼

cured a range of diseases using the local mineral-rich brine and mud from the saltpans, the same health-inducing properties that led to the development of Portorož as a popular resort in the nineteenth century. The resort's first hotel – originally intended to accommodate the military – went up in 1830, followed by the once magnificent *Palace Hotel* in 1912, built in expectation of a visit by Emperor Franz Jozef. While the town remains a popular health and treatment centre, most visitors to Portorož today come here for the more traditional **beach** diversions.

Arrival and information

From Piran it's a gentle thirty-minute **walk**, via the Bernadin complex, to Portorož. The main **bus stop** is located midway along Obala, the main coastal strip and the point for all things of interest, though buses doing the loop between Piran and Koper stop at regular intervals along here. The **tourist office** is in the large building across the road from the bus stop at Obala 16 (July & Aug daily 9am–8pm; Sept–June Mon–Sat 9am–5pm, Sun 10am–2pm; ☎05/674-2220, ⓦwww.portoroz.si). The **post office** is at K Stari cesta 1 (Mon–Fri 8am–7pm, Sat 8am–noon), next to the *Grand Hotel Portorož*, while the best place for **internet access** is the *Cacao* café, Obala 14 (see p.207). **Bikes** can be rented from the Atlas agency at Obala 55 (€12 for half a day, €18 for a day).

Accommodation

As befits Slovenia's major beach resort, Portorož is awash with **hotels**, though most are managed by small groups of companies, resulting in a characterless uniformity to most; furthermore, there is nothing which could remotely be termed budget. This being the case, your best bet is **private accommodation**, for which you should head to Maona at Obala 14b (daily June–Aug Mon–Sat 9am–8pm, Sun 10am–1pm & 5–8pm; Sept–May Mon–Fri 9am–5pm; ☏05/674-0363, ⓦwww.maona.si), or Turist Biro at Obala 57 (June–Sept daily 9am–1pm & 4–7pm; Oct–May Mon–Fri 10am–1pm & 4–6pm; ☏05/674-1055, ⓦwww.turistbiro-ag.si); both have a good stock of rooms (❶–❷) and apartments (❸–❼), all of which are priced according to category and distance from the sea. The town's large **campsite** is 2km south of the main bus stop in the small suburb of Lucija (☏05/690-6000; April–Oct).

The village-like **Bernardin complex** on the western edge of town (midway between Portorož and Piran) incorporates three contrasting, but all very expensive, places: the *Grand Hotel Bernardin* (☏05/695-0000, ⓦwww.h-bernardin .si; ❾), a monstrous-looking building sloping down to the sea, but which has quite spectacular rooms and sea views and all the attendant facilities of a five-star hotel; the very well-appointed *Histrion* (same tel; ❾); and the unfortunately named, but extremely comfortable, *Vile Park* (same tel; ❽) – guests of all three receive free entry to the complex's Waterpark (see below).

Fronted by tall palms and silky lawns, the imposing *Kempinski Palace*, at Obala 45 (☏05/692-7000, ⓦwww.kempinski-portoroz.com; ❾), is the coast's most opulent hotel; originally built in 1912, its recent restoration is nothing less than majestic, reflected in stunningly appointed rooms and first-rate facilities including a gorgeous pool and a wonderful breakfast terrace. Close by, at Obala 33, the almost identical *Riviera* (☏05/692-6020, ⓦwww.lifeclass.net; ❾) and *Slovenija* (☏05/692-5020, same website; ❾) are two of the more characterful hotels along the main strip; the former has an authentic Thai Massage Centre. Of the cluster of Metropol-owned hotels at Obala 77, the family-friendly *Lucija* (☏05/690-3000, ⓦwww.metropol-resort.com; ❾) and the *Roža* (☏05/690-2000, same website; ❽), behind, are the only ones with any semblance of charm – guests of these hotels receive free use of the tennis courts and the swimming pool, both of which are opposite the *Lucija*.

Beaches and activities

The main **beach**, an incongruous mix of sand, grass and concrete, is clean and well maintained, with lifeguards dispersed along the shore and a wide range of facilities available. Parasols and sunbeds can be rented (€4), as well as cabins and safes (same price plus €5 deposit). Inevitably, it can get tremendously crowded, though there's usually enough space to go around; otherwise you could head to one of several **private beaches** (around €5) – in effect those owned by the hotels – the best of which is the one in front of the *Hotel Slovenija*. All these designated beaches are roped off and it is forbidden to swim outside the boundary. There are other spots along the beachfront (essentially concrete banks) where you can bathe without restriction.

There are activities aplenty to be had on the main beach. The **water sports centre** in the central kiosk offers, among other activities, kayaks (€15 for 1hr), water-skiing (€35 for 15min) and jet-skiing (€55 for 15min), while the Nemo dive centre, inside the Bernardin complex, has a range of reef and wreck **dives** (€35 for one dive including equipment). The Laguna Waterpark (daily 7am–8pm) in the Bernardin Complex has an appealing **swimming pool** (€6 for 2hr, €12 for the day), with a great section for kids, and Turkish and Finnish saunas (€12 for 2hr). There's also a good pool opposite the *Metropol Hotel* (daily 9am–6pm; €4), next door to which are **tennis** courts (€10 for 1hr). The Terme Portorož **spa**, at the *Hotel Portorož* at Obala 33 (☎05/696-8060, ⓦwww .lifeclass.net), offers a huge range of treatments and therapies, as well as two thermal pools and two whirlpools.

Seča

If you want to leave the crowds behind, take a stroll over to **Seča**, 2km south of town. Dispersed among thick rows of olive trees throughout the western end of this knobbly peninsula is the **Forma Viva Sculpture Park** (accessible via the road behind the campsite or via a set of steps partway through the campsite), one of several such sculpture parks in Slovenia (each park demonstrates works of art made from a different material). This particular grouping, opened in 1961, consists of over one hundred greying, weather-worn pieces carved from stone; though the odd piece might interest, a better reason for coming here is for the views back to Portorož and the sea. On the other side of the peninsula are the famous Sečovlje saltpans (see below).

Eating, drinking and entertainment

Obala is lined with an endless succession of indistinguishable **restaurants**, pizzerias and snack joints, few of which stand out. One restaurant worth trying, however, is *Staro Sidro*, 100m east of the Maona agency at no. 55 (closed Mon); it's a restful, rather old-fashioned place, but its fish, the mainstay of a reasonably pricey menu, comes highly recommended. Away from here, one place definitely worth venturing to is *Tomi*, 500m north of the main bus stop, just by the bend in the road at Letoviška 1; accommodating both a smart interior and a sunny, canopied terrace, the strong menu features fish – including exotic starters such as truffles and crab – and stomach-busting, meat-heavy Serbian dishes. There's also *Miranda*, halfway up the hill towards Piran, at Vilfanova 10, with a good mix of fish and meat dishes, and a tidy stone terrace from which to enjoy the sea views.

Drinking possibilities are eminently more enticing, with an array of upbeat cafés, bars and clubs scattered along Obala. The pick of the cafés are *Cacao*, near the tourist office at Obala 14, which sports a cool, loungey interior and deck terrace facing the beach, and the similarly designed *Coco*, 200m further along. Out in the Bernardin complex to the west of town, there is a reasonable selection of bars, the best of which is the *News Café*, a capacious American-style saloon bar.

The most popular of the open-air **beach bars** is *Alaya*, a sprawling, tropically themed hangout located at the southern end of the beach, which also stages regular live music and party nights. In a similar vein, but much smaller, there's the cabana-like *Playa*, just beyond the old salt warehouses out towards the Bernardin complex. Clubbers should make a beeline for the flash *Paprika* club, 200m back up the beach from *Alaya*, whose nightly themed events range from Latin and salsa to house and dance. Also look out for films and concerts at the **open-air theatre** (Portorož Avditorij), behind the bus station at Senčna pot 10.

Sečovlje saltpans

Located right along the border with Croatia, some 3km south of Portorož, are the **Sečovlje saltpans** (Sečoveljske soline; daily: April–Oct 8am–8pm; Nov–March 9am–6pm; €5; ⓦwww.soline.si), once the most extensive saltpans in Slovenia, but now a designated Regional Park. Although salt is still harvested in the northern section of the park (Lera), the larger southern part (Fontanigge) – traversed by vast grids of canals, dykes and pools – has been out of commission since the late 1960s. There are two official **entrances** to the park; the main one is at Lera, reached via a road which branches off in the village of Seča. On reaching the hut, it's an 800m walk to the park's souvenir shop, stocking all manner of beautifully packaged, salt-related paraphernalia, then another 800m to the **visitor centre**, which gives detailed explanations into the salt-making process in the form of a multi media presentation and relief maps. The second entrance is at Fontanigge; from the main road (for how to get here see opposite), a long, dusty track runs alongside the Dragonje River, which marks the border between Slovenia and Croatia. After the first kilometre or so (by which point you'll probably have despaired at the monotony of the walk), you'll reach the entrance (this is also as far as cars can go), before dozens of deserted saltpanners' houses inch into view. It makes for an eerie sight, these stark, crumbling, grey-stone houses randomly strewn across the pancake-flat landscape. A further 2km down the track, it comes as some relief to see the **Saltworks Museum** (Muzej Solinarstva), easily spotted as this comprises the only two intact buildings in the park, having been completely renovated for the purposes of housing the museum. As interesting as the exhibits are, including a store of salt-making equipment and techniques and, upstairs, a mock-up of a saltpanner's living quarters, more fascinating is the detailed explanation of the salt-making process given by the helpful guide (see box below).

Among the most important heritage sites in the country – it is, along with the Škocjan Caves, on the Ramsar List of internationally protected wetlands – the rich, salt-impregnated soil supports a wide variety of saltwater (halophytic) **flora**, sheltering over forty species of plant, many of which feature on the "Red List" (Slovenia's list of endangered plant and animal species), and a range of land vertebrates, including *Suncus etruscus*, a tiny shrew alleged to be Europe's smallest mammal. **Bird-life**, too, is prominent; the warm, sub-Mediterranean climate

---

Salt of the earth

Salt harvesting has been practised along the Slovenian coast since the first saltpans were introduced in Piran some time in the fourteenth century. Although the pans remain at Strunjan, Sečovlje is now the only place where harvesting still takes place, albeit on a much smaller scale than in its heyday during the first half of the last century, when over forty thousand tonnes of salt were yielded annually – today around five thousand tonnes are harvested each year.

The **saltpans** are supplied by seawater funnelled along several large channels, before settling in dammed crystallization basins lined with "petola" (artificially grown crust consisting of algae, gypsum and clay), a method used so as to prevent the salt mixing with sea mud and other sediments. The water is then slowly removed with the aid of large wind-powered pumps, while the remainder evaporates in the sun as the salt crystallizes. After being drained and washed, the salt would be carted off to large warehouses (*skladišča soli*) sited along the coast, before being distributed; there's a good example of one of these (now disused) warehouses in Portorož, near the Bernardin complex.

Saltpanners' (*solinarji*) dwellings – inhabited by the entire family, but only during the harvesting season (April to September) – were extremely modest, comprising a large downstairs storage room and, upstairs, living quarters, divided into a couple of bedrooms and a joint living and kitchen area; the most important aspects of the building, however, were the windows and doors, positioned on both sides of the house so that changes in the weather could be carefully observed.

▲ Šecovlje saltpan

and abundance of food in the basins attracts large numbers of migratory birds, such as the common coot and great cormorant, while herons, gulls and egrets have established themselves as permanent residents.

If you haven't got your own transport, **getting here** is a little tricky: travelling to the Lera part, get the bus driver to drop you off by the road down to the entrance; if heading to Fontanigge the nearest you can get by bus is the village of Sečovlje itself, around 1km before the border crossing, though you'd do just as well jumping on a Croatia-bound bus and getting off at the border crossing; either way, take your passport as a precaution, as you will have to pass through Slovenian customs. One hundred metres beyond the crossing (but before the Croatian border – you are now in "no man's land"), a sign on your right points to the museum.

Travel details

Trains

Divača to: Koper (4–7 daily; 50min); Ljubljana (5–8 daily; 1hr 30min); Postojna (4–7 daily; 35min); Sežana (13 daily; 10min).
Koper to: Divača (5–7 daily; 50min); Ljubljana (5–7 daily; 2hr 30min); Postojna (5–7 daily; 1hr 30min).
Most na Soči to: Bled Jezero (4–7 daily; 1hr); Bohinjska Bistrica (4–7 daily; 50min); Jesenice (4–7 daily; 1hr 15min); Nova Gorica (4–7 daily; 40min).
Nova Gorica to: Ajdovščina (2 daily; 40min); Bled Jezero (4–7 daily; 1hr 30min); Bohinjska Bistrica (4–7 daily; 1hr 15min); Jesenice (4–7 daily; 1hr

50min); Most na Soči (4–7 daily; 40min); Sežana (3–5 daily; 1hr).
Sežana to: Divača (13 daily; 10min); Ljubljana (7 daily; 1hr 35min–2hr); Nova Gorica (4–6 daily; 1hr).

Buses

Ajdovščina to: Ljubljana (Mon–Fri 8 daily, Sat & Sun 3 daily; 1hr 20min); Nova Gorica (Mon–Fri hourly, Sat 5 daily, Sun 3 daily; 40min); Postojna (Mon–Fri hourly, Sat 5 daily, Sun 2 daily; 40min); Vipava (Mon–Fri hourly, Sat 5 daily, Sun 2 daily; 10min).

Bovec to: Kobarid (Mon–Fri 5 daily, Sat 2 daily, Sun 1 daily; 35min); Kranjska Gora (June & Aug 4 daily; 1hr 45min); Tolmin (Mon–Fri 5 daily, Sat 2 daily, Sun 1 daily; 1hr 10min).

Cerkno to: Bovec (2 daily; 1hr 15min); Idrija (Mon–Fri hourly, Sat 6 daily, Sun 4 daily; 25min); Ljubljana (Mon–Fri 5 daily, Sat & Sun 3 daily; 1hr 25min); Tolmin (Mon–Fri 3 daily; Sat & Sun 2 daily; 40min).

Divača to: Koper (Mon–Fri 9 daily, Sat & Sun 2 daily; 1hr 15min); Ljubljana (Mon–Fri 7 daily, Sat & Sun 4 daily; 1hr 45min).

Idrija to: Bovec (1 daily; 1hr 30min); Cerkno (Mon–Fri hourly, Sat 6 daily, Sun 4 daily; 25min); Ljubljana (Mon–Fri 8 daily, Sat 6 daily, Sun 4 daily; 1hr 15min); Tolmin (Mon–Fri 4 daily, Sat 2 daily, Sun 1 daily; 1hr).

Kobarid to: Bovec (Mon–Fri 5 daily, Sat & Sun 3 daily; 35min); Tolmin (Mon–Fri 6 daily, Sat & Sun 3 daily; 30min).

Koper to: Ljubljana (5 daily; 2hr 20min); Piran (every 20–30min; 25min); Postojna (6 daily; 1hr 20min).

Nova Gorica to: Ajdovščina (Mon–Fri hourly, Sat 4 daily, Sun 3 daily; 40min); Bovec (Mon–Fri 4 daily, Sat & Sun 2 daily; 1hr 15min); Kobarid (Mon–Fri 4 daily, Sat & Sun 2 daily; 50min);

Ljubljana (Mon–Fri 8 daily, Sat & Sun 4 daily; 2hr 30min); Postojna (Mon–Fri 8 daily, Sat & Sun 4 daily; 1hr 10min); Tolmin (Mon–Fri 6 daily, Sat 4 daily, Sun 2 daily; 40min); Vipava (Mon–Fri hourly, Sat & Sun 3 daily; 45min).

Piran to: Koper (every 20–30min; 25min); Ljubljana (Mon–Fri 6 daily, Sat & Sun 4 daily; 2hr 40min).

Sežana to: Ajdovščina (Mon–Sat 1 daily; 40min); Divača (Mon–Sat 1 daily; 15min); Ljubljana (1 daily; 1hr 40min); Nova Gorica (Mon–Fri 4 daily, Sat & Sun 1 daily; 1hr 10min); Štanjel (Mon–Fri 5 daily, Sat & Sun 1 daily; 30min); Postojna (Mon–Fri 2 daily, Sat 1 daily; 40min).

Tolmin to: Bovec (Mon–Fri 4 daily, Sat & Sun 2 daily; 1hr 10min); Cerkno (Mon–Fri 3 daily, Sat & Sun 2 daily; 40min); Kobarid (Mon–Fri 4 daily, Sat & Sun 2 daily; 30min); Most na Soči (Mon–Fri 6 daily, Sat & Sun 2 daily; 15min); Nova Gorica (Mon–Fri 6 daily, Sat & Sun 2 daily; 40min).

International trains

Divača to: Pula (1 daily; 2hr 45min).
Sežana to: Trieste (Mon–Fri 4 daily, Sat 3 daily; 1hr 40min).

International buses

Koper to: Trieste (10 daily; 1hr).

Southern Slovenia

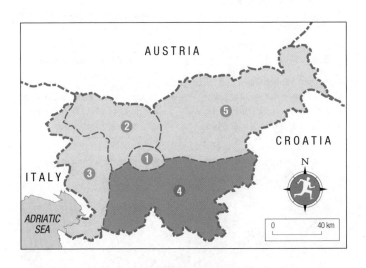

CHAPTER 4 # Highlights

✳ **Postojna Caves** Vast chambers and dazzling formations in one of the world's truly great cave systems. See p.218

✳ **Predjama Castle** Visit Slovenia's most dramatically sited castle, and discover the legend of Erasmus Lueger. See p.221

✳ **Lake Cerknica** Europe's largest intermittent lake is another of Slovenia's great natural wonders. See p.224

✳ **Križna Water Cave** Discover cave-bear bones and over a dozen lakes in one of Europe's finest water caves. See p.226

✳ **Walking in Kočevski Rog** Explore Slovenia's finest expanse of forest, and catch some wildlife along the way – mind the bears though. See p.233

✳ **Kayaking on the Kolpa River** The beautiful, twisting, Kolpa River is a great spot for kayaking and other water sports. See p.234

✳ **Pleterje Monastery** Visit the atmospheric church and grounds of Slovenia's only functioning Carthusian monastery. See p.246

✳ **Repnice wine cellars** Down a few glasses of wine in unique cellars hewn from sand. See p.252

▲ Kayaking on the Kolpa River

Southern Slovenia

The three regions comprising southern Slovenia: Notranjska, Dolenjska and Bela Krajina, offer an attractive mix of darkly forested hills, karstic rock formations, river valleys, castles, monasteries and spas, not to mention several outstanding wine-producing regions. Unsurprisingly, there are opportunities aplenty for hiking, cycling and other leisurely pursuits.

The province of **Notranjska** encompasses an expanse of terrain extending south from the Ljubljana marshes to the Croatian border, bound by Primorska and the Karst to the west and by the Velika Gora hills to the east. Characterized by karst fields, underground rivers and thickly forested limestone hills and plateaus pocked by innumerable cave systems, its most celebrated attractions are the astonishing **Postojna Caves** and the majestically sited **Predjama Castle**. Largely ignored by most travellers, Notranjska's lesser-known sites include **Lake Cerknica**, Europe's largest intermittent lake, and the wonderful **Križna Water Cave**. Pressed up hard against the Croatian border, the **Snežnik Mountains** offer some of the country's best non-alpine hiking.

The thick forests of Notranjska extend eastwards into the neighbouring province of **Dolenjska**, the largest of the three regions and the one possessing the lion's share of southern Slovenia's historical sites. Its westernmost flank centres around the towns of **Ribnica** and **Kočevje**, close to both the massive forests of Velika Gora and **Kočevski Rog**, and the **Kolpa River Valley** on the Croatian border, the latter offering an exciting complement of fantastic scenery and superb walking, cycling and adrenaline-fuelled sports.

The only town of any real size is **Novo Mesto**, a handy base from which to take in any number of local attractions, foremost of which is the beautiful **Krka River Valley**, which extends northwest to the village of **Muljava**, itself just a few kilometres from the ancient **Stična Monastery**. Following the course of the Krka River eastwards from Novo Mesto brings you to **Otočec Castle**, the secluded **Pleterje Monastery** and the sleepy island town of **Kostanjevica na Krki**. Beyond here the road and river continue to **Brežice**, setting for one of the country's most celebrated classical music festivals; **Čatež**, the country's largest spa centre; and the **Bizeljsko wine region**, perhaps the most appealing of the area's four winegrowing centres.

Quietly tucked away in the far southeastern corner of the country and bound by the forests of Kočevjski Rog to the west and the Croatian border to the south and east is **Bela Krajina**. It is easily the smallest of southern Slovenia's regions, a gentle landscape where hilly slopes raked with lush vineyards descend to flatlands strewn with the region's famous white birch trees.

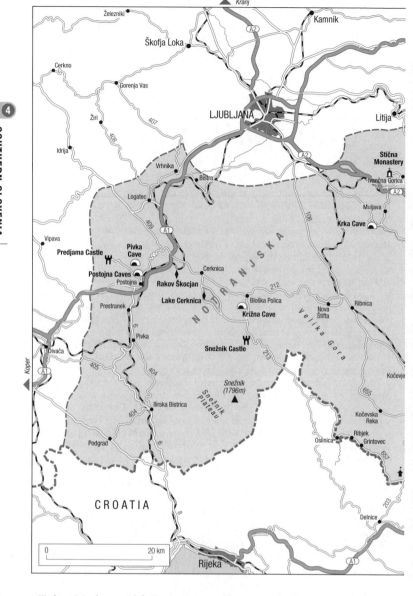

Today, viticulture and fruit growing are the main agricultural activities in this region, and it's these, along with strong folk traditions, that entice any visitors the region receives. Of the province's two main towns, **Črnomelj** and **Metlika**, the latter is more appealing by dint of its architecture and museums as well as its proximity to the fabulous Gothic pilgrimage shrine of **Tri Fare** (Three Parishes) and some lovely **wine villages**.

SOUTHERN SLOVENIA

Getting around by **public transport** is more difficult here than in any other part of the country, so it's the one region where having your own wheels is particularly advantageous; trains serve relatively few places outlined in this chapter, while local bus services are patchy at best.

Notranjska and Western Dolenjska

Most visitors to **Notranjska** head straight to Slovenia's number one tourist attraction, the **Postojna Caves**, and follow that with a visit to the nearby **Predjama Castle**, perched miraculously halfway up a cliff. However, the region contains other, less-visited subterranean delights in the form of the **Pivka and Black Caves**, a mere stone's throw from their more famous counterparts. To the north of the caves, a worthwhile diversion en route to or from Postojna/Ljubljana is the **Bistra Technical Museum**; containing a massive collection of agricultural and industrial machines, trams, carriages and cars, this is a must for any vehicle enthusiast.

South of Postojna, the **Snežnik mountains** offer both tremendous hiking and the opportunity to spot some of Slovenia's most spectacular wildlife. Further east, the **Rakov Škocjan Regional Park** presents more rambling possibilities. Close by is one of Slovenia's most unusual landmarks, the extraordinary **Lake Cerknica** – by winter a lake, by summer a field; permanent, though underground, lakes can be explored at **Križna Water Cave**, where skeletons of prehistoric cave-bears have been discovered. Finally, for the less energetic, **Snežnik Castle** offers lovely landscaped gardens and a fine art collection.

Although the main towns in **Western Dolenjska** are nothing special, they are useful jumping-off points for **Velika Gora** and the stunning virgin forests of **Kočevjski Rog**. Other worthwhile places to visit are **Ribnica** whose fine woodenware tradition is in evidence in the town's museum and at the annual fair, and nearby Nova Štifta, home to one of Slovenia's main pilgrimage churches. Furthermore, **Kočevje**, once home to the country's German-speaking minority, contains Slovenia's first parliament building. Straddling the Croatian border south of Kočevje, the beautiful **Kolpa Valley** is the region's centre for river-based activities, all of which can be organized from the valley's main village, **Osilnica**.

Bistra Technical Museum

Twenty-two kilometres southwest of Ljubljana, close to the small settlement of Vrhnika in the hamlet of Bistra, is the former **Bistra Monastery**, a large complex that is now home to the **Technical Museum of Slovenia** (Tehniški muzej Slovenije; July & Aug Tues–Fri & Sun 10am–6pm, Sat 8am–5pm; March–June & Sept–Nov Tues–Fri 8am–4pm, Sat 8am–5pm, Sun 10am–6pm; €4). The museum is divided into several sections, though such is the size of the place you're best off making a beeline for a select few, particularly if time is short. As interesting as the voluminous displays of textiles, forestry, agriculture and engineering are, it's the massive road vehicle department – comprising a magnificent collection of pre-World War II automobiles, carriages (including a fine Ljubljana tram from 1901), bicycles and tractors – which demands greatest attention.

The highlight of the collection is some two dozen cars given as gifts to Tito by various government offices and heads of state, which were used for his many travels throughout Yugoslavia and abroad, including India and Burma; there are some splendid models on display, notably a magnificent Rolls Royce Silver Wraith, a Mercedes Benz (from the Croatian Home Office), and an armour-plated 1937 Packard Twelve, presented to Tito by Stalin in 1945 – ironically, just three years before Yugoslavia's expulsion from Cominform. There's also a 1953 Fiat Zastava, just one of Tito's many hunting vehicles.

Although undoubtedly worth a special visit from Ljubljana, the museum is more conveniently done as a trip en route to Postojna. Moreover, without your own transport, getting here is fairly time-consuming; take one of the regular buses from Ljubljana (stand 29 at the bus station) to Vrhnika, and alight by the *Hotel Mantova* in the centre; from here, it's a signposted three-kilometre walk along a winding country road to the museum – however, many cars travel this road, so there's a good chance of hitching a ride.

Postojna and around

The town of **POSTOJNA**, 66km south of Ljubljana, would be an eminently forgettable place were it not the location of one of Slovenia's most popular tourist attractions, the amazing **Postojna Caves**, whose vast chambers and dazzling formations have been pulling in the punters for nearly two centuries. The town itself is pretty much devoid of character and you'll not want to hang around once you've visited the caves and the **Predjama Castle** (see p.221), just a few kilometres away. Located on the main road and rail routes to the coast, the caves are easily managed as a half-day trip from Ljubljana, or as a stop-off en route to the coast itself.

Arrival, information and accommodation

From the **bus station** on Titova cesta, it's a five-minute walk to the main square, Titov trg, while the **train station** is less conveniently 1km southeast of town on Kolodvorska cesta – from the station exit, take the stairs down to Pod Kolodvorom, then walk along Ulica 1 Maja until you reach the main square. The **tourist office** (May–Sept daily 9am–6pm; ☎05/720-1610, ⓦwww .turizem-kras.si) is out by the caves, though you can get the same information from the Kompas agency at Titov trg 2a (April–Oct Mon–Fri 8am–7pm, Sat 9am–1pm; Nov–March Mon–Fri 8am–6pm, Sat 9am–1pm; ☎05/721-1480, Ⓔinfo@kompas-postojna.si) – they also offer a five percent discount on tickets to the caves. There's **internet access** in the library, 100m behind the *Hotel Kras* on Trg Padlih borcev (July & Aug Mon & Wed 10am–6pm, Tue, Thu & Fri 7am–3pm; rest of year Mon–Fri 7.30am–5.30pm, Sat 7am–noon; free), and the **post office** (Mon–Fri 8am–7pm, Sat 8am–noon) is at Ulica 1 Maja 2a, across from the main square.

The town's principal **hotel** is the *Kras* (☎05/700-2300, ⓦwww.hotel-kras .si; ❼), a flashy glass structure on Titov trg concealing pricey but good-sized and extremely stylish rooms. More affordable is the *Hotel Sport* at Kolodvorska 1 (☎05/720-2244, ⓦwww.sport-hotel.si; ❻), a simple yet colourful and welcoming place offering singles and doubles, as well as hostel accommodation in multi-bedded rooms (❷–❸) – they've also got bikes for rent (€9 for half a day, €15 per day). Cheaper still, but far more basic, is the *Dijaški Dom* in the Forestry and Woodworking School at Tržaška cesta 36 (☎05/726-5291), which has triples all with shared bathroom (€15 including breakfast). Alternatively you can book **private rooms** (❷) through the Kompas agency. Finally, if you've got your own transport, the *Hudičevec* tourist farm, 10km west of town just outside

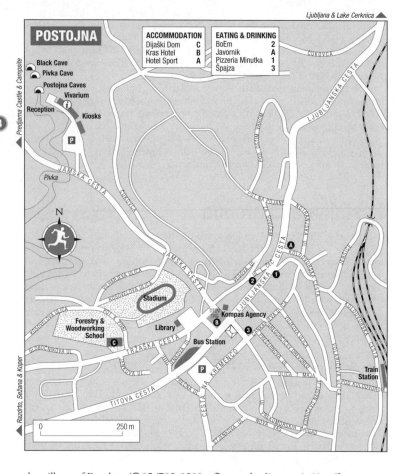

POSTOJNA

ACCOMMODATION	
Dijaški Dom	C
Kras Hotel	B
Hotel Sport	A

EATING & DRINKING	
BoEm	2
Javornik	A
Pizzeria Minutka	1
Špajza	3

the village of Razdrto (☎05/703-0300, ⓦwww.hudicevec.si; ❸), offers warm, homely rooms and its own organically grown food – the farm (it's signposted) stands in a field just off the main road.

Scenically located in a pine forest 4km north of the cave (go 1.5km along the road to Predjama, take a right and the site is 2.5km further on) is the large *Pivka* **campsite** (☎05/720-3993; April–Oct), which also has simple four-bed bungalows with bathrooms (❻), some with a kitchen (❼). During July and August the full rate is applicable, regardless of the number of people staying; at other times, it's half-price if there are two of you.

Postojna Caves

Located an easy walk (1.5km) northwest of town along the road to Predjama the 19km of tunnels, chambers and passages which constitute the **Postojna Caves** (Postojnska jama; ⓦwww.postojna-cave.com) lie under the slopes of a broad karstic limestone plateau on the eastern fringes of the Postojna basin. Millions of years of erosion and corrosion by the Pivka River, coupled with abundant rainfall seeping through the cave's permeable limestone ceilings, have created a fantastic jungle of stalactites and stalagmites, Gothic-like chiselled columns and translucent stone draperies.

Although parts of the cave had been continually visited since the Middle Ages, it was the brilliant seventeenth-century polymath Valvasor (see box, p.237), inevitably, who first reported upon this immense grotto, commenting, "in some places you see terrifying heights, elsewhere everything is in columns so strangely shaped as to seem like some creepy-crawly, snake or other animal in front of one". The caves were pronounced open to tourists on the occasion of a visit by Emperor Franz Ferdinand in 1819, the first in a long line of distinguished visitors to Postojna. Within six years of his visit, the caves had been illuminated with oil lamps and professional guides had been employed. The famous cave train, meanwhile, entered service in 1872, a rather crude model in which tourists were shunted along in hand-pushed wagons. These carriages were superseded by gas-powered trains in 1914, themselves replaced by the electric version (used today) in 1959.

The Cave Tour

Tours take place throughout the year (daily: Jan–March & Nov–Dec 10am, noon & 3pm; April & Oct 10am, noon, 2pm & 4pm; May & Sept hourly 9am–5pm; June–Aug hourly 9am–6pm; €22 plus €4 to park), but to get the most out of your visit, try and make one of the first or last tours of the day to avoid the crowds. Dress warmly, as it can get quite chilly.

The tour begins with a ride on the **cave train**, which whisks you along 2km of preliminary systems before the tour proper begins. As the train hurtles forth keep an eye out for several interesting features: a shaft of blackened walls, the result of a Nazi fuel dump blown up by Partisan saboteurs during World War II; the **Congress Hall**, a beautifully lit chamber so-named following the staging of a Speleological Congress here in 1965; and the **Curtain**, a transparent, wafer-thin formation precariously angled on a sloping wall.

Alighting at the **Great Mountain** (Velika Gora), you'll break off into the group of your chosen language before the one-hour guided tour begins. The most

▲ Postojna Caves

impressive formations in this vast hall – a 45-metre-high stone-block mound formed when the ceiling collapsed and which, in time, became smothered in calcite – are the so-called **Natural Curtains**, whose shape and colour is akin to that of dried tobacco leaves. Crossing the **Russian Bridge**, built in 1916 by Russian prisoners of war, you enter the most enchanting part of the system, a series of chambers collectively known as the **Beautiful Caves** (Lepe jame), whose names are suggestive of some of the lustrous formations and colours on display, such as the **Spaghetti Hall**, with its dripping, needle-like formations, the calcium-rich **White Hall**, and the **Red Room**, stained a rich ochre by iron oxides. Continuing in a circuitous route, you pass back under the Russian Bridge through several more chambers, one of which, the **Winter Chamber** (Zimska dvorana), is home to the two formations that have become symbols of the cave: one called the **Pillar**, and another dubbed **Brilliant**, the latter on account of its dazzling snow-white colour and peculiar shape, which resembles something like a stack of giant cauliflowers. The main attraction in the next gallery has less to do with the formations on display and more to do with the contents of the large tank located in the centre, which contains **Proteus Anguinus**, the largest permanent cave-dwelling vertebrate known to man (see the Subterranean Slovenia colour section). The tour concludes a little further on in the **Concert Hall** (Koncertna dvorana), the largest open space in the system, and which, you are told, can hold some ten thousand people – the odd concert is still held here.

You can see more Proteus Anguinus, as well as other cave flora and fauna – such as crickets, beetles and spiders – in the Speleobiology Station, or **Proteus Vivarium** (daily: May–Sept 9.30am–5.30pm; Oct–April 9.30am–3.30pm; €8 or €25 with entrance to caves), a short walk from the cave entrance by the kiosks. You'll do well, though, to spot more than a handful of these tiny creatures, as most are apt to hide themselves away. The exhibition is housed inside the Gallery of Signatures, so-called because of the many signatures scrawled over the cave walls, the oldest of which (no longer visible) is thought to date from 1213.

Pivka and Black caves

If you'd rather avoid the crowds, then more low-key subterranean alternatives are the **Pivka Cave** (Pivka jama) and **Black Cave** (Črna jama; both June–Aug daily 9am & 3pm; €8). The entrance to the former is via a sixty-metre-deep collapsed chasm near the Pivka camping ground, some 4km north of the main Postojna entrance (follow the signs to the camp). Descending nearly three hundred steps, the route then follows a specially constructed walkway cut into the wall just above the level of the Pivka River. Beyond an iron door and a short tunnel is the Black Cave (also known as the Magdalena Cave), a modestly sized, dry gallery, which takes its name from the large amount of black calcite present.

Eating and drinking

There is a trio of commendable **restaurants** in Postojna, led by *Špajza*, at Ulica 1 Maja 1, an elegant little trattoria offering Mediterranean cuisine (mostly fish) alongside some imaginative local dishes such as pasta with truffles, and Karst risotto. *Pizzeria Minutka*, up from the main square at Ljubljanska cesta 14, has (aside from a range of pizzas and fresh salads) a superb choice of Serbian stews, such as *Prebranac* (oven-baked beans), and grilled meats, notably *Čevapi* and *Pljeskavica*, both served with *Lepinja*, a deliciously doughy bread – the service is good too. Just up from here, the good-looking *Javornik* restaurant in the *Hotel Sport* has a great tourist menu with four-course meals from as little as €8. Opposite *Minutka*, the café-cum-bar *BoEm* is about as exciting as it gets for **drinking**.

Predjama Castle

Second only to Postojna as the region's main tourist attraction is the fabulously dramatic **Predjama Castle** (Predjamski grad; daily: Jan–March & Nov–Dec 10am–4pm; April & Oct 10am–6pm; May, June & Sept 9am–6pm; July & Aug 9am–7pm; €8), 9km north of the caves in the village of the same name. Pressed into a huge cavern, hollowed out of the high, flat rock face over the karstic swallow hole of the Lokva stream, its setting is as unforgettable as it is improbable. Stopping here in 1802 en route to Italy, the German architect Karl Schinkel recalled, "it was with the wildest bravery that man was ordered to settle in this place. There is nothing more stirring than to look upon the castle, wondrously composed of tower-like structures which, built under the dark vault of the cavern, need not their own ramparts, as the dark cavern's huge bulk hangs far beyond them."

Among its many aristocratic residents, the most infamous was the castle's last owner, knight and brigand **Erasmus Lueger** (see box below), who inhabited the castle during the second half of the fifteenth century, and whose life – in particular the manner of his death – has intrigued historians for centuries.

With origins dating back to around the twelfth century, the castle manifests a number of styles, from Romanesque through to Gothic, although its predominant form is Renaissance following heavy renovation in the sixteenth century. With a total of some fifteen rooms, as well as numerous passageways, galleries and alcoves, all condensed into five floors, there's much to see, though little of what's on display is original. Before you start, take one of the useful accompanying leaflets to guide you through the numbered rooms. On the second floor, keep an eye out for a portrait of the suitably gruff Erasmus (one of the few pictures of him known to exist), and the cupboard in the dining room – made by an inmate of a local prison using just his pocket-knife. Located on the same (third) floor where Erasmus came to grief is the tiny castle **chapel**, containing a fifteenth-century Gothic pietà. Next door is the chaplain's room, from where he could witness the punishments being meted out in the torture chamber one floor below. From the natural apertures on each floor there are fine panoramas of the flower-speckled Vipava Valley ahead.

At the very top of the castle – across the drawbridge and up some uneven steps – lie the ruins of the Cave Castle, beyond which is the **secret natural passage**; tours of the latter are possible during the summer, but you should call a couple of days in advance. Easier to visit is the **cave under the Castle**

The death of Erasmus Lueger

The beginning of what proved to be a rather sticky ending for **Erasmus** began after he killed one of the Austrian emperor Frederick III's kinsmen, in revenge for the decapitation of a friend. Hot on his heels as he fled to Predjama was the governor of Trieste, Caspar Ravbar, whose mission it was to capture Erasmus. For more than a year Ravbar and his men laid siege to Predjama, attempting to starve out its defenders. However, Ravbar hadn't reckoned on a **secret natural passage**, located beyond the castle walls, through which came a constant supply of fresh food that Erasmus would occasionally hurl down into the valley to taunt his besiegers. Finally betrayed by a double-dealing servant, Erasmus's **death**, when it finally came, was an ignoble one. The poor fellow was blasted to bits by a large projectile while settling down to answer nature's call. Local legend has it that he is buried under the linden tree, supposedly planted by his lover, next to the **Church of Our Lady of Sorrows**, just down from the castle.

(Jama pod Predjamskim gradom), which extends for some 13km (much of it still unexplored) to the Vipava Valley, though only around 700m of walking is possible for the casual visitor. Bar the odd stalactite, there's not an awful lot to see, but it's one of the few caves around that hasn't been artificially lit, so it's quite good fun wandering around with torches. Scheduled tours, lasting 45 minutes, take place between May and September (11am, 1pm, 3pm & 5pm; €8 or €13 if combined with the Castle); contact the ticket office in the castle. If you're around in July try and make it for the annual **jousting tournament**, which takes place on the narrow strip of grass just below the castle on the last, or second to last, Sunday of that month.

The Snežnik Mountains

Thirty-three kilometres south of Postojna, and just 11km from the Croatian border, the nondescript market town of **ILIRSKA BISTRICA** holds no specific appeal, but it's a good place from which to strike out into the wonderful **Snežnik Mountains**, a densely forested karst plateau cloaked in spruce, beech, fir and dwarf pine, and traversed by a number of well-marked trails, including a section of the European footpath E6. From Ilirska Bistrica, it's a good three-hour walk to **Sviščaki** (1242m), where the *Dom na Sviščakih* (☎051/222-212) has a handful of beds available between June and mid-September as well as at weekends throughout the rest of the year; from here it's a further two-hour trek to the cone-like **Mount Snežnik**, where there are more beds at the *Koča na Velikem Snežniku* (☎050/615-356; May–Oct Sat & Sun, Aug daily). Usually topped with snow until late spring, Slovenia's highest non-Alpine mountain (1796m) offers fantastic views of the Alps to the north, and the Croatian seaboard, dotted with its many islands, to the south. From Mount Snežnik, the path continues to **Mašun** (1024m; 4hr), and down through the Leskova Valley towards Snežnik Castle (see p.227). If you have a car, you could drive to Sviščaki and walk to Snežnik from there – from Sviščaki, the deteriorating mountain road continues to Mašun (13km), before descending to Snežnik Castle. If you're doing this route in reverse – from Snežnik Castle – you could drive to Mašun and walk to Snežnik from there. The plateau also shelters numerous large mammals, including lynx, wolf and a significant bear population. In Ilirska

---

Brown bears

The majority of Slovenia's estimated six hundred or so **brown bears** are to be found in the heavily forested regions of southern Slovenia, and in particular, those forests surrounding Kočevje and Snežnik.

The country's **indigenous brown bear population** was almost decimated during the nineteenth century, thanks to intensive farming, deforestation and excessive hunting practices. But stricter environmental protection standards since the end of World War II have contributed to a sharp increase in their number over the past few decades, numbers that were boosted during the wars in Bosnia in the early 1990s when many bears sought to escape their disturbed habitats. Today around one hundred bears are culled each year, while small numbers are regularly transferred to France, Spain and other European countries in order to repopulate certain areas.

The most likely time to **see bears** – not that you really want to – is from March to June, and during October and November. In any case, you'd do well to follow the cardinal rules: store food and rubbish properly, make sure bears know you're there (make lots of noise as you're walking along), and, clearly, do not approach them – also watch out for fresh tracks, diggings and droppings.

Bistrica, the **tourist office**, at Bazoviška cesta 12 (Mon–Fri 8am–3pm, plus Sat in summer 9am–noon; ☎05/710-1384, ✉razvojni.center@siol.net), can organize **private accommodation** if you wish to stick around.

East of Postojna

The area east of Postojna is blessed with several first-rate attractions. The first of these is the **Rakov Škocjan Regional Park**, an enjoyable walking spot from where it's a short distance to the small town of **Cerknica**, of little interest itself but which is close to one of the country's most extraordinary geographical features, the intermittent **Lake Cerknica**, sometimes lake, sometimes field depending on the season. East and south of here respectively is the must-see **Križna Water Cave** and **Snežnik Castle**, the latter tucked away under the shadow of the Snežnik Mountains. This is lovely cycling country, and there are a few places in Postojna from where bikes can be rented. This is just as well, as public transport is extremely limited; without your own wheels, careful planning is required, particularly if you wish to see more than one of these places in the same day.

Rakov Škocjan Regional Park

A couple of kilometres north of Postojna, the secondary road running parallel to the main E70/E61 Ljubljana–Koper highway breaks off sharply to the right in the direction of Cerknica. After a further 5km, the road passes the **Rakov Škocjan Regional Park**, a small, lush karst valley popular with local walkers. There's an easy, well-marked, circular trail around the park, which should take no more than a couple of hours to complete.

The park's focal point is the short, well-defined **Rak Gorge**, which begins at the **Small Natural Bridge** (Mali Naravni Most) – the first of two stunning natural rock bridges sited at either end of the gorge – just below which lurks the **Zelške Cave** (Zelške Jama) and the Rak Spring, from whence the babbling **Rak River** emerges. The river, which carries water from Cerknica Polje to the Planina Polje, winds its way down the gorge to the immaculately cut arch of the **Great Natural Bridge** (Veliki Naravni Most), underneath which is the **Tkalca Cave** (Tkalca Jama). On the far side of the bridge a crumbling heap of stone ruins, including parts of a stone altar, are all that remain of the **Church of St Kancijan**. During periods when the river is low, or completely dry, it is possible to explore both cave entrances, but caution should be exercised as it's likely to be slippery. Right in the heart of the park is the *Hotel Rakov Škocjan* (☎01/709-7470, ⓦwww.h-rakovskocjan.com; ❻), a small and cosy lodge-style residence with warm, pine-furnished rooms – there's also a restaurant and café here, as well as bikes for rent (€3 for 1hr, €15 per day).

Cerknica

Located approximately 4km east of Rakov Škocjan, the town of **CERKNICA** is a drab place, enlivened only during the **Pust Festival** each February – one of Slovenia's better organized carnivals – but it does offer a smattering of accommodation, useful if you're planning to spend a day or two anywhere in the vicinity of the **lake**.

There is a **train station** 4km northwest of Cerknica in **Rakek**, which may be a more feasible option if you don't mind walking or hitching the rest of the way, given the paucity of buses to Cerknica. The **bus station** is on Čabranska ulica, from where it's a short walk to the **tourist office**, situated next to the post office at Cesta 4 maja 51 (Mon–Fri 8.30am–3pm, Sat 8.30am–1pm; ℡01/709-3636, ✉info@notranjska.eu). They might be able to help out with **private rooms** but otherwise *TeliCo*, 500m east of the tourist office up the hill at Brestova 9 (℡01/709-7090, ✉vilma.telic@guest.arnes.si; ❸), has a couple of **rooms** with great views out towards the lake. Pretty much the only place in town to eat is the *Valvasorjev hram* **restaurant** opposite the tourist office, which knocks up cheap, good food in a roomy, if rather unatmospheric, cellar bar.

Cerknica is also the starting point for trails to the **Slivnica Plateau**, ranged across the lake's northern shore. If the lake looks impressive from ground level, the views from atop its highest peak, **Velika Slivnica** (1114m; 2hr from Cerknica), are superlative; Velika Slivnica is also known as witch mountain, owing to its associations with witchcraft in the Middle Ages. Once at the top, you can enjoy refreshments at the *Dom na Slivnici* (℡01/709-4140) just below the summit, which also has beds available (May–Sept Sat & Sun only).

Lake Cerknica

There are several ways to approach a visit to **Lake Cerknica** (Cerkniško Jezero), but what you see, and how you see it, will largely be determined by which time of the year you visit, and which mode of transport, if any, you use. The most direct route across the lake (or field) is via an unsurfaced north–south road that shaves the lake's western shore. Beginning at **Dolenje Jezero**, a small village 2km south of Cerknica, the road bisects a group of sink holes, before passing by the small wooded island of Gorica and continuing southwards to **Otok** (Island) which, when the lake is full, magically becomes the

The disappearing lake

Although the so-called **"disappearing lake"**, located about 2.5km south of Cerknica, had been the subject of much postulation and fascination on the part of researchers and explorers long before Valvasor's time, it was left to the great polymath himself to unravel the lake's eccentricities, concluding as he did: "I think there is no lake so remarkable either in Europe or in any other of the three corners of the world…no lake has as many exceptional features." As a result of his efforts, which included the publication of a map of the lake in 1689, Valvasor was granted honorary membership of the Royal Society in London. There were other significant contributions, too, most notably from the botanist Balthazar Haquet and the Jesuit Tobijas Gruber, both of whom offered thoroughgoing accounts of the lake's extraordinary hydrological functions.

The lake functions thus: once water from the Slivnica and Bloke Plateaus to the east, and the Javornik mountains to the west, enters the permeable limestone surface of the lakebed, it begins to percolate through the lake's many sink holes, into the subterranean area, and when more water enters the lake than can be depleted, the waters of the main channel, the Stržen (itself fed by a number of tributaries and streams), overflow and the shallow lake is created, sometimes in a matter of days. At its fullest, the lake can extend for some 10km in length and nearly 5km in width – that's roughly three to four times the size of Lake Bohinj, Slovenia's largest permanent body of water. The disappearing act takes a little longer, usually between three and four weeks. There have been numerous, hitherto unsuccessful, attempts at **human intervention** over the years – either to prevent the lake filling (in order to grow more hay for livestock), or, conversely, to preserve a permanent body of water (in order to prolong the fishing season and encourage tourism).

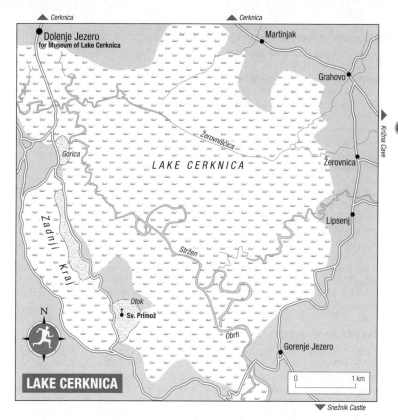

country's sole inhabited island. From Otok you can either head back in a northerly direction via the forest road which skirts the western shore of the **Zadnji kraj inlet**, or take the longer route along the lake's eastern shore through the settlements of Laze, Gorenje Jezero, Lipsenj and Žerovnica, winding up at Grahovo on the main road.

As a rule the lake is usually present between October and June, and at its most voluminous during spring, following snowmelt from both the Snežnik and Slivnica plateaus. During this period, the lake becomes a vast playground for a multitude of **activities**, the most popular of which is fishing – pike, tench and chub are the main stock here – as well as swimming, rowing, windsurfing, and even skiing and skating when it's cold enough. With over two hundred species of bird, including corncrake, lapwing and field lark, either migrating or nesting among the wide expanse of reeds, the lake is something of a haven for birdwatchers.

The most enjoyable way to see the lake is on a **bike**, which can be rented from *TeliCo* in Cerknica (see opposite) and from the *Hotel Sport* (see p.217) in Postojna. Should you wish to **stay** near the lake, there are two good possibilities in the village of **Žerovnica** on the eastern side: the modern *Logar* tourist farm at no. 16 (℡01/709-6071, ✉logar.katarina@volja.net; ❹) and the pleasantly isolated *Miškar* house at no. 66 (℡040/646-285, 🌐www.miskar.si; ❹) – it's actually outside the village on the road to Bloška Polica – which has three rooms and self-catering facilities.

If you plan to spend any length of time around the lake, arm yourself with a copy of the 1:25,000 *Notranjska Cerkniško jezero* map, which outlines a good range of walks and cycle routes in the area.

Museum of Lake Cerknica

For a better understanding of the lake's peculiarities, pay a visit to the **Museum of Lake Cerknica** (Muzej Cerkniškega Jezera; €4.50) in **Dolenje Jezero** (at no. 1e). The centrepiece of this family-run museum is an enormous 1:2500-scale **map-relief** of the lake and its surrounding features, constructed by the museum's indefatigable owner over the course of three years. By way of the lake's most salient features – tributaries, springs, sink holes, as well as settlements and roads, and complemented by live recordings of bird and other animal sounds – the map illustrates how the lake performs and what it looks like during both dry and wet periods.

There's also a 25-minute slide show, featuring some beautifully shot images of the lake in its various guises, and a collection of tools and implements tradition-ally used by local fishermen – wooden skates, nets, baskets and the like – as well as models of the long wooden canoes (*drevak*) that were used, until the 1970s, for transporting cattle and other livestock across the lake. In theory the museum is only open to visitors at 3pm on Saturdays, but if you call in advance a visit should be possible at other times (☎01/709-4053, ⓦwww.jezerski-hram .si). The adjoining café (closed Tues) is a useful place to stop off for **refresh-ments** en route to the lake.

Križna Water Cave

Utterly different from Postojna and that ilk of cave, the eight-kilometre-long **Križna Water Cave** (Križna jama), 12km southeast of Cerknica, is one of the world's great lake caves, and *the* cave to visit in Slovenia if it's a more authentic caving experience you're after. Entering the cave via a small aperture hollowed out of the rock face, you immediately descend into a rocky, dry gallery, also known as the **Bear's Corridor** (Medvedji rov) owing to the many cave-bear (*ursus spelaeus*) that sheltered here thousands of years ago. The first cave-bear excavations – carried out some 130 years ago – uncovered around two thousand fossil remains from over one hundred animals, mainly mandibles, skulls and other bone fragments; there are still many fragments, typically part of a jaw or a tooth, embedded within the rock, some of which you'll see as you walk around. There's also an almost-complete cave-bear skull on display, next to a much smaller skull of a brown bear; the difference in size is striking, though this will be of little comfort should you have the misfortune to encounter one in the surrounding forests, which is by no means improbable. Less alarmingly, the cave is home to a large number of bats, drawn here by the relatively warm temperature of around 8°C.

First explored in 1926, the chain of 22 lakes that comprise the **Lakes and Stream Passages** (Jezerski rov), should you decide to go this far, is the undeni-able high point of a visit to Križna. Separated by calcite barriers, the lakes are fed with water from the nearby Bloke Plateau, via a number of springs in the eastern part of Lake Cerknica; groups of more than four people cannot go any further than the first lake, but smaller groups can venture to the thirteenth and most decorative of all the lakes, the **Calvary** (Kalvarija), a wonderful grotto comprising a huge mound of collapsed material and a shimmering array of stalactites and stalagmites, many of which lie submerged under water. **Visits** to the cave take place at 3pm on Sundays between May and September, and should be arranged at least two or three days in advance – visits at other times may be possible by arrangement; trips just to the dry part (including a paddle on the first lake) cost €6 per person, whereas a trip across the lakes to the Calvary (around four hours) costs €38 per person if there are two of you, €32 each if there are three, and €26 each if there are four people. All equipment (helmet, flashlight and boots) is supplied by the **cave guide**, Alojz Troha, who lives in the tiny village of Bloška Polica, at no.7 (T041/632-153, W www.krizna-jama .si), approximately 1km north of the turning off the main road towards the track which leads to the cave (it's signposted).

Snežnik Castle

Sitting in the middle of a luscious landscaped park of chestnut trees and silky lawns, some 7km south of Križna Jama and just beyond the village of **Kozarišče**, is **Snežnik Castle** (Snežnik Grad; daily: May–Aug 10am–7pm; Sept–May 10am–4pm; visits are by guided tour only, which take place on the hour; €4), a handsome, three-storey Renaissance building impressively girdled by ramparts, towers and a high grey wall.

Entered via a graceful stone-arch bridge spanning a small brook, the castle was originally the thirteenth-century domain of the Aquilean patriarchs, and their subjects the Snežniški lords, after which time it changed hands on many occasions. As a result of a court assessment in 1832 the castle was recovered from the heavily-in-debt Lichtenberg family and declared a lottery prize; however, its winner, a Hungarian blacksmith, opted for a cash prize instead, leaving the entire estate up for grabs. Snapped up by Prince Oton Schönburg at an auction in 1853, the castle remained under the ownership of the family until World War II, when it was appropriated by the state. Unlike many other castles in Slovenia during World War II, Snežnik was fortunate enough to retain most of its original nineteenth-century bourgeois furnishings and other works of art, most of which is on display in a dozen or so rooms, the pick being an exotic hoard of deities, sphinxes and pharaohs in the Egyptian Room.

Housed in one of the former dairy buildings across the way from the castle is the **Dormouse Hunting Museum** (Lovski Polharski muzej; same times; €2), where you can learn more about one of Slovenia's more unusual customs. A unique tradition in Notranjska, the dormouse (*polh*) has long been hunted for commercial purposes – its fur for caps and its fat for machine oil – though it's also something of a culinary speciality in these parts. The first Saturday after September 25, known as **Dormouse Hunting Night** (Polharska noč), is given over to a frenzied night of hunting activity. There's also a small information point located here (same times as castle). The grounds around the castle are a lovely spot for a picnic, with or without dormice.

Without your own transport getting here is awkward: the closest you can get by one of the few buses heading this way is the village of **Stari Trg**, 4km north of Kozarišče – from here there's little option but to hitch a ride or walk. The castle is also the main starting point for **hiking trails** and **cycle routes** up into the Snežnik plateau (see p.222), while those with a car can take the mountain road, which winds its way across the plateau to Ilirska Bistrica.

From Lake Cerknica to Ribnica

From Lake Cerknica the road heads eastwards across the **Bloke Plateau** – a flat, wide and largely featureless karst plateau whose abundant streams feed Lake Cerknica and Križna Cave to the southwest. The name of the plateau gave rise to one of Slovenia's most enduring cultural symbols, the **Bloke skis**; these short, fat skis, made of beech or birch wood and bound to the foot by a leather strap, were used principally as a means of transportation across the snowy plateau during winter. Valvasor, for one, was suitably impressed, proclaiming: "they descend into the valley with incredible speed...one such strip of wood is strapped under each foot, they take a stout cudgel into their hands and push it into their armpit, and use it as if it were some sort of a rudder to slide off...no less swift than those who use skates in Holland to glide on ice". Although downhill skiing as a sport all but died out here after World War I, the plateau is now a popular cross-country skiing venue.

Ribnica and around

Pitched in the centre of a lovely flat-bottomed river valley, between the pine-beech covered ridges of Velika Gora and Mala Gora some 40km south of Ljubljana, **RIBNICA** is an idyllic, diminutive town known throughout Slovenia for its woodenware, pottery and witchcraft legends. Like many other towns and villages in the Dolenjska region, Ribnica suffered mercilessly at the hands of the Turks during the fifteenth century: records recount some 27 raids in all though, ironically, it was as a result of these incursions that the town's woodenware, or *suha roba* (dry goods), industry flourished. In order to kick-start the local economy, Emperor Frederick III issued a decree allowing peddlers from Ribnica, Kočevje and surrounding areas to trade freely throughout the Austrian territories. Such was their aptitude for a good sell, however, that these indomitable characters began to trade as far afield as Africa and Asia. Ribnica is a good place to break up a journey en route to the forests of Kočevje and other attractions further south.

Pretty much everything of interest (and of a practical nature) lies along, or just off, the town's main street, **Škrabčev trg**, a fetching thoroughfare preserving a neat ensemble of grey, cream and white two-storey tenements. Running parallel to the main street is the slender Bistrica River, spanned by three exquisite stone bridges, each of which crosses over to **Ribnica Castle** on the left bank. Originally built around the tenth or eleventh century, it later assumed a Renaissance form, though all that remains now – two defensive towers linked by a residential passageway – is the result of the building having been occupied, and subsequently wrecked, during Word War II. More commonly known as the **Cultural Activists' Park**, the surrounding grounds feature busts and memorial stones of prominent local achievers such as Jakob Gallus (composer) and Stanislav Škrabec (linguist; see opposite).

Now a cultural centre, the castle holds the collection of the **Ribnica Town Museum** (May–Oct 10am–1pm & 4–7pm; €2), a hit-and-miss affair, but worth a visit to view its Woodenware Collection. This activity was traditionally split into nine or ten branches, each branch – for example, frame making, vessel making, wickerwork and sieve making – linked to a particular household, village, or type of wood (typically pine, beech or lime-tree wood). Although somewhat haphazardly arranged, there's much to admire here, from wicker baskets, drinking vessels and farm tools to less orthodox items such as mouse-traps, ski-shoes and backpacks, plus all the appliances used for making these items, every single one of which was hand-made. There's also a tidy little collection of ceramic goods from nearby Dolenja Vas, the valley's principal pottery centre. The best time to see the full array of products is at the **Ribnica Fair**, held each year on the first Sunday in September, which entails much buying and selling of wares along the main street.

The museum's other exhibitions merit just a brief look: the first documents the lives of those emigrants who left Dolenjska, mainly for North America, during the late nineteenth and early twentieth centuries in search of a more fruitful life, while the second features a group of mock-up implements and nasty-looking contraptions – gallows, spiked chairs and the like – used in the torture and killing of witches in these parts between the fifteenth and eighteenth centuries.

Back on Škrabčev trg stands the **Parish Church of St Stephen** (Cerkev Sv Štefan), the third church on this site, built in 1868. Its drab exterior was given a sharp contemporary twist shortly after World War II by Jože Plečnik (see box, p.60), who designed the crown-like steeples atop the twin bell towers – an odd, but effective, amalgamation of triangular arches, spiked cones and pillars. Originally designed for an unnamed cathedral, this was Plečnik's last ever project, though it was actually completed by one of his students after his death. Its interior stars a ceiling painting of the Holy Trinity, a couple of sculptures of St Peter and St Paul, and some terrific paintings by the likes of Langus and Koželj. If the church is closed, call in at the priest's house next door (no. 15) for the key. The **Šteklíček House**, opposite the church at no. 26, is where Slovenia's most esteemed poet, France Prešeren (see box, p.121), was schooled between 1810 and 1812.

Located 1km south of town in Hrovača (no. 42) is the enjoyable **Škrabec Homestead** (Škrabčeva Domačija; contact the tourist office to visit; €2), ancestral home of the Škrabec family for more than two centuries. Widely regarded as the country's premier nineteenth-century linguist, Stanislav Škrabec (1844–1918) published his first work in 1870 – a text on the vocal properties and dialect of Slovene literary language and writing – followed by a number of other important treatises, critiques and religious texts. Moreover, he taught several languages at a monastic school in Gorizia. The renovated house comprises the traditional setup of "black" kitchen, living room and bedroom, each room having retained its outstanding original furnishings. The thoroughly modern-looking barn, formerly used for threshing wheat and millet, displays a number of objects made from glass, clay and, of course, wood.

Practicalities

Although there is a train station at Ribnica, this line nowadays carries only freight traffic. All **buses** stop outside the church on Škrabčev trg, from where it's a two-minute walk to the **tourist office**, on the same street at no. 40 (Mon–Fri 9am–3pm; ☎01/836-9335, ⊛www.ribnica.si). The **post office** is just off Škrabčev trg at Kolodvorska ulica 2 (Mon–Fri 8am–6pm, Sat 8am–noon), and there's **internet** in the library a few paces along from the tourist office (Mon–Fri 9am–7pm, Sat 8am–1pm).

There's no **accommodation** in town, but a couple of possibilities exist just outside: 4km south of town in the village of Prigorica, *Pension Izlaty* at no. 115 (☎01/836-4515; ❸), has six boxy rooms sleeping between one and three people – breakfast is not available; buses en route to Kočevje stop 50m from the pension opposite the church. A more rural alternative is the *Boltetni* tourist farm (☎01/836-0208; ❷), located on the edge of a forest in the tiny village of Dane (no. 9) 4km west of town, and hence only really accessible if you're driving.

You'll not fare much better if looking for somewhere to **eat**, though the *Gostilna Mihelič*, opposite the church at Škrabčev trg 22 (closed Mon), can sustain you with a range of fish, grills and salads, as well as dumplings and cottage cheese dishes for vegetarians; and, in a similar vein, there's the *Pri Pildarju* at no. 27 (daily till 3pm). The oddly named *Pub Hotel* (there is no hotel), just around the corner on Kolodvorska ulica, is a surprisingly lively place, equally good for a daytime coffee or late-night beer.

Six kilometres west of Ribnica in the hamlet of **Nova Štifta**, at the foothills of Velika Gora, the **Church of the Assumption** (Vnebovzetje Device Marije) is one of Slovenia's foremost pilgrimage churches, a fine-looking Baroque structure built between 1641 and 1671 and noteworthy for its unorthodox octagonal form and unusual arcaded portico embracing the south and east facades.

Its interior, meanwhile, would ordinarily be considered unremarkable were it not for the blisteringly colourful, gold, red and green wood-carved altars, ornamented with dazzling spiral columns. Around a century after the church was built, the **Holy Steps** (Sancta Sanctorum) were constructed on the north side in order to allow greater numbers of pilgrims into the church; unless you're here for Sunday mass, the steps are usually out of bounds, though you can just catch a glimpse of them, and the frescoes lining the side walls, through the windows. Although the church is usually kept locked, there should be someone with the key in the monastery building adjacent. You really need your own transport to get here.

Kočevje and around

From Ribnica, hourly buses trundle the 16km south to **KOČEVJE**, whose first inhabitants were German settlers way back in the fourteenth century, the result of a policy of systematic colonization introduced by the then ruling Ortenburgs – the name Kočevje is actually derived from the German word Gottschee, the name of the region (and the German-language speaking, Slovene, minority) during the interwar years. Historically, Kočevska (the name of the region) has always been a sparsely populated area, the legacy of poor transportation links, a programme of mass resettlement of the majority ethnic German population towards the end of World War II, and the closure of a large part of the region for military purposes following the end of the same war – a regulation that was lifted following independence in 1991. Although the town itself is not particularly appetizing, its proximity to **Kočevski Rog**, the country's finest uninterrupted expanse of forest, and the **Kolpa Valley** on the Croatian border, means that there's a good chance you'll pass through here if either of these places are your intended destination.

As hard as it is to imagine, a castle stood on the site of the present main square, Trg Zbora Odposlancev, until as recently as World War II, when it was obliterated and its remains removed. From the **World War II monument to freedom** in the centre of this same square, it's a short walk to the enormous neo-Gothic **Parish Church of St Fabian and St Sebastian**, completed in 1903 and announced by two searing 65-metre-high spires. Inside, the bright and beautiful paintings of the Holy Trinity on the presbytery ceiling, the 24 old men of Israel underneath, and the kings and angels to the side, were executed by Slavko Pengov in 1932, while the large wooden statue of Saint Jernej next to the high altar was completed by popular local sculptor, Stane Jarm, a native of Osilnica (see p.234).

If you've got some time to pass, then head to the **Kočevje Regional Museum** (Pokrajinski Muzej Kočevje; Mon–Fri 9am–3pm; €2), a ten-minute walk east of the main square at Prešernova 11. Of particular interest – indeed of some historical importance for Slovenes – is the building itself: built in 1937, the monstrously dull **Šeškov House** (Šeškov Dom) staged the Assembly of the Delegates of the Slovene Nation in October 1943, the first elected parliament in Slovenia's history. The only remaining original feature of the hall is the heavily pockmarked bright red insignia above the stage, which reads "Narod si bo pisal Sodbo Sam" ("The people will make their own judgement"). The walls of the hall are now framed with a fine selection of sketches and drawings by Dolenjska native **Božidar Jakac**, an artist whose work you'll come across time and again in this region; completed during the sessions of the 1943 assembly, his drawings depict local landscapes, portraits and the lives of the Rog inhabitants – notably the Partisans, for whom he acted as pictorial chronicler.

The museum's core exhibition deals with the plight of the **Kočevje Germans** who, until the Italian occupation during the winter of 1941–42, had been the region's majority population for some six hundred years. The effect of the occupation was catastrophic; most of the population was relocated into homes of previously deported Slovenes in the lower Posavje region (which was then under German control), more than half of the 170 or so German-speaking settlements in the region were abandoned, demolished or renamed, while nearly one hundred churches were razed. The absence of English captioning, however, makes this part of the museum a frustrating and frankly rather dull experience.

Practicalities

The **bus station** is 200m south of the main square, Trg Zbora Odposlancev (abbreviated to TZO on signs), location for pretty much everything else of a practical nature – that said, tourist facilities here are negligible and there's no tourist office. The town's sole **hotel** is the very reasonable *Valentin* (☎01/895-1286, ⓦwww.hotel-valentin.com; ❺) in the centre of the square.

Eating possibilities are dreadfully unexciting, with options limited to a couple of pizzerias: the bright *Luigi*, just across from the bus station, or the larger but wholly characterless *Briški*, a few paces along from the *Hotel Valentin*. For a daytime or evening **drink**, the colourful and loungey *Kavarna*, on the main square, is a good spot, as is *Café Medo* a few paces away, which also has a superb choice of cakes and pastries.

Kočevski Rog

One of the country's most secluded karst landscapes, **Kočevski Rog** is a massively forested 35-kilometre-long mountain range bordering Kočevje to the east, and extending in a northwest–southeast direction (a typical Dinaric range) towards the Kolpa River and Croatian border. During World War II Kočevski Rog offered perfect sanctuary for Partisan activities, sheltering military and political offices, workshops, hospitals, printing presses and schools. The centre of operations was **Baza 20** (Base 20), which consisted of some 26 wooden shacks occupied by members of both the Central Committee of the Communist Party of Slovenia, and the Executive Committee of the Liberation Front. At the height of operations, nearly two hundred people were ensconced here.

As an attraction it can't compare with the old Franja Partisan Hospital near Cerkno (see p.181), but if you want to see inside a couple of the huts (save for some bunk beds and a small exhibition there's not much to see), contact the tourist office in Dolenjske Toplice (see p.241). Baza 20 is sited on the eastern ridge of Kočevski Rog, and is actually easier to get to from the small town of Dolenjske Toplice, at the foot of Rog, than it is from Kočevje. From Dolenjske Toplice take the road south for 1km to Podturn, then head up the mountain road to the car park, a further 7km distant; from here it's a fifteen-minute walk through the forest to Baza 20. There's also a small **restaurant** by the car park.

▲ Kočevski Rog

It was in these forests, too, that several thousand anti-communist forces – mostly members of the notorious Slovene Home Guard (Domobranci) returned by British military authorities at the war's conclusion – were summarily executed and dumped into limestone pits. The existence of these **mass graves** remained a secret until 1975, when the dissident writer and politician Edvard Kocbek revealed the grim details in an interview to a Trieste newspaper. It was only recently, however, that the victims of these "silent killings" were acknowledged, with the passing of the 2003 War Graves Act, which effectively made provision for the management and marking of burial sites at the appropriate spots.

The Kolpa Valley

The main Ljubljana–Ribnica–Kočevje road continues south towards the stunning **Kolpa Valley**, a contorted, gorge-like river valley named after the beautiful 120-kilometre-long **Kolpa River** (Kupa in Croatian), which forms the border with Croatia. For the most part, the valley remains well off the main tourist track, thanks both to the popularity of more-established destinations further north and the paucity of public transport hereabouts. This is, though, wonderful driving and cycling country, and if you have wheels or are prepared to hitch then you could do a lot worse than spend a day taking in the scenery, partaking in any number of water activities, or just resting up at one of the many delightful riverside picnic spots. Although quite different in character and temperament from the Soča River, the Kolpa, with its picturesque rapids and dams, is a big draw for adventure-sports enthusiasts, while swimmers and bathers flock to its warm waters in the summer months.

Before you reach the border, it's worth taking a minor detour to the dramatically sited ruins of the thirteenth-century **Kostel Castle**, perched atop a lofty promontory about 20km south of Kočevje, and just 6km shy of the Petrina border crossing. The castle is currently undergoing extensive renovation works (and hence, partly closed off), but you can scramble up to the entrance, a great spot from which to soak up the magnificent views. A good time to visit is at

Hiking in Kočevski Rog and the virgin forests

Kočevski Rog offers some of the best non-alpine hiking in the country and, though not especially demanding, the walks here are no less enjoyable. You'd do well, however, to stick closely to the trails; not only are you likely to get completely lost if you stray, but it's not inconceivable that you'll encounter brown bear, a large number of whom inhabit these parts – as do lynx, wolf, boar and red deer. Not surprisingly, Kočevksi Rog is a popular destination with hunters. The circular **Rog Footpath** (Roška Pešpot) – somewhat ominously marked out by bear paws – totals some 60km. While it's unlikely you'd want to tackle the whole thing as this would take around three days, you can easily do parts of it; one possibility is to drive to the highest point, **Veliki Rog** (1099m), where there's a viewing tower, and hike a section of the trail from there.

Three kilometres south of Veliki Rog is **Rajhenavski Rog**, one of Kočevski's six **virgin forests** – there are a total of fourteen in the country. The trees here are manifestly higher, thicker, and older (four- and five- hundred-year-old trees are not uncommon) than those of your average forest, while strictly administered rules forbid the cutting or removal of any trees, dead or alive; moreover, as protected and preserved areas, virgin forests are strictly off limits to the general public, though trails are laid out around the periphery. The best known of the forests' trees, and the symbol of Kočevski Rog, is the **Queen of Rog**, a magnificent fifty-metre-high, five-hundred-year-old fir sited 2km south of Rajhenavski Rog. There are beds at two **forest huts**: Luža at the northernmost point of the path (approx 16km from the start in Kočevje) and Podstene, 2km south of the Queen of Rog.

An excellent alternative to the above is the Stojna Highland south and west of town, in particular the popular trail which leads up to **Mestni Vrh** (1034m; 1hr) and the **ruins of Friedrichstein Castle** (970m), built in the early fifteenth century but abandoned around 1650. The 1:50,000 *Kočevsko* map is an essential aid if you plan to take any hikes in these forests.

the end of August, when the **Tamburanje Festival**, a showpiece for local folk bands, is staged in and around the castle's grounds.

The Upper Kolpa Valley

The valley is at its most impressive between the hamlet of **Dol** – some 26km east of the Petrina border crossing – and the village of Osilnica, 20km west of the same crossing, a stretch known as the **Upper Kolpa Valley** (Zgornja Kolpska Dolina).

Approximately 10km west of the border crossing, just beyond the village of Srobotnik (stop off at the small parking bay), a short gravel path sneaks its way up to the redundant **Church of Saint Anne** (Cerkev Sv Ana); the church is closed but the stupendous views are more than ample compensation. Back on the road, shortly after the church, the entrance to the uppermost part of the valley – **Osilnica Valley** (Osilniška Dolina) – is marked by a hulk-sized **wooden statue** of the local mythological folk hero **Peter Klepec**, whose feats of strength and daring against the Turks are the stuff of legend in these parts. A further 4km on from here, the village of **GRINTOVEC PRI OSILNICI** is the starting point for an energetic hike up to the formidable bluff of **Loška stena** (875m; 5hr).

The first building you see on entering the village of **RIBJEK**, some 2km on from Grintovec and sited almost directly beneath Loška stena, is the preposterously pretty roadside **Church of St Egidius** (Cerkev Sv Egidija), the valley's most important historical monument. Built around 1680 but substantially renovated a few years ago, this dinky Renaissance structure manifests some absorbing detail: whitewashed walls, painted window frames, shingled gable roof and portico and a flat bell tower. Its interior, meanwhile, stars a wood-coffered

Sport and activities

As far as **activities** go, there's just about everything on offer in the Kolpa valley, most of which is available at Kovač Sports (see below) between April and October – be sure to call at least a day in advance to organize. Activities include rafting, kayaking and canoeing, each costing around €20 per person for a three-hour trip; archery (€12 for 1hr) and paintballing (€20 for 3hr), while there's also an Adrenaline Park (€25 for 3hr). Guided hikes are also possible on request, and there are bikes for rent (€8 for half a day, €12 per day). If you've got your passport, you could also hike to the **source of the Kolpa** in Croatia, which should take around five hours (round trip).

ceiling and elaborately carved wooden altars dating from around the same time. If the church is locked the key can be obtained from no. 2, just a few paces away.

Osilnica

At the confluence of the Kolpa and Čabranka rivers, 3km beyond Ribjek, **OSILNICA** is the valley's largest settlement, and pretty much the end of the line as far as things to see and do are concerned. Aside from harbouring most of the valley's practical facilities, the reason you're most likely to wind up here is to have a crack at one of the many sports and activities on offer. A good time to be in the village is on the last Saturday in July (**St Peter's Day**), a day of live music, food and drink in honour of Peter Klepec.

A short walk uphill from the tourist office, at no. 19, is the **Stane Jarm Gallery**, named after the sculptor who was born here in 1931. He used wood as his principal medium (see also his dramatic sculpture of Saint Jernej in the Parish Church in Kočevje, p.230), and the small gallery is chock-full of the master sculptor's haunting, rigidly cut faces.

The helpful little **tourist office** (which you should contact if you wish to visit the gallery) is located on the small main square at no. 16 (Mon–Fri 8am–3pm; ☎01/894-1594, ⓦwww.osilnica.si); if it's closed, pop across the road to the municipal building (Občina), where someone will be able to help. While here, it's quite likely that you'll end up at Kovač Tourism and Sports, a large family-run affair five minutes' walk away at Sela 5 (☎01/894-1508, ⓦwww.kovac-kolpa .com), as this is virtually where everything in the village happens. They also run a lovely and very comfortable **hotel** (❺), and **apartments** sleeping between four and six people (❹–❺) – there's a tidy little **campsite** here too. The classy **restaurant** offers superb home-style cooking and the terrace is a splendid place to eat in the summer months.

Eastern Dolenjska

The eastern half of Dolenjska holds the majority of its sights. These are by and large ranged along the **Krka River**, which emanates from a cave near the village of the same name and flows eastwards towards the Croatian border, joining up with the mighty Sava River near Brežice. Approximately midway between Ljubljana and the beginning of the Krka, both **Stična Monastery** and **Bogenšperk Castle** are well worth visiting.

From its source, the Krka continues east towards the ruins of **Žužemberk Castle** and **Soteska Manor**, before turning north just prior to the atmospheric little spa town of **Dolenjske Toplice**. A little further on, **Novo Mesto** hoves into view; comfortably southern Slovenia's largest town, it merits a leisurely half-day visit. East of Novo Mesto, the river continues past the beautifully set **Otočec Castle**, and the delightfully slumberous town of **Kostanjevica na Krki**, itself close to another of Slovenia's ancient monasteries, **Pleterje**. The region's easternmost attractions are the small market town of **Brežice**, and the country's largest spa centre in **Čatež**.

Stična Monastery

Some thirty kilometres southeast of Ljubljana, just off the Ljubljana–Novo Mesto highway near the village of **Ivančna Gorica**, stands **Stična Monastery** (Cistercijanski Samostan Stična). Slovenia's oldest monastery, it was established in 1136 as part of the European network of Cistercian monasteries. Within a few years of its foundation Stična had assumed the role of Dolenjska's chief centre of culture and learning, with several important religious manuscripts having been drawn up in the monastery's scriptorium; these are now kept at the NUK library in Ljubljana and the Austrian National Library in Vienna.

The thick walls and towers you see today were erected as a result of repeated Turkish raids during the fifteenth century, a period of otherwise relative prosperity for Stična. Dissolved by Emperor Joseph II in 1784 as part of his sweeping reforms, the monastery remained defunct until 1898, at which point it was revived by Cistercians from the monastery at Bodensee (Lake Constance). It is currently home to eleven monks (including the abbot), and while not as asocial as Pleterje Monastery (see p.246), the monks at Stična remain strictly governed by the motto of Saint Benedict, "*Ora et labora*" ("Pray and Work"), and so must devote themselves to between six and eight hours of prayer each day, and all meals are taken in complete silence. A visit to Stična entails a **guided tour** (Tues–Sat 8.30am, 10am, 2pm & 4pm, Sun 2pm & 4pm; €5) of the monastery's religious museum, the church and cloister.

The nearest **train station** is in Ivančna Gorica (on the Ljubljana–Novo Mesto line), about 2.5km south of the monastery, while buses can set you down on the highway running parallel to the rail track. If you need to stay, there's **accommodation** at the homely *Grofija* tourist farm, about 1.5km southeast of the monastery in the village of Vir pri Stični, at no. 30 (☎01/787-8141, ⓦwww .grofija.com; ❷).

The Slovene Religious Museum

On the north side of the courtyard (to the right as you enter), the two-storeyed, Renaissance-era **Old Prelature**, formerly the monastery's administrative centre, now houses the **Slovene Religious Museum**; its first floor is a treasure-trove of monastic riches – antique furniture, liturgical vessels, vestments and so on – while the second floor (entitled Christianity in Slovenia) chronicles the many disparate groups and movements that have shaped the development of the Slovene Church throughout the centuries, including Protestants, Jesuits, Capuchins and Ursulines. The museum's impressive art and cultural history section has fresco remains by the renowned fifteenth-century artist Janez Ljubljanski, paintings by Langus and Metzinger, and a typically exuberant chalice designed by architect Jože Plečnik as a gift for Simon Ašič, a former abbot who also happened to be one of Slovenia's most eminent herbalists; you can purchase some of his medicinal herbs and teas from the shop by the entrance.

The Abbey Church and Cloister

Adjacent to the Prelature, the twelfth-century **Abbey Church** betrays few signs of its Romanesque origins, having been extensively reworked in Baroque style during the seventeenth and eighteenth centuries. Its vast, white tripartite nave is fairly naked, save for a larger than usual number of side altars – one for each priest to pray to – although there are some fine artistic treasures to admire, most notably the fourteen Stations of the Cross painted by Fortunat Bregant in 1766; a marble tabernacle by Plečnik; and some beautifully worked tombstones – look out for the red stone tombstone of Abbot Jacob Reinprecht, the chief architect of the church's present Baroque appearance.

Abutting the church at the heart of the complex is the thirteenth-century Gothic **cloister**, a splendid rib-vaulted space complete with lancet windows and several layers of just about discernible frescoes, the best of which are those by master painter Janez Ljubljanski in the north wing. Elsewhere, look out for the figural keystones in the western wing depicting human faces, and the two superbly restored bifora (double-arched windows), the cloister's most obvious Romanesque remains. On the south side of the cloister, the **refectory**'s pink vaulted ceiling is decorated with some marvellous stuccowork (it's forbidden to enter, but you can see it from the doorway), as is the ceiling of the **Upper Tower**, located on the opposite side of the Prelature; the compositions on the latter depict scenes from the Crucifixion and Last Judgement, as well as images of the four Church Fathers.

Bogenšperk Castle

Surrounded by the densely forested Dolenjska hills some 20km north of Stična, close to the large village of Šmartno pri Litiji, **Bogenšperk Castle** (April–Oct Tues–Sat 10am–5pm, Sun 10am–6pm; March & Nov Sat & Sun 10am–5pm; €3.50) is a descendant of a twelfth-century medieval fortification, though the present structure dates from around 1511. Built by the lords of Wagen (Wagensperg is German for Bogenšperk), the castle is synonymous with the great polymath Janez Vajkard Valvasor (see box opposite), who lived and worked here between 1672 and 1692, during which time he compiled his immense opus *The Glory of the Duchy of Carniola*.

The building is a classic Renaissance-era chateau featuring three cylindrical towers and a partly arcaded inner courtyard. The interior, meanwhile, has been refurbished – the castle's entire contents were plundered at the end of World War II – so as to evoke the atmosphere of Valvasor's day. His **library** is now used as a wedding venue, while the old hunting room contains an odd, and rather mundane, mishmash of exhibits: hunting trophies, geological and folk-costume displays, as well as an exposition on seventeenth-century witch trials, a subject Valvasor wrote about in his aforementioned work. Of greater interest are the two rooms packed with fascinating maps and sketches, including original works by Valvasor and eminent Slovene cartographer Peter Kosler, and a cylinder printing press of the type Valvasor used – the original is in Mainz, Germany. Valvasor's **study** contains the museum's principal exhibit, an original copy of *The Glory of the Duchy of Carniola*.

Bogenšperk is not the easiest place to get to; if you're coming from Ivančna Gorica, you'll have to get here under your own steam, be it by bike or car. By **public transport** you must take a bus or train from Ljubljana as far as Litija, though from here it's still another 6km slog uphill to the castle.

Janez Vajkard Valvasor

Arguably Slovenia's greatest scholar, **Janez Vajkard Valvasor** – historian, topographer and ethnologist – was born in Ljubljana in 1641 of a noble family from Bergamo in Italy. Following extensive travels throughout Europe and North Africa, Valvasor purchased Bogenšperk in 1672, assembling a rich library and establishing important graphics and printing workshops within the castle. Having devoted his entire life to research, he spent the next fifteen years compiling and writing his monumental baroque topography *The Glory of the Duchy of Carniola*, four illustrated encyclopaedic volumes weighing in at 3532 pages. In it, Valvasor offered the first thoroughgoing presentation of the then province of Carniola, as well as several neighbouring provinces, expounding on the region's extraordinary natural phenomena, such as the caves at Postojna and Škocjan, and the disappearing Lake Cerknica, as well as extolling the virtues of the people who shaped these lands. Following the book's publication, Valvasor lectured to the Royal Society in London on the miraculous workings of the lake, an occasion that saw him rewarded with a fellowship from the society. However, such was the debt accumulated by Valvasor during the process of compiling and publishing the book, that he was eventually forced to sell the castle and all its contents. He died, destitute, in the town of Krško in 1693.

Trebnje

Back on the main Ljubljana–Zagreb E70 highway, 18km east of Stična (it's also on the Ljubljana–Novo Mesto rail line), it's worth stopping off at the small town of **TREBNJE** to visit the **Gallery of Naïve Artists** (Galerija Likovnih Samorastnikov; Mon–Fri 10am–noon & 3–6pm, Sat 10am–2pm 3pm; €3), the only museum of its kind in the country. Modelled on the famous Hlebine school in northern Croatia, the gallery presents an outstanding collection of naïve art principally from Slovenia and other countries of the former Yugoslavia, but also from Africa, Asia and Latin America. The origins of self-taught painting in Slovenia can be traced back to the popular nineteenth-century folk art of beehive panel painting (see box, p.109), itself believed to have derived from the widely practised discipline of painting farm furniture and glass. These wonderfully authentic expressions of indigenous peasant culture later manifest themselves in the colourful world of the naïve painters during the 1930s and 1940s.

The pictures here – painted on wood, canvas or glass – are typically fresh and vibrant, occasionally kitsch or sometimes just plain bizarre, but in nearly all cases touch on themes pertaining to everyday village life; there are also some wonderfully bucolic landscape paintings, such as *Eve* by the Bosnian Sekula Dugandič, and *Two Blooms*, by eminent Croatian village painter Ivan Rabuzin. Works by Slovenian artists to look out for include scenes from the Kurent by Boris Žohar, and several portraits by Irena Polanec. If you're here at the end of June there's a week-long festival starring international artists working live inside the gallery.

The museum is in the centre of town on Goliev trg – from the **train station** on Kolodvorska ulica, walk up to the main road, turn left and continue for some 150 metres. The **bus station** is next to the church, which is opposite the museum, as is the small **tourist office** (Mon–Fri 9am–3pm; ☏07/304-4717, ⓦwww.trebnje.si). A simple but decent place to **eat** here is *Gostilna Šeligo* (closed Sun), 150m back down from the tourist office on the corner of Kolodvorska ulica and Goliev trg. If you're looking to **stay** hereabouts, there's the classy *Gostilna Rakar* (☏07/346-6190, ⓦwww.rakar.si; ❻),

3km southeast of town in the village of Gorenje Ponikve, at no. 8; it offers a dozen or so very tidy rooms as well as a handsome restaurant (closed Tues).

The Krka River Valley

The **Krka River Valley** is one of the country's most picturesque valley regions, yet it's little visited by tourists, many of whom inadvertently bypass it travelling on the main road or rail routes just to the north. The valley's defining feature is its wide, languid river, richly stocked with brown trout, pikeperch and grayling; issuing forth from a spring in the Krka Cave, it continues beyond the valley's lower reaches to Novo Mesto, and then onwards to Brežice where it discharges into the Sava River. The Krka is also known for its attractive calc-tufa falls and rapids, step-like waterfalls composed of porous rock formed from calcium carbonate, which you can see at regular intervals along the entire stretch of the river. Natural attractions aside, there's much of historical importance to see within the valley, including castle remains at **Žužemberk** and **Soteska**, the village of **Muljava** – birthplace of one of Slovenia's great writers – and, at the tail end of the valley, the quaint spa town, **Dolenjske Toplice**.

Muljava and the source of the Krka

Due south of Ivančna Gorica, on the other side of the highway, **MULJAVA** is an attractive little village known throughout the country as the birthplace of popular Slovene novelist and journalist Josip Jurčič (1844–81), the man credited with writing Slovenia's first full-length novel *Deseti Brat* (*The Tenth Brother*), in 1866. The house in which he was born (Jurčičeva Domačija; Tues–Sat 9am–noon & 2–5pm, Sun 2–5pm; €3), and lived in until the age of 12, was built by his grandfather in 1826 and is as interesting for its architectural detail – a traditional "black" kitchen, living room, bedroom and cellar – as it is for the memorabilia on display pertaining to Jurčič's life. In the garden stands a beehive, furnished with the traditional painted panels, while to the rear of the house there's a granary and a Krjavelj Hut, a timber shack dwelling usually inhabited by a *bajtar* – a poor villager. The house, at no. 11, is signposted from the main square.

Each year, on two or three consecutive weekends at the end of June/beginning of July several of Jurčič's works are staged in the fabulous natural amphitheatre at the edge of woodland behind the house; tickets (around €8) can be purchased one hour before each performance. Muljava also marks the starting point for the very scenic and very popular **Jurčičeva Pot walk**; the walk (3–4hr) winds up at the lovely little medieval settlement of Višnja Gora (550m) some 15km further north.

One section of the walk takes in the village of **Krka**, 2km south of Muljava, and the **source of the Krka River** (Pri Izviru), another 2km further on. The source (a seventeen-metre-deep siphon lake) is actually located inside the small, two-hundred-metre-long **Krka Cave** (Krška jama), an unexciting spectacle which does, however, hold a specimen of Proteus Anguinus (the Human Fish – see the Subterranean Slovenia colour section). To visit, head to the kiosk located 200m before the entrance, from where you will be escorted to the cave and given a short guided tour; although opening times can be erratic, the cave is usually open daily between 9am and 6pm (4 or 5pm in winter), but it's best to call in advance to make sure (☎041/276-252; €2).

Žužemberk Castle and Soteska Manor

The valley's major settlement is the market town of **ŽUŽEMBERK**, which is dominated by the formidable bulk of **Žužemberk Castle** (July & Aug Fri 9am–7pm, Sat & Sun 10am–6pm; free), much of which was razed during World War II; although a programme of renovation has been ongoing for years, the restoration of the five huge towers and bastions aside, you'd hardly notice. Dramatically sited on a steep bank high above the Krka River and buffered by a thick clump of trees which slope down to the water, the original castle dates from the thirteenth century, with piecemeal development over the ensuing centuries, including the aforementioned towers, as well as defensive walls, arcades and vaulted cellars, most of which you can still see.

Today, the castle's large inner courtyard is the atmospheric venue for summer concerts and plays, all of which are usually free; the key event is the **Market Town Days Festival** (Trški dnevni) in mid-July, a weekend of medieval jousting, exhibitions, food and craft stalls and the like. To find out what else is on, contact the municipal building (Občina) opposite the castle at Grajska trg 33 (Mon–Fri 8am–4pm; ☎07/388-5180, ✉obcina.zuzemberk@zuzemberk.si). In the centre of this main square is a fine little cast-iron fountain, forged at the ironworks in the nearby village of Dvor and worth a look for its splendidly crafted animal heads, which still spout water. For the best views of the castle, walk down to the river and across to the opposite bank; standing on the bridge gives you head-on views of the calc-tufa falls. The town's position on the Krka allowed for the extensive development of water-powered installations during the sixteenth and seventeenth centuries, most commonly iron foundries and sawmills. At one stage there were around forty of the latter lining this stretch of river, though by the end of the twentieth century most had ceased functioning. The Zajčev Mill, located a little way upstream near Prapreče, is the only mill still in operation

▲ Žužemberk Castle

and can be visited if you contact the municipal building (see p.239). The Krka River is also popular with watersports enthusiasts; canoes and kayaks (€4 per hour) can be rented from the *Koren* tourist farm, down by the river at Dolga Vas 5 (℡07/308-7260, ⓦwww.turizem-koren.com; ❸) – they also have one- to five-bed **rooms** and camping space, and offer solid home-cooked food. Delicious river fish is also served up at the *Gostilna Zupančič*, Grajski trg 5, whose terrace overlooks the river.

Some 9km downriver from Žužemberk are the less complete ruins of **Soteska Manor** (Dvorec Soteska), built between 1664 and 1689 by Duke Jurij Gallenberg but which, for the greater part of its existence, was the domicile of the Auersperg counts. Today, a fairly unbroken outer shell incorporating two of the four original corner towers and the entrance gate are all that remain of the manor following its destruction in 1943 by Partisan units, an act of deliberate sabotage carried out in order to prevent German troops from appropriating it.

From the former entrance to the manor, a path cuts across the main road towards a field (formerly a walled-in park), in the centre of which stands the park pavilion, otherwise known as the **Devils Tower** (Hudičev turn); its empty interior is illuminated with murals of mythological figures, pillared architecture and other fantastical compositions painted by the Almanach workshop in the seventeenth century. Before the manor's destruction, the path was lined with three stone portals, one of which – and it's a particularly fine piece of craftsmanship – now marks the entrance to the field. If you wish to see inside the tower, contact the tourist office in Dolenjske Toplice (see opposite).

Dolenjske Toplice

Just where the river turns sharply in the direction of Novo Mesto is **DOLENJSKE TOPLICE**, a classic, neat and orderly spa town, whose elegant Habsburg-era buildings give it an authentic *fin-de-siècle* ambience. Exploited since medieval times for curative purposes, the town's springs were first channelled into a bathhouse by Ivan Vajkard, a member of the Auersperg family, in the seventeenth century, although it wasn't until the late nineteenth century that Dolenjske Toplice (then called Strascha Toplitz) prospered as a fashionable, modern spa resort, utilized to treat a wide range of disorders and illnesses. During both World Wars the resort was pressed into action as an emergency military treatment centre and hospital.

The town's main **thermal pools** are part of the super-modern Balnea Wellness Centre (daily 9am–9pm, Fri & Sat till 11pm; weekdays €8 for 3hr, €10 day & weekends €10 for 3hr, €13 day), which has both indoor and outdoor (May–Sept) thermal pools, complete with water massages, water-walls and geysers, as well as an array of saunas and baths. Elsewhere, the modern complex inside the *Vital* hotel (see opposite) houses three pools (weekdays €9 for three hours, €10 day & weekends €10 for 3hr, €12 day) – all these pools are free to hotel guests. If you fancy doing something a little more energetic than wallowing, pop into the K2M agency, just across the road from the tourist office at Pionirska cesta 3 (Mon–Fri 9am–4pm, Sat 9am–1pm; ℡07/306-6830, ⓔinfo@k2m.si); they organize rafting (€20 per person for 2hr 30min) and kayaking (€30 per person for 3hr) on the Krka, and you can also rent canoes (€14 per hour, €20 for 3hr) and bikes (€5 per hour, €14 per day).

Practicalities

Buses stop off along Zdraviliški trg, the town's main street and from where nothing is more than a ten-minute walk away. From the bus stop it's a short walk beyond the *Kristal* hotel and across the bridge to the **tourist office** at Sokolski trg 4 (June–Aug Mon–Fri 9am–6pm, Sat 9am–3pm, Sun 9am–noon; Sept–May Mon–Fri 9am–3pm, Sat & Sun 9am–noon; ☎07/384-5188, ⓦwww .dolenjske-toplice.si), which has free **internet**, and the **post office** at no. 3 (Mon–Fri 8–9.30am & 10am–5pm, Sat 8am–noon).

Clustered around Zdravilíski trg's southern, square-like space are the town's three spa **hotels** (all ☎07/391-9400, ⓦwww.terme-krka.si); by far the most superior is the wood- and glass-panelled *Balnea* (⑨), whose rooms are as luxurious as they come; appreciably less appealing, though not that much cheaper, are the lime-green *Kristal* (❽) and, opposite, the pink coloured *Vital* (❽) hotels.

There's much cheaper accommodation at the *Gostišče Račka* (☎07/306-5510, ⓦwww.gostisce-racka.si; ❹), 200m east of Zdravilíski trg at Ulica Maksa Henigmana 15, which has a handful of perfectly decent rooms plus a couple of apartments. Alternatively, take your pick from one of the many private rooms (❷) advertised throughout town; either the tourist office or the K2M agency can help out if you're struggling to find a place. The town's small **campsite** is nicely located at the northern end of Zdravilíski trg, at the foot of the wooded slopes by the Sušica stream (☎07/391-9400; May–Sept – reception is at the *Balnea* hotel).

The town's main **restaurant** is the vaguely countrified *Gostilna Rog* at Zdravilíski trg 22 (closed Mon), beyond which there are a cluster of informal places to eat and drink just across the bridge: the lodge-like *Lovec* is a decent pizzeria, as is *Ošterija* a bit further down – its shaded little courtyard does the job for a beer, as does the *Illy Pub*, opposite, which is a more heads-down drinking venue. For a better class of coffee, and cake, pop into the shiny café inside the *Balnea* hotel.

Novo Mesto

As Dolenjska's cultural and religious centre since the Middle Ages, **NOVO MESTO** (New Town) is easily the largest town in southeastern Slovenia. Continuously settled since the Bronze Age – as attested to by the numerous archeological sites hereabouts – Novo Mesto was granted city rights in 1365, thereafter evolving into a prosperous market town and trade centre and, following the establishment of a collegiate chapter around the same time, a centre of ecclesiastical importance too. In recent times, Novo Mesto has established itself as one of the country's leading industrial heartlands, home to the major pharmaceutical enterprise Krka, and the highly productive vehicle manufacturer Revoz (a subsidiary of Renault), formerly the largest plant in Yugoslavia.

The town's sights are few, but its personable old core, attractively sited on a rocky promontory in a hairpin bend of the Krka River, does possess a couple of noteworthy monuments, while its museum keeps a first-rate collection of archeological treasures; moreover, it's handy as a springboard for the many attractions – rivers, castles, spas and monasteries – close at hand.

Most of the out-of-town sights are situated along the E216 (west from Novo Mesto) and E419 (east from Novo Mesto) roads, both of which run south of and parallel to the main E70 Ljubljana–Zagreb highway. However, without your own transport, you will have to rely on a modest bus service. The rail line from Ljubljana follows the same course as the highway, although only as far as Novo Mesto, before continuing south into Bela Krajina.

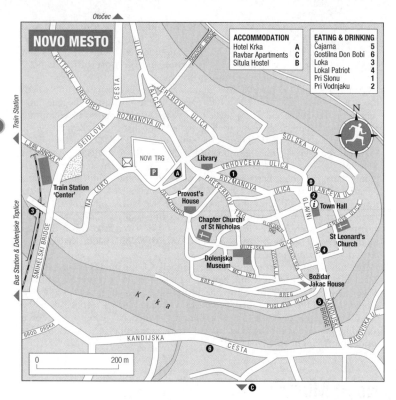

Arrival, information and accommodation

The **bus station** is on Topliška Cesta, a ten-minute walk southwest of the town centre, and there are two **train stations** – the main one, Novo Mesto, is 800m west of town on Ljubljanska cesta; the second one, Center, is on the north side of Šmihelski bridge, just five minutes' walk into town; all trains stop at both stations, so alight at Center. The **tourist office** is next to the town. All at Glavni trg 6 (June–Sept Mon–Fri 9am–7pm, Sat 9am–4pm, Sun 9am–noon; Oct–May Mon–Fri 9am–6pm, Sat 9am–2pm; ℡07/393-9263, ⊛www.novomesto.si). The **post office** (Mon–Fri 8am–7pm, Sat 8am–1pm) is on Novi trg, and there's free **internet** at the library, Rozmanova ulica 26 (Mon–Fri 8am–7pm, Sat 8am–1pm).

Located in the heart of the Old Town, the *Situla* **hostel**, at Dilančeva 1 (℡07/394-2000, ⊛www.situla.si), is a fabulously conceived place; with a nod to the town's archeological heritage, this artfully designed outfit has three- to eight-bed dorms (€17–19), as well as a single (€25), double (€22) and family room (€60) – it also has canoes for rent, a very respectable restaurant and wine cellar. A decent alternative is the family-run *Ravbar Apartments* (℡07/373-0680, ⊛www.ravbar.net), a fifteen-minute walk east of the bus station at Smrečnikova ulica 15–17, which has eight apartments sleeping two to six people (④–⑥) and a couple of rooms (④), all of which are large, modern and immaculately kept. The town's sole **hotel**, meanwhile, is the business-like, and hence outrageously expensive, *Krka* on Novi trg (℡07/394-2100, ⊛www.terme-krka.si; ⑨).

The Town

Most things of a practical nature are in or around modern and charmless **Novi trg**, while the city's main sights – the **Chapter Church**, **Franciscan Church** and **Town Museum** – are a short walk east in the pleasantly compact Old Town.

Chapter Church and Dolenjska Museum

Commanding the summit of Kapiteljski hrib, a five-minute walk from Novi trg up Dalmatinova and then Kapiteljska Ulica, the **Chapter Church of St Nicholas** (Cerkev sv Miklavza) is the town's oldest monument. Encompassing a chequered mix of Gothic, neo-Gothic and Baroque elements, the most striking thing about the church is its fifteenth-century presbytery, constructed at a peculiar seventeen-degree angle to the nave. Inside, the church has some outstanding works of art, most notably the high-altar painting *St Nicholas* by Tintoretto, one of the country's most celebrated church paintings and, allegedly, one of only two of the Venetian master's works in Slovenia. Elsewhere, look out for the copy of *Maria Pomagaj* (*Mary Help*) in the first altar on the left and several works by Metzinger adorning other altars. To the right of the presbytery a flight of steps leads down to a chilly, Gothic-vaulted **crypt**, the only one of its kind in the country and somewhat unusual in that there's actually no one buried here as it was built rather as a support for the presbytery which was constructed on a slight down slope. The crypt is usually locked, but if you want to have a look try calling at the provost's house just across from the church.

Housed in a complex of several buildings a short walk down from the church at Muzejska ulica 7, the **Dolenjska Museum** (Dolenjski muzej; Tues–Sat 9am–5pm, Sun 9am–1pm; €5) keeps one of the finest stockpiles of archeological treasures in Slovenia. The core of the collection comprises grave finds unearthed from hundreds of burial sites on the slopes of Marof and Mestne njive, two modest rises located a short way north of the town centre. The earliest artefacts, from the late Bronze Age (the so-called Urnfield culture), comprise a superb display of large ceramic urns, into which the remains of the deceased, together with their personal belongings – bronze needles, jewellery, beads and the like – were placed.

The **Hallstatt** period (the early Iron or late Bronze Age, approximately 8th–4th BC) is represented by more vessels and jewellery, including earrings, bracelets and anklets, as well as several pieces of armour – the star exhibits are a beautifully well-preserved Bronze Age helmet and breast plate. The most impressive items, however, are the specimens of **Situla Art**, bronze buckets, or pails, ornately embossed with festive or hunting scenes, a collection which represents the greatest achievement in prehistoric art in Slovenia. The larger grave urns from the Celtic period were somewhat more sophisticated, suggesting that the deceased were from a higher social rank. Rounding off this veritable treasure trove is a hoard of Roman grave goods, typically cups, coins, wine pitchers and oil lamps, as well as a stash of Roman legionary weapons. The remainder of the museum, comprising ethnological and modern history collections is, by comparison, distinctly underwhelming.

Glavni trg and around

From the museum a number of narrow alleyways descend through town to cobbled **Glavni trg** (Main Square). Actually more street than square, this is the city's focal point, once the haunt of merchants and craftsmen but today profiled with two rows of handsome town houses, shops and cafés. The square's most striking feature is its elegant arcades, although its most prominent building, located midway down the left-hand side at no. 6, is the grey, mock-Renaissance **Town Hall** (Rotovž), built in 1905.

Lurking just behind the Town Hall on Frančišk trg (accessed via Jenkova ulica) stands **St Leonard's Franciscan Church** (Frančiškanska cerkev sv Lenarta), whose elegant, mustard-coloured neo-Gothic gabled facade dating from around 1880 was just one of the church's many piecemeal additions following a fire in 1664. From the original church, built in 1472 as a place of refuge for Franciscan monks from Bosnia (who had initially sheltered at the Tri Fare Parish in Metlika, see p.259), only the Gothic presbytery was retained, although its wooden altars were lost and replaced with the current neo-Gothic editions. The adjoining **monastery** boasts a fine library with some superb manuscripts, a tiny prayer book from 1450, and a psalm book made from animal skin and featuring Gothic and Baroque text dating from 1418 (visits to the monastery are possible by prior arrangement only; contact the tourist office).

At the square's southern end, just above the picturesque **Breg** embankment (turn right just before the bridge), the **Božidar Jakac House** (Jačkev Dom; Tues–Sat 9am–5pm, and last Sunday in the month 9am–1pm; €3) holds the eponymous artist's largest collection of sketches and drawings outside Kostanjevica (see p.247); there's also a terrific selection of watercolours and oils depicting town scenes and local landscapes. Formerly a hotel, this building was actually the house of his father – Jakac was born 100m further up the street at Cvelbarjeva ulica 9. Crossing the **Kandijski Bridge** (Kandijski Most) gives you some lovely views back to Breg and the bright orange-tiled rooftops of the Old Town.

Eating, drinking and entertainment

The town is somewhat lacking in decent places to **eat**, although *Loka*, a good-looking restaurant down by the river (under the Šmihelski Bridge), does offer a classy Slovene and international menu – there's a terrific outdoor terrace in the summer. Otherwise there's the cosy, cellar-like cavern *Gostilna Don Bobi*, out on the busy main road Kandijska cesta (no. 14), which knocks up steaming plates of pastas; or the sleek-looking restaurant in the *Situla* hostel, whose lunchtime *malica* (€6) is worth dropping by for.

Similarly, exciting **drinking** venues are few and far between, though there is a cluster of places at the northern end of Glavni trg, notably the pubby *Pri Vodnjaku*, and the café inside the *Situla* hostel, which has wi-fi. A short walk away, at Rozmanova ulica 22, the old-style café, *Pri Slonu* (At the Elephant), is an enjoyable venue, as is *Čajarna*, a sweet little teahouse down by the Kandijski bridge. Midway along Glavni trg, the enterprising student club *Lokal Patriot* offers a varied mix of club nights, film showings and rock and jazz concerts, occasionally starring some of Slovenia's top acts.

Otočec Castle

Picturesquely sited on an elongated, tree-covered island in the middle of another attractive stretch of the Krka river, 7km east of Novo Mesto, is **Otočec Castle**. Surrounded by dozens of tiny islets and the Krka's distinctive calc-tufa falls, the country's only island castle was originally occupied by the knights of Otočec during the thirteenth century, thereafter passing through the hands of various noble families. Fortified with high walls and four chunky towers during persistent fifteenth-century Turkish raids, the castle was purchased in 1560 by Ivan Lenkovič, commander of the Austrian Empire's Vojna Krajina region, during which time it acquired its present, largely Renaissance appearance, albeit heavily renovated following extensive World War II damage.

The castle now functions as the five-star *Hotel Grad Otočec* (☎07/384-8900, Ⓦwww.terme-krka.si; ❾), whose apartment-style rooms are fitted out in

Cviček

While in Novo Mesto, it would be remiss not to try the local speciality, **Cviček** (pronounced tsveechek), one of the country's most distinctive and unusual wines. Cultivated only here in southeast Dolenjska, Cviček is produced from a blend of red and white grapes – said to be more than a dozen, but this is considered an exaggeration – giving it a cranberry-juice-like appearance. Despite its dry, rather sour taste, it's a surprisingly refreshing wine, made all the more drinkable thanks to its low alcoholic content of around nine percent. Although most Cviček is produced for home consumption, it's the first drink you'll be offered in the local restaurants and bars. The wine is also given due prominence in the **Cviček Week** festival at the end of May.

faux-Gothic furniture and enormous bathrooms with oversized baths. The hotel's elegant and, inevitably, pricey **restaurant** offers some wonderfully creative dishes, though its fish (red trout, pikeperch, smoked swordfish) is the best reason to come. If your wallet can't stretch to a meal, then settle for a coffee in the courtyard café.

There's more accommodation back across the main road (under the bridge on the other side of the highway) in the shape of the *Hotel Šport* (same contact details as the *Grad Otočec*; ❼), whose bland exterior belies some good-looking and comfortable rooms; they've also got cheaper, en-suite bungalows (❺) opposite. Guests of both hotels receive complimentary use of the thermal pools in Šmarješke Toplice (see below), and there's an adjoining **tennis centre** with indoor and outdoor courts (€24 & €8 per hour respectively). The small and very basic **campsite** (☎040/466-589; April to mid-Oct) is located a few hundred metres east of the castle on the river's south bank. Just uphill from here is the superb eighteen-hole Otočec **golf course** (☎07/307-5627; 18 holes €45 or €50 at weekends, 9 holes €25 or €30 at weekends; March–Oct).

There's a smattering of other accommodation hereabouts, the best of which is the fabulous ⚑ *Šeruga* **tourist farm**, secreted away in an isolated wooded area some 3km south of Otočec (just off the main road to Kostanjevica) at Sela pri Ratežu 15 (☎07/334-6900, ⓦwww.seruga.si; ❻); its ten homely, yet modern, rooms are complemented by exceptional home cooking and local wines. Back on the main road, 2km further east at Ratež 48, the roadside inn *Gostilna Vovko* also has a handful of good-value rooms (☎07/308-5603; ❹), but if you're heading this way anyway don't pass up the opportunity to try out its terrific **restaurant** (Tues–Sat 10am–10pm, Sun 11am–4pm), which specializes in barbecued meats and Slovene dishes such as buckwheat, *žljikrofi* and *štruklji*.

During the last weekend in June or the first weekend in July, Otočec is awoken from its slumber by the **Rock Otočec Festival** (ⓦwww.rock-otocec.com), the country's largest rock festival featuring the biggest names from Slovenia and the ex-Yugoslav republics, as well as the odd big name international outfit.

Šmarješke Toplice

From Otočec, five daily buses (Mon–Fri) make the short trip to **ŠMARJEŠKE TOPLICE** some 5km to the northeast. Although far smaller and more low-key than Dolenjske Toplice (see p.240), Šmarješke Toplice has been a spa centre of sorts since the eighteenth century, only developing into a serious resort after World War II, when it served the needs of ailing Communist Party members. Located a short way north of the village, the complex now counts five thermal pools – two indoor (€10 for the day, €8.50 for 3hr) and three outdoor (€8.50 for the day, €7 for 3hr), all averaging 32°C. Even if you don't plan on taking a dip, the forest-fringed park is a lovely place for a gentle stroll or a picnic.

Accommodation comes in the form of three inter-connected hotels (☎07/384-3400, ⓦwww.terme-krka.si; all ❾), the most upmarket of which is the *Vitarium*, with huge, immaculately furnished rooms and heated bathroom floors, while the *Šmarjeta* and *Toplice* are both clinical and characterless. Although the hotels are primarily concerned with serious therapy treatments, they also offer all manner of health and fitness facilities. In addition to the regular pools (free of charge to hotel guests) there are steam baths, saunas and massage pools. A much cheaper alternative is the *Domen Pension*, located 1.5km back down the road towards Otočec at Družinska Vas 1 (☎07/307-3051; ❸), and there's very good home cooking in the adjoining *Pri Jovotu* restaurant.

Pleterje Monastery and Skansen

Beautifully set in a secluded valley at the foot of the Gorjanci forests, **Pleterje Monastery** is Europe's easternmost Carthusian monastery, and the only one of Slovenia's four charterhouses still functioning. Shut off from the outside world by a formidable 2600-metre-long, three-metre-high enclosure wall, the monastery has endured a chequered history, one not that dissimilar to that of Stična (see p.235). Founded in 1407 by Count Herman II of Celje, Pleterje was fortified during the fifteenth century in advance of Turkish raids, before its dissolution and subsequent appropriation by the Jesuits at the end of the sixteenth century. Following the reforms of Emperor Joseph II, the monastery was disbanded again in 1784, only to be repurchased and rebuilt by the Carthusian order in 1899.

While the main church is open to visitors, the rest of the monastery is strictly out of bounds. Rooted in the anchorite traditions of Early Christianity, the fourteen Pleterje's monks here live according to a precisely defined schedule, completely devoted to prayer and work. While here, make time to visit the **Skansen** (see below), located just down from the monastery.

Church of the Holy Trinity

Rated as one of the best-preserved examples of early French Gothic in Central Europe, the single-nave **Church of the Holy Trinity** (built in 1420) is astonishingly simple and, though almost completely devoid of furniture or ornamentation, has some wonderfully subtle detail. Entering through the low, stone rood screen which separates the nave and chancel, have a look up at the splendid cross rib-vaulted ceiling, embellished with numerous bosses bearing a range of motifs, and the seventy or so clay vessels (also known as acoustical pottery) spotted along the walls. You can't really miss the high altar, a smooth slab of grey stone placed on two stone stools. On the exterior the badly pockmarked wall was the result of heavy shelling during World War II.

You can learn more about the Carthusian order by watching the informative, 25-minute **presentation** set up in the sacristy to the side of the church. Information and tickets (€4, though this is based on a minimum of five people paying) for this can be obtained from the monastery **shop** (Mon–Sat 7.30am–5.30pm), located just down from the church; they've also got a terrific stock of wines and brandies produced at the monastery's own distillery – take your pick from juniper (*brinovec*), pear (*hruška*) and plum (*slivovka*) – as well as honey and propolis (another bee-produced substance).

The Skansen

Spread out across a lovely green field at the bottom of the road leading up to the monastery is a fabulous little **Skansen**, or open-air museum (Pleterje

Skansen; daily 9am–5pm; €2.50), whose handful of buildings, representing a typical farmyard from this region, were relocated partly in order to draw visitors away from the monastery itself. As well as its classic thatched wooden house, dating from 1833 and fully equipped with authentic domestic furniture and a black kitchen, the complex includes a threshing floor, fruit and flax dryer, and a superb double hayrack; you can also buy pottery and ceramics.

Time and energy permitting, you can partake in the **Pleterje Way**, a circular footpath that skirts the hills above the monastery, and which affords views of the complex you wouldn't normally get to see; allow around ninety minutes to complete it. Unless you've got your own transport, getting here entails taking a bus to Šentjernej (6km west of Kostanjevica along the road to Novo Mesto), from where it's a 3km walk south to the monastery.

Kostanjevica na Krki

Compacted into a tight loop of the Krka River, the island settlement of **KOSTANJEVICA NA KRKI** is one of the country's smallest towns, a once thriving commercial centre with its own mint but now a rural backwater, possessed of a ghostly charm. From the main bus stop on Ljubljanska cesta, it's a five-minute walk north to the bridge, which in turn leads you onto the tranquil, palette-shaped island, comprising of two main streets that join to form a circle around a cluster of buildings variously spruced up or in an advanced state of decay. Aside from a couple of small Gothic churches sited at either end, there's actually very little to see or do on the island, but if you've got an hour to spare following a visit to the out-of-town attractions, it's worth taking a leisurely stroll around.

The Božidar Jakac and Jože Gorjup galleries

A fifteen-minute walk southwest of town (head down Ljubljanska Cesta and follow the signs) is the former **Cistercian Monastery**, founded in 1234, disbanded in 1784 and largely destroyed during World War II. All but completely renovated now, there are some interesting masonry fragments – vaulted ribs, keystones and so on – from the previously damaged church in the **lapidarium**, located in the eastern arcaded passage of the monastery's immense three-sided cloister. The cloister's numerous rooms now accommodate the **Božidar Jakac Gallery** (Galerija Božidar Jakac; April–Oct Tues–Sun 9am–6pm; Nov–March 9am–4pm; €3) which, with the works of no fewer than eight of Slovenia's most prominent artists to plough through, requires no little stamina.

The most obvious place to start is the collection by the versatile Jakac, whose prolific stock of prints and graphics, many of which document his time spent with the Partisans, are complemented by some exquisite pastels and oils, featuring land or townscapes from both Slovenia (*Hayrack*) and Prague where he studied – keep an eye out for the lovely *Midnight Mass on Hradčani*. After Jakac, make a beeline for the rooms holding the extensive collections of the Kralj brothers, France and Tone, both key figures in the interwar Slovene avant-garde but whose later works veered towards the realm of Socialist Realism. Tone's later work, in particular, is biased towards themes of war, revolt and daily peasant life (*Black Gold*). Family portraits feature heavily too, such as the disturbing *My Mother*, which depicts their mother standing over his dead pilot brother's body.

Of the other artists, try not to miss the fabulously creative bronze sculptures of Janez Boljka, whose work evolved from sculpting simple motifs from Ribnica, to more adventurous subject matter, such as the animal kingdom (*Bull, Chimpanzee*) and the human form – in particular, eminent Slovenes (*Ivan Cankar and his Muse, Rihard Jakopič Seated*); there are further sculptures (and oils) by France Gorše and Jože Gorjup – Gorše also specialized in portraits of noteworthy Slovenes, such as Primož Trubar. Worth a peek, too, is a rather dusty collection of Old European Masters (German, Italian and Flemish) from Pleterje Monastery. The monastery's gardens are used to exhibit some one hundred oak-wood sculptures, otherwise known as the **Forma Viva** (Living Form), one of several such sculpture parks around Slovenia, each of which demonstrates works of art made from a different material.

If you've still got the appetite, there's more work by some of the same artists at the **Jože Gorjup Gallery**, housed in the primary school of the same name at Gorjanska ulica, 2200m east of the bridge. Take a look at the wall on the side of the school's gym building, which features a brilliant mosaic of the 1573 Battle on Krško Plain, in which the counts do battle with peasants amid a fierce snowstorm.

Kostanjevica Cave

One and a half kilometres southeast of town, in a small wooded area bound by a stream, is **Kostanjevica Cave** (Kostanjeviška jama), the largest and most impressive of Dolenjska's cave systems. Speleologists were first drawn to the possibility of the cave's existence following a flood in 1937, after which time systematic exploration uncovered numerous other shafts, chambers and lakes. Fifty-minute guided tours of the old part of the cave take in approximately 250m of the 1800m discovered to date, beginning at the sixty-metre-long entrance tunnel. Beyond here a series of tight passages and staircases wend their way through several chambers, past two lakes, the **Watershed Cavern** (Razvodna dvorana) and the **Intermittent Lake** (Presihajoče jezero), and up to the **Cross Cavern** (Križna dvorana). The tour winds up at the **Stalactite Cavern** (Kapniška dvorana), a relatively narrow hall that, true to its name, is replete with dozens of shimmering stalactites, the tallest of which, the pillar, stands twelve metres high. The remainder of the cave is accessible only to experienced cavers. There are bats here, too, lots of them, including the southern horseshoe bat, which is found only in this cave. **Guided tours** (€6) take place every two hours between 10am and 6pm each day in July and August, and at the same times but only at weekends between April and June, and September and October.

Practicalities

The main **bus stop** is opposite the *Green Bar* on Ljubljanska cesta, from where it's a five-minute walk to the island. The small **tourist office**, however, is located out at the entrance to the Božidar Jakac Gallery (same opening times; see p.247). The old-fashioned *Gostilna Žolnir*, 500m north of St James Church, across the bridge at Krška cesta 4 (☏07/498-7133, ⓦwww.zolnir-sp.si; ❹), is the only place in town to **sleep**, while its **restaurant** is reasonable enough. There's better Slovene food, though, at the rustically styled *Kmečki Hram*, back on the island at Oražnova ulica 11 (closed Mon).

Brežice

The town of **BREŽICE**, a moderately important regional economic and cultural centre, sits at the confluence of the Krka and Sava rivers in the middle of the hill-fringed Krško Plain 15km east of Kostanjevica na Krki. Granted its town charter in 1354, Brežice retains a distinctive, small-town atmosphere, its single concession to grandeur a fine Renaissance Castle now housing a very good museum. Beyond this one major sight there's little else to see or do here, but if you want to make good use of a night's stopover you have the option of several not too distant trips; the **Čatež Spa** and **Mokrice Castle** a few kilome-tres to the south, and the **Bizeljkso wine region** to the north, though the latter is served by just a few buses.

Arrival, information and accommodation

From the **bus station**, around 800m east of town on Cesta Svobode, it's a ten-minute walk to the centre: heading south take a right down Bizeljska Ulica, then past the Water Tower to the main street Cesta prvih borcev. Less conveniently, the **train station** is located 2.5km north of town on Trg Vstaje, in the village of Šentlenart; buses depart from the station forecourt roughly every 45 minutes on weekdays, and every two hours on Saturdays between 6.15am and 2.15pm – there are none on Sundays. If walking, exit the station, turn left and follow the road around; you'll eventually end up on Cesta prvih borcev. This is the location for the **tourist office**, at no. 22 (Mon–Fri 8am–4pm; ℡07/496-6995, ⓦ www .zpt-brezice.si), which has free **internet**. The **post office** is on the street behind, at Ulica Stare pravade 34 (Mon–Fri 8am–6pm, Sat 8am–noon).

Accommodation in town is limited to the comfortable *Splavar* pension at Cesta prvih borcev 40a (℡07/499-0630, ⓔinfo@splavar.si; ❻), which has quite small, but tidy, air-conditioned rooms, all with wi-fi. Two options out of town are *Gostilna Les* (℡07/496-1100, ⓦwww.gostilna-les.com; ❹), south of the river in Čatež ob Savi, which also has a range of differently sized apart-ments across the road (❹–❻); and the very welcoming *Pri Martinovih* tourist farm (℡07/496-1057, ⓦwww.martinovi.com; ❸) in Globočice; heading back along the road to Kostanjevica, the village is signposted after about 4km, from where it's another 4km uphill to the farm.

Brežice Castle and the Posavje Museum

Prominently positioned at the extreme southern end of the town's long and attractive main street, Cesta prvih borcev, the foundations of present-day **Brežice Castle** were laid in 1529, when it was also fortified with robust, red-tiled conical towers. Following its purchase by the counts of Attems in the seventeenth century, the castle underwent a major style renovation – the courtyard was arcaded with Tuscan columns and several of its most important spaces, such as the stairway, chapel and, most famously, the Knight's Hall, were decorated with splendid Baroque frescoes.

The castle is now home to the **Posavje Museum** (Posavski Muzej; Mon–Fri 8am–2.30pm, Sat & Sun 10am–2pm; €2.50), as comprehensive a regional museum as you'll come across; there are useful information sheets in each room to guide you. The first ten of the museum's twenty or so rooms are given over to archeological and ethnological collections; the former is crammed with ancient skeletons, weapons, jewellery and equine equipment extricated from over four hundred Celtic graves at Dobova on the Croatian border. The latter documents life in the Posavje region, with due prominence given to wine-making, featuring a weighty display of viticultural implements including two large wine presses.

Located in two small vaulted rooms in the northeastern tower is a small medieval history section documenting the Slovene and Croatian peasant struggles of the sixteenth century, as well as items and literature related to the Reformation in Dolenjska; the key exhibit, and the museum's most precious item, is the Dalmatin Bible from 1584, the first complete translation of the Bible from German into Slovene. Of the 1500 copies originally printed, only around eighty survive. The several rooms constituting the Baroque Art collection are taken up with portraits of the aristocracy, some fine sacral

The Brežice Festival

One of the country's most celebrated musical and cultural events, the Brežice Festival (mid-June to mid-Aug; Ⓦ www.festivalbrezice.com) is an outstanding series of ancient and Baroque music concerts, featuring some of Europe's finest musicians. Although the majority of concerts are staged here in Brežice – some in the superb Knight's Hall – many events take place in other castles and churches throughout Slovenia, such as Dobrovo Castle in Brda, Fužine Castle in Ljubljana, and the Church of the Annunciation in Skofja Loka. Tickets (€10–30), available online or by phone (Ⓣ07/420-5000), usually go on sale at the beginning of May.

art (paintings by Metzinger and wooden sculptures) and, best of all, a magnificent eighteenth-century wooden sled made in Vienna and donated to Brežice by Empress Maria Theresa.

The museum's centrepiece is the **Knight's Hall** (Viteška dvorana), awash with typically florid Italian Baroque paintings featuring scenes from classical myth and legend, the arts and sciences and portraits of the Attems family; the hall is now used for weddings, high-level state functions and as one of the principal venues for concerts of the Brežice Festival.

Eating and drinking

Given its modest size, the town has a surprisingly healthy number of places to **eat and drink**. The most accomplished place is the cool ✻ *Ošterija Debeluh* restaurant and wine bar at Trg Izgnancev 7 (closed Sun), whose attractive pastel painted walls and elegantly set tables make it an enjoyable place to tuck into the very juicy Balkan grills – the bar has a terrific selection of wines from the local Bizeljsko region (see p.252). The popular *Santa Lucia*, at Cesta prvih borcev 15, has similarly comfortable surrounds, including a straw-covered terrace to the rear, while the extensive, predominantly Italian, menu is very creditable.

The two most popular **drinking** venues in town are *Rafters Pub*, part of the *Splavar* pension (see p.249), and the *Jazz Club*, further down at Trg Izgnancev 2, though there is no jazz. The most original place, however, is *Aquarius*, with four small circular floors inside the pink Water Tower on Bizeljska ulica. The bright *Kavarna*, just down from the castle at Cesta prvih borcev 14, has a good selection of **coffee**, teas and cakes to indulge in.

Čatež

From Brežice, hourly buses (five on Saturdays) run the 3km southeast (across the Sava) to **ČATEŽ**, Slovenia's largest and most popular **spa centre** (Terme Čatež; Ⓦ www.terme-catez.si). Hot springs were first discovered at Čatež in 1797, only to be flooded by the Sava, then rediscovered some fifty years later, around which time the first private spa – a basic wood cabin and pool – was built by Father Edvard Zagorc. A fledgling resort in the 1920s, offering numerous therapies and treatments to a wide variety of disorders, Čatež only really began to develop as a serious spa centre in the 1960s, with the construction of the first large pools and hotels. Today this more or less self-contained village, incorporating restaurants, shops, a bank and post office, is as much a recreational park as it is a therapeutic and treatment centre.

Water and sauna parks

The huge **Thermal Riviera water park** (daily mid-April to mid-Oct 9am–7pm, July & Aug 8am–8pm; weekdays €10.50, weekends €13) comprises some ten thermal pools and bathing areas (average temperature 30°C), with a fantastic array of wave machines, waterfalls and slides. If it gets a bit cool, there's indoor action at the *Toplice*'s modern **Winter Thermal Riviera** (daily 9am–9pm; weekdays €12, weekends €15), which has a multitude of slides, wave pools, whirlpools and water massage machines; guests of the *Toplice* have unlimited free use of this pool, while guests of the other two hotels have free usage once a day.

If you fancy sweating off a few pounds, then the **sauna park** (weekdays €12, weekends €16), also inside the *Toplice*, incorporates eight different saunas – the Indian sauna, Salt sauna and Finnish Aroma sauna, to name but three. If that's not enough, the **spa and wellness centre** inside the *Hotel Čatež* accommodates a plethora of modern and exotic massages and treatments. There are more activities in the shape of indoor and outdoor tennis (€7–13 per hour), badminton (€7 per hour) and squash (€8 for 45min), in addition to bikes for rent (€6.50 for half a day, €9 for the day).

Practicalities

The **tourist office** (June–Aug Mon–Fri 8am–7pm, Sat 8am–4pm, Sun 8am–2pm; Sept–May Mon–Fri 9am–5pm, Sat 9am–4pm, Sun 9am–2pm; ☎07/493-6777) is located opposite the *Hotel Toplice*. Unless you're here for more than a few days, it's unlikely you'll need or want to stay on site. If you do, the complex incorporates three pricey **hotels** (all ☎07/493-6700; ❾); the *Čatež*, an attractive atrium-style building with exquisitely appointed rooms, and the slightly more expensive *Toplice* and *Terme* hotels, both of which offer similarly luxurious rooms – the former also has rooms in a 1920s Swiss-style chalet. At the eastern end of the complex, alongside the clean and well-equipped **campsite** (☎07/493-5010; open all year), is the holiday village, which has dozens of large, two- and four-bed apartments (❼–❽). Much more fun is the **Indian village** (May–Sept; ❻), a cluster of some 25 tepees, each equipped with four beds, kitchen and other furnishings; modern bathroom facilities are shared. Hotel **restaurants** aside, there are a number of snack bars and cafés sprinkled around the complex.

Mokrice Castle

At the end of the secondary road which runs parallel with the E70 highway to Zagreb, 8km southeast of Čatež, stands **Mokrice Castle**, a beautifully proportioned Renaissance chateau, which once functioned as a defensive outpost against the Turks. Today, and like Otočec Castle (see p.244), it has been converted into a luxury **hotel**, the *Grad Mokrice* (☎07/493-6700, ⓦwww.terme-catez.si; ❾), and very posh **restaurant**; those staying receive free use of the pools at Čatež. During the golf season (March–Nov) there are some superb-value golf **apartments** (❺) available, each sleeping up to four people.

Both the restaurant and the long and hilly eighteen-hole **golf course** (☎07/457-4246; 18 holes €40 or €48 at weekends, 9 holes €26 or €32 at weekends – thirty percent discount for guests staying at the hotel here and the hotels at Čatež Spa) are popular with the moneyed middle classes, a good number of whom make the short trip up from Zagreb in Croatia. Those with neither the time nor wallet for a meal or a round of golf can take a stroll around the impressively manicured lawns of the stately landscaped English Park, whose pear-tree orchards provide the fruits for the fiery local brandy, *Viljamovka*. There's more affordable **accommodation** out along the road to

Mokrice in Dvorce, at the very smart *Penzion Čateški Dvorec* (☎07/499-4870, ⓦwww.cateski-dvorec.com; ⑥), which also has a sauna, wine cellar and **restaurant**.

Bizeljsko-Sremič wine region and Podsreda Castle

Tracking the Croatian border, the road heading north out of Brežice heads up through the **Bizeljsko-Sremič wine region**, renowned for its characteristic blended wines, such as the dry whites *Bizeljčan* and *Sremičan*. Although the odd **bus** trundles this way (Mon–Fri, 3 daily), it's difficult to get the most out of the region unless you've got your own wheels. Wine can be sampled anywhere where you see the sign *vinska klet* (wine cellar) of which there are many; however, to be sure of getting a visit in, it's best to call in advance – reckon on paying around €5 for three or four wines, a little more for sparkling wine.

The wine road doesn't really begin until the village of **Stari Vas**, some 10km north of Brežice, where you can sample sparkling wines at the renowned *Istenič* cellar at no. 7 (☎07/495-1559, ⓦwww.istenic.si); they've also got a comfortable little pension on site (④). Two kilometres further up the road, there's more tasting and similar accommodation at the countrified roadside inn *Pri Peču* (☎07/452-0103; ④; restaurant closed Tues).

From the *Istenič* cellar, a footpath (Pot k Repnicam) winds its way across the shallow hills up to the village of **BREZOVICA**, some 5km distant. Spotted around this area are some 150 unique cellars called *repnice*, small sand caves hewn from the surrounding flint-stone hills, their walls and ceilings wonderfully patterned with obliquely laid layers of sand. *Repnice* were traditionally used for the storage of turnips (*repa* means turnip) and other produce, before local vintners discovered that the caves' climatic conditions (a constant 7–11°C) and humidity were ideal for the maturing and storage of wine. Around thirty *repnice* are still in use today, the greatest concentration of which are in Brezovica itself; particularly worth trying are *Kovačič* at no. 29 (☎07/495-1091), *Kelhar* at no. 31 (☎07/495-1551), which was dug out in 1825, and, most impressively, *Najger* at no. 32 (☎07/495-1115) – all three are located approximately 1.5km from the main road up the hill.

The next village along is **Bizeljsko** itself, the region's main settlement, where there's the well-regarded *Gostilna Šekoranja* at no. 72 (closed Mon), a real old-fashioned eatery serving up heavy home-made Slovene fare such as smoked bacon, chunky sausages and black pudding, and, some 800m further up the road at no. 115, the outstanding *Pinterič* cellar (☎07/495-1266). Beyond here, the road gently ascends to **Bistrica ob Sotli**, whereupon a branch road cuts west to the village of **PODSREDA**, above which looms the resplendent **Podsreda Castle** (April–Oct Tues–Sun 10am–6pm; €2.50). Originally a thirteenth-century fortification, its fine Romanesque core remains splendidly intact, although systematic and comprehensive renovation work on the interior has left few visible traces of its former state, with just the old medieval kitchen and single-cell jail remaining from the original building. Its empty rooms are now used almost exclusively as exhibition and gallery spaces, and there are currently collections devoted to glassworks and prints.

The castle can be reached by road (5km from Podsreda) or, if you're walking, via a steep trail (45min) beginning south of the village – look for the signs to Levstikov Mlin (Levstikov Mill) and the trail starts there.

Bela Krajina

Bela Krajina acquired its name – meaning White Carniola, derived partially from the ubiquitous birch tree, and the white costumes worn by its inhabitants, the **Bela Kranjci** (White Carniolans) – during the fifteenth century, when the lands were incorporated into the province of Carniola. Its frontline position ensured that, around the same time, the region's towns and villages suffered a fair battering at the hands of the Turks, whose unremitting drive up through the Balkans also led to an influx of Croat and Serb refugees and renegades (Uskoks) from Bosnia. A period of cultural and economic efflorescence eventually gave way to regional decline, as the closure of many important industrial plants was compounded by a catastrophic bout of phylloxera at the end of the nineteenth century, which destroyed almost all the region's vineyards. Much of the local population was forced to emigrate, mainly to North America, while those who remained continued to engage in traditional cottage industries as a means of eking out a living. Its two main towns, **Črnomelj** and **Metlika**, are fairly low-key places but are convenient for the more interesting sites close at hand.

The best of Bela Krajina, however, is to be found in the surrounding countryside, amid the birch trees and vineyards; history and culture buffs can get their kicks at the **Mithraeum shrine** at Rožanec, and the fabulous **Three Parishes Pilgrimage Centre** at Rosalnice, near Metlika; those seeking more relaxing fare should make a beeline for the **Lahinja Landscape Park** or the numerous wine villages sprinkled around the region, such as **Drašiči** with its pleasant vineyard-clad surrounds.

Črnomelj and around

Sitting plumb in the geographical centre of Bela Krajina, 45km east of Kočevje, **ČRNOMELJ** is both the capital, and the largest, of the province's towns. Frankly, though, it's not much to get excited about, and the only reason you might contemplate a visit here is to indulge in the town's marvellous folklore **festival** in June, or to use it as a springboard for visits to surrounding attractions.

Unlike many settlements in the region, Črnomelj was spared widespread devastation by the Turks, owing to its naturally strong fortifications, although its strategic importance was stripped away in the mid-sixteenth century following the erection of a fort and the relocation of the command of the military frontier across the border in Karlovac, Croatia. Its decline continued for several centuries thereafter, though its fortunes were partially revived following the opening of the Novo Mesto–Karlovac rail line in 1914.

Bela Krajina's rich folk-music heritage is joyously celebrated each year here in the form of the **Jurjevanje** (St George's Day Festival), which features a tremendous, and usually very accomplished, line-up of both local and international folkloric groups and dance troupes. Usually taking place during the third week of June, it's a great opportunity to see rarely used folk instruments – such as the *tamburica*, *bisernica* (lute) and *berdo* (contrabass) – being played live.

What little there is of interest is centred on an elongated promontory in a tight loop of the Dobličica and Lahinja rivers to the south of town. Consuming the eastern side of the main square, Trg Svobode, is the town's rather low-key **castle**, originally built in the twelfth century but rebuilt, modified and tinkered with by numerous owners over the years, the result being that it doesn't much look like a castle at all now, instead just another regular building on the square. There's little of interest to see, inside or out, and even the small **town museum** (Mon–Fri 8am–3.30pm, Sat 9am–noon plus Sun 9am–noon in summer; €1) offers not much more than a weary collection of local photographs, though there are a few drawings by Božidar Jakac (see p.247) to admire. A few paces south of the castle, at the beginning of Ulica Staneta Rozmana – the main traffic thoroughfare – the Baroque **Church of St Peter** is fairly standard issue, but look out for an oversized fresco of St Christopher on the exterior west wall. Perched above the confluence of the two rivers at the end of Ulica Mirana Jarca, the street running parallel to Ulica Staneta Rozmana, is the late-fifteenth-century **Church of the Holy Spirit**, now restored to something like its former glory.

Practicalities

The town's **train station** is located 1km due north of the centre on Železničarska cesta, from where it's a twenty-minute walk due south to the Old Town core. More conveniently, all **buses** stop on the main square, Trg Svobode, from where it's a quick hop across the road to the **tourist office**, inside the castle at no. 3 (same times as museum; ☏07/305-6530, Ⓦwww.belakrajina.si). The **post office** is some 500m north of here on Kolodvorska ulica (Mon–Fri 8am–7pm, Sat 8am–noon).

Town **accommodation** is scant: there are dorm beds available all year round in the *Dijaški Dom*, 400m north of the tourist office at Otona Župančičeva 7 (☏07/306-2160; €15), while *Gostilna Muller*, south of the main square, and along the road below the bridge at Ločka cesta 6 (☏07/356-7200, Ⓔgostilnstvo .muller@siol.net; ❹) has four large, spotless and reasonably priced rooms.

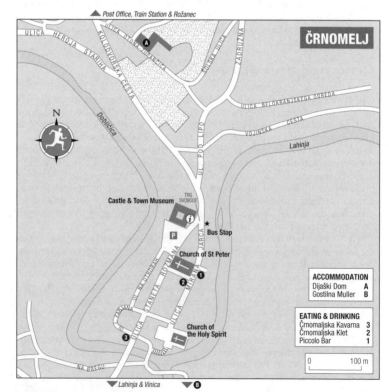

Eating options are scarcely better, the one possibility being the rustically styled restaurant in the *Gostilna Muller*, offering a generous choice of seafood, game and vegetarian dishes (closed Mon). The quiet and pleasant *Črnomaljska Kavarna*, under the bridge at the end of Ulica Staneta Rozmana, has good coffee and thick hot chocolate, while the *Piccolo Bar*, down some steps directly opposite the Church of St Peter, does for a beer. Wine buffs should check out the *Črnomaljska Klet* wine cellar, next to the church at Ulica Mirana Jarca 2 (contact the tourist office), where you can partake in some tasting of the regional wines, and buy bottles too.

Rožanec and the Mithraeum

Just after the village of Lokve, beyond a couple of Romany settlements, a left turn takes you up to the smaller village of **Rožanec**; from the parking place, a signposted path leads you up to and across the rail track, then into a chestnut forest, at the edge of which is a small, picturesque hollow. Hewn into the rock face of one wall is the **Mithraeum** (Mitrej), a second-century Roman shrine dedicated to the invincible sun god Mithras (see box, p.305).

The centrepiece of the rock-cut relief (first excavated in 1921) is the sacrifice of the bull, which has Mithras kneeling on, and plunging a dagger into, its back. The spilling of the bull's blood supposedly gave rise to the plant kingdom, while its semen gave rise to the animal kingdom, the latter represented here by the presence of a dog, a snake and a scorpion. The sacrificial scene is accompanied by personifications of the sun and the moon (light and darkness), as well as two priests, Cautopates and Cautes. The inscription, meanwhile, is an address to Mithras from three brothers (Nepos, Prokulus and Firminus), appealing for health and prosperity. The Mithraeum's presence at this particular site is unsurprising given that a Roman road once ran from Črnomelj to Semič, a small town some 5km further north, at which point it divided with one road continuing to Emona (Ljubljana), the other towards present-day Novo Mesto. A copy of the relief is held in the Bela Krajina Museum in Metlika.

Lahinja Landscape Park

A couple of kilometres south of Črnomelj – along the road to Vinica and the Kolpa River – you'll pass another Romany settlement, 7km beyond which is the **Lahinja Landscape Park**, a protected area of fields, marshy groves, streams and karstic springs. The park can be accessed from any one of several hamlets clustered in or around its boundary, though the best and most convenient point of entry is at **Pusti Gradac**, the park's northernmost settlement, located up a gravel-track 1.5km beyond the village of **Dragatuš** (see p.256); if you're travelling by bus get the driver to set you down on the main road, from where it's a twenty-minute walk.

Pusti Gradac also happens to be the park's most culturally well-endowed patch: not only have several extremely important archeological finds been unearthed here – including a remarkable gold coin featuring an imprint of Hungarian King Matthias Corvinus (which dates from around the fifteenth century) – but it's also the site of one of the country's few remaining working **water mills**. The mill still operates according to traditional methods, its grinders powered by an impressively large water wheel, itself propelled by waters from the nearby Lahinja River. Demonstrations of the mill are organized by the Klepec family, who live in the house next door at no. 10 (☎07/305-7660, ✉klepec@siol.net). They can also provide information and assistance on the park and its facilities, as well as arrange two- to four-hour-long **guided tours** of the park (€3); in theory these tours are only available to groups, but arrangements can be made for individuals as long as you contact the family at least a day or two in advance. There's also **accommodation** here in the renovated family house near the mill, which can sleep between three and six people (❸–❹). A leisurely circular walk around the park takes around three hours.

Vinica

There's more comfortable accommodation in Dragatuš, at the *Pri Štefaniču* tourist farm (☎07/305-7347, ✉stefanic@siol.net; ❹), which also possesses a very accomplished restaurant – the *Župančičev Hram* – named after the poet, playwright and essayist Oton Župančič, who was born in the small fishing village of **VINICA**, 10km further south right on the Croatian border. Along with Ivan Cankar, Župančič (1878–1949) was regarded as the principal exponent of the so-called Moderna movement, a Slovene literary trend which appeared at the end of the nineteenth century, and which was closely aligned to the tenets of Slovene national and socio-historical identity; his principal contribution was a collection of poetry entitled *Čaša opojnosti* (*Intoxicating Cup*). A prolific wordsmith, Župančič also wrote and translated numerous plays (including Shakespeare), composed poems for the Partisan press, and wrote many children's stories; above all he is known to every Slovene as the creator of the children's character, *Ciciban*. His **birthplace** is located on the main road in the centre of the village at no. 9 (get the key from no. 6, opposite; €1.50); on display, albeit in Slovene only, are copies of his work, his death mask and a beautiful sketch portrait completed by Božidar Jakac just two years before Župančič's death. He is buried at Žale cemetery in Ljubljana. A short way beyond the house is the derelict sixteenth-century **castle**, which now offers little more than terrific views across the Kolpa towards Croatia.

There are two **campsites** (both May–Sept) down by the river on the southern fringe of the village, close to the border crossing; the better of the two is the clean, green and spacious *Katra* (☎07/364-6034, ✉katra@siol.net), but if that's full, there's the *Kolpa-Vinica* (☎031/513-060, ⓦwww.kamp-kolpa.si) right next door, which also has tidy four-person chalets (❺).

Metlika and around

Pressed up hard against the Croatian border just 15km northeast of Črnomelj, **METLIKA** is Bela Krajina's second centre of population. It's a mellow town, but palpably more interesting than its neighbour, thanks to a couple of fine museums, some lovely architecture, and a strong viticultural tradition.

Founded in the thirteenth century when the province (then an important frontier region) was known as Metlika March, it acquired its town rights and developed into a prosperous medieval centre the following century. However, as one of Austria's border strongholds it found itself at the sharp end of Hungarian, then Turkish, attacks – it was razed no fewer than sixteen times. Almost entirely gutted by fire in 1705, its historic centre was swiftly rebuilt, although it received another battering at the hands of its Italian occupiers during World War II, which makes the survival of its attractive old core all the more remarkable.

The town's principal annual event is the **Spring Wine Festival** (Vinska Vigred) on the third weekend of May, a booze-fuelled three days of wine-related events taking place throughout the Old Town's three squares.

Arrival, information and accommodation

The **bus station** is right on the main crossroads at the southern entrance to town, from where it's a fifteen-minute walk to the Old Town; the **train station**, meanwhile, is 1km southeast of the same crossroads, on the road towards the Croatian border crossing on Kolodvorska ulica. The helpful **tourist office** is handily situated in the Castle courtyard (May–Aug Mon–Fri 8am–5pm, Sat 9am–noon; Sept–April Mon–Fri 8am–4pm, Sat 9am–noon; ☎07/363-5470, Ⓦwww.metlika-turizem.si). The **post office** (Mon–Fri 8am–6pm, Sat 8am–noon) is in the small complex across the road from the bus station.

The town's only **hotel** is the brightly coloured and very decent *Bela Krajina*, situated just down from the old town on the main through road, Cesta Bratstva in Enotnosti (☎07/305-8123; ❻). The nearest **campsite**, *Podzemelj ob Kolpi* (☎07/306-9572; May–Sept), is 7km southwest of town, just off the main Črnomelj–Metlika road down by the Kolpa River – the waters are good for swimming here; buses heading in either direction can drop you off on the main road, from where it's about 1km to the site. Five hundred metres prior to the campsite, at Podzemelj 17, the *Gostišče Veselič* has a handful of very small, basic rooms (☎07/306-9156; ❸).

The Town

Everything of interest in Metlika is located within the confines of the **Old Town**, sited on a low elevation between the main thoroughfare, Cesta Bratstva in Enotnosti and the River Obrh, and reached via Ulica na Trg, opposite the *Hotel Bela Krajina*. On the north side of **Trg Svobode**, the largest and most

3 Parishes Pilgrimage Centre

METLIKA

Metlika Castle & Bela Krajina Museum

Firefighting Museum

TRG SVOBODE

Town Hall

Church of St Nicholas

Commandery

Metlika Wine Cellar

Bus Station

Novo Mesto

N

EATING & DRINKING
Gostilna Budački	3
Grajska Klet	1
Vinoteka Pinot	2

ACCOMMODATION
Hotel Bela Krajina	A

0   150 m

Črnomelj & Campsite

❸ & Train Station

central of the three irregularly shaped squares which form the backbone of the Old Town, stands the neat, triangular-shaped **Metlika Castle**, whose vaulted tracts house the **Bela Krajina Museum** (Belokranjski muzej; Tues–Fri 9am–2pm, Sat & Sun 9am–noon; €3.50), one of Slovenia's finest regional museums. Following an informative fifteen-minute film about the region, the collection kicks off with an impressive haul of Bronze and Iron Age artefacts – vessels, armour, jewellery and the like – and a stash of Roman finds, many of which were unearthed from Pusti Gradac south of Črnomelj (see p.255); there's also a copy of the Mithraic relief at Rožanec on display (see p.255). The most enjoyable part is the section devoted to the region's inhabitants, Bela Kranjci, and features a fine display of homespun attire, as well as items and artefacts pertaining to the local traditional cottage industries, typically pottery, spinning, weaving, cart- and barrel-making and an exhibition of one of the more delicate Slovenian folk-arts, *Pisanice* (egg-painting).

The development of viticulture – as important to the local economy today as agriculture was prior to World War II – is also given due prominence, as is the role of local societies and associations in Bela Krajina during the nineteenth and twentieth centuries. Foremost among these was the Metlika Fire Brigade, whose heroics are documented in the **Firefighting Museum** (Slovenski gasilski muzej; Mon–Sat 9am–1pm, Sun 9am–noon; €1.50), in the building next to the castle. Opened on the occasion of the Metlika firefighting brigade's centenary anniversary in 1969, the museum proudly displays an assortment of photographs, awards, helmets and uniforms, klaxons and other memorabilia. Best of all, though, are the old firefighting machines – the oldest of which is a model from Cerknica dating from 1836 – located in both this building and the pavilion opposite.

Trg Svobode segues into **Mestni Trg**, an elongated square bound by an attractive blend of beige, cream and mint-coloured buildings, the most distinguished being the neo-Gothic **Town Hall** at no. 24. Positioned atop the building is a slightly askew town coat of arms, featuring two ravens perched either side of a castle tower – no doubt on the look-out for rampaging Turks. The bottom end of the square is consumed by the box-like **Church of St Nicholas** (Cerkev Sv Nikolaj), a uniform Baroque structure resurrected in 1759 following a fire some fifty years earlier. The statues of St Nicholas and the pope adorning the high altar were carved by an unknown sculptor, while the frescoes were executed by the Friulian Domenico Fabrio. Just behind the church stands the

Wine villages

The triangle of land between Metlika and the pretty wine villages of **Drašiči**, **Vinomer** and **Radovica** to the northeast is classic Krajina countryside swathes of copse-like *steljniki* – birch tree and fern – set against the backdrop of soft, gently sloping vineyards. The majority of wines cultivated here are blends, the trademark one being *Metliška Črnina*, a rich, velvety and very dark red; others worth trying include the lighter reds, *Modra Portugalka* and *Modri Pinot*, and, if you're prepared to spend that little extra, the sparkling white *Metliška Penina*.

Of the aforementioned villages, Drašiči (6km northeast of Metlika) offers most to the wine connoisseur, with a number of cellars providing tasting: a good one for starters is the *Simonič* tourist farm at no. 56 (☏07/305-8185); otherwise, take your pick from the many cellars advertised – these can be approached direct or, alternatively, contact the tourist office in Metlika, who will happily fix something up for you. The 1:50,000 *Bela Krajina* map, available from either of the tourist offices, should help you navigate your way around the villages.

Commandery (Komenda), the one-time residence of the knights of the Teutonic Order, but which is now an old people's home; its impressive size is best appreciated from below the Old Town.

Eating and drinking

Eating options in Metlika are almost nonexistent and you may well spend more time drinking in the local wine cellars than you had initially intended. The only worthwhile restaurant is the *Gostilna Budački*, awkwardly located in a residential area out near the train station at Ulica Belokranjskega odreda 14, featuring a decent grill menu and fish from the nearby Kolpa. Two places to sample the local **wine** are the classy little *Grajska Klet* café, inside the castle courtyard, and *Vinoteka Pinot*, a cramped cellar bar at Trg Svobode 28.

For a more sophisticated bout of wine appreciation, *Vinska Klet Metlika*, across the road from the bus station, arranges organized visits of their extensive cellars with a tasting session to boot; they are, though, heavily inclined towards groups, so you may end up having to pay the group rate even if there are only a couple of you (☎07/363-7000). There's a shop here, too (Mon–Fri 8am–3pm, Sat 7am–noon).

The Three Parishes Pilgrimage Centre

Two kilometres east of Metlika in the village of **ROSALNICE**, the **Three Parishes Pilgrimage Centre** (Tri Fare) – comprising three fourteenth- and fifteenth-century Gothic churches – is the region's most outstanding ecclesiastical monument. From the few historical documents that existed, it was ascertained that the original churches were likely to have been built by the Knights Templar some time during the twelfth century. Following the arrival of a group of refugee Franciscan monks from Bosnia shortly after the completion of the middle church in the fifteenth century, the complex evolved into an important pilgrimage site. It reached its apogee a century or two later when followers of many different faiths, including Orthodox, journeyed here regularly.

The largest and oldest of the three churches, the **Lady of Our Sorrows** (Žalostna Mati božja) features a superb Gothic interior with Baroque append- ages, decorated with a splendid array of frescoes: the presbytery is covered with scenes from the New Testament, the side walls with images of the Apostles and, on the triumphal arch, scenes representing the Ten Commandments. The main altar is ornamented with a fine statuette of Mary with Seven Swords (the Seven Sorrows), the story of which is relayed in the middle church, while the Rococo side altars – dedicated to St John Nepomuk and St Francis of Paola – are no less impressive. Of the three churches this is the only one where Mass is still held.

Next to Our Sorrows, the **Ecce Homo Church** (Glej človek) is the smallest of the three and the only one with a bell tower. It, too, boasts a marvellous Gothic presbytery and high altar, but the show-stealer is its cupola ceiling, painted with wildly colourful frescoes depicting the story of Mary's Seven Sorrows. Completing the trilogy is the poorly preserved **Church of Our Lady of Lourdes** (Lurška Devica Marija), almost completely devoid of colour or ornamentation. Its singular highlight is the neo-Gothic high altar featuring a statue of Mary of Lourdes, while it's just about possible to detect the fragments of a fresco of the Crucifixion, from around 1500.

There is a **train station** in Rosalnice, one stop along the line from Metlika, but few trains actually stop here and you're just as well off walking: the most direct route is along Cankarjeva cesta, which begins from a point some 100m north of the main crossroads in the south of town (on Cesta Bratstva in

Enotnosti), and winds its way to the village. If you plan to visit the churches, make sure you call the tourist office in Metlika in advance (see p.257), so that arrangements for the keys can be made.

Travel details

Trains

Brežice to: Ljubljana (Mon–Fri hourly, Sat & Sun 6 daily; 1hr 30min–2hr).
Črnomelj to: Ljubljana (Mon–Fri 6 daily, Sat & Sun 3 daily; 2hr 10min–2hr 45min); Metlika (Mon–Fri 8 daily, Sat & Sun 3 daily; 20min); Novo Mesto (Mon–Fri 8 daily, Sat & Sun 3 daily; 45min–1hr).
Metlika to: Črnomelj (Mon–Fri 7 daily, Sat & Sun 3 daily; 20min); Ljubljana (Mon–Fri 5 daily, Sat & Sun 3 daily; 2hr 30min–3hr); Novo Mesto (Mon–Fri 7 daily, Sat & Sun 3 daily; 1hr–1hr 15min).
Novo Mesto to: Črnomelj (Mon–Fri 9 daily, Sat & Sun 3 daily; 45min–1hr); Ljubljana (Mon–Fri 10 daily, Sat & Sun 4 daily; 1hr 20min–2hr); Metlika (Mon–Fri 8 daily, Sat & Sun 3 daily; 1hr–1hr 15min); Trebnje (Mon–Fri 12 daily, Sat & Sun 4 daily; 20min).
Postojna to: Divača (every 40min–1hr 30min; 30min); Koper (5–7 daily; 1hr 30min); Ljubljana (every 40min–1hr 30min; 1hr); Sežana (hourly–1hr 30min; 45min).

Buses

Brežice to: Bizeljsko (Mon–Fri 3 daily; 30min); Ljubljana (3 daily; 2hr 30min); Novo Mesto (Mon–Fri 6 daily, Sat & Sun 3 daily; 50min).
Cerknica to: Ljubljana (Mon–Fri 8 daily, Sat 4, Sun 2; 1hr 15min); Stari Trg (Mon–Fri 7 daily, Sat & Sun 2 daily; 25min).
Črnomelj to: Metlika (Mon–Fri 3 daily; 25min); Novo Mesto (Mon–Fri 3 daily; 50min); Vinica (Mon–Fri hourly, Sat & Sun 5 daily; 35min).
Dolenjske Toplice to: Novo Mesto (Mon–Fri hourly, Sat 3 daily; 20min); Žužemberk (Mon–Fri 4 daily; 30min).
Kočevje to: Ljubljana (Mon–Fri hourly, Sat & Sun 6 daily; 1hr 30min); Ribnica (Mon–Fri hourly, Sat & Sun 6 daily; 30min).

Kostanjevica na Krki to: Brežice (Mon–Fri 7 daily, Sat & Sun 2 daily; 25min); Ljubljana (Mon–Fri 3 daily, Sat & Sun 2 daily; 2hr 30min); Novo Mesto (Mon–Fri 7 daily, Sat & Sun 3 daily; 35min).
Metlika to: Črnomelj (Mon–Fri 6 daily; 25min); Novo Mesto (Mon–Fri 3 daily; 25min).
Novo Mesto to: Brežice (Mon–Fri 7 daily, Sat & Sun 3 daily; 50min); Črnomelj (Mon–Fri 1 daily; 50min); Dolenjske Toplice (Mon–Fri 10 daily, Sat 3 daily; 25min); Kostanjevica na krki (Mon–Fri 7 daily, Sat & Sun 3 daily; 40min); Ljubljana (Mon–Fri 5 daily, Sat 3 daily, Sun 2 daily; 1hr 10min); Metlika (Mon–Fri 2 daily; 25min); Otočec (Mon–Fri 7 daily, Sat 3 daily; 15min); Šmarjeske Toplice (Mon–Fri 7 daily, Sat 3 daily; 15min); Trebnje (Mon–Fri 6 daily, Sat & Sun 3 daily; 30min); Žužemberk (Mon–Fri 1 daily; 40min).
Postojna to: Ajdovščina (Mon–Fri 10 daily, Sat & Sun 5 daily; 40min); Ilirska Bistrica (Mon–Fri 5 daily; 40min); Koper (Mon–Fri 6 daily, Sat & Sun 3 daily; 1hr 15min); Ljubljana (Mon–Fri hourly, Sat & Sun 7 daily; 1hr); Nova Gorica (Mon–Fri 10 daily, Sat & Sun 5 daily; 1hr 10min); Piran (Mon–Fri 4 daily, Sat & Sun 3 daily; 1hr 40min); Sežana (Mon–Fri 2 daily; 40min).
Trebnje to: Ljubljana (Mon–Sat 3 daily, Sun 2 daily; 45min); Novo Mesto (Mon–Sat 4 daily, Sun 2 daily; 30min).

International trains

Postojna to: Pula (1 daily; 3hr); Rijeka (2 daily; 1hr 35min); Trieste (1 daily; 2hr); Venice (3 daily; 3hr).

International buses

Novo Mesto to: Zagreb (1 daily; 1hr 20min).

Eastern Slovenia

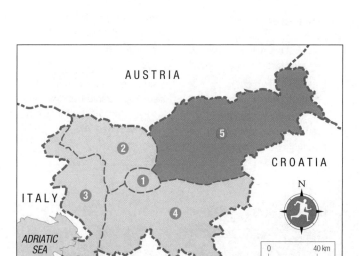

CHAPTER 5 # Highlights

* **Logar Valley** Gorgeous alpine valley in the heart of the Kamniške-Savinja Alps, ideal for a number of leisurely pursuits. See p.279

* **Pohorje Massif** Skiing, cycling and hiking are just three sporting possibilities on this thickly wooded plateau. See p.287

* **Lent Festival, Maribor** Fantastically lively and colourful two-week gathering, featuring street theatre, music and dance all over town. See p.297

* **Ptuj** Slovenia's oldest and prettiest town, stuffed with remnants of its Roman and medieval past, and famed as the home of the Kurent Carnival. See p.298

* **Church of the Virgin Mary, Ptujska Gora** Sublime Gothic church featuring the masterful *Virgin with Mantle* relief. See p.305

* **Ljutomer Wine Road** Spend the day cycling through the rolling, stepped vineyards of this beautiful wine road. See p.306

* **Prekmurje** Quaint villages, churches, farmhouses and storks characterize Slovenia's distinctively flat northeastern region. See p.308

▲ The Ljutomer wine road

5

Eastern Slovenia

Taken as a whole, eastern Slovenia receives relatively few visitors, which is a shame, as there's some enticing countryside and a wealth of interesting sites to explore, while many towns and villages host excellent spring and summer festivals, as well as carnivals. The region's history is certainly writ large: **Štajerska**, the country's largest province, was part of Austrian Styria prior to World War I, while **Koroška** was once the centre of the oldest Slovene state, Karantanija, from the seventh century, and later part of the former Habsburg duchy of Carinthia. Whereas Koroška and Štajerska came under the sway of the Austrians, **Prekmurje**, in many ways the country's most distinctive region, was subject to around a thousand years of Hungarian rule before being divided between Hungary and the new Yugoslav state in 1920.

Beyond the smattering of central Štajerska's small towns lie **Maribor** and **Celje**, the second- and third-largest cities in Slovenia, respectively. Neither town, however, can match the historic resonance of **Ptuj**, Slovenia's oldest and most appealing town, which is also a short ride away from the stunning Gothic Church of the Virgin Mary in **Ptujska Gora**. Eastern Slovenia is, however, chiefly known for its spas – notably **Rogaška Slatina**, the country's most quintessential spa town – and its wine. Štajerska harbours the largest of the country's three wine-growing regions, **Podravje**, whose six districts each yield a superb range of predominantly white wines. The region's main activity centre is the **Pohorje Massif**, a broad, arcing plateau which extends some 50km west from the foothills of Maribor, and offers plentiful recreational opportunities including two of the country's largest and best-equipped ski resorts.

Lying to the west of the Massif and bordering Austria to the north, **Koroška**, Slovenia's smallest region, marks a return to the alpine peaks of the west. The former mining and iron-working towns of the region now make useful bases for forays into the surrounding hills and mountains, which are mapped out with an excellent series of hiking and cycling routes. The most attractive town here is the region's economic and cultural centre, **Slovenj Gradec**.

Spread across the edge of the Pannonian basin, bordering Austria, Croatia and Hungary, **Prekmurje** is the country's easternmost province and the polar opposite of mountainous western Slovenia. It's also the least visited, yet its mellow tranquillity offers a surprisingly enchanting mix of neat, flower-bedecked villages, such as **Bogojina**, **Filovci** and **Beltinci**, ancient churches, as at **Martjanci** and **Selo** and lush, green countryside, whose flat, wide open spaces provide the ideal terrain for cyclists with an aversion to hills. Although

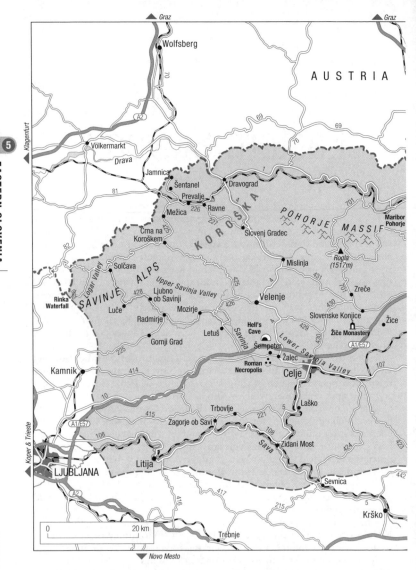

sparsely populated – the only settlements of any conspicuous size are **Murska Sobota** and **Lendava** – Prekmurje is one of the most multifarious regions in Slovenia, home to the country's largest Roma community.

Transport links in this part of the country are pretty good: the main rail line serves quite a few places and a well-integrated bus system links remoter towns and villages.

HUNGARY

Selo
Martjanci   Moravske
Murska   Toplice
Sobota   Bogojina
              Filovci
Radenci
                Beltinci
Lenart
                Črenšovci   Velika
                              Polana   Lendava
                      Mura
              Ljutomer
          Jeruzalem
Maribor

Bolfenk

Pragersko   Mithra
Slovenske   Shrines   Ptuj
Bistrica   Ormož   Čakovec
          Ptujska Gora   Cirkulane
                    Drava   Varaždin
              Haloze Hills

Rogaška   Rogatec
Slatina
Olimia Spa   Krapina   Novi Marof
Podčetrtek
Olimje
Monastery

                                          N
                    C R O A T I A

                            EASTERN SLOVENIA

Novo Mesto   Zagreb

Celje and around

From Ljubljana, several main roads – the fastest of which is the A1 highway – head eastwards to **CELJE**, which lies at the heart of the **Lower Savinja Valley** (Spodnja Savinjska Dolina), a predominantly flat, fairly densely populated landscape raked with vast hop plantations and wheat fields.

Slovenia's third-largest city after Ljubljana and Maribor, though with a population that still just barely tops the fifty thousand mark, Celje derives its name from the Roman settlement, Celeia, a key administrative centre of the Roman province of Noricum. Economically and culturally the town peaked in the Middle Ages under its overlords, the counts of Celje, who, for three centuries, staked their claim as one of Central Europe's foremost ruling dynasties – one of their last acts before the Habsburgs assumed control was to award Celje its town rights in 1451. As in much of the Štajerska region, Celje faced formidable Germanizing pressures during the late nineteenth and early twentieth centuries, culminating in German occupation during World War II, during which time the town was heavily bombed by Allied planes. Despite its heavy industry, modern-day Celje is not an unattractive place, and worthy of a full day's sightseeing thanks to its clutch of impressive churches and buildings, and one of the largest castles in the country.

Aside from Celje, the area's sites are relatively few, though there's an impressive **Roman necropolis** west of Celje, in Šempeter, and you could spend an entertaining couple of hours in the towns of **Velenje** and **Laško**, located a short way north and south of Celje respectively.

Arrival and information

Both the **train** and **bus stations** are smack-bang in the centre of town, the former just across the road from Krekov trg, the latter 400m north of here; you'll also find left-luggage facilities at the bus station (Mon–Fri 6am–8pm; €2). From the train station it's a short hop across the road to the very helpful **tourist office**, based inside the striking Celje Hall (Mon–Fri 9am–5pm, Sat 9am–1pm; ☏03/428-7936, ⓦwww.celje.si). The **post office** (Mon–Fri 8am–7pm, Sat 8am–1pm) is a few paces north of Krekov trg, and there's **internet access** 200m further north of here in the café of the Celje Youth Centre (CMC), at Mariborska cesta 2 (daily 7am–10pm).

Accommodation

The limited stock of **private accommodation** in town can be booked through the tourist office. Otherwise, there's the **student dorm** (Dijaški Dom) about 500m west of the centre at Ljubljanska 21 (☏03/426-6600), which has one-, two- and three-bed rooms available throughout the year (€17 per person); and the *Castle View* **hostel**, a tiny place with just a couple of doubles and one four-bed room (€15 per person) 400m south of town at Breg 21 (☏070/220-069, ⓔhostel@elfa-sp.si.

Of Celje's three **hotels**, the most central is the expensive *Evropa* on Krekov trg (☏03/426-9000, ⓦwww.hotel-evropa.si; ⑦–⑧), whose rooms are all smartly decorated in striking chocolate brown and cream. Just across from the bus station, at Mariborska cesta 3, the *Hotel Štorman* (☏03/426-0426, ⓔrecepcija.storman@siol.net; ⑤–⑦) is popular with visiting business folk, though its poky rooms are very ordinary; while the vaguely Egyptian-themed *Hotel Faraon*, 1km north of the centre on the road to Šempeter at Ljubljanska 39 (☏03/545-2018, ⓦwww.hotel-faraon.si; ⑥), is a motel-style building concealing modern, crisply furnished rooms.

The City

The castle aside, all the main sights – churches, squares and museums – are compacted together in the **Old Town**, itself bounded by the Savinja River to

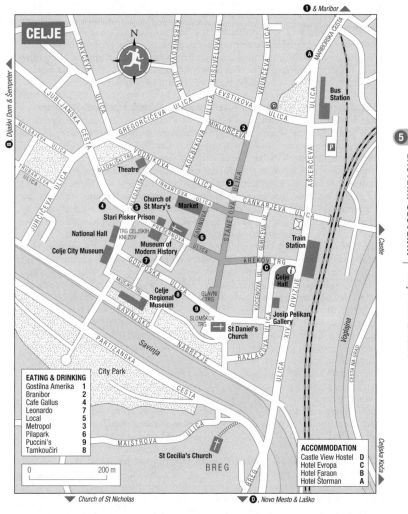

EATING & DRINKING
Gostilna Amerika	1
Branibor	2
Cafe Gallus	4
Leonardo	7
Local	5
Metropol	3
Pilapark	6
Puccini's	9
Tamkoučiri	8

ACCOMMODATION
Castle View Hostel	D
Hotel Evropa	C
Hotel Faraon	B
Hotel Štorman	A

the south, the railway line to the east and a chain of main streets to the north and west. The best way to take in the town is to follow a roughly circular route from Krekov trg through to Prešernova ulica and Trg Celjskih Knezov, then down Muzejski trg and along the riverside promenade to Glavni trg.

Krekov trg and around

Facing the busy main street on Krekov trg is **Celje Hall** (Celjski Dom), a red and cream brick building erected in 1906 as a cultural centre for the town's German citizens – it's now the location for the tourist office. Further along the street, where Krekov trg segues into Prešernova ulica, take a short diversion down Stanetova ulica for a quick glance at the **Bank of Celje**, whose curving balconies and distinctive pillar and column motifs are instantly recognizable as the work of the great Jože Plečnik (see box, p.60).

A two-minute walk south of Krekov trg at Razlagova ulica 5, the **Josip Pelikan Gallery** (Tues–Fri 10am–2pm, Sat 9am–noon, Sun 2–6pm) holds an extensive number of the photographer's studio portraits, mountain landscapes (he was a mountaineer himself) and pictures of Celje and surrounds. The gallery is actually part of the glass photo studio in which Pelikan (1885–1977) worked, so there's plenty of his original equipment on display too.

Museum of Modern History and Stari Pisker Prison

Just beyond the pedestrianized portion of Prešernova ulica, the former town hall, at no. 17, now accommodates the **Museum of Modern History** (Muzej Novejše Zgodovine; Tues–Fri 10am–6pm, Sat 9am–noon, Sun 2–6pm; €3 includes entry into Stari Pisker Prison), an enjoyable and imaginatively presented trawl through twentieth-century Celje. Numerous items from different fields, such as education, work and war, are presented through the eyes of three fictitious characters, each from a different generation. Upstairs, the "Streets of Craftsmen" show mock-up workshops representing goldsmiths, clockmakers, milliners, tailors and so on, who thrived here during the interwar period. There are further such models of the main square, Glavni trg, and the northeastern working-class suburb of Gaberje, which is now a sprawling industrial zone. The museum also incorporates **Herman's Den** (Hermanov Brlog), the country's only dedicated children's museum with plenty of gadgets and gizmos to keep the kids entertained, as well as a small play area to mess around in while the parents go off and enjoy the rest of the museum in peace.

Across the road, at Prešernova 20, is the **Stari Pisker Prison** (same times as museum), where, during World War II, 374 civilian prisoners were executed by occupying German forces. The courtyard where the shootings took place is now a memorial yard, with the names of those killed identified on one wall alongside a bronze relief, while the old torture chamber now contains various items from that time, including clothing, shackles, farewell letters and objects made by prisoners – note, too, on the wall, several photos of the shootings, which were taken by Josip Pelikan (see above). During Slovenia's ten-day war of independence in 1991 a large number of Yugoslav army soldiers were briefly held here, while today the prison functions as a young offenders centre. In order to visit you should call in at the Museum of Modern History first.

The Roman Road and Celje Regional Museum

Prešernova ulica continues up to the grandly named **Trg Celjskih knezov** (Dukes of Celje Square), a large irregularly shaped space dominated by the late nineteenth-century, neo-Renaissance **Narodni Dom** building (National House), now the headquarters of the town council. A few paces further down the square is the **Roman Road** (Rimska cesta; Tues–Fri 10am–noon & 4–6pm, Sat 10am–noon; €2); almost exclusively used for military purposes during the twentieth century – excavations of the underground site began in 1992, revealing some extraordinary Roman and, to a lesser extent, Gothic remains. Running through the heart of the site is a Roman road (part of which has wheel tracks embedded), while there are also extensive foundations of two houses, one of which bears some remarkable wall frescoes. Best of all, however, is a stunning white marble statue (minus the head and arms), believed to be the figure of an aristocratic woman.

From the square's southern end, walk down Muzejski trg until you come to the arcaded Old Manor House, now home to the **Celje Regional Museum** (Pokrajinksi Muzej Celje; March–Oct Tues–Sun 10am–6pm; Nov–Feb Tues–Fri 10am–4pm, Sat 10am–noon; €4). If you only see one thing in this museum,

For more than three hundred years the **counts of Celje** ranked among the great Central European ruling dynasties. The dynastic line began with Gebhard I de Saun in 1130, before it morphed into the lords of Žovnek in the thirteenth century and the counts of Celje in 1341. As their status and wealth grew, the counts established their own court system, minted their own money and built castles and churches around the Savinja region. They reached the zenith of their powers under the reign of Hermann II around the end of the fourteenth century, a period during which they extended their sphere of control outside Slovenia into neighbouring lands, at the same time establishing important ties with other European ruling aristocratic houses. Raised to the rank of dukes of the province in 1436, the counts were, for a short period, the equal of their great adversaries and former feudal overlords, the Habsburgs. Their sudden demise followed Ulrich II's assassination by his long-time Hungarian adversary, László Hunyadi, in Belgrade in 1456.

make it the **Celje Ceiling**, a dramatic, illusionist tempera painting discovered under another wooden ceiling in 1926. Completed around 1600 by an unknown author (the piece has been attributed to Almanac, although this is disputed), this splendid Renaissance composition comprises eleven panels featuring the four seasons, four gods, two battle scenes, and, in the central panel, a tangle of pillars and columns rising upwards to an imaginary sky. As a measure of protection, the room is kept in a permanent state of near darkness.

The remainder of the museum is taken up with several rooms of not very exciting furniture, the odd painting and a bit of sculpture. Its saving grace is the room given over to the deeds of the counts of Celje, its star exhibit a glass cabinet holding eighteen of the counts' grisly skulls, including that of its last ruler Ulrich II, easily identifiable as it's the one with the jaw missing.

Slomškov trg, Glavni trg and the City Park

From the Celje Regional Museum, continue along the promenade, past a section of medieval walls, to cobbled **Slomškov trg**, a small square named in honour of the saint Anton Slomšek – there is statue of him nearby (see box, p.293). Standing in the middle, the fourteenth-century **Abbey Church of St Daniel** (Cerkev Sv Danijel) is the town's most impressive ecclesiastical monument. Invested with some outstanding Gothic architecture, including a fine rib-vaulted ceiling and a towering arch at the entrance to the presbytery, the church also features numerous high-quality wall frescoes, most notably in the **Chapel of Our Lady of the Sorrows**, which also keeps a fifteenth-century pietà of the Madonna cradling the dead body of Jesus. The chapel dedicated to Slomšek was added in 2000, one year after his beatification in Maribor.

From Slomškov trg a narrow path leads through to **Glavni trg**, a lovely square flush with Baroque and Renaissance buildings, and a convivial place to enjoy a drink during the warmer summer months. In the centre stands **St Mary's Column**, adorned with statues of Sts Rok, Joseph and Florian. Heading north out of the square brings you to the intersection with Krekov trg and Prešernova ulica.

For a bit of peace and quiet, head across the river to the **City Park** (Mestni Park), a tranquil green expanse where you can ramble, play tennis or ice-skate (in winter) in the recreation centre. Also on this side of the river is the **Church of St Cecilia** (Cerkev Sv Cecilija), reached via a long covered walkway (though it's often closed) and, further up the hill, the **Church of St Nicholas**

(Cerkev Sv Miklavž); although this, too, is almost always closed, there are some superlative **views** of the castle opposite.

The Old Castle and around

Once the largest fortification in the country, the windswept ruin of Celje's **Old Castle** (Stari Grad; daily: summer 9am–9pm, winter 10am–5pm; €2) sits atop a four-hundred-metre rise 2km southeast of town. Originally a twelfth-century structure, the castle acquired its present layout in the fourteenth century during the rule of the counts of Celje, who reinforced the walls and invested the interior with residential quarters; ad-hoc additions followed, before its eventual demise and descent into ruin during the seventeenth century. Although there are vestigial Romanesque and Gothic remains, years of renovation have quashed much of the castle's historical charm; nevertheless it remains an impressive site, particularly when viewed from afar. While here it would be remiss not to climb the enormous **Friedrich Tower** (Friderikov Stolp), originally a four-storey defence tower built by the counts in the fourteenth century but now a roofless structure offering stupendous **views** of the rust-red and orange tiled town rooftops, and the hump backed hills of the Lower Savinja Valley. The castle also has a **café** and information centre. It stages a regular programme of medieval themed events throughout the summer, though the principal happening takes place on the last Saturday in August. To reach the castle, head through the underpass by the train station and follow the signs; beyond the old football stadium, the quickest walking route is to cut through the woods and rejoin the road at the top, from where it's a further 1km or so.

The castle is also a good starting point for several short to medium length **hikes** in the area, with signposted trails to Celjska koča (651m; 2hr 30min or 1hr 30min), Svebotnik (700m; 2hr) and the delightful little hill village of Svetina (679m; 2hr 30min). At the first of these, there's excellent accommodation at the *Celjska Koča* **hotel** (☏05/907-0405, Ⓦwww.celjska-koca.si), a large, alpine-like lodge with spotless and very comfortable **rooms** (❺), as well as dorm beds (❷). There's a very accomplished **restaurant** here, too, with fantastic views down to the Savinja valley, well worth visiting even if you're not planning to sleep over. If you're here in the summer, try the **bobkart** (€2 for one run, €5 for three runs), located just up behind the hotel. The lodge can also be reached by car (or bicycle) from Celje; take the road east towards the castle, before continuing south along Cesta na Grad, from where there are signs up to the hotel. If you are planning to do some walking, pick up a copy of the 1:50,000 *Celjska Kotlina* **map**, available from the tourist office.

Eating and drinking

There are few really decent **restaurants** in town; occupying a handsome white and grey coloured town house at the bottom end of Glavni trg, *Puccini's* has a super menu, in the main featuring home-made pasta and risotto, but also offering fish, steak and other treats; both the elegant, faux-Gothic interior and the raised, wood-decked terrace are equally enjoyable settings in which to dine (closed Sun). *Pilapark*, at Savinova ulica 9, is a comfortable Mexican place with dark red and bright yellow painted walls and a brick vaulted ceiling, serving up the usual suspects – between 11am and 5pm they offer a good selection of *malica* dishes (bargain two- or three-course set meals) for around €6. Despite its awkward location 1km north of the centre at Mariborska cesta 79, opposite the City Center shopping complex, the oddly named *Gostilna Amerika* is worth trekking to for its huge portions of southern Balkan specialities such as bean stews, *čevapi* (rolls of minced meat) and *ražnjiči* (a combination of meats on a skewer).

Celje has a healthy sprinkling of cafés and pubs to choose from. Of the town **cafés**, take your pick from the restful *Café Gallus*, secreted away in a passageway just off Ljubljanska cesta; *Leonardo* on Gosposka ulica, whose mouthwatering selection of cakes and pastries are quite likely to draw you in; or the loungey café inside the Metropol art-house cinema at Stanetova ulica 17. Between June and September the grassy riverbank area in front of the Regional Museum becomes the *Mestna Plaža* (City Beach), a nicely shaded, open-air café-cum-bar with hammocks strung between the trees; there's also a daily programme of fun events staged here, such as dancing, theatre and puppetry.

For evening **drinking** your first stop should be the well-frequented *Tamkoučiri*, an artsy, laid-back brick vaulted bar with tall wooden tables and stools; the beer's good too. Alternatively, there's *Local*, a long, coolly lit cellar bar attracting a mixed crowd enjoying the regular DJ nights of jazz, funk, soul and swing – it's located through a small passageway opposite the National Hall on Prešernova ulica. No less enjoyable is the roomy, pub-like *Branibor* at Stanetova ulica 27.

Entertainment

The **Slovenian People's Theatre** (Slovenski Ljudsko Gledališče), at Gledališki trg 5 (box office Mon–Fri 9–11am & 5–7pm, plus one hour prior to each performance; closed July & Aug), is one of the best professional theatres in Slovenia. The theatre is also the venue for the **Days of Comedy** festival in February, though surmounting the language barrier might prove a little tricky. The town puts on a couple of other festivals, foremost of which is **Summer in Celje**, a two-month programme of small concerts and gigs at various venues around town, while **medieval-themed events** (markets, jousting and the like) take place regularly up at the castle during the summer months.

Šempeter and the Roman Necropolis

Approximately 12km west of Celje along the main road running parallel to the A1 highway, the small urban settlement of **ŠEMPETER** is the setting for a **Roman Necropolis** (Rimski Nekropoli; mid-April to Sept daily 10am–6pm, Oct Sat & Sun 10am–4pm; €4). One of the most important archeological sites in this part of Europe, the necropolis, excavated and reconstructed over a fifteen-year period during the 1950s and 1960s, served as a burial ground for the nobles of Celeia (Roman Celje) until it was swamped by floodwaters from the Savinja River around 270 AD. Four marble mausolea, emblazoned with relief portraits of the families they commemorate, as well as scenes from classical mythology, were re-erected, and dozens more plinths, columns and fragments were unearthed.

The largest and grandest of the four monuments is the **Spectatii** family tomb, its members represented by three headless statues; the funerary plinths are arrayed with mythical figures and various seasonal scenes, while the head of Medusa juts out over the gable. The most arresting tomb is that of the **Ennii** family, depicted here by three shallow relief portraits of the mother, father and daughter, Kalendina, though curiously there's not one of the son, Vitulus. On the front-facing plinth there's a fine relief of *Europa Riding the Bull* and, on the Baldachin ceiling, sculpted caskets bursting with rosettes. By way of contrast, the other two mausolea are less fanciful: the altar-shaped tomb of **Vindonius** – understood to be the oldest of the four – features reliefs of *Hercules and Alcestis* and, on the side panels, two hunters, one with a hare draped around his neck, the other carrying a shepherd's staff and a basket of birds. Built in the form of a chapel, the tomb of **Secundinii** is largely devoid of ornamentation.

▲ Roman Necropolis, Šempeter

To get here take one of the hourly **buses** from Celje, alight in the centre, and backtrack 100m to the traffic lights; from here walk up Ob Rimski Nekropoli towards the church, opposite which is both the necropolis and the small **tourist association office** (April–Oct Tues–Sun 10am–6pm; ☏03/700-2056, Ⓦwww .td-sempeter.si). From Šempeter, buses continue west along the main road, stopping after 2km at the road which branches south to the village of **Dolenja Vas** (which is actually part of **Prebold**). At no. 147 the family-run, little *Dolina* **campsite** (☏03/572-4378, Ⓦwww.dolina.si; April–Oct) also has four simple rooms (❸) and two apartments (❺). Some 800m further on from here, at Graščinska ulica 9, the *Garni Šport Hotel* (☏03/703-4060, Ⓦwww.garnisporthotel .com; ❾) has comfortable, clean and warm rooms.

Hell's Cave

If you don't manage to get down to the Karst region, you can content yourself with a visit to the **Pekel (Hell's) Cave** (Jama Pekel; hourly tours April–Sept daily 9am–6pm, March & Oct Sat & Sun til 5pm; €6. Located 5km north of Šempeter, across the main A1 highway near the isolated hamlet of **Podlog**, this atmospheric little cave takes its name from the devilish figure carved into the rock face above the entrance. Inside, it's split between two levels; the first, lower gallery tracks the Peklenščica (Hell Stream) past several lakes towards a small subterranean waterfall. Thereafter it's a steady climb to the stalactite-infested upper gallery, and then onwards to the exit, positioned some 40m higher than the entrance. If you don't have your own transport, **bikes** (€5 per day) can be rented from the *Dolina* campsite (see above).

Laško

Eleven kilometres south of Celje, the small spa town of **LAŠKO** has been brewing beer since 1825, and is today one of the two largest breweries in the country – the Union brewery in Ljubljana is the other – and formerly one of the largest in Yugoslavia. Visits to the **brewery** (pivovarna), which take in the

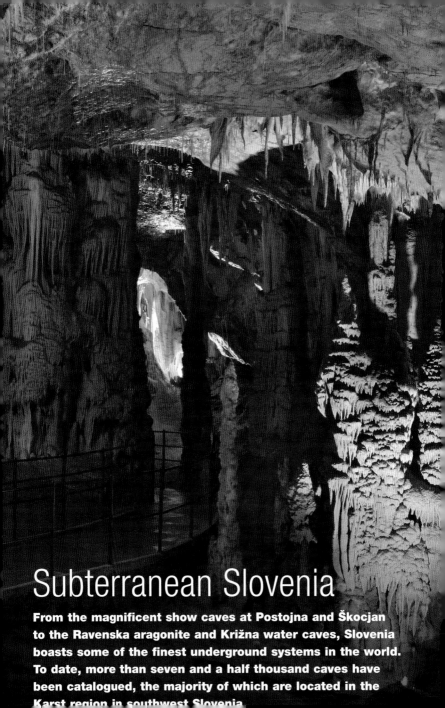

Subterranean Slovenia

From the magnificent show caves at Postojna and Škocjan to the Ravenska aragonite and Križna water caves, Slovenia boasts some of the finest underground systems in the world. To date, more than seven and a half thousand caves have been catalogued, the majority of which are located in the Karst region in southwest Slovenia.

Križna cave ▲
Postojna cave ▼

Caving on Migovec mountain ▼

Cave exploration

Although caves have been visited since the Middle Ages, it wasn't until the seventeenth century that systematic exploration and documentation of Slovenia's caves began. Foremost among the scholars of that time was the celebrated Slovene polymath Janez Vajkard Valvasor, who explored and wrote extensively on the mysterious subterranean phenomena. However, it was only after a visit to Postojna by Emperor Franz Ferdinand in 1819 that caves came into fashion as a mass tourist destination. Today there are around two dozen caves open to the general public, some of which rank among Slovenia's most popular tourist attractions. A visit to one of these natural wonders could have you traversing an underground canyon, floating on a subterranean lake or even engaging with a cave's animal inhabitants.

Visiting Slovenia's caves

Visits to Slovenia's two classic show caves, Postojna and Škocjan, take place all year round, with tours usually lasting around ninety minutes; those expecting long walks and steep climbs need not worry, as there are well laid-out paths catering to the less dynamic, and nothing other than warm clothing and half-decent shoes are required. However Slovenia also offers longer and more adventurous caving at places such as Križna, where visitors are kitted out with flashlight, helmet and boots, and Babji Zob, which requires a reasonable degree of physical exertion. If you fancy a truly authentic cave visit – complete with all the gear (rope, harness and so on) – try your luck with one of the many caving clubs located throughout the country, details of which can be found at ⓦ www.jamarska-zveza.si.

Proteus anguinus – the Human Fish

There are an estimated two hundred animal species in Slovenia's caves, but none is as enigmatic as **Proteus anguinus**, the Human Fish. This peculiar-looking creature is a 25cm-long amphibian with pigment-less skin, bright red gills and atrophied eyes; it is snake-like in appearance, with two tiny pairs of legs (the front ones have three digits, the rear two – hence the "human" part of its name) and a flat, pointed fin to help propel itself through water. The fact that the Human Fish is completely blind matters little, as the creature spends almost all of its one hundred years' existence entirely in the dark. While it usually consumes insect larvae, it's not uncommon for *Proteus* to indulge in a spot of cannibalism; conversely, it can go years without food, leaving researchers stumped. The most vexing questions, however, concern its habits of reproduction, which remain a mystery.

▲ *Proteus anguinus*

▼ The Karst

The Karst

The Karst, a limestone plateau in southwest Slovenia, is one of the country's most fascinating geographical features. The incredible underground formations that characterize this landscape are the consequence of millions of years of erosion and corrosion of the soluble limestone rock by rainwater. The results are spectacular: weird and wonderfully formed caves and tunnels, often with fantastically shaped and richly coloured stalactites and stalagmites, subterranean rivers and lakes, and deep-sided depressions, the best examples of which can be seen at the amazing Škocjan Caves.

The Škocjan Caves Park ▲

Stalactites and stalagmites at Postojna caves ▼

Slovenia's top ten caves

▶▶ **Škocjan** This awesome natural wonder features dozens of passages and chambers, plus an underground canyon that's truly something to behold. See p.188

▶▶ **Križna** A helmet, flashlight and boots are required to visit this magnificent water cave, riddled with lakes, streams and passages, and home to a stack of cave-bear remains. See p.226

▶▶ **Postojna** Slovenia's premier show cave begins with a ride on the cave train, before you enter a vast network of chambers crammed with a dazzling array of stalagmites and stalactites. See p.218

▶▶ **Vilenica** A beautiful karst cave featuring classic formations, which is also the unlikely setting for a prestigious annual literary festival. See p.187

▶▶ **Babji Zob** Although it's a tough little trek to get here, it's worth it to see this modest cave's highly unusual and rarely seen helictite formations. See p.119

▶▶ **Kostanjevica** Chambers, lakes and dozens of tight passages and stair-cases characterize this cave, which is inhabited by thousands of southern horseshoe bats. See p.248

▶▶ **Krka** This is one of the smallest caves open to the public, but you will get to see *Proteus anguinus* (the Human Fish). See p.238

▶▶ **Pekel** Named after the devilish-looking figure cut into the rock face, the ominously nicknamed "Hell's Cave" features split-level galleries and a lovely subterranean waterfall. See p.272

▶▶ **Ravenska** A relative minnow of a show cave, Ravenska is known for its flourish of brilliant white aragonite crystals. See p.182

▶▶ **Pivka** The small and atmospheric Pivka Cave is named after the river that created the neighbouring Postojna cave system. See p.220

filtration and bottling plants, a modest museum and a spot of sampling, are usually only available for groups, but if you call well in advance it should be possible to arrange a tour (contact the tourist office).

However, there's more to Laško than just beer. Known to have existed since Roman times, the town's thermal springs have been attracting a more contemporary crowd since 1854 when the first formal baths were built. Today the **Laško spa** (Zdravlišče Laško; ⓦ www.thermana.si), a ten-minute walk north of the tourist office on Zdravališče cesta, is a thoroughly modern affair, incorporating two complexes; with its huge glass cupola, the **Wellness Park Laško** (ⓣ 03/423-2000; daily 9am–9pm, Fri & Sat till 10pm; weekdays €12, €10 after 6pm; weekends €14, €10 after 6pm) has a myriad of indoor and outdoor thermal baths, comprising whirlpools, massage pools, water slides and wave machines, in addition to a sauna centre and a smart hotel (❼); next door the **Zdravlišče Laško** complex (ⓣ 03/734-5178; daily 9.30am–10pm; weekdays €9 for 3hr, €11 all day; weekends €10 for 3hr, €12 all day) also has a wide range of indoor and outdoor baths, plus its own hotel (❻).

The town's **Beer and Flowers Festival** (Pivo-Cvetje) in early/mid-July is one of the most enjoyable provincial events in the Slovene calendar, four manic days of music, sports and games, flower displays and, of course, lots of beer.

The town's **train** and **bus stations** are positioned side by side on Trg Svobode on the west bank of the Savinja River, and just a few paces from the **tourist office** (Mon–Fri 8am–5pm, Sat 8am–noon; ⓣ 03/733-8950, ⓦ www.stik-lasko.si), housed in a modern glass building by the bridge – they've got **bikes** to rent (€3 for 1hr, €9 for the day). Spa **hotels** aside (see above), there's the *Hotel Savinja*, across the river in the old part of town at Valvasorjev trg 1 (ⓣ 03/734-3030, ⓔ storman.savinja@siol.com; ❺), whose ten large and fantastically luxurious rooms are superb value. Back across the bridge, opposite the tourist office, the polished *Hotel Hum* (ⓣ 03/734-8800, ⓦ www.thermana.si; ❻) is similarly good value.

Eating possibilities are more or less limited to the *Pizzeria Špica* on the corner of the bridge opposite the tourist office, though the *pivnica* in the basement of the *Hotel Savinja* is good fun, serving up draught beer and snacks. Beautifully set on the slopes of Mount Hum (583m) 1km north of town is **Tabor Castle** (Grad Tabor), whose two renovated towers – one round, one square – now accommodate a wedding hall and a seriously posh and expensive **restaurant**; the food, however, is exemplary, featuring an exotic menu of meats and fish (deer, duck, cuttlefish and lobster) alongside some intriguing local specialities such as beer soup and beer mousse. From the castle there's a well-marked footpath to the top of Mount Hum, where you'll be rewarded with some splendid views (45min).

Velenje

Opened with great ceremonial pomp in 1959, **VELENJE**, 24km northwest of Celje and well connected by both bus and train, is Slovenia's youngest town. Formerly known as Titov Velenje – the Yugoslav president Tito visited here no fewer than four times, on one occasion with Brezhnev – modern-day Velenje was designed as a model industrial workers' town, characterized by a uniform series of grim high-rise apartments and wide streets broken up by the odd splash of greenery. Today, Slovenia's fifth largest city is still sustained by major industry, including coal mining, which employs around two thousand people, and the major domestic appliances producer, Gorenje, which employs more than five thousand people. Amid this oddly appealing Socialist-Realist aesthetic are two worthwhile attractions: the town castle and museum, and the coal mining museum.

Velenje Castle and the Velenje Coal Mine

Sited on a high, rounded hill above Velenje's small, almost forgotten, Old Town quarter is the beautifully renovated **Velenje Castle** (Velenjski Grad), most of which dates from the sixteenth century. The castle now houses the **town museum** (Tues–Sun 9am–6pm, €3), which comprises several disparate but interesting exhibitions: the most enthralling section is the collection of African art donated to the museum by Czech-born sculptor František Foit, who spent more than twenty years living in and travelling around the continent. During this time he accumulated some terrific stuff, most of which is on display here, including jewellery, furniture, musical instruments, tribal masks and puppets, as well as some of his own wood-carved sculptures. The two other major exhibitions are those on twentieth-century Slovene art, featuring big-hitters such as Pilon, Kralj, Mihelič and Tisnikar, and an exposition on the region in medieval times, comprising lots of sacral artwork, a reconstruction of a seventeenth-century house, and items culled from the area – look out for an exquisite, and extremely rare, ivory watch. A couple of rooms are also given over to the development of Velenje post-World War II though, for the most part, it's little more than a shrine to socialist-era figureheads such as Tito and Edvard Kardelj. The castle can be reached via a path just across from the sports hall and by road from the old part of town.

Coal has been excavated at the **Velenje Coal Mine** in Škale, 1.5km north of town, since the mid-eighteenth century, although it was the drilling of the main lignite layer around a century later that really put the town on the map. Although the mine remains operational, it's possible to visit certain parts of it as part of an organized **tour** (daily at 9am, noon & 3pm; €9). The ninety-minute visit – enlivened by audiovisual presentations and puppets of assorted mine characters – takes in sections of both the old and new mine shafts, the latter first used after World War II; you also get to tuck in to a hearty miner's lunch in the underground canteen. Once done you can view the **coal mining exhibition** (price included in the tour ticket, €2 for exhibition only). However, in order for an ad-hoc visit to take place, there needs to be a minimum of seven people, so you should ring in advance to see when tours are scheduled (℡03/587-0997). Unless you have your own transport, it's a good thirty-minute walk to the mine; from the Old Town, head north up Cesta Talcev, cross the rail tracks and continue along Kidričeva cesta, which loops round and becomes Koroška cesta.

If you've got a moment to spare, pop over to Titov trg, opposite the *Hotel Paka*, to see the oversized **monument of Tito** – one of very few statues of the former Yugoslav president remaining in Slovenia. On the opposite side of this monstrous concrete square is a more sobering monument commemorating some 668 victims of fascist oppression during World War II.

Practicalities

The **bus station** is located in the centre of town midway along Šaleška cesta, while the **train station** is 1km northeast of here, just off Cesta Talcev near the industrial zone. The informative **tourist office** is inside the sports centre 200m west of the bus station (Mon–Fri 8am–6pm, Sat & Sun 9am–1pm & 3–6pm; ℡03/896-1860, @tic@velenje.si) – they've also got **bikes** for rent.

The most agreeable **place to stay** in town is the *Hotel Ražgoršek*, below the castle on Stari trg (℡03/898-3630, Ⓦwww.hotelrazgorsek.com; ❻), whose brazenly colourful – if slightly over the top – rooms are fashioned in Baroque style, with plush carpets, oversized paintings and gold trimmings. Across the road from the tourist office, at Rudarska 1, is the formidably dull and slightly overpriced *Hotel Paka* (℡03/898-0700, Ⓦwww.hotelpaka.com; ❻); while, up behind the bus station at Kopališka cesta 1, the upmarket, nineteenth-century *Vila Herberstein* (☎03/896-1400, ⓦwww.gorenjegostinstvo.si; ❼) possesses seven large rooms furnished in period style. The small *Jezero* **campsite** (☎03/586-2776) is sited 2km west of town, beyond the coal mining museum by the lake. The best **eating** option is the fanciful restaurant inside the *Ražgoršek* hotel.

Koroška

From Velenje, two roads forge their way into the heart of **Koroška**, a mountainous, heavily forested region crossed by three river valleys and scattered with isolated highland farmsteads and small valley settlements. One road heads north up the Mislinja Valley to the pretty town of **Slovenj Gradec**, and beyond to **Dravograd**, while the other road straggles across a mountain pass northwest to the ex-mining towns of **Črna na Koroškem** and **Mežica**; the former is also a key starting point for forays into the heart of the Koroška mountains themselves.

Slovenj Gradec

In stark contrast to Velenje, the spruce little town of **SLOVENJ GRADEC**, 27km further north in the Mislinja Valley and the largest settlement in Koroška, preserves a delightful medieval core. The town is renowned for its rich cultural heritage, thanks to the likes of prominent Slovene artists, Bogdan Borčič and Jože Tisnikar, and the Austrian composer Hugo Wolf, all of whom were born here.

Everything of interest is spread out along **Glavni trg**, a wide, smoothly curving street that forms the heart of the town's beautifully preserved historic medieval core. The town's two principal sites are both inside the former town hall at no. 24; on the first floor is the **Koroška Gallery of Fine Arts** (Koroška Galeriji Likovnih Umetnosti; Tues–Fri 9am–6pm, Sat & Sun 10am–1pm & 2–5pm; €2.50), one of the largest and most progressive art centres in the country. The gallery dotes almost exclusively on the works of artists from Koroška, namely Franc Berneker, the first modern Slovene sculptor, Bogdan Borčič, painter of brightly coloured abstract pieces – though several darker works were influenced by his time spent in Dachau – and Jože Tisnikar, whose overwhelmingly bleak and moody paintings, defined as "dark modernism", undoubtedly owe much to the time he spent in a hospital pathology department.

Installed in the cells of the former town prison (last used during World War II by the Germans) across the courtyard is a fine little **archeological collection** (Arheologija Krajine; same times; €2), whose finds, from the Mislinja, Mežica and Drava valleys, span several periods: the earliest exhibits include cave-bear remains, a bone harpoon, and Stone and Iron Age tools, while from the Roman and Slavic period there is a stack of grave goods (signet rings and bronze fibula brooches) and, from the Middle Ages, tiles and clay pots; further treasures – ceramics, coins and jewellery – were unearthed in 2000 during the building of a new school. Some 200m down the street, the muddy-green, neo-Renaissance house at no. 40 was the birthplace of Austrian composer **Hugo Wolf** (1860–1903), a bust of whom sits just above the entrance; appropriately it's now a music school.

Situated on Trg Svobode directly opposite the town hall, the thirteenth-century, but several times rebuilt, **Parish Church of St Elizabeth** (Cerkev sv Elizabete) honours the Hungarian princess Elizabeth. Although the exterior is largely of Gothic appearance, the interior showcases an abundance of Baroque extravagances, most notably a sumptuously overblown high altar – the central painting of Elizabeth was executed by the Baroque workshop of

Franz Strauss – and a richly gilded pulpit. Also keep your eye out for numerous liturgical items, Gothic knight's tombstones, and, to the right as you enter, a painting of St Anton Slomšek (see box, p.293), completed in 2000. Standing in its shadow is the lovely wood-shingled **Church of the Holy Spirit** (Cerkev sv Duha), beautifully ornamented with a fine array of fifteenth-century frescoes – note, too, the fragment of a Roman tombstone embedded into the exterior wall on the north side. The church is usually closed, so contact the tourist office to arrange a visit.

Practicalities

The town's **bus station** is on Pohorska cesta, from where it's a ten-minute walk south to Glavni trg and the **tourist office**, situated on the ground floor of the old town hall at no. 24 (May–Sept Mon–Fri 9am–6pm, Sat & Sun 9am–noon; Oct–April Mon–Fri 8am–4pm; ℡02/881-2116, ⊛www.slovenj-gradec.si).They can also arrange private **accommodation**, which may be your preferred choice given that the town has just one rather dull hotel, the *Slovenj Gradec* (℡02/883-9850; ❺), a short walk up from the tourist office at no. 43. Somewhat oddly located out at the small airport 3km south of town on the road to Velenje, the hotel *Aerodrom* (℡02/885-0500, ⊛www.aerodrom-sg.si; ❻) has smart, sunny, air-conditioned rooms, and a **campsite** (mid-March to mid-Oct) with bungalows sleeping three people (❺).The best option, however, is the delightful *Rotovnik-Plesnik* **tourist farm** (℡02/885-3666, ✉info@rotovnik-plesnik.si; ❸), 4km east of town in Legen, on the road up to the Kope ski resort; on offer is warm accommodation, super home-cooked food, and a still-functioning 1970s jukebox.

The town is devoid of a single worthy place to **eat**, so head for *Gostilna Murko* on the northern outskirts of town (on the road to Dravograd) at Francetova cesta 24.There are several appealing **cafés** spread along Glavni trg, in particular *Mestna kavarna* opposite the tourist office, and *Fragolissima*, adjoining the *Slovenj Gradec* hotel, which serves up fabulous, big bowls of ice cream.

Dravograd, Šentanel and Jamnica

Eleven kilometres north of Slovenj Gradec and just 4km shy of the Austrian border, the old market town of **DRAVOGRAD** sits at the junction of Koroška's three valleys – the Drava, the Meža and the Mislinja – as well as several key road routes and the Maribor–Klagenfurt rail line. Although it's likely that the only reason you might end up here is to take an onward connection, there are a couple of minor sights worth checking out if you've got an hour or so to spare, both of which lie across the river in the old town.

Some 50m along the main street,Trg 4 julija, in the basement of the municipal town building at no. 7, is a World War II **Gestapo prison** (Muzej Zbirka Gestapovski; Mon–Fri 8am–2pm; free), whose half a dozen dingy, cobwebbed cells now display a dusty collection of uniforms and artefacts belonging to both the captives and their captors. The Gestapo controlled the prison on two occasions, the first time between the beginning of the occupation and July 1941, and the second time between January 1944 and the end of the war. Five minutes' walk further along the street stands the attractive twelfth-century **Church of St Vitus** (Cerkev Sv Vid), one of the few Carinthian-style Romanesque structures remaining in this region, and unusual in that it features a bell tower at its eastern end – it's usually closed so if you'd like a look, contact the tourist office.

The **train** and **bus stations** are just 200m apart, on the south bank of the river near the bridge. From here, it's a ten-minute walk across the bridge and along Trg 4 julija to the **tourist office** at no. 50 (daily: May–Oct 10am–7pm; Nov–April 11am–2pm & 3–6pm; ☎02/871-0285, ✉info@dravograd.si). Just up from here at Koroška cesta 48 is the town's one **hotel** (and just about the only place to **eat**), the very dull *Hesper* (☎02/878-4440, ⓦwww.hesper.si; ❻).

From Dravograd, one road (and the rail line) threads its way through the scenic Drava Valley eastwards to Maribor some 60km away, while the road west passes through the uninteresting towns of **Ravne na Koroškem** (the "capital" of Koroška) and **Prevalje**. About 2km beyond Prevalje, a road branches off up towards the villages of **ŠENTANEL** (4km distant) and **JAMNICA** (7km distant), two picturesque mountain settlements known for their abundance of **tourist farms** (all ❸); two of the best in Šentanel are *Ploder* at no. 3 (☎02/823-1104, ✉kmetijaploder@hotmail.com) and *Marin Miler* at no. 8 (☎02/824-0550, ✉marin@koroska.org) – the latter has a terrific *gostilna* too. In Jamnica, at no. 10, there's the large *Bike Hotel-Koroš* tourist farm (☎02/870-3060, ⓦwww.mtbpark.com), a dedicated **cyclists' hotel** offering simple, but warm and comfortable double rooms; they're also the main cycling centre for the region (see box, p.278).

Mežica and Črna na Koroškem

A short way south of Prevalje is the town of **MEŽICA** where, up until a few years ago, lead and zinc had been mined for over three hundred years. Although mining began here way back in 1665, it wasn't until Napoleon's arrival in 1809 that intensive, heavy-duty production took place. Further modernization of the mine during the early twentieth century saw the introduction of electricity in addition to pneumatic drilling methods, though the gradual depletion of ore reserves after World War II led to a decline in production and the mine finally closed in 2000. Part of it, however, was kept open for **tours** (April–Nov Tues–Sun 11am, plus 3pm in July & Aug; Dec–March Sat at 11am; ☎02/870-0180, ⓦwww.podzemljepece.com; €8). Kitted out with jacket, helmet and light, you clamber aboard the very small and rickety mine train (not for the claustrophobic), which transports you 3.5km along a shaft into the heart of the mine complex, the area known as Moring. During the one-hour tour you walk through numerous large galleries on two levels (there are twenty in total, each approximately 30m apart), where you'll get to see the calling room, where miners would gather at the beginning of the shift before dispersing to their stations, various mining equipment and machinery preserved *in situ* and a series of audiovisual demonstrations.

After resurfacing, head to the adjacent **mine museum** (Tues–Sun: April–Oct 9am–5pm; Nov–March 9am–3pm; €3), where you can view a fine display of minerals and fossils, mine survey maps and mapping instruments and a mock-up miner's home, a typically cramped living space which would be expected to accommodate up to eight members of the same family.

For something a little more adventurous, you can participate in **underground bike rides** through a section of the mine, which takes you through 5km of illuminated tunnels constructed for the transportation of lead ore and waste materials. Tours (€22 for two to three people, €20 for four to seven people) take place at 10am daily except Monday, but you should contact the bike hotel in Jamnica first (see above).

During the mine's heyday, most of the population of **ČRNA NA KOROŠKEM**, a sedate little town 7km south of Mežica in the Upper Meža Valley, were also employed at Mežica, as well as in the local ironworking, forestry and timber industries. Črna is chiefly of interest as a springboard for

Cycling and hiking around Črna na Koroškem

The mountains encircling Črna na Koroškem, also known as King Matjaž Park, offer some of the best **cycling** in the country, with twelve circular routes adding up to around 1000km of marked trails – each of which is marked out by yellow animal footprints. Everything you need to know about cycling in the region can be obtained from the *Cycling Hotel* at the Koroš tourist farm in Jamnica (see p.277), where you can also **rent bikes** (€15 per day) and get repairs done. As well as organizing guided mountain bike tours, the hotel arranges combined biking and climbing, and biking and kayaking excursions – check out ⓦwww.mtbpark.com for more details.

From Črna there are a number of good **hiking** possibilities, the most popular of which is the trek northwest up to **Mala Peca** (1731m; 3hr 15min), just below which is the *Dom na Peci* hut (April–Oct daily; Nov–March Sat & Sun only; ☎02/823-8406); fifteen minutes' walk from the hut is the **cave of King Matjaž** (Matjaževa jama), the alleged sleeping place of the mythological folk hero named after the Hungarian king, Matthias Corvinus – there's a bronze statue of Matjaž inside the cave entrance. From the hut, you can continue via one of two paths towards Kordeževa glava (2125m) and the Austrian border. From Črna there are shorter hikes, too, including a ninety-minute trail north to the year-round *Koča na Pikovem* hut (992m), which has just a handful of beds (☎02/823-8525), and another trail south to **Najevska Lipa** (1hr 45min), the site of an enormous Linden tree, alleged to be one of the largest trees in Slovenia. Whatever activity you plan to undertake, you'll find the 1;50,000 *Koroška* **map** available from the tourist office, a useful aid.

onward ventures into the mountains, while there are a couple of tourist facilities here. If you've got some time to kill, there are a couple of minor collections to nose around: across from the bus stop, the **ethnological museum** (€2) comprises a modest assortment of everyday household items and farming implements used by local peasants, and hewn into the rock face a few metres from the bus station, the **mining museum** (€2) presents mine trucks, drilling equipment and tools used in the Mežica mine before its closure.

To view either collection contact the helpful **tourist office** (June–Sept Mon–Fri 8am–6pm, Sat 9am–1pm; Oct–May Mon–Fri 8am–3pm, Sat 9am–1pm; ☎02/870-3066, ✉pkm@siol.net), just around the corner from the **bus stop** at Center 100. There's nowhere to stay here, but if you're looking for something to **eat**, try one of the several gostilna dotted around town, the most central of which is *Rešer*, directly opposite the tourist office at Center 101.

Črna is also known throughout Slovenia for its **Snow Castle Festival**, staged 6km from town up at Pod Peca on the last weekend of January, and which sees over a hundred teams compete to see who can design the highest, grandest or most dazzling ice castle. How long these constructions remain intact is, naturally enough, dependent on the weather, though most are still standing about a week or so after the event.

The Upper Savinja Valley

Named after the **Savinja River**, which flows from the heart of the Kamniške-Savinja Alps, down through Celje and beyond to Zidani Most, where it joins the Sava River, the **Upper Savinja Valley** (Zgornja Savinjska Dolina) is a pristine landscape of towering alpine peaks, river valleys and undulating slopes. The territory it covers extends roughly from between the aforementioned Alps to Letuš, a small village just north of Šempeter. The region's settlements are mainly large villages and a couple of small towns; picturesque as some of them are, such as the administrative centre of **Mozirje**, they're not really worth a special visit. In any case, the chances are that you'll be keen to push on to the surrounding hills and mountains.

The Logar Valley

The region's siren draw is the extraordinarily beautiful **Logar Valley** (Logarska dolina), a seven-kilometre-long alpine valley situated along the western margins of the Upper Savinja in the cradle of the Kamniške-Savinja Alps. Formed during the Ice Age, the U-shaped glaciated valley manifests a level, green valley floor covered with flower-speckled meadows and beech woods, enclosed by step-like cliff sides riddled with glacial boulders, waterfalls, springs, streams and a majestic wreath of jagged grey peaks, most of which top 2000m.

From the entrance to the valley (April–Oct; €6 per car), it's about 2km to the **information hut** (May–Oct daily 9am–6pm; ☎03/838-9004, ⓦwww .logarska-dolina.si) and a couple of hotels (see below), beyond which point the road continues for a further five kilometres up to the head of the valley and Logarska's most popular site, the ninety-metre-high **Rinka Waterfall** (Slap Rinka); if you're walking, there's a trail (6km) to the waterfall beginning approximately 1km along the road after you've entered the valley. Although the mountains look formidable, they can be traversed via a trail which starts at Rinka and climbs to **Okrešelj** (1396m), where there's the *Frischaufov* hut (☎03/838-9070; May–Oct), before continuing to **Kamniško Sedlo** (1864m) and another hut (☎051/241-639; mid-June to mid-Oct); from here the trail continues down to Kamniška Bistrica (see p.92).

The staff at the information hut organize three-hour guided walks of the valley (€3.50 per person for a group of up to ten people), as well as a number of other activities including **horseriding** (€15 for 1hr), **rock climbing** (€25 for 1hr), **archery** (€10 for 1hr) and tandem **paragliding** (€60); you can also rent **bikes** (€3 for 1hr, €12 for 4hr plus) – usefully these can also be rented back up at the entrance to the valley.

Out of season, you can get information at the alpine-style *Hotel Plesnik* (☎03/839-2300, ⓦwww.plesnik.si; ❾) across the road; this extremely comfort-able, and very expensive, place also has a pool and sauna, but it's not as homely as the neighbouring *Vila Palenk* (same tel as *Plesnik*; ❽), which has some rooms with a fireplace, lovely if you're here during the winter. Otherwise, there's plenty more affordable accommodation elsewhere throughout the valley: 500m along the road from the *Plesnik* is the *Plesnik* tourist farm (☎03/838-9009, ⓦwww.plesnik.si; ❸), and, another 500m further on from here, sheltered among tall pines and with a super play area for kids, the smart *Pension Na Razpotju* (☎03/839-1650, ⓦwww.logarska-narazpotju.si; ❻). Back down in the opposite direction, roughly midway between the valley entrance and the *Hotel Plesnik*, there's the small *Juvanija* tourist farm (☎03/838-9080, ✉juvanija@email.si; ❸), with just four rooms.

The one major approach to Logarska is via the road from **Ljubno ob Savinji**, a small town 34km east of Kamnik and 26km northwest of the Ljubljana–Celje highway. Logarska can also be reached from Črna na Koroškem (see p.277), via a relatively short (20km), but difficult and mostly unsurfaced, mountain road – the road actually emerges in Solčava from where it's a short drive to Logarska. Indeed, unless you've got your own **transport**, getting to Logarska will prove difficult; although there are a handful of (weekday) buses from Celje and Velenje to Ljubno ob Savinji, Luče and Solčava (the nearest settlements to Logarska), only one of these continues to Logarska, and even then, that's only between

April and October (10.45am from Luče & 11.06am from Solčava). During this same period one bus (weekdays at 12.40pm) departs Logarska for Celje.

Around the Logar Valley

Although most cars and buses pile into Logarska, the two glaciated valleys flanking Logarska Dolina, **Robanov Kot** to the east and **Matkov Kot** to the west (and just a couple of kilometres from the Austrian border), are no less magnificent, and should appeal to those seeking more solitudinous recreation. There's beautifully sited **accommodation** in both valleys, with the *Govc-Vršnik* tourist farm in Robanov Kot, at no. 34 (☎03/839-5016, ⊛www.govc-vrsnik .com; ❸), and the *Gradišnik* tourist farm (☎03/838-9012, ⊛www.gradisnik.si; ❸), high up in Matkov Kot, which also has archery for its guests.

The nearest settlements to Logarska are the villages of **Solčava**, 4km to the east, where there's a **tourist office** at no. 30 (daily: July & Aug 8am–6pm; April–June & Sept–Oct 8am–3pm; ☎03/839-0710), and **LUČE**, 10km further along the same road, which also has a tourist office at no. 106 (same times; ☎03/839-3555). Luče is the best place to stock up on provisions (there are a few shops, a bank and post office here) prior to heading on to Logarska; there's **accommodation** in the form of the *Pension Raduha* at no. 67 (☎03/838-4000, ⊛www.raduha.com; ❺), which also has a very well-regarded **restaurant**, and the beautifully sited *Spodnji Jerovčnik* tourist farm (☎03/584-4087, ⓔrebeka .kumer@volja.net; ❸), 1.5km south of Luče in the hillside hamlet of Krnica – follow the signs for Podvolovljek. The only **campsite** in the area, *Camp Šmica* (☎03/584-4330, ⊛www.camp-smica.com; May–Sept), is 1km back out along the road towards Solčava by the Savinja River.

East of Celje

The region east of Celje is dominated by spas, the best known of which are **Rogaška Slatina** and **Olimia**, the former once one of Europe's grandest resorts, the latter a relatively recent addition to the scene. There is also a brace of cultural diversions to enjoy – the Skansen-like **Rogatec open-air museum** near Rogaška Slatina, and **Olimje Monastery**, not far from the Olimia spa.

Rogaška Slatina

Thirty kilometres east of Celje, **ROGAŠKA SLATINA** was built around several mineral-rich springs (Donat, Styria and Tempel) discovered during the sixteenth century, and was once one of the most fashionable spa resorts in Central Europe – some of its more illustrious visitors included the Habsburg ruler Franz Jozef, the French Bonapartes and King Karađorđevič of Serbia.

Arrival, information and accommodation

The town's **train station** is on Kidričeva ulica, some 500m south of town, while the **bus station** is closer to the centre on Celjska cesta, from where it's a five-minute walk to the main square Zdravliški trg. The **tourist office** (July & Aug Mon–Fri 9am–7pm, Sat & Sun 11am–5pm; Sept–June Mon–Fri 8am–4pm, Sat 8am–noon; ☎03/581-4414, ⓔtic.rogaska@siol.net), on the southwestern corner of the square, can arrange private **accommodation** if you can't afford, or don't fancy, one of the many hotels in town. By some distance the grandest of these are the *Grand Hotel Rogaška* (❾), *Styria* and *Strossmayer* (both ❽), adjoining each other on the square's eastern side (reception for all three is in the *Grand* ☎03/811-2000, ⓦwww.terme-rogaska.si); all three are supremely comfortable, with big square beds, thick pile carpets, and gowns and bottled water supplied. There are further, marginally more affordable options on Celjska cesta, the town's other main street, running adjacent to Zdravilíski trg; the *Slovenija* (☎03/811-5000; ❼), a large yellow building 100m north of the tourist office, distinctive for its Plečnik-designed frontage, and the good-value *Slatina* (☎03/818-4100, ⓔinfo@hotelslatina.com; ❼), a short walk further along, which also has some apartments (❽). The **post office** (Mon–Fri 8am–6pm, Sat 8am–noon) is next to the bus station.

Between May and October you can jump on a **tourist train** (*turistíni vlak*), one of which runs to the Olimia spa and onwards to Olimije Monastery (€10), and another to the glass factory (€7); the times are irregular, however, so check with the tourist office first. **Bikes** can be rented from the *Sava* and *Donat* hotels, both located at the northern end of Zdravilíski trg (€10 for the day).

The Town

Despite the addition of a couple of beastly looking hotels, the town has managed to preserve its quintessential spa ambience. This is particularly true around its central square, **Zdravilíski trg**, a broad, immaculately kept landscaped park neatly framed by gravel walkways and grand buildings, the pick of which is the stately **Zdravilíski Dom** (now the *Grand Hotel Rogaška*), one of the finest Neoclassical buildings in the country.

Although its curative properties have long been used to treat a wide range of disorders – typically gastrointestinal complaints and metabolic problems – the water is tapped first and foremost for commercial purposes, and you'll find many bottled waters from Rogaška in bars and restaurants throughout the country; in its purest form, however, it is incredibly metallic, and hence barely drinkable. You can sample the magnesium-laden Donat mg, the spa's most famous water, and others, in the large **pump room** (daily 7am–1pm & 3–7pm; €1.50) located at the northern end of Zdravilíski trg near the **Temple**, an oval pavilion sitting on top of the spa's main spring; head towards reception, grab a cup and away you go.

The main therapeutic baths and treatment centres are in the Terapija building adjoining the pump room. However, casual visitors tend to make a beeline for the **Riviera swimming complex** (Termalna Riviera; daily 9am–8pm, Sat till 11pm; weekdays €9 for the day, €7.50 for 3hr, weekends €10/€8), indoor and outdoor pools (average temperature 30°C) halfway along Celjska cesta; guests of some hotels receive free entry to these pools so check with yours.

The town is also known for its crystal glassware, the production of which has been taking place since 1665; the **Glass Factory** (Steklarska šola; ⓦwww .steklarna-rogaska.si) is located 2km south of town, with tours of the factory possible by prior arrangement – contact the tourist office; there's a shop here too (Mon–Fri 8am–7pm, Sat 8am–noon).

Eating and drinking

The town's eating and drinking options are not bad at all; the pick of the **restaurants** is *Sonce*, a short walk beyond the Riviera swimming complex on Celjska cesta, with a menu heavily skewed towards fish from the Dalmatian coast, but where you can also find other, rarely found delicacies such as horsemeat and ostrich – they've got a fine stock of wines here too. Back down the street at no. 6, the cute little cellar pizzeria, *La Gondola*, also has some good salads and pasta dishes; or there's *Bohor*, near the bus station on Kidričeva ulica, a simple, old-fashioned place serving standard grills. The most enjoyable of the several **cafés** in town is the cool *Café Attems*, housed in the lovely, mint-coloured building at the southern end of Zdraviliški trg; alternatively there's the sprawling, terraced *Central Café* a few paces away, or the cosy, old-style *Teater Café*, inside the cultural centre opposite *La Gondola*.

Rogatec Open-Air Museum

Regular buses and some trains make the short trip east to the ancient little market village of **ROGATEC**, known for its delightful **Open-Air Museum** (Muzej na Prostem Rogatec; April–Nov Tues–Sun 10am–6pm; €3), a modest gathering of vernacular architecture from Štajerska's sub-Pannonian plain. Standing either side of the entrance gate are the **forge** and **general store** (*Lodn*), the former a single-room building built from sandstone in 1930, and stuffed with tools and semi-finished products, the latter a typical Rogatec grocer's store, furnished with a counter surrounded by weighing and measuring machines, containers and jars full of goodies. The museum's central space is taken up by the early nineteenth-century wooden **house** which once belonged to the local poet Jože Šmit from the nearby village of Tlake. Comprising a traditional setup of *lojpa* (entrance hall), *kuhna* ("black" kitchen) and *hiša* (living room), this type of house had unusual sleeping arrangements: while young, the children would sleep with their parents in the larger bedroom, but once grown-up, the girls would move to another bedroom, which had smaller windows barred with an iron cross, in case of any unwanted male visitors; the boys, meanwhile, had to make do with the barn.

The double **hayrack** is of the type found all over Slovenia, though, curiously, this one comes from Croatia. There's also a working well, a beehive and a thatched-roof pigsty, which doubles up as a storage rack for turnip and carrot leaves, used as fodder for the swine during winter months. To the rear of the museum the old **winegrower's house** now serves as a catering centre. Regular workshops are held here during the summer, whereby you can watch, or participate in, such pursuits as bread making, corn braiding and nail forging. Next door to the museum is the Strmol **riding centre** (☏070/279-249), offering trail riding and regular lessons (both around €15 per hour).

The museum is a little awkward to get to; from the train station, head due north using the church as a marker; at the main road turn right and walk to another road junction where you should turn left following the signs for Ptuj. The museum is about 1km along the road from here. Buses from Rogaška usually stop at the *Gostilna Jelša*, from where you must backtrack until you reach the road junction – again, from here, follow signs to Ptuj.

Podčetrtek and Olimia Spa

A somewhat more contemporary spa resort than Rogaška Slatina is **Olimia**, 1km northeast of the border village of **PODČETRTEK**, 15km south of Rogaška Slatina. The spa (daily 8am–10pm, Sat until midnight; weekdays €10.50 for the day, €8.50 for 3hr; weekends €12.50 for the day, €10.50 for 3hr; ⓦwww .terme-olimia.com) is essentially geared towards package tourists – most day-trippers head to the water park a short way to the north (see opposite). However, if you want to stay, there's plenty of **accommodation** (all ☏03/829-7000), all of which is of a uniformly high standard: the upmarket and very pricey *Sotelia* and *Breza* (both ➒) hotels – the latter has its own pool; the *Rosa* apartments (➐–➒); and the *Vas Lipa* tourist village, comprising two dozen apartment buildings holding four separate units each, and sleeping two to five people (➏–➑);

there's a restaurant, supermarket and so on in the village, too; guests of all three receive free entrance to the pools and the water park.

There are more thrills and spills less than 1km further north of the spa at the large **Water Park Aqualuna** (daily May–Sept 9am–7pm; weekdays €10.50 for the day, €7.50 after 3pm; weekends €12.50, €9 after 3pm), which is a great place to take the kids. Spread across a field next door is the large and well-equipped *Natura* **campsite** (☎03/829-7833; mid-April to mid-Oct). Back out on the main road, opposite the campsite, *Gostišče Ciril* (☎03/582-9109, ⓔgostisce .ciril@siol.net) is a hostel offering cheap beds (❷) with shared shower facilities, and simple food.

From a distance, the much-remodelled twelfth-century **Podčetrtek Castle** high above Podčetrtek looks very impressive, but on closer inspection it is, sadly, nothing of the sort. Ravaged by looters and now littered with debris and crumbling masonry, it's a depressing site and you're best off just admiring it from afar. The village itself holds little of interest, though is useful for practical means: there's a **tourist office**, in a small hut at Škofja Gora 1 (Mon–Fri 8am–3pm, Sat 8am–1pm; ☎03/810-9013, ⓦwww.turizem-podcetrtek.si), and on the main road opposite the entrance to the village, the *Aparthotel Pirc* (☎03/818-3802, ⓦwww.aparthotel-pirc.com), which has large, modern and well-furnished rooms (❹) and apartments sleeping two- to five people (❹–❺), as well as a decent restaurant and pizzeria.

If you're coming by **train** (Podčetrtek is on the Celje–Imeno line), then make sure you get off at the appropriate stop: for Podčetrtek get off at the station of the same name; for the spa it's "Atomske Toplice" (the old name for the spa); and for the campsite and water park, it's "Podčetrtek Toplice". **Buses** also stop in all three places.

Olimje Monastery

From Podčetrtek, a smooth, winding valley road snakes through some gorgeous countryside to **Olimje Monastery**, 4km to the southwest. Originally built as a castle in 1550, on the site of a former fortification possibly dating from the eleventh century, the building was acquired by Pauline monks from Croatia in 1663. They proceeded to convert it into a monastery, enlarging the premises and augmenting it with a church before the order's dissolution in 1782. The Minorite order returned here in 1990.

Tacked on to the left-hand side of the monastery, the **Church of the Assumption** was completed in 1675 by the monks as part of the monastery's rebuilding programme. Preceded by two jet-black and gold marble altars – the one to the left holds a painting of Christ's Passion, the one to the right honours St Paul the Hermit, regarded as the founding father of the monastery – the small presbytery is almost entirely filled by an immense three-tiered golden altar, finished with several paintings and a dozen statues of saints. The side chapel, dedicated to St Francis Xavier and featuring a majestic, caramel-coloured late Baroque altar, was a later addition (1766) to the church. Note, too, the fine upright organ in the choir loft.

Reputedly the third-oldest preserved pharmacy in Europe, after ones in Paris and Dubrovnik, the Pauline **pharmacy** (daily 10am–noon & 1–6pm; €1), located on the ground floor of the left round tower as you face the monastery, was founded in the mid-eighteenth century, functioning until 1782 when the monastery was disbanded. There's now little left in the way of fittings and fixtures or pharmaceutical goods (these were all removed when the monastery was dissolved), but its frescoes – executed around 1789 by local painter Anton

Lerchinger, and depicting Sts Cosmas and Damian, patron saints of physicians and pharmacists, eminent physicians Aesculapius and Paracelsus and scenes of Christ healing – are worth the small entrance fee. If it's not open, ring the bell on the door a few paces along the cloister for admission. There's also a shop where you can buy herbal teas and brandies, honey, oils and creams, most of which is cultivated in the surrounding gardens.

Just behind the monastery is the fantastic **Syncerus chocolateria** (April–Oct 10am–7pm; Nov–March till 5pm) where you can indulge your wildest sweet-toothed fantasies with an eye-popping selection of the finest chocolates, all of which are produced in the factory to the rear of the shop.

After visiting the monastery you could take a short walk up the hill to the *Jelenov Greben* tourist farm (☎03/582-9046, ⓦwww.jelenov-greben.si; ❹) to grab some refreshments, while, if you wish to stay, they've got some lovely rooms, a number of which overlook the valley; the family also cultivate their own foodstuffs, such as mushrooms, jams, fruits and nuts, all available in the large shop. There are further places to **sleep** and **eat** along the road between Podčetrtek and the monastery; approximately midway between these two points, the roadside *Domačija Haler* pub and brewery brews its own beer (*Haler Pivo*) on the premises, the perfect foil for its bistro, which features a selection of beer dishes alongside a more sophisticated *à la carte* menu. In a separate building behind the pub, the *Pension Katja* (☎03/812-1202, ⓦwww.haler-sp.si) has cheap, but very smart, rooms (❸) and apartments (❹–❻), sleeping four to six people; there's also a small basement swimming pool, sauna and gym.

The *Gostišče Amon* (☎03/818-2480, ⓦwww.amon.si), 1.5km further on, was one of the first private **wineries** in the country and is renowned for its Laški Rizling and Chardonnay; tasting costs around €5 for four or five wines. Its **restaurant**, too, is of the highest order, with specialities of the house including roast duck and oyster mushrooms, and baked snails, while the interior looks great, the chunky oak tables and chairs having been recycled from old wine presses. Close by is the tight little nine-hole **golf course** (☎03/810-9066; €25 for 18 holes, €20 for 9 holes).

If you don't have your own wheels, you'll have to walk, which is no great hardship as it's a very enjoyable short trek. If you'd like to do more extensive **walking**, pick up a copy of the 1:18,000 *Podčetrtek* map from the tourist office, which maps out several local walks between one and four hours long, one of which is the walk to Olimje.

From Celje to Maribor

There are several worthwhile sites between Celje and Maribor, most of which are easily reached by public transport. Just off the main highway, the charming little town of **Slovenske Konjice** lies close to the enchanting ruins of **Žiče Monastery**. A few kilometres further on, the small spa town of **Zreče** is the jumping-off point for the ski and sports resort of **Rogla**, which nestles at the heart of the **Pohorje Massif** mountain range.

Slovenske Konjice

Nineteen kilometres northeast of Celje, just off the main highway to Maribor, is **SLOVENSKE KONJICE**, the self-styled town of "Wine and Flowers", owing to recent triumphant efforts in Europe-wide floral competitions and a strong tradition of wine-making. The centre of town is shaped by Stari trg, a lovely, gently inclining street framed by a neat kernel of yellow, apricot and lime-green town houses, and bisected by the Gospodična (Miss) stream, itself straddled by a series of tiny wooden bridges.

At no. 15, the **Riemer Gallery** (Mestna Galerija Riemer; Tues & Thurs noon–3pm, Wed till 4pm, Fri & Sat 10am–noon; €3) is a private collection of art and period furniture amassed by wealthy local businessman Franc Riemer. As impressive as his collection of Old Masters, paintings by Ivana Kobilica and sketches by Rihard Jakopič are, the show-stealer is a fourteenth-century fresco of the Crucifixion, retrieved from Žiče Monastery in 1996, and held to be the only fresco from the monastery still in existence. Fifty metres further up the street on the opposite side, at no. 24, is a **wine shop**, where you can partake in some tasting – however, there are no regular opening hours, so you should contact the tourist office first.

There's tasting of a very different kind further north at the **Trebnik Manor House** (Dvorec Trebnik; Mon–Fri 8am–3pm, Sat 8am–noon), located up beyond the **Church of St George** (Cerkev Sv Jurij). The one renovated part of this otherwise dilapidated building has been transformed into a herbal shop and gallery, displaying and selling a range of products such as honey, oils, creams, shampoos and brandies, all of which have been cultivated from the beautifully tended herb garden to the rear of the manor. There are free brandy-tasting sessions, though an acquired palate is most definitely required. From behind the manor house, it's a two-hour walk up a marked path to **Konjiška Gora**, from where there is a superlative panorama of the town and vineyards below, and the Pohorje Massif in the distance.

Practicalities

The **bus station** is located on Liptovska cesta, from where it's just a couple of minutes' walk north to Mestni trg and beyond (across the bridge) to the centre of town, which is essentially the main street, Stari trg. About two-thirds of the way along Stari trg, at no. 29, is the small **tourist office** (Mon–Fri 7am–6pm, Sat 10am–noon; ☎05/759-3110). The town's one **hotel** is the welcoming, but plain and over-priced, *Dravinja* (☎05/757-5700, @ hotel-dravinja@siol.net; ❼), down by the bridge on Mestni trg.

The town's one truly outstanding **restaurant**, the 🍴 *Zlati Grič*, is a fifteen-minute walk north of the centre, planted among the impossibly lush Škalce vineyards; the food (roast lamb and smoked meats) and wine on offer is of a high standard, but really it's a place to come and enjoy the setting. To get here from Mestni trg, walk through the small park-like area to the traffic lights, cross the road and walk up Škalska cesta, from where it's a further ten minutes. Weaving its way through these same vineyards is a gorgeous nine-hole **golf course** (☎05/758-0362; 9 holes €20, 18 holes €30; March–Nov).

There are few other places to **eat or drink** in this quiet town; the *Beli Konj* (White Horse) at the lower end of Stari trg (no. 6) is a colourful and energetic pub, or there's the slightly more laid-back *Tattenbach* café next to the Riemer Gallery. The smart little *Patriot* bar, in the **Youth Club** (Mladinski Center) north of Stari trg, behind the fire station at Žička 4, occasionally has live music at weekends – they've also got free **internet access**.

Žiče Monastery

Fringed by ancient woodland in the isolated splendour of the Valley of St John, some 12km southwest of Slovenske Konjice, lie the mist-swathed ruins of **Žiče Monastery** (Žička Kartuzija; May–Oct Mon–Fri 9am–7pm, Sat & Sun

▲ Žiče Monastery

9am–7pm; Nov & Feb–April Mon–Fri 10am–6pm; €4, which includes an audio guide). Founded around 1160 by Otakar III of Traungau, the margrave of Styria, Žiče was the first of four Carthusian monasteries to be chartered on Slovenian territory, and fairly prospered until its dissolution under the reforms of Joseph II in 1782. Although part of the complex has been renovated (and work is ongoing), the rest is pretty much as it was, including the twelfth-century Romanesque **Church of St John the Baptist**, now hollowed out – its vaults and roof collapsed around 1840 – but still exuding a befitting sense of authority. In one restored wing you can view a fine collection of thirteenth- and fourteenth-century keystones, consoles and other stone fragments from the original building, alongside some beautifully illustrated ancient texts and manuscripts. A healing place of repute during the thirteenth century, Žiče remained an important medicinal centre for locals and travellers alike until the monastery's dissolution; there's now a reconstructed **apothecary** on the site of the old one, offering the opportunity to sample some powerful home-made herbal brandies. The small, grass-covered mounds just behind the pharmacy were the former monks' cells.

Standing at the entrance to the monastery is the *Gostišče Gastuž*, dating from 1467 and reputedly one of the oldest guesthouses in Central Europe; it now houses a **tourist office** (same times as monastery), as well as a very good **restaurant**, which also has excellent wines, and downstairs a small inn-style room where you can get tea and mulled wine. Getting to Žiče entails taking a local bus from Slovenske Konjice to the village of **Špitalič**, 2km shy of the monastery, and then it's a gentle walk from here.

Zreče

From Slovenske Konjice hourly buses make the short five-kilometre journey north to the small industrial town of **ZREČE**, a relatively recent addition to the country's growing number of spa resorts. The spa aside, there's nothing else of interest here, though you may find yourself passing through if Rogla and the Pohorje Massif are your intended destinations. The **Terme Zreče spa** (ⓦwww.terme-zrece.eu) has an excellent complement of facilities, including indoor and outdoor therapeutic and recreational pools (daily 9am–9pm, Fri & Sat till 10pm; weekdays €10 for the day, €8 for 3hr; weekends €12 for the day, €9 for 3hr), with temperatures ranging between 28 and 34°C, a sauna village (Mon–Thurs 11am–9pm, Fri–Sun 10am–9pm), gym and a Thai massage centre (Mon–Sat 10am–noon & 3–9pm).

The spa also accommodates the very modern *Dobrava Hotel* (☎03/757-6000; ➒), and, more appealingly, the *Terme Zrece Villas* (➐–➑), a series of lodge-like apartments located 200m across the park on the edge of the forest, which sleep two to six people. There are also a couple of very agreeable, pension-like places opposite the **bus station**, itself adjacent to the spa: the jolly *Smogavc* (☎03/757-6600, Ⓔhotel@smogavc.com; ➏–➐) and the almost identical, but slightly cheaper, *Zvon* (☎03/757-3600, Ⓔinfo@hotelzvon.com; ➏) next door. Both offer good-looking rooms with all mod cons and are also decent places to eat. There's a small **tourist office** (Mon–Fri 7am–3pm, Wed till 5pm, Sat 9am–noon; ☎03/759-0470; Ⓔtic .zrece.lto@siol.net) directly behind the bus station inside the small shopping mall (PTC Tržnica).

The two best **places to stay**, however, are out of town, and are really only reachable if you've got your own transport. Three kilometres north of Zreče on the road up to Rogla, in the tiny hamlet of **Loška Gora**, the *Hotel Pod Roglo* (☎03/757-6800, ⓦwww.hotelpodroglo.com; ➏) has beautifully warm, colourful rooms fitted with plush carpets and large beds. They also brew their own beer on the premises, which complements the large, buzzy pizzeria here superbly. A couple of kilometres southwest of town in the hillside village of **Križevec**, the *Urška* tourist farm at 11a (☎03/759-0410, ⓦwww.kmetija-urska.com; ➍) offers cosy rooms, delicious home cooking and charming hospitality.

Rogla and the Pohorje Massif

From Zreče the road zigzags steeply for 16km to **Rogla** (1517m), one of Slovenia's premier ski and sports resorts sited on the eastern margins of the **Pohorje Massif**, a fifty-kilometre-long, sparsely populated plateau, arcing between Dravograd in the west and Maribor in the east. Geologically, the massif is an extension of the Alps, although physically it's quite different, a series of gently rounded ridges – few peaks top 1500m – riddled with peat marshes and small swampy lakes, and where the only settlements are isolated farmsteads and tiny upland churches. The massif was once home to sawmills, forges and *glažute* (glass-making workshops), but it is now tourism that rules the roost, with ski runs, hiking paths and other recreational facilities complemented by a good number of mountain huts and tourist farms.

Rogla's extensive **sports facilities** – an outdoor stadium, huge sports hall and indoor swimming pool – are frequently used by Slovenian and Croatian Olympic

Hiking and skiing in Pohorje

Rogla, in the heart of the Pohorje Massif, and **Mariborsko Pohorje,** further east on the doorstep of Maribor, are consistently rated two of the best **ski and snowboard** resorts in the country. Rogla has around 12km of ski trails, most of which are suited to intermediate skiers, though there are a few slopes for the less experienced. You can also take a ride on a **snowmobile** here (€8 for a circular track ride, or €60 for a safari with a guide). At 1347m, Mariborsko Pohorje is a slightly lower mountain range, but has one of the largest capacities of all Slovenia's ski resorts, with more than 60km of trails, almost half of which are beginners' slopes. It also claims to have the longest night-time (floodlit) slope in Europe. Moreover, it possesses far more tourist facilities, particularly accommodation, than Rogla. The ski season at both resorts usually runs from December to March, and the presence of snow cannons along the main runs ensures that it's possible to ski throughout this period, regardless of snowfall. **Day passes** at both cost around €30 and **weekly passes** around €150. The main piste at Mariborsko Pohorje is also the venue for the women's World Cup slalom race, the "Golden Fox", at the end of January, an event not to be missed if you're in the region around this time.

Skiing aside, the massif also has some excellent **hiking.** The trails on Rogla are numbered from PP1 to PP7, and range in distance from just a few kilometres to more than thirty. If you're short on time, there's a nice and easy 45-minute walk north from the *Planja* hotel to the *Koča na Pesku* mountain hut (1386m), which has accommodation and food available year-round (☎031/415-612). From here you can either continue northwest to the beautiful **Lovrenc Marsh Lakes** (Lovrenška jezera; 1hr), and then further onwards to *Ribniška Koča* hut (1507m; 2hr), where there's more accommodation (☎02/876-8246; closed April & Nov); or east to **Osankarica** (1193m) and the *Dom na Osankarica,* where there are refreshments only – the trail continues east to the **Black Lake** (Črno jezero), one of the largest lakes in the massif. The 1:25,000 *Zreče* map, available from the tourist office in Zreče (see p.287), marks out a number of hiking and cycle routes around both Zreče and Rogla.

teams, but all are available for use by the general public when they're not in residence; some sample prices (hourly rates) include: badminton €15; tennis €16; squash €10 (45min); gym €10; and swimming €8. Despite all these facilities, it's **skiing** that's the real draw (see box above). The resort possesses three package-type **hotels** (☎03/757-7100) within one building, the comfortable *Planja* (❽) and the slightly less expensive *Rogla* and *Brinje* (both ❼), as well as modern chalets (❺) sleeping up to four. Although the main restaurant is for hotel guests only, there is the comely inn-style *Stara Koča* in the same building, serving up wholesome, filling meals, and there's also good food at the *Koča na Jurgovem* mountain hut, sited at the top of the Jugovo chairlift a few kilometres east of the *Planja.* In winter there's a **ski bus** from Zreče to Rogla (and return) five times a day.

Maribor and around

Located at the easternmost foothills of the Pohorje Massif, **MARIBOR** is Slovenia's second city of culture, commerce and education. Yet despite its position as such, the city remains small, with a modest population of around one hundred thousand, about a third that of the capital. Despite lacking Ljubljana's sophistication and cultural appeal, Maribor still offers much to enjoy; the prevailing industrial sprawl is countered by an incoherent, yet appealing, Austrianate old core, patchworked with an elegant confection of architectural styles, colourful squares and streets, monuments and churches. Furthermore, if you tire of the city, there's plenty to see and do on the outskirts, including a couple of enjoyable wine roads to the north, and the **Pohorje Massif** to the south, where it's possible to ski, hike or partake in any number of other sporting and adventure activities.

Some history

The seeds of present-day Maribor were sown around the **twelfth century**, when the Carinthian duke, Spanheim, instructed a fort to be built (known as Marchburg, later Marburg and eventually Maribor) on Piramida, a low hill to the north of town, in order to protect the town from Hungarian raiders from Pannonia. During the **fourteenth century**, a large Jewish population established important commercial ties with major European cities, Milan, Prague and Dubrovnik; unfortunately their expulsion from the city in 1497, in addition to Hungarian and Turkish sieges, fires and recurrent plague epidemics, led to a sudden and long-term decline in the city's fortunes. The key to its revival in the **nineteenth century** was the arrival of the rail line from Vienna in 1846 (which would later be extended to Ljubljana and Trieste), together with the relocation of the seat of the Lavantine diocese from St Andraz in Austria to Maribor. Meanwhile, the establishment of a raft of major cultural and financial institutions further heightened the city's importance around this time.

Ongoing nationalist struggles between the city's German and Slovene populations towards the end of the nineteenth century culminated in outright warfare at the tail end of **World War I** following German attempts to incorporate the city into Austrian lands. However, a resounding defeat for the Germans at the hands of the Slovenes, led by General Rudolf Maister, resulted in the incorporation of Slovenian Styria into Slovene lands, and the establishment of the present-day border with Austria. Despite Maribor's assimilation into the **Kingdom of Yugoslavia**, German expansionist tendencies continued and the city eventually succumbed to German forces during **World War II**, with the mass expulsion of thousands of Slovenes and the demolition of nearly half of the city's buildings. As one of the most industrialized cities in the former Yugoslavia, Maribor was among the hardest hit by the **break-up of the federation** in 1991, the sudden loss of important inter-republic trade resulting in tremendous economic hardship and high levels of unemployment. However, thanks to a booming local wine trade, its proximity to one of the largest ski resorts in the country, not to mention some terrific festivals, this under-rated city is today a vibrant and excellent destination.

Arrival and information

The **bus** and **train stations** are handily located just 400m apart on Partizanska cesta, from where it's just a ten-minute walk into the city centre, and the **tourist office**, near the Church of St Mary at Partizanska cesta 6 (Mon–Fri 9am–7pm, Sat & Sun 9am–6pm; ☎02/234-6611, ⓦwww.maribor.travel); they have **bikes** for rent (€5 per day). The main city **post office** is at Slomškov trg 10 (Mon–Fri 8am–7pm, Sat 8am–1pm), but there's another next to the train station (same times). There's **internet** at the *Kibla* multimedia centre in the Narodni Dom at Ulica Kneza Kozlja 9 (see p.295), and at the *KIT* Cyber Café (Mon–Sat 9am–10pm) on Glavni trg.

Accommodation

The city centre is poorly served with **places to stay**, but there are further possibilities in Zgornje Radvanje, at the foot of the **Maribor Pohorje** ski

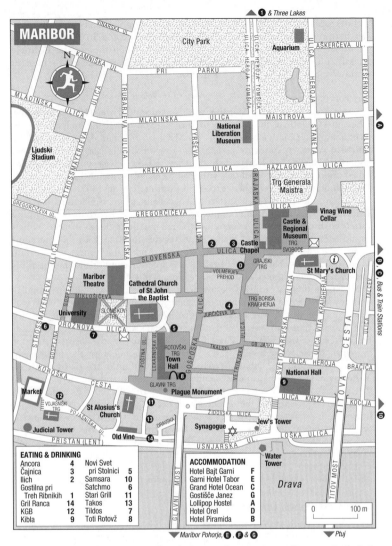

MARIBOR

City Park

Aquarium

National
Liberation
Museum

Ljudski
Stadium

Trg Generala
Maistra

Vinag Wine
Cellar

Castle &
Regional
Museum

Castle
Chapel

St Mary's Church

Maribor
Theatre

Cathedral Church
of St John
the Baptist

University

Town
Hall

National Hall

Plague Monument

Market

St Alosius's
Church

Judicial Tower

Old Vine

Synagogue

Jew's Tower

Water
Tower

Drava

EATING & DRINKING			
Ancora	4	Novi Svet	
Čajnica	3	pri Stolnici	5
Ilich	2	Samsara	10
Gostilna pri		Satchmo	6
Treh Ribnikih	1	Stari Grill	
Gril Ranca	14	Gostišče Janez	
KGB	12	Takos	13
Kibla	9	Tildos	7
		Toti Rotovž	8

ACCOMMODATION	
Hotel Bajt Garni	F
Garni Hotel Tabor	E
Grand Hotel Ocean	C
Gostišče Janez	G
Lollipop Hostel	A
Hotel Orel	D
Hotel Piramida	B

0   100 m

Maribor Pohorje, E, F & G

Ptuj

www.roughguides.com

resort 7km southwest of town; for purposes of convenience these are included along with the city hotels here. To get to any of the places in Zgornje Radvanje, take bus #6 from the train station to its last stop, which is the cable car station. The hotels at the top of Pohorje itself are listed on p.297.

The city's principal **youth hostel** is the bright and clean *Lollipop Hostel*, a five-minute walk from the stations at Maistrova ulica 17 (☎040/243-160, ✉lollipophostel@yahoo.com; €20), which has a couple of multi-bed dorms, a kitchen available for breakfast, laundry and internet. A second option is the *Uni Hostel*, which is actually part of the *Hotel Orel* (see opposite); although mostly occupied by lecturers and students, it does have a limited number of beds available (€27) between June and August. The only **campsite** hereabouts is the small and very basic one just up from the cable car station in Radvanje (☎02/614-0950; March–Nov).

Hotel Arena Pot k mlinu 57, Maribor Pohorje ☎02/614-0950, ⊛www.pohorje.org. A super location right at the bottom of the piste, this revamped hotel comprises two categories of room, some of which have terrific balconies overlooking the slope. ⑥–⑧

Hotel Bajt Garni Radvanjska 106 ☎02/332-7650, ⊛www.hotel-bajt.com. Extremely pleasant, family-run place across the river en route to Pohorje, with fairly simple, but modern and bright rooms, all with a/c and wi-fi – they've also got some cheaper rooms in the building across the road. Bus #6. ⑥

Hotel Habakuk Pohorska cesta 59, Maribor Pohorje ☎02/300-8100, ⊛www.termemb.si. Featuring all the luxuries you'd expect of a five-star hotel, the *Habakuk*, just across from the cable car station, simply oozes class; fantastically comfortable, richly furnished rooms, indoor and outdoor pools, sauna and fitness facilities. ⑨

Gostišče Janez Ciril-Metodova 4 ☎02/420-4404, ⓔjanez.antolinc@triera.net. Great-value pension 1km west of the centre across the river near Koroški most. Doubles, triples and one quad available. Take bus #4 along Valvasorjeva ulica and alight at the junction with Ruška cesta. ④

🏃 **Grand Hotel Ocean** Partizanska cesta 39 ☎059/077-120, ⊛www.hotelocean.si. Located across from the train station, and so-named after the first locomotive to pass through

Maribor in 1846, this elegant and quiet hotel possesses 22 immaculately presented rooms, each decorated in gentle cream, beige and orange colours, with cool wood furnishings and sumptuous beds. ⑨

Hotel Orel Volkmerjev prehod 7 ☎02/250-6700, ⊛www.termemb.si. Cracking location overlooking Grajski trg, though its smart, well-furnished rooms are steeply priced; also incorporates a hostel (see opposite). ⑧–⑨

Hotel Piramida Ulica heroja Šlandra 10 ☎02/234-4400, ⊛www.termemb.si. Very much the city's business hotel, this expensive, charmless place has disappointingly bland rooms (smoking and no-smoking), though they do have tea and coffee making facilities. ⑨

Pohorska Kavarna Ob Ribniku 1, Maribor Pohorje ☎02/614-1500, ⊛www.pohorska-kavarna.com. Clean, bright and modern pension with nine two- and three-bed rooms located about 500m before the cable car. Excellent value, and with a good coffee house too. ⑤

Garni Hotel Tabor Ulica heroja Zidanška 18 ☎02/421-6410, ⊛www.hoteltabor.podhostnik.si. Frequented by sporty types using the neighbouring facilities, this reasonable place, 400m north of the *Bajt Garni*, has boxy, but modern two-, three- and four-bed rooms. Bus #6. ⑥

The City

Almost all of the city's sights are grouped around the city's three principal squares – **Grajski trg**, **Slomškov trg** and **Glavni trg** – and the Lent water-front district on the north bank of the **Drava River**. Beyond these areas, possibilities exist for more leisurely diversions, such as the city park and lakes to the north of town, and a small island retreat and spa complex out to the west. There's nothing of interest to see on the residential, south side of the Drava, and the only reason you might need to cross the river is to visit the huge shopping mall, or if you're heading out to the ski resort in **Maribor Pohorje**. Wine aficionados, meanwhile, can content themselves with a visit to one of the city's outlying wine roads.

Grajski trg and around

Although not especially interesting itself, the best place to start a walking tour of the city is **Grajski trg** (Castle Square), so-named after the fifteenth-century town **castle** on the square's northeastern corner. Most of the castle's rooms are now taken up with the **Maribor Regional Museum** (Muzej Pokrajinski; Tues–Sat 9am–4pm, Sun 9am–2pm; €3); there are excellent information sheets in English in each room. Following the standard display of archeological bits and bobs, the ethnological section presents some fine rafts and cargo boats – of the type that used to dock along the Drava waterfront in the nineteenth century – beautifully painted chests and wardrobes, beehive panels and the famous *pust* masks from Ptuj. No less absorbing is the cultural history section, and in particular its voluminous collection of costumes representing the multifarious regions of Slovenia – the most celebrated piece of attire, however, is a military uniform that belonged to Tito.

The upper floor is mostly given over to the history of Maribor, and although much of it is not that stimulating, the displays of locally produced wrought ironwork and glassware are worth a lengthy pause. There's some impressive artwork here, too, the best of which is the group of smooth humanist sculptures by **Jožef Straub** (1721–83), Slovenia's leading exponent of Baroque sculpture. Also worth a glance is a wonderfully fanciful Rococo staircase, ornamented with sculptures by **Straub**, while the ceiling is strewn with stuccoed swirls and vines. Facing the square is the **castle chapel** (Grajski kapeli), built some time around 1660, its blackened interior so small it barely seats twenty people; it's usually closed however.

Looming large over the square to the east is the massive red-brick **Franciscan Church of St Mary** (Cerkev Sv Marija; daily 6am–noon & 3–7.45pm), commissioned by Viennese architect Richard Jordan in 1903 and built at the same time as the Franciscan monastery complex behind. The only concession to grandeur inside the capacious and gloomy interior is the high altar, featuring four statues in niches and some contemporary, almost cartoonish, wall paintings, completed by Catholic priest and artist Stane Kregar, one of Slovenia's foremost post-World War II church painters.

Heading south, Grajski trg funnels down to Vetrinjska ulica, a busy pedestrianized thoroughfare whose houses are now mainly ramshackle, dark and crumbling – memories of an earlier, more fanciful past, when the street served as a major route for traffic en route from Vienna to Ljubljana; the standout building is the richly stuccoed, mint-coloured Vetrinje Mansion at no. 16, dating from 1725.

Trg Svobode to the City Park

On the castle's east side is **Trg Svobode**, a large, nondescript space containing little of note save for an ugly, bulbous-shaped bronze memorial to Partisans killed during World War II, and the Vinag wine cellar on the east side, at no. 3 (see box, p.298). Trg Svobode segues into grassy Maistrov trg, from where it's another five-minute walk to the **National Liberation Museum** (Muzej Narodne Osvoboditve; Mon–Fri 8am–6pm, Sat 9am–noon; €3), housed in a handsome late-nineteenth-century terracotta and grey villa at Ulica heroja Tomšiča 5. Although there is currently no permanent display, it will eventually hold an exhibition about the city's cultural and industrial heritage; in the meantime, it does stage some excellent temporary exhibitions.

The broad, lamp-lined promenade across the road from the museum marks the entrance to the **City Park** (Mestni Park), a large, well-groomed expanse of greenery laid out in 1872 and carved up by concrete strips of pathway. For kids, there's a rather downbeat **aquarium-terrarium** (Akvarij-Terarij; Mon–Fri 8am–7pm, Sat & Sun 9am–noon & 2–7pm; €3) on the park's east side, its tanks filled with the usual suspects, including fish, snakes, lizards, turtles and spiders. Beyond here the park tapers towards the slender chain of the **Three Lakes** (Trije Ribniki). If you fancy a slightly more strenuous walk, take the path that peels off of Ribniška ulica (the road skirting the park's eastern side), and continue uphill through the almost vertically pitched vineyard to **Piramida** (386m), at the top of which is a tiny chapel; from here there are fine views of

Anton Slomšek

Bishop, poet and scribe, **Anton Martin Slomšek** was born in the small parish of Ponikva, near Celje, in 1800. Ordained in 1824, just three years into his theological studies, Slomšek took his first Mass in Olimje that same year, before returning to his studies in Celovec. He spent the next few years devoting his time to the development of Slovene schooling – in particular Sunday schools – in rural areas, and writing prayer and hymn books; by the time of his death, Slomšek had had some fifty books published.

His greatest achievement, however, was to transfer the seat of the Lavantine diocese from St Andraz, in Austria, to Maribor, thus uniting all Styrian Slovenes in one diocese, as well as effecting an upgrade in the status of the parish church to a cathedral. Slomšek was also instrumental in setting up the Catholic Society of St Hermagoras (Družba Sv Mohorja), a publishing house established in 1851 in order to help Slovenes read and write. His second great contribution was the establishment of Maribor's Theological High School in 1859, the forerunner to today's university. Slomšek died in 1862, and was beatified by the pope in September 1999.

the bright red and terracotta-coloured rooftops of the city, and the broad slopes of the Pohorje mountains in the distance.

Slomškov trg
Named after St Anton Slomšek (see box above), **Slomškov trg** is the largest, greenest and grandest of the city's three squares, endowed with some venerable old buildings and site of Maribor's premier ecclesiastical monument. The lumpish **Cathedral Church of St John the Baptist** (Cerkev Sv Janez Krstnik) was originally built as a single-naved Romanesque structure in the twelfth century, though later modifications gave it its present, predominantly Gothic and Baroque appearance. The highlight of what is otherwise a rather plain interior is the splendid Gothic presbytery, featuring exquisitely carved choir stalls inlaid with reliefs showing scenes from the life of the patron saint. The north side **Chapel of the Holy Cross** holds the tomb of the beatified Slomšek, while the stained-glass windows depicting images of Pope John Paul II were crafted on the occasion of his second visit to Maribor, in 1999 – his first was in 1996. There's further homage to Slomšek in front of the church, in the form of a large bronze statue.

The neo-Renaissance bulk at the square's western end is the former City Savings Bank, now the **university building**. Of a similar ilk, but appreciably smaller, is the splendid, pea-green-coloured **post office** (Pošta Slovenije) building at no. 10 on the square's south side. Although aesthetically less pleasing, the one other building of note is the **National Theatre**, adjacent to the university on the north side. From the square's southeastern corner, a narrow path leads into the lovely arcaded courtyard, Rotovški trg, and then into Glavni trg.

Glavni trg and around
Bounded on one side by a sweep of elegant buildings, and on the other by one of the city's busiest thoroughfares, cobbled **Glavni trg** is a fine-looking Renaissance square that functioned as the city's market area during the Middle Ages. Standing in the centre of the square, and arguably one of the finest monuments of its type in Central Europe, the **Plague Monument** was originally raised in 1681 as a memorial to the thousands that perished during the great plague. This second version was erected in 1743, its smooth column topped with a gold-leaf statue of

Mary, and its base with six saintly intercessors, the entire project masterfully sculpted by **Jožef Straub**.

Opposite, at no. 9, the Renaissance **town hall** was originally built in 1515, though reworked several times over before it attained its present appearance, featuring an exquisite Venetian stone balcony emblazoned with a two lion-relief and the city coat of arms. Recessed between two buildings on the opposite side of the road is the former Jesuit **Church of St Aloysius**.

A short walk east of Glavni trg, **Židovska ulica** (Jewish street) was the centre of the Jewish ghetto during the Middle Ages, its focal point the now beautifully restored **synagogue** (Sinagoga; Mon–Fri 8am–4pm, Sun 9am–2pm) at no. 4. The first Jewish presence in the city was recorded around 1290, at around the same time the synagogue was built, but, following a decree in 1496 banishing Jews from Maribor, the synagogue was converted into a Catholic Church. It operated as such until it was closed down under the reforms of Emperor Joseph II at the end of the eighteenth century; thereafter it functioned variously as a factory, warehouse and residential quarters. A decade-long renovation programme, during which four wooden boxes containing the remains of ancient skeletons were unearthed, has restored the synagogue to something like its former glory, and it's now used as a cultural centre and exhibition venue.

Erected in 1465, the **Jews' Tower** (Židovski stolp), just across from the synagogue, was once an integral part of the city's defence walls – it's now a photographic gallery (Mon–Fri 10am–1pm & 3–7pm, Sat 10am–1pm) – as was the immaculately restored sixteenth-century **Water Tower** (Vodni stolp) down by the river, now the venue for a lovely wine bar.

Lent

Across the busy main street, Koroška ulica, several alleyways slope down to the **Drava River** and the **Pristan** (Pier) district, or, as it's more commonly known, **Lent** (Port). Until the construction of the railways in the 1860s, the Drava was the city's principal transport artery, and Lent the main docking station for the hundreds of rafts and small cargo vessels that would stop here en route to the Danube and the Black Sea. Today, it's a bustling promenade and *the* place to kick back with a beer on summer evenings.

Lent's star attraction, and the city's most celebrated symbol, is the four-hundred-year-old **Vine** (Stara trta), which runs along the facade of the **Old Vine House** (Hiša Stare trte; Tues–Sun 10am–6pm). Reputedly the world's oldest vine, it still yields the evocatively titled *Žametna Črnina* (Black Velvet), 35 litres of which are harvested each year, although, unfortunately, this is usually bottled up for visiting dignitaries. The house itself – originally dating from the sixteenth century when it was part of the southern defence wall – holds a small exhibition relaying the history of the vine, while it's possible to sample some of the local vintages. Two of the city's main events, the pruning of the vine, and its ceremonial harvesting, take place here in March and September respectively.

A five-minute walk further west along the embankment stands the rotund, whitewashed **Judicial Tower** (Sodni stolp), though this name is something of a misnomer given that it was erected as a defensive bastion in 1310; this present structure dates from 1830. Up behind the tower, Vojašniški ulica (Army Street) and Vojašniški trg (Army Square) – essentially one and the same – are scattered with a shabby fusion of half-wrecked buildings, one of which, the former **Minorite Church and Monastery**, once functioned as a barracks and warehouse, though it's now defunct and decaying. Just beyond here is Vodnikov trg and the city's open-air market place. The best views of Lent can be garnered from **Glavni most** (Main Bridge), an elegant, rich-red structure completed in 1913.

Eating and drinking

What Maribor's **restaurant** scene may lack in quantity, it makes up for in quality, with a select core of excellent and diverse places to eat. On summer evenings, the **cafés and bars** of the Lent waterfront spill out onto the street with the hectic atmosphere of a mass open-air bar. Otherwise, there are several excellent bar-cum-club places scattered elsewhere throughout town.

Restaurants

Ancora Jurčičeva ulica 7. Buzzy, sprawling split-level pizzeria also offering lots of salads, pasta, risotto and seafood dishes; great kids menu too. Also incorporates a popular pub.

Gostilna pri Treh Ribnikih Ribniška 3. Though not quite in the same league as *Novi Svet*, this inn-style restaurant out by the Three Lakes is, nevertheless, an enjoyable place to sample fish dishes and good wine. Good set menus (€8–15), including one for vegetarians.

Gril Ranca Dravska 10. Attractively sited down on Lent, this is fast-food Balkan style, with a menu exclusively devoted to gut-busting Serbian meats, *Čevapčiči* and *Pljeskavica*, all for around €6–8. Closed Sun.

Novi Svet pri Stolnici Slomškov trg 5. In the style of a Dalmatian *konoba* (pub), this superb, homely restaurant – with fishing gear strung along the walls – has fresh fish flown in daily from the Adriatic. They've a fine wine list too. Right on the corner of Slomškov trg and Rotovški trg.

Samsara Slovenska cesta 1. Despite its bland location inside the *Kolosej* (cinema) building, this neat and colourful restaurant offers a very decent choice of well-cooked and stylishly presented Italian food; the wines aren't bad either.

Stari Gril Glavni trg 5. In the same vein as *Grill Ranca*, this cosy little place serves hunks of juicy beef with raw onion and *kajmak* (cheese) wedged inside a deliciously doughy *lepinja* (bread roll) – sit down or takeaway. Closed Sun.

Takos Mesarski prehod 3. Tucked away down a narrow passage on the south side of Glavni trg, this cool, understated restaurant offers well-cooked and well-presented Mexican dishes. The place takes on a clubby feel as the evening wears on. Closed Sun.

Toti rotovž Glavni trg 14. Top-class restaurant boasting three separate kitchens: Slovene (Pohorje steak, boar, chamois and pheasant), Japanese (sushi, vegetable tempura) and Thai (red/green curry, steamed shrimps, fish with coconut milk or chilli). The fantastic cellar bar (where you can also eat) rocks to live music at weekends. Closed Sun.

Cafés and bars

Čajnica Slovenska 4. The cosy, wooded interior of this charming teahouse is a delightful spot to indulge in some of the many world teas (and pastries) on offer – you even get given a timer to tell you when your brew is ready.

Ilich Slovenska 6. Not only does this laid-back, contemporary café offer the best range of coffees, cakes and ices in town, it's also one of the most relaxing places to while away an hour or so.

KGB Vojašniški trg. Opposite the Minorite church on a ramshackle square just west of Lent, this small, but brilliant underground cellar bar/club (check out the fantastic door as you enter) is the funkiest place in town, with regular live music to boot. A guaranteed good time. Closed Sun.

Kibla Ulica Kneza Kozlja 9 (inside the Narodni Dom; ⓦ www.kibla.org) Cool and relaxing internet café, bookshop and multimedia centre all rolled into one – the centre is highly regarded for the quality of contemporary art exhibitions staged here. Closed Sun.

Klub MC Pekarna Ob Zeleznici 16. Located across the river in a former military bakery (*Pekarna* means bakery), this is the city's foremost underground club/bar venue, its four interconnected rooms used for a range of concerts, exhibitions and other innovative cultural happenings.

Satchmo Jazz Klub Strossmayerjeva ulica 6. Good-time jazz club with a top-class rota of gigs, though the summer programme is irregular – count on around one gig every two weeks during this period; otherwise, ideal for a bout of mellow drinking.

Tildos Slomškov trg 13. Energetic, youthful place just across from the university building; just a few paces along from *Tildos* is *Toto Café,* another good little drinking spot, though rather less raucous.

Entertainment and activities

The highly regarded **Slovenian National Theatre** (Slovensko Narodno Gledališče, SNG) on Slomškov trg stages a regular top-class diet of plays, opera and ballet; theatre tickets cost around €10–15, operatic and ballet performances around €15–20 (☎02/250-6100; box office Mon–Fri 10am–1pm & 3–7.30pm and 1hr before each performance; ⓦwww.sng-mb.si). The **Puppet Theatre** (Lutkovno gledališče) at Rotovški trg 1 (☎02/228-1970) puts on performances, in Slovene, every Saturday at 10am (€3.50; closed July & Aug).

About 3km west of the centre (bus #15), the **Terme Fontana** spa and recreation complex at Koroška cesta 172 (daily 9am–9pm; ☎02/234-4100) offers a raft of activities – swimming (€10 for 4hr, €14 for the day), sauna and solarium, gym facilities and aerobics. A further 1.5km along the road, a left turning leads to **Maribor island** (Mariborski Otok), a pleasant rambling and bathing spot in the summer; if you don't fancy taking to the Drava, there's a large outdoor pool in the centre of the island (daily June–Sept 9am–8pm; €5).

Maribor Pohorje

From Maribor bus #6 runs regularly to Zgornje Radvanje, 7km southwest of town at the foot of the popular ski resort, **Maribor Pohorje**. The last stop is at the **cable car** station (vzpenjača; April–Nov hourly 7am–9pm;

▲ Lent Festival, Maribor

Maribor festivals

Maribor puts on a great range of festivals and events throughout the year, the biggest and best of which is the **Lent Festival** at the end of June/beginning of July. Second only to Ljubljana's Summer Festival in size, this is arguably Slovenia's most exuberant gathering, comprising two fabulous weeks of street theatre, comedy, modern and classical dance and jazz, pop and classical music along the waterfront and in the squares and streets around town. The Lent Vine is the site of the **Pruning of the Vine** at the beginning of March, and the **Embrace of the Vine** in late September, the latter entailing the harvesting of the grapes, though both are actually little more than excuses for a good old jolly-up.

Musically, the key event is the **Festival Maribor** at the beginning of September, ten days of high quality classical concerts (including numerous celebrated international artists) taking place in diverse venues. There's also the **National and International Choir Competition** in April, and at the end of August the **No Border Jam Festival**, a gathering of international punk acts. For kids (and adults too), the terrific **International Puppet Festival** runs throughout July and August and features a huge variety of acts from all over Europe.

The **Golden Fox** (Zlata Lisica) slalom race on the slopes of Maribor Pohorje at the end of January is one of the country's major sporting occasions, attracting the world's top women skiers, not to mention some 25,000 spectators, for a weekend of top-class sporting action and lots of drinking.

Dec–March nonstop 7am–10pm; €10 return), from where the small four-seater cabins transport skiers and hikers to the upper station (1040m) on **Bolfenk** in fifteen minutes.

Aside from **skiing** (see box, p.288), there are plenty more exciting activities on offer at the **Adrenaline Park**, which is not a park as such, but rather the collective name for a range of **activities** taking place at different locations around the mountain. Take your pick from, among other things, the bike park (€25 for the day, €19 for half a day), summer tobogganing (€5 per hour), paint-balling (€20 per person – minimum group of eight required) and horseriding (€13 for 1hr, €60 for 5hr). For more information, contact the Sports Centre (Športni Centre Pohorje) in Maribor, at Mladinska ulica 29 (℡02/220-8825, Ⓦwww.pohorje.org), or the tourist office in Maribor. Pohorje offers terrific woodland **cycling**, with numerous cycle paths carving their way across the massif. There's a free cycle map outlining numerous trails, while another useful aid (whether hiking or cycling) is the 1:50,000 *Pohorje* **map** – both of these are available from the tourist office in Maribor.

There's stacks of **accommodation** on top of the mountain: beside the cable car station is the *Hotel Bellevue* (℡02/607-5100, Ⓦwww.termemb.si; ⑧), a smart, glass-fronted chalet-type place with fabulous rooms and a fine restaurant and bar; just behind here, and offering similar comfort, is the *Hotel Bolfenk* (℡02/603-6505, Ⓦwww.pohorje.org; ⑦), which also has a large complex of apartments (⑦–⑧) sleeping between four and eight people; 500m southwest of here the *Pension Martin* (℡02/603-6510) has both rooms (⑥) and apartments (⑧).

Approximately 2km along the road to **Areh**, the *Aparthotel Pohorje* (℡02/603-6700, Ⓦwww.aparthotel-pohorje.com) offers a range of excellent apartments sleeping two to four people (⑦–⑧). In Areh itself, a further 4km distant, there's the very basic *Hotel Areh* (℡02/603-5040; Nov–March; ③) and the *Ruška koča* **mountain hut** (℡02/603-5046; €16) just across the field and open all year. There's another hut, the *Mariborska koča* (℡02/603-2731), 45 minutes' walk from the church at Bolfenk (or one hour from *Ruška koča*). Across from the mountain

Maribor's wine roads

Maribor is one of the **Podravje** wine region's six wine-producing areas, and counts two **wine roads** with the **Kamnica** road to the west, and the more-visited **Malečnik** road to the east. Although a couple of reds are produced here (Žametna Črnina and Modri Pinot), this is overwhelmingly white wine territory – Laški and Renski Rizling, Chardonnay and Sauvignon, as well as the blended Mariborčan. One of the region's best wineries is at the *Joannes* tourist farm (the Protner winery) in the hamlet of **Vodole** (no. 34), in Malečnik (☎02/473-2100, ⊛www.joannes.si), where you can also sample grilled blood sausages with sauerkraut; they've also got several very comfortable rooms (❸). Although having your own wheels is certainly an advantage, it is feasible to walk at least part of these routes from Maribor. The 1:50,000 *Podravje* **map**, available from the tourist office in Maribor, should help you negotiate your way around.

If you have neither the time nor the means to head out into the countryside, make your way to the **Vinag Wine Cellar** in Maribor at Trg Svobode 3, one of the largest cellars in Central Europe; its 2.5km of tunnels hold some 150 wooden, concrete and aluminium barrels, with a storage capacity of some seven million litres. For a **tour** of the cellar and a tasting session (around €5 for four wines), you should contact them a day or two in advance (☎02/220-8111, ⊛www.vinag.si). You can also buy their wines at the adjoining shop (Mon–Fri 9am–7pm, Sat 8am–1pm).

---

hut is the **Church of St Areh**, a simple, late seventeenth-century Baroque building, which is now in a rather sad state of decrepitude; if it's closed, get the key from the hut. During the winter hourly **buses** (9am–4pm) from Bolfenk to Areh depart from the car park next to the cable car station. Note that if driving, or cycling, to Bolfenk you should take the road south to Ljubljana before turning at the village of Hoče, from where it's a further 10km uphill.

Ptuj and around

If you've only got time to visit one place in eastern Slovenia, make it **PTUJ**. Set 26km southeast of Maribor on the broad, flat Drava Plain between the Slovenske Gorice and Haloze hills, Ptuj is the oldest continuously settled site in Slovenia and is historically the most important settlement outside Ljubljana. The town and its surrounds are run through with two thousand years of history, its squares, streets and buildings rampant with architectural and archeological riches – Romanesque and medieval town houses, built-in Roman monuments and tombstones, and ancient Mithras shrines. Moreover, Ptuj is home to the wonderful Shrovetide **Kurent Carnival**, Slovenia's most famous, and entertaining, folkloric event. Though not the easiest to reach without your own transport, two further places worth venturing to are the beautiful Church of the Holy Virgin in **Ptujska Gora**, and the **Haloze wine region**, bordering Croatia to the south.

Some history

Settled as far back as the late **Stone Age**, and later populated by the **Celts**, Ptuj began life around 69 AD, when a **Roman** legionary camp was established on the south bank of the Drava River. The result of expansion across the river was the creation of a self-governing, civilian entity called Poetovio, which functioned as a major staging post linking the Roman provinces of Pannonia and Noricum. Occupied successively by **Avars**, **Magyars** and then **Slavs**, Ptuj received its town rights in 977 AD, at which point it passed into the hands of the **Salzburg** archdiocese, whose members grew rich from the trade between Pannonia and the Italian peninsula. During the **Middle Ages**, the town developed around the solidly fortified castle, and established itself as a commercial centre of some considerable importance. Until the death of **Frederick XI** in 1438, the town remained under the jurisdiction of the Ptuj nobility, vassals of the Salzburg archdiocese, though subsequent incursions by the Turks and wars with the Hungarians undermined the town's development. It recovered sufficiently to re-establish itself as a small provincial town, which it remains to this day.

Arrival and information

Ptuj's **train station** is 500m northeast of the centre on Osojnikova cesta, the **bus station** 200m nearer town on the same road. From both stations, continue down Osojnikova to the junction with ulica Heroja Lacka: a right turn here lands you straight in the centre. The **tourist office** is at Slovenski trg 5 (daily: May–Sept 9am–8pm; Oct–April 9am–6pm; ℡02/779-6011, Ⓦwww.ptuj-tourism.si), though you can get the same information at the welcoming **Centre for Free Time Activities** (CID), just across from the bus station in the modern building at Osojnikova 9 (Mon–Thurs 8am–6pm, Sat 10am–1pm; ℡02/780-5540); both places offer free **internet**. The **post office** is opposite the Minorite church at Vodnikova ulica 12 (Mon–Fri 8am–6pm, Sat 8am–noon). **Bikes** can be rented (€8 for half a day, €11 for the day) from the bike shop across from the *Eva* hostel (see p.300), worth considering if you'd like to visit either the Mithra Shrines (see p.305) or the Haloze wine region (see p.306).

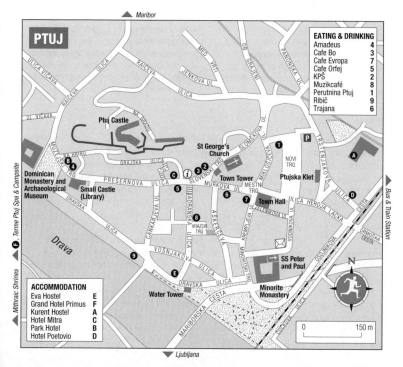

PTUJ

▲ Maribor

▼ Ljubljana

EATING & DRINKING
Amadeus	4
Cafe Bo	3
Cafe Evropa	7
Cafe Orfej	5
KPŠ	2
Muzikcafé	8
Perutnina Ptuj	1
Ribič	9
Trajana	6

ACCOMMODATION
Eva Hostel	E
Grand Hotel Primus	F
Kurent Hostel	A
Hotel Mitra	C
Park Hotel	B
Hotel Poetovio	D

Ptuj Castle

St George's Church

Dominican Monastery and Archaeological Museum

Small Castle (Library)

Town Tower

Ptujska Klet

Town Hall

SS Peter and Paul

Water Tower

Minorite Monastery

Drava

◀ Mithraic Shrines   ◀ Terme Ptuj Spa & Campsite   Bus & Train Station ▶

0   150 m

N

Accommodation

There's a limited, but high quality, spread of **hotels** in town, in addition to a couple of hostels, while there are plenty of private rooms to go around – the tourist office can advise on this, as well as accommodation on local tourist farms (③). The *Kurent* **youth hostel**, at Osojnikova 9 (☎02/771-0814, ⓔyhptuj@csod.si), has modern and colourful rooms sleeping between two and six people, each with its own shower (€18 per person including breakfast); they've also got a laundry. More appealingly located down near the water tower at Jadranska 20 is the clean and tidy *Eva* hostel (☎02/771-2441, ⓦwww.bikeek.si), which has two-, four- and six-bed rooms (€13–16), all with shared shower facilities; reception is in the bike shop opposite. The town's year-round **campsite** (☎02/749-4500, ⓦwww.terme-ptuj .si) is 2km east of town across the river next to the **thermal baths**; they've also got modern chalets (⑥) sleeping up to four people. Within this large spa complex (which includes the *Grand Hotel Primus*) there are spacious, well-furnished **apartments** (⑥–⑧) sleeping up to six, as well as more basic **bungalows** (④) sleeping up to three. Guests staying in any of this accommodation receive free use of the spa's pools.

Hotel Mitra Prešernova ulica 6 ☎02/787-7455, ⓦwww.hotel-mitra.si. Slovenia's first Story Hotel – each room is themed after historical characters (St George, Mithras, Lords of Ptuj, Habsburgs, etc) – is absolutely first rate; the seductive white and silver rooms are furnished with elegant drapes, gorgeous beds and thick duvets and pillows – moreover, there's a brick vaulted spa centre, atrium/courtyard, wine cellar and coffee house to enjoy. ❼

Park Hotel Prešernova ulica 38 ☎02/749-3300, ⓦwww.parkhotel-ptuj.si. In much the same vein as the *Mitra*, this wonderfully renovated sixteenth-century house (which has retained much of its stunning original architectural features) conceals fifteen imaginatively conceived,

individually styled rooms, each of which is titled after a historical character; breakfast down in the old wine cellar is a treat. ❽

Hotel Poetovio Vinarski trg 5 ☎02/779-8201, ⓔmemorija@volja.net. Dour place in a good location on the edge of the Old Town; its occasionally careworn rooms lack any semblance of style or character, though they are clean and fairly priced. ❻

Grand Hotel Primus Pot v toplice 9 ☎02/749-4500, ⓦwww.terme-ptuj.si. Located 2km east of town, out by the thermal baths, this large, flashy hotel possesses all the requisite four-star comforts, with immaculately turned-out rooms, while the bathrooms are sourced with thermal water. Guests receive free use of the baths. ❾

The Town

Ptuj is a compact town and a leisurely half-day should be enough to cover the main sights, although you could quite easily use up the best part of a day admiring the wealth of architectural detail. Pretty much everything of interest is situated on or just off the two main squares, **Mestni trg** and **Slovenski trg**, and the old main street, **Prešernova ulica**, which curls under the base of the castle-topped hill.

Mestni trg and around

The ideal place to start is fourteenth-century **Mestni trg** (Town Square), a charming little square ringed by several stately buildings, the most prominent of which is the muddy-green **Town Hall**, a large neo-Gothic German pile raised in 1907 on the site of a late-Renaissance structure built by the Dominicans in 1571. Remnants of this earlier building are still just about visible in the form of a pair of dragon reliefs and a reclining nude on one of the corner prominences. The colourful, heavily stuccoed eighteenth-century **corner house**, opposite at no. 2, is now the popular *Café Evropa* (see p.304); above the entrance is a slender corner niche holding a statue of Mary with Child. At the heart of the square, the regulation **plague column**, featuring a posturing St Florian dressed in military attire, is a copy, erected in 1993.

There's more architecture to admire along Krempljeva ulica – the street heading south from Mestni trg – notably at no. 1, whose peeling paintwork can't detract from some marvellous stuccowork, and in particular, the beehive relief between the windows on the prominence. At no. 7, the entrance to the old **Court House** is framed by a superb sixteenth-century Renaissance portal, either side of which sit a pair of lions holding escutcheons. West from Mestni trg, up Murkova ulica, check out the portal with griffins at no. 2, and the Patrician Mansion, opposite at no. 1.

The Minorite Church

Krempljeva ulica segues into Minoritski trg, site of the late thirteenth-century **Minorite Monastery** (Minoritski Samostan), which, unlike the majority of Slovenia's monasteries, wasn't closed down under the reforms of Emperor Joseph II at the end of the eighteenth century. Instead, it continued to prosper as a centre of learning until World War II, when it was confiscated by the Germans, then bombed by the Allies. The most feted part of the complex is the first-floor **summer refectory**, thanks to its thickly stuccoed ceiling, decorated by Italians Quadrio and Bettini, and oval and rectangular panels depicting scenes from the lives of the monastery's patrons, Sts Peter and Paul. The prize exhibit in the monastery's richly stocked **library** is one of three original copies of the New Testament translated into Slovene by Primož Trubar in 1561 – the other two reside in the National Library in Ljubljana, and in Vienna. If you wish to visit the monastery, contact the tourist office.

The adjoining Church of St Peter and St Paul was one of Slovenia's greatest ecclesiastical losses during World War II. The only part of the church to survive the raids was the presbytery, slightly shortened after the war in order to accommodate, rather insensitively, a post office on the site of the bombed-out nave. Look out for the beautifully worked relief of a lamb on a keystone by the high altar, and the gargoyle-like animal heads on the exterior buttresses. Reconstructed in 2005, the nave stands in stark contrast, a large, austere space worked over in glass and marble.

A short walk east along Dravska ulica – the street running parallel to the river – brings you to the bulky **Drava Water Tower** (Drava stolp), the largest of six former defensive towers that once formed the core of the town's fortification system; contrary to popular legend the stone balls built into the upper section of the walls were not those fired by Turks, but rather were placed there by local enthusiasts who had a penchant for this kind of architecture. The tower's two floors now function as the **France Mihelič Gallery** (Miheličeva galerija; Tues–Sun 10am–1pm & 4–7pm; €2), holding a selection of works by the graphic artist as well as other rotating exhibitions. During the Middle Ages Dravska ulica was known for its butcher's shops and tanneries, as indicated by the numerous portals embedded with the traditional tanners' symbols of a bucket with two crossed scrapers.

Slovenski trg: the Town Tower and St George's Church

The centre of triangular-shaped **Slovenski trg** is dominated by the chunky, five-storey **Town Tower** (Mestni stolp), originally a sixteenth-century bell tower, then a seventeenth-century watchtower, before retiring gracefully in the eighteenth, when it was embellished with an onion-bulb spire. Embedded within the tower's lower reaches are numerous civil and military tombstones, relief votive slabs and sacrificial altars, though the most impressive tombstone is the freestanding **Orpheus Monument** in front of the tower (it's covered up in winter). Cut from Pohorje marble, the thick rectangular column commemorates Marcus Verus, former mayor of Poetovio, although during the Middle Ages it was used as a pillory, whereby petty criminals were chained to iron rings fastened to the bottom of the block – the poor state of the inscriptions is down to the wear and tear caused by the chains.

Outwardly austere, the twelfth-century Gothic **Church of St George** (Cerkev Sv Jurij) conceals some exceptional works of art. The first thing you see as you enter is a small glass cabinet on the left, containing a fragile and rather foppish-looking fourteenth-century wooden **sculpture of St George** nonchalantly slaying a dragon. From here proceed into the central nave, arranged with incongruously placed frescoes, altars and chapels, such as the **Crucifixion**, framed with an elaborately decorated banner, immediately to the left, and opposite, the **Altar of the Three Kings**, featuring a relief of the Coronation of St Mary inside a Baroque casing. The church's most renowned piece of work, **Laib's winged altar**, is positioned to the rear of the south aisle; dating from around 1460, the gilded paintings depict, in the centre, Mary's death, and to the left and right respectively, St Hieronymous with a church model in one hand and a book in the other, and St Mark writing the Gospel held by a lion. Of the several chapels dotted around the church, the most important is the **Chapel of Our Lady of Sorrows** at the end of the north aisle, the centrepiece of which is a fifteenth-century stone pietà sculpture. Just to the right of the chapel, a splendid, high lancet-arch fronts the bright fourteenth-century cross-vaulted presbytery, and a magnificent long choir, lined either side by two long rows of oak-wood pews ornamented with figures of animals.

Prešernova ulica

The Old Town's central artery, **Prešernova ulica**, is an attractive, peaceful thoroughfare, lined with tightly packed ranks of medieval town houses, almost every single one furnished with a Renaissance stone portal or some other beautifully crafted feature. For starters take a look at house no. 1, whose corner prominence is supported by a so-called Parlerian mask, a black painted head of a grinning, curly-haired man; and, opposite, at no. 4, the Romanesque Bratonič house, the oldest tenement along the street and which now accommodates the tourist office. Before continuing, take a quick look down **Jadranska ulica**, and in particular nos. 4 and 6, the facades of which are decorated with *Kurent*-style masks worked in flat relief (see box, p.304).

Back on Prešernova, beyond the colourful neo-Baroque *Hotel Mitra* at no. 6, the house at no. 16 is notable for some marble fragments jutting out of the passageway wall, which, on closer inspection, reveal themselves to be parts of dedication blocks or tombstones – there are more complete blocks embedded into the back wall of the run-down courtyard. On the opposite side of the road, at no. 27, take a peek inside the courtyard, where there's another grey marble relief, this one of a prostrate, headless lion. The building on the corner of Prešernova and Cafova ulica used to be the **Small Castle** (Mali Grad), and the seat of the lords of Ptuj; it is now a library.

The Dominican Monastery and Archeological Museum

A few paces on from the Small Castle, the **Dominican Monastery** (Dominikanski Samostan) stands in a small park-like area on Muzejski trg, its bright pink facade hung with spidery stuccowork and pocked with five niches containing statues of saints. Founded in 1230, the monastery was forced to disband as part of Joseph II's reforms in 1786, after which time it was used alternately as a barracks and a residential building, before eventually falling into a state of disrepair.

The monastery is now home to the town's **Archeological Museum** (daily: mid–April to Nov 10am–5pm; €3), an impressive hoard of archeological treasures held within several separate areas of the building. Begin with the monastery's gloriously dishevelled **cloisters** – painted with early fourteenth-century frescoes (restored during the interwar period) and vaulted around a century later – and which are now cluttered with an array of statuary and fragments, some of which were brought across from the demolished Minorite church after World War II. The **small archeological collection** on the upper floor comprises a fabulous store of Celtic and Roman grave finds, mostly urns and vessels, but also gold jewellery, exquisite bronze and clay statuettes and oil lamps. The **lapidarium**, meanwhile, contains a matchless collection of marble and sandstone sarcophagi, statues and busts, mosaic floors and beautiful votive altars dedicated to various deities. There are also memorials from Mithra shrines II (in the church crypt) and IV (see box, p.305). The **old refectory** now keeps a modest collection of Celtic and Roman coins (also look out for the clay piggy banks), but is more interesting for its gorgeous vaulted and stuccoed ceiling – not dissimilar to that of the summer refectory in the Minorite Monastery, and similarly painted with venerated saints.

Ptuj Castle and Regional Museum

Lording it over the flutter of red roofs and cobbled streets below, **Ptuj Castle** (Grad Ptuj) is the town's showpiece attraction. It began life around 69 AD when the inhabitants of Roman Poetovio built a fortress and temple atop this very hill. The oldest archives date the present structure to some time in the twelfth century, when the castle was owned by the archbishops of Salzburg, who in turn leased it to the lords of Ptuj. Fortified ahead of anticipated Turkish raids in the sixteenth century, the castle was further modified in Baroque fashion during the seventeenth century.

Whether approaching from the path opposite the monastery, or via Grajska ulica, a narrow street just off Prešernova ulica near the *Hotel Mitra*, you enter the castle grounds through the thick-set **Charles portal**, which opens up into the lower courtyard, once the location for the castle stables and military outbuildings, but now empty save for a weatherbeaten statue of a one-armed St Florian dousing yet another fire – the views from this platform, however, are fantastic. Walk on up through the fine Renaissance **Peruzzi portal** into the immaculate inner courtyard, enclosed by a horseshoe-shaped, three-tiered **residential palace**. Before entering the museum take a look at the splendid, red Salzburg marble tombstone of Frederick IX, the last lord of Ptuj, embedded into the wall on the left-hand side of the courtyard.

The castle's **regional museum collection** (daily: May to mid-Oct 9am–6pm, plus July & Aug Sat & Sun 9am–8pm; mid-Oct to April 9am–5pm; €4) comprises a mixed bag of exhibitions. The most stimulating are the colourful displays of *Kurenti* masks and associated carnival paraphernalia (see box, p.304), and a fascinating section on musical instruments; supplemented by sound recordings, the exhibition charts the history of Ptuj's military and town brass bands, though more intriguingly there are some Greek and Roman artefacts, including a tibia fragment believed to have been used as a pipe to be played at funerals, social dances and the like. After your visit, you can savour the marvellous views of the Drava River and Haloze Hills beyond, or have a coffee in the small courtyard café.

The Kurent

One of the oldest, most unusual and celebrated folklore events in the Slovene calendar is the **Kurent**, a kind of fertility rite and celebration of the awakening of spring confused together, which takes place in the ten days up to Shrove Tuesday (late February/early March). Wearing spooky masks made of sheepskin and feathers with a coloured beak for a nose, white beads for teeth and long, bright red tongues, the Kurenti proceed from house to house, warding off evil spirits with the incessant din from the cowbells and other instruments tied to their weighty costumes. Leading the procession is the Devil (*Hudič*), pitchfork in hand and wrapped in a net to symbolize his capture: behind the *Kurenti*, the ploughers (*Orači*) pull a small wooden plough, scattering sand around to represent the sowing of seed, while the other participants smash clay pots at their feet in return for good luck and health. Although several similar carnivals, known as *pust*, take place in other towns throughout Slovenia – most famously in Cerkno and Cerknica – and in neighbouring countries such as Hungary and Croatia, most are pale imitations of the events that take place here in Ptuj.

Eating and drinking

The town counts on a handful of decent **restaurants** and there is no shortage of **cafés** around town: the number one hangout is the fabulous *Muzikafé*, down Jadranska ulica on Vrazov trg, which combines a summery stone terrace with a loungey, richly painted interior where you can chill out to various sounds and dip into books and magazines – the cool, bare-brick cellar is regularly used for events. Elsewhere there's *Café Evropa* on Mestni trg, by day a fairly relaxed place for coffee, by night a noisy, frenetic bar, and, similarly, the student bar, *KPŠ*, at Slovenski trg 7, which puts on film screenings and concerts on the terrace in front of the town tower in the summer. More sedate options are *Café Bo*, at Slovenski trg 7, and *Café Orfej*, at Prešernova ulica 5, while, no less enjoyable than any of these places are the quaint little coffee houses in the *Mitra* and *Park* hotels, both of which have superb cakes. It's also worth checking out what's going on at the Centre for Free Time Activities (see p.299), as it occasionally stages the odd gig in its basement bar.

If you haven't time to visit the Haloze winegrowing region (see p.306), the next best option is to call in at the **Ptuj wine cellar** (Ptujske klet) at Vinarski trg 1 (☎02/787-9810); call in advance to arrange a visit – this incorporates a fifteen-minute film presentation, a tour of the labyrinthine cellars (complete with sound and light effects) and a sampling session (€12). There's also a shop (Mon–Fri 7am–7pm & Sat 8am–noon).

Restaurants

Amadeus Prešernova 36. Warm, classy place with big glass windows, offering an upscale take on Slovene standards, in addition to a terrific steak menu and some unusually appealing vegetarian options. Top-notch hospitality too.

Perutnina Ptuj Novi trg 2. Cheap and cheerful canteen-style joint knocking up fast and filling daily specials (around €6) – including vegetarian – though it's known for its local chicken dishes. Mon–Fri 8am–7pm, Sat 8am–1pm.

Pri Ernestu Rabelcja vas 15. Despite its awkward location in a residential district fifteen-minutes walk north of town, this exceptional, modern-looking place conjures up a scrumptious range of beautifully presented meat and seafood dishes. To get here head down Volkmerjeva cesta then Peršonova ulica.

Ribič Dravska ulica 9. Enticingly positioned on the bank of the Drava, this smartly decorated and hugely popular restaurant has a menu almost exclusively devoted to fish (freshwater and sea), with some top-rate wines to boot – the riverside terrace is a wonderful spot to dine in summer. Expensive. Closed Mon.

Mithra Shrines

Approximately 1km west of town, across the river in **Zgornji Breg**, the **Mithra III Shrine** is one of four shrines in Ptuj dedicated to the sun god and warrior Mithra. The Mithras III shrine, housed in a small pavilion just off Mariborska cesta (it's signposted), dates from 3 AD and comprises the remains of a three-naved temple, around which are scattered sacrificial altars carved with votive inscriptions. The plate on the far wall is a copy of an altar relief of the sacrificial bull from the Mithraeum in Osterburken, in Germany, though there are a few surviving fragments from the original in the right-hand corner. The rest of the room is neatly arranged with dedication blocks, chunky slabs of marble carved with reliefs from the Mithras cult – his birth from a rock, his slaying of a bull, and another that depicts him shooting water from a rock with an arrow. The most impressive stone, however, is the one positioned in front of the main altar, which depicts two figures taking an oath over the fire on the sacrificial altar.

A twenty-minute walk southwest of Mithra III, across a dusty field in the tiny settlement of **Spodnja Hajdina**, a smaller building holds the remains of the **Mithra I Shrine**, discovered in 1898 and considered to be the oldest of the Mithra temples located in the Roman Empire's northern province; this one dates from around the second half of the second century. The most interesting of the dozen or so haphazardly arranged stone dedication blocks are statues of Mithras dragging the sacrificial bull, and a snake coiled around a torso emerging from a rock mass. Both temples are usually closed, but the keys can easily be obtained from the neighbouring houses, the numbers of which are given on the respective doors.

Church of the Virgin Mary

In the village of **Ptujska Gora** (twelve kilometres southwest of Ptuj along the road to Rogatec), the Gothic **Church of the Virgin Mary** (Cerkev Sv Marija) ranks alongside the churches at Brezje and Sveta Gora as one of the country's premier pilgrimage destinations. Built some time around 1400, the church's

---

Mithraism

Mithraism, the ancient religion of Mithras the sun god, is believed to have originated in Persia, before spreading west during the time of the Roman Empire. However, it was never officially recognized as a Roman religion, in all probability because the Romans believed that Mithraism consisted of elements of the religion of their bitter enemies, the Persians. For this reason the first Mithras shrines, such as those in Ptuj, were built outside town boundaries. By the second half of the third century, however, Mithraism – with Ptuj as one of its leading centres – had almost established itself as the state religion, rivalling Christianity as the dominant faith. However, with Emperor Constantine's ascension to the throne in the fourth century, Mithraism, along with other pagan religions, was outlawed and most of its temples destroyed.

Little is known of its rituals and believers, although it's likely that meetings took place within confined religious communities, dominated exclusively by male members; Initiates were typically imperial administrators, slaves of the customs administration or soldiers, and would number around one hundred. Members would be grouped and divided into several ranks, ranks that were depicted in relief. Although stone dedication blocks and relief depictions of Mithras were widely distributed throughout the Roman Empire, few match the calibre of those in Ptuj. There's another excellent Mithraeum shrine in Rožanec, near Črnomelj (see p.255).

beautifully cool interior manifests some outstanding Gothic architecture, most notably in the form of the three arches which presage the tripartite nave, whose aisles are separated by smooth slender columns. But nothing in this, or any other church in Slovenia, comes close to the splendour of the **high altar**, a majestic, towering work of art whose focal point is the *Virgin with Mantle* relief, which features seven angels lifting a dusky green cloak to reveal ranks of some eighty figures, each carved in remarkable life-like detail; mingling among the cast of the rich and the poor are several of the counts of Celje. So compelling is this piece that it somewhat detracts from the rest of the altar's ornamentation, most notably some extraordinary sculptural work.

To the right of the high altar, in the southern aisle, the canopied **Celje Altar** pays further homage to the counts of Celje, its baldachin ceiling and pillars beautifully ornamented with sculpted flowers, animal figures and the counts' coats of arms. Also worthy of close inspection are the frescoes depicting scenes from *Christ's Passion* by John Bruneck, located under the organ loft, and a fine statue of St James standing on the console of a pillar in the southern aisle. To get here take one of the seven daily buses (Mon–Fri) heading to **Majšperk**, and alight on the main road just below the church, from where it's a five-minute walk.

Haloze hills

Rearing up from the iron-flat Drava Plain south of Ptuj, the **Haloze hills** present further opportunities to sample Slovenia's fine wines. Extending for some 30km east, from the village of Makole (just beyond Ptujska Gora), along the Croatian border to Zavrč, the Haloze are divided into two diverse landscapes – the Vinorodne (winegrowing) region to the east, and the Gozdnate (forested) region to the south and west, both regions spotted with solitary farms, orchards and hamlets.

Although the many cellars here can be visited independently, you can, alternatively, head to the accommodating Halo Agency in **Cirkulane**, 12km southwest of Ptuj. Located in the centre of the village across from the church at no. 56 (℡02/795-3200, ✉info@halo.si), the agency can provide information, arrange accommodation (⑤), and organize guided visits to a selection of the cellars; many of these produce their own goat's cheese, bread and pastries, and other home made treats. Between Monday and Friday there are three daily buses (hourly during school term-time) from Ptuj to Cirkulane, but otherwise there's no public transport around the region.

The Ljutomer wine road

Twenty-three kilometres east of Ptuj, the anonymous town of Ormož is the starting point for the Ljutomer **wine road**, which extends north to Ljutomer, some 20km distant. Despite being the smallest of Podravje's six winegrowing districts, the region possesses a high density of viticultural sites. Moreover, it vies with the Goriška Brda region in Primorje for the title of Slovenia's most beautiful wine-producing region, a fabulously picturesque and sunny landscape shaped by horizontal rows of curving, terraced vineyards set against the backdrop of *Klopotec*, wooden wind-powered rattles designed to scare off birds and, according to local superstition, to drive snakes out of the vineyards. Of the predominantly white wines harvested here, the smooth and slightly sweet Beli Pinot is regarded as the finest, followed by Laški Rizling, Šipon and Traminec, while the blended wines Jeruzalemčan and Ljutomerčan are popular alternatives. The numerous **cellars** lining the route are marked by brown and cream signposts – although you can call in on the off-chance, most prefer advance notice of your arrival.

The midway point of the route is the delightful little hilltop village of **JERUZALEM**, so-named after crusaders visiting here in the thirteenth century became so enamoured with the wine and the people that they decided to name the settlement after the holy city. At the centre of the village is the Baroque **Church of Our Lady of Sorrows**, whose painting of Our Lady of Sorrows on the high altar is a late seventeenth-century copy of the original, which was brought here by the aforementioned crusaders, but later stolen. Look out, too, for the imprint of a horse hoof which, according to local legend, was left here by one of the marauding Turks during seventeenth-century raids. Just across from the church is the **tourist office** (daily: April–Oct 10am–6pm; Nov–March 10am–4pm; ⓦwww.jeruzalem.si), where you can sample some of the local wines, but which is also a useful source of advice on the best cellars to visit, as well as places to stay. Also sited here is the very posh, ten-room *Dvorec* **hotel** (ⓣ02/719-4805, ⓔdvorec.jeruzalem@siol.net; ⓪), though if that's a bit pricey, 500m back down the road there's the *Vinski Hram* guesthouse (ⓣ02/719-4504, ⓦwww.brenholc.com; ⓪), which has really good value rooms; whether staying here or not, its vine-covered terrace overlooking the hills is a terrific spot to lunch. Just beyond the village, heading towards Ljutomer, there's an **observation tower**, from where there are superlative views of the surrounding hills – on a clear day it's possible to see as far as Lake Balaton in Hungary.

The route is made for **cycling**, and you may not have much choice anyway, as what buses that do travel between Ormož and Ljutomer, and vice versa, take the main road running parallel to the east, passing through Ivanjkovci. If you're planning to cycle the entire route, you should allow for around four to five hours, a little more, of course, if cellar-hopping is on the agenda. The stretch between Jeruzalem and Ljutomer is slightly tougher going than the stretch between Jeruzalem and Ormož, which flattens out markedly after Vinski Vir. **Bikes** can be rented at the tourist offices in both Jeruzalem and Ljutomer.

Ljutomer

LJUTOMER, the economic and cultural centre of the region, is the last town before you cross the Mura River into Prekmurje. Although it's unlikely you will need or should want to stay here, there are a couple of interesting diversions; it also has excellent rail connections, including the Budapest–Venice InterCity train, which passes through here once a day. The wine connections aside, the town is best known for its horse racing, having staged trotting races since 1874. Today, the **hippodrome** – located around 500m northwest of the town's main square, Glavni trg – stages some ten **horse-trotting races** a year. These usually take place on Sundays and public holidays between April and September (around €5), but check with the tourist office first for schedules. If you can't manage to get here for a race day, you can still visit the track and stables, and you may also get to see the horses in training; the tourist office should be able to fix something up for you.

Otherwise fairly limited, the small **town museum** (Mon–Fri 8am–3pm, €2), located in the town hall on Glavni trg, is worth visiting to view some original footage of the first-ever films to be produced in Slovenia, *People Leaving the Church* and *The Fair at Ljutomer*, which were shot by Karol Grossmann in 1905 (see p.336). There's also an interesting exhibition on the so-called "Tabor Movement"; between 1868 and 1870, numerous groups of young intellectuals living in Slovene ethnic territories initiated regular mass open-air forums (*tabors*) to publicize and rally support for a united Slovenia, whose very existence as a national group around that time appeared seriously threatened. Although they were subsequently banned by Vienna, the influence of the *tabors* continued to be felt in later years whenever questions concerning the Slovene national movement were raised.

Practicalities

All the town's practical facilities are fairly close to each other: Ljutomer has two **train stations**: Ljutomer, and the smaller Ljutomer Mesto on Rajh nade ulica, where you should alight for the town centre and from where it's a ten-minute walk south to the **bus station** and the town centre. The most helpful tourist office is at Jureša Cirila 4 (Mon–Fri 9am–5pm, Sat 8am–noon; ☎02/584-8333), a few paces away inside the courtyard of the town hall. As well as supplying information on the Ljutomer wine road (see p.306), the staff here can arrange private **accommodation** along the route, and rent out **bikes** (€10 per day). Glavni trg is also the site for the town's only **hotel**, the bland but modern *Hotel Jeruzalem* (☎02/581-1211; ❺); as well as the only place in town worth **eating** at, the *Galileo* pizzeria/spaghetteria, which is inside the courtyard of the town hall.

Prekmurje

Cut off by the fast-flowing Mura River to the south, and bounded on the remaining three sides by the Austrian, Hungarian and Croatian borders, **Prekmurje** (Pomurje) is a region quite apart from the rest of the country. Known as Slovenia's breadbasket, it is, for the most part, a relentlessly flat landscape, carved up by grids of smooth green fields, picturesque villages and little white churches. Prekmurje's relative isolation is rooted in over a thousand years of Magyar rule, a situation that changed only after World War I when it was incorporated into Yugoslav lands, although there was another brief period of Hungarian imposition during World War II. Physically, economically and culturally distanced from the rest of the country prior to World War I – there was no bridge crossing the Mura until 1924 – Prekmurje is still regarded by many Slovenes as something of a backwater. However, thanks largely to Hungary's long-term rule, Prekmurje remains one of Slovenia's most ethnically diverse regions, embracing a sizeable Hungarian minority, as well as the country's largest Roma community. Prior to World War II it also accounted for over half of the country's Jewish population.

Prekmurje has one of the richest culinary traditions in Slovenia, and you shouldn't leave without trying *bograč*, a steaming goulash pot of mixed meats, onions and potatoes, or its most famous product, *gibanica*, a delicious sweet pie stuffed with cottage cheese, poppy seeds, walnut and apple.

There's a fairly regular **bus service** linking the region's only two towns, **Murska Sobota** and **Lendava**, via most of the villages in between, including **Martjanci**, **Bogojina** and **Beltinci**. However, services are dramatically reduced (if non existent) at weekends, so try and coincide a visit with a weekday. Alternatively, the best way to explore the region is by bike (see box, p.312).

Murska Sobota

Located in the geographical centre of Prekmurje, **MURSKA SOBOTA** is the largest settlement in the province, a one-horse town where nothing very much ever happens. However, it is the region's main road and rail hub, so there's a good chance you'll wind up here if you're planning to explore the surrounding countryside. The town developed alongside the Ledava River, in the plains north of the Mura River, during the eleventh century, and was almost immediately incorporated into the Hungarian state, under whose administration it remained until 1920. Another, brief period of Hungarian control during World War II was ended by the Red Army, who liberated the town in April 1945.

With the reopening, in 2001, of the rail line between Puconci, a few kilometres north of Murska Sobota, and Hodoš, on the Hungarian border, the town once again found itself the first major stop, in Slovenia, for intercity trains travelling from Budapest to Ljubljana. If you do have an hour or two to spare while waiting for buses to the outlying villages, there's a very worthwhile museum, as well as a pleasant park to laze around in.

Arrival, information and accommodation

Both the **bus** and **train stations** are centrally located, the former on Slomškova ulica, the latter to the east at the end of Ulica Arhiteka Novaka. The **tourist office** is inside the town library on Trg Kulture (Mon–Fri 9am–6pm, Sat 8am–1pm; ☏02/534-1130, Ⓔtic.sobota@siol.net), while the **post office** is to the north of here on Trg Zmage (Mon–Fri 8am–7pm, Sat 8am–1pm), and there's **internet** in the *Pomaranča* café, just across from the tourist office. The town's one **hotel** is the *Diana* at Slovenska ulica 52 (☏02/514-1200,

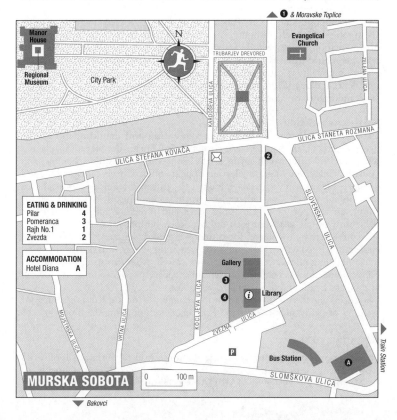

ⓔ recepcija@zvezda-diana.si; ⓖ), which has slick rooms with cool furnishings and large beds; there's also a pool, sauna, solarium and gym.

The Town

The town's only real point of interest, and its saving grace, is the **Regional Museum** (Pokrajinksi muzej; Mon–Fri 9am–5pm, Sat 9am–1pm; €3), housed inside an eighteenth-century Renaissance mansion in the centre of the leafy **City Park** west of the town's main square Trg Zmage (Victory Square). The museum's fifteen or so rooms (there are comprehensive English captions) offer an impressive narrative of life in the town and Prekmurje from prehistory to the present. Selected highlights from the earliest periods include Roman burial mounds and the remnants of a medieval forge discovered in Grad na Goričkem in 1990. The medieval period is further represented by some superb Gothic architecture, including a stone tabernacle, as well as some fresco fragments. Trades such as shoe-making, milling and wheel-making, all make an appearance, though the greatest emphasis is on pottery, one of the region's most important nineteenth-century cottage industries, and a tradition that just about survives to this day in old potters' settlements such as Filovci (see p.312). The last few rooms document the town's liberation by the Red Army in 1945, including a short film of the unveiling of the Liberation Monument on Trg Zmage, erected on August 12, 1945, less than two months after the Red Army left Murska Sobota; the exhibition concludes with a slightly tacky presentation on contemporary life in the region.

On the opposite side of City Park stands the slender, whitewashed neo-Gothic **Evangelical Church**. Although there's little in the way of traditional church ornamentation, its paintwork is striking, the cream-coloured walls splattered with geometric patterns of burgundy, green and blue; note the presbytery, too, which, unusually, is carpeted. There's a touch more culture courtesy of the town's **art gallery** (Mon–Fri 10am–6pm, Sat 9am–noon; €2) on Trg Kulture, a large and impressive space showcasing contemporary artwork.

Eating and drinking

There's little choice here when it comes to **eating and drinking**, though the lively *Zvezda* on the southeastern corner of Trg Zmage doubles up nicely as a restaurant and pub; worth trying is the game (particularly the chamois) and goulash, while there's a good selection of light and dark beers on tap, all brewed on site – before you enter, take a look at the stuccoed reliefs of moustachioed men on the facade. One other place worth considering is *Rajh no 1* (closed Mon), on the corner of Lendavska ulica and Cvetkova ulica, which offers deliciously simple salad and pasta dishes at rock-bottom prices.

If you're prepared to travel for your food, then make tracks for the 🍴 *Rajh* restaurant (closed Mon), 5km south of town in the village of **Bakovci**; the food here, including pheasant, lamb and goose, as well as Serbian specialities such as *Sarma* (minced meat wrapped inside cabbage leaves), is exceptional. It's located at the very beginning of the village, at Soboška ulica 32.

For drinking, the majority of townsfolk congregate on Trg Kulture, setting for a cluster of **cafés**, such as *Pilar* and *Pomaranča*, both opposite the library.

Martjanci

Heading north out of Murska Sobota along the road to Moravske Toplice, it's worth taking a moment to stop off at the roadside **Parish Church of St Martin** in the village of **MARTJANCI**. Distinguished by an elegant high belfry, the church was designed and painted by Janez Aquila, a frequent contributor to religious monuments in the Prekmurje region. Arguably the most beautifully frescoed church in Prekmurje, its gorgeous, cross-ribbed vaulted presbytery is smothered with some fine paintings – Apostles (including the *Masters of the Apostles*), saints and prophets, as well as a painting of the author himself (supposedly one of the oldest self-portraits known to exist in European art). On the inner wall of the triumphal arch there's a fabulous fresco of George and the Dragon. The simple high altar, meanwhile, featuring a statue of St Martin, is the work of Jože Plečnik, a modest contribution by the architect in comparison to his work at Bogojina (see below).

Moravske Toplice

From Martjanci, buses continue for a further 3km to **Moravske Toplice**, dominated by the **Terme 3000 Spa** (Ⓦwww.terme3000.si), a sprawling, modern complex incorporating one of the largest recreational centres in the country. Starting out in the 1960s, when thermal springs were discovered during a search for oil, the spa now comprises some twenty separate indoor and outdoor bathing areas featuring water and air massage pools, geysers and waterfalls, a diving pool, wave machines and enormous water slides (daily 8am–9pm; daily ticket €12, after 3pm €10).

There's plenty of accommodation on site, though none of the spas three adjoining **hotels**, all of which are inclined to package visitors, is particularly inspiring: top of the range, though not really warranting its billing, is the five-star *Livada* (Ⓣ02/512-1200; ❾), followed by the shiny four-star *Ajda* (❽) and the very similar but slightly cheaper *Termal* (❼). A far more pleasant alternative is the lovely thatched-roof, Prekmurje-style **bungalows** (❻) sheltered among trees on the opposite side of the complex (reception is in the *Ajda* hotel); or the huge *Prekmurska Vas* complex adjacent, which has **apartments** sleeping between two and five people (Ⓣ02/538-1520; ❻–❽) – reception is across the road from the bungalows. There's an excellent year-round **campsite** here, too. Guests of all the above accommodation receive free access to the spa pools.

The **tourist office** (Mon–Fri 8am–6pm, summer till 8pm, Sat 7am–3pm, Sun 8am–2pm; Ⓣ02/538-1520, Ⓦwww.moravske-toplice.com) is situated among the small complex of shops as you enter the village (if coming by bus backtrack 200m from the bus stop at the entrance to the spa); they can assist in finding **private accommodation** (❷) in the area, of which there is plenty, and there are bikes for rent. The *Flisar* tourist farm, 4km northwest of Moravske Toplice at Dolga ulica 216 (Ⓣ02/538-1320, Ⓔtur.kmetija-flisar@siol.net; ❸), is a terrific rural retreat, combining homely accommodation with fabulous domestic cooking. Likewise, there's the *Tremel* tourist farm (Ⓣ02/545-1017, Ⓦwww.kmetija-tremel.si; ❸), a lovely renovated farmstead located further north in the village of Bokrači, at no. 28 (from Murska Sobota follow signs for Hodoš, then Sebeborci).

Bikes can be rented from the Freerider Bike Center (see box, p.312), near the campsite entrance, while there's **tennis** (€5 for 1hr) and an eighteen-hole **golf course** (€30 for 9 holes, €40 for 18 holes); reception is under the *Livada* hotel and there's a twenty percent discount for guests of the hotels.

Bogojina, Filovci and Beltinci

BOGOJINA, some 5km east of Moravske Toplice, is the location for what is perhaps Prekmurje's best-known church, the **Church of the Ascension** (Cerkev Vnebovhod). Visible from miles around – owing to its slight elevation above the

Cycling In Prekmurje

Given the region's predominantly flat terrain, **cycling** around Prekmurje is a joy, and there's an excellent network of well-marked and well-maintained cycle paths to choose from. Moreover, with no two villages more than a few kilometres apart, there are plenty of opportunities to rest up before pushing on to the next destination.

If you do plan to do some cycling, there's plenty of information and materials to assist. The best place to start is the excellent Freerider Bike Center (☎02/538-1238), whose shop is within the grounds of the Terme 3000 spa in Moravske Toplice; as well as **renting out bikes** (€10 per day), they also organize bicycle excursions (€15), though a minimum of five people is usually required.

The *Cycling Around Prekmurje* pamphlet, available from the tourist office in Moravske Toplice, details eight routes, each one indicating sights of interest, places to sleep and eat as well as bike rental and repair shops; the 1:75,000 *Pomurje* map (€7) is also a useful aid.

rest of the village – the church was redesigned by Slovenia's greatest architect, Jože Plečnik (see box, p.60), between 1925 and 1927, and clearly manifests his trademark characteristics, from the high cylindrical tower to the columns, pillars and fanciful oddments gracing the interior. At the heart of this bright, single-nave hall-church is a monumental black marble column, from which four equally striking vaults emanate, built to help support the beautiful oak timber ceiling. In typically idiosyncratic fashion, Plečnik furnished the church with numerous flamboyant accessories, such as the ceramic plates and jugs ornamenting the ceiling and high altar. The village itself is exceptionally pretty, and it's an enjoyable fifteen-minute walk from the bus stop on the main road to the church, past rows of colourful Prekmurje-style farmhouses – L-shaped homesteads built on narrow strips of land perpendicular to the traffic routes.

The so-called *črna keramika*, or **black pottery**, industry flourished in several villages hereabouts from the late eighteenth century onwards, and especially in **FILOVCI**, 2km further along the road from Bogojina. In the centre of the village, at no. 29 – walk across the small bridge and beyond the church – the Bojnec family offers pottery demonstrations in their workshop; they've also got a shop selling a wide range of earthenware. Contact the tourist office to arrange a visit.

If you're around during the last weekend of July, then don't miss the **Beltinci International Folklore Festival**, which takes place in the large village of **BELTINCI**, about 10km south of Bogojina – it is actually easier to reach the village via the faster road from Murska Sobota to Lendava. For over thirty years this superb festival has consistently attracted a high-calibre roster of both domestic and foreign folk groups, musicians and dance troupes, who perform over four days on several stages in the village's large and leafy manor park – Saturday is generally reckoned to be the best day. It's also a great opportunity to try out some traditional Prekmurje dishes at the many stalls spread out around the grounds.

The focal point of the park itself is the seventeenth-century L-shaped **Manor House**, now mostly decrepit and decaying, but which does house a **pharmacy exhibition** in one renovated room; on display are the original early twentieth-century fixtures and fittings, including some gorgeous wood-carved cabinets, painted ceramic jars, and other vessels. In opposing corners on the ground floor, there's a **tourist office** (Mon–Fri 8am–3pm; ☎02/541-3580, ⓔbeltinci .info@siol.net) and the *Grajskem Stolpu* **restaurant**, a tidy, friendly place offering regional specialities (Mon–Sat 8am–10pm, Sun 7am–4pm).

Selo

From the village of **Tešanovci**, a kilometre or so east of Moravske Toplice, a road breaks left and climbs slowly up to the scattered settlement of **SELO**, some 10km distant. Standing in a field below the main road is the pinkish **Chapel of St Nicholas** (Rotunda Sv Nikolaj; €2), a superb Romanesque rotunda built in the mid-thirteenth century. Its interior is adorned with some exceptional, albeit badly effaced, wall paintings, the upper half covered in scenes from the Adoration of the Magi and the Passion Cycle, and the dome smothered with evangelical symbols. To gain entrance to the church, you will need to call in at the **information hut** (April–Oct Tues–Sun 9am–5pm). Out of season, you can get the key from the house at no. 61. Located 1km back along the road (before the church), the roadside gostilna, *K Rotundi* (Mon–Sat 11am–10pm, Sun 10am–4pm), is one of the region's best **restaurants**; as well as the standard Prekmurje specialities, it's known for its game and roast goat dishes.

Lendava and around

Wedged into the southeastern corner of Prekmurje, 31km from Murska Sobota and just a stone's throw from the Croatian and Hungarian borders, **LENDAVA** (Lendva in Hungarian) is Slovenia's easternmost town and also one of the largest bilingual settlements in the country, its sizeable Hungarian minority accounting for nearly half of the town's population. Despite this harmonized ethnic union, it's a fairly low-key place, its relative isolation ensuring that few visitors make it to this remote little corner of the country.

Lendava's major **festival** is the fun *Bogračfest* on the last Saturday in August, a culinary affair where dozens of teams line up along Glavna ulica to prepare the tastiest, meatiest goulash, accompanied by lots of wine and music.

Arrival, information and accommodation

Arriving at the **bus station** on Kolodvorska ulica make your way across the ugly concrete square towards the *Hotel Elizabeta*, through the small complex of shops to the park; take a right here, up past the town hall to the triangle in the middle of the road. At this point turn left and you'll find yourself on the main street, Glavna ulica, location for the **tourist office** at no. 38 (Mon–Fri 8am–4pm, Sat & Sun 10am–1pm; ☎02/578-8390, ⓦwww.lendava-turizem.si).

Aimed at nonexistent business travellers, the **hotel** *Elizabeta* (☎02/577-4600, ⓦwww.terme-lendava.si; ❼) is a gleaming glass block at Mlinska ulica 5 – the rooms are perfectly fine and comfortable, albeit pricey. The only other hotel hereabouts is the unattractive and absurdly expensive *Lipa* (☎02/577-4100, ⓦwww.terme-lendava.si; ❽), which is actually part of the Lendava spa complex 1km south of town at Tomšičeva 2; more appealingly, they've got good-looking apartments sleeping two to four people (❻–❽), and a year-round **campsite**.

The Town

The town's major attraction is the **castle**, reached via a steep path next to the **Parish Church of St Catherine**, midway along Glavna ulica. Although a fortification of sorts stood here as early as the twelfth century, the present castle was rebuilt by the noble Hungarian Esterházy family between 1712 and 1717, remaining within their possession until the beginning of World War II. It now houses a modest **museum** (Mon–Fri 8am–4pm, Sat 10am–2pm; €2.50), containing a rather ordinary collection of Bronze Age artefacts, weaponry from battles with the Turks, and a small ethnographic collection.

The only other two sites of note are located on the opposite side of Glavna ulica near the town park. Built in 1866, the **synagogue** (Mon–Fri 9am–3pm, Sat & Sun 9am–1pm) on Župančičeva ulica was cleared out, along with the town's several-hundred-strong Jewish population, during World War II. Although there is no longer a Jewish community in town, the synagogue has been restored to something like its former self, and now accommodates a few exhibits – mainly photo documentation and religious items – from the pre-World War II period. The extraordinary building in the park opposite – designed by the renowned, and controversial, Hungarian architect **Imre Makovecz** – functions as the town's cultural centre, the centerpiece of which is a fine theatre, with Slovene and Hungarian productions sharing equal billing.

Nestled among the winegrowing **Lendava Hills** (Lendavske Gorice), less than 1km southeast of town, is the **Church of the Holy Trinity** (Cerkev Sv Trojice), a standard Baroque issue built in 1728. The church is notable, however, for holding the grisly, mummified body of local warrior Mihael Hadik, slain by the Turks in 1603, but whose immaculately preserved body – take a peek if you wish – was miraculously discovered in a casket during construction of the castle chapel in 1728. If you wish to visit the church contact the tourist office, and a member of staff will accompany you. If you fancy a wallow, head over to the **Terme Lendava Spa** (daily 7am–8pm, Fri & Sat till 11pm; €8.50 for the day, €6.50 after 1pm), 1km south of town at Tomšičeva 2; one of the country's warmest spas, it has two indoor and three outdoor (May–Sept) pools, with temperatures between 29 and 37 degrees.

Eating and drinking

The decent *Gostilna Krona* **restaurant**, within the town hall at Glavna ulica 20, is pretty much the only place to eat in town (closed Mon). The best spot for a drink is the *Teater Café* inside the cultural centre, while there's also good coffee, and **internet**, at *Banffy*, a lovely, restful spot just along from the tourist office on Glavna ulica. **Wine** buffs may care to visit the Cuk Wine Cellar at Lendavske Gorice 217 (☏02/575-1815, ⓦwww.hisa-vina-cuk.si), a pretty little hillside cellar 1km southeast of town on the fringe of the Lendava Hills. As well as

---

Slovenia's Roma

Most of Slovenia's estimated seven thousand **Gypsies**, or **Roma**, many of whom settled in the country following the wars in Croatia and Bosnia, live in small, scattered settlements throughout Prekmurje. The majority of the remainder of the Roma community live in southeast Dolenjska and Bela Krajina. Although the lot of the Roma in Slovenia is considerably better than that of those in many other countries of the former Eastern Bloc – Slovenia is one of the few European countries that have included the Roma in the constitution – discrimination is still commonplace. Moreover, living conditions remain, on the whole, substandard, with many settlements still lacking basic infrastructure, while standards of education are low and unemployment remains unacceptably high.

However, the situation is improving. In recent years, the state has made concerted attempts to integrate the Roma community into the majority culture. The most significant piece of legislation, adopted in 2002, allowed for Romany community representatives to be elected to local councils in more than twenty municipalities. The Roma community, too, have made concentrated efforts to organize themselves into coherent groups, such as the Union of Roma of Slovenia (the country's major Roma organization), which was formed in 1991 following Slovene independence. Among its many artistic activities, it publishes the magazine *Romano Them* (Romany News).

wine-tasting, they've also got a handful of rooms (❸) and apartments (❹) if you wish to stop over.

Velika Polana

If you've got your own transport, there are two villages of interest a short way from Lendava. **VELIKA POLANA**, around 10km west, is one of Europe's officially designated **stork villages** thanks to the dozen or so storks that pitch up here each spring. Attracted by the abundance of food, especially frogs and toads, to be found in the nearby marshes and swamplands, the storks usually return to the same nest (improbably bulky constructions perched atop telegraph poles or chimneys) each year. Whether kicking back in their nests, or skulking around the fields foraging for food, these birds offer irresistible photo opportunities.

Around five kilometres further west of Velika Polana, the dusty village of **Kamenci** is home to one of the largest **Roma settlements** in Prekmurje. Organized visits, which include a programme of entertainment featuring traditional Roma music and dance, are available – contact the tourist office in Lendava. There is also a small **Gypsy Museum** here, the only one of its kind in the country.

Travel details

Trains

Celje to: Laško (every 45min–2hr; 10min); Ljubljana (every 45min–2hr; 1hr–1hr 40min); Maribor (every 45min–2hr; 45min–1hr 10min); Podčetrtek (Mon–Fri 5 daily; 45min); Rogaška Slatina (Mon–Fri 6 daily; 45min); Velenje (Mon–Fri 9 daily, Sat 2 daily; 50min).
Dravograd to: Maribor (Mon–Fri 5 daily; 1hr 40min).
Ljutomer to: Ljubljana (Mon–Fri 6 daily, Sat & Sun 3 daily; 3hr 10min); Murska Sobota (Mon–Fri 9 daily, Sat & Sun 3 daily; 20min); Ormož (Mon–Fri 8 daily, Sat & Sun 3 daily; 25min).
Maribor to: Celje (every 45min–2hr; 45min–1hr 10min); Dravograd (Mon–Fri 5 daily; 1hr 40min); Ljubljana (every 45min–2hr; 1hr 45min–2hr 45min).
Murska Sobota to: Ljubljana (Mon–Fri 6 daily, Sat & Sun 3 daily; 3hr 30min); Ljutomer (Mon–Fri 9 daily, Sat & Sun 3 daily; 20min); Ormož (Mon–Fri 9 daily, Sat & Sun 3 daily; 45min); Ptuj (Mon–Fri 7 daily, Sat & Sun 4 daily; 50min–1hr 10min).
Ormož to: Ljubljana (Mon–Fri 8 daily, Sat & Sun 3 daily; 2hr 50min); Ljutomer (Mon–Fri 8 daily, Sat & Sun 3 daily; 25min); Murska Sobota (Mon–Fri 9 daily, Sat & Sun 3 daily; 45min); Ptuj (Mon–Fri 12 daily, Sat & Sun 5 daily; 25min).
Podčetrtek to: Celje (Mon–Fri 6 daily; 45min).
Ptuj to: Ljubljana (Mon–Fri 8 daily, Sat & Sun 3 daily; 2hr 30min–3hr); Murska Sobota (Mon–Fri 7 daily, Sat & Sun 4 daily; 50min–1hr 10min); Ormož (Mon–Fri 12 daily, Sat & Sun 5 daily; 25min).

Rogaška Slatina to: Celje (Mon–Fri 5 daily; 45min).
Velenje to: Celje (Mon–Fri 9 daily, Sat 2 daily; 50min).

Buses

Celje to: Laško (Mon–Fri 9 daily, Sat 5 daily; 15min); Ljubljana (Mon–Fri 8 daily, Sat & Sun 2 daily; 1hr 30min); Maribor (Mon–Fri 7 daily, Sat & Sun 2 daily; 1hr 15min); Murska Sobota (1 daily; 2hr 30min); Rogaška Slatina (Mon–Fri 8 daily, Sat 4 daily, Sun 3 daily; 40min); Slovenske Konjice (Mon–Fri hourly, Sat & Sun 2 daily; 25min); Velenje (Mon–Fri hourly, Sat 5 daily, Sun 2 daily; 25min); Zreče (Mon–Fri 6 daily; 25min).
Črna na Koroškem to: Dravograd (Mon–Fri hourly, Sat 8 daily, Sun 4 daily; 45min); Maribor (3 daily; 1hr 50min); Slovenj Gradec (Mon–Fri hourly, Sat 8 daily, Sun 4 daily; 50min); Velenje (Mon–Fri 6 daily, Sat & Sun 4 daily; 50min).
Dravograd to: Celje (1 daily; 1hr 10min); Črna na Koroškem (Mon–Fri every 30min–hourly, Sat 7 daily, Sun 5 daily; 45min); Maribor (Mon–Fri 6 daily, Sat & Sun 5 daily; 1hr 15min); Slovenj Gradec (Mon–Fri every 30min–hourly, Sat hourly, Sun 8 daily; 20min); Velenje (Mon–Fri every 45min–hourly, Sat & Sun 6 daily; 40min).
Lendava to: Črenšovci (Mon–Fri hourly; 25min); Moravske Toplice (Mon–Fri 6 daily, Sat 1 daily; 15min). Murska Sobota (Mon–Fri hourly, Sat 2 daily; 40min);

Ljutomer to: Murska Sobota (Mon–Fri 8 daily; 40min); Ormož (Mon–Fri 5 daily; 30min).
Maribor to: Celje (Mon–Fri 8 daily, Sat & Sun 4 daily; 1hr 15min); Dravograd (Mon–Fri 9 daily, Sat & Sun 6 daily; 1hr 15min); Ljubljana (Mon–Fri 6 daily, Sat & Sun 4 daily; 2hr 30min–3hr); Ljutomer (Mon–Fri 3 daily, Sat & Sun 1 daily; 1hr 20min); Murska Sobota (Mon–Fri every 30min, Sat 7 daily, Sun 3 daily; 1hr 10min); Ormož (Mon–Fri 4 daily, Sat & Sun 1 daily; 50min); Ptuj (Mon–Fri every 45mins hourly, Sat hourly, Sun 6 daily; 30min) Radenci (Mon–Sat every 30–45min, Sat 8 daily, Sun 6 daily; 1hr); Slovenske Konjice (Mon–Fri 8 daily, Sat & Sun 3 daily; 50min).
Moravske Toplice to: Bogojina & Filovci (en route to Dubrovnik) (Mon–Fri 8 daily; 10min); Lendava (Mon–Fri 3 daily; 30min); Murska Sobota (Mon–Fri 10 daily; 10min).
Murska Sobota to: Bakovci Mon–Fri 10 daily, Sat 3 daily; 15min); Beltinci (Mon–Fri every 20–30min, Sat 5 daily, Sun 2 daily; 15min); Bogojina (Mon–Fri 9 daily; 20min); Filovci (Mon–Fri 9 daily; 25min); Lendava (Mon–Fri hourly, Sat 4 daily, Sun 2 daily; 40min); Ljutomer (Mon–Fri 6 daily; 40min); Maribor (Mon–Fri hourly, Sat & Sun 5 daily; 1hr 10min); Moravske Toplice (Mon–Fri 10 daily; 10min); Radenci (Mon–Fri every 20–30min, Sat 7 daily, Sun 5 daily; 15min).
Ormož to: Ljutomer (Mon–Fri 7 daily; 30min); Maribor (Mon–Fri 2 daily, Sat 1 daily; 50min); Ptuj (Mon–Fri 8 daily, Sat 4 daily; 30min).
Podčetrtek to: Bistrica ob Sotli (Mon–Fri 6 daily; 25min); Celje (Mon–Fri 5 daily; 45min); Rogaška Slatina (Mon–Fri hourly, Sat 4 daily; 20min).
Ptuj to: Ljutomer (Mon–Fri 2 daily; 1hr 10min); Maribor (Mon–Sat every 30min, Sat 10 daily, Sun 6 daily; 30min); Ormož (Mon–Fri 9 daily, Sat 1 daily; 30min); Ptujska Gora (Mon–Fri 7 daily; 20min); Rogaška Slatina (Mon–Fri 1 daily; 1hr 5min).
Rogaška Slatina to: Celje (Mon–Fri 9 daily, Sat & Sun 2 daily; 40min); Maribor (Mon–Fri 2 daily; 1hr 10min); Podčetrtek (Mon–Fri hourly, Sat & Sun 4 daily; 20min); Rogatec (Mon–Fri 8 daily, Sat 4 daily, Sun 3 daily; 15min).
Rogatec to: Celje (Mon–Fri 6 daily, Sat 2 daily; 50min); Ptuj (Mon–Fri 1 daily; 1hr 20min); Rogaška Slatina (Mon–Fri 4 daily, Sat 2 daily; 15min).
Slovenj Gradec to: Celje (1 daily; 45min); Črna na Koroškem (Mon–Fri every 1hr–1hr 30min, Sat 5 daily, Sun 3 daily; 50min); Dravograd (Mon–Fri every 45min–hourly, Sat & Sun 10 daily; 20min); Ljubljana (Mon–Fri 3 daily, Sat & Sun 1 daily; 2hr); Maribor (2 daily; 1hr 20min); Velenje (Mon–Fri every 45min–hourly, Sat & Sun 10 daily; 25min).
Slovenske Konjice to: Celje (Mon–Fri hourly, Sat & Sun 2 daily; 25min); Ljubljana (Mon–Fri 5 daily, Sat & Sun 2 daily; 2hr); Maribor (Mon–Fri 4 daily, Sat & Sun 2 daily; 50min); Zreče (Mon–Fri every 45min–hourly; 10min).
Velenje to: Celje (Mon–Sat hourly, Sat 8 daily, Sun 2 daily; 25min); Črna na Koroškem (Mon–Fri hourly, Sat & Sun 4 daily; 50min); Dravograd (Mon–Fri hourly, Sat 6 daily, Sun 5 daily; 40min); Ljubljana (Mon–Fri 3 daily, Sat & Sun 2 daily; 1hr 30min); Slovenj Gradec (Mon–Fri hourly, Sat & Sun 8 daily; 25min).
Zreče to: Celje (Mon–Fri 8 daily; 25min); Slovenske Konjice (Mon–Fri hourly; 10min).

International trains

Maribor to: Graz (4 daily; 1hr 15min); Vienna (3 daily; 3hr 45min).
Murska Sobota to: Budapest (2 daily; 5hr 15min).

International buses

Lendava to: Čakovec (Croatia) (Mon–Sat 1 daily; 40min).
Ptuj to: Zagreb (Mon–Sat 1 daily; 1hr 45min).
Maribor to: Graz (Mon–Fri 1 daily at 7.20am; 1hr).

Contexts

Contexts

History

Although recorded history of the area now covered by Slovenia begins with the arrival of the Romans, archeological finds suggest that this territory was already settled in the **Paleolithic** and **Neolithic** eras. The most intriguing discovery from the Paleolithic era was a bone flute unearthed from a cave in Šebrelje near Cerkno in 1995, while the most compelling evidence of the existence of a Neolithic culture comes from the Ljubljana Marshes south of the capital. Here, the inhabitants built wooden huts on stilts, made coarse pottery and raised livestock.

The early Iron Age, or **Hallstatt**, period (eighth to fourth centuries BC) coincided with the arrival of the region's first identifiable peoples – Illyrian-speaking tribes, possibly called Veneti, who settled in the Alpine region. The major Hallstatt settlements were located in Most na Soči and throughout the region of Dolenjska, as indicated by some superb archeological finds in these areas, such as armour, jewellery and *situlae* (ornately embossed pails or buckets). More generally, this was a period of great economic and cultural advancement. Around the third century BC the Hallstatt cultures were superseded by the Celts who, led by the Norics, established a protostate called **Noricum**, the centre of which was located in the eastern Alps, while a second centre grew up in the area of present-day Celje, then called **Celeia**.

The Romans

Noricum was subsumed into the Roman Empire around 10 BC, which more or less marked the beginning of **Roman occupation** in this territory. Settled by colonists from Aquileia (a small town in the Gulf of Trieste established by the Romans in 181 BC), Emona (Ljubljana) was the first Roman town to develop on the territory of present-day Slovenia, followed by Poetovio (Ptuj) and Celeia (Celje). Trade, administration and culture grew up around these garrison towns and spread along the roads constructed to link the imperial heartland with Pannonia and beyond. Some of the country's best-preserved **Roman remains** include vestigial ruins in Ljubljana, a wealth of monuments in Ptuj, and a superb Roman necropolis in Šempeter, just outside Celje. The most significant legacy of the Roman occupation was the partition of the Byzantine and Roman spheres into separate civilizations, a division that would later result in a critical split between the Eastern Orthodox and Roman Catholic churches. The disintegration of the Roman Empire in the fifth century corresponded with a series of incursions into the region by a multitude of warring tribes, such as the Huns, Ostrogoths and Lombards, and the all-powerful **Avars**, a Turkic people from Central Asia whose empire survived well into the eighth century, before it was crushed by the Franks.

From the first Slav state to Habsburg rule

Although there is no definitive record as to when, or from where, the ancestors of today's Slovenes first entered the territory of present-day Slovenia, the most widespread theory is that migrating Slav tribes (loosely divided into two different, but related, groups, Slaveni and Antes) arrived from the Carpathian Basin in the middle of the sixth century. As Avar power waned, these tribes, along with others, united into a loose confederation, resulting in the first Slav political entity, the **Duchy of Karantanija**, located near present-day Klagenfurt in Austria. This brief period of autonomy lasted until 745 AD, when the Duchy was subsumed into the Carolingian Empire of the Franks, thus subjecting the Karantanian Slav population to a Germanic domination that would continue for several centuries more. Around the same time, an influx of western missionaries and the establishment of a formal church paved the way for the **Christianization of the Slovenes**.

In the tenth century, the Magyars, led by the feared Arpad clan, invaded and settled in the Slovenian regions of Pannonia. Before they were able to advance any further, however, they ran into the imperial forces of the German king, Otto I, who promptly routed them in a counter-offensive just outside Augsburg in 955 AD. German victory instigated the reorganization of Karantanian territory into frontier marches, namely, Carinthia (Koroška), Carniola (Kranjska), Styria (Štajerska), Gorica (Goriška) and Bela Krajina, the boundaries of which would essentially remain the same for the next thousand years.

The first chartered towns on Slovene territory – Kamnik, Piran, Ptuj, Škofja Loka and the capital Ljubljana – began to develop a short while thereafter, around the beginning of the twelfth century. By the fourteenth century there would be some 27 chartered towns and countless other market towns, many of which developed trade and crafts industries as an adjunct to agricultural activity. Cultural life during this period, meanwhile, was mostly centred around the newly established monasteries, such as the Carthusian orders at Pleterje and Žiče, and the Cistercian orders at Kostanjevica and Stična. Although primarily schools for the education of the clergy, they also served a wider educational purpose, functioning as key centres of learning for intellectuals, musicians and so on. Meanwhile, the prominent ruling entities of this time – the Bamberg, Spanheim and Premysl dynasties – were confronted with the spectre of the Habsburgs who, by 1270, had already established a stronghold in the eastern Alps and would soon rule across most of the Slovene lands.

Habsburg rule, Turkish invasions and the Reformation

The **Habsburg dynasty** established its first feudal holdings in Slovene lands in 1282, holding sway across most of the territory until the end of World War I, while small geographical areas in the eastern and western peripheries were governed by Hungary and Venice respectively. The only serious political rivals to the Habsburgs at this time were the **counts of Celje**, an aristocratic dynasty who, through a combination of fortuitous politics and skilfully arranged marriages into distinguished European feudal houses, managed to acquire great swathes of territory and wield tremendous influence across the country. Although the assassination of Count Ulrik II in Belgrade in 1456 nullified this particular threat, the Habsburgs now had to contend with other problems.

Having already conquered much of the Balkan peninsula in the first half of the fifteenth century, the **Ottoman Turks** resumed their advance north towards Slovene territories around 1470. Despite repeated raids, which reached their peak during the reign of Sultan Suleyman I "the Magnificent" (1520–66), the defining moment was the **Battle of Sisak** in 1593, where the Turks were crushed by combined Habsburg-Croatian forces, an episode which effectively put the lid on Turkish aspirations in Habsburg-occupied lands.

The economic pressures engendered as a result of these assaults, coupled with the transformation of the old feudal tax system into less favourable forms, precipitated a series of violent and widespread **peasant revolts**. The most famous of these was the 1573 uprising, during which some ten thousand Slovene and Croatian peasants (*puntarji*) participated. In the event, the rebellion was crushed and its leader, Matija Gubec, met a somewhat ignominious fate (crowned with a red-hot metal rod in Zagreb Cathedral), while the peasants were bound to perpetual serfdom. The prevalence of serfdom meant that there was little other economic activity to speak of around this time, though pockets of proto-industrialization existed in parts of the country, for example, the Idrija mercury mine and the forges in Kropa.

The **Germanization** of culture, education and administration had been a key policy of Habsburg rule since the tenth century, yet despite this, Slovenes managed to preserve both their language and cultural identity. This was largely down to **Protestant reformers** such as **Primož Trubar** (the "Slovene Luther"), who wrote and published the first book in the Slovene language, and **Adam Bohorič**, who compiled the first Slovene grammar book. It would, however, be another two centuries before written Slovene would be appropriated for secular use. Having seen off the Turks, the Austrians, under Archduke Ferdinand, turned their attention to the religious revolts taking place throughout Habsburg lands, and by the end of the century the **Counter-Reformation** was in full swing. The ensuing period of recatholicization and absolutism resulted in a lengthy spell of political, economic and cultural regression for Slovenes.

The eighteenth century: reform and the Enlightenment

Prospects looked decidedly brighter at the turn of the eighteenth century owing to strong economic growth and modernization, manifest in the development of manufacturing industries – forges in Bohinj and Jesenice, textile mills in Ljubljana, improved transport links between Vienna and Trieste (via Maribor, Celje and Ljubljana) and the declaration of Trieste as a free port. These developments were taken a stage further under the centralized, state-building reforms of **Maria Theresa** and her son **Joseph II** during the second half of the century: judicial reforms were introduced, primary schooling was made compulsory and religious tolerance was decreed. More tendentiously, German replaced Latin as the language of government, a move that caused some alarm among the emerging national groups, many of whom preferred to use their own language.

Led by the cultural innovator **Baron Žiga Zois** and a small coterie of Slovene intellectuals (the so-called "Zois Circle"), the **Slovene Enlightenment** (roughly 1760–1820) was the first sustained period of cultural advancement since the work of the sixteenth-century Protestant reformers. This celebrated group featured the historian/playwright **Anton Linhart**, poet/journalist **Valentin Vodnik** – founder of the first Slovene newspaper, *Ljublanske Novice* (*The Ljubljana News*) – and the priest, **Marko Pohlin**, whose 1768 publication, *Kranjska gramatika* (*Carniolan Grammar*), was the forerunner to a modern Slovene literary language. In addition, theatres in Ljubljana, Maribor and Celje were built, public and private libraries became the focus for Slovene cultural life, and the establishment of assorted professional and cultural societies and institutions, including the Philharmonic Music Society (1794) and the literary and linguistic society, Academia Operosorum, affirmed Slovenia's integration into the circle of cultured European nations. It was also a time of great **Baroque** extravagance, particularly in the fields of architecture, painting and sculpture. Nowhere was this more so than in Ljubljana, which acquired several beautiful churches, church paintings and buildings. Leading Baroque contributors included the painters Valentin Metzinger and Giulio Quaglio, architect Andrea Pozzo, and sculptor Francesco Robba.

The nineteenth century: nationalism and reform

Following **Napoleon's** dissolution of the Venetian republic in 1797, the French were drawn into several wars against the Austrians, culminating in a hard-fought victory for the French at Wagram in 1809. Subsequent to this, Napoleon cut the Austrians off from the Adriatic and created a quasi-ethnic state, stretching from Graz in Austria down to the Bay of Kotor in Montenegro, a region known as the **Illyrian Provinces**. Over the next four years, and with Ljubljana designated as the provinces' administrative centre, Slovenes enjoyed a series of liberating French reforms, the most important of which was free use of the Slovene language in administration and schools. Following Napoleon's defeat in 1813, and the subsequent collapse of the French Empire, Slovene territory was reincorporated into the Habsburg domain and all the old political and feudal systems were restored. Nevertheless, four years of French rule was long enough for Slovene intellectuals to be made aware of their ethno-national identities; moreover the inclusion of Croats, as well as a minority Serb population, within the same state gave rise to the notion that some form of common Slav union might one day be realized. These embryonic national sentiments were powerfully reinforced through the work of Slovenia's pre-eminent Romantic poet and greatest-ever literary figure, **France Prešeren** (see box, p.121), who refashioned Slovenian as a literary language and raised it to the level of other European languages. It was no surprise, therefore, when Prešeren's poem, *Zdravljica* (*A Toast*), was adopted as the Slovene national anthem in 1991.

The **1848 Revolution** was the catalyst for tremendous upheaval across continental Europe, including Austria, where the tenets of absolutism and serfdom had reigned since the demise of the Illyrian provinces in 1813. Fired by the literary brilliance of Prešeren and the pedagogic reforms of **Anton Slomšek** (the bishop of Maribor), **Slovene nationalism** became increasingly vocal around this time, culminating in calls for a **United Slovenia programme** (*Zedinjena Slovenija*), whose prime objectives were to unite all ethnic Slovene territories within one autonomous region and to promulgate the use of the Slovene language. Although the programme was never realized, its basic tenets informed much of Slovene political life well into the next century. By and large, though, most Slovenes remained committed to Austria and few envisaged a future outside the Habsburg Empire.

According to the terms of the **Compromise of 1867**, the Habsburg state became the **Dual Monarchy of Austria–Hungary**, whereby the two became constitutionally separate entities, albeit with the same Habsburg ruler, Franz Jozef – emperor in Austria and king in Hungary. In practice this meant shared common foreign and defence policies, but internally each was governed by its own constitution. As a result of the compromise most Slovenes remained within Austria, though a small, yet significant, number were incorporated into Hungarian and Italian sectors. Around this time Slovenes began to make important strides politically, organizing themselves into distinct and identifiable political groupings, and by the end of the century three core parties had been established: the liberal **National Progressive Party**, the conservative, or clerical **Slovene People's Party**, and the socialist **Yugoslav Democratic Party**. Each of these parties presented alternative political philosophies, but they collectively espoused a common commitment to some form of pan-Slavism, or **Yugoslavism**, a political concept that had initially taken root earlier that century. However, despite adopting broadly nationalist agendas, all three parties remained firmly committed to their Austrian overlords, aware that they were too small and there were too few of them (even with their Slav allies) to go it alone. Instead, they concluded that **Trialism** – the notion that a third element, a South Slav component, would be created within the Habsburg Empire – could be the only possible framework for any form of Slovene self-determination. The latter part of the century was also a time of cultural efflorescence for Slovenes, manifest in the establishment of **reading societies** (*čitalnice*), the **Slovene Literary Society** (Slovenska Matica) and the **Sokol** (Falcon) association, a patriotic gymnastic society which advocated the cult of the healthy body as well as Slavonic brotherhood.

In the two decades prior to World War I, Slovene political life became increasingly preoccupied with the idea of Yugoslavism, and while most Slovenes ostensibly remained loyal to Austria, there were those who felt increasingly uneasy with regard to Austria's domestic and foreign policies, and in particular its progressively cosy alliance with Germany. Championing the Yugoslav cause was the celebrated novelist **Ivan Cankar**, who posited that some form of linguistic and cultural merging was both practical and desirable. Cankar was closely associated with the avowedly anti-Austrian student organization **Preporod** (Rebirth), which, along with other South Slav groups, including the ultra-nationalist Young Bosnian movement from Sarajevo, advocated an independent Yugoslav state. Following the **assassination of Archduke Franz Ferdinand** in Sarajevo in 1914 by Gavrilo Princip (a member of the Young Bosnians), Austria declared war on Serbia. Within a matter of days, Europe's major alliance systems had been activated – Germany joined forces with Austria, while their opponents, who supported Serbia, were the Entente powers of Russia, France and Britain.

World War I and the Kingdom of Serbs, Croats and Slovenes

During the formative stages of **World War I**, Slovenes fought in several arenas on behalf of the Austrian crown, including the Serbian and Russian fronts, though the prospect of fighting fellow Slavs appealed to few Slovenes and defections were common. The single most important factor affecting Slovenia during the war was the **1915 London Pact**, which persuaded Italians to join the Entente forces in return for promises of land populated by Slovenes and Croats. Galvanized into action, Slovenes pitched in with the Austrians along the Western **Soča front**, which extended for some 90km from Mount Rombon, near Bovec, along the course of the Soča river down to a position just north of Trieste on the Adriatic coast. The Soča Front was one of the bloodiest battlegrounds of the entire war, with catastrophic losses on both sides, though particularly for the Italians who were routed during the famous twelfth and final offensive in the Krn mountain range above Kobarid in October 1917.

With an increasingly mutinous Slovene military, and the Habsburg Empire on the verge of collapse, a group of South Slav delegates, led by Slovene Anton Korošec, presented the **May 1917 declaration** to Vienna demanding the creation of an autonomous, democratic Slav state within the Habsburg monarchy. The demand was dismissed, but support for a unitary state continued apace and in October 1918, Serb, Croat and Slovene political leaders convened in Zagreb to form the **National Council**, at the same time declaring their independence from Budapest and Vienna. Little more than a month later, on December 1, 1918, in Belgrade, Serbian Prince Alexander Karađorđevič declared the establishment of the **Kingdom of Serbs**, **Croats and Slovenes**, which also incorporated the territories of Bosnia, Montenegro and Macedonia.

At the end of the war, Slovenia's ethnic territory was subject to widescale dismemberment: while the greater part of Slovenia was incorporated into the kingdom, a significant portion of southern Carinthia was ceded to Austria and, under the terms of the **1920 Treaty of Rapallo**, almost a third of Slovene territory – which included the economically important cities of Trieste and Gorizia – was annexed to Italy. The first few years under Italian jurisdiction were bearable, but the situation worsened considerably following Mussolini's ascent to power: political and cultural institutions were banned, public use of the Slovene language was abolished (except in Catholic churches), and all Slavic geographical names were Italianized. While large numbers of Slovenes chose to emigrate during this heightened period of Italian irredentism, many more established political, social and cultural organizations and underground movements, in order to fight for minority rights – some, such as the terror group, **TIGR** (Trst, Istra, Reka, Gorica), had several of its members executed.

For Slovenes living within the new kingdom, the situation was not much better than it was for those in Italy or Austria, and certainly not what they had in mind when they cast their lot with that of their fellow southern Slavs. The centralistic **1921 Vidovdan Constitution**, which established a parliamentary, constitutional monarchy for the kingdom, with Belgrade as its capital and Karađorđevič as head of state, immediately buried any aspirations Slovenes (and other constituent groups within the state) may have had for political autonomy. Although traditional liberties were largely protected by the constitution, the rights of liberals and communists were frequently infringed and the king wielded almost absolute power. Years of political chaos – ineffectual governments, high-profile assassinations and persistent attempts to undermine Serb rule – culminated in the suspension of the constitution in January 1929. A **royal dictatorship** was imposed and the Kingdom of Serbs, Croats and Slovenes was recast as the **Kingdom of Yugoslavia**, ostensibly to foster Yugoslav political unitarism but which was ultimately a disaster for all non-Serbs. Increasingly violent nationalist strains began to emerge among the constituent groups, particularly in Croatia, where the ultranationalist, proto-fascist **Ustaše** movement were particularly prominent – it was they who masterminded the assassination of King Alexander Karađorđević in Marseille in 1934. Authority, thereafter, passed to Prince Paul, whose regime merely escalated anti-Serb sentiment.

Another organization opposed to the unitary Yugoslav state was the **Communist Party of Yugoslavia** (CPY), which, from the time of its formation in 1919 until the mid-1930s, had remained a largely underground movement, with many of its congresses held abroad and most of its activity supervised from Moscow. With the appointment, in 1937, of **Josip Broz Tito** as its leader, the party began to reorganize itself into a federation of national units – hence the birth of the **Communist Party of Slovenia** (CPS). Of immediate concern to Slovenia was the menacing presence of Italian Fascism and German imperialism, for both Italy and Germany had territorial designs on Slovene lands.

World War II

Whereas in World War I Slovenia and the other Slav states found themselves embroiled in combat from the very start, it was over eighteen months after the start of **World War II** before Yugoslavia (and by implication, Slovenia) became involved. By this time much of continental Europe had already fallen under the sway of Germany and Italy. After initially being cowed into joining the Axis powers' orbit, Yugoslavia renounced the decision following a governmental coup, a decision they paid for on April 6, 1941, when Germany blitzed Belgrade. The king fled in exile to London and within a matter of days the country had capitulated. For its part, Slovenia was partitioned between Germany, which claimed the northern and eastern areas, Hungary, which took Prekmurje, and Italy, which annexed the rest. While the Italians were more or less sympathetic to Slovenes, allowing them a measure of cultural autonomy, those in the German and Hungarian occupied territories were subject to aggressive denaturalizing policies – arrests, torture, execution and deportation.

In response, **resistance groups** took up arms almost immediately. Organized by the CPY, with Tito as chief military commander, a **Yugoslav Partisan resistance** movement was established. In Slovenia, the **Liberation Front** (OF – Osvobodilna Fronta) was formed, organized and controlled by the CPS; it comprised Christian Socialists, the liberal Sokols and leftist intellectuals, as well as party members. The Liberation Front was broken up into smaller Partisan units, dispersed throughout the cities and countryside – circumstances, however, dictated that in the early stages at least, the Slovenes and Tito's Partisans were mostly detached from each other. The Slovene Partisan army continued in a fairly independent manner until 1944, when they joined forces in a wider pan-Yugoslav resistance movement, which had by now received official recognition from the Allies. By this stage Tito had already moved to establish a provisional government, the **Anti-Fascist Assembly for the National Liberation of Yugoslavia** (AVNOJ), which laid down the principles for the eventual Yugoslav state. For the most part, the terms of the programme – one of which made provision for a republic's right to self-determination (this was later dropped) – were welcomed by the Slovenes, as confirmed by their participation at the second AVNOJ meeting in Jajce, Bosnia, in 1943.

Communist resistance was complicated by conflicting political ideologies within Slovenia, which was manifested by the emergence of several armed organizations. The most prominent of these was the **Home Guard** (Domobranci), a major anti-Communist organization formed in Ljubljana in September 1943 with the approval and assistance of the Germans. Its resistance, however, didn't last long. Faced by overwhelming Partisan force, the Guard was forced to retreat into Austrian Carinthia, where it was met by the British and disarmed as German collaborators. Following their repatriation to Slovenia and the waiting Partisans, thousands of guardists and anti-Communist civilians (estimates suggest up to ten thousand in total) were executed and thrown into pits close to the Liberation Fronts' wartime headquarters in the forests of Kočevski Rog in southern Slovenia. The grisly secrets were only revealed to the wider Slovene public some thirty years later, when politician and writer Edvard Kocbek spilled the beans in an interview with a Trieste newspaper.

Having finally driven the occupying forces from Slovene territory in May 1945, the Partisans liberated Trieste that same month, but just two months later the Western Allies issued an ultimatum requiring Yugoslav forces to leave. At the 1946 Paris Peace Conference the region was partitioned into two zones: Zone A (Trieste and hinterland), controlled by the Allies, and Zone B (Slovene coast and Istria), controlled by Yugoslavia. The **1954 London Agreement** restored Zone A to Italy, thus bringing an end to a bitter and long-standing dispute, though many Italians returned to Italy, as others had done at the end of the war.

The second Yugoslavia: Tito and socialism

Following the émigré government's recognition of Tito as *de facto* leader, **elections** were held towards the end of 1945, though these were something of a foregone conclusion, given that the only party standing was the **People's Front**, an organization dominated by the Communist Party. Following these elections, the monarchy was abolished and in November the **Federal People's Republic of Yugoslavia** was proclaimed, comprising six federal republics – Serbia, Croatia, Bosnia, Macedonia, Montenegro and Slovenia.

Power was now incontrovertibly held in the hands of the Communists, who sought to emulate the Soviet model of control, a system shaped by central planning, nationalization of property and ideological conformity – this also included a substantial amount of **forced industrialization** throughout the entire country, although the speed with which this was done created numerous problems, not least the decline in agricultural practices, as individual and large institutional landowners were expropriated without compensation. A critical rift over political and ideological differences between the Soviet Union and Yugoslavia in 1948 resulted in the latter's **expulsion from the Cominform**, the Soviet-controlled organization of European Communist countries. The split effected an almost immediate (albeit cosmetic) change in name of both the

Communist Party of Yugoslavia, renamed the **League of Communists of Yugoslavia** (LCY), and the Communist Party of Slovenia, renamed the **League of Communists of Slovenia** (LCS).

More importantly it presented Tito with an opportunity to fashion his own, alternative brand of Communism, one that featured a mix of socialist and capitalist ideals. The basic institution at the heart of "Titoism", as it was known, was a system of **workers' self-management** with the slogan "Factories to the workers!" Such an approach, however, invited dissent in the form of strikes and political criticism, particularly in Slovenia. In the international arena, Tito manoeuvred carefully, his policy of **non-alignment** enabling Yugoslavia to secure prestigious international endorsement. Meanwhile, those party members suspected of collaborating with Stalin (known as "Conformists") were immediately purged and packed off to concentration camps, such as the notorious Goli Otok (Bare Island) camp in the Adriatic. With regard to this there were few dissidents on the Slovene side, the Slovene Communists well aware that supporting a federal Yugoslav republic was their only option, especially given that such a Yugoslavia would support Slovenia's claims to ethnic territory in Italy and Austria.

The 1960s and 1970s

Yugoslavia in the **1960s** was characterized by strong economic growth and improved living conditions, particularly for Slovenes, many of whom could travel freely abroad, a liberty denied to citizens of most other countries in the Eastern bloc, including many within the Yugoslav federation itself. That said, Slovenes were becoming increasingly resentful at the federal bureau's centrally planned means of redistribution, whereby money was siphoned off to support the less wealthy republics in the federation, thereby stifling their own economic development. The so-called **Road Affair** of 1969 was indicative of such problems. Having solicited funds from the World Bank for the development of its road network – in order to better facilitate trade and increase tourism opportunities – the federal authorities redistributed the money to road projects in other republics instead, triggering widespread protests throughout Slovenia. The federal bureau merely dismissed the protest as nothing more than the work of a bunch of renegade Slovene nationalists. In any case, the Road Affair signalled the end of the **liberalization movement** of the 1960s, whose members had pushed for major market economic reforms throughout Yugoslavia. Fearful of losing control, the conservative Communists purged the party of its stronger liberal elements, before turning their attention to those in other institutions – universities, intellectual journals and the media.

Numerous **constitutional amendments and changes** repeatedly brought to the surface old arguments about decentralization and the need for greater autonomy, with Slovenia invariably at the forefront of these disputes. The **1974 constitution** went a stage further than previous ones, giving more autonomy to Vojvodina and Kosovo, and making provision for each republic to assume greater responsibility for its own internal affairs. However, the issue of centralism versus federalism, a recurring theme since the formation of the Kingdom of Serbs, Croats and Slovenes back in 1918, remained at the forefront of Slovene and Yugoslav political life up to and following **Tito's death** in 1980.

The 1980s

With the death of its founding father, the federal construct began to fall apart in dramatic fashion: Yugoslavia had racked up enormous foreign debt and unemployment, inflation had reached unacceptably high levels and **inter-republic relations** were at an all-time low. Of particular concern were the worsening relations between the Serbs and the Albanian majority in the auton-omous province of Kosovo in southern Serbia, where riots in 1981 were followed by further draconian anti-Albanian measures, culminating in the annulment of the province's autonomy in 1989. On the domestic front, in 1986, Milan Kučan was elected president of the League of Communists of Slovenia, who were by now struggling to reconcile the political and ideological doctrines of the Yugoslav League of Communists with the increasingly widespread pluralistic inclinations pervading Slovenian society around this time.

In particular it was the emergence of **avant-garde and alternative movements** (also known as new social movements) – foremost among these were the arts collective **Neue Slowenische Kunst** (New Slovene Art), one of whose members was the legendary punk rock group Laibach (see p.337) – that paved the way for the democratization of Slovene society. No less influential were the countercultural **magazines** *Nova Revija* (*New Review*) and *Mladina* (*Youth*), both of which provided broad-based platforms for cultural and intellectual expression and exchange, as well as political dialogue and debate. In *Nova Revija's* infamous issue no. 57 (February 1987), the magazine published "Contributions to a Slovene National Programme", a collection of papers that outlined provisions for Slovenian self-determination (this essentially echoed and amplified the content of *Revija 57*, a document which had appeared exactly thirty years earlier). Despite intense pressure from the federal government, the Slovene authorities refused to acquiesce to Belgrade's demands for those responsible to be prosecuted. *Mladina*, meanwhile, continued to provoke with its fearless and often humorous attacks on key groups and individuals within the Yugoslav federation, and articles on social taboos such as homosexuality and World War II massacres. In 1988, three of the magazine's members, along with an officer, were hauled up before a military court on trumped-up charges of betraying state secrets (widely believed to be a plan for military intervention in Slovenia), an affair known as the **Ljubljana Four Trial**. Conducted entirely in secret and in Serbo-Croatian, the trial was considered unconstitutional by most Slovenes, and served only to radicalize political opinion towards Belgrade. The trial, and the mass rallies that it inspired, represented the last hurrah for these movements, which became increas-ingly marginalized thereafter. However, despite fewer and less obvious targets these days, *Mladina* remains an influential and topical political journal.

The fall of the Berlin Wall in November 1989 set in motion a chain of events which convulsed Eastern Europe, culminating in the bloody overthrow of Ceaușescu in Romania. These events, though, had little direct effect on Yugoslavia, which was readying itself for its own, spectacular implosion.

The road to independence

At the fourteenth and final Congress of the Yugoslav League of Communists in January 1990, Slovenian calls for absolute independence for the respective Communist parties were given short shrift by the Serbs. In response, the

Slovene delegation walked out of the assembly, an incident that effectively spelt the end of the Yugoslav Communist Party. Just three months later, in April 1990, the country's first ever multiparty elections were won by the coalition Demos Party (Democratic Opposition of Slovenia), while **Milan Kučan**, the reformed Communist leader of the Party of Democratic Renewal (SDP) – formerly the League of Communists of Slovenia – was sworn in as president. Immediately after the elections, a number of constitutional amendments were implemented, thus paving the way for eventual separation from the Yugoslav federation.

The one remaining obstacle was Serbia which, with Slobodan Milošević in charge and championing a greater Serbia, now had control of four of the eight votes on the federal presidency (those of Vojvodina, Kosovo and Montenegro, in addition to its own), prompting Slovenes, somewhat mischievously, to coin the phrase "Serboslavia". Undaunted, Slovenia pressed on, and in December that year a **plebiscite for independence** was held, the result of which was an overwhelming 88 percent vote (the turn-out was 93 percent) for a split with the federation. Six months later, on June 25, 1991, the Slovene Parliament passed a constitutional law declaring independence, thus triggering the **Ten-Day War** (see box below). Slovene independence was formally recognized by the European Union on January 15, 1992, and the country was officially admitted into the United Nations on May 22.

The Ten-Day War

Even as Slovenes were celebrating the declaration of independence in Ljubljana on the night of June 26, 1991, the Serb-dominated **Yugoslav army** (JNA) had begun manoeuvring tank units towards Ljubljana's Brnik airport, and some thirty border posts that Slovenia had taken over following the declaration. The well-drilled Slovenian defence comprised the Territorial Defence (which itself was removed from the JNA's jurisdiction in a constitutional amendment the previous year) and the police, and was orchestrated by Minister of Defence Janez Janša – ironically one of those implicated in the Ljubljana Four Trial three years earlier.

As Slovene soldiers and officers began **deserting** the Yugoslav army in droves, the first strikes took place, though the capture of Brnik and threatened assault on the capital itself never materialized. In the end, there were few major clashes, with the majority of engagements being small-scale skirmishes at key traffic points and border positions. Nevertheless, and much to the surprise of the Yugoslav army – as well as neutral observers and many Slovenes themselves – the Slovene forces proved themselves to be more than competent adversaries, forcing around 2500 JNA troops to desert or **surrender**, while many more were captured. Following a flurry of diplomatic activity and several attempts to mediate by European Union representatives, the ten-day conflict was brought to an end on July 7, following the brokering of the Brioni Agreement, which provided for an **immediate ceasefire** and **withdrawal** of the Yugoslav army. Moreover, it stipulated that Slovenia put its declaration of independence on hold for a further three months. In human terms, the price was relatively low: officially, 21 Slovenes (military and civilian) were killed and a further 100 wounded, while 39 Yugoslav troops were killed and around 160 wounded.

The reason for Belgrade's confused and rather diffident policy in Slovenia was unclear, though most analysts concurred that it was based on an (ill-founded) assumption that a short, sharp show of force would be enough to cow the Slovenes into submission – failing that, they could resort to a policy of escalation. Their humiliating climbdown, meanwhile, was attributed to the fact that Serbia had no strong territorial or ethnic claims to Slovenia.

The 1990s

While the war continued to savage effect for another four years in Croatia and Bosnia, Slovenia was facing up to the **difficult transition** from communist to market economy. Despite possessing an already relatively sound economy, Slovenia still faced considerable problems, namely, rising unemployment, low salaries and high inflation, while additional strains were being placed on the economy as a result of the influx of refugees fleeing the chaos in Croatia and Bosnia. The task of economic restructuring was further complicated by the necessary imposition of **trade barriers** with the other republics, hitherto its most important markets. Moreover, potential foreign investors were frightened off by the perceived political risks associated with the ongoing **hostilities in the region**. It was for this reason that tourist numbers remained well below the levels the country experienced prior to the war, when it was one of the most popular destinations in Yugoslavia. However, the introduction of a **new currency** (the *tolar*), coupled with reforms in the banking and public service sectors, and the creation of new institutions, gradually smoothed the path to economic stability.

Slovenia's first **multiparty elections** as an independent nation took place in December 1992, by which stage internal discord within the Demos coalition had seen that party disband. Of the eight parties to win seats in the ninety-member parliament, it was the reform-oriented centre-left Liberal Democratic Party, led by the introverted yet competent **Janez Drnovšek** (he was also president of the Yugoslav Federation from May 1989 to May 1990), who secured the greatest number of votes (22 percent), followed by the centre-right Slovene Christian Democrats. Drnovšek himself was elected head of the coalition government. That same month saw the popular and avuncular Kučan returned as president, thus cementing his considerable standing in Slovene politics. Four years down the line, the 1996 elections yielded similar results, with the Liberal Democrats once again topping the polls, leaving Drnovšek to form a coalition government with seven other parties, despite the clear ideological differences between them. However, as in 1992, the overriding agenda was economic and political modernization. In November the following year, the unassailable Kučan was re-elected president for a second and final term.

One of the key issues dominating the political agenda was Slovenia's prospective membership of **NATO**, to which the country had aspired since 1994. With high hopes going into the Madrid summit in June 1997, Slovenia was somewhat dismayed to find itself omitted from the invitation list. This sense of grievance was compounded when Hungary, Poland and the Czech Republic formally joined NATO in March 1999, just as the alliance was preparing to launch strikes on Serbia following the collapse of diplomatic talks aimed at ending the escalating violence in Kosovo. While relations with Serbia had more or less normalized by this stage, most Slovenes shed few tears over the country's plight, regarding the bombing campaign as just desserts for the events of 1991. Yet the bombing cast yet another long shadow over the region, precipitating, among other things, another alarming drop in visitor numbers to the country.

Europe and the New Millennium

Since the early 1990s, Slovenia was always regarded as one of the outstanding candidates for EU accession among the central and east European countries, which was in part a reflection of the country's relatively strong economic and political standing. Accession talks were arguably of greater importance than NATO membership, given the wider economic opportunities that potential membership afforded. Obstacles remained, however, not least a simmering feud between Slovenia and **Italy** over disputed property rights, and in particular the issue of **restitution of property** to Italian owners who had emigrated from Yugoslavia after World War II, an issue Slovenes claimed had been resolved in 1983 following the Treaty of Rome.

Relations with **Croatia** were no less troubled, with disputes over the question of outstanding debt of the Zagreb branch of Slovenia's now defunct Ljubljanska Bank, as well as questions over the Krško nuclear reactor in southern Slovenia, which was built to provide energy for both republics. By far the thorniest issue concerned the long-standing dispute over **sea borders** in the Bay of Piran. The initial problem arose because no sea border ever existed during the time of Yugoslavia, and neither was one defined once the two countries had seceded from the federation. Following a series of incidents in the disputed waters, the situation reached crisis point in the summer of 2003, when Croatia unilaterally announced its intention to declare an Exclusive Economic Zone (EEZ), a move vehemently opposed by Slovenia, which argued that it would be impossible to create such a zone if the boundaries of the territorial waters hadn't been defined. Moreover, any such zone would effectively invalidate Slovenia's right to access international waters. Following much diplomatic activity and attempts at bilateral border agreements, the interminable dispute over the Bay of Piran all but came to a close in 2009, when an internationally brokered solution was endorsed by both sides, with Slovenia simultaneously stating that it would no longer block Croatia's negotiations to join the European Union.

During **parliamentary elections** in October 2000, the ruling Liberal Democrats, with Drnovšek still firmly in command, once again eased to victory, their third in succession. Two years later, in December 2002, the **presidential elections** saw an end to the decade-long Kučan-Drnovšek union, for Kučan was obliged to stand down having served the maximum two terms allowed in the constitution. His retirement paved the way for Drnovšek as his successor and opened the door for a new prime minister, a post duly taken up by finance minister and vice-president of the senior coalition party (Liberal Democrats), Anton Rop. Rop was immediately assigned the task of forming a new government from a broad-based coalition of four parties.

On the international front, final accession negotiations to both NATO and the EU were wrapped up at the tail end of 2002, with referendums held the following March. As predicted, support for the former was far from overwhelming, though a 66 percent "yes" vote was much higher than anticipated; support for the EU, meanwhile, was more or less unequivocal, with the "yes" camp accounting for almost 90 percent of the vote. **NATO membership** was finally confirmed in March 2004, and was followed just over a month later, on May 1, by the country's **admission into the European Union** alongside nine other central-eastern European countries. Although EU membership had little direct impact on the general population, Slovenia did claim a minor coup when it became the first of the ten new member states to **introduce the euro currency**, in January 2007.

Other key political subjects came to the fore in 2004, the most controversial of which was the issue of the so-called '**erased**', some eighteen thousand citizens from other countries of the former Yugoslavia who were removed from the population registry after the country obtained independence in 1992. Having declined the offer of citizenship at the time, most of the 'erased' immediately lost their jobs and were stripped of any health and pension rights. In a highly charged referendum in April 2004, Slovenes decided overwhelming to deny full citizenship rights to the 'erased', a decision that prompted many observers to suggest that nationalism was still alive and kicking in the region.

Parliamentary elections in October later that year – the fourth since independence, which also saw the lowest-ever turnout – resulted in a surprisingly comfortable victory for the opposition Slovenian Democratic Party (SDS) over the Liberal Democrats, the first time that the latter had been ousted since independence. Anton Rop was replaced as prime minister by **Janez Janša**, best known as one of the defendants in the infamous Ljubljana Four Trial in 1988 (see p.328), which resulted in his imprisonment for six months. Following his release, Janša helped found the Slovenian Democratic Union (SDZ), after which he became defence minister, a position he held during the ten-day war of independence.

Owing to increasing ill-health, Drnovšek did not run for the 2007 presidential elections, and was succeeded by the leftist former diplomat, **Danilo Tuerk**. Having since turned his attention to environmental issues, Drnovšek – one of the key figures in Slovenia's drive for both independence and EU membership – died in February 2008. Tuerk, meanwhile, was sworn in just in time for Slovenia's assumption of the EU presidency in January 2008, the first former Communist state to have had this honour bestowed. Parliamentary elections later that year saw Janša and his Slovenian Democratic Party narrowly defeated by the Social Democrats, led by the hitherto little known **Borut Pahor**, who headed up a centre-left coalition comprising three other parties.

Books, film and music

T here's a real dearth of books about Slovenia in the English language, in every genre. What recent titles there are – particularly travelogues and historical or political publications – tend to revolve almost exclusively around the other countries of the former Yugoslavia. Slovenia's literary heritage, however, is strong, and while there's little available in translation, there are several impressive anthologies to choose from. Likewise, in film and music, Slovenia has yielded some terrific, and influential, artists and producers in recent years, though few are known beyond the country's borders.

Books

The number of publications dedicated to the break-up of Yugoslavia is considerable, yet in most cases there is scant coverage of Slovenia's involvement in the conflict. While you'll find some reference to Slovenia in the titles below, the following are excellent reads in their own right, and well worth dipping into if you're travelling more widely around the region: Misha Glenny *The Fall of Yugoslavia*; John Allcock *Explaining Yugoslavia*; John Lampe *Yugoslavia as History – Twice There Was a Country*; Branka Magas & Ivo Žanič *The War in Croatia and Bosnia-Herzegovina 1991–1995*; Dejan Djokič *Elusive Compromise: A History of Interwar Yugoslavia*.

Jill Benderley and Evan Craft *Independent Slovenia: Origins, Movements, Prospects* (Macmillan). Enjoyable and wide-ranging collection of essays pertaining to the country's historical development up to and including independence. The most interesting accounts are those which chart the development of the so-called new social movements of the 1980s (trade unions, women's organizations and the local punk scene), all of which helped fashion a strong and independent civil society in the run-up to independence.

Janez Bogotaj *Handicrafts of Slovenia: Encounters with Contemporary Slovene Craftsmen* (Rokus). Beautifully illustrated work covering Slovenia's rich tradition of crafts, including ceramists, potters, lace-makers, weavers and glass painters.

Justi Carey and Roy Clark *The Julian Alps of Slovenia* (Cicerone Press). Useful pocket-sized book detailing over fifty trails throughout the Julian Alps, with treks starting from Bled, Bohinj, Bovec, Kobarid and Kranjska Gora. Although essentially a guide to the French/Italian/Swiss Alps, Kev Reynolds' *Walking in the Alps* (Cicerone Press) also features a short chapter on hiking in the Julian Alps.

John Corsellis and Marcus Ferrar *Slovenia 1945: Memories of Death and Survival after World War II* (IB Tauris). Sympathetic and superbly accomplished account documenting the fate of the large Catholic, non-Communist Slovene migrant community (including members of the anti-Communist Home Guard) both during and after World War II.

Aleš Debeljak *Twilight of the Idols: Recollections of a Lost Yugoslavia* (White Pine Press). Better known for fiction and poetry (see p.335), the Slovene novelist turns his attention here to politics in this critical reflection on the disintegration of Yugoslavia, though his portrayal of the Serbs as outright aggressors is overly subjective.

James Gow and Cathie Carmichael *Slovenia and the Slovenes: A Small State and the New Europe* (Hurst). This is the most thoroughgoing assessment of twentieth-century Slovenian history currently available. The introductory chapter sets the tone with an illuminating overview of the country, and is followed by very readable accounts of Slovenia's cultural, economic and political maturation; the book concludes with a revealing insight into the events surrounding the country's drive for independence and the Ten-Day War.

Andrej Hrausky and Janez Koželj *Architectural Guide to Ljubljana* (Rokus). Insightful guide to one hundred of the capital's buildings, from its castles and churches to its many Baroque and Secessionist splendours, as well as most of the projects conceived by Slovenia's greatest urban planner, Jože Plečnik. For more on Plečnik, try the more detailed *Plečnik's Ljubljana* and *National and University Library Ljubljana*.

Oto Luthar (Ed) *The Land Between: A History of Slovenia* (Peter Lang). Written by a team of Slovene scholars, this is a solid, well-researched history of the country, with particularly enlightening chapters on the early Slav settlements through to the Middle Ages. A welcome addition to the historiography of the country.

Tine Mihelič *Mountaineering in Slovenia* (Cordee). Excellent and easy-to-follow guide to tackling Slovenia's most important summits, in the Julian, Kamnik and Savinja Alps, and the Karavanke mountains. Complete with diagrams and lots of shiny pictures.

Alexei Monroe *Interrogation Machine: Laibach and NSK* (MIT Press). Thoroughgoing and fascinating insight into the workings of the provocative avant-garde Slovene collective NSK, the most famous and controversial component of which was the rock band Laibach (see p.337).

Julij Nemanič and Janez Bogataj *Wines of Slovenia* (Rokus). This comprehensive handbook, featuring some beautifully illustrated pictures, is the definitive guide to the country's wines (with ratings for each) and wine growing districts; a must for anyone serious about Slovenian wine.

Nigel Thomas *The Yugoslav Wars: Slovenia and Croatia 1991–95* (Osprey). Authoritative and well-illustrated guide – including some rare photos – documenting the roles played by the various combatant armies on Slovenian and Croatian territory during the wars of the early 1990s.

Slavoj Žižek and Glyn Daly *Conversations with Žižek* (Polity Press). In this entertaining series of conversations, the renowned Slovene theorist elaborates on various aspects of popular culture and politics, including topics such as Marxism, Nazism and the films of Stanley Kubrick; a far more accessible introduction to the mindset of Žižek than his other work.

Literature

Although written records in Slovenian appeared as early as the tenth century, **Slovenian literature** began to systematically develop during the **sixteenth-century Reformation**. This development was thanks to leading reformers

Primož Trubar (writer of the first Slovene book, the primer *Abecedarium*, in 1550), Jurij Dalmatin (the first Slovene translation of the Bible, in 1584), and linguist Adam Bohorič, whose *Arcticae Horulae* (*Winter Hours*) was the first Slovene grammar book, written in Latin and published the same year as Dalmatin's Bible. Around a century later Janez Vajkard Valvasor (see box, p.237) wrote and published (in German) the *Glory of the Duchy of Carniola*, a seminal work that synthesized the country's history, sights and peoples in one encyclopedic, four-volume work; to this day it remains the single most important document written about the Slovene lands.

It was during the period of **romanticism** in the early nineteenth century that Slovene literature reached its first peak, thanks to the poet France Prešeren (see box, p.121), the most iconic literary figure in Slovenia's history. Very little of Prešeren's work has been translated into English, but the audio CD, *Sonnets of Unhappiness*, is a beautifully read collection (by Vanessa Redgrave, Katrin Cartlidge and Simon Callow) of the poet's key works. The next writers to make their mark were the **realists**, led by the playwright Josip Jurčič, whose enduringly popular *Deseti Brat* (*The Tenth Brother*) was the first full-length Slovene novel to be published (1866) – an abridged version is available in English. Literary trends at the start of the twentieth century were shaped by the so-called **Moderna movement**, whose two main representatives were Oton Župančič and Ivan Cankar, the second of whom is regarded as Slovenia's finest prose writer; one of the few novels available in English translation, *Martin Kačur: The Biography of an Idealist* is Cankar's expressive tale of a young schoolteacher and his misguided attempts to enlighten his fellow countrymen as he travels around provincial Slovenia. A prolific and highly politicized essayist and polemicist, Cankar was also one of the first to champion a southern Slav union.

The coexistent movements of expressionism and social realism that had dominated both the artistic and literary landscape prior to, and just after, World War II eventually gave way to western literary trends, notably **symbolism and existentialism**. Foremost among these writers was the dissident politician and ex-Partisan Edvard Kocbek, whose opposition to Communist ideology and socialist repression manifested itself in a short-story collection, *Strah in Pogum* (*Fear and Courage*), and the diaries *Tovarišija* (*Comrades*) and *Listina* (*The Document*) – it also landed him a spell in prison. Similar critiques of the resistance movement were the preserve of other commentators at that time, too, including Dane Zajc and Tomaž Šalamun, the doyens of Slovene postwar poets.

Prominent among the **new generation** of writers are essayist and poet Aleš Debeljak – *The City and the Child* is one of his best volumes of poetry; post-modern fiction writer Andrej Blatnik, whose collection of short stories, *Skinswaps*, is a good introduction to his work; and poet and gay rights activist Brane Mozetič. Given that there's only a limited amount of Slovenian **literature in translation**, you're best off starting with one of the several excellent anthologies available: *A Bilingual Anthology of Slovene Literature* includes poems and prose by a panoply of Slovenia's literary greats, from Trubar and Prešeren to Kocbek and Šalamun, while *The Imagination of Terra Incognita: Slovenian Writing 1945–1995* is the best available anthology of essays, poems and fiction by authors from the second half of the last century. A useful reference book is *Key Slovenia: Contemporary Slovenian Literature in Translation*.

Film

Cinematography in Slovenia made its mark as early as 1905, with the short documentaries *The Fair at Ljutomer* and *People Leaving the Church*, shot by the pioneer of Slovene film, Karol Grossman. The development of the industry continued apace after World War II, a golden period for Slovene film thanks to the state-financed Triglav Film house, which produced several classics, such as *Kekec*, Jože Gale's enduringly popular 1952 film about a clever shepherd boy, and France Stiglič's 1956 film, *Dolina Miru* (*Valley of Peace*). Despite the fact that Slovenia has one of the lowest outputs among central-eastern European countries, a fine crop of movies have been released in recent years; by far the most successful and celebrated of these – it was actually a joint Belgian–French–Italian–Slovenian project, and shot in the village of Bač near Postojna – was the Oscar-winning (Best Foreign Film 2001) *Nikogaršnje Ozemlje* (*No Man's Land*) by Bosnian director Danis Tanovič. Featuring a Bosnian and a Serb as the two protagonists trapped together in a trench somewhere between enemy lines, it's an acute, compassionate, and darkly comic dissection of a pitiless conflict, and without doubt one of the most affecting movies ever made about the Yugoslav wars. Another **landmark Slovenian film**, and winner of the prestigious Golden Lion award at the 2001 Venice Film festival, *Kruh in Mleko* (*Bread and Milk*) is the outstanding debut film by Jan Cvetkovič, a brooding social commentary on the effects of alcoholism and alienation in small-town Slovenia.

Other films to look out for include Damjan Kožole's *Rezervni Deli* (*Spare Parts*), a gritty, sobering drama about human trafficking across Slovenia; the humorous *Kajmak in Marmelada* (*Cheese and Jam*), which explores race, immigration and happiness in contemporary Slovenia – directed by and starring the respected Bosnian actor Branko Djurič (also the lead actor in *No Man's Land*); *Varuh Meje* (*Guardians of the Frontier*), a creepy, atmospheric tale of sexual discovery down on the Kolpa river; the wonderfully titled *Petelinji Zajtrk* (*Rooster's Breakfast*), a sympathetic love story set in a village in Prekmurje; and the dense, moody thriller, *9:06*.

Music

As in other spheres of the arts and culture, Slovenia's musical heritage is surprisingly strong, manifest in ancient **folk** traditions and a **punk/rock** scene that, during the 1980s, spawned some of the most exciting and controversial music in the former Yugoslavia. Although Slovenia has few **jazz** artists of its own, the genre has a small, yet devout following, as evidenced by the increasing number of bars with live music and a world-class summer jazz festival in Ljubljana. In general there's no shortage of events, chief among which is the **world music** festival, Druga Godba, while there are some superb **classical** music gatherings around the country each summer, notably festivals in Brežice, Piran and Radovljica.

Folk music

The most traditional forms of **Slovenian folk music** are based on age-old folk literature and poems and utilizes instruments such as the *okarina* (clay flute), *trstenka* (panpipe), *drumlja* (Jew's Harp) and *gudalo*, a small clay pot over the top of which a pig's bladder is stretched – the bass sound emitted is made by rubbing the straw rod which extends up through the membrane. Although its role in everyday life has largely diminished you are likely to come across traditional music during local festivals.

Some of the best Slovene folk music in recent years has come out of the small village of Beltinci in Prekmurje, in particular from the remarkable **Beltinška Banda Kociper**, a kind of Mitteleuropean Buena Vista Social Club, whose members, playing the fiddle (a stock Prekmurje instrument), violin, clarinet, cimbalom, double bass and accordion, have been delighting audiences for more than half a century. The baton has now been passed down to a new generation of musicians from the same village, namely the four-strong **Marko Banda**, and the ten-strong, teenage **Mlada Beltinska Banda**. Another folk band to listen out for are the stunning all-female vocal group **Katice**, who specialize in interpreting classic harmonies from the Rezija mountain valley region on the Italian side of the Julian Alps.

No self-respecting gathering is complete without some form of **dancing** which, like songs, varies greatly from region to region. The oldest dances developed in Bela Krajina during the sixteenth century and were heavily influenced by the Uskoks, bands of renegades from Serbia and Croatia who fled the Turks and settled in the region. The most popular dance is the *kolo*, an energetic, circular group dance performed to both musical and vocal accompaniment. The dances of Prekmurje are less exuberant affairs – typical is the *tkalecka* (weaver's dance), a kind of skipping dance whereby handkerchiefs are waved under the knees (reminiscent of an English Morris dance) – while those of Primorska are of an altogether more refined bent, having been established in bourgeois circles.

Although not strictly folk, Slovenia's best-known band internationally is **Terra Folk**, a group of four academically and classically trained musicians, whose free-ranging repertoire of Balkan, Gypsy, Folk, Klezmer, Irish and classical pretty much defies any standard form of categorization. Featuring an eclectic set of violin, flute, guitar, drums, accordion and double bass, Terra Folk's reputation has largely been built on their entertaining live shows, which combine ebullient musicianship with a roguish sense of humour. Another fine live prospect is the marvellous six-piece ensemble **Katalena**, another slightly unorthodox outfit who marry traditional folk forms with souped-up jazz and blues to beautiful effect.

Rock and pop

Although a number of creative bands emerged throughout Yugoslavia in the 1970s, Ljubljana was the first of all the Yugoslav cities to develop an authentic, home-grown musical scene of its own. In particular, it was the emergence of a local punk subculture in the late 1970s, alongside other so-called new social movements, that set the tone for the next few years. The most prominent of the first generation of punk bands were **Pankrti** (The Bastards). They, like the majority of punk groups and their followers at that time, were deemed a threat to civil society by the authorities, who attempted to associate the movement with Nazism; concerts were prohibited and persecution by the police was commonplace. Dismantled by the state in the early 1980s, the punk scene was eventually supplanted by other social movements, most notably an avant-garde collective called **Neue Slowenische Kunst** (New Slovene Art, or NSK), whose core members included the rock group Laibach.

Conceived in the industrial mining town of Trbovlje in 1980, shortly after Tito's death, **Laibach** produced some of the most uncompromising music and art ever to come out of the former Yugoslavia. Following an interview on national television in June 1983 – six months after the band's original singer, Tomaž Hostnik, committed suicide – Laibach were summarily banned from appearing in public. The authorities argued that the band's use of the German language (Laibach is the German name for Ljubljana, used during both Habsburg rule and the Nazi occupation) and their apparent appropriation of Nazi images was just a cover for the resurgence of fascism. Laibach, meanwhile, maintained that rather than espousing totalitarianism, they were in fact exposing its ugliest facets. Ostracized, the group embarked on the "Occupied Europe Tour" later that year, a tour that took them to countries on both sides of the Iron Curtain and exposed them for the first time to audiences outside their own country. In 1987, Laibach marked the lifting of the ban with a series of homecoming gigs (the "Bloody Ground-Fertile Soil" tour) in several Yugoslav cities, including Zagreb and Belgrade. Returning to Belgrade two years later, the group delivered a typically incendiary speech, warning against the inflammatory rhetoric of Slobodan Milošević, alongside a screening of a 1941 German propaganda film on the bombing of the Serbian capital.

Since their eponymously titled debut in 1985, Laibach have released more than a dozen albums. Their earlier recordings were wilfully experimental, avant-garde exercises, which drew heavily on the electronic minimalism of Kraftwerk and DAF – as a result they do not make for easy listening. Towards the end of the 1980s the group moved towards a more overt and accessible rock sound, thanks in part to their predilection for doing cover albums, namely the Beatles' *Let it Be*, and the Stones' *Sympathy for the Devil*, neither of which will sound quite the same again once you've heard Laibach's version. The group returned to familiar ground with the 1994 release, *NATO*, which pointedly anticipated the expansion of western influence in the region, and included covers of Status Quo's *You're in the Army Now* and Pink Floyd's *Dogs of War*, while 1996's metal-driven *Jesus Christ Superstars* marked another shift in musical direction. After a seven-year hiatus, Laibach returned with *WAT* (We Are Time), as direct and aggressive a record as any previously released and one that marked a return to the heavy techno/industrial rhythms of earlier albums. Their two most recent records, *Volk* and *LaiBachKunstDerFuge*, are typically audacious concept albums, the former a collection of surprisingly melodic interpretations of national anthems, the latter an uncompromising reworking of Bach's *The Art of Fugue*.

Spearheading Slovenian **pop music** these days is the youthful, six-piece band, **Siddharta**, whose melodic brand of stadium rock has made them the most successful and popular home-grown outfit since Laibach. Other current pop acts range from mainstream groups (**The Elevators** and **Big Foot Mama**), to dance and techno-inspired performers like the multi-rooted **DJ Umek**, a regular on the European club circuit. Two stalwarts of the Slovenian music scene are the singer-songwriter **Vlado Kreslin**, who has kept legions of fans in thrall for nearly two decades with his folksy brand of guitar-based rock, and the perennially popular poet and songwriter **Zoran Predin**, who first came to prominence some twenty years ago as the founder of the rock group Lačni Franz (Hungry Franz). In addition to writing film and theatre scores, Predin now spends most of his time collaborating with other artists, such as **Šukar**, Slovenia's outstanding Romany group, with whom he has recorded an album of gypsy music.

Discography

The following list is merely a pointer to some of the recordings available, a few, but not many of them, internationally; rooting around stores and record shops in Slovenia will yield the many more CDs that don't have international distribution.

Folk music

Katalena *(Z)godbe* (RTV Slovenija). Luscious sounding album of traditional songs from Slovenia's most important folk regions, Prekmurje, Istria and Bela Krajina. While remaining faithful to their folk roots, the two subsequent releases, *Babje Leto* and *Kmečka ohcet* (Dallas), feature a denser, rockier sound, while *Cvik Cvak!* (Dallas) is exclusively dedicated to the musical heritage of the Rezija Valley in Italy.

Mlada Beltinska Banda *Prekmurje Musical Heritage* (KUD Beltinci). Traditional folk music from the Prekmurje region, as performed by the young Beltinci Band.

Modern Folk Music in Slovenia Volumes I & II (Folk Slovenia Cultural Society). This enjoyable two-disc set is the best introduction to Slovenia's contemporary folk artists, including the female vocal group Katice, Styrian folk trio Kurja Koža, and the Marko Banda from Prekmurje.

Slovenian Folk Songs (RTV Slovenija). Four-disc set of narrative folk music recorded on-site by the Institute of Ethnomusicology in Ljubljana. Drawing on themes of heroes, legends and love, this voluminous collection brings together poems, songs and instruments from the country's multifarious regions. The excellent sleeve notes help make some sense of it all.

Terra Folk Packed with their trademark effervescent tunes, the band's first two releases, *StereoFolk Live* and *Jumper of Love*, are both live outings, recorded in clubs across Slovenia. The third (studio) album, *N'taka*, is in a similar vein and features the gorgeous female voices of Katice. Following a return to the live arena with *Live at Queen's Hall*, the diverse and entertaining *Full Circle* features a rather novel reworking of *You Are My Sunshine* (All Music Net).

Rock/pop music

Laibach The band's earliest works are cassette-only affairs, and very difficult to get hold of. Selected albums available on CD include: *Laibach* (Ropot, 1985); the double box-set *Rekapitulacija 1980–1984* (Mute, 2002); *Nova Akropola* (Cherry Red, 1987); *Opus Dei* (Mute, 1987); *Krst Pod Triglavom* (the soundtrack to NSK's theatre performance that same year; Sub Rosa, 1987); *Let it Be* (Mute, 1988); *Sympathy for the Devil* (Mute, 1990); *Nato* (Mute, 1994); *Jesus Christ*

Superstars (Mute, 1996); *The John Peel Sessions* (recordings from two sessions, in 1986 and 1987, with the legendary DJ; Strange Fruit, 2002); *WAT* (Mute, 2003); *Volk* (Mute, 2006); *LaiBachKunstDerFuge* (Mute, 2008). For an overview, there's the best of album, *Anthems* (Mute, 2004), which also contains a superb forty-page booklet.

Siddharta *ID*, *Nord* and *Rh-* (Menart). Released between 1999 and 2003, these are the band's three albums to date. A limited edition English version of

the third, and best, album, *Rh-*, is also available.

Romany music

Šukar *Prvo Ti* (*First Snow*; Nika) and *En Concert 1990–2002* (Etno Karavana). These two offerings (the second a live album) by this five-piece tamburica ensemble from Ljubljana, feature sumptuous

reworkings of traditional gypsy dance songs and ballads. *Mentol Bombon* is an album of songs recorded with singer songwriter, Zoran Predin.

Language

Language

Slovenian

Although the earliest written records in Slovene date from around 1000 AD, it has existed as a literary language since the middle of the sixteenth century, when the first printed books – including a translation of the Bible – came into being. Today it's spoken by nearly two million people within Slovenia, and around half a million more outside the country's borders. Slovenian is a Slavic language, a branch of the Indo-European linguistic family, and is most closely related to Croatian and Serbian, with which it shares quite a few identical words and phrases.

While attempting the odd word or phrase of Slovenian will be appreciated, and can be a fun experience in itself, generally speaking there will be little call for it, as the standard of English among Slovenes – especially the young – is exceptionally high. Many older generation Slovenes speak Serbo-Croatian (as it was formerly called), while Italian is widely spoken in the Primorska region, and Hungarian in Prekmurje. Regional variations of Slovene abound, and the language is characterized by nearly fifty dialects and subdialects.

Basic grammar

Slovenian is grammatically complex with **six cases** for nouns, adjectives and pronouns, **three genders** (masculine, feminine and neuter) and **four verb tenses** (although only three are used in everyday language). Besides the singular and plural in the Slovene grammar, the dual number is also used (for two persons or objects): for example, not only *gora* (mountain) and *gore* (mountains), but also *dve gori* (two mountains). Matters become very complex when one considers special endings for gender, numbers and different cases. In Slovenian the **prepositions** are important because the forms or the following noun, pronoun and adjectives are dependent on them. Slovenian has no **articles** (such as "a" or "the") and the gender of the word is defined by its ending. The script is Roman and there are 25 letters, the speciality being s, c, and z, with a caron (a small "v" or hook) on top of each, which indicates sh, ch and zh sounds.

Pronunciation

Slovenian has free stress – it may fall on any syllable of a word. Like English, there are different values for vowels; vowels can be stressed or unstressed, long or short, open or closed, with further subtle variations in the pronunciation. The Slovenian consonants are mostly pronounced as they are spelt. Letters not included below are pronounced as in English. There are no explosive or aspirated consonants.

A short a as in cat, long a as in father

C ts as in bats

Č ch as in church

D d as in dog (*dan*), t as in sit (*grad*)

E short e as in met (*več*), ea as in pear (*mleko*)

I short i as in hit (*ris*), long ee as in been (*sin*)

J y as in yet

L l as in **l**eap

O short o as in h**o**t (*voda*), long o as in sh**o**rt (*sok*)

R r pronounced with the tip of the tongue like a Scottish "r"

Š sh as in **sh**op

U oo as in f**oo**t (*kruh*)

V v as in **v**at (*voda*), w as in **w**ord (*avto*)

Ž zh as in mea**s**ure

Words and phrases

Slovenian distinguishes between formal and informal means of address. The formal (polite) way is very often used. The informal way is used among friends and people you know well. In the phrases below the polite form of address has been used.

Basics

Yes	Ja
No	Ne
I am from	Sem iz
Britain/Ireland/ America/Canada/ Australia/New Zealand	Velike Britanije/ Irske/Amerike/Kanade/ Avstralije/Nove Zelandije
Slovenian	Slovensko
Slovenian person	Slovenec (male)/ Slovenka (female)
Slovenian language	Slovenščina
Do you speak…?	Govorite…?
English	Angleško
German	Nemško
French	Francosko
What's your name?	Kako ti je ime?
My name is	Ime mi je
I (don't) understand	(Ne) Razumem
Please	Prosim
Excuse me	Oprostite
Two beers, please	Dve pivi, prosim
Thank you (very much)	Hvala (lepa)
You're welcome	Prosim/ni za kaj
Hello (informal)	Živijo
Goodbye	Nasvidenje
See you later (informal)	Adijo
Good morning	Dobro jutro
Good day	Dober dan
Good evening	Dober večer
Good night	Lahko noč

How are you?	Kako ste?
Could you speak more slowly?	Lahko govorite počasneje?
What do you call…?	Kako se reče…?
Please write it down	Lahko prosim napišete
Hurry up!	Pohitite!
Entrance	Vhod
Exit	Izhod
Arrival	Prihod
Departure	Odhod
Open	Odprto
Closed	Zaprto
Free admission	Prost vstop
Toilet	Stranišče/WC (women's – ženske, men's – moški)
Shop	Trgovina
Market	Trg
Hospital	Bolnica/bolnišnica
Pharmacy	Lekarna
Police	Policija
Caution/beware	Previdno/pozor
Help!	Na pomoč!
I'm ill	Bolan (bolna) sem
No smoking	Kajenje prepovedano
No bathing	Kopanje prepovedano
Where is/are?	Kje je/so?
What?	Kaj?
Why?	Zakaj?
When?	Kdaj?
Who?	Kdo?

Accommodation

I'd like/we'd like	Rad(a)**/radi bi		Do you have a student discount?	Ali imate študentski popust?
when speaker is male	**rad		Is everything included?	Je vse vključeno v ceno?
when speaker is female	**rada		Is breakfast included?	Ali je zajtrk vključen v ceno?
How much is it?	Koliko stane?		Full board	Polni penzion
Per night	Na noč		Half board	Pol penzion
Per week	Na teden		Can we camp here?	Ali lahko tukaj kampiramo?
Single room	Enoposteljna soba			
Double room	Dvoposteljna soba		Can I see the room?	Ali lahko vidim sobo?
Rooms for rent	Sobe/oddaja sob		I have a reservation	Imam rezervacijo
Hot (cold) water	Topla (mrzla) voda		The bill please	Račun prosim
Shower	Tuš		We're paying separately	Plačamo posebej
It's very expensive	Zelo drago je			
Do you have anything cheaper?	Ali imate kaj cenejšega?			

Getting around

Where's the...?	Kje je...?		When does the next train/bus leave for...?	Kdaj odpelje naslednji vlak/avtobus v...?
Campsite	Kamp			
Hotel	Hotel		Do I have to change trains?	Ali moram prestopiti?
Railway station	Železniška postaja			
Bus station	Avtobusna postaja		Towards	Proti
Bus stop	Avtobusno postajališče		On the right (left)	Na desni (levi)
Inland	Notranji promet		Straight ahead	Naravnost
International	Mednarodni promet		(Over) There/here	Tam/tukaj
Is it near (far)?	Ali je blizu (daleč)?		Where are you going?	Kam greste?
Which bus goes to...?	Kateri avtobus pelje v...?		Is that on the way to...?	Ali je to na poti v...?
A one-way ticket to... please	Enosmerno vozovnico za... prosim		I want to get out at...	Rad(a) bi izstopil(a) v...
			Please stop here	Prosim ustavite tukaj
A return ticket to...	Povratno vozovnico za...		I'm lost	Izgubil(a) sem se
			Arrivals	Prihodi
Can I reserve a seat?	Ali lahko rezerviram sedež?		Departures	Odhodi
			To/from	V/iz
What time does the train/bus leave...?	Kdaj odpelje vlak/ avtobus...?		Change	Prestop

Numbers

1	Ena		6	Šest
2	Dva		7	Sedem
3	Tri		8	Osem
4	Štiri		9	Devet
5	Pet		10	Deset

11	Enajst	80	Osemdeset
12	Dvanajst	90	Devetdeset
13	Trinajst	100	Sto
14	Štirinajst	101	Stoena
15	Petnajst	150	Stopetdeset
16	Šestnajst	200	Dvesto
17	Sedemnajst	300	Tristo
18	Osemnajst	400	Štiristo
19	Devetnajst	500	Petsto
20	Dvajset	600	Šesto
21	Enaindvajset	700	Sedemsto
30	Trideset	800	Osemsto
40	Štirideset	900	Devetsto
50	Petdeset	1000	Tisoč
60	Šestdeset	Half	Pol
70	Sedemdeset	Quarter	Četrt

Time, days and dates

Either the 24- or 12-hour clock is used. When the 12-hour clock is used, "in the morning" (*dopoldan*), or "in the afternoon" (*popoldan*), is usually added. Halves and quarters are used: 4.30 is either *štiri trideset* or *pol petih* (half five), the latter being more common; 4.15 is either *štiri petnajst* or *četrt čez štiri* (quarter past four). Duration is expressed by the prepositions *od* (from) and *do* (to). To ask the time, say: *Koliko je ura?*

Day	Dan	Wednesday	Sreda
Week	Teden	Thursday	Četrtek
Month	Mesec	Friday	Petek
Year	Leto	Saturday	Sobota
Today	Danes		
Tomorrow	Jutri	January	Januar
The day after tomorrow	Pojutrišnjem	February	Februar
		March	Marec
Yesterday	Včeraj	April	April
The day before yesterday	Predvčerajšnjim	May	Maj
		June	Junij
In the morning	Zjutraj	July	Julij
Before noon	Dopoldan	August	Avgust
Noon	Opoldan	September	September
Afternoon	Popoldan	October	Oktober
In the evening	Zvečer	November	November
At midnight	Ob polnoči	December	December
At night	Ponoči		
		Spring	Pomlad
Sunday	Nedelja	Summer	Poletje
Monday	Ponedeljek	Autumn	Jesen
Tuesday	Torek	Winter	Zima

Food and drink

Basics

Bedro	Leg
Dober tek!	Bon appétit!
Dunajsko	Vienna-style (deep fried in breadcrumbs)
Dušeno	Steamed
Gorčica/senf	Mustard
Kis	Vinegar
Kisla smetana	Sour cream
Kruh	Bread
Kuhano	Boiled
Malo krvavo	Underdone/rare
Maslo	Butter
Med	Honey
Na žaru	Grilled
Na zdravje!	Cheers!
Ocvrto	Fried
Pariško	à la Parisienne (deep fried without breadcrumbs)
Pečeno	Baked
Poper	Pepper
Praženo	Roasted
Prsi	Breast
Sladkor	Sugar
Smetana	Cream
Sol	Salt
Žemlja/Štrucka	Bread roll
Zapečeno	Well done (fried)

Soups (juhe) and stews (enolončnice)

Fižolova juha	Bean soup
Gobova juha	Mushroom soup
Goveja juha	Beef broth
Jota	Sauerkraut soup
Kisla juha	Sour soup
Krompirjeva juha	Potato soup
Mineštra	Minestrone (mixed vegetable stew)
Paradižnikova juha	Tomato soup
Prežganka	Soup made by browning flour on lard and adding water
Ribji brodet	Istrian fish soup
Ričet	Barley and pork broth
Telečja obara	Veal stew
Zelenjavna juha	Vegetable soup

Appetizers – cold or hot (predjedi – hladne ali tople)

Jetrca	Liver
Narezek	Slices of cold meats
Olive	Olives
Pašteta (jetrna, račja, ribja)	Pâté (liver, duck, fish)
Pršut	Dry-cured Italian ham/smoked ham
Rižota	Risotto
Sir (kozji, kravji, ovčji)	Cheese (goat, cow, sheep)
Šunka	Ham
Tatarski biftek	Raw mince with spices spread on toast
Testenine	Pasta

Salads (solate)

Salads are usually served with vinegar and oil (vegetable, olive or pumpkin). Other dressings often include yogurt. Many restaurants have salad bars.

Fižolova solata	Bean salad
Hobotnica v solati	Octopus salad
Krompirjeva solata	Potato salad
Kumarična solata	Cucumber salad
Mešana solata	Mixed salad
Motovilec	Lamb's lettuce
Paradižnikova solata	Tomato salad
Radič	Radicchio
Rdeča pesa	Beetroot
Regrad	Dandelion
Sezonska solata	Fresh salad or whatever is in season
Šopska solata	Mixed tomatoes, cucumbers, red/green peppers and cheese
Zelena solata	Lettuce
Zeljnata solata	Cabbage salad

Fish dishes (ribje jedi) and seafood (morski sadeži)

Brancin	Seabass
Lignji	Squid
Losos	Salmon
Morski list	Sole
Ocvrta riba	Fried fish
Orada	Dorada
Oslič	Variety of cod
Postrvi	Trout
Rakci	Prawns
Sardele	Anchovies
Škampi	Shrimps
Školjke	Mussels
Skuša	Mackerel
Tuna	Tuna

Meat dishes (mesne jedi)

Čevapčiči	Minced meat, grilled in rolled pieces
Divjačina	Venison
Dunajski zrezek	Wiener schnitzel
Golaž	Goulash
Gos	Goose
Govedina	Beef
Goveji zrezek	Rumpsteak
Jagnjetina	Lamb
Kranjska klobasa s kislim zeljem	Sauerkraut with sausage
Mesne kroglice	Meatballs
Meso na žaru	Assorted grilled meat
Ovčetina	Mutton
Perutnina	Poultry
Piščanec	Chicken
Polnjene paprike	Peppers stuffed with meat and rice
Puran	Turkey
Raca	Duck
Sarma	Cabbage stuffed with meat and rice
Svinjina	Pork
Svinjski kotlet	Pork chop
Telečja (svinjska) krača	Veal (pork) shank
Telečja (svinjska) pečenka	Roast veal (pork)
Telečji zrezek	Roast cutlet

Teletina	Veal
Vampi	Tripe
Zajec	Rabbit
Žrebičkov zrezek	Horse steak

Sauces (omake)

Gobova omaka	Mushroom sauce
Paradižnikova omaka	Tomato sauce
Sirova omaka	Cheese sauce
Smetanova omaka	Cream sauce
Tatarska omaka	Sauce made of mayonnaise, mustard, garlic and parsley
Vinska omaka	Wine sauce

Accompaniments (priloge)

Ajdovi žganci	Buckwheat porridge
Krompir	Potatoes
Krompirjevi cmoki	Potato dumplings
Kruhovi cmoki	Bread dumplings
Kuhan	Boiled
Kuhana zelenjava	Boiled vegetables
Pečen	Roasted
Pire	Mashed
Pommes frittes (pomfri)	French fries
Riž	Rice
Testenine	Pasta
Žlinkofi	Slovene type of ravioli

Vegetables (zelenjava)

Artičoka	Artichoke
Beluši/šparglji	Asparagus
Brstični ohrovt	Brussels sprouts
Bučke	Courgette
Čebula	Onions
Česen	Garlic
Cvetača	Cauliflower
Fižol	Beans
Gobe	Mushrooms
Grah	Peas
Hren	Horseradish
Jajčevec/melancana	Aubergine/eggplant
Korenje	Carrots
Koruza	Sweetcorn
Krompir	Potatoes

Kumara	Cucumber
Paprika	Red/green peppers
Paradižnik	Tomato
Peteršilj	Parsley
Por	Leek
Rdeča pesa	Beetroot
Redkev	Radish
Repa	Turnip
Špinača	Spinach
Zelena	Celery
Zelje	Cabbage

Fruit (sadje) and nuts (oreski)

Ananas	Pineapple
Breskev	Peach
Češnja	Cherr
Figa/smokva	Fig
Grozdje	Grapes
Hruška	Pear
Jabolko	Apple
Jagoda	Strawberry
Lešnik	Hazelnut
Limona	Lemon
Lubenica	Watermelon
Malina	Raspberry
Mandelj	Almond

Marelica	Apricot
Melona	Melon
Oreh	Walnut
Pomaranča	Orange
Ribez	Currant
Sliva	Plum

Desserts (sladice)

Gibanica Pastry filled with apples, cheese and poppy seeds baked in cream

Palačinke z orehi, čokolado ali marmelado Pancakes with walnuts, chocolate or jam

Potica (orehova ali pehtranova) Cake (walnut or tarragon)

Štruklji (ajdovi, orehovi ali sirovi) Rolls (buckwheat, walnut or cheese)

Zavitek (jabolčni ali sirov) Strudel (apple or cheese)

Drinks (pijace)

Pivo	Beer
Sok	Juice
Vino (belo, rdeče)	Wine (white, red)
Voda	Water
Mineralna voda	Mineral water, usually with gas

Glossary of Slovenian words and terms

Avto	Car
Avtobusna postaja	Bus station
Avtobusna postajališče	Bus stop
Avtocesta	Highway
Banka	Bank
Bolnica	Hospital
Center	Centre
Cerkev	Church
Cesta	Road
DDV	Goods tax, equivalent to VAT
Denar	Money
Dolina	Valley
Dom/Koča	Mountain hut
Gledališče	Theatre
Gora	Mountain

Gostilna	Inn
Gozd	Forest
Grad	Castle
Hiša	House
Hrib	Hill
Jama	Cave
Jezero	Lake
Kino	Cinema
Kmečki turizem	Farm tourism
Letališče	Airport
Mestna hiša	Town hall
Mesto	Town, city
Morje	Sea
Most	Bridge
Muzej	Museum
Nakupovalni center	Shopping centre
Optik	Optician

Otok	Island	Stadion	Stadium
Peron	Platform (at the station)	Toplice	Spa or mineral baths
Plavalni bazen	Swimming pool	Trajekt	Ferry
Plaža	Beach	Trg	Square, market
Pokopališče	Cemetery	Trgovina	Shop
Polje	Field	Ulica	Street
Pošta	Post office	Vas	Village
Pot	Path/way	Veloposlaništvo	Embassy
Pristanišče	Port	Vodnjak	Fountain
Reka	River	Vozni red	Timetable (bus and train)
Restavracija	Restaurant		
Samostan	Monastery	Vrt	Garden
Sejem	Fair	Zdravnik	Doctor
Slap	Waterfall	Železniška postaja	Railway station
Šola	School	Zemljevid	Map

Travel store

Holidays on a farm – an unforgettable experience

Spend your vacation in close contact to nature in the homely and hospitable surrounds of more than 200 tourist farms. The countryside offers ideal opportunities for hiking, cycling, horseback riding, skiing, water sports and more, while farms are excellent starting points for excursions around Slovenia. Enjoy, too, delicious specialities from the Slovenian kitchen, accompanied by excellent wines.

Price per person per day for half board on a tourist farm of highest category (4 apples) is: 30 – 40 EUR.

Information, catalogues:
Association of Tourist Farms of Slovenia
Trnoveljska c. 1, SI-3000 Celje
Tel.: +386 3 491 64 81
Fax: +386 3 491 64 80
e-mail: ztks@siol.net
www.farmtourism.si
www.slovenia.info/touristfarms

Travel

Andorra The Pyrenees, Pyrenees & Andorra Map, Spain
Antigua The Caribbean
Argentina Argentina, Argentina Map, Buenos Aires, South America on a Budget
Aruba The Caribbean
Australia Australia, Australia Map, East Coast Australia, Melbourne, Sydney, Tasmania
Austria Austria, Europe on a Budget, Vienna
Bahamas The Bahamas, The Caribbean
Barbados Barbados DIR, The Caribbean
Belgium Belgium & Luxembourg, Bruges DIR, Brussels, Brussels Map, Europe on a Budget
Belize Belize, Central America on a Budget, Guatemala & Belize Map
Benin West Africa
Bolivia Bolivia, South America on a Budget
Brazil Brazil, Rio, South America on a Budget
British Virgin Islands The Caribbean
Brunei Malaysia, Singapore & Brunei [1 title], Southeast Asia on a Budget
Bulgaria Bulgaria, Europe on a Budget
Burkina Faso West Africa
Cambodia Cambodia, Southeast Asia on a Budget, Vietnam, Laos & Cambodia Map [1 Map]
Cameroon West Africa
Canada Canada, Pacific Northwest, Toronto, Toronto Map, Vancouver
Cape Verde West Africa
Cayman Islands The Caribbean
Chile Chile, Chile Map, South America on a Budget
China Beijing, China,

Hong Kong & Macau, Hong Kong & Macau DIR, Shanghai
Colombia South America on a Budget
Costa Rica Central America on a Budget, Costa Rica, Costa Rica & Panama Map
Croatia Croatia, Croatia Map, Europe on a Budget
Cuba Cuba, Cuba Map, The Caribbean, Havana
Cyprus Cyprus, Cyprus Map
Czech Republic The Czech Republic, Czech & Slovak Republics, Europe on a Budget, Prague, Prague DIR, Prague Map
Denmark Copenhagen, Denmark, Europe on a Budget, Scandinavia
Dominica The Caribbean
Dominican Republic Dominican Republic, The Caribbean
Ecuador Ecuador, South America on a Budget
Egypt Egypt, Egypt Map
El Salvador Central America on a Budget
England Britain, Camping in Britain, Devon & Cornwall, Dorset, Hampshire and The Isle of Wight [1 title], England, Europe on a Budget, The Lake District, London, London DIR, London Map, London Mini Guide, Walks In London & Southeast England
Estonia The Baltic States, Europe on a Budget
Fiji Fiji
Finland Europe on a Budget, Finland, Scandinavia
France Brittany & Normandy, Corsica, Corsica Map, The Dordogne & the Lot, Europe on a Budget, France, France Map, Languedoc & Roussillon, The Loire, Paris, Paris DIR,

Paris Map, Paris Mini Guide, Provence & the Côte d'Azur, The Pyrenees, Pyrenees & Andorra Map
French Guiana South America on a Budget
Gambia The Gambia, West Africa
Germany Berlin, Berlin Map, Europe on a Budget, Germany, Germany Map
Ghana West Africa
Gibraltar Spain
Greece Athens Map, Crete, Crete Map, Europe on a Budget, Greece, Greece Map, Greek Islands, Ionian Islands
Guadeloupe The Caribbean
Guatemala Central America on a Budget, Guatemala, Guatemala & Belize Map
Guinea West Africa
Guinea-Bissau West Africa
Guyana South America on a Budget
Holland see The Netherlands
Honduras Central America on a Budget
Hungary Budapest, Europe on a Budget, Hungary
Iceland Iceland, Iceland Map
India Goa, India, India Map, Kerala, Rajasthan, Delhi & Agra [1 title], South India, South India Map
Indonesia Bali & Lombok, Southeast Asia on a Budget
Ireland Dublin DIR, Dublin Map, Europe on a Budget, Ireland, Ireland Map
Israel Jerusalem
Italy Europe on a Budget, Florence DIR, Florence & Siena Map, Florence & the best of Tuscany, Italy, The Italian Lakes, Naples & the Amalfi Coast, Rome, Rome DIR, Rome Map, Sardinia, Sicily, Sicily Map, Tuscany & Umbria, Tuscany Map,

Venice, Venice DIR, Venice Map
Jamaica Jamaica, The Caribbean
Japan Japan, Tokyo
Jordan Jordan
Kenya Kenya, Kenya Map
Korea Korea
Laos Laos, Southeast Asia on a Budget, Vietnam, Laos & Cambodia Map [1 Map]
Latvia The Baltic States, Europe on a Budget
Lithuania The Baltic States, Europe on a Budget
Luxembourg Belgium & Luxembourg, Europe on a Budget
Malaysia Malaysia Map, Malaysia, Singapore & Brunei [1 title], Southeast Asia on a Budget
Mali West Africa
Malta Malta & Gozo DIR
Martinique The Caribbean
Mauritania West Africa
Mexico Baja California, Baja California, Cancún & Cozumel DIR, Mexico, Mexico Map, Yucatán, Yucatán Peninsula Map
Monaco France, Provence & the Côte d'Azur
Montenegro Montenegro
Morocco Europe on a Budget, Marrakesh DIR, Marrakesh Map, Morocco, Morocco Map,
Nepal Nepal
Netherlands Amsterdam, Amsterdam DIR, Amsterdam Map, Europe on a Budget, The Netherlands
Netherlands Antilles The Caribbean
New Zealand New Zealand, New Zealand Map

DIR: Rough Guide DIRECTIONS for short breaks

Available from all good bookstores

ROUGH GUIDES
Don't Just Travel

NOTES

Small print and

Index

A Rough Guide to Rough Guides

Published in 1982, the first Rough Guide – to Greece – was a student scheme that became a publishing phenomenon. Mark Ellingham, a recent graduate in English from Bristol University, had been travelling in Greece the previous summer and couldn't find the right guidebook. With a small group of friends he wrote his own guide, combining a highly contemporary, journalistic style with a thoroughly practical approach to travellers' needs.

The immediate success of the book spawned a series that rapidly covered dozens of destinations. And, in addition to impecunious backpackers, Rough Guides soon acquired a much broader and older readership that relished the guides' wit and inquisitiveness as much as their enthusiastic, critical approach and value-for-money ethos.

These days, Rough Guides include recommendations from shoestring to luxury and cover more than 200 destinations around the globe, including almost every country in the Americas and Europe, more than half of Africa and most of Asia and Australasia. Our ever-growing team of authors and photographers is spread all over the world, particularly in Europe, the US and Australia.

In the early 1990s, Rough Guides branched out of travel, with the publication of Rough Guides to World Music, Classical Music and the Internet. All three have become benchmark titles in their fields, spearheading the publication of a wide range of books under the Rough Guide name.

Including the travel series, Rough Guides now number more than 350 titles, covering: phrasebooks, waterproof maps, music guides from Opera to Heavy Metal, reference works as diverse as Conspiracy Theories and Shakespeare, and popular culture books from iPods to Poker. Rough Guides also produce a series of more than 120 World Music CDs in partnership with World Music Network.

Visit www.roughguides.com to see our latest publications.

Rough Guide travel images are available for commercial licensing at www.roughguidespictures.com

Rough Guide credits

Text editor: Hazel Meek
Layout: Sachin Tanwar
Cartography: Katie Lloyd-Jones and Maxine Repath
Picture editor: Harriet Mills
Production: Rebecca Short
Proofreader: Susannah Wight
Cover design: Dan May and Chloë Roberts
Photographer: Tim Draper
Editorial: Ruth Blackmore, Andy Turner, Keith Drew, Edward Aves, Alice Park, Lucy White, Jo Kirby, James Smart, Natasha Foges, Róisín Cameron, James Rice, Lara Kavanagh, Emma Traynor, Emma Gibbs, Kathryn Lane, Monica Woods, Mani Ramaswamy, Harry Wilson, Lucy Cowie, Alison Roberts, Joe Staines, Peter Buckley, Matthew Milton, Tracy Hopkins, Ruth Tidball; **Delhi** Madhavi Singh, Karen D'Souza, Lubna Shaheen
Design & Pictures: **London** Scott Stickland, Dan May, Diana Jarvis, Mark Thomas, Nicole Newman, Sarah Cummins, Emily Taylor; **Delhi** Umesh Aggarwal, Ajay Verma, Jessica Subramanian, Ankur Guha, Pradeep Thapliyal, Anita Singh, Nikhil Agarwal, Sachin Gupta.

Production: Liz Cherry
Cartography: **London** Ed Wright **Delhi** Rajesh Chhibber, Ashutosh Bharti, Rajesh Mishra, Animesh Pathak, Jasbir Sandhu, Karobi Gogoi, Alakananda Bhattacharya, Swati Handoo, Deshpal Dabas
Online: **London** Faye Hellon, Jeanette Angell, Fergus Day, Justine Bright, Clare Bryson, Aine Fearon, Adrian Low, Ezgi Celebi; **Delhi** Amit Verma, Rahul Kumar, Narender Kumar, Ravi Yadav, Debojit Borah, Rakesh Kumar, Ganesh Sharma, Shisir Basumatari
Marketing & Publicity: **London** Liz Statham, Louise Maher, Jess Carter, Vanessa Godden, Vivienne Watton, Anna Paynton, Rachel Sprackett, Laura Vipond; **New York** Katy Ball, Judi Powers; **Delhi** Ragini Govind
Reference Director: Andrew Lockett
Operations Assistant: Becky Doyle
Operations Manager: Helen Atkinson
Publishing Director (Travel): Clare Currie
Commercial Manager: Gino Magnotta
Managing Director: John Duhigg

Publishing information

This 3rd edition published April 2010 by
Rough Guides Ltd,
80 Strand, London WC2R 0RL
14 Local Shopping Centre, Panchsheel Park, New Delhi 110017, India
Distributed by the Penguin Group
Penguin Books Ltd,
80 Strand, London WC2R 0RL
Penguin Group (USA)
375 Hudson Street, NY 10014, USA
Penguin Group (Australia)
250 Camberwell Road, Camberwell, Victoria 3124, Australia
Penguin Group (Canada)
195 Harry Walker Parkway N, Newmarket, ON, L3Y 7B3 Canada
Penguin Group (NZ)
67 Apollo Drive, Mairangi Bay, Auckland 1310, New Zealand
Cover concept by Peter Dyer.

Typeset in Bembo and Helvetica to an original design by Henry Iles.
Printed in Singapore
© Norm Longley 2010
Maps © Rough Guides

368pp includes index
A catalogue record for this book is available from the British Library
ISBN: 978-1-84836-483-7

The publishers and authors have done their best to ensure the accuracy and currency of all the information in **The Rough Guide to Slovenia**, however, they can accept no responsibility for any loss, injury, or inconvenience sustained by any traveller as a result of information or advice contained in the guide.

1   3   5   7   9   8   6   4   2

Help us update

We've gone to a lot of effort to ensure that the third edition of **The Rough Guide to Slovenia** is accurate and up-to-date. However, things change – places get "discovered", opening hours are notoriously fickle, restaurants and rooms raise prices or lower standards. If you feel we've got it wrong or left something out, we'd like to know, and if you can remember the address, the price, the hours, the phone number, so much the better.

Please send your comments with the subject line "**Rough Guide Slovenia Update**" to ©mail @roughguides.com. We'll credit all contributions and send a copy of the next edition (or any other Rough Guide if you prefer) for the very best emails.

Have your questions answered and tell others about your trip at ®www.roughguides.com

Acknowledgements

A very special thanks go to:
Hazel for excellent and enthusiastic editing; Monica for continued support; Tatjana Radovič in Ljubljana for friendship; Renata Kosi and Vesna Čuček at the Association of Slovenian Tourist Farms for their continued assistance; Tina Križnar and Lucija Jager at the Slovenian Tourist Board for their invaluable help; Joanna Chandler in Ljubljana for support and for putting me up wherever, whenever; Ana Roš and Valta Kramar in Kobarid for wonderful food and hospitality; Janez Fajfar in Bled for the brandy and the pletna; Špela Jurak for fine tuning the language section; Jurij Šarman in Ptuj; Clive Judge and Myrna Santos in Bohinjska Bela; Gaby Lukič in Murska Sobota; Lisa Spratling in Trnje; Nika and Ian Middleton in Ljubljana; Petra Stušek at the Ljubljana Tourist Board; Ingrid Cercek in Ljubljana.

Thanks are also due to:
Edi Polh in Škocjan; Gregor Protner in Malečnik; Breda Durcik in Pliskovica; Ljuba Bagar in Nova Gorica; Lila Šeruga in Sela pri Ratezu; Helena Rotovnik in Šmartno pri Slovenj Gradcu; Damjana and Jože Mulej in Selo pri Brdu; Breda Časar in Logarska; Jana Kovač in Ljubljana; Karin Tomažič in Brussels; Ana Tušar at Slovenian Railways; Mojca Špiler in Kranj; Tomaž Lukančič in Žiri; Miha Mlinar in Most na Soči; Barbara Žlender in Ljubljana; Uroš Mijosek in Celje; Mojca Zupanič; Graeme Higgs; Zoe Miller.

And finally, Luka, Christian and Tim.

Readers' letters

Thanks to all the readers who have taken the time to write in with comments and suggestions (and apologies if we've inadvertently omitted or misspelt anyone's name):

Joanna Jeanes, Ian Jones, Andrew Guest, Margaret Deith, Malcolm & Jenny Inglis, Winnie Wong, John Bilsland, Kirstie Kemp, Joshua Geake, Sarah Woollam, Ivan Valencic, Reinier Bergwerf, Graham & Julia Sharp, Angus Stewart, Rachel Harper

Photo credits

All photos by Tim Draper © Rough Guides except the following:

Introduction
Ljubljana Cafés © Photolibrary/Cuboimages/ Michele Bella
Mountain biking, Triglav National Park © Hermann Erber/Getty

Things not to miss
03 Planica ski-jumping © Srdjan Zivulovic/ Reuters
05 Škocjan Caves © D.Mladenovič/www.slovenia .info
07 Kurent festival © Nina Zaplotnik/istockphoto .com
09 Vineyard near Ljutomer © David Robertson/ Alamy
12 Hiking in Triglav National Park © Don Fuchs/ LOOK-foto/Photolibrary
17 Skiing, Krvavec © J. Skok/www.slovenia.info

The Great Outdoors colour section
Ski slope, Vogel © A. Fevžer/www.slovenia.info
Climbing in the Julian Alps © Urban Golob/Alamy
Fishing, Krka river © Bobo/www.slovenia.info

Subterranean Slovenia colour section
Postojna Caves © Arhiv Postojnske jame/www .slovenia.info
Caving on Migovec mountain © Anthony Baker/ Alamy
Proteus anguinus © Arhiv Postojnske jame/www .slovenia.info
Škocjan church and caves © B. Kladnik/www .slovenia.info

Black and whites
p.296 Lent Festival folk dancing © Archive Narodni dom Maribor

Map symbols

maps are listed in the full index using coloured text

▪▪▪▪	International boundary	🏛	Monument
▪▪▪	Chapter divisions boundary	🏛	Mansion/stately home
▬▬▬	Motorway	🔆	Lighthouse
═══	Main road	♰	Church (regional maps)
═══	Minor road	♰	Monastery
▬▬▬	Pedestrianized road	✡	Synagogue
⊞⊞⊞	Steps	⚐	Campsite
-----	Footpath	♰	Gardens
··········	Mountain trail	∩	Arch
▪━▪━	Railway	⊠—⊠	Gate
++++++	Funicular railway/cable-car	✈	Airport
────	River/canal	⛴	Boat transfer
▬▬▬	Wall	★	Bus stop
♦	Point of interest	🅿	Parking
♦	Border crossing	ⓘ	Tourist office
/|\\	Hill	⊠	Post office
⌂	Mountains	@	Internet access
▲	Peak	▪	Building
⬟	Mountain refuge	─┼	Church (town maps)
⚐	Skiing	▫	Market
⌒	Cave	◯	Stadium
⚒	Waterfall	▨	Park/forest
⌣	Bridge	⊡	Cemetery
∴	Ruins	▨	Beach
♙	Castle	▭	Marshland
♜	Fortress	▭	Saltpan
♦	Museum		

So now we've told you about the things not to miss, the best places to stay, the top restaurants, the liveliest bars and the most spectacular sights, it only seems fair to tell you about the best travel insurance around

WorldNomads.com
keep travelling safely

Recommended by Rough Guides

www.roughguides.com
MAKE THE MOST OF YOUR TIME ON EARTH

ROUGH
GUIDES